To my children, Em
considerable time w
in completion of thi
but so much joy los

Specification, Estimation, and Analysis of Macroeconometric Models

Ray C. Fair

Harvard University Press
Cambridge, Massachusetts, and London, England 1984

10 9 8 7 6

This book is prin
have been chose

Library of Cong

Fair, Ray C.
Specification,
macroeconomet

Bibliography:
Includes inde
1. Economet
models. I. Tit
HB141.F34 1
ISBN 0-674-83

Acknowledgments

The beginnings of this book go back to my graduate student days, and thus my indebtedness to others is substantial. My thesis advisers at MIT, Robert Solow, Franklin Fisher, and Edwin Kuh, were important in shaping my research interests. Later, at Princeton University, I benefited greatly from my association with Gregory Chow, Stephen Goldfeld, and Richard Quandt. Although what is commonly referred to as "Yale macro" is quite different in emphasis from my own work (see the discussion in Section 3.1.1), I have clearly profited from the lively and stimulating environment at Yale University.

Regarding the work for this book, I am indebted to Barry Bosworth, Gregory Chow, Angus Deaton, William Parke, Peter Phillips, and John Taylor for comments on various drafts. Part of the work in Chapter 6 was done jointly with William Parke, and much of that in Chapter 11 was done jointly with John Taylor. I am also grateful to a number of students, in particular to Lewis Alexander and Tae Dong Kim, for helpful comments. None of these individuals should, of course, be held accountable for the material; all errors are mine. Christopher Baum and Jack Ciccolo provided considerable assistance in the use of the VAX computer at Boston College. Glena Ames, as usual, provided outstanding typing; all the tables in this volume were typed by her. Much of my research, including the work for this book, has been funded by the National Science Foundation (current grant number SOC77-03274).

Contents

Specification, Estimation, and Analysis of Macroeconometric Models

Abbreviations

ARMC	Autoregressive model (MC)
ARUS	Autoregressive model (US)
BFGS	Broyden-Fletcher-Goldfarb-Shanno nonlinear maximization algorithm
DFP	Davidon-Fletcher-Powell nonlinear maximization algorithm
DW	Durbin-Watson statistic
Fed	Federal Reserve Bank of the United States
FFA	Flow of Funds Accounts
FIML	Full information maximum likelihood
FSR	First-stage regressor
LAD	Least absolute deviations
LHS	Left-hand side
LINUS	A twelve-equation linear model (US)
MAE	Mean absolute error
MC	Multicountry
NIA	National Income and Product Accounts
OLS	Ordinary least squares
RHS	Right-hand side
RMSE	Root mean squared error
SARUS	Sargent's classical macroeconomic model (US)
SE	Estimated standard error of an equation
S&L	State and local
US	United States
USRE1	US model with rational expectations in the bond market
USRE2	US model with rational expectations in the bond and stock markets
VAR1US	Vector autoregressive model 1 (US)
VAR2US	Vector autoregressive model 2 (US)
2SLAD	Two-stage least absolute deviations
2SLS	Two-stage least squares
3SLS	Three-stage least squares

1 Introduction

There is currently little agreement among macroeconomists about the structure of the economy. The recent popularity of the assumption of rational expectations has, for example, led to the construction of a number of new econometric models that differ considerably from previous models. Even among models without rational expectations, there are considerable differences in the specification of many equations, as any casual glance at them will reveal. This lack of agreement also manifests itself in quite different monetary and fiscal policy recommendations that are generally made at any one time by different economists.

At the beginning of large-scale model construction in the early 1950s, one might have thought that there would be a gradual and fairly systematic improvement in the accuracy of the specification of the equations, so that by the early 1980s there would exist a generally agreed upon model. Obviously this is not the case, and in fact there has been a movement in the last decade among people doing macroeconomic research away from large-scale models to much smaller ones. Also, as the large-scale models have become commercially successful, interest among the model practitioners in what one would call scientific research has waned. Estimation and analysis of these models are computationally expensive, and the commercial payoff from extensive testing and analysis of them is not likely to be very large, given that the models are subjectively adjusted before being used.

My research has been concerned with large-scale models and is thus contrary to the general trend of the last decade. The implicit premise on which this work is based is that a few equations are not sufficient to give a good approximation of the structure of the economy. Part of this book is a summary of this work and an attempt to stimulate more people to move into the field.

I have had three goals in writing this book. The first is to provide a reference book for advanced graduate students on the tools needed to construct and analyze macro models. Estimation techniques are discussed in Chapter 6. The emphasis in this chapter is on nonlinear methods, since most macroeconometric models are nonlinear, and on computational problems.

Chapters 7–11 are concerned with techniques that are used to analyze models once they have been estimated. Chapter 7 discusses deterministic and stochastic simulation techniques that are used to solve models. The evaluation of predictive accuracy is discussed in Chapter 8, and Chapter 9 covers the evaluation of static and dynamic properties. Optimal control techniques are considered in Chapter 10. Chapter 11 discusses the special techniques that are needed for the estimation and analysis of rational expectations models. Tools are also considered to some extent in Chapter 2, which is concerned with the methodology of macroeconomics. In particular, the transition from theoretical to econometric models is discussed in this chapter. In a loose sense this transition can be considered to be a "tool" of the trade, although it is seldom discussed.

The second goal is to present my current macroeconometric model, both the theory behind it and the actual equations. The theoretical basis of the model is discussed in Chapter 3, and the econometric model is presented in Chapter 4. The data for the model are discussed in Appendixes A and B. The model is used in Chapters 6–11 to illustrate the various techniques. After a technique is explained, it is applied to the model. This procedure helps in understanding the techniques and provides information on the computational costs of each technique.

The second goal is a complement to the first in that it provides the student with an actual example of the specification, estimation, and analysis of a model. This may be particularly helpful in understanding topics such as the transition from theoretical to econometric models. This knowledge is more easily conveyed by means of examples than it is by discussion in the abstract. It should be stressed, however, that the model presented in this book is not meant solely for illustration; it is not a "textbook" model in the sense of being deliberately simplified for expository purposes. The model is the actual model that I am working on, and it is currently my best attempt at approximating the structure of the economy.

The third goal is to argue, partly by way of example, for a particular methodology. This is dangerous business, and I hasten to add that I do not mean to be particularly rigid on this matter. The world of scientific discourse is at times chaotic, and it is probably not sensible to try to characterize this world as one with a single methodology. Nevertheless, it seems to me that macroeconomics has suffered in the past from too few attempts to test alternative theories, and the methodology that is discussed in this book stresses the testing of theories in a particular way.

Testing alternative theories or models in macroeconomics is difficult. It is relatively easy with aggregate time series data to fit the data well within the sample period, and thus a good within-sample fit is no guarantee that the particular equation or model is a good representation of the actual process generating the data. It is also difficult to make comparisons of predictive accuracy across models because of differences in the number and types of variables that are taken to be exogenous. The existence of these problems is undoubtedly one of the main reasons there has been so little progress in narrowing the disagreements within macroeconomics. I have, however, recently proposed a method for comparing alternative models that does take account of these problems, and the methodological approach of this book centers around the use of this method.

The method is discussed in detail in Chapter 8, but it will be useful to give a brief outline of it here. The method estimates variances of prediction errors, and in doing so it accounts for the four main sources of uncertainty of a prediction: uncertainty due to (1) the error terms, (2) the coefficient estimates, (3) the exogenous variable predictions, and (4) the possible misspecification of the model. Because the method accounts for all four sources, it can be used to make comparisons across models. The method, in other words, puts each model on an equal footing and thus allows comparisons to be made. Of particular importance is the accounting for the possible misspecification of the model. By doing this, the method has the potential for weeding out models that fit the data well within sample, but are in fact poor approximations of the structure.

The major methodological theme of this book is that one should be able in the long run to use the method to weed out inferior specifications and to begin to narrow the range of disagreements in macroeconomics. By "long run" in this case is meant more than, say, the next five or ten years. Much work remains to be done on the specification of different theoretically based econometric models, and the method itself requires some time to learn to use. It is also possible that better methods will be developed in the future for making comparisons. At any rate, it seems too early to draw strong conclusions regarding which model best approximates the structure, and no such conclusions have been made in this book. The method has been used in this book to compare my US model to four other models: an autoregressive model, two vector autoregressive models, and a twelve-equation linear model. (These four models are presented in Chapter 5.) Although the results of these comparisons, which are discussed in Chapter 8, may be useful reference material for others, many more comparisons with other models are needed before one can draw any strong conclusions about my model.

It will be obvious in what follows that this "wait and see" theme plays an important role in this book. Whenever a theory or approach is discussed that is different from mine, a statement is made to the effect that the differences can be tested in the long run. A computer program is available for carrying out the tests (that is, for using the method to compare alternative models), and I hope that this book will stimulate work of this kind.

It is important to note that the method tests econometric models, not theoretical models. Another important methodological question, which is also considered in this book, is what the results of testing econometric models have to say about theoretical models. Given that the transition from theoretical to econometric models is usually not very tight in macroeconomics, the question remains after, say, a particular econometric model has been chosen to be the best approximation of the structure what the results say about the theory on which the econometric model is based. Does this mean, for example, that the theory is "confirmed?" This issue is discussed in Section 2.3.

There are many computational problems involved in dealing with large-scale nonlinear models, and this may be one reason that research on these models has declined in recent years. Many of these problems are, however, much less serious now than they were a few years ago, and I have tried to indicate in the text, primarily by way of example, the computational costs of each technique. A computer program has been written that handles all the techniques discussed in this book. An outline of the logic of this program is presented in Appendix C, and the program is available for distribution. It has the advantage that once a model has been set up in the program, all the techniques can be applied to it with no further programming. For the more advanced techniques, this can represent a considerable saving in research time.

This book is not a survey of the field and is not a textbook in the usual meaning of this word. The subject matter spans many areas — methodology, macroeconomic theory, specification of econometric models, estimation techniques, other econometric techniques, optimal control issues, rational expectations models, computational issues — and it is not my intention to provide a textbook treatment of each area. I have instead selected and discussed those topics within an area that I think are important for macroeconometric work. This approach is by nature idiosyncratic. I make no apologies for this, since I do not mean this to be the usual kind of textbook, but the reader should be warned what not to expect.

1.1 Guide to the Book

A subset of this book is a book on my United States (US) model, and another subset is a book on my multicountry (MC) model. They are located in the following sections:

US Model

Theory: Section 3.1
Specification and Estimation: Section 4.1
Further Estimation: Sections 6.5 and 6.6
Testing and Analysis: Sections 7.5.1, 8.5, 9.4, 10.4, and 11.7
List of Equations: Sections 4.1.4 through 4.1.9 and Appendix A

MC Model (other than the US Model)

Theory: Section 3.2
Specification and Estimation: Section 4.2
Testing and Analysis: Sections 7.5.2, 8.6, and 9.5
List of Equations: Tables 4-1 through 4-13 and Appendix B

Sections 9.4 and 9.5 are of particular importance in understanding the properties of the models.

If one is interested only in the US or the MC model, the rest of the book can be omitted. The cost of doing this is that none of the techniques that are applied to the models will have been explained. If, on the other hand, the reader is interested only in the techniques, the sections listed above can be omitted. The cost of doing this is that no applications of the techniques will have been discussed. In particular, one loses from this latter approach an example of the transition from a theoretical to an econometric model, which is a tool that is best described by means of examples.

Chapter 7 on the solution of models is a prerequisite for Chapters 8–11. The discussion of the FIML estimation technique in Chapter 6 is required for the discussion of the estimation of rational expectations models in Chapter 11. The discussion of the various models in Chapter 5 is required for some of the applications. Otherwise the individual chapters are self-contained.

1.2 Conventions Adopted

The number of symbols used in Chapters 3 and 4 is fairly large, and for ease of reference the symbols have been listed in alphabetical order in tables. The symbols for the variables in the theoretical model in Chapter 3 are listed in Table 3-1, and the symbols for the variables in the econometric model in

Chapter 4 are listed in Table A-4 of Appendix A and in Table B-2 of Appendix B. Table A-4 presents the variables for the United States, and Table B-2 presents the variables for the other countries. The variables used for the econometric models in Chapter 5 are also used for the econometric model in Chapter 4, and thus Tables A-4 and B-2 are also relevant for Chapter 5.

I have tried to keep the notation simple. One or two letters usually denote a variable, and subscripts have generally been used only when the reference would otherwise be ambiguous. For example, there are three housing investment variables in the US model in Chapter 4, one each for the household, firm, and financial sectors, and therefore subscripts *h*, *f*, and *b* have been used for the housing investment variable *IH*. There is, however, only one housing stock variable (denoted *KH*), and although this variable pertains to the household sector, no subscript *h* has been used for it. A *t* subscript has been used for the variables in Chapter 3 to denote the period in question, but, with a few exceptions, this has not been done for the variables in Chapter 4. Some confusion might have resulted had the subscript not been used for the theoretical model because of the multiperiod nature of the maximization problems; no confusion is likely to result from not using the *t* subscript for the econometric model.

A coefficient estimate will be said to be "significant" if its absolute value is greater than or equal to twice the size of its estimated standard error. An explanatory variable will be said to be significant if its coefficient estimate is significant. Although this convention facilitates the discussion of results, no precise statistical statement is implied by its use. Given the searching for equations with good statistical properties that is done in macroeconometric work, classical statistical tests are not applicable. In practice these tests are generally not used in a rigorous way to decide on the final specification of a model.

By "*t*-statistic" in this book is meant the absolute value of a coefficient estimate divided by its estimated standard error. In other words, the minus sign has been dropped from what is conventionally referred to as the *t*-statistic. This should cause no confusion, and it makes the results somewhat easier to present.

Unless otherwise stated in the text, none of the goodness of fit measures have been adjusted for degrees of freedom. For example, in computing the standard error of an estimated equation, the sum of squared residuals has been divided by the number of observations, not the number of observations minus the number of coefficients estimated. For the general model considered in this book (nonlinear, simultaneous, dynamic), only asymptotic results are available, and so if any adjustments were made, they would have to be based on analogies to simpler models. In many cases there are no obvious analogies, and it seemed best simply to forgo any adjustments. Fortunately, in most cases the number of observations is fairly large relative to numbers that might be used in the subtraction, and therefore the results are not likely to be sensitive to the present treatment.

The phrase "rational expectations" is used in this book in the sense of Muth (1961). An expectation of a variable is said to be "rational" if, given a set of exogenous variable predictions, it is what the model predicts the variable to be. This definition requires that there be a model and a set of exogenous variable predictions. In practice an expectation is sometimes said to be rational if "all available information" has been used in forming it. The problem with this definition is that it is vague concerning what "all available information" means, and so I have not used it. In the Muth sense it is clear what this means, "all available information" means using the model (including all the nonlinear restrictions involved in going from the structural coefficients to the reduced form coefficients) to solve for the expectation.

In discussing the properties of a model, I have used statements to the effect that a change in variable *A* "leads to" or "results in" a change in variable *B*, where both variables *A* and *B* are endogenous. In a simultaneous equations model, which is what most of the models considered in this book are, the use of statements like this is not precise, since in general every endogenous variable affects every other one. This way of discussing the results is, however, helpful in explaining the properties of a model, and as long as one is aware of its loose nature, no confusion should result. On a related matter, I have referred to the "matching" of variables to equations when discussing the solution of a model. This is again only for pedagogical purposes, since in general every equation influences the determination of every variable in a simultaneous equations model.

1.3 Computer Work

This book went through two main drafts. For the first draft nearly all the computer work was done on a VAX 11/780 at Boston College. For the second draft all the econometric models were updated and the computer work was done over on an IBM 4341 at Yale University. Only the updated results are presented in this book, but whenever possible, both the VAX times for the old results and the IBM times for the new results are presented. The computer times that are presented, especially the IBM times, are fairly rough. Sometimes more than one set of results was obtained in a single job, and some sets of results required parts of many jobs. It was not always easy to keep track of exactly how much computer time each task took. This was particularly true on the IBM, which did not allow elapsed times to be computed within a single job. Also, the basic sample period used for the IBM work was slightly larger than that used for the VAX work (115 versus 107 observations), and this adds to the imprecision of the comparisons of the estimation jobs. Nevertheless, the times reported here are not likely to be off by more than about 25 percent, which is adequate for giving a general idea of the computational costs of each technique. Relative to the IBM, the VAX is faster at reading from and writing to the disk than it is at numerical computations. The VAX times would thus not be a constant proportion of the IBM times even without measurement error; the relative speeds vary depending, among other things, on the amount of reading and writing that is done.

To give an indication of the likely times on faster computers, the IBM 4341 is about five times slower than the IBM 3033, which in turn is about four times slower than one of the fastest computers currently available, the CRAY-1. The times reported in this book for the IBM 4341 are thus likely to be about twenty times less for a CRAY-1. This comparison is, however, very rough, and it could be off by a factor of 2 or more. The relative speeds of computers vary considerably depending on the type of job. Moreover, the time for the same job on the same type of computer can vary across installations depending on the other features of the installations. To give an example, near the end of the computer work for the first draft of this book, Boston College installed a second VAX 11/780, which I began using. This VAX seemed to be roughly twice as fast as the other one. There are undoubtedly subtle reasons for this difference, but the main point here is that any comparison of time between computers is very rough unless one has actually run the job on both computers. All the VAX times reported in this book are for the first (slower) VAX. Some of the computer work for the results in Chapter 11 was done on an IBM 360/91 at Columbia University. This machine is about 2.5 times faster than an IBM 4341.

It seems clear that time is on our side with respect to computer costs. It is likely that in, say, ten years, computer costs for results like those in this book will be trivial. At the same time, many of the problems that it was not feasible to solve for this book should become soluble.

1.4 References

Although part of this book is a summary of my previous work, the present volume is self-contained in that it does not require that any of the earlier literature have been read. I have indicated in a note to each chapter (given at the end of the book) the references to my prior research that the chapter draws upon, but otherwise little mention of these references is made. This is not true, however, of references to other authors, which are scattered in the usual way throughout the chapters.

2 Macroeconomic Methodology

2.1 Macro Theoretical Models and the Role of Theory

2.1.1 Ingredients of Models

Broadly speaking, an economy consists of people making and carrying out decisions and interacting with each other through markets. Theories provide explanations of how the decisions are made and how the markets work. The ingredients of a theory include the choice of the decision-making units, the decision variables and objective function of each unit, the constraints facing each unit, and the amount of information each unit has at the time the decisions are made. Possible constraints include budget constraints, technological constraints, direct constraints on decision variables, and institutional or legal constraints. If expectations of future values affect current decisions, another ingredient of a theory is an explanation of how expectations are formed.

A theory of how markets work should explain who sets prices and how they are set. If there is the possibility of disequilibrium in certain markets, the theory should explain how quantities are determined each period and why it is that prices are not set to clear the markets. Institutional constraints may play an important role in some markets.

In macroeconomics there are also a number of adding-up constraints that should be met. In particular, balance-sheet and flow-of-funds constraints should be met. An asset of one person is a liability of someone else, and income of one person in a period is an expenditure of someone else in the period. These two constraints are not independent, since any deviation of income from expenditure for an individual in a period corresponds to a change in at least one of his or her assets or liabilities.

2.1.2 The Traditional Role of Theory

An important issue in the construction of a model is the role that one expects theory to play. If the aim is to use the theoretical model to guide the specification of an empirical model, the issue is how many restrictions one can expect theory to provide regarding the specification of the equations to be estimated. In practice, the primary role of theory has been to choose the variables that appear with nonzero coefficients in each equation. (Stated another way, the primary role of theory has been to provide "exclusionary" restrictions on the model, that is, to provide a list of variables *not* to include in each equation.) In most cases theory also chooses the signs of the coefficients. Much less often is theory used to decide things like the functional forms of the estimated equations and the lengths of the lag distributions. (This is not to say that theory could not be used for such purposes, only that it generally has not been.) This role of theory—the choice of the variables to include in each equation—will be called the "traditional" role or approach.

An interesting question within the traditional approach is whether theory singles out one variable per equation as the obvious dependent or "left-hand-side" (LHS) variable, where the other variables are then explanatory or "right-hand-side" (RHS) variables. In this way of looking at the problem, the LHS variable is the decision variable and the RHS variables are the determinants of the decision variable. If the theoretical problem is to explain the decisions of agents, this way seems natural. Each equation is a derived decision equation (derived either in a maximization context or in some other way) with a natural LHS variable. The alternative way of looking at the problem is that theory treats all variables in each equation equally. These two interpretations have important implications for estimation. In particular, full information maximum likelihood (FIML) treats all variables equally, whereas two-stage least squares (2SLS) and three-stage least squares (3SLS) require an LHS variable to be chosen for each equation before estimation (see, for example, Chow 1964). One might thus be inclined to choose 3SLS over FIML under the first interpretation, although there are other issues to consider in this choice as well. This issue is discussed in more detail in Section 6.3.4, where FIML and 3SLS are compared. For the remainder of this chapter it will be assumed that within the traditional approach the LHS variable is also chosen.

2.1.3 The Hansen-Sargent Approach and Lucas's Point

An alternative role for theory is exemplified by the recent work of Hansen and Sargent (1980). In this work the aim is to estimate the parameters of the objective functions of the decision-making units. In the traditional approach these parameters are never estimated. The parameters of the derived decision equations (rules) are estimated instead, where these parameters are functions of the parameters of the objective function and other things. The Hansen-Sargent approach imposes many more theoretical restrictions on the data than does the traditional approach, especially considering that the traditional approach imposes very few restrictions on the functional forms and the lag structures of the estimated decision equations.

The advantage of the Hansen-Sargent approach is that it estimates structural parameters rather than combinations of structural parameters and other things. The problem with estimating combinations is that if, say, one wants to examine the effects of changing an exogenous variable on the decision variables, there is always the possibility that this change will change something in the combinations. If so, then it is inappropriate to use the estimated decision equations, which are based on fixed estimates of the combinations, to examine the effects of the change. This is the point emphasized by Lucas (1976) in his classic article. (Note that the validity of the point does not depend on expectations being rational. Even if expectations are formed in rather naive ways, it may still be that the coefficients of the decision equations are combinations of things that change when an exogenous variable is changed.)

There are two disadvantages of the Hansen-Sargent approach, one that may be temporary and one that may be more serious. The temporary disadvantage is that it is extremely difficult to set up the problem in such a way that the parameters can be estimated, especially if there is more than one decision variable or if the objective function is not quadratic. Very restrictive assumptions have so far been needed to make the problem tractable. This disadvantage may gradually be lessened as more tools are developed. At the present time, however, this approach is a long way from the development of a complete model of the economy.

A potentially more serious disadvantage, at least as applied to macroeconomic data, is the possibility that the approach imposes restrictions on the data that are poor approximations. Macroeconomic data are highly aggregated, and it is obviously restrictive to assume that one objective function pertains to, say, the entire household sector or the entire firm sector. Although both the traditional approach and the Hansen-Sargent approach are forced to make assumptions like this when dealing with macroeconomic data, the Hansen-Sargent approach is much more restrictive. If because of aggregation problems the assumption that a sector behaves by maximizing an objective function is not correct, models based on both approaches will be misspecified. This misspecification may be more serious for models based on the Hansen-Sargent approach because it uses the assumption in a much stronger way. To put it another way, by not requiring that a particular objective function be specified, the traditional approach may be more robust to errors regarding the maximization assumption.

It is difficult to argue against the Hansen-Sargent approach without sounding as if one is in favor of the use of ad hoc theory to explain macroeconomic data. Arguments against theoretical purity are generally not well received in the economics profession. There are, however, as just discussed, different degrees to which theory can be used to guide econometric specifications. There is a middle ground between a completely ad hoc approach and the Hansen-Sargent approach, namely what I have called the traditional approach. An example of this approach is given in Chapters 3 and 4.

It should also be noted that the Hansen-Sargent approach can be discussed without reference to how expectations are formed. It is typically assumed within this approach that expectations are rational, but this is not a necessary assumption. It is clearly possible within the context of a maximization problem to assume that expectations of the future variable values that are needed to solve the problem are formed in simple or naive ways. The possible problems with the Hansen-Sargent approach discussed earlier exist independently of the expectational assumptions that are used. The problems are perhaps potentially more serious when the rational expectation assumption is used because of the tighter theoretical restrictions that are implied, but this is only a matter of degree. The treatment of expectations is discussed in Section 2.2.2.

Whether the Hansen-Sargent approach will lead to better models of the economy is currently an open question. As noted in Chapter 1, a major theme of this book is that it should be possible in the long run to decide questions like this using methods like the one discussed in Chapter 8. The method in Chapter 8 allows one to compare different models in regard to how well they approximate the true structure. If the Hansen-Sargent approach leads eventually to the construction of complete models of the economy, it should be possible to compare these models to models based on the traditional approach.

If because of the limitations just discussed the Hansen-Sargent approach does not lead to econometric models that are good approximations, this does not invalidate Lucas's point (1976). The point is a logical one. If parameters that are taken to be constant change when an exogenous variable is changed, the estimated effects of the change are clearly in error. The key question for any given experiment with an econometric model is the likely size of this error. There are many potential sources of error, and even the best econometric model in the future (as judged, say, by the method in Chapter 8) will be only an approximation to the structure. It may be that for many experiments the error from the Lucas point is quite small. The question is how much the parameters of estimated decision equations, such as consumption and labor supply equations of the household sector, change when a government policy variable changes. For many policy variables and equations these changes may not be very great. The errors in the multipliers that result from not accounting for the parameter changes may be much smaller than, say, the errors that result from aggregation. At any rate, how important the Lucas point is quantitatively is currently an open question.

One encouraging feature regarding the Lucas point is the following. Assume that for an equation or set of equations the parameters change considerably when a given policy variable changes. Assume also that the policy variable changes frequently. In this case the method in Chapter 8 is likely to weed out a model that includes this equation or set of equations. The model is obviously misspecified, and the method should be able to pick up this misspecification if there have been frequent changes in the policy variable. It is thus unlikely that a model that suffers from the Lucas criticism will be accepted as the best approximation of the structure.

One may, of course, still be misled regarding the Lucas point if the policy variable has changed not at all or very little in the past. In this case the model will still be misspecified, but the misspecification has not been given a chance to be picked up in the data. The model may thus be accepted when in fact it is seriously misspecified with respect to the effects of the policy variable on the endogenous variables. One should thus be wary of drawing conclusions about the effects of seldom-changed policy variables unless one has strong reasons for believing that the Lucas point is not quantitatively important for the particular policy variable in question.

2.1.4 The Sims Approach

Another role for theory in the construction of empirical models has been stressed recently by Sims (1980). This role is at the opposite end of the spectrum from that advocated by Hansen and Sargent—namely, it is very limited. Sims does not trust even the exclusionary restrictions imposed by the traditional approach; he argues instead for the specification of vector autoregressive equations, where each variable is specified to be a function of its own lagged values and the lagged values of other variables. (An important early study in this area is that of Phillips 1959.) Although this approach imposes some restrictions on the data—in particular, the number of variables to use, the lengths of the lags, and (sometimes) cross-equation restrictions on the coefficients—the restrictions are in general less restrictive than the exclusionary ones used by the traditional approach.

Although it is again an open question whether Sims's approach will lead to better models, it should be possible to answer this question by comparing models based on this approach to models based on other approaches. Some results that bear on this question are presented in this book. The method in Chapter 8 is used to compare my US model to two vector autoregressive models. The vector autoregressive models are presented in Section 5.2, and the comparison is discussed in Section 8.5.

2.1.5 Long-Run Constraints

In much macroeconomic modeling in which theory is used, various long-run constraints are imposed on the model. Consider, for example, the question of the long-run trade-off between inflation and unemployment. Economists with such diverse views as Tobin and Lucas seem to agree with the Friedman-Phelps proposition that there is no long-run trade-off. (See Tobin 1980, p. 39, and Lucas 1981, p. 560. For the original discussion of the Friedman-Phelps proposition see Friedman 1968 and Phelps 1967.) Accepting this proposition clearly colors the way in which one thinks about macroeconomic issues. Lucas, for example, points out that much of the recent work in macroeconomic theory has been concerned with trying to reconcile this long-run proposition with the observed short-run fluctuations in the economy (1981, p. 561). The imposition of long-run constraints of this type clearly has important effects on the entire modeling exercise, including the modeling of the short run.

Although it is difficult to argue this in the abstract, my feeling is that long-run constraints may be playing too much of a role in recent macroeconomic work. Consider the two possible types of errors associated with a particular constraint. The first is that an incorrect constraint is imposed. This error will lead to a misspecified model, and the misspecification may be large if the constraint has had important effects on the specification of the model and if it is a poor approximation. The second type of error is that a correct constraint is not imposed. Depending on the setup, this type of error may not lead to a misspecified model, but only one in which the coefficient estimates are inefficient. At any rate, it is my feeling that the first type of error may be more serious in practice than the second type, and if this is so, long-run constraints should be imposed with considerable caution. It is not obvious, for example, that the assumption of no long-run trade-off between inflation and unemployment warrants so much confidence that it should be imposed on models, given the severe restrictions that it implies.

This argument about long-run constraints will be made clearer in Section 3.1.6 in the discussion of my theoretical model. Again, however, this issue of the imposition of long-run constraints can be tested (in the long run) by comparing models based on different constraints.

2.1.6 Theoretical Simulation Models

With the growth of computer technology there has been an increase in the number of theoretical models that are analyzed by simulation techniques. The main advantage of using these techniques is that much larger and more complicated models can be specified; one need not be restricted by analytic tractability in the specification of the model. A disadvantage of using the techniques is that the properties of the model may depend on the particular set of parameters and functions chosen for the simulation, and one may get a distorted picture of the properties. Although one can guard against this situation somewhat by performing many experiments with different sets of parameters and functions, simulation results are not a perfect substitute for analytic results.

The relationship between simulation exercises and empirical work is not always clearly understood, and it will be useful to consider this issue. If simulation techniques are merely looked upon as a substitute for analytic techniques when the latter are not feasible to use, then the relationship between simulation exercises and empirical work is no different from the relationship between analytic exercises and empirical work. The results of analyzing theoretical models are used to guide empirical specifications, and it does not matter how the theoretical model is analyzed. An example of the use of simulation techniques in this way is presented in this book. The theoretical model discussed in Chapter 3 is analyzed by simulation techniques, and the results from this model are used to guide the specification of the econometric model in Chapter 4. Had it been feasible to analyze the model in Chapter 3 by analytic techniques, this would have been done, and provided no new insights about the model were gained from this, the econometric specifications in Chapter 4 would have been the same. In this way of looking at the issue, the difference between simulation and analytic techniques is not important: the methodology is really the same in both cases.

Note with respect to empirical work that the type of theoretical simulation model just discussed is not an end in itself; it is merely a stepping-stone to the specification of the equations to be estimated. The data are used in the estimation and analysis of the derived empirical model (derived in a loose sense—see Section 2.2), not in the theoretical model itself. This type of theoretical simulation model is quite different from the type that has come to be used in the field of applied general equilibrium analysis. A good discussion of the methodology of this field is contained in Mansur and Whalley (1981), and it will be useful to review this methodology briefly to make sure there is no confusion between it and the methodology generally followed in macroeconomics.

There are two main steps in the construction of an applied general equilibrium model. The first is to construct for a given period (usually a particular year) a "benchmark equilibrium data set," which is a collection of data in which equilibrium conditions of an assumed underlying equilibrium model are satisfied. Considerable data adjustment is needed in this step because the existing data are generally not detailed enough (and sometimes not conceptually right) for a general equilibrium model. The data, for example, may not be mutually consistent in the sense that the model equilibrium conditions are not satisfied in the data. Most benchmark equilibrium data sets satisfy the following four sets of equilibrium conditions: (1) demand equals supplies for all commodities, (2) nonpositive profits are made in all industries, (3) all domestic agents (including the government) have demands that satisfy their budget constraints, and (4) the economy is in zero external balance. Condition (3) usually involves treating the residual profit return to equity as a contractual cost.

The second step is to choose the functional forms and parameter values for the model. These are chosen in such a way that the model is "calibrated" to the benchmark equilibrium data set. The fundamental assumption involved in this calibration is that the economy is in equilibrium in the particular year. The restriction on the parameter values is that they replicate the "observed equilibrium" as an equilibrium solution of the model. The values are determined by solving the equations that represent the equilibrium conditions of the model, using the data on prices and quantities that characterize the benchmark equilibrium. Depending on the functional forms used, the observed equilibrium may not be sufficient to determine uniquely the parameter values. If the values are not uniquely determined, some of them must be chosen ahead of time (that is, before the model is solved to get the other values). The values chosen ahead of time are generally various elasticities of substitution; they are often chosen by searching the literature for estimated values.

Once the parameters are chosen, the model is ready to be used for policy analysis. Various exogenous variables can be changed, and the model can be solved for these changes. The differences between the solution values and the values in the data set are the estimates of the effects of the policy change. These estimates are general equilibrium estimates in the sense that the entire general equilibrium model is solved to obtain them.

The difference between this second type of theoretical simulation model and the first type should be clear. The second type is an end in itself with respect to empirical work: models of this type are used to make empirical statements. The main problem with this methodology, as is well known by people in the field, is that there is no obvious way of testing whether the model is a good approximation to the truth. The models are not estimated in the usual sense, and there is no way to use a method like the one in Chapter 8 to compare alternative models. Each model fits the data set perfectly, usually with room to spare in the sense that many parameter values are typically chosen ahead of time. This is contrasted with models of the first type, which can be indirectly tested by testing the empirical models that are derived from them (see the discussion in Section 2.3).

It is unclear at this stage whether the applied general equilibrium models will become more like standard econometric models and thus more capable of being tested or whether they will remain in their current "quasi-empirical" state. Whatever the case, the main point for this book is that the methodology followed here is quite different from the methodology currently followed in applied general equilibrium analysis.

2.2 The Transition from Theoretical to Econometric Models

The transition from theoretical models to empirical models is probably the least satisfying aspect of macroeconomic work. One is usually severely constrained by the quantity and quality of the available data, and many restrictive assumptions are generally needed in the transition from the theory to the data. In other words, considerable "theorizing" occurs at this point, and it is usually theory that is much less appealing than that of the purely theoretical model. Many examples of this will be seen in Chapter 4 in the discussion of the transition from the theoretical model in Chapter 3 to the econometric model in Chapter 4. This section contains a general discussion of the steps that are usually followed in the construction of an econometric model.

2.2.1 Step 1: Data Collection and the Choice of Variables and Identities

The first step is to collect the raw data, create the variables of interest from the raw data, and separate the variables into exogenous variables, endogenous variables explained by identities, and endogenous variables explained by stochastic equations. The data should match as closely as possible the variables in the theoretical model. In macroeconomic work this match is usually not very close because of the highly aggregated nature of the macro data. Theoretical models are usually formulated in terms of individual agents (households, firms, and the like), whereas the macro data pertain to entire sectors (household, firm, and the like). There is little that can be done about this problem, and for some it calls into question the usefulness of using theoretical models of individual agents to guide the specification of macroeconometric models. It may be, in other words, that better macroeconometric models can be developed using less micro-based theories. This is an open question, and it is another example of an issue that can be tested in the long run by comparing different models.

There are many special features and limitations of almost any data base that one should be aware of, and one of the most important aspects of macroeconometric work, perhaps the most important, is to know one's data well. Knowledge of how to deal with data comes in part through experience and in part from reading about how others have done it; it is difficult to learn in the abstract. Appendixes A and B of this book provide an example of the collection of the data for my model.

It is important, if possible, to have the data meet the adding-up constraints that were mentioned at the beginning of this chapter. In addition to such obvious things as having the data satisfy income identities, it is useful to have the data satisfy balance-sheet constraints. For the US data, this requires linking the data from the Flow of Funds Accounts to those from the National Income and Product Accounts. This is discussed in Chapter 4 and in Appendix A. The linking of these two data bases is a somewhat tedious task and is a good example of the time-consuming work that is involved in the collection of data.

The data base may be missing observations on variables that are essential for the construction of the model. In such cases, rather than giving up, it may be possible to construct estimates of the missing data. If, for example, the data for a particular variable are annual, whereas quarterly data are needed, it may be possible, using related quarterly variables, to create quarterly data from the annual data by interpolating. There are also more sophisticated procedures for constructing missing observations (see, for example, Chow and Lin 1971). Appendix B provides a number of examples of the construction of missing data for my multicountry model.

Although it is easiest to think of the division of endogenous variables into those determined by stochastic equations and those determined by identities as being done in the first step, the choice of identities is not independent of the choice of explanatory variables in the stochastic equations. If a given explanatory variable is not exogenous and is not determined by a stochastic equation, it must be determined by an identity. It is thus not possible to list all the identities until the stochastic equations are completely specified.

2.2.2 Step 2: Treatment of Unobserved Variables

Most theoretical models contain unobserved variables, and one of the most difficult aspects of the transition to econometric specifications is dealing with these variables. Much of what is referred to as the "ad hoc" nature of macroeconomic modeling occurs at this point. If a theoretical model is explicit about the determinants of the unobserved variables and if the determinants are observed, there is, of course, no real problem. The problem is that many models are not explicit about this, and so "extra" modeling or theorizing is needed at this point.

Expectations

The most common unobserved variables in macroeconomics are expectations. A common practice in empirical work is to assume that expected future values of a variable are a function of the current and past values of the variable. The current and past values of the variable are then used as "proxies" for the expected future values. Given the importance of expectations in most models, it will be useful to consider this procedure in some detail.

Consider first the following example:

$$y_t = \alpha_0 + \alpha_1 E_{t-1} x_{t+1} + u_t, \tag{2.1}$$

where $E_{t-1}x_{t+1}$ is the expected value of x_{t+1} based on information through period $t-1$. A typical assumption is that $E_{t-1}x_{t+1}$ is a function of current and past values of x:

$$E_{t-1}x_{t+1} = \lambda_1 x_t + \lambda_2 x_{t-1} + \ . \ . \ . \ + \lambda_n x_{t-n+1}, \tag{2.2}$$

where it is assumed that x_t is observed at the beginning of period t. Given (2.2), two procedures can be followed to obtain an estimatable equation. One is to substitute (2.2) into (2.1) and simply regress y_t on the current and past values of x. (Other variables can also be used in 2.2 and then substituted into 2.1. If, say, z_t affects $E_{t-1}x_{t+1}$, then z_t would be used as an explanatory variable in the y_t regression.) A priori restrictions on the λ_i coefficients (that is, on the shape of the lag distribution) are sometimes imposed before estimation. Lagged values of time series variables tend to be highly correlated, and it is usually difficult to get estimates of lag distributions that seem sensible without imposing some restrictions. If no restrictions are imposed on the λ_i coefficients, α_1 cannot be identified.

The other procedure is to assume that the lag distribution is geometrically declining, in particular that $\lambda_i = \lambda^i$, $i = 1, \ldots, \infty$. Given this assumption, one can derive the following equation to estimate:

$$(2.3) \qquad y_t = \alpha_0(1-\lambda) + \lambda\alpha_1 x_t + \lambda y_{t-1} + u_t - \lambda u_{t-1}.$$

The coefficient of the lagged dependent variable in this equation, λ, is the coefficient of the lag distribution. It appears both as the coefficient of the lagged dependent variable and as the coefficient of u_{t-1}, and although this restriction should be taken into account in estimation work, it seldom is. Sometimes equations like (2.3) are estimated under the assumption of serial correlation of the error term (that is, an assumption like $v_t = \rho v_{t-1} + \epsilon_t$, where v_t denotes the error term in 2.3), but this is not the correct way of accounting for the λ restriction.

There is a nonexpectational model that leads to an equation similar to (2.3), which is the following simple lagged adjustment model. Let y_t^* be the "desired" value of y_t, and assume that it is a linear function of x_t:

$$(2.4) \qquad y_t^* = \alpha_0 + \alpha_1 x_t.$$

Assume next that y_t only partially adjusts to y_t^* each period, with adjustment coefficient γ:

$$(2.5) \qquad y_t - y_{t-1} = \gamma(y_t^* - y_{t-1}) + u_t.$$

Equations (2.4) and (2.5) can be combined to yield

$$(2.6) \qquad y_t = \lambda\alpha_0 + \lambda\alpha_1 x_t + (1-\gamma)y_{t-1} + u_t.$$

Equation (2.6) is in the same form as (2.3) except for the restriction on the error term in (2.3). As noted earlier, the restriction on the error term in (2.3) is usually ignored, which means that in practice there is little attempt to distinguish between the expectations model and the lagged adjustment model. It may be for most problems that the data are not capable of distinguishing between the two models. The problem of distinguishing between the two is particularly difficult if the u_t error terms in (2.1) and (2.5) are assumed to be serially correlated, because in this case the differences in the properties of the error terms in the derived equations (2.3) and (2.6) are fairly subtle. At any rate, it is usually the case that no attempt is made to distinguish between the expectations model and the lagged adjustment model.

Two other points about (2.3) should be noted. First, if there is another variable in the equation, say z_t, the implicit assumption that is being made when this equation is estimated is that the expectations of z are formed using the same coefficient λ that is used in forming the expectations of x. In other words, the shape of the two lag distributions is assumed to be the same. This may be, of course, a very restrictive assumption. Second, if there is another future expected value of x in (2.1), say $\alpha_2 E_{t-1}x_{t+2}$, and if this expectation is generated as

$$(2.7) \qquad E_{t-1}x_{t+2} = \lambda E_{t-1}x_{t+1} + \lambda^2 x_t + \lambda^3 x_{t-1} + \ . \ . \ . \ ,$$

then (2.3) is unchanged except for a different interpretation of the coefficient of x_t. The coefficient in this case is $\lambda(\alpha_1 + 2\alpha_2\lambda)$ instead of $\lambda\alpha_1$. The same equation would be estimated in this case, although it is not possible to identify α_1 and α_2.

It should be clear that this treatment of expectations is somewhat unsatisfying. Agents may look at more than merely the current and past values of a variable in forming an expectation of it, and even if they do not, the shapes of the lag distributions may be quite different from the shapes usually imposed in econometric work. The treatment of expectations is clearly an important area for future work. An alternative treatment to the one just presented is the assumption that expectations are rational. This means that agents form expectations by first forming expectations of the exogenous variables (in some manner that must be specified) and then solving the model using these expectations. The predicted values of the endogenous variables from this solution are the expected values. The assumption of rational expectations poses a number of difficult computational problems when one is dealing with large-scale nonlinear models, but many of these problems are now capable of solution. Chapter 11 discusses the solution and estimation of rational expectations models.

It is by no means obvious that the assumption that expectations are rational is a good approximation to the way that expectations are actually formed. The assumption implies that agents know the model, and this may not be realistic for many agents. It would be nice to test assumptions that are in between the simple assumption that expectations of a variable are a function of its current and past values and the assumption that expectations are rational. One possibility is to assume that expectations of a variable are a function not only of its current and past values but also of the current and past values of other variables. To implement this, the variable in question could be regressed on a set of variables and the predicted values from this regression taken to be the expected values. In other words, one could estimate a small model of how expectations are formed before estimating the basic model. Expectations are not rational in this case because they are not predictions from the basic model, but they are based on more information than merely the current and past values of one variable. An example of the use of this assumption is presented in Section 4.1.3. Although, as will be seen, this application was not successful, there is clearly room for more tests of this kind.

Other Unobserved Variables

In models in which disequilibrium is a possibility, there is sometimes a distinction between "unconstrained" and "constrained" (or "notional" and "actual") decisions. An unconstrained decision is one that an agent would make if there were no constraints on its decision variables other than the standard budget constraints. A constrained decision is one in which other constraints are imposed; it is also the actual decision. In the model in Chapter 3, for example, which does allow for the possibility of disequilibrium, a household may be constrained in how much it can work. A household's unconstrained consumption decision is the amount it would consume if the constraint were not binding, and the constrained decision is the amount it actually chooses to consume given the constraint. In models of this type the unconstrained decisions are observed only if the constraints are not binding, and so this is another example of the existence of unobserved variables. The treatment of these variables is a difficult problem in empirical work, and it is also a problem for which no standard procedure exists. The way in which the variables are handled in my model is discussed in Section 4.1.3.

2.2.3 Step 3: Specification of the Stochastic Equations

The next step is to specify the stochastic equations, that is, to write down the equations to be estimated. Since the stochastic equations are the key part of any econometric model, this step is of crucial importance. If theory has not indicated the functional forms and lag lengths of the equations, a number of versions of each equation may be written down to be tried, the different versions corresponding to different functional forms and lag lengths. If the theoretical approach is the traditional one, theory has presumably chosen the LHS and RHS variables. The specification of the stochastic equations also relies on the treatment of the unobserved variables from step 2; the extra theorizing in step 2 also guides the choice of the RHS variables.

Theory generally has little to say about the stochastic features of the model, that is, about where and how the error terms enter the equations. The most common procedure is merely to add an error term to each stochastic equation. This is usually done regardless of the functional form of the equation. For example, the term $+ u_{it}$ would be added to equation i regardless of whether the equation were in linear or logarithmic form. If the equation is in log form, this treatment implies that the error term affects the level of the LHS variable multiplicatively. This somewhat cavalier treatment of error terms is generally done for convenience; it is another example of an unsatisfying aspect of the transition to econometric models, although it is probably not as serious as most of the other problems.

2.2.4 Step 4: Estimation

Once the equations of a model have been written down in a form that can be estimated, the next step is to estimate them. Much experimentation usually takes place at this step. Different functional forms and lag lengths are tried, and RHS variables are dropped if they have coefficient estimates of the wrong expected sign. Variables with coefficient estimates of the right sign may also be dropped if the estimates have *t*-statistics that are less than about two in absolute value, although practice varies on this.

If at this step things are not working out very well in the sense that very few significant coefficient estimates of the correct sign are being obtained, one may go back and rethink the theory or the transition from the theory to the estimated equations. This process may lead to new equations to try and perhaps to better results. This back-and-forth movement between theory and results can be an important part of the empirical work.

The initial estimation technique that is used is usually a limited information technique, such as 2SLS. These techniques have the advantage that one can experiment with a particular equation without worrying very much about the other equations in the model. Knowledge of the general features of the other equations is used in the choice of the first-stage regressors (FSRs) for the 2SLS technique, for example, but one does not need to know the exact features of each equation when making this choice. If a full information technique is used, it is usually used at the end of the search process to estimate the final version of the model. If the full information estimates are quite different from the limited information ones, it may again be necessary to go back and rethink the theory and the transition. In particular, this may indicate that the version of the model that has been chosen by the limited information searching is seriously misspecified.

Sometimes ordinary least squares (OLS) is used in the searching process even though the model is simultaneous. This is a cheap but risky method. Because the OLS estimates are inconsistent, one may be led to a version of the model that is seriously misspecified. This problem presumably will be caught when a consistent limited information or full information technique is used, at which point one will be forced to go back and search using the consistent limited information technique. It seems better merely to begin with the latter in the first place and eliminate this potential problem. The extra cost involved in using, say, 2SLS over OLS is small.

2.2.5 Step 5: Testing and Analysis

The next step after the model has been estimated is to test and analyze it. This step, it seems to me, is the one that has been the most neglected in macroeconomic research. Procedures for testing and analyzing models are discussed in Chapters 7–10; they will not be discussed here except to note the two that have been most commonly used. First, the principal way that models have been tested in the past is by computing predicted values from deterministic simulations, where the accuracy of the predictions is usually examined by calculating root mean squared errors (Sections 8.2 and 8.3). Second, the main way that the properties of models have been examined is by computing multipliers from deterministic simulations (Section 9.2). As will be seen, both of these procedures, especially the first, are subject to criticism.

It may also be the case that things are not working out very well at this testing and analysis step. Poor fits may be obtained, and multipliers that seem (according to one's a priori views) too large or too small may also be obtained. This may also lead one to rethink the theory, the transition, or both, and perhaps to try alternative specifications. In other words, the back-and-forth movement between theory and results may occur at both the estimation and analysis steps.

2.2.6 General Remarks

The back-and-forth movement between theory and results may yield a model that fits the data well and seems on other grounds to be quite good, when it is in fact a poor approximation to the structure. If one searches hard enough, it is usually possible with macro time series data to come up with what seems to be a good model. The searching for models in this way is sometimes called "data mining" and sometimes "specification searches," depending on one's mood. A number of examples of this type of searching are presented in Chapter 4. Fortunately, there is a way of testing whether one has mined the data in an inappropriate way, which is to do outside sample tests. If a model is poorly specified, it should not fit well outside of the sample period for which it was estimated, even though it looks good within sample. It is thus possible to test for misspecification by examining outside sample results, and this is what the method in Chapter 8 does in testing for misspecification. (There is, however, a subtle form of data mining that even the method in Chapter 8 cannot account for. This is discussed in Section 8.4.5.)

Because of the dropping of variables with wrong signs and (possibly) the back-and-forth movement from multiplier results to theory, an econometric model is likely to have multiplier properties that are similar to what one expects from the theory. Therefore, the fact that an econometric model has properties that are consistent with the theory is in no way a confirmation of the model. Models must be tested using methods like the one in Chapter 8, not by examining the "reasonableness" of their multiplier properties.

It should also be emphasized that in many cases the data may not contain enough information to decide a particular issue. If, for example, tax rates have not been changed very much over the sample period, it may not be possible to discriminate between quite different hypotheses regarding the effects of tax rate changes on behavior. It may also be difficult to discriminate between different functional forms for an equation, such as linear versus logarithmic. In Chapter 4 a number of examples are presented of the inability to discriminate between alternative hypotheses. When this happens there is little that one can do about it except to wait for more data and be cautious about making policy recommendations that are sensitive to the different hypotheses.

2.3 Testing Theoretical Models

This is a good time to consider the second methodological question mentioned in Chapter 1, namely, what do econometric results have to say about the validity of theories? It should be clear by now that transitions from theoretical models to econometric models are typically not very tight. It may be that more than one theoretical model is consistent with a given econometric model. If this is so, then finding out that an econometric model is, say, the best approximation among all econometric models is not necessarily a finding that a particular theory that is consistent with the model is valid. One may thus be forced to make weaker conclusions about theoretical models than about econometric models.

If it is possible to test the assumptions of a theoretical model directly, it may not be the case that one is forced to make weaker conclusions about theoretical models. The problem in macroeconomics is that very few assumptions seem capable of direct tests. Part of the problem is the aggregation; it is not really possible to test directly assumptions about, say, the way an entire sector chooses its decision variables. A related problem is that many macroeconomic assumptions pertain to the way in which agents interact with each other, and these assumptions are difficult to test in isolation. Assumptions about expectations are also difficult or impossible to test directly because expectations are generally not observed. Even if expectations were observed, however, it would not be possible to test the rational expectations assumption directly. In this case one needs a complete model to test the assumption. One is thus forced in macroeconomics to rely primarily on testing theories by testing econometric models that are derived (however loosely) from them. This procedure of testing theories by testing their implications rather than their assumptions is Friedman's view (1953) about the way theories should be tested. One does not, however, have to subscribe to Friedman's view about economic testing in general in order to believe that it holds for macroeconomics. Macroeconomic theories are tested indirectly not always out of choice, but out of necessity.

Given the indirect testing of theories and the sometimes loose transitions from theories to empirical specifications, it is not clear that one ought to talk in macroeconomics about theories being "true" or "false." Macroeconomics is not like physics, where on average theories are linked more closely to empirical tests. I have suggested (Fair 1974d) that it may be better in macroeconomics to talk about theories being "useful" or "not useful." A theory is useful if it aids in the specification of empirical relationships that one would not already have thought of from a simpler theory and that turn out to be good approximations. Otherwise, it is not useful. Although how one wants to label theories is a semantic question, the terms "useful" and "not useful" do highlight the fact that theories in macroeconomics are not as closely linked to empirical tests as are many theories in physics.

2.4 Expected Quality of Macroeconometric Models in the Long Run

An interesting question is how good one expects macroeconometric models to be in the long run, say in twenty or thirty years. It may be that behavior is so erratic and things like aggregation problems so severe that no model will be very good. This will show up in large estimated variances of prediction errors by the method in Chapter 8 and probably in large estimates of the degree of misspecification. Another way of stating this is that the structure of the economy may be too unstable or our potential ability to approximate closely a stable structure too poor to lead to accurate models. If this is true, models will never be of much use for policy purposes. They may be of limited use for short-run forecasting, but even here probably only in conjunction with subjective adjustments.

My research is obviously based on the premise that there is enough structural stability to warrant further work on trying to approximate the structure of the economy well. This is, of course, a premise that can only be verified or refuted in the long run, and there is little more that can be said about it now. It is interesting to note that the extensive use of subjective adjustments by the commercial model builders and their lack of much scientific research on the models may indicate lack of confidence in a stable structure.

It is also interesting to note, as mentioned in Chapter 1, that the lack of confidence in large-scale models has led to research on much smaller ones. In one sense this may be a reasonable reaction, and in another sense not. If the lack of confidence is a lack of confidence in a stable structure, the reaction does not seem sensible. It seems quite unlikely that the structure would be unstable in such a way as to lead small models to approximate it less poorly than large models. One should instead just give up the game and do something else. If, on the other hand, the lack of confidence in large-scale models is a feeling that they have gone in wrong directions, it may be sensible to back up for a while. In this case the premise is still that the structure is stable, and the issue is merely how best to proceed to try to approximate it well.

2.5 Nonlinear Optimization Algorithms

It may seem odd to put a section on nonlinear optimization algorithms in a chapter on macroeconomic methodology, but the solution of nonlinear optimization problems is an important feature of current macroeconomic research. In this book the following problems arise. (1) In the theoretical model in Chapter 3 the decisions of the agents are based on the solutions of nonlinear multiperiod maximization problems. (2) The estimation techniques discussed in Chapter 6 require the solution of nonlinear optimization problems. (3) The optimal control problems discussed in Chapter 10 are set up as standard nonlinear maximization problems. (4) The estimation of rational expectations models discussed in Chapter 11 requires the solution of a nonlinear maximization problem.

For many nonlinear optimization problems, general-purpose algorithms are sufficient. One of the most commonly used is the Davidon-Fletcher-Powell (DFP) algorithm, which is discussed later in this section. For a number of problems, however, general-purpose algorithms do not work or do not work very well, and for these problems special-purpose algorithms must be written. As discussed in Section 6.5.2, the DFP algorithm does not seem to work for moderate to large FIML and 3SLS estimation problems. These problems must instead be solved using an algorithm designed particularly for them, the Parke algorithm. The other problems in this book for which special-purpose algorithms were written are the least absolute deviations (LAD) and two-stage least absolute deviations (2SLAD) estimation problems in Section 6.5.4 and the multiperiod maximization problems in Sections 3.1.2 and 3.1.3. The DFP algorithm does not work for the LAD and 2SLAD problems, and it was not tried for the multiperiod maximization problems because it seemed likely to be too expensive.

When general-purpose algorithms are used, it is not really necessary to know how they find the optimum as long as they do. They can, in other words, be treated as black boxes as long as things are going well. If the algorithms are not working well, knowledge of what they are trying to do may help either in modifying them for the particular problem or in designing new algorithms. In the remainder of this section a brief explanation of the DFP algorithm will be presented.

Consider the problem of minimizing $f(x)$ with respect to the elements of the $n \times 1$ vector $x = (x_1, x_2, \ldots, x_n)'$. (The problem of maximizing $f(x)$ is merely the problem of minimizing $-f(x)$.) The function f is assumed to be twice continuously differentiable. Approximating $f(x)$ by a second-order Taylor series about some point x^0 yields

$$f(x) \approx f(x^0) + g(x^0)'(x - x^0) + \frac{1}{2}(x - x^0)'G(x^0)(x - x^0), \tag{2.8}$$

where $g(x^0)$ is the $n \times 1$ vector of the gradient of $f(x)$ evaluated at x^0 and $G(x^0)$ is the $n \times n$ matrix of the second derivatives of $f(x)$ evaluated at x^0.

Minimizing the RHS of (2.8) by setting the partial derivatives with respect to x equal to zero yields

$$g(x^0) + G(x^0)(x - x^0) = 0 \tag{2.9}$$

or

$$x = x^0 - [G(x^0)]^{-1}g(x^0). \tag{2.10}$$

Equation (2.10) forms the basis for many algorithms. Letting x^k denote the value of x on the kth iteration, one can iterate using (2.10):

$$x^k = x^{k-1} - [G(x^{k-1})]^{-1}g(x^{k-1}), \tag{2.11}$$

where some initial guess is used for x^0. If (2.11) is used exactly, the algorithm is called Newton's method, or Newton-Raphson's method. The matrix $[G(x^{k-1})]^{-1}$ is called the Hessian matrix.

Newton's method can be expensive because it requires calculating the Hessian matrix at each iteration, and much of the recent work in this area has been concerned with algorithms that do not require this calculation. The general formula for many of these algorithms can be written

$$x^k = x^{k-1} - \lambda^{k-1}H^{k-1}g(x^{k-1}), \tag{2.12}$$

where H^{k-1} is an $n \times n$ matrix and λ^{k-1} is a scalar. Algorithms based on (2.12) do two things at each iteration: (1) they choose a search direction $H^{k-1}g(x^{k-1})$, and (2) they choose a value for λ^{k-1} by carrying out a line search in this direction. (Newton's method is, of course, one of these algorithms, where $H^{k-1} = [G(x^{k-1})]^{-1}$ and $\lambda^{k-1} = 1$.) After the direction is chosen, the line search usually consists of fitting a second-degree polynomial to three points along the direction and then minimizing the resulting polynomial.

The algorithms differ in their choice of search directions. The DFP algorithm, which is of primary concern here, is a member of a class of methods called "matrix-updating" methods. Other names for this class include "quasi-Newton" and "variable metric." These methods never compute the Hessian, but instead build up an approximation to it during the iterative process by successive additions of low-rank matrices. The updating equation for the DFP algorithm is

$$H^0 = I, \tag{2.13}$$

$$H^{k-1} = H^{k-2} + \frac{\delta\delta'}{\delta'\gamma} - \frac{H^{k-2}\gamma(H^{k-2}\gamma)'}{\gamma' H^{k-2}\gamma}, \qquad k = 2, 3, \ldots,$$

where $\delta = x^{k-1} - x^{k-2}$ and $\gamma = g(x^{k-1}) - g(x^{k-2})$. There are a number of ways to motivate (2.13), but to do so here would take us too far afield; the interested reader is referred to Huang (1970) and Dennis and More (1977). (The original discussion of the DFP algorithm is contained in Davidon 1959 and Fletcher and Powell 1963.) It can be shown that if f is quadratic and if accurate line search is used, $H^n = G^{-1}$, where n is the dimension of x. Note that although algorithms like DFP do not require the computation of second derivatives, they do require the computation of first derivatives.

Another update that is sometimes used is

$$(2.14) \qquad H^0 = I,$$

$$H^{k-1} = H^{k-2} + \frac{\delta\delta'}{\delta'\gamma}\left(1 + \frac{\gamma' H^{k-2}\gamma}{\delta'\gamma}\right) - \frac{\delta\gamma' H^{k-2} + H^{k-2}\gamma\delta'}{\delta'\gamma}, \qquad k = 2, 3, \ldots,$$

where δ and γ are as above. This algorithm is called the Broyden-Fletcher-Goldfarb-Shanno (BFGS) algorithm. (See Dennis and More 1977 for references.) Once a program for the DFP algorithm has been written, the extra coding for the BFGS algorithm is small, and therefore many nonlinear optimization packages offer a choice of both the DFP and BFGS updating equations. My experience is that it generally does not make much difference which of the two updating equations is used. An example of the use of the two algorithms is reported in Section 10.4.

Another option that is sometimes available in nonlinear optimization packages is the method of steepest descent. This method simply uses $H^{k-1} = I$ for all k. It has very slow convergence properties, and it is not in general recommended.

The DFP algorithm has turned out to work well for many problems, and it is widely used. It does not, however, by any means dominate all other algorithms for all problems. There are also many problems for which it does not work in the sense that it does not find the optimum. My experience with the DFP algorithm is mixed but on the whole is fairly good. It has worked extremely well for the solution of optimal control problems, where in one case it was used to solve a problem of 239 unknowns (that is, $n = 239$). These results are reported in an earlier paper (Fair 1974a), where it can be seen that DFP easily dominated two other algorithms, one that required no derivatives (Powell's no-derivative algorithm; Powell 1964) and one that required both first and second derivatives (the quadratic hill-climbing algorithm of Goldfeld, Quandt, and Trotter 1966). The solution of optimal control problems in this way is discussed in Section 10.2.

As noted earlier, DFP does not work for moderate to large FIML and 3SLS estimation problems, which seem to require special-purpose algorithms like the Parke algorithm. It also does not work for the minimization problem associated with the LAD and 2SLAD estimators. I have found it to work fairly well for the OLS or 2SLS estimation of a single equation that is nonlinear in coefficients.

My general strategy for dealing with nonlinear optimization problems is the following. If I choose to obtain and code analytic first derivatives, which is usually not the case, I merely solve the first-order conditions using the Gauss-Seidel technique (discussed in Section 7.2). In other words, I solve the equation system

(2.15) $g(x) = 0$

using Gauss-Seidel. I have had very good success with the Gauss-Seidel technique (with damping sometimes required), and the procedure of solving (2.15) avoids having to use any optimization algorithm. If first derivatives are instead computed numerically, then I usually begin with the DFP algorithm and only try other procedures if this does not work.

When first derivatives are computed numerically, they can be either "one-sided" or "two-sided." Consider the derivative of f with respect to x_1. One-sided derivatives are computed as $[f(x_1 + \epsilon, x_2, \ldots, x_n) - f(x_1, x_2, \ldots, x_n)]/\epsilon$, where ϵ is a small number. Two-sided derivatives are computed as $[f(x_1 + \epsilon, x_2, \ldots, x_n) - f(x_1 - \epsilon, x_2, \ldots, x_n)]/2\epsilon$. Since $f(x_1, x_2, \ldots, x_n)$ is available at the time the derivatives are computed, one-sided derivatives require only one function evaluation per unknown, whereas two-sided derivatives require two. Both one-sided and two-sided derivatives were used for the results of solving the optimal control problems in Fair (1974a), and these results indicate that two-sided derivatives are not worth the extra cost. Little or no change in the number of iterations needed for convergence was obtained by the use of the two-sided derivatives. For the optimal control results in Chapter 10, on the other hand, slightly more accurate answers were obtained using two-sided derivatives, because the stopping criterion that was used for the Gauss-Seidel technique in solving the model was not small enough to allow highly accurate one-sided derivatives to be computed. This example is discussed in Section 10.4.

Note that the use of the DFP algorithm in conjunction with numerical derivatives requires very little work to set up the problem. One merely needs to write a program (a subroutine when using FORTRAN) to compute f for a given value of x. Once this is done, the DFP algorithm merely calls this program many times in the iterative process. Each iteration requires n calls for the derivatives plus a few more for the line search. The calculations for each iteration other than the calculations involved in computing the function are generally very minor, so most of the computer time is taken in computing the function values. The estimates in Fair (1974a) for the one-sided derivative results show that this time is between 78 and 97 percent of the total time. For two-sided derivatives the percentages are even higher. It is thus important to code the function program efficiently. If numerical derivatives are used, it is easy to see why methods that require the calculation of second derivatives are likely to be expensive: $(n^2 + n)/2$ evaluations of the function are needed to calculate the second-derivative matrix, and for large n this is obviously expensive.

For purposes of the Fair-Parke program, I have coded the DFP and BFGS algorithms from scratch. The coding is straightforward except for the line search, which was coded as follows. (1) $\lambda = 1$ is tried. If this results in an improvement (a lower value of $f(x)$ than that of the previous iteration), $\lambda = 1.25$ is tried. If this results in an improvement, $\lambda = (1.25)^2$ is tried, and so on through $\lambda = (1.25)^9$. At the point of no improvement or at $\lambda = (1.25)^9$, a quadratic is fit to the three points $.8\lambda_s$, λ_s, and $1.2\lambda_s$, where λ_s is either the last value of λ that resulted in an improvement or $(1.25)^9$. The quadratic is minimized. The function is then evaluated for $\lambda = \lambda^*$, where λ^* is the minimizing value. A second quadratic is then fit to the three points $.95\lambda_{ss}$, λ_{ss}, and $1.05\lambda_{ss}$, where λ_{ss} is either $.8\lambda_s$, λ_s, $1.2\lambda_s$, or λ^*, depending on which one has yielded the smallest value of the function. This quadratic is minimized, and the function is evaluated for $\lambda = \lambda^{**}$, where λ^{**} is the minimizing value. The final value of λ is then taken to be $.95\lambda_{ss}$, λ_{ss}, $1.05\lambda_{ss}$, or λ^{**}, depending on which one yielded the smallest value of the function. (2) If $\lambda = 1$ does not result in an improvement, $\lambda = .5$ is tried. If this does not result in an improvement, $\lambda = (.5)^2$ is tried, and so on through $\lambda = (.5)^9$. At the point of improvement or at $\lambda = (.5)^9$, the quadratic fitting discussed in (1) is done.

The algorithm is stopped for one of five reasons: (1) no improvement is found for any value of λ tried at the current iteration; (2) the prescribed maximum number of iterations is reached; (3) the successive estimates of x are within some prescribed tolerance level; (4) at the current iteration the gradient values as a percentage of the respective x values are less than some prescribed tolerance level in absolute value; or (5) the improvement in the function from one iteration to the next is within some prescribed tolerance level.

There is nothing subtle or sophisticated about this code, but it seems to work quite well for the types of problems I have dealt with. It may be that one could get by with fewer function evaluations for the line search (there is now a maximum of sixteen per iteration), but for problems with a large number of unknowns, these function evaluations are a small percentage of the function evaluations required to get the derivatives. With respect to the derivatives, the user has the option of deciding whether to use one-sided or two-sided derivatives and what step size to use.

3 A Theoretical Model

3.1 The Single-Country Model

The purpose of this chapter is to discuss the theoretical model that has guided my empirical work. The single-country model is discussed in this section, and then the model is expanded to two countries in Section 3.2. As noted in Section 2.1.6, the model is a simulation model in the sense that its properties are analyzed using simulation techniques. It should be repeated, however, that the model is not a simulation model of the kind that is used in applied general equilibrium analysis. The simulation results are only meant to be used to learn about the qualitative properties of the model; no significance is attached to the size of any of the effects. Knowledge of the qualitative properties of the model is used to guide the econometric specifications in Chapter 4. For ease of reference, the symbols for the variables in the model are listed in alphabetical order in Table 3-1.

3.1.1. Introduction

Nature of the Model

The model is an attempt to integrate three main ideas. The first is that macroeconomics should be based on better microeconomic foundations. In particular, macroeconomics should be consistent with the view that decisions are made by maximizing objective functions. The second idea is that macroeconomic theory should allow for the possibility of disequilibrium in some markets. The third, and perhaps somewhat less important, idea is that a model should account explicitly for balance-sheet and flow-of-funds constraints.

Relation to Previous Work

The implications of the first two ideas have generally been worked on together, beginning with the work of Patinkin (1956, chap. 13) and Clower (1965). Studies that have followed these two include Leijonhufvud (1968,

TABLE 3-1. The variables in the theoretical model in alphabetical order

Subscripts:

b	bank
f	firm
g	government
h	household
i	machine of type i (i = 1, ..., M)
k	firm
p	private (sum of b, f, k, and h)
t	time period
m	number of periods a machine lasts

Symbols:

A	end-of-period assets (+) or liabilities (-)
BO	bank borrowing from the monetary authority
BR	bank reserves
C	consumption
CF	cash flow
CG	capital gain or loss
D	dividends
d_1	personal income tax rate
d_2	profit tax rate
DEP	depreciation
e	exchange rate (spot)
F	forward exchange rate
g_1	reserve requirement rate
I	total investment in units of goods
IM	investment in units of the number of machines of the given type
K	actual number of machines of the given type on hand
KH	machine-hour requirements
KMIN	minimum number of machines of the given type required to produce the output
L	labor supplied or demanded
LA	aggregate constrained supply of labor to the firms
LAUN	aggregate unconstrained supply of labor to the firms
L^*	labor constraint
LL'	labor requirements
LMAX	maximum amount of labor to employ
LMIN	minimum amount of labor required to produce the output
LUN	aggregate unconstrained supply of labor to the firms and the government
M	money holdings
N	amount of time spent taking care of money holdings
P	price level
P'	price of investment goods
$\overline{P}$	average price
PS	value of stocks
Q	international reserve
R	interest rate
RD	discount rate
S	savings
T	taxes
T'	taxes due to fluctuations in the work force
TH	total number of hours in the period
TR	transfer payments
U	utility
UR	unemployment rate
V	stock of inventories, end of period
W	wage rate
$\overline{W}$	average wage rate
X	sales
XA	aggregate demand for goods
Y	total production for firms, taxable income for households
YY	production on machines of the given type
Π	profits

1973), Tucker (1968, 1971a, 1971b), Barro and Grossman (1971, 1976), and Grossman (1971, 1972a, 1972b). (Two related studies are Solow and Stiglitz 1968 and Korliras 1972, although the models developed in these papers are not constructed on a choice-theoretic basis and so are not concerned with the first idea.) This work has provided a more solid theoretical basis for the existence of the Keynesian consumption function and for the existence of unemployment; it has thus made the standard, textbook Keynesian theory somewhat less ad hoc. The existence of excess supply in the labor market is a justification for including income as an explanatory variable in the consumption function, and the existence of excess supply in the commodity market is a justification for the existence of unemployment.

The main problem with these disequilibrium studies is that they have not provided an explanation of why it is that prices and wages may not always clear markets. Prices and wages are either taken to be exogenous or are determined in an ad hoc manner. This is particularly restrictive in a disequilibrium context, since one of the key questions in this area is why there are market failures. Barro and Grossman are quite explicit in their book about this problem: "We provide no choice-theoretic analysis of the market-clearing process itself. In other words, we do not analyze the adjustment of wages and prices as part of the maximizing behavior of firms and households. Consequently, we do not really explain the failure of markets to clear, and our analyses of wage and price dynamics are based on ad hoc adjustment equations" (1976, p. 6).

This problem has persisted in the related work on fixed price equilibria (see Grandmont 1977 for a survey of this work). In a discussion of some of this work, for example, Malinvaud states: "A dynamic theory that would correctly describe the successive adjustments [of prices and wages] occurring in the real world is still more difficult to build than a long-run equilibrium theory under short-run rationing. At the present stage in the development of economic theory, one cannot expect to do more than provide a model of the first few steps of the dynamic adjustments initiated by demand pressures in the markets for goods and labour and by unwanted inventories, excess capacities or unemployment" (1977, pp. 101–102).

My model does provide a choice-theoretic explanation of market failures. The explanation is based on two postulates, both of which draw heavily on the studies in Phelps et al. (1970) and related work, which in turn have been influenced by Stigler's classic article (1961) on imperfect information and search. The first postulate is that firms have a certain amount of monopoly power in the short run in the sense that raising their prices above prices charged by other firms does not result in an immediate loss of all their customers, and lowering their prices below prices charged by other firms does not result in an immediate gain of everyone else's customers. There is, however, a tendency for high-price firms to lose customers over time and for low-price firms to gain customers. A similar statement holds for wages. This postulate can be justified on the basis of imperfect information about prices and wages on the part of customers and workers. The second postulate is that prices and wages are decision variables of firms, and firms choose these variables (along with others) in a profit-maximizing context.

If a firm's market share is a function of its price relative to the prices of other firms, then a firm's optimal price strategy is a function of this relationship. Models of this type have been developed by Phelps and Winter (1970) and Maccini (1972) for prices and by Phelps (1970) and Mortensen (1970) for wages. My model expands on this work by considering the price and wage decisions together (along with other decisions) and by assuming that firms expect that the future prices and wages of other firms are in part a function of their own past prices and wages.

It should be clear that disequilibrium can occur in models of this type. In the Phelps and Winter model, for example, disequilibrium occurs if the average price set by firms differs from the expected average price (1970, p. 335). In my model, as will be seen, disequilibrium also occurs because of expectation errors. The difference is that expectation errors in my model have much wider effects. In the Phelps and Winter model there is a straightforward way in which the system returns to equilibrium, whereas this is not true in my case. This is, I believe, an important difference between models of the Phelps and Winter type and more general models, something that will be stressed later. If the effects of expectation errors spill over into other markets, the effects of shocks and errors may be much more serious (larger and longer) than would seem to be implied by models of the Phelps and Winter type.

With respect to the previous literature, it is surprising that the studies in Phelps et al. (1970) and related work have had no impact on the work on fixed price equilibria, given the admittedly restrictive assumption of fixed prices or ad hoc price determination in the latter. In a 1980 study Malinvaud argues against the view that "price and wage changes are decided by firms as a rational reaction to the situation confronting them" (1980, p. 52). He argues that by following this approach "we may be fairly certain that we shall end up with a very partial representation of the real world; the representation will be so partial that the adequacy of the derived dynamic specification will be quite doubtful" (p. 53). This view seems so far to have prevailed in the fixed price equilibria literature. My view is obviously contrary to this: the linking of the Phelps et al. work to the disequilibrium models does seem to me to be an appealing way to close the disequilibrium models. At any rate, one should be able to test this in the long run by comparing models based on this idea with other models.

With regard to the third idea (the accounting for balance-sheet and flow-of-funds constraints), one of the main advantages of doing this is that it means that the government budget constraint is automatically accounted for. Christ (1968), among others, has emphasized this constraint. Accounting explicitly for balance-sheet constraints also means that it is easier to keep track of wealth effects.

I was also concerned with making the model general enough to include the main variables of interest in a macroeconomic context. The endogenous variables include sales, production, employment, investment, prices, wages, interest rates, and financial assets and liabilities. Previous disequilibrium models have not been this general.

A weakness of the model is that search has not been treated as a decision variable of any agent. As noted earlier, the existence of imperfect information and search can be used to justify the short-run monopoly power of firms with respect to prices and wages. It is thus a weakness of the model not to explain search and thus derive the degree of monopoly power of the firms. A much more complicated model would be needed to treat search as endogenous, and this has not been attempted.

Treatment of Expectations

Since the treatment of expectations is critical in any macro model, it will be useful to explain at the beginning how expectations have been handled. Individual agents in the model are assumed to form their expectations on the basis of a limited set of information. Agents do not know the complete model, and their expectations are in general different from the model's predictions. Expectations, in other words, are not rational. (The simulation model is deterministic, so "rational expectations" in this case means perfect foresight.) The nonrationality of expectations leads to expectation errors, which in turn lead to the system being in disequilibrium.

Another feature regarding expectations should be noted: expectations are assumed to be treated with certainty by the individual agents. In other words, agents ignore the fact that their expectations are uncertain when solving their optimization problems. The variables that are stochastic from the point of view of the individual agent are replaced with their expected values before the optimization problem is solved. Although this "certainty equivalent" treatment is only correct for linear models, it has been used here even though the models facing the individual agents are nonlinear. This is a common procedure in the optimal control literature (see, for example, Athans 1972), and it may provide a reasonable approximation in many cases. It does, however, rule out potentially important effects of uncertainty on decisions.

Treatment of Different Kinds of Financial Securities

The model treats different kinds of financial securities in a fairly simple way. The financial assets of households include demand deposits in banks, which will be called "money"; corporate stocks; and an all-other category, which will be called "bonds." The bonds are one-period securities. The expected one-period rate of return on bonds and stocks is assumed to be the same, and thus households are indifferent as to whether they hold bonds or stocks. Households have no financial liabilities. Firms have financial assets in the form of demand deposits and financial liabilities in the form of bonds. The government has financial assets in the form of bank borrowing; its liabilities consist of bonds and bank reserves. The liabilities of banks are demand deposits and borrowing from the government; their assets are bonds and bank reserves.

Comparison to the "Pitfalls" Approach of Brainard and Tobin

Because of the assumption that the expected one-period rate of return on bonds and stocks is the same, there are really only two securities in the model with respect to the maximization problem of households: bonds-stocks and money. This treatment ignores the main thrust of the "pitfalls" approach of Brainard and Tobin (1968). (Tobin's 1982 Nobel lecture provides a good review of this approach.) Brainard and Tobin stress the lack of perfect substitutability of different securities and develop a model for explaining the different rates of return on different securities.

There is little doubt that there is lack of perfect substitutability among many securities in the real world, and thus the pitfalls approach has considerable appeal. There are at present, however, some costs to adopting the approach, and it is an open question whether the potential gains are greater than these costs. The general strategy of the pitfalls approach has been to regard income account variables as exogenous for balance sheet behavior, and although this assumption can be relaxed, it is not trivial to do so given the basic strategy. It is also not easy within the approach to account for the effects of expected future short-term rates on current long-term rates and for the effects of expected future dividends on current stock prices. There is also a practical difficulty in trying to estimate pitfalls models. Different interest rates are highly collinear (because there is considerable substitutability among different securities, even though possibly not perfect substitutability), and it is difficult to get precise estimates of the effects of interest rate differences on security holdings. (See, for example, Smith and Brainard 1976, who attempt to get around this problem by the use of a Bayesian procedure.) It may be that the degree to which different securities are not perfect substitutes is too small to be capable of being picked up with the use of macro time series data.

It will be useful in understanding my model to consider another important difference between my approach and the pitfalls approach. This can best be explained by seeing how consumption is determined in the two approaches. As just mentioned, income account variables are generally taken to be exogenous by the pitfalls approach, but Tobin's 1982 Nobel lecture provides an example of the endogenous treatment of these variables within the context of the pitfalls approach.

Consider the following two specifications. The first is

(3.1) $C = f(Y, R, A_{-1}, \ldots) + \epsilon,$ [consumption]

(3.2) $Y = W \cdot L + R \cdot A_{-1},$ [income]

(3.3) $S = Y - C,$ [savings]

(3.4) $A = A_{-1} + S,$ [end-of-period assets]

where C is consumption, Y is income, S is savings, A is end-of-period assets, R is the interest rate, W is the wage rate, L is the number of hours worked, A_{-1} is beginning-of-period assets, and ϵ is an error term. The price level is assumed to be fixed and equal to 1. W, L, and R are taken to be exogenous. The second specification is

(3.5) $A = g(Y, R, \ldots) + \mu,$ [end of period assets]

(3.6) $Y = W \cdot L + R \cdot A_{-1},$ [income]

(3.7) $S = A - A_{-1},$ [savings]

(3.8) $C = Y - S,$ [consumption]

where the variables are as before and μ is an error term.

The first set of equations is consistent with my treatment. Consumption is determined by an estimated equation, (3.1). Income, savings, and end-of-period assets are determined by identities. In particular, end-of-period assets are "residually" determined by (3.4), given the consumption decision and Y. (In practice, as will be seen in Section 3.1.2, both consumption and labor supply are determined jointly in my model of household behavior, which means that income is not exogenous and does not belong on the RHS of 3.1. For the sake of the present argument, however, nothing is lost by taking labor supply to be exogenous. Also, the income definition in my model uses $R \cdot A$ instead of $R \cdot A_{-1}$ for the interest revenue term, but this difference is of no consequence for the present argument. If $R \cdot A$ were used in 3.2, then A would be determined, given C, by the solution of 3.2, 3.3, and 3.4 rather than by 3.4 alone.) The variables on the RHS of (3.1) are the exogenous variables (that is, exogenous to the household) that affect the consumption decision. In my model consumption decisions are derived from multiperiod utility maximization, and so the RHS variables are variables that affect the solution of the maximization problem, including expectations of future variables.

The second set of equations is consistent with Tobin's treatment. End-of-period assets are determined by an estimated equation, (3.5). Income, savings, and consumption are determined by identities. In particular, consumption is "residually" determined by (3.8), given the asset decision and Y. The variables on the RHS of (3.5) are variables that affect the asset decision.

From the point of view of a utility-maximizing model, Tobin's treatment is awkward. In the simple model with labor supply exogenous, one maximizes utility with respect to consumption. The natural decision variable to consider is consumption, not assets. Given that $C = Y - A + A_{-1}$, one can, of course, replace C with this expression in the utility function and maximize with respect to A (remember that Y is exogenous), but this is not the natural thing to do.

If the only problem with the Tobin approach were a certain awkwardness of interpretation, there would be no real issue involved in choosing between the above two specifications. In practice, however, quite different models are likely to result from the two approaches. In the first approach much time is spent searching for the estimated equation that best explains C, whereas in Tobin's approach the time is spent searching for the estimated equation that best explains A. For example, C_{-1} is a natural variable to use in the consumption equation to try to capture expectational and lagged adjustment effects, whereas A_{-1} is the natural variable to use in the asset equation. If different RHS variables are chosen for the two equations, it is likely that the behavior of consumption implied by Tobin's approach will be considerably different from the behavior implied by the first approach. If this is true, the awkwardness of Tobin's approach becomes a real issue, and it may argue against its use. (Note that if the same set of RHS variables is used for both equations, if this set includes Y and A_{-1}, and if the equations are linear, then the same equation is being estimated by both approaches. The argument here is that this is unlikely to be the case in practice.)

The main thrust of the pitfalls approach is, of course, to disaggregate A into many different kinds of securities, which means estimating an equation like (3.5) for many different securities. It is straightforward to disaggregate A following this approach, whereas it is not straightforward to do so following the first approach. On the other hand, it is straightforward to disaggregate consumption into different categories following the first approach, whereas it is not following the pitfalls approach. There is again likely to be a real issue here regarding which is the better approach in practice.

Although the example just given is for household behavior, similar considerations apply to models of firm behavior. From the point of view of a profit-maximization model, the pitfalls approach is awkward. In my profit-maximization model, for example, which is discussed in Section 3.1.3, it would be awkward to treat end-of-period assets (or liabilities) as a direct decision variable and thus in the empirical work to estimate an equation with this variable on the LHS. If this were done, it is likely that the estimated model of firm behavior would be quite different from the one that is in fact estimated.

These difficulties with the pitfalls approach may be overcome in future work and, in the spirit of the methodology of this book, it should be possible in the long run to compare pitfalls and non-pitfalls models. The foregoing discussion indicates that the two types of models are likely to have important quantitative differences, which should increase the chances of choosing between them.

It should finally be noted that an approach that is in between the two just discussed would specify that both the consumption and asset equations have errors, where the covariance matrix of the errors would be singular because of the adding up constraints. I do not find this approach particularly appealing, since the theoretical arguments against it are the same as those against the Tobin approach, but it is a possible area for future research.

3.1.2 Household Behavior

There are four types of agents in the model: households *(h)*, firms *(f)*, banks *(b)*, and the government *(g)*. The behavior of each type of agent will be discussed in turn, beginning with households in this section. The complete model is discussed in Section 3.1.5.

In order to simplify the notation, no special symbols have been used to denote expectations. This is unlikely to cause any confusion, since it will be made clear in the discussion which variables are expectation variables and which are decision variables. Note also that the use of the certainty equivalent assumption discussed earlier means that the household decision problem can be analyzed as a deterministic problem.

The Decision Problem

The model of household behavior is fairly straightforward. The utility of household h in period t is a function of consumption and leisure:

(3.9) $$U_{ht} = f_9(C_{ht}, TH - L_{ht} - N_{ht}),$$ [utility function]

where C_{ht} is consumption, L_{ht} is the amount of labor supplied, N_{ht} is the amount of time spent taking care of money holdings, and TH is the total number of hours in the period. The objective of the household is to maximize

(3.10) $$OBJ_h = g_{10}(U_{h1}, U_{h2}, \ldots, U_{hN}),$$ [objective function]

where period 1 is the current period and N is the remaining length of life of the household.

Since the expected one-period rate of return on bonds and stocks is the same, one can deal with only one security when analyzing the decision problem of a household. Let A_{ht} denote the security holdings of the household. Before-tax income (Y_{ht}) is

(3.11) $$Y_{ht} = W_{ht}L_{ht} + R_t A_{ht},$$ [before-tax income]

where W_{ht} is the wage rate and R_t is the one-period interest rate. This equation merely states that before-tax income is equal to wage plus nonwage income. The tax-transfer schedule is

(3.12) $$T_{ht} = d_{1t}Y_{ht} - TR_t,$$ [net taxes]

where d_{1t} is the (proportional) income tax rate, TR_t is the level of transfer payments to the household (TR_t can be interpreted as a minimum guaranteed level of income), and T_{ht} is the amount of net taxes paid. The level of savings (S_{ht}) is equal to income minus taxes minus consumption expenditures:

(3.13) $$S_{ht} = Y_{ht} - T_{ht} - P_{ht}C_{ht},$$ [savings]

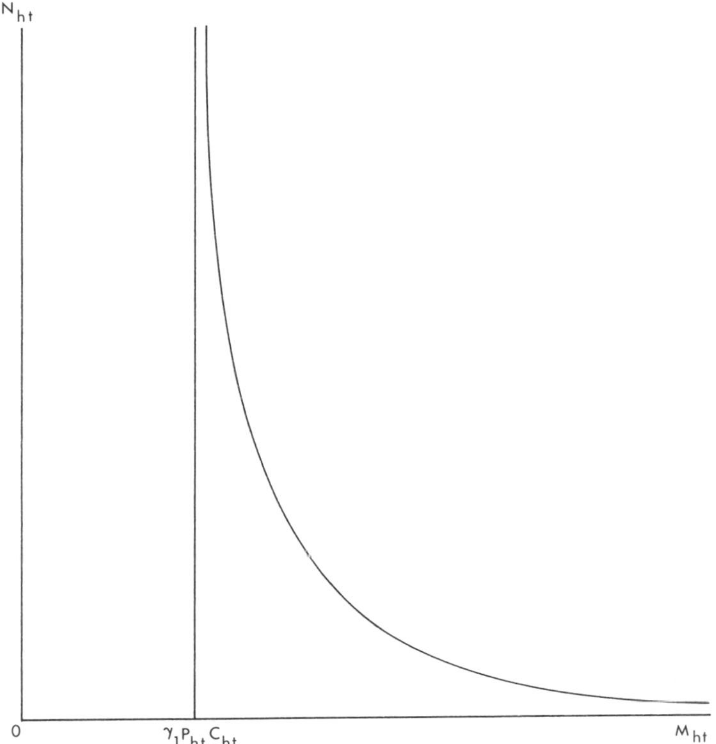

Figure 3-1 Relationship between N_{ht} and M_{ht}

where P_{ht} is the price of goods. The household budget constraint is

$$0 = S_{ht} - \Delta A_{ht} - \Delta M_{ht}, \qquad \text{[budget constraint]} \tag{3.14}$$

where M_{ht} is the level of money holdings. The budget constraint states that any nonzero level of savings must result in a change in holdings of securities or money.

The relationship between the level of money holdings and the amount of time spent taking care of these holdings is depicted in Figure 3-1. For large values of M_{ht}, N_{ht} is small (few trips to the bank needed), whereas for values of M_{ht} that are small in the sense of being close to some proportion of expenditures, $\gamma_1 P_{ht} C_{ht}$, N_{ht} is large. This specification captures the idea that work is involved in keeping money balances small. The functional form that was used for the relationship in Figure 3-1 is

$$(3.15) \qquad N_{ht} = \frac{\gamma_2}{M_{ht} - \gamma_1 P_{ht} C_{ht}}.$$

[time spent taking care of money holdings]

Equations (3.9)–(3.15) hold for each period ($t = 1, \ldots, N$). The decision variables are C_{ht}, L_{ht}, and N_{ht} ($t = 1, \ldots, N$). The exogenous variables to the problem are W_{ht}, P_{ht}, R_t, d_{1t}, and TR_t ($t = 1, \ldots, N$). If future values of the exogenous variables are not known, expectations of these values must be made before the optimization problem is solved. In the solution of the complete model in Section 3.1.5 it is assumed that the household knows the values of the exogenous variables for period t, but not for periods $t + 1$ and beyond. There are two initial conditions: the initial stocks of securities and money, A_{h0} and M_{h0}. There is also assumed to be an exogenous terminal condition:

$$(3.16) \qquad A_{hN} + M_{hN} = \overline{AM}, \qquad \text{[terminal condition]}$$

where $\overline{AM}$ is exogenous. This means that bequests are exogenous.

There is a possible "disequilibrium" constraint on the household, which is that it may not be able to work as many hours as it would like:

$$(3.17) \qquad L_{ht} \leq L^*_{ht}, \qquad \text{[labor constraint]}$$

where L^*_{ht} is the maximum amount that the household can work in period t.

The decision problem of the household is to choose the paths of the decision variables to maximize (3.10), given the actual and expected values of the exogenous variables, the initial conditions, the terminal condition, and the possible labor constraint.

Simulation Results

The following values and functional forms were used for the simulation results. The functional form of the utility function was taken to be the constant elasticity of substitution (CES) form:

$$(3.9)' \qquad U_{ht} = [\alpha_1 C_{ht}^{-\alpha_2} + (1 - \alpha_1)(TH - L_{ht} - N_{ht})^{-\alpha_2}]^{-1/\alpha_2},$$

where $\alpha_1 = .5$ and $\alpha_2 = -.5$. The elasticity of substitution is $1/(1 + \alpha_2)$, which in the present case is 2.0. The length of the decision period, N, was taken to be 3, and the objective function was taken to be

$$(3.10)' \qquad OBJ_h = U_{h1} U_{h2}^{\lambda} U_{h3}^{\lambda^2},$$

where λ is the discount rate.

The exogenous variable values for period 1 were taken to be: $W_{h1} = 1.0$, $P_{h1} = 1.0$, $R_1 = .07$, $d_{11} = .2$, and $TR_1 = 0$. The household was assumed to know these values at the beginning of the period and to expect them to remain unchanged in periods 2 and 3. In other words, expectations were assumed to be static.

The values of the initial conditions were as follows: $A_{h0} = 1000.0$ and $M_{h0} = 100.0$. The value of the terminal condition was $\overline{AM} = 1100.0$. The remaining parameter values were chosen so as to lead to a flat optimal path of each decision variable; these were $\lambda = .944$, $TH = 1004.72366$, $\gamma_1 = .255905$, and $\gamma_2 = 1.0$. The value of λ is one minus the after-tax interest rate, where the after-tax interest rate is $.07 \times .8$.

The maximization problem of the household is to choose the three values of each of the decision variables, L_{ht}, C_{ht}, N_{ht} $(t = 1, 2, 3)$, so as to maximize (3.10)′, subject to the terminal condition (3.16). This problem was solved by calculating the first-order equations analytically and then solving these equations using the Gauss-Seidel technique. The first-order equations were obtained as follows. The terminal condition allows one to write one of the nine decision variables as a function of the others, and this was done for C_{h3}. This expression was then substituted for C_{h3} in the objective function, leaving eight variables to be determined. The derivatives of the objective function with respect to the eight variables were taken, and the resulting eight first-order equations were used to solve for the eight unknowns. Some damping of the Gauss-Seidel technique was needed to solve the equations, but the time taken to solve them was trivial. A damping factor of .1 was generally used (although larger values also worked), and the time taken to solve a typical problem was about .75 seconds on the IBM 4341 at Yale. This procedure was chosen over the use of the DFP algorithm because it was undoubtedly much cheaper in terms of computer time and because the analytic work involved in obtaining the first-order equations was not very large.

The solution values are presented in the first column of Table 3-2. As noted in the table, the values are the same in each of the three periods. The choice of λ as one minus the after-tax interest rate means that the household has no incentive to save or dissave in any period, and thus the optimal value of savings each period is zero. Note that the variables just discussed, other than L_{ht}, C_{ht}, and N_{ht}, are "indirect" decision variables in the sense that they are residually determined given (1) the first three decision variable values, (2) the exogenous variable values, and (3) the parameter values.

The simulation experiments consisted of changing a particular variable from the value used for the base run, solving the household maximization

TABLE 3-2. Simulation results for household h

Variable	Base run values 1[a]	Experiment 1 $W_{ht}(+)$ 1 2 3	2 $P_{ht}(-)$ 1 2 3	3 $A_{h0}(+)$ 1 2 3	4[c] $R_t(+)$ 1 2 3	5 $d_{1t}(+)$ 1 2 3	6 $TR_t(-)$ 1 2 3	7 $L^*_{h1}(-)$ 1 2 3
L_{ht}	400.0	+ + +	+ + +	- - -	+ - -	- - -	+ + +	- + +
C_{ht}	376.0	+ + +	+ + +	+ + +	- + +	- - -	- - -	- - -
N_{ht}	26.0	- - -	0 0 0	0 0 0	+ + +	0 0 0	0 0 0	+ 0 0
M_{ht}	100.0	+ + +[b]	+ + +[b]	+ + +[b]	- - +	- - -[b]	- - -[b]	- - -[b]
S_{ht}	0.0	0 0 0	0 0 0	- - -	+ + -	- - +	0 0 0	- + +
A_{ht}	1000.0	- - -[b]	- - -[b]	+ + -[b]	- - -	+ + +[b]	+ + +[b]	- - +[b]
U_{ht}	483.48	+ + +	+ + +	+ + +	- + +	- - -	- - -	+ - -
OBJ_h	17.524	+	+	+	+	-	-	-

Notes: a. Values for periods 2 and 3 are the same as those for period 1.
b. Change in $M_{h3} + A_{h3} = 0$ since $M_{h3} + A_{h3} = 1100.0$.
c. For experiment 4 both A_{h0} and $\overline{AM}$ were lowered by 86.07.

- The +'s and -'s refer to changes from the values for the base run, not changes from period to period.
- The amounts of the changes were: .05 for W_{ht}, -.05 for P_{ht}, 50.0 for A_{h0}, .01 for R_t, .1 for d_{1t}, and -20.0 for TR_t. L^*_{h1} for the last experiment was 390.0.

problem using the new value, and observing the resulting changes in the optimal values. Seven experiments were performed: each of the five exogenous variables was changed, the initial condition A_{h0} was changed, and the labor constraint was made binding. The results are presented in Table 3-2. For the last experiment the labor constraint was binding, but for the others it was not. The five exogenous variables were changed for all three periods, which means that the household expected the changes to be permanent. In the last experiment the labor constraint was only made binding for the first period; the household was unconstrained in periods 2 and 3. The following paragraphs give a brief discussion of the results. Since only qualitative properties of the model are important, only pluses and minuses are presented in Table 3-2. This makes the results somewhat easier to discuss. When a quantitative result is needed in order to understand a property of the model, it is mentioned in the text. All the pluses and minuses are changes from the base run values, not changes from period to period.

Experiment 1: W_{ht} (+). The increase in the wage rate led the household to work and consume more. This is, of course, not an unambiguous result since d the difference between the number of machines on hand f machines required to produce the output will be called

firm behavior is somewhat tedious to present, since the blem is complicated. In the following discussion, subscript f nd subscript i refers to a machine of type i. The number of f machines is M, and i always runs from 1 through M. All positive unless indicated otherwise.

se for the model of household behavior, no special symbols to denote expectations. It should be clear in the discussion s are decision variables and which are expectation variables. t because of the certainty equivalence assumption, the maxi- blem can be analyzed as a deterministic one.

gy

ful to present the equations representing the technology first. The o equations reflect the putty-clay nature of the technology:

$$L'_{fit} = \frac{YY_{fit}}{\lambda_i}, \qquad \text{[labor required to produce } YY_{fit}]$$

$$KH_{fit} = \frac{YY_{fit}}{\mu_i}. \qquad \text{[machine hours required to produce } YY_{fit}]$$

e amount of output produced on machines of type i in period t. er that i always runs from 1 through M. There is assumed to be no progress, so that λ_i and μ_i are not functions of time. The machines ned to wear out completely after m periods, but they are assumed not bject to physical depreciation before that time. λ_i and μ_i are thus not ns of the age of the machines.

next equation defines the minimum number of machines of type i d to produce YY_{fit}:

$$KMIN_{fit} = \frac{KH_{fit}}{\overline{H}}.$$

[minimum number of machines required to produce YY_{fit}]

ssumed that $\overline{H}$, the maximum number of hours that each machine can ed each period, is constant across time. The actual number of machines ch type on hand in period t is

there are both income and substitution effects operating. Given the particular parameter values chosen, the substitution effect dominates. The increase in the wage rate also led the household to spend less time taking care of money holdings. This is because an increase in the wage rate increases the opportunity cost of time spent both in leisure and in taking care of money holdings. Money holdings increased both because N_{ht} decreased and because consumption increased. Savings remained unchanged at zero each period. A_{ht} fell by the same amount that M_{ht} rose.

Experiment 2: P_{ht} (−). The signs of the results for the decrease in the price level are the same as those for the increase in the wage rate, with the exception of those for N_{ht}. Although N_{ht} did not change for this experiment, it fell for the wage rate increase. The change in price does not affect the opportunity cost of spending time taking care of money holdings, and so N_{ht} is not affected. Money holdings increased because consumption increased by a larger percentage than the price level decreased.

Experiment 3: A_{h0} (+). The increase in the initial value of assets led the household to work less and consume more. The terminal condition was not changed for this experiment, and so the household dissaved each period by enough to have the value of assets fall to the terminal condition value. The value of A_{ht} was lower in period 3 by the amount that M_{ht} was higher; M_{ht} was higher because consumption was higher.

Experiment 4: R_t (+). This experiment requires a little more explanation. Since part of the household's wealth is in the form of stocks, an increase in the interest rate implies a capital loss on stocks and thus a fall in wealth. In the base run for the complete model in Section 3.1.5, the value of stocks is equal to $48.2/R_t$, where 48.2 is the expected stream of after-tax cash flow. The interest rate for the present experiment was increased from .07 to .08, which implies a capital loss on stocks of 86.07. A_{h0} was thus lowered by this amount before the maximization problem was solved. The terminal value of wealth, $\overline{AM}$, was also lowered by this amount. Had the terminal value remained unchanged, the household would have had to save 86.07 over the three periods to make up for the loss. Instead, the household was merely assumed to lower its bequests by the amount of the loss.

The increase in the interest rate led the household to save in periods 1 and 2 and dissave in period 3. Work effort was higher in period 1 and lower in periods 2 and 3, consumption was lower in period 1 and higher in periods 2 and 3, and time spent taking care of money holdings was higher in all three periods. This last variable was higher because an increase in the interest rate increases the opportunity cost of holding money and thus increases the reward from keeping money holdings low. M_{ht} was lower in periods 1 and 2 and higher in period 3. It was higher in period 3 even though N_{ht} was higher because the positive effect from the increase in consumption dominated the negative effect from the increase in N_{ht}.

Experiment 5: d_{1t} (+). The increase in the tax rate led the household to work less and consume less. It worked less because the after-tax return to work was lower. It dissaved in periods 1 and 2 and saved in period 3. It dissaved in the first two periods because the after-tax interest rate was lower. The increase in the tax rate had no effect on N_{ht}. Although an increase in the tax rate lowers the after-tax return to work, which increases N_{ht}, it also lowers the after-tax interest rate, which decreases N_{ht}. These two effects exactly cancel each other out, and so a change in the tax rate has no effect on N_{ht}. Money holdings decreased for this experiment because consumption decreased.

Experiment 6: TR_t (−). The decrease in transfer payments led the household to work more and consume less. N_{ht} was not affected. Money holdings decreased because consumption decreased. Since a decrease in transfer payments is an increase in net taxes, experiments 5 and 6 show an important difference between raising net taxes by increasing the tax rate and raising net taxes by decreasing transfer payments. In both cases consumption is lower, but in the first case work effort is less, whereas in the second case work effort is greater.

Experiment 7: L^*_{h1} (−). Making the labor constraint binding forced the household to work less in period 1. It consumed less and dissaved in period 1. It also spent more time taking care of money holdings. It then worked more in periods 2 and 3 to make up in part for the forced cutback in period 1. It saved in periods 2 and 3 to make up for the dissaving in period 1. Consumption was less in all three periods.

Other Experiments. Experiments 1–6 were also performed with the signs of the changes reversed. The signs of the changes in the optimal values were opposite to those given above. The quantitative results were almost, but not quite, symmetric. For example, L_{ht} responded slightly more to a wage rate decrease than to a wage rate increase. Also, L_{ht} responded more to a change in the wage rate than to a change in the price level.

Summary of Household Behavior

The maximization problem of the household is fairly standard, and so its optimal behavior is not surprising. When the wage rate increases or the price level decreases, the household works more and consumes more. When the

initial value of wealth inc
interest rate increases, it
responds to an increase in
and it responds to a decre
consuming less. A binding l
and leads it to consume less.
The only unusual feature a
of N_{ht}, time spent taking care
responds negatively to the wa
other words, the household spe
when the wage rate is low or the i
an explanation of the interest ser

3.1.3 Firm Behavior

General Features

There are a number of features of the
distinguish it from others. One is th
discussed in Section 3.1.1, firms are ass
in the short run in their price and wage se
to set prices and wages in a profit-ma
decision variables of the firm is also larg
and wages, the variables include productio
The assumptions about technology and
The underlying technology of a firm is assu
where at any one time there are a number of
can be purchased. The machines differ in pric
must be used with each machine per unit of tim
that can be produced per machine per unit of ti
is assumed to be fixed for each type of machine
are assumed to be costs involved in changing the
size of the capital stock. Because of these costs, it
operate some of the time below capacity and "off
This means that some of the time the number of wo
greater than the number of hours that the workers
Similarly, some of the time the number of machine
may be greater than the number of machine ho
difference between hours paid for by a firm and hour

"excess labor," an
and the number o
"excess capital."
The model of
optimization pro
refers to firm f a
different types o
coefficients are
As was the c
have been used
which variable
Again note th
mization prob

The Technolo

It will be use
following tw

(3.18)

(3.19)

YY_{fit} is th
Rememb
technical
are assu
to be su
functio
The
require

(3.20)

It is
be u
of e

$$(3.21) \qquad K_{fit} = K_{fit-1} + IM_{fit} - IM_{fit-m}.$$

[actual number of machines of type i on hand]

Machines purchased in a period are assumed to be able to be used in the production process in that period. IM_{fit} is the number of machines of type i purchased in period t, and IM_{fit-m} is the number that wear out at the end of period $t-1$ and thus cannot be used in the production process in period t. The firm is subject to the restriction

$$(3.22) \qquad K_{fit} \geq KMIN_{fit},$$

[number of machines of type i on hand must be greater than or equal to the minimum number required]

which says that the actual number of machines of type i on hand must be greater than or equal to the minimum number required.

There is one good in the model, which can be used for either consumption or investment. In the following equation the number of machines purchased in period t is translated into the equivalent number of goods purchased:

$$(3.23) \qquad I_{ft} = \sum_{i=1}^{M} \theta_i IM_{fit}.$$

[number of goods purchased for investment]

θ_i is the number of goods it takes to create one machine of type i.

The total amount of output is

$$(3.24) \qquad Y_{ft} = \sum_{i=1}^{M} YY_{fit},$$

[total amount of output]

and the stock of inventories is

$$(3.25) \qquad V_{ft} = V_{ft-1} + Y_{ft} - X_{ft}.$$

[stock of inventories]

Equation (3.25) merely states that the stock of inventories is equal to last period's stock plus production minus sales. X_{ft} is the level of sales of the firm.

The next three equations define various adjustment costs facing the firm, with the costs taking the form of increased labor requirements:

$$(3.26) \qquad LL'_{fM+1t} = \beta_2 |V_{ft} - \beta_1 X_{ft}|,$$

[labor required to maintain deviations of inventories from β_1 times sales]

$$(3.27) \qquad LL'_{fM+2t} = \beta_3 (\Delta X_{ft}),^2$$

[labor required to handle fluctuations in sales]

$$(3.28) \qquad LL'_{fM+3t} = \beta_4 \left(\sum_{i=1}^{M} K_{fit} - \sum_{i=1}^{M} K_{fit-1} \right)^2.$$

[labor required to handle fluctuations in the capital stock]

Equation (3.26) reflects the assumption that there are costs in having inventories that are either greater than or less than a certain proportion of sales. Equations (3.27) and (3.28) reflect the assumptions that there are costs in having sales and the capital stock fluctuate. The minimum amount of labor required is

$$LMIN_{ft} = \sum_{i=1}^{M+3} LL_{fit}^{\prime}. \tag{3.29}$$

[minimum amount of labor required]

The firm is subject to the restriction that labor paid for must be greater than or equal to labor requirements:

$$L_{ft} \geq LMIN_{ft}. \tag{3.30}$$

[labor paid for must be greater than or equal to the minimum required]

It is also assumed that there are adjustment costs in having the work force fluctuate. These costs take the form of increased taxes:

$$T_{ft}^{\prime} = \beta_5 |L_{ft} - L_{ft-1}|, \tag{3.31}$$

[taxes due to fluctuations in the work force]

where $T_{ft}^{\prime}$ is the amount of taxes paid as a result of fluctuations in the work force.

The Financial Variables and Objective Function

The next set of equations pertains to the financial variables of the firm and to the firm's budget constraint. Depreciation is assumed to be straight line:

$$DEP_{ft} = (1/m) \sum_{j=1}^{m} P_{ft-j+1}^{\prime} I_{ft-j+1}. \tag{3.32}$$

[depreciation]

The price of investment goods in (3.32) is denoted $P^{\prime}$ rather than P. The variable P is the price that the firm sets, and the firm is assumed not to buy its own goods for investment purposes. The variable $P^{\prime}$ is the price that it pays for these goods from other firms.

The value of before-tax profits on an accounting basis is

$$\pi_{ft} = P_{ft} Y_{ft} - W_{ft} L_{ft} - DEP_{ft} + R_t A_{ft} + (P_{ft} - P_{ft-1}) V_{ft-1}. \tag{3.33}$$

[before-tax profits]

If the firm is a debtor, the term $R_t A_{ft}$ is negative; it represents the interest costs of the firm. Negative values of A are liabilities, and so $-A_{ft}$ is the amount of borrowing of the firm. The last term in (3.33) is the gain or loss on the stock of inventories due to a price change. The level of taxes paid is

(3.34) $T_{ft} = d_{2t}\pi_{ft} + T'_{ft}$, [taxes paid]

where d_{2t} is the profit tax rate and T'_{ft} is the amount of taxes paid because of fluctuations in the work force. T'_{ft} is determined by (3.31).

The firm is assumed not to retain any earnings, and thus the level of dividends is merely the difference between before-tax profits and taxes:

(3.35) $D_{ft} = \pi_{ft} - T_{ft}$. [dividends paid]

The value of cash flow before taxes and dividends is

(3.36) $CF_{ft} = P_{ft}X_{ft} - W_{ft}L_{ft} - P'_{ft}I_{ft} + R_t A_{ft}$,
[cash flow before taxes and dividends]

and the value of cash flow after taxes and dividends is

(3.37)
$$\begin{aligned} S_{ft} &= CF_{ft} - T_{ft} - D_{ft} \\ &= CF_{ft} - \pi_{ft} \\ &= P_{ft}(X_{ft} - Y_{ft}) - P'_{ft}I_{ft} + DEP_{ft} - (P_{ft} - P_{ft-1})V_{ft-1} \\ &= -P_{ft}V_{ft} + P_{ft-1}V_{ft-1} - P'_{ft}I_{ft} + DEP_{ft}. \end{aligned}$$
[savings: cash flow after taxes and dividends]

Cash flow after taxes and dividends is the savings of the firm. Since all after-tax profits are paid out in dividends, cash flow after taxes and dividends is merely cash flow minus profits, which is depreciation minus investment minus the change in the value of inventories. The budget constraint is

(3.38) $0 = S_{ft} - \Delta A_{ft} - \Delta M_{ft}$. [budget constraint]

M_{ft} is the level of money holdings of the firm. The budget constraint says that any nonzero value of savings must result in a change in A_f or M_f. The demand for money by the firm is simply assumed to be proportional to the value of sales:

(3.39) $M_{ft} = \gamma_3 P_{ft} X_{ft}$.

Equations (3.18)–(3.39) hold for each period of the horizon ($t = 1, \ldots, T$). The objective of the firm is to maximize the present discounted value of after-tax cash flow, where the discount rates are the after-tax interest rates:

(3.40) $$OBJ_f = \sum_{t=1}^{T} \frac{CF_{ft} - T_{ft}}{[1 + R_t(1 - d_{2t})]^t}.$$ [objective function]

$R_t(1 - d_{2t})$ is the after-tax interest rate for period t. The firm is assumed to be subject to the following two terminal conditions:

$$V_{fT} = \overline{V}, \qquad \text{[terminal condition for the stock of inventories]} \tag{3.41}$$

$$\sum_{i=1}^{M} K_{fiT} \geq \overline{K}. \qquad \text{[terminal condition for the capital stock]} \tag{3.42}$$

The first condition states that the stock of inventories at the end of the decision horizon is equal to a given number $\overline{V}$, and the second condition states that the number of machines held at the end of the horizon is greater than or equal to a given number $\overline{K}$. These conditions were imposed to avoid quirks that would otherwise occur in the optimal paths near the end of the horizon.

The decision problem of the firm is to choose paths of the decision variables to maximize (3.40), subject to the two terminal conditions and a number of initial conditions. The main decision variables are the firm's price, P_{ft}, its wage rate, W_{ft}, the number of each type of machine to buy, IM_{fit}, production, Y_{ft}, and the amount of labor to employ, L_{ft} $(t = 1, 2, \ldots, T)$. The main exogenous variables are the interest rate, R_t, the tax rate, d_{2t}, and the price of investment goods, P'_{ft} $(t = 1, 2, \ldots, T)$. The decision problem also requires that a number of expectations be formed, and these will now be discussed.

Determination of Expectations

The main expectations of a firm are those regarding other firms' prices and wages. For simplicity it will be assumed that there are just two firms, firm f and firm k. All expectations are firm f's. All values for the period prior to the first period of the decision horizon are known. Values for all other periods are either decision values or expectations.

The first equation pertains to firm f's expectation of firm k's price-setting behavior:

$$\frac{P_{kt}}{P_{kt-1}} = \left(\frac{P_{ft-1}}{P_{kt-1}}\right)^{\beta_6} \left(\frac{V_{kt-1}}{\beta_1 X_{kt-1}}\right)^{\beta_7}, \qquad \beta_7 < 0. \tag{3.43}$$

[expected price of firm k]

The first term in parentheses on the RHS of this equation reflects the assumption that firm f expects its price-setting behavior in period $t - 1$ to have an effect on firm k's price-setting behavior in period t. The second term represents the effect of market conditions on firm f's expectation of firm k's price. If firm k's stock of inventories at the end of period $t - 1$, V_{kt-1}, is greater than a certain proportion of sales, $\beta_1 X_{kt-1}$, firm f is assumed to expect that firm k will respond to this by lowering its price in period t in an effort to increase sales and draw down inventories.

The second term in (3.43) is assumed to pertain only to the first period of the horizon; (3.43) for periods $t+1$ and beyond includes just the first term:

$$(3.43)' \quad \frac{P_{kt+j}}{P_{kt+j-1}} = \left(\frac{P_{ft+j-1}}{P_{kt+j-1}}\right)^{\beta_6}, \qquad j = 1, \ldots, T.$$

[expected price of firm k for period $t+j$]

Equation (3.43)′ means that firm f expects that firm k is always adjusting its price toward firm f's price. If firm f's price is constant over time, then firm f expects that firm k's price will gradually approach this value. Firm f's expectation of the average price level is assumed to be the geometric average of its price and its expectation of firm k's price:

$$(3.44) \quad \overline{P}_t = (P_{ft} P_{kt})^{\frac{1}{2}}.$$

[expected average price]

The next equation determines firm f's expectation of the aggregate demand for goods, XA_t. This expectation is a function of the expected average price level:

$$(3.45) \quad XA_t = XA_{t-1}\left(\frac{\overline{P}_t}{\overline{P}_{t-1}}\right)^{\beta_8}, \qquad \beta_8 < 0.$$

[expected aggregate demand for goods]

Firm f's expectation of its market share of goods is

$$(3.46) \quad \frac{X_{ft}}{XA_t} = \frac{X_{ft-1}}{XA_{t-1}}\left(\frac{P_{ft}}{P_{kt}}\right)^{\beta_9}, \qquad \beta_9 < 0.$$

[expected market share of goods]

This equation reflects the assumption that a firm expects that its market share is a function of its price relative to the prices of other firms. The equation states that firm f's expected market share is equal to last period's share times a function of the ratio of its price to firm k's price.

This completes the equations regarding prices and demand. The next five equations pertain to wages and labor supply. The first determines firm f's expectation of firm k's wage rate:

$$(3.47) \quad \frac{W_{kt}}{W_{kt-1}} = \left(\frac{W_{ft-1}}{W_{kt-1}}\right)^{\beta_{10}}.$$

[expected wage rate of firm k]

This equation is similar to (3.43) for prices, but without the second term in

(3.43). Firm f's expectation of the average wage rate is

$$\overline{W}_t = (W_{ft} W_{kt})^{\frac{1}{2}}. \qquad \text{(3.48)} \quad \text{[expected average wage rate]}$$

This equation is similar to (3.44) for prices.

Firm f's expectation of the aggregate unconstrained supply of labor is

$$LAUN_t = LAUN_{t-1}\left(\frac{\overline{W}_t}{\overline{W}_{t-1}}\right)^{\beta_{11}}\left(\frac{\overline{P}_t}{\overline{P}_{t-1}}\right)^{\beta_{12}}, \quad \beta_{12} < 0. \qquad \text{(3.49)}$$

[expected aggregate unconstrained supply of labor]

$LAUN_t$ is the amount of labor that firm f expects will be supplied to the firm sector if the labor constraint is not binding on households. Equation (3.49) states that firm f expects that this amount is a positive function of the average wage rate and a negative function of the average price level. The next equation reflects the assumption that firm f expects households to be unconstrained in their labor supply decisions:

$$LA_t = LAUN_t, \qquad \text{(3.50)} \quad \text{[expected aggregate constrained supply of labor]}$$

where LA_t denotes the actual amount of labor that firm f expects will be supplied. This assumption is discussed below. The final equation regarding wages and labor supply determines firm f's expectation of its market share of labor:

$$\frac{L_{ft}}{LA_t} = \frac{L_{ft-1}}{LA_{t-1}}\left(\frac{W_{ft}}{W_{kt}}\right)^{\beta_{13}}. \qquad \text{(3.51)} \quad \text{[expected market share of labor]}$$

This equation is similar to (3.46) for goods. Firm f expects that its share is a function of its wage rate relative to firm k's wage rate.

This completes the expectational equations regarding prices, wages, demand, and labor supply. One last point in this regard concerns the firm's response to the possibility that it underestimates the supply of labor available to it at the wage rate that it sets. A firm is assumed to prepare for this possibility by announcing to households not only the wage rate that it will pay, but also the maximum amount of labor that it will employ, denoted $LMAX_{ft}$. This maximum is assumed to be set equal to the amount of labor that the firm expects to pay for, L_{ft}:

$$LMAX_{ft} = L_{ft}. \qquad \text{(3.52)} \quad \text{[maximum amount of labor to employ]}$$

L_{ft} is determined by (3.51). By setting $LMAX_{ft}$ equal to L_{ft}, the firm is assured that it will never have to hire more labor than it expects to hire. This treatment is one exception to the general practice discussed in Section 3.1.1 of ignoring the effects of uncertainty on decisions. Note the similarity between (3.52) and (3.50). According to (3.52) the firm does not expect to turn any workers away, and according to (3.50) it does not expect any workers to be turned away in the aggregate.

Note that (3.49) implicitly assumes that firm f observes the lagged aggregate unconstrained supply of labor. If the labor constraint is binding on households, firms will be turning away workers, which should give firms some idea of the unconstrained supply. Firms are not, however, assumed to observe the lagged aggregate unconstrained demand for goods. If the labor constraint is binding on households, they will demand fewer goods than otherwise, and so the aggregate unconstrained demand for goods will be greater than the aggregate constrained demand. In this case there is no mechanism comparable to turning workers away for firms to observe the unconstrained demand, and thus it has been assumed that they do not observe it. In other words, firms have no way of knowing, say, how much (if any) of a drop in demand occurs because households are constrained in their labor supply. This assumption means that (3.45) is in terms of the actual (perhaps constrained) aggregate demand, not the unconstrained aggregate demand.

Characteristics of the Maximization Problem

The maximization problem of the firm is fairly complicated, and it may help to outline its main features. A key decision variable is the firm's price. The firm expects that it will gain customers by lowering its price relative to the expected prices of other firms. The main expected costs from doing this, in addition to the lower price it is charging per good, are the adjustment costs (3.26), (3.27), (3.28), and (3.31) involved in increasing sales, investment, and employment. The firm also expects that other firms will follow it if it lowers its price, so it does not expect to be able to capture an ever-increasing share of the market without further and further price reductions.

The firm expects that it will lose customers by raising its price relative to the expected prices of other firms. The main costs from doing this, aside from the lost customers, are the adjustment costs. On the plus side, the firm expects that other firms will follow it if it raises its price, so it does not expect to lose an ever-increasing share of the market without further and further price increases.

The firm expects that it will gain workers if it raises its wage rate relative to the expected wage rates of other firms and lose workers if it lowers its wage rate relative to the expected wage rates of other firms. The firm also expects that other firms will follow it if it raises (lowers) its wage rate, so it does not expect to capture (lose) an ever-increasing share of the market without further and further wage rate increases (decreases).

Because of the various adjustment costs, the firm, if it chooses to lower production, may choose in the current period not to lower its employment and capital stock to the minimum levels required. In other words, it may be optimal for the firm to hold either excess labor or excess capital or both during certain periods.

It may help in understanding the maximization problem to consider the algorithm that was used to solve it. The algorithm first searched over different price paths. For a given price path, the expected sales path can be computed using (3.43), (3.44), (3.45), and (3.46). For a given expected sales path, different output paths were tried. Two extreme output paths were tried: one in which the level of output remains as close as possible to the level of sales each period, and one in which the level of output remains as close as possible to the level of the previous period. In other words, for the first path output fluctuates roughly as sales do, and for the second path output fluctuates very little. The paths must satisfy the terminal condition (3.41) for inventories, and for each path production was adjusted to have this condition met. There is also a constraint that the stock of inventories cannot be negative in any period, and production was also adjusted if necessary to have this constraint met. The other output paths that were tried were weighted averages of the two extreme paths.

At the beginning of the first period there are a certain number of machines of each type on hand. If it is assumed, say, that only machines of type 1 are purchased, it is possible to compute for a given output path the number of machines that must be purchased to produce the output each period. This is done by first calculating the amount of output that can be produced with the current number of machines of all types on hand and then calculating the number of machines of type 1 required to produce the remaining output. These calculations are done using (3.19), (3.20), and (3.21). For a given output path, each of the M types of machines was tried, which means that it was first assumed that only type 1 machines are purchased, then only type 2 machines, and so on through type M machines.

For a given output path and a given type of machine, different investment paths were tried. Again, two extreme paths were tried: one in which the number of machines purchased equals the number required to produce the output and meet the terminal condition (3.42), and one in which the number of machines purchased remains as close as possible to the amount required to keep the number of machines unchanged from the previous period. The first path is one in which the capital stock fluctuates as much as the amount required, and the second path is one in which the capital stock fluctuates very little. The second path is subject to the constraint (3.22) that the number of machines must be sufficient to produce the output each period and to the terminal condition (3.42), and investment was adjusted if necessary to meet these conditions. Other paths were tried as weighted averages of the two extreme paths.

For each investment path different employment paths were tried. Given all the paths just mentioned, including the paths of the amount of output produced on each type of machine, it is possible to compute the amount of labor required to produce the total output. This is done using (3.18) and (3.26)–(3.29). Two extreme employment paths were tried: one in which the amount of labor equals the amount required, and one in which the amount of labor remains as close as possible to the amount of the previous period. The first path is one in which the amount of labor fluctuates as much as the amount required to produce the output, and the second path is one in which the amount of labor fluctuates very little. The second path is subject to the constraint (3.30) that the amount of labor must be sufficient to produce the output, and the amount of labor was adjusted if necessary to meet this. Other paths were tried as weighted averages of the two extreme paths.

Given the price path and the employment path, it is possible from (3.43)–(3.44) and (3.47)–(3.51) to compute the wage path that is necessary to have the employment path met. In other words, it is possible to compute the wage path that the firm expects is necessary to attract the amount of labor that it wants.

Given all these paths, it is possible to compute the objective function of the firm. This is done using (3.31)–(3.40). Since the algorithm consists of many layers of searching, the objective function is computed many times in the process of searching for the optimum. If, say, 5 output paths are tried for each sales path, if there are 3 types of machines, if 5 investment paths are tried for each output path and type of machine, and if 5 employment paths are tried for each investment path, then 375 objective function values ($5 \times 3 \times 5 \times 5$) are computed in the process of finding the optimum for the given sales path. If, say, 25 price paths (and thus 25 sales paths) are tried, the total number of objective function evaluations is 9,375 (25×375). Searching for the optimum price path was done by changing a price for a given period or a set of prices for a number of periods until the objective function stopped increasing and then trying another price or set of prices. The base price path that was used was the one in which the firm expects its market share of goods to remain unchanged. In other words, the base price path is one in which the firm is not trying to increase or decrease its market share.

Simulation Results

The length of the decision horizon, T, was taken to be 3 for the simulation results. The number of different types of machines, M, was taken to be 3, and the length of life of a machine, m, was taken to be 2.

The following values of the initial conditions were used.

Initial Conditions

$(t = 1)$

$A_{ft-1} =$	-100.0	$M_{ft-1} =$	25.0
$I_{ft-1} =$	27.0	$P_{ft-1} =$	1.0
$IM_{f1t-1} =$	0.0	$P'_{ft-1} =$	1.0
$IM_{f1t-2} =$	0.0	$P_{kt-1} =$	1.0
$IM_{f2t-1} =$	27.0	$\bar{P}_{t-1} =$	1.0
$IM_{f2t-2} =$	27.0	$V_{ft-1} =$	50.0
$IM_{f3t-1} =$	0.0	$V_{kt-1} =$	50.0
$IM_{f3t-2} =$	0.0	$W_{ft-1} =$	1.0
$K_{f1t-1} =$	0.0	$W_{kt-1} =$	1.0
$K_{f2t-1} =$	54.0	$\bar{W}_{t-1} =$	1.0
$K_{f3t-1} =$	0.0	$X_{ft-1} =$	263.0
$L_{ft-1} =$	185.0	$X_{kt-1} =$	263.0
$LA_{t-1} =$	370.0	$XA_{t-1} =$	526.0
$LAUN_{t-1} =$	370.0		

Note that all machines on hand were assumed to be type 2 machines.

With respect to the exogenous variables, the interest rate for period 1, R_1, was taken to be .07, and the tax rate for period 1, d_{21}, was taken to be .5. The firm was assumed to know these values at the beginning of period 1 and to expect them to remain unchanged for periods 2 and 3. The firm was assumed to expect the price of investment goods for periods 1, 2, and 3 to be unchanged from its initial value given above of 1.0 (that is, $P'_{ft} = 1.0$, $t = 1, 2, 3$).

The two terminal-condition values were taken to be $\bar{K} = 54.0$ and $\bar{V} = 50.0$. The following parameter values were used.

Parameter Values

$\overline{H} = 1.0$	$\gamma_3 = 25.0/263.0 = .095057$
$\beta_1 = 50.0/263.0 = .190114$	$\lambda_2 = 263.0/185.0 = 1.421622$
$\beta_2 = .08$	$\lambda_1 = 1.006\lambda_2 = 1.422475$
$\beta_3 = .08$	$\lambda_3 = \lambda_2/1.006 = 1.413143$
$\beta_4 = .04$	$\mu_2 = 263.0/54.0 = 4.870370$
$\beta_5 = .04$	$\mu_1 = \mu_2$
$\beta_6 = .5$	$\mu_3 = \mu_2$
$\beta_7 = -.03$	$\theta_1 = 1.0315$
$\beta_8 = -1.0$	$\theta_2 = 1.0$
$\beta_9 = -5.0$	$\theta_3 = .97$
$\beta_{10} = .5$	
$\beta_{11} = 1.0$	
$\beta_{12} = -1.0$	
$\beta_{13} = 5.0$	

Note that all three types of machines have the same μ_i value. Type 1 machines are the most efficient with respect to labor requirements (that is, λ_1 is the largest) and cost the most (that is, θ_1 is the largest). Type 3 machines are the least efficient with respect to labor requirements and cost the least.

The algorithm discussed in the previous section was used to solve the maximization problem. In the search for the optimal price path, the smallest change in a price that was allowed was .001. For each price path, five output paths were tried (the two extreme paths and three weighted averages). For each output path and each type of machine, five investment paths were tried (the two extreme paths and three weighted averages). For each investment path, five employment paths were tried (the two extreme paths and three weighted averages). The weights were .5, .5; .1, .9; and .9, .1. It is clear that it would be necessary to try more paths in order to obtain the exact optimum, but for present purposes it is unlikely to matter that the exact optimum was not reached. Enough searching was done to make it likely that the computed optimum is close to the exact optimum, and for qualitative purposes this should be sufficient.

Each solution of the maximization problem took about 38 seconds on the IBM 4341 at Yale. Neither the DFP algorithm nor the procedure of obtaining first-order conditions analytically and solving them using Gauss-Seidel was tried, since the problem is really too complex for these methods. The problem has an inequality constraint, (3.42), which the methods cannot handle directly, but even if adjustments could be made for this, the problem is still too involved. It is not obvious that the DFP algorithm could have found the optimum given that it takes no advantage of the structure of the problem, and it seemed too risky to try. With respect to the other method, considerable work would have been required to obtain the first-order conditions, and this did not seem worth the effort.

The solution using the initial conditions and parameters just given was one in which the value of each decision variable was the same in all three periods. The values for selected variables are presented in the first column of Table 3-3. The ratio $L_{ft}/LMIN_{ft}$ in row 20 is a measure of the amount of excess labor held, where a value of 1.0 means no excess labor held. Likewise, the ratios $K_{fit}/KMIN_{fit}$, $i = 1, 2, 3$, in rows 21–23 are measures of the amount of excess capital held.

The simulation experiments consisted of changing initial conditions or exogenous variable values or parameter values, solving the maximization problem again, and observing the changes in the solution values from those for the base run. Results for nine experiments are presented in Table 3-3. The following paragraphs provide a discussion of these results.

Experiment 1: Increase in P_{k0}, the initial value of firm k's price. From (3.43), P_{k0} has a positive effect on firm f's expectation of firm k's price for period 1 and beyond (row 2). Firm f responded to the increase in P_{k0} by raising its own price (row 1). Had it raised its price by the same amount that it expected firm k's price to be raised, its expected market share would have remained constant (Eq. 3.46). In fact, its expected market share increased in all three periods (row 4). Although this is not shown in the table, firm f raised its price less in period 1 and slightly more in periods 2 and 3, the net result being an increase in market share for all three periods.

The expected aggregate demand for goods decreased because of the increase in prices (row 3; Eq. 3.45). Since firm f's expected market share rose and the expected aggregate demand for goods fell, firm f's expected sales could go either way. In fact, expected sales rose in period 1 and fell in periods 2 and 3 (row 5). Although this is not shown in the table, the sum of sales over the three periods rose. Production was smoothed relative to sales and was higher in all three periods (row 6). The stock of inventories was lower in periods 1 and 2 and equal to the terminal condition of 50.0 in period 3 (row 7).

The firm retained its investment in type 2 machines (rows 8–13). Investment was higher in periods 1 and 3 to meet the increased production (rows 12 and 14). Employment was also higher (row 15). Firm f's wage was higher to attract the extra employment (row 16). This in turn led firm f to expect that firm k's wage would be higher in periods 2 and 3 (row 17; Eq. 3.47). The expected aggregate supply of labor was lower because (although not shown) prices rose more than wages (row 18; Eqs. 3.49 and 3.50). Firm f's expected market share of labor rose because it had to attract the extra employment (row 19).

The firm planned to hold no excess labor or excess capital (rows 20–23). Profits and cash flow were higher because of the expansion and the higher prices relative to wages (rows 25 and 28). The level of savings was lower (row 30), primarily due to the fact that the increase in prices led to an increase in the value of inventories, which increases profits but not cash flow (Eqs. 3.33 and 3.36). Since the level of savings equals cash flow minus profits, it falls, other things being equal, when prices rise (Eq. 3.37). Money holdings rose because prices and sales rose (row 32; Eq. 3.39). The level of borrowing, which is $-A_{ft}$, rose because savings fell and money holdings rose (row 31; Eq. 3.38).

Although this is not shown in Table 3-3, roughly the opposite happened when P_{k0} was decreased rather than increased. Firm f did not lower its price as much as it expected firm k to do, and therefore it lost some market share. Its level of sales was lower in all three periods, as was its production. Investment and employment were lower; the wage rate was lower; profits and cash flow fell. The results were not exactly opposite in sign because the level of sales of firm f was lower in all three periods, whereas in Table 3-3 it is higher only in period 1. Moreover, the level of inventories, which is lower in periods 1 and 2 in Table 3-3, was also lower when P_{k0} was decreased. In both experiments firm f chose to produce less than it sold in period 1.

Experiment 2: Increase in W_{k0}, the initial value of firm k's wage. From (3.47), W_{k0} has a positive effect on firm f's expectation of firm k's wage in period 1 and beyond. The increase in W_{k0} thus led firm f to expect firm k's wage to be higher (row 17). Firm f responded to this by raising its wage (row 16). Although this is not shown in the table, firm f raised its wage less than it expected firm k to do. Its expected market share thus fell (row 19; Eq. 3.51). The expected aggregate supply was higher because of the higher wage rates (row 18; Eqs. 3.49 and 3.50). Profits and cash flow were lower because of the higher labor costs. The increase in W_{k0} had no effect on firm f's price, output, and investment decisions.

Although this is not shown in Table 3-3, the opposite signs were obtained when W_{k0} was decreased rather than increased.

Experiment 3: Increase in the λ_i's, the labor efficiency parameters. An increase in the λ_i's means that labor is now more efficient. With no other changes, this means that the firm is now holding excess labor. It responded to

TABLE 3-3. Simulation results for firm f

Row no.	Variable	Base run values 1[a]	Experiment 1: Increase in P_{k0}	2: Increase in W_{k0}	3: Increase in λ_i's	4: Increase in μ_i's	5: Interest rate increase to .20	6: Interest rate increase to .15	7: Tax rate increase	8: Sales decrease	9: Sales increase
			1 2 3	1 2 3	1 2 3	1 2 3	1 2 3	1 2 3	1 2 3	0 1 2 3	0 1 2 3
1	P_{ft}	1.0	+ + +	0 0 0	0 0 0	0 0 0	0 + +	0 + +	0 0 0	0 - - -	0 + + +
2	P_{kt}	1.0	+ + +	0 0 0	0 0 0	0 0 0	0 0 +	0 0 +	0 0 0	0 - - -	0 + + +
3	XA_t	526.0	- - -	0 0 0	0 0 0	0 0 0	0 - -	0 - -	0 0 0	- - - -	+ + + +
4	X_{ft}/XA_t	.5	+ + +	0 0 0	0 0 0	0 0 0	0 - -	0 - -	0 0 0	0 0 0 0	0 0 0 0
5	X_{ft}	263.0	+ - -	0 0 0	0 0 0	0 0 0	0 - -	0 - -	0 0 0	- - - -	+ + + +
6	Y_{ft}	263.0	+ + +	0 0 0	0 0 0	0 0 0	- - -	- - -	0 0 0	- - - -	- + + +
7	V_{ft}	50.0	- - 0	0 0 0	0 0 0	0 0 0	- - 0	- - 0	0 0 0	+ + + 0	- - - 0
8	Y_{f1t}	0.0	0 0 0	0 0 0	0 0 0	0 0 0	0 0 0	0 0 0	0 0 0	0 0 0 0	0 0 0 0
9	Y_{f2t}	263.0	+ + +	0 0 0	0 0 0	0 0 0	- - -	- - -	- - -	- - - -	- + + +
10	Y_{f3t}	0.0	0 0 0	0 0 0	0 0 0	0 0 0	+ + +	0 0 0	+ + +	0 0 0 0	0 0 0 0
11	IM_{f1t}	0.0	0 0 0	0 0 0	0 0 0	0 0 0	0 0 0	0 0 0	0 0 0	0 0 0 0	0 0 0 0
12	IM_{f2t}	27.0	+ 0 +	0 0 0	0 0 0	0 0 0	- - -	- 0 0	- - -	0 - 0 0	0 + 0 +
13	IM_{f3t}	0.0	0 0 0	0 0 0	0 0 0	0 0 0	+ + +	0 0 0	+ + +	0 0 0 0	0 0 0 0
14	I_{ft}	27.0	+ 0 +	0 0 0	0 0 0	- 0 0	- - -	- 0 0	- - -	0 - 0 0	0 + 0 +
15	L_{ft} ($= LMAX_{ft}$)	185.0	+ + +	0 0 0	- - -	+ 0 +	- + +	- - -	+ + +	0 - - -	0 + + +
16	W_{ft}	1.0	+ + +	+ + +	- - -	+ - +	- + +	- - -	+ + +	0 - - -	- + + +
17	W_{kt}	1.0	0 + +	+ + +	0 - -	0 + 0	0 - +	0 - -	0 + +	0 0 - -	0 0 + +
18	LA_t ($= LAUN_t$)	370.0	- - -	+ + +	- - -	+ 0 +	- - -	- - -	+ + +	0 + + +	0 - - -

19	L_{ft}/LA_t	.5	+ + +	- - -	- - -	+ 0 +	- + +	- - -	+ + +	0 - - -	0 + + +
20	$L_{ft}/LMIN_{ft}$	1.0	0 0 0	0 0 0	0 0 0	0 0 0	0 0 0	0 0 0	0 0 0	0 0 0 0	0 0 0 0
21	$K_{f1t}/KMIN_{f1t}$ [b]	1.0	0 0 0	0 0 0	0 0 0	0 0 +	0 0 0	0 0 0	0 0 0	0 0 0 0	0 0 0 0
22	$K_{f2t}/KMIN_{f2t}$ [b]	1.0	0 0 0	0 0 0	0 0 0	0 0 0	0 0 0	0 0 +	0 0 0	+ 0 0 0	+ 0 0 0
23	$K_{f3t}/KMIN_{f3t}$ [b]	1.0	0 0 0	0 0 0	0 0 0	0 0 0	0 0 +	0 0 0	0 0 0	0 0 0 0	0 0 0 0
24	DEP_{ft}	27.0	+ + +	0 0 0	0 0 0	- - 0	- - -	- - 0	- - -	0 - - 0	0 + + -
25	Π_{ft}	44.0	+ + +	- - -	+ + +	+ + -	- - -	- - -	- - -	- - - -	- + + +
26	T_{ft}	22.0	+ + +	- - -	+ + +	+ + -	- - -	- - -	+ + +	- - - -	- + + +
27	D_{ft}	22.0	+ + +	- - -	+ + +	+ + -	- - -	- - -	- - -	- - - -	- + + +
28	CF_{ft}	44.0	+ + +	- - -	+ + +	+ + -	- - -	- - -	+ - -	- + - -	+ - + -
29	$CF_{ft} - T_{ft}$	22.0	+ + +	- - -	+ + +	+ - -	- - -	- - -	- - -	- + - +	+ - - -
30	S_{ft}	0.0	- - -	0 0 0	0 0 0	+ - 0	+ + -	+ - -	+ 0 0	- + + +	+ - - -
31	$-A_{ft}$	100.0	+ + +	0 0 0	0 0 0	- 0 0	- - -	- - -	- - -	+ + + -	- - - +
32	M_{ft}	25.0	+ + +	0 0 0	0 0 0	0 0 0	0 - -	0 - -	0 0 0	- - - -	+ + - +
33	OBJ_f	61.636	+	-	+	+	-	-	-	+	-

Notes: a. Values for periods 2 and 3 are the same as those for period 1.

b. If no capital of type i is held, then both K_{fit} and $KMIN_{fit}$ are 0. In this case 0/0 is defined to be 1.

- For experiment 1, P_{L0} was increased to 1.05.
- For experiment 2, W_{L0} was increased to 1.05.
- For experiment 3, each λ_i was increased by 2.0 percent.
- For experiment 4, each μ_i was increased by 2.0 percent.
- For experiment 7, the tax rate (d_{2t}) was increased to .75 (t = 1, 2, 3).
- For experiment 8, XA_0 was decreased to 525.0.
- For experiment 9, XA_0 was increased to 527.0.
- For both experiments 8 and 9, firm f expected XA_0 to be 526.0 when it made its decision for period 0.

this by lowering employment (row 15); its wage rate was lower because it needed to attract less labor (row 16). The firm chose to hold no excess labor (row 20), which means that all excess labor was eliminated in period 1. Profits and cash flow were higher because of the lower labor costs.

Experiment 4: Increase in the μ_i's, the capital efficiency parameters. An increase in the μ_i's means that the machines are now more efficient, which with no other changes means that the firm is holding excess capital. It responded to this by lowering investment enough in period 1 to eliminate all excess capital (rows 14 and 21). Although excess capital was not held in period 1, it was held in period 3 (row 21). The amount of capital held in period 3 was the amount required by the terminal condition (3.42), which was more than the amount required to produce the output. (The terminal condition was not changed for this experiment.)

Experiment 5: Interest rate increase to .20. In this case the firm switched to the cheaper, more labor-intensive type 3 machines (rows 8–13). It also raised its price in periods 2 and 3 and contracted. Investment was lower in all three periods (row 14). Employment was lower in period 1, but it was higher in periods 2 and 3 because of the increased labor requirements on the type 3 machines. The increase in the interest rate thus led to higher prices and lower investment and output.

Experiment 6: Interest rate increase to .15. In this case the interest rate increase was not large enough to lead the firm to switch to the type 3 machines. It was still optimal, however, for the firm to raise its prices in periods 2 and 3 and contract. Note that sales are unchanged in period 1, but that production is lower (rows 5 and 6), which means that the stock of inventories is lower (row 7). Since the interest rate contributes to the opportunity cost of holding inventories, an increase in the interest rate may lead the firm to hold fewer inventories, which is what happened here. The stock of inventories was unchanged in period 3 because of the terminal condition. Since the initial stock of inventories and the terminal condition are the same, any optimal plan of the firm must have the sum of production across the three periods equal the sum of sales. The way in which the firm can bring this about and still have the stock of inventories be less in periods 1 and 2 is to sell more in period 1 than in periods 2 and 3 and yet produce the same amount in all three periods. This is what the firm did in this experiment.

Although this is not shown in Table 3-3, the firm responded to an interest rate decrease (to .04) by switching to the type 1 machines and increasing investment. It did not, however, change its price and production plans, so there was no planned change in inventories. Employment was lower even though production was unchanged because of the use of the less labor-intensive machines.

Experiment 7: Tax rate increase. The increase in the profit tax rate led the firm to switch to the cheaper type 3 machines. Investment was lower because of this. Prices and production were unchanged. The main reason for the switch to the cheaper type 3 machines is the following. The objective of the firm is to maximize the present discounted value of after-tax cash flow. Two of the terms in the expression for after-tax cash flow are $-P'_{ft}I_{ft} + d_{2t}DEP_{ft}$, which means that investment lowers after-tax cash flow but depreciation raises it. The higher the tax rate d_{2t}, the more advantageous it is for the firm to have investment be low relative to depreciation. One way in which this can be done is to switch to the cheaper type 3 machines. This change lowers investment but does not require a lowering of production as long as more labor is hired. Depreciation does not fall as much as investment because it is a function of investment lagged one period as well as of current investment (Eq. 3.32). Although depreciation is lower in Table 3-3 (row 24), it is not as low as investment in period 1. (Note that from row 15 employment is higher, and that from row 16 the wage is higher, in order to attract the extra labor.) This negative effect of the tax rate on investment would, of course, not exist if investment expenditures could be written off completely in the current period. The effect is simply due to the firm's taking advantage of the effect of past investment expenditures on current depreciation.

Although this is not shown in Table 3-3, a decrease in the tax rate led the firm to switch to the type 1 machines, raise investment, and lower employment. The results were exactly opposite in sign to those for the increase in the tax rate.

Experiment 8: Unexpected decrease in sales. This experiment requires somewhat more explanation than the others. As will be discussed in Section 3.1.5, a firm solves its maximization problem at the beginning of the period before any transactions have taken place. Once transactions have taken place, many of the variables will be different from what the firm expected them to be. For experiment 8 the firm was first assumed to solve its maximization problem with no changes in any variables, so the decision values were those for the base run. The level of sales was then decreased. The effects of this change on the variables for the current period are presented in column 0 in Table 3-3 under experiment 8. The sales decrease took the form of a drop in aggregate demand (XA_t), and thus there is a negative sign in row 3. The firm's market share was assumed to remain unchanged, so its sales dropped (row 5). Because a change in sales increases labor requirements (Eq. 3.27) and because the firm was not planning to hold any excess labor, production had to be cut slightly from its planned level in order to meet the employment constraint (3.30). This is the reason for the minus sign in row 6. Production was cut less than sales fell, and therefore inventories rose (row 7). Because of the lower level of production, the firm ended up with slightly more capital than it needed to produce the output (row 22). In other words, meeting the labor constraint resulted in some excess capital being held. Profits and cash flow were lower because of the drop in production and sales. The drop in aggregate demand was also assumed to affect firm *k*, the other firm in the model. Firm *k* is assumed to be identical to firm *f*, and so the results are the same for firm *k*.

Any variable in column 0 that is not changed is a decision variable or an expectation variable that is not affected by the transactions of the period. The important decision variables for which this is true are the firm's price, investment, employment, and wage rate. Given the new set of initial conditions, the firm's maximization problem was solved again, where the horizon was still assumed to be three periods. The results are in columns 1, 2, and 3 in the table under experiment 8.

The firm responded to the sales decrease by lowering its price, production, investment, employment, and wage rate. Firm *f* expected firm *k* to lower its price because it knew that firm *k*'s stock of inventories exceeded $\beta_1 X_{k0}$. Firm *f* lowered its price by the same amount that it expected firm *k* to, thus leaving its market share unchanged (row 4). The lower prices have a positive effect on expected aggregate demand, but the lower initial level of aggregate demand has a negative effect (Eq. 3.45). The net effect was negative (row 3). Given the unchanged market share, the level of sales of firm *f* was lower (row 5). This then led to lower production, investment, employment, and the like.

Cash flow after taxes was larger for two of the three periods (row 29), and the objective function was larger (row 33). This is, however, somewhat misleading in that the firm is not better off because of the sales decrease. The firm suffered a loss of cash flow after taxes in period 0, and the objective function sign in row 33 pertains only to periods 1, 2, and 3. The firm started off at the beginning of period 1 with a higher level of inventories than was the case for the base run, and it gained cash flow by selling these off over the periods to reach the terminal condition of 50.0.

Experiment 9: Unexpected increase in sales. For this experiment sales were increased rather than decreased. The results are roughly the opposite to those for the sales decrease, but there is one important exception: production in period 0 was lower in both cases. This occurred because of the increased labor requirements due to the change in sales, which in both cases required cutting production in period 0.

Summary of Firm Behavior

The results of these experiments give a fairly good idea of the properties of the model of firm behavior. Some of the main effects are the following.

1. A change in the expected price (wage) of firm *k* leads firm *f* to change its own price (wage) in the same direction.
2. Excess labor on hand leads to a fall in employment, and excess capital on hand leads to a fall in investment.
3. An increase (decrease) in the interest rate leads to a substitution away from (toward) less labor-intensive machines and a decrease (increase) in investment expenditures. Changes in the interest rate also affect the opportunity cost of holding inventories, and thus the interest rate may affect the price and production decisions through this channel.
4. The firm responds to a decrease in aggregate demand by lowering its price and contracting. It responds to an increase in aggregate demand by raising its price and expanding.

It should be stressed that the results in Table 3-3 are for a particular set of parameter values. At least slightly different qualitative results are likely to be obtained for different sets. It seems unlikely, however, that the general properties of the model would be much affected by changes in the parameters. For the purpose of using the model to guide the specification of the econometric model, the results seem sufficient.

One point to note about the results is that for none of the experiments did the firm plan to hold excess labor. Similarly, the firm never planned to hold excess capital except in the last period. There are at least two reasons for this. One is that the cost-of-adjustment parameters regarding labor and capital, β_5 and β_4, are fairly small; the second is that it is relatively easy for the firm to smooth production, and with a smooth production path the employment and investment paths can be fairly smooth without deviating from the required amounts. Production can be smoothed not merely by using inventories as a buffer, but also by smoothing the expected sales path through changes in prices. In order for the results to show excess labor and excess capital being routinely held, the costs of smoothing production would have to rise relative to the costs of adjusting labor and capital. Again, however, for present purposes the results given above seem adequate.

3.1.4 Bank and Government Behavior

Bank Equations

Banks play a passive role in the model in the sense that no maximization problem is specified for them. Each bank, say bank b, receives money from households and firms in the form of demand deposits. Let $-M_{bt}$ denote the amount of demand deposits held in bank b, where M_{bt} is negative because demand deposits are a liability of a bank. Banks must hold a proportion g_{1t} of their demand deposits in the form of bank reserves:

(3.53) $\quad BR_{bt} = -g_{1t}M_{bt},$ [bank reserves]

where BR_{bt} is the level of bank reserves and g_{1t} is the reserve requirement rate.

Bank borrowing from the monetary authority, BO_{bt}, is assumed to be a function of the difference between the discount rate, RD_t, and the interest rate, R_t:

(3.54) $$\frac{BO_{bt}}{BR_{bt}} = \gamma_4(RD_t - R_t), \qquad \gamma_4 < 0.$$ [bank borrowing]

No interest is assumed to be paid on demand deposits, and thus the level of before-tax profits of a bank is the difference between the interest revenue from its loans and the interest costs of its borrowing from the monetary authority:

(3.55) $\quad \pi_{bt} = R_tA_{bt} - RD_tBO_t,$ [before-tax profits]

where A_{bt} is the amount of loans of the bank. The amount of taxes is

(3.56) $\quad T_{bt} = d_{2t}\pi_{bt},$ [taxes paid]

where T_{bt} is the amount of taxes and d_{2t} is the profit tax rate. A bank is assumed to pay all of its after-tax profits in dividends:

(3.57) $\quad D_{bt} = \pi_{bt} - T_{bt},$ [dividends paid]

where D_{bt} is the amount of dividends paid.

A bank's after-tax cash flow is merely its after-tax profits. Because it pays all of its after-tax profits in dividends, its level of savings is always zero, which means that a savings variable for a bank does not have to be specified. The bank's budget constraint is

(3.58) $\quad 0 = \Delta A_{bt} + \Delta M_{bt} + \Delta BR_{bt} - \Delta BO_{bt}$

or

(3.58)′ $\quad 0 = A_{bt} + M_{bt} + BR_{bt} - BO_{bt}.$ [budget constraint]

Government Equations

The government is defined here to be both the fiscal authority and the monetary authority. It collects taxes from households, firms, and banks, and it earns interest revenue on its loans to banks. If the government is a net debtor, which is assumed here, it pays interest on its borrowings. The other costs are wage costs and costs of goods purchased. The level of savings of the government, S_{gt}, is

$$(3.59) \qquad S_{gt} = \Sigma_h T_{ht} + \Sigma_f T_{ft} + \Sigma_b T_{bt} + RD_t \Sigma_b BO_{bt} + R_t A_{gt} - W_{gt} L_{gt} - P_{gt} C_{gt}. \qquad \text{[savings]}$$

The respective summations are over all the households, all the firms, and all the banks. A_{gt} is the value of net assets of the government (not counting $\Sigma_b BO_{bt}$), and it is negative if the government is a net debtor. The term $R_t A_{gt}$ is thus negative. L_{gt} is the amount of labor employed by the government, and W_{gt} is the wage rate paid by the government. C_{gt} is the amount of goods purchased, and P_{gt} is the price paid per good.

The budget constraint of the government is

$$(3.60) \qquad 0 = S_{gt} + \Sigma_b \, \Delta BR_{bt} - \Sigma_b \, \Delta BO_{bt} - \Delta A_{gt}. \qquad \text{[budget constraint]}$$

This equation states that any nonzero level of savings of the government must result in a change in nonborrowed reserves (that is, high-powered money) or government borrowing, $-A_{gt}$. For convenience, $-A_{gt}$ will be referred to as "the amount of government securities outstanding," even though there is no distinction in the model between government securities and any other type of securities.

Government behavior with respect to the tax-rate and expenditure variables is taken to be exogenous. In other words, fiscal policy is exogenous. The exogenous fiscal policy variables are d_{1t}, d_{2t}, TR_t, L_{gt}, and C_{gt}.

The three monetary policy variables are g_{1t}, RD_t, and A_{gt}. If all three of these variables are taken to be exogenous, the interest rate is implicitly determined in the model. Its value must be such as to have (3.60) satisfied, and in this loose sense it can be matched to (3.60). An alternative treatment is to assume that the government follows some reaction function with respect to its monetary policy. The reaction function that was assumed here is an interest rate reaction function:

$$(3.61) \qquad R_t = f(\; . \; . \; . \;), \qquad \text{[interest rate reaction function]}$$

where the arguments of the function are variables that affect the interest rate decision. Another possible reaction function is one in which the money supply, M_{bt}, is on the LHS, and another is one in which the variable nonborrowed reserves, $\Sigma_b BR_{bt} - \Sigma_b BO_{bt}$, is on the LHS. If a reaction function is postulated, one of the three monetary policy variables must be taken to be endogenous, where the most likely candidate is A_{gt}. If A_{gt} is taken to be endogenous, this means that open-market operations are used to meet the target LHS variable each period.

3.1.5 The Complete Model

There are two main questions to consider when putting together a model like the present one. One is how the agents are to be aggregated, and the other is the order in which the transactions take place. Aggregation will be discussed first.

One way in which the model could be put together would be to specify a number of different households, firms, and banks; have each one make its decisions; and then have them trade with each other. In order to do this one would have to specify mechanisms for deciding who trades with whom, and one would have to keep track of each individual trade. Questions of search behavior invariably arise in this context, as do distributional questions.

The other way is to ignore search and distributional issues. Even here, however, there are at least two ways in which these issues can be ignored: one is to postulate only one firm and treat it as a monopolist; the other is to postulate more than one firm but treat all firms as identical. This latter approach is the one that was taken. The advantage of postulating more than one firm is that models can be specified in which the behavior of an individual firm is influenced by its expectations of the behavior of other firms. Models like this, in which market share considerations can play a role, seem more reasonable in macroeconomics than do models of pure monopoly behavior.

An apparent disadvantage of postulating more than one firm and yet treating all firms as identical is that whenever a firm expects other firms to behave differently from the way it plans to behave, the firm is always wrong. Although firms always behave in the same way, they almost always expect that they will not. Firms never learn, in other words, that they are identical. Fortunately, this disadvantage is more apparent than real. If one is ignoring search and distributional questions anyway, there is no real difference (as far as ignoring the questions is concerned) whether one postulates one firm or many identical firms. Both postulates are of the same order of approximation, namely the complete ignoring of search and distributional questions, and if one feels that a richer model can be specified by postulating more than one firm, one might as well do so. The added richness will be gained without losing any more regarding search and distributional issues than is already lost in the monopoly model.

The aggregation that was used here consists of one household, two identical firms, and one bank. The household will be denoted h, the firms f and k, and the bank b. With respect to the order of transactions, information flows in one direction in the model: from the government, to the firms, to the household. Decisions are made at the beginning of the period before any transactions take place, and transactions occur throughout the rest of the period. A brief outline of the information flows will be given, and then the complete model will be set up. Note that the order of transactions is important in a model like the present one in which there can be disequilibrium. If transactions take place at nonmarket clearing prices, it is necessary to postulate who goes unsatisfied. In an equilibrium model in which no transactions take place until the market clearing prices are determined, the order of transactions does not matter.

A Brief Outline

Let t be the period under consideration. Before transactions take place, the following events occur. (1) The government determines the fiscal and monetary policy variables for period t. This includes the determination of the interest rate, which means that whatever variables are in the interest rate reaction function (3.61) are assumed to be known by the government at the beginning of period t. (2) Each firm receives information on the profit tax rate and the interest rate for period t from the government, forms expectations of these two variables for all relevant future periods, and solves its maximization problem. Determined by this solution are, among other things, its price, wage rate, and the maximum amount of labor to employ. (3) The household receives information for period t on the tax rate, the level of transfer payments, the interest rate, the wage rate, the price of goods, and the maximum amount that it will be able to work. It forms expectations of these variables for all relevant future periods and then solves its maximization problem. Determined by this solution are, among other things, its labor supply and consumption. (4) After the household makes its decision, transactions take place.

Note that the model is recursive in the sense that information flows in only one direction. The firms are not given an opportunity to change their decisions for the current period after the household has made its decisions; the firms only find out the decisions of the household after transactions have taken place. Note also that because the household makes its decisions after receiving information on the labor constraint, the system is guaranteed that the amount of labor supplied will not exceed the maximum allowed.

If the model is to be solved for more than one period, the whole procedure is repeated for period $t+1$ after the transactions have taken place for period t. The decisions for period $t+1$ are based on knowledge of the transactions for period t. Although values of the decision variables are computed for all periods of the horizon each time a maximization problem is solved, it is important to keep in mind that only the values for the current period are used in computing the transactions that take place. In each period new time paths are computed, based on the transactions that have taken place in the previous period, and thus the optimal values of the decision variables for periods other than the current period are of importance only insofar as they affect the optimal values for the current period.

The Model

When the complete model is put together a distinction must be made between the stock holdings and the bond holdings of the household. This distinction was unnecessary in the discussion of the household maximization problem because the expected rates of return on stocks and bonds are the same. The actual rates of return are not in general the same, and so this must be modeled.

The household owns all the stock in the model. Let PS_{t-1} denote the value of this stock at the end of period $t-1$ or the beginning of period t. PS_{t-1} is assumed to be equal to the present discounted value of expected future after-tax cash flow of the firms and the bank, where the discount rates are the expected future one-period interest rates. Let ${}_{t-1}E_{t-1}$ denote the expected value of after-tax cash flow for period $t-1$ that was made at the beginning of period $t-1$, and let ${}_tE_t$ denote the expected value of after-tax cash flow for period t that is made at the beginning of period t. The variable ${}_tE_t$ is assumed to be a weighted average of ${}_{t-1}E_{t-1}$ and the actual value of after-tax cash flow in period $t-1$:

$$(3.62) \qquad {}_tE_t = \lambda({}_{t-1}E_{t-1}) + (1-\lambda)(CF_{ft-1} - T_{ft-1} + CF_{kt-1} - T_{kt-1} + D_{bt-1}), \qquad 0 < \lambda < 1.$$

[expected value of after-tax cash flow for period t]

The expected values of after-tax cash flow for periods $t+1$ and beyond are all assumed to be equal to ${}_tE_t$. Similarly, the expected values of the interest rate for periods $t + 1$ and beyond are all assumed to be equal to the rate for period t, R_t. R_t is known at the beginning of period t. These expectational assumptions imply that

(3.63) $$PS_{t-1} = \frac{{}_tE_t}{R_t}.$$ [value of stocks at the beginning of period t]

Let A'_{ht-1} denote the bond holdings of the household at the beginning of period t. Then the total value of stock and bond holdings at the beginning of period t, which was denoted A_{ht-1} in the discussion of the household maximization problem in Section 3.1.2, is $A'_{ht-1} + PS_{t-1}$. These variables will be used in the equations that follow.

There is a potential constraint on the output of the firms, which was briefly discussed in Section 3.1.3. Although the firms expect that they will be able to produce the amount of output that is computed from the maximization problem, this may not be the case. If the level of sales and the stock of inventories turn out to be different from what they were expected to be, labor requirements in (3.26) and (3.27) will be different from what they were expected to be. If the requirements are higher and if the firm was not planning to hold any excess labor, output will have to be cut from its planned value. Also, the firm may not get as much labor as it expected, and this will force it to cut output unless there is excess labor on hand to make up the difference. These adjustments are included in the model below.

The complete description of the model is as follows. The government determines

(M1) $$d_{1t}, d_{2t}, TR_t, L_{gt}, C_{gt}, R_t, g_{1t}, RD_t.$$

These decisions are exogenous except for the decision regarding R_t. R_t is determined by the reaction function (3.61). The value of stocks for the beginning of period t is determined by (3.63):

(M2) $$PS_{t-1}.$$

The value of the stock and bond holdings of the household at the end of period $t - 1$ or the beginning of period t is

(M3) $$A_{ht-1} = A'_{ht-1} + PS_{t-1},$$

where A'_{ht-1} is determined in period $t - 1$.

Given d_{2t} and R_t, firms f and k solve their maximization problems. Since the firms are identical, only the values for firm f need to be noted. The following variables, among others, are determined from this solution:

(M4) $P_{ft}, IM_{fit}, K_{fit}, I_{ft}, LMAX_{ft}, W_{ft}.$

All the different prices in the model are assumed to be equal to P_{ft}, and all the different wage rates are assumed to be equal to W_{ft}:

(M5) $P_{ht} = P_{gt} = P'_{ft} = P_{ft},$

(M6) $W_{ht} = W_{gt} = W_{ft}.$

The maximum amount that the household can work, L^*_{ht}, is

(M7) $L^*_{ht} = LMAX_{ft} + LMAX_{kt} + L_{gt}.$

Given d_{1t}, TR_t, R_t, A_{ht-1}, P_{ht}, W_{ht}, and L^*_{ht}, the household solves its maximization problem. Determined from this are

(M8) $L_{ht}, C_{ht}, N_{ht}, M_{ht}.$

The household can also be thought of as solving its maximization problem under the assumption of no labor constraint. Let LUN_{ht} denote the amount of labor that would be supplied if the constraint were not binding. Firms are assumed to observe this value after transactions have taken place, and therefore it is a variable of the model:

(M9) $LUN_{ht}.$

After the household makes its decisions, transactions take place. The rest of the model describes these transactions. The level of total sales is

(M10) $XA_t = C_{ht} + I_{ft} + I_{kt} + C_{gt}.$

Each firm receives half the sales:

(M11) $X_{ft} = X_{kt} = .5XA_t.$

The total amount of labor supplied to the firms is

(M12) $LA_t = L_{ht} - L_{gt}.$

This assumes that the government gets its labor first; what is left over goes to the firms. Each firm gets half the labor:

(M13) $L_{ft} = L_{kt} = .5LA_t.$

If the household were unconstrained, the amount of labor that would be supplied to the firms would be

(M14) $LAUN_t = LUN_{ht} - L_{gt}.$

Given X_{ft} and L_{ft}, it can now be seen whether firm f can produce the amount of output that it expected when it solved its maximization problem. If it cannot, output is cut back by the necessary amount. This is done in the most efficient way possible, which is by using the most labor-efficient machines first, the next most labor-efficient machines second, and so on. Y_{ft} will be used to denote the actual amount of output produced:

(M15) $\quad Y_{ft}.$

Given d_{2t}, R_t, P'_{ft}, I_{ft}, L_{ft}, X_{ft}, Y_{ft}, and the various lagged values, the following variables are determined by (3.25) and (3.31)–(3.39):

(M16) $\quad V_{ft}, T'_{ft}, DEP_{ft}, \pi_{ft}, T_{ft}, D_{ft}, CF_{ft}, S_{ft}, A_{ft}, M_{ft}.$

Because A_{ft} appears in (3.36) as well as in the budget constraint (3.38), the solution for some of these variables requires solving a small linear model.

The bank variables are determined next. The following equation determines M_{bt}:

(M17) $\quad M_{bt} = -M_{ht} - M_{ft} - M_{kt},$

where the RHS variables are determined above. This equation merely states that the demand deposits of the household and firms are held in the bank. Given d_{2t}, g_{1t}, R_t, RD_t, M_{bt}, and various lagged values, the following variables are determined by (3.53)–(3.58):

(M18) $\quad BR_{bt}, BO_{bt}, \pi_{bt}, T_{bt}, D_{bt}, A_{bt}.$

In order to complete the variables for the household, the value of stocks at the end of period t must be known. This can be done if R_{t+1} is known, and so it is assumed that the government sets this rate at the end of period t but before the remaining variables for the household are determined:

(M19) $\quad R_{t+1}.$

Given that CF_{ft}, T_{ft}, CF_{kt}, T_{kt}, and D_{bt} have already been determined, ${}_{t+1}E_{t+1}$ can be computed from (3.62) with the time subscript moved ahead one period. ${}_{t+1}E_{t+1}$ is the expected value of after-tax cash flow for period $t+1$ made at the beginning of period $t+1$ (or the end of period t). Given R_{t+1} and ${}_{t+1}E_{t+1}$, PS_t can be computed from (3.63) with the time subscript moved ahead one period:

(M20) $\quad PS_t.$

The value of capital gains on stocks for period t, denoted CG_t, is

(M21) $\quad CG_t = PS_t - PS_{t-1}.$

Capital gains are assumed to be taxed like regular income. Given d_{1t}, TR_t, R_t, W_{ht}, P_{ht}, D_{ft}, D_{kt}, D_{bt}, M_{ht}, CG_t, M_{ht-1}, and A'_{ht-1}, the following four equations are used to solve for the four LHS variables:

(M22) $\quad Y_{ht} = W_{ht}L_{ht} + R_tA'_{ht} + D_{ft} + D_{kt} + D_{bt},$

(M23) $\quad T_{ht} = d_{1t}(Y_{ht} + CG_t) - TR_t,$

(M24) $\quad S_{ht} = Y_{ht} - T_{ht} - P_{ht}C_{ht},$

(M25) $\quad A'_{ht} = A'_{ht-1} + S_{ht} - \Delta M_{ht}.$

Equation (M22) is like (3.11), where nonwage income is now disaggregated into interest and dividend income. Equation (M23) is like (3.12), where capital gains are now included in the taxable income base. Equation (M24) is the same as (3.13). The budget constraint (M25) is like (3.14) except for the replacement of A' for A. Because A'_{ht} appears in both (M22) and (M25), the solution for the four LHS variables requires solving a linear model.

The last two variables to be determined are the government variables S_{gt} and A_{gt}. These are determined by (3.59) and (3.60):

(M26) $\quad S_{gt}, A_{gt}.$

There is one important redundant equation in the model, which states that the sum of bond holdings across all agents is zero:

(M27) $\quad 0 = A'_{ht} + A_{ft} + A_{kt} + A_{bt} + A_{gt}.$

This equation is redundant because the sum of savings across all agents is zero, and each agent's budget constraint has been used to solve for its bond holdings.

This completes the solution for period t. Given the solution values for this period, the model can be solved for period $t+1$. The initial conditions for period $t+1$ are the solution values for period t.

Simulation Results

Before the model is solved, the interest rate reaction function (3.61) must be specified. It is taken to be

$$(3.61)' \quad R_t = R_{t-1} - .1UR_t + \frac{P_{ft} - P_{ft-1}}{P_{ft-1}},$$

where UR_t is the unemployment rate. The unemployment rate is defined to be one minus the ratio of the constrained to the unconstrained supply of labor:

$$(3.64) \qquad UR_t = 1 - \frac{L_{ht}}{LUN_{ht}}. \qquad \text{[unemployment rate]}$$

Equation (3.61)′ is a "leaning against the wind" equation. The government raises the interest rate when unemployment falls and inflation rises, and it lowers the rate when unemployment rises and inflation falls. Given that the reaction function is used, A_{gt} it taken to be endogenous. The other two monetary policy variables, RD_t and g_{1t}, are exogenous.

The initial conditions and parameter values that were presented earlier for the household and firms were used for the results for the complete model. The other initial conditions and parameter values that are needed are the following.

$$(t = 1)$$

$$\begin{aligned}
A'_{ht-1} &= 311.42857 \\
D_{bt-1} &= 4.2 \\
BR_{bt-1} &= 30.0 \\
BO_{bt-1} &= 0.0 \\
A_{gt-1} &= -231.42857 \\
{}_{t-1}E_{t-1} &= 48.2 \\
CF_{ft-1} &= 44.0 \\
CF_{kt-1} &= 44.0 \\
T_{ft-1} &= 22.0 \\
T_{kt-1} &= 22.0 \\
R_{t-1} &= .07 \\
UR_{t-1} &= 0.0 \\
\gamma_4 &= -1.0 \\
\lambda &= .9
\end{aligned}$$

The reason for the choice of the above value for A'_{ht-1} is the following. From (M3) the value of wealth of the household at the beginning of period t, A_{ht-1}, is equal to $A'_{ht-1} + PS_{t-1}$, where from (3.63) $PS_{t-1} = {}_tE_t/R_t$. Given the above initial conditions, ${}_tE_t$ equals 48.2 and R_t equals .07, which implies a value of PS_{t-1} of 688.57143. This value plus the above value of 311.42857 for A'_{ht-1} equals 1,000, which is the value of A_{ht-1} used in Section 3.1.2 for the simulation results for the household.

With respect to the terminal value of wealth of the household, $\overline{AM}$ in (3.16), it was taken to be $311.42857 + PS_{t-1}$ for all of the experiments with the complete model, where PS_{t-1} is the value of stocks at the end of the previous period. If the model has been solved for at least one period, then the value of PS_{t-1} will in general differ from 48.2/.07, since in general both ${}_tE_t$ and R_t will be different. The terminal value of wealth thus differs from period to period depending on the value of stocks.

The government values that were used for the base run are as follows.

$(t = 1)$

$$
\begin{aligned}
d_{1t} &= .2 \\
d_{2t} &= .5 \\
TR_t &= 0.0 \\
L_{gt} &= 30.0 \\
C_{gt} &= 96.0 \\
g_{1t} &= .2 \\
RD_t &= .07
\end{aligned}
$$

The results of solving the model for the above values are presented in the first column of Table 3-4. A solution of the model for, say, period 1 requires running through steps (M1)–(M26). This entails the household and firms solving their maximization problems for periods 1–3, although only the decision values for period 1 ever get used. Once the model is solved for period 1, it can be solved for period 2. As the model is solved forward, it is assumed that the length of the decision horizon for the household and firms always remains at 3.

The cost of solving the complete model for one period is dominated by the cost of solving the maximization problem of the firm, since the other calculations are more or less trivial. The time taken on the IBM 4341 at Yale for the solution of the model for one period was about 39 seconds, of which about 38 seconds was used for the firm's maximization problem.

When the household solves its problem in, say, period 1, it must form expectations of W_{ht}, P_{ht}, R_t, d_{1t}, and TR_t for periods 2 and 3. In the analysis of household behavior in Section 3.1.2 it was assumed that the household expects these variables to remain unchanged in periods 2 and 3 from the observed period 1 values, and this assumption has been retained for the solution of the complete model. Regarding the labor constraint, it was assumed for experiment 7 in Table 3-2 that the household expected the constraint to be binding only for period 1, and this assumption has also been retained for the solution of the complete model. The labor constraint is thus binding on the household for at most the first period. In the analysis of firm behavior in Section 3.1.3 it was assumed that the firm expects the interest rate (R_t) and the tax rate (d_{2t}) to remain unchanged from the observed period 1 values, and the price of investment goods (P'_{ft}) to remain unchanged from the observed period 0 value. This assumption has been retained here.

When the model is solved period after period using the above initial conditions and parameter values and the above set of government values, the same solution value is obtained for each variable for each period. In other words, a "self-repeating" run is obtained. The values for selected variables from this run are presented in Table 3-4 in the column headed "Base run values." The self-repeating run is an equilibrium run in the sense that all the expectations are equal to the actual values. No errors are made anywhere in the model.

The experiments consisted of changing one of the government values and solving the model again. The value was changed for the current and all future periods. Most of the important properties of the model can be discovered by analyzing just two experiments: an increase in the interest rate and a decrease in government purchases of goods. For the interest rate experiment, the interest rate reaction function was dropped from the model and the interest rate was taken to be exogenous. This allows the interest rate to be taken to be a policy variable and changed exogenously. The results of the two experiments are presented in Table 3-4. Both the pluses and minuses and the actual numbers are presented for each experiment. Although the numbers have no empirical content, knowledge of them sometimes helps in understanding the results. The following paragraphs present a discussion of the results.

Experiment 1: An increase in the interest rate. The reader should remember that for this experiment there is no interest rate reaction function. The interest rate is exogenous, and the experiment consists of increasing it to .071 from its base period value of .070. Call the first period of the experiment period 1. The increase in the interest rate in period 1 causes the household to suffer a capital loss on its stocks at the beginning of the period (Eq. 3.63). Although this is not shown in the table, the value of stocks is $48.2/.071 = 678.87$, which compares to the base run value of $48.2/.07 = 688.57$.

The increase in the interest rate was not large enough to affect the firms' decisions for period 1 (rows 1, 6, 8–12). The household wanted to work more (row 19), but it was constrained from doing so because the firms did not want to hire any more labor. The household thus worked the same amount (row 13). It consumed less, spent more time taking care of money holdings, and planned to save more (rows 14, 15, 17). When transactions took place, sales were less (row 2) because of the drop in demand from the household. Production was slightly less (row 3) because the firms were forced to cut production from the planned values due to the increased labor requirements resulting from the change in sales. This cut was small, and sales dropped more than production. The level of inventories thus rose (row 4). The firms' profits

TABLE 3-4. Simulation results for the complete model

Row no.		Base run values 1[a]	Experiment $R_t(+)$ Signs 1 2 3 4 5	$R_t(+)$ Values 1	2	3	4	5	$C_{gt}(-)$ Signs 1 2 3 4 5	$C_{gt}(-)$ Values 1	2	3	4	5
Some key variables:														
1	P_{ft}	1.0	0 - - - -	1.0	.9999	.9998	.9997	.9996	0 - - - -	1.0	.9998	.9996	.9994	.9991
2	X_{ft}	263.0	- - - - -	262.82	262.78	262.83	262.86	262.93	- - - - -	262.75	262.61	262.54	262.38	262.21
3	Y_{ft}	263.0	- - - - -	262.97	262.79	262.75	262.82	262.83	- - - - -	262.96	262.70	262.56	262.47	262.29
4	V_{ft}	50.0	+ + + + -	50.16	50.17	50.09	50.05	49.96	+ + + + +	50.21	50.30	50.31	50.40	50.49
5	UR_t	0.0	+ + + + 0	.00052	.00068	.00056	.00018	0.0	0 + + + +	0.0	.00086	.00159	.00217	.00307
6	W_{ft}	1.0	0 - - - -	1.0	.9997	.9796	.9995	.9995	0 - - - -	1.0	.9998	.9995	.9991	.9985
7	R_{t+1}	.07	+ + + + +	.071	.071	.071	.071	.071	0 - - - -	.07	.0698	.0694	.0689	.0683
Firm f's decisions (other than P_{ft} and W_{ft}):														
8	X^e_{ft}	263.0	0 - - - -	263.0	262.85	262.81	262.85	262.87	0 - - - -	263.0	262.79	262.67	262.61	262.46
9	Y^e_{ft}	263.0	0 - - - -	263.0	262.80	262.75	262.82	262.85	0 - - - -	263.0	262.72	262.57	262.50	262.33
10	V^e_{ft}	50.0	0 + + + +	50.0	50.10	50.11	50.06	50.03	0 + + + +	50.0	50.14	50.20	50.21	50.27
11	I_{ft}	27.0	0 - - - -	27.0	26.96	26.99	26.97	27.00	0 - - - -	27.0	26.94	26.97	26.93	26.93
12	L^e_{ft} ($= LMAX_{ft}$)	185.0	0 - - - -	185.0	184.87	184.84	184.88	184.91	0 - - - -	185.0	184.82	184.73	184.67	184.56
Household's decisions:														
13	L_{ht}	400.0	0 - - - -	400.0	399.74	399.68	399.76	399.77	0 - - - -	400.0	399.64	399.44	399.35	399.12
14	C_{ht}	376.0	- - - - -	375.64	375.63	375.68	375.77	375.85	0 - - - -	376.0	375.84	375.65	375.41	375.04
15	N_{ht}	.2646	+ + + + +	.2665	.2665	.2666	.2665	.2665	0 + - - -	.2646	.2647	.2643	.2637	.2629
16	M_{ht}	100.0	- - - - -	99.88	99.87	99.87	99.88	99.90	0 - - - -	100.0	99.94	99.88	99.80	99.69
17	S^e_{ht}	0.0	+ + + + +	.66	.41	.32	.31	.26	0 - - - -	0.0	-.18	-.27	-.31	-.40
18	A^e_{ht}	1000.0	- - - - -	991.08	990.99	991.20	991.54	991.83	0 - + + +	1000.0	999.29	1000.70	1003.25	1006.30
19	LUN_{ht}	400.0	+ + - - -	400.21	400.01	399.90	399.83	399.77	0 - + + +	400.0	399.98	400.08	400.22	400.35

	Transactions-determined variables (other than X_{ft}, Y_{ft}, V_{ft}, UR_t):												
20	L_{ft}	185.0	0 - - - -	185.0	184.87	184.84	184.88	184.88	0 - - - -	185.0	184.82	184.72	184.67	184.56
21	T_{ft}	44.0	- - - - -	43.86	43.85	43.85	43.88	43.88	- - - - -	43.95	43.88	43.88	43.90	43.93
22	D_{ft}	22.0	- - - - -	21.93	21.92	21.93	21.94	21.94	- - - - -	21.97	21.93	21.94	21.95	21.96
23	$CF_{ft} - T_{ft}$	22.0	- - - - +	21.78	21.93	21.99	21.99	22.02	- - - - -	21.76	21.89	21.92	21.89	21.89
24	S_{ft}	0.0	- + + + +	-.16	.02	.07	.05	.08	- - - - -	-.21	-.04	-.01	-.06	-.07
25	$-A_{ft}$	100.0	+ + + - -	100.14	100.12	100.05	100.00	99.92	+ + + + +	100.19	100.22	100.22	100.25	100.30
26	M_{ft}	25.0	- - - - -	24.98	24.98	24.98	24.98	24.98	- - - - -	24.98	24.96	24.95	24.93	24.90
27	$-M_{bt}$	150.0	- - - - -	149.85	149.82	149.82	149.84	149.87	- - - - -	149.95	149.86	149.77	149.65	149.49
28	BR_{bt}	30.0	- - - - -	29.97	29.96	29.96	29.97	29.97	- - - - -	29.99	29.97	29.95	29.93	29.90
29	BO_{bt}	0.0	+ + + + +	.030	.030	.030	.030	.030	0 0 - - -	0.0	0.0	-.007	-.019	-.032
30	D_{bt}	4.2	+ + + + +	4.256	4.255	4.255	4.255	4.256	- - - - -	4.199	4.196	4.179	4.153	4.121
31	A_{bt}	120.0	- - - - -	119.91	119.89	119.89	119.90	119.92	- - - - -	119.96	119.89	119.81	119.70	119.56
32	PS_t	688.57	- - - - -	678.32	678.26	678.38	678.48	678.67	- + + + +	687.89	690.03	693.64	697.95	703.97
33	CG_t	0.0	- - + + +	-.55	-.06	.12	.10	.19	- + + + +	-.68	2.14	3.61	4.31	6.02
34	S_{ht}	0.0	+ + + + +	.70	.36	.25	.25	.19	+ - - - -	.10	-.71	-1.10	-1.28	-1.72
35	A'_{ht}	311.43	+ + - + +	312.25	312.62	312.87	313.11	313.28	+ - - - -	311.53	310.88	309.84	308.63	307.02
36	A_{ht}	1000.0	- - - - -	990.58	990.89	991.26	991.59	991.95	- + + + +	999.42	1000.90	1003.48	1006.59	1011.00
37	S_{gt}	0.0	- - - - -	-.39	-.39	-.38	-.36	-.36	+ + + + +	.33	.80	1.13	1.39	1.87
38	$-A_{gt}$	231.43	+ + + + +	231.28	232.28	232.66	233.01	233.36	- - - - -	231.11	230.33	229.21	227.83	225.98

Notes: a. Values for all future periods the same as those for period 1.

- Superscript e denotes an expected value at the time the maximization problem was solved. The actual value that is determined when transactions takes place may differ from the expected value.
- For experiment 1, R_t was increased to .071 for all t.
- For experiment 2, C_{gt} was decreased to 95.0 for all t.

and cash flow were down because of the decrease in production and sales (rows 21, 23). The level of profits of the bank was higher because of the higher interest rate (row 30). The sum of after-tax cash flow of the firms and after-tax profits of the bank was lower, and this caused a fall in the value of stocks at the end of period 1 (rows 32 and 33). This capital loss, contrary to the capital loss at the beginning of the period, was caused by a fall in cash flow rather than a rise in the interest rate. The government ran a deficit in period 1 (row 37). There are a number of reasons for this. Firms' taxes were lower because of the fall in profits, and the household's taxes were lower because of the capital loss; the government's interest payments were higher because of the higher interest rate. The increase in the bank's taxes works the other way, but this increase was quite small, and thus the net effect on the government's budget was negative.

The response of a firm to a decrease in sales has been discussed in Section 3.1.3. The decrease in sales in period 1 led the firms in period 2 to lower prices, expected sales, planned production, investment, employment, and wage rates (rows 1, 6, 8–12). The household was again constrained in its labor supply, but this time because of the decrease in labor demand by the firms. (Unconstrained, the household wanted to work essentially the same amount as the base run value; see row 19.) The unemployment rate was higher in period 2 than in period 1 (row 5) because of the more severe labor constraint on the household. Sales were again lower in period 2 because of the lower consumption of the household.

The system continued at a lower level of sales and production throughout the five periods presented in the table. The main reason for this is the lower level of consumption of the household resulting from the higher interest rate. By period 5 the firms had reduced their inventories to essentially the base run value (row 4). The unemployment rate was back to zero by period 5. Given the particular parameter values used, the wage rate falls more than the price level each period (rows 1 and 6). This fall in the real wage leads the household to want to work less, and by period 5 its unconstrained supply of labor (row 19), while lower than the base run value, is no longer greater than the maximum amount allowed. The drop in the real wage is also the main reason that after-tax cash flow is higher than the base run value in period 5 (row 23) even though sales are lower. The government budget is in deficit throughout the period.

Experiment 2: A decrease in government purchases of goods. Part of this experiment has been discussed in Section 3.1.3 in the analysis of firm behavior. The decrease in goods purchases has no effect on anyone's decisions in period 1, but it does lead to lower sales, slightly lower production, and a higher level of inventories. The lower production is again due to the increased labor requirements resulting from the change in sales. Profits are lower, which causes a capital loss on stocks. Dividends are also lower. The reaction function does not change the interest rate at the end of period 1 (row 7) because the unemployment rate is zero and prices are unchanged.

In period 2 the firms responded to the sales decrease in the same manner as discussed in Section 3.1.3, namely by contracting. Although the price level and wage rate are the same to four digits in Table 3-4, the wage rate dropped slightly more. This led the household to lower very slightly its unconstrained supply of labor (row 19), but it was forced to supply even less because of the drop in the demand for labor from the firms (row 13). This is the main reason for the decrease in consumption in period 2. Sales were thus even lower in period 2 than they were in period 1 because of the consumption decrease. At the end of period 2 the reaction function lowered the interest rate (row 7) because of the positive level of unemployment and the fall in prices. This resulted in a capital gain at the end of period 2 (rows 32–33).

The system continued at the lower level of sales and production throughout the five periods in the table. The main factor that prevents the system from falling more than it does and that will eventually lead it to stop falling is the interest rate. As the unemployment rate rises and prices fall, the interest rate falls. A falling interest rate leads the household to consume more, both because of the fall in the interest rate itself (the intertemporal substitution effect) and the rise in wealth due to the capital gains on stocks. A fall in the interest rate may also lead the firms to switch to more expensive, less labor-intensive machines, which increases investment. Although this happened in the analysis of firm behavior in Table 3-3, the interest rate decreases were not large enough in Table 3-4 for this to take place in the current experiment. Although this is not presented in Table 3-4, the firms did switch to the more expensive machines in period 6 and thus increased their investment expenditures. It should be noted that one consequence that this switch has is to lower the demand for employment, which further constrains the household and leads it to lower consumption further. The substitution of more expensive machines is thus not in itself enough to stop the system from falling.

Other Contractionary Experiments

Given an understanding of the two experiments in Table 3-4, other contractionary experiments are easy to follow. If for any reason demand is lowered

—either government demand, firm demand, or household demand—a contractionary situation is likely to develop in which firms lower employment, the household lowers consumption because of the labor constraint, the firms lower employment more because of the further fall in sales, and so on.

Two of the experiments that were run involved an increase in the personal income tax rate, d_{1t}, and a decrease in the level of transfer payments, TR_t. Both led to decreased consumption by the household. The main difference between the two experiments is that the increase in d_{1t} leads, other things being equal, to a decrease in the unconstrained supply of labor, whereas the decrease in TR_t leads to an increase in the supply. The unemployment rate, which is a positive function of the unconstrained supply of labor, is thus higher in the transfer payment experiment than it is in the other.

An increase in the profit tax rate, d_{2t}, led to a fall in after-tax cash flow, dividends, and the price of stocks. The lower dividends and wealth of the household led it to consume less, which then started a contraction. This is the main channel through which an increase in the profit tax rate affects the economy, namely by first affecting the income and wealth of the household. As discussed in Section 3.1.3, an increase in d_{2t} may also lead the firm to switch to the less expensive machines, which lowers investment, but this is of rather minor importance.

An increase in the discount rate, RD_t, lowered the profits and dividends of the bank and thus the price of stocks. The lower dividends and wealth of the household led it to consume less. To the extent that bank profits are a small fraction of total profits in the economy, this effect on households is not likely to be a very large one in practice. A change in RD_t has no direct effect on the interest rate since it does not appear in the interest rate reaction function. An increase in RD_t does lead to a decrease in bank borrowing from the government, BO_t, which from (3.60) means that there are fewer government securities outstanding than otherwise (that is, $-A_{gt}$ is smaller). Remember that A_{gt} is the instrument by which the government achieves the target interest rate each period as dictated by the interest rate reaction function. Because of the interest rate reaction function, RD_t has little effect on R_t. The government merely offsets any changes in bank borrowing that result from changes in RD_t by changes in A_{gt}.

An increase in the reserve requirement rate, g_{1t}, also lowered bank profits and dividends, which then affected the household. Again, this effect is likely to be small in practice if bank profits are a small fraction of total profits. Bank reserves were higher because of the higher requirement rate, which from (3.60) means that there were fewer government securities outstanding than otherwise. g_{1t}, like RD_t, has little effect on R_t because the government merely offsets any changes in bank reserves that result from changes in g_{1t} by changes in A_{gt}.

Expansionary Experiments

Two "expansionary" experiments that were run involved a decrease in the interest rate and an increase in government purchases of goods. Expansionary experiments from a position of equilibrium are of somewhat less interest than contractionary ones in terms of learning about the properties of the model. When the system is in equilibrium, as it is in the base run, there are only two ways in which more output can be produced: one is for the household to work more, and the other is for the firms to switch to less labor-intensive machines. The household's work effort is a positive function of the real wage and the interest rate; it is a negative function of the initial value of wealth, the tax rate, and the level of transfer payments. The firms' switching to less labor-intensive machines is a positive function of the real wage and a negative function of the interest rate. The disequilibrium features of the model are thus not likely to be apparent for expansionary experiments, and the effects on output hinge on the labor supply response of the household and the investment response of the firms. The following is a brief discussion of the expansionary experiments.

When the interest rate was decreased, the household worked less in period 1. The real wage was unchanged because the interest rate decrease was not large enough to affect the firms' decisions in period 1. Given this and given the lower interest rate and the higher initial value of wealth from the interest rate decrease, the effect on household work effort was negative. Household consumption was higher in period 1, and thus sales were higher. Production was lower because of the increased labor requirements due to the change in sales and because of the decrease in labor supply. The stock of inventories was thus lower at the end of period 1. The lower work effort and higher consumption meant that the household dissaved in period 1.

The firms responded in period 2 to the higher sales, lower inventories, and lower labor supply by raising prices and wages. The price level was raised less than the wage rate, and this increase in the real wage led the household to increase its work effort in period 2 compared to the base run value. It continued to dissave in period 2. The real wage began to fall in period 3, but labor supply remained higher than its base run value. The main reason for this has to do with the saving behavior of the household. As noted, the lower interest rate led the household to dissave; this decreases wealth, which has a positive effect on labor supply in the next period. By period 3 the positive effect from the lower wealth outweighed the negative effects from the lower interest rate and the lower real wage.

The unemployment rate was zero for the first four periods, but in period 5 it was positive. Although labor supply and production were higher than they were in the base run, the household wanted to work slightly more than the labor constraint allowed, and so the unemployment rate was positive.

For the experiment in which government purchases of goods were increased, labor supply was the same in period 1, higher in period 2, and lower in periods 3 and beyond. It was unchanged in period 1 because the increase in goods purchases has no effect on the decisions in period 1. It was higher in period 2 primarily because the real wage was higher, and it was lower in periods 3 and beyond primarily because the real wage was lower.

The unemployment rate was zero throughout the five periods of the experiment; production was lower because of the lower labor supply; and prices and wages were higher because of the increase in sales and decrease in inventories. The interest rate was higher beginning in period 3 because of the increase in prices. Capital losses on stocks began occurring at the end of period 2 because of the higher interest rate.

3.1.6 Summary and Further Discussion

1. One of the main properties of the model is that disequilibrium can occur because of expectation errors. Once the system is in disequilibrium in the sense that expected values differ from actual values, it will remain so. In particular, a multiplier reaction can take place in which the firms constrain the household in its labor supply; the household responds by lowering consumption and thus sales of the firms; the firms respond by lowering production and their demand for labor, which further constrains the household; the household responds by lowering consumption even more; and so on.

2. Contrary to a model like the one of Phelps and Winter that was discussed in Section 3.1.1, the present model does not return to equilibrium in a straightforward way once it is shocked. In fact, the model never returns to equilibrium. No agent knows or ever learns the complete model, and thus decisions are always being made on the basis of expectations that turn out not to be correct. There is no convergence of expectations to the true values. This feature of the model does not depend on the expectations being formed in simple ways; it would be true even if agents formed their expectations on the

basis of predictions from sophisticated models as long as the models were not the true model and did not converge to the true model.

This feature of less than perfect expectations seems sensible in the present context. In order for agents to form correct expectations, they would have to know the maximization problems of all other agents. They also would have to know the exact way that transactions take place once the decisions have been solved for. In a model like the present one it seems unreasonable to assume that agents have this much information. (This is contrary to simple models of the Phelps and Winter type, where the assumption does not necessarily seem implausible.) It also seems unreasonable to assume that agents all learn the correct model over time. At the least, if they did finally learn it, the length of time needed to do so seems so long as to be for all practical purposes infinity.

The imposition of long-run constraints on models was discussed in Section 2.1.5, where it was noted that these constraints can play a critical role in the development of a model. It can now be seen why I believe that long-run constraints may be playing too much of a role in recent work. In order for a model like the present one to return to equilibrium once it is shocked, one has to make what seem to be unreasonable assumptions about the ability of agents to learn the complete model. Unless these assumptions are made, no long-run equilibrium constraints can be imposed on the model.

3. No price and wage rigidities have been postulated in the model. If this were done, it would provide another explanation of the existence of disequilibrium aside from expectations errors. One reason this was not done is to show that disequilibrium phenomena can easily arise without such rigidities.

4. The interest rate is the key variable that prevents the system from contracting indefinitely. As unemployment increases or prices fall, the interest rate is lowered by the interest rate reaction function. A fall in the interest rate results in a capital gain on stocks. Both the lower interest rate and the higher wealth have a positive effect on the consumption of the household. The lower interest rate may also lead the firms to switch to more expensive, less labor-intensive machines, which increases investment expenditures.

5. The fact that the interest rate has such important effects in the model means that monetary policy is quite important. With the interest rate reaction function included in the model, monetary policy is endogenous, and therefore monetary policy experiments cannot be run. One can, however, drop the reaction function and take the interest rate as exogenous. Monetary policy experiments can then be run by changing the interest rate, and, as just noted, this will have important effects on the system.

With the reaction function dropped, it is possible to take all three monetary instruments—the amount of government securities outstanding $(-A_{gt})$, the reserve requirement rate (g_{1t}), and the discount rate (RD_t)—as exogenous. In this case R_t is endogenous and is implicitly determined. Monetary policy experiments can then be run by changing one or more of these variables. The primary way that these changes would affect the system is through their effect on the interest rate.

6. The unemployment rate is a positive function of the supply of labor, which in turn is a function of variables such as the real wage, the interest rate, the income tax rate, and the level of transfer payments. The effects of a policy change on the unemployment rate thus depend in part on the labor supply response to the policy change. For example, increasing the income tax rate lowers labor supply, whereas decreasing the level of transfer payments raises it. Given the many factors that affect labor supply, there is clearly no stable relationship in the model between the unemployment rate and real output and between the unemployment rate and the rate of inflation. There is, in other words, no stable Okun's law and no stable Phillips curve in the model.

7. An interesting question about the long-run properties of the model is whether it is possible to concoct a self-repeating run in which there exists unemployment. It can be seen from (3.50) that this is not possible. The firm expects the unconstrained and constrained aggregate supplies of labor to be the same. If this is not true for, say, period t, which the firm knows at the beginning of period $t+1$, the firm will not make the same decisions in period $t+1$ as it did in period t.

The key assumption that allows there to be no self-repeating run with unemployment is that the firms observe the unconstrained as well as the constrained aggregate supplies of labor. Assume instead that the firms do not observe the unconstrained supply, and consider a self-repeating run with no unemployment. Now change the utility function of the household in such a way that it desires to work more and consume more, but keep the same levels of money holdings and wealth. Assume also that when constrained by the old self-repeating value of labor supply, the household chooses the same labor supply, consumption, and money holdings as it did before (and thus the same value of wealth as before). If the firms do not know the unconstrained supply of labor, there is no way for the information on the change in the utility function to be communicated to them. They only observe the actual demand for goods and supply of labor, which are the same as before. The firms thus make the same decisions as before, the household is subject to the same labor constraint as before (and so makes the same decisions as before), and so on. A self-repeating run will thus exist, but now in a situation where there is unemployment. Although this result is artificial, it does help to illustrate a feature of the model regarding information flows.

3.1.7 Comparison of the Model to the IS-LM Model and to a Class of Rational Expectations Models

The IS-LM Model

It may help in understanding the present model to compare it to two well-known models. The first is the IS-LM model, which has undoubtedly been the most popular model of the last three decades. A standard version of the IS-LM model consists of the following ten equations: (1) a consumption function in income and assets (the level of assets is exogenous), (2) an investment function in the rate of interest and income, (3) an income identity, where income is consumption plus investment plus government spending, (4) a real money demand function in the rate of interest and income, (5) a money supply function in the rate of interest (or the money supply taken to be exogenous), (6) an equilibrium condition equating money supply to money demand, (7) a production function in labor and the capital stock (the capital stock is exogenous), (8) a demand for labor equation equating the marginal product of labor to the real wage rate, (9) a labor supply function in either the money wage (the "Keynesian" version) or the real wage (the "classical" version), (10) an equilibrium condition equating the supply of labor to the demand for labor. These ten equations determine the following ten unknowns: consumption, investment, income, demand for money, supply of money, demand for labor, supply of labor, the price level, the wage rate, and the interest rate.

One of the main differences between my model and the IS-LM model is the treatment of consumption and labor supply. In my model the consumption and labor supply decisions are jointly determined. Both are a function of the same variables: the wage rate, the price level, the interest rate, the tax rate, the level of transfer payments, and wealth. In the IS-LM model, on the other hand, the decisions are not integrated. Labor supply is a function of the money wage or the real wage, and consumption is a function of income and assets. From a microeconomic point of view these decisions are not consistent. The only justification for using income as an explanatory variable in the consumption function is if the households are always constrained in their labor supply decisions. This is, however, inconsistent with the labor supply equation, where it is implicitly assumed that the households are not constrained.

Another important difference is the treatment of investment and employment. In my model the investment and employment decisions are jointly determined. Both decisions are a function of the various factors that affect the solutions of the firms' maximization problems. These decisions are not integrated in the IS-LM model. Investment is a function of the interest rate and income, and the demand for employment is a function of the real wage rate and the shape of the production function.

A third difference is that the IS-LM model is a static equilibrium one, whereas my model is dynamic and allows for the possibility of disequilibrium. Because of its static nature, there are no wealth, inventory, or capital-stock effects in the IS-LM model. These effects play an important role in my model. Wealth effects are easy to handle in the model because of the accounting for the flow-of-funds and balance-sheet constraints. This also means that there is no confusion regarding the government budget constraint: the constraint is automatically accounted for, so that any savings or dissavings of the government must result in a change in at least one of its assets or liabilities. This constraint is not part of the IS-LM model, and it has caused considerable discussion (see, for example, Christ 1968).

The equilibrium nature of the IS-LM model means that there is no unemployment. In the Keynesian version of the model it is possible to increase output by increasing government spending, but this comes about not by lessening some disequilibrium constraint but by inducing the households to work more by increasing the money wage. As discussed in the previous sections, disequilibrium effects can be quite important in my model. Unemployment can exist, and multiplier reactions can take place over time.

One of the key variables that affect consumption in my model is the interest rate. This comes about because of the multiperiod nature of the utility maximization problem, where intertemporal substitution effects are allowed. There are no such effects in the IS-LM model because it is static, and thus the interest rate does not affect consumption.

A Class of Rational Expectations Models

A class of rational expectations (RE) models has recently been developed that has become quite popular. This class includes the models in Lucas (1973), Sargent (1973, 1976), Sargent and Wallace (1976), and Barro (1976). Although the models in these five studies are not identical, they are similar enough to be able to be grouped together for purposes of the present comparison.

Three characteristics of the RE models are (1) the assumption that expectations are rational, (2) the assumption that information is imperfect regarding the current state of the economy, and (3) the postulation of an aggregate supply equation in which aggregate supply is a function of exogenous terms plus the difference between the actual and the expected price level. The models have the important property that government actions affect real output only if they are unanticipated. Because information is imperfect, unanticipated government actions can affect the difference between the actual and the expected price level, and so they can affect, for at least one period, aggregate supply. Anticipated government actions, on the other hand, do not affect this difference (because, since expectations are rational, all the information regarding anticipated government actions has already been incorporated into the actual and expected price levels), and so they cannot affect aggregate supply.

A key difference between the RE models and my model is that expectations are not rational in my model. The implications of the nonrationality of expectations have already been discussed and will not be repeated here. There is, however, another important difference between the models, which is that the RE models are not choice-theoretic. While agents are assumed to be rational in the sense that they know the model and use all the available information in the system in forming their expectations, they are at the same time irrational in the sense that their decisions are not derived from the assumption of maximizing behavior.

To the extent that the aggregate supply equation in the RE models has any microeconomic justification, it is based on the Lucas and Rapping (LR) model (1969). In this model a household is assumed to maximize a two-period utility function in consumption and leisure subject to a two-period budget constraint. Current labor supply is a function of the current wage rate and price level, the discounted future wage rate and price level, and the initial value of assets. The discount rate is the nominal interest rate. The signs of the derivatives of this function are ambiguous for the usual reasons. If it is assumed, as Lucas and Rapping do, that current and future consumption and future leisure are substitutes for current leisure and that income and asset effects are small, then current labor supply is a positive function of the current wage rate and a negative function of the current and future price level and the future wage rate. This model is used to justify, in at least a loose sense, the assumption in the RE models that the difference between the actual and the expected price level has a positive effect on aggregate supply. An actual price level higher than expected is analogous to an increase in the current wage rate relative to the current and future price level and the future wage rate.

Although the LR model is used in part as a justification for the aggregate supply equation in the RE models, there are some important features of the LR model that are not incorporated into the supply equation. One variable that is omitted is the interest rate. As just discussed, the interest rate has an effect on the current supply of labor in the LR model, and thus it should be included in the supply equation in the RE models. The interest rate clearly belongs in an equation whose justification is based in part on an appeal to intertemporal substitution effects. The RE models, with the exception of Barro's (1976), also exclude from the supply equation any asset variables, even though the initial value of assets has an effect on the current supply of labor in the LR model. Another omission of both the LR and RE models is the exclusion of personal tax rates from the analysis. It is well known that personal tax rates have an effect on the labor supply of a utility-maximizing household.

It is also true that many of the other equations of the RE models are not based on the assumption of maximizing behavior. Sargent and Wallace, for example, note that their model is ad hoc, where "by *ad hoc* we mean that the model is not derived from a consistent set of assumptions about individuals' and firms' objective functions and the information available to them" (1976, p. 241).

The RE models can thus be criticized on theoretical grounds in that it seems odd to postulate rationality with respect to the formation of expectations (in particular that agents are sophisticated enough to know the complete model) but not with respect to overall behavior.

Regarding policy effects, it seems likely that in models in which there are both rational expectations and maximizing agents, anticipated government actions will affect the economy. To the extent that the government affects, directly or indirectly, variables that influence the solutions of the households' utility maximization problems, real output will be affected. It would be an unusual model that insulated the households' decision problems from everything that the government affects. The policy property of the RE models that anticipated government actions do not affect real output is thus not likely to be true in a model in which there are rational expectations and maximizing agents.

3.2 The Two-Country Model

3.2.1 Introduction

The way in which I approached the construction of a two-country model was to consider how one would link my single-country model to another model exactly like it. Because the flow-of-funds and balance-sheet constraints are met in the single-country model, they are also met in the two-country model, which distinguishes it in an important way from previous models. Stock and flow effects are completely integrated in the model. There is, for example, no natural distinction between stock-market and flow-market determination of the exchange rate, a distinction that has played an important role in the literature on the monetary approach to the balance of payments. (See, for example, Frenkel and Rodriguez 1975; Frenkel and Johnson 1976; Dornbusch 1976; Kouri 1976; and the survey by Myhrman 1976.) The exchange rate is merely one endogenous variable out of many, and in no rigorous sense can it be said to be *the* variable that clears a particular market. In other words, there is no need for a stock-flow distinction in the model. (Other studies in which the stock-flow distinction is important include Allen 1973; Black 1973; Branson 1974; and Girton and Henderson 1976.)

In the following sections capital letters denote variables for country 1, lowercase letters denote variables for country 2, and an asterisk (*) on a variable denotes the other country's purchase or holding of the variable. The exchange rate, denoted e_t, is the price of country 2's currency in terms of country 1's currency. There is assumed to be an international reserve, denoted Q_t for country 1's holdings and q_t for country 2's holdings, which is denominated in the currency of country 1. The total amount of this reserve is assumed to be constant across time. There is assumed to be one good per country

3.2.2 Trade Linkages

A way of introducing trade in the model is to add c^*_{ht} to the utility function (3.9) of the household:

$$(3.9)'' \qquad U_{ht} = f_{9''}(C_{ht}, TH - L_{ht} - N_{ht}, c^*_{ht}),$$

where c^*_{ht} is household h's consumption of the foreign good. The term $-e_t p_{ht} c^*_{ht}$ is then added to the savings equation, (3.13):

$$(3.13)'' \quad S_{ht} = Y_{ht} - T_{ht} - P_{ht}C_{ht} - e_t p_{ht} c^*_{ht},$$

where p_{ht} is the price of the foreign good. This adds one decision variable, c^*_{ht}, and two exogenous variables, e_t and p_{ht}, to the maximization problem of the household. The demand for the home good will be, among other things, a function of the two prices and the exchange rate, and similarly for the demand for the foreign good.

3.2.3 Price Linkages

In addition to the obvious trade linkages between countries, there may be price linkages. In particular, prices of domestic goods may be influenced by the prices of foreign goods. One way of introducing this into the model is to modify the equation determining firm f's expected aggregate demand for (domestic) goods, (3.45). Since a household's demand for domestic goods is a function of the price of domestic goods and the price of foreign goods, it is reasonable to assume that a firm expects that the aggregate demand for domestic goods is a function of the average price of domestic goods and the average price of foreign goods:

$$(3.45)'' \quad XA_t = XA_{t-1}\left(\frac{\bar{P}_t}{\bar{P}_{t-1}}\right)^{\beta_8}\left(\frac{e_t\bar{p}_t}{e_{t-1}\bar{p}_{t-1}}\right)^{\beta_{14}}, \qquad \beta_8 < 0, \qquad \beta_{14} > 0,$$

where $\bar{p}_t$ is the average price of foreign goods.

Replacing (3.45) with (3.45)″ adds two exogenous variables to the maximization problem of the firm: the exchange rate and the average price of foreign goods. If the product of these two, which is the average price of foreign goods in domestic currency, increases, the firm expects, other things being equal, that the demand for domestic goods will increase. An increase in the domestic currency price of foreign goods is thus like a demand increase, and the firm responds to a demand increase by raising its price. Higher import prices thus lead to higher domestic prices through this channel.

3.2.4 Introduction of a Foreign Security

Although it is easy to introduce a foreign good into the model, it is not as easy to introduce a foreign security; the model is not set up to handle different securities in a convenient way. One way of introducing a foreign security is the following. Assume that only banks hold foreign securities, and let a^*_{bt} denote the amount of the security held by bank b. Foreign securities, like domestic securities, are assumed to be one-period bonds. Bank b's demand for foreign securities is assumed to be a function, among other things, of each country's interest rate:

$$(3.65) \qquad a^*_{bt} = f_{65}(R_t, r_t, \ldots),$$

where r_t is country 2's interest rate. This assumption is ad hoc in that the equation is not derived from the solution of a maximization problem for bank b, but for present purposes it is sufficient for illustrating the main features of the model. In the empirical work this assumption is not used because perfect substitutability between foreign and domestic securities is assumed.

The introduction of a^*_{bt} to the model requires that (3.55) determining bank profits be modified:

$$(3.55)'' \qquad \pi_{bt} = R_t A_{bt} - RD_t BO_t + r_t e_t a^*_{bt},$$

where the last term is the interest revenue in domestic currency on the foreign security holdings. The bank's budget constraint (3.58) is also modified:

$$(3.58)'' \qquad 0 = \Delta A_{bt} + \Delta M_{bt} + \Delta BR_{bt} - \Delta BO_{bt} + e_t \Delta a^*_{bt}.$$

Finally, (M27) is modified to reflect foreign holdings of domestic securities:

$$(M27)'' \qquad 0 = A'_{ht} + A_{ft} + A_{kt} + A_{bt} + A_{gt} + A^*_{bt}.$$

3.2.5 Determination of the Exchange Rate

The basic feature of the two-country model with respect to the determination of the exchange rate can be most easily seen by aggregating the household, firms, and bank into one sector, called the "private sector." Let S_{pt} denote the level of savings of the private sector, which is the sum of the savings of the household and firms. (As discussed in Section 3.1.4, the savings of the bank is always zero.) Let A_{pt} denote the sum of A'_{ht}, A_{ft}, A_{kt}, and A_{bt}. Also, change the b subscript on BR_{bt}, BO_{bt}, and a^*_{bt} to p to keep the notation consistent. The same aggregation hold for country 2, with capital and lowercase letters reversed.

Although the level of savings of an agent is determined by a definition in the model, it will be convenient to represent the determination of savings in the following way:

$$(T1) \qquad S_{pt} = f_{T1}(\ldots),$$

$$(T2) \qquad S_{gt} = f_{T2}(\ldots),$$

$$(T3) \qquad s_{pt} = f_{T3}(\ldots),$$

$$(T4) \qquad s_{gt} = f_{T4}(\ldots).$$

Equation (T1) represents the determination of the savings of the private sector of country 1. Almost every variable in the model, including the variables that pertain to country 2, has at least an indirect effect on savings, and thus the argument list of the function in (T1) is long. This is also true of (T2), which represents the determination of the savings of the government of country 1. Equations (T3) and (T4) are similar equations for country 2.

The next thing to be done is to aggregate the budget constraints of the individual agents into a budget constraint of the private sector. This cancels out the securities that are only held within the private sector, which in the present case are money holdings. Adding the budget constraints (3.14) for the household, (3.38) for each firm, and (3.58)″ for the bank yields:

$$\text{(T5)} \qquad 0 = S_{pt} - \Delta BR_{pt} + \Delta BO_{pt} - \Delta A_{pt} - e_t \Delta a^*_{pt}.$$

The government budget constraint (3.60) in the present notation is

$$\text{(T6)} \qquad 0 = S_{gt} + \Delta BR_{pt} - \Delta BO_{pt} - \Delta A_{gt} - \Delta Q_t,$$

where the term ΔQ_t, which is the change in holdings of the international reserve of the government, is added to the equation. Similar equations hold for country 2:

$$\text{(T7)} \qquad 0 = s_{pt} - \Delta br_{pt} + \Delta bo_{pt} - \Delta a_{pt} - \frac{1}{e_t}\Delta A^*_{pt},$$

$$\text{(T8)} \qquad 0 = s_{gt} + \Delta br_{pt} - \Delta bo_{pt} - \Delta a_{gt} - \frac{1}{e_t}\Delta q_t.$$

The level of bank reserves, BR_{bt}, is determined by (3.53). It is equal to $-g_{1t}M_{bt}$, where g_{1t} is the reserve requirement rate and $-M_{bt}$ is the level of demand deposits. M_{bt} drops out of the model in the aggregation to the private sector, and so an equation like (3.53) cannot be written down for BR_{pt}. BR_{pt} is, of course, still determined in the model, and for the purpose of the equations here its determination can be represented in the same manner as in (T1)–(T4) for the savings variables:

$$\text{(T9)} \qquad BR_{pt} = f_{T9}(\ldots).$$

This equation stands for the determination of BR_{pt}, where nearly every variable in the model is in the argument list. Bank borrowing from the monetary authority is determined by (3.54), which in the present notation is

(T10) $\quad \dfrac{BO_{pt}}{BR_{pt}} = \gamma_4(RD_t - R_t), \qquad \gamma_4 < 0.$

Similar equations hold for country 2:

(T11) $\quad br_{pt} = f_{T11}(\ldots),$

(T12) $\quad \dfrac{bo_{pt}}{br_{pt}} = \gamma_4(rd_t - r_t).$

Equation (3.65), the equation determining the domestic demand for the foreign security, in the present notation is

(T13) $\quad a^*_{pt} = f_{T13}(R_t, r_t, \; . \; . \; . \;).$

A similar equation holds for country 2's demand for country 1's security:

(T14) $\quad A^*_{pt} = f_{T14}(R_t, r_t, \; . \; . \; . \;).$

The following three definitions close the model:

(T15) $\quad 0 = A_{pt} + A_{gt} + A^*_{pt},$

(T16) $\quad 0 = a_{pt} + a_{gt} + a^*_{pt},$

(T17) $\quad 0 = \Delta Q_t + \Delta q_t.$

Equation (T15) states that the sum of the holdings of country 1's bond across holders is zero. (Remember that liabilities are negative values.) Equation (T16) is the similar equation for country 2. Equation (T17) states that there is no change in total world reserves.

The savings variables satisfy the property that $S_{pt} + S_{gt} + e_t s_{pt} + e_t s_{gt} = 0$, and therefore one of the equations (T1)–(T8) and (T15)–(T17) is redundant. It will be useful to drop (T17); this leaves 16 independent equations. There are 19 variables in the model: S_{pt}, S_{gt}, s_{pt}, s_{gt}, A_{pt}, a^*_{pt}, a_{pt}, A^*_{pt}, BR_{pt}, br_{pt}, BO_{pt}, bo_{pt}, Q_t, q_t, e_t, R_t, r_t, A_{gt}, and a_{gt}. In the case of fixed exchange rates e_t is exogenous and Q_t is endogenous, and in the case of flexible exchange rates e_t is endogenous and Q_t is exogenous. Given that one of these two variables is taken to be exogenous, the model can be closed by taking A_{gt} and a_{gt} to be the exogenous monetary policy variables.

It should be clear from this representation that e_t is not determined solely in stock markets or in flow markets; it is simultaneously determined along with the other endogenous variables. This, as discussed earlier, is an important difference between this model and previous models.

3.2.6 Properties of the Model

I have not obtained any simulation results for the two-country model. Given the results for the single-country model and given (as will be seen in Section 4.2.2) the special case of the two-country model that had to be used to guide the econometric specifications, simulation results for the two-country model seemed unnecessary. The main features to be remembered about the model are the following.

1. Adding a foreign good to the utility function of the household means that the demand for the foreign good will be a function of the same variables that affect the household's consumption decision in the single-country model plus two new variables: the price of the foreign good and the exchange rate.

2. Adding the price of the foreign good to the equation determining the firm's expected aggregate demand for the domestic good means that the price of the foreign good and the exchange rate will affect the domestic price level.

3. Any model of exchange rate determination that is used for the empirical work should be consistent with (T1)–(T17). In particular, no distinction should be necessary between stock-market and flow-market determination of the exchange rate.

4 An Econometric Model

4.1 The United States (US) Model

4.1.1 Introduction

The construction of an econometric model is described in this chapter. This model is based on the theoretical model in Chapter 3, and thus the discussion in this chapter provides an example of the transition from a theoretical model to an econometric model. It will be clear, as stressed in Chapter 2, that this transition is not always very tight, and I will try to indicate where I think it is particularly weak in the present case. I have tried to maintain the three main features of the theoretical model in the econometric specifications, namely, the assumption of maximizing behavior, the explicit treatment of disequilibrium effects, and the accounting for balance-sheet constraints. The United States (US) model is discussed in this section, and the multicountry (MC) model is discussed in the next section. The presentation of the models in this chapter relies fairly heavily on the use of tables, especially the tables in Appendixes A and B. Not everything in the tables is discussed in the text, so for a complete understanding of the models the tables must be read along with the text.

4.1.2 Data Collection and the Choice of Variables and Identities

The Data and Variables

As discussed in Section 2.2.1, the first step in the construction of an empirical model is to collect the raw data, create the variables of interest from the raw data, and separate the variables into exogenous variables, endogenous variables explained by identities, and endogenous variables explained by estimated equations. I find it easiest to present this type of work in tables, which in the present case are located in Appendix A at the back of the book.

Table A-1 lists the six sectors of the model and some frequently used notation. The sectors are household *(h)*, firm *(f)*, financial *(b)*, foreign *(r)*, federal government *(g)*, and state and local government *(s)*. The household sector is the sum of three sectors in the Flow of Funds Accounts: (1) households, personal trusts, and nonprofit organizations; (2) farms, corporate and noncorporate; and (3) nonfarm noncorporate business. The firm sector comprises nonfinancial corporate business, excluding farms. The financial sector is the sum of commercial banking and private nonbank financial institutions. The federal government sector is the sum of U.S. government, federally sponsored credit agencies and mortgage pools, and monetary authority.

If the balance-sheet constraints are to be met, the data from the National Income and Product Accounts (NIA), which are flow data, must be consistent with the asset and liability data from the Flow of Funds Accounts (FFA). Fortunately, the FFA data are constructed to be consistent with the NIA data, so the main task in the collection of the data is merely to ensure that the data have been collected from the two sources in the appropriate way to satisfy the constraints. To review what these constraints are like, consider (3.13) and (3.14) of the theoretical model, which are repeated here:

$$(3.13) \qquad S_{ht} = Y_{ht} - T_{ht} - P_{ht}C_{ht},$$

$$(3.14) \qquad 0 = S_{ht} - \Delta A_{ht} - \Delta M_{ht},$$

where S denotes savings, Y denotes income, T denotes taxes, P denotes the price level, C denotes consumption, A denotes net assets other than money, and M denotes money. The data on S, Y, T, P, and C are NIA data, and the data on A and M are FFA data. The data must be consistent in the sense that both (3.13) and (3.14) must hold: the S_{ht} that satisfies (3.13) must be the same as the S_{ht} that satisfies (3.14). An additional restriction on the FFA data is that the sum of the A's across all sectors must be zero, since an asset of one sector is a liability of some other sector. Likewise, the sum of the M's across all sectors must be zero.

Table A-2 presents all the raw-data variables. The variables from the NIA are presented first in the table, in the order in which they appear in the *Survey of Current Business.* The variables from the FFA are presented next, ordered by the code numbers on the Flow of Funds tape. Some of these variables are NIA variables that are not published in the *Survey* but that are needed to link the two accounts. Interest rate variables are presented next, followed by employment and population variables. All the raw-data variables are listed in alphabetical order at the end of Table A-2 for ease of reference.

Given Table A-2 and the discussion of it in Appendix A, it should be possible to duplicate the collection of the data with no help from me.

Although one would seldom want to do this, since a tape of the data set can be easily supplied, this kind of detail should be presented if at all feasible; it has the obvious scientific merit of allowing for the reproducibility of the results, and in general it helps to lessen the "black box" nature of the discussion of many econometric models, especially large models.

Table A-3 presents the balance-sheet constraints that the data satisfy. This table provides the main checks on the collection of the data. If any of the checks are not met, one or more errors have been made in the collection process. Although the checks in Table A-3 may look easy, considerable work is involved in having them met: all the receipts from sector I to sector J must be determined for all I and J (I and J in the present case run from 1 to 6). Once the checks have been met, however, one can have considerable confidence that this part of the data base is correct.

Table A-4, the key reference table for the variables in the model, lists all the variables in alphabetical order. These are not in general the raw-data variables, but variables that have been constructed from a number of the raw-data variables. With a few exceptions, which are noted in the table, the variables that are not defined by identities are defined solely in terms of the raw-data variables. I have found that coding the variables in this way lessens the chances of error, since the order in which the variables are constructed does not matter. The present procedure also has the advantage of providing a clear indication of the links from the raw data to the variables in the model. Order does in general matter, of course, for the variables in the table that are defined in terms of the identities, so one must be careful with respect to these.

The Identities

Table A-5 lists all the equations of the model. There are 128 equations; the first 30 are stochastic and the remaining 98 are identities. One of the equations is redundant, and it is easiest to take Eq. 80 to be the redundant one. The 30 stochastic equations are discussed in Sections 4.1.4–4.1.9.

The identities in the table are of two types. One type simply defines one variable in terms of others. The identities of this type are Eqs. 31, 33, 34, 43, and 58–128. The other type defines one variable as a rate or ratio times another variable or set of variables, where the rate or ratio has been constructed to have the identity hold. The identities of this type are Eqs. 32, 35–42, and 44–57. Consider, for example, Eq. 49:

49. $T_{fg} = d_{2g}\pi_f,$

where T_{fg} is the amount of corporate profit taxes paid by f to g, π_f is the level of corporate profits of f, and d_{2g} is a "tax rate." Data exist for T_{fg} and π_f, and d_{2g} was constructed as T_{fg}/π_f. The variable d_{2g} is then interpreted as a tax rate and is taken to be exogenous. This rate, of course, varies over time as tax laws and other things that affect the relationship between T_{fg} and π_f change, but no attempt is made in the model to explain these changes. This general procedure was followed for the other identities involving tax rates.

A similar procedure was followed to handle relative price changes. Consider Eq. 38:

38. $$PIH = \psi_5 PD,$$

where PIH is the price deflator for housing investment, PD is the price deflator for total domestic sales, and ψ_5 is a ratio. Data exist for PIH and PD, and ψ_5 was constructed as PIH/PD. ψ_5, which varies over time as the relationship between PIH and PD changes, is taken to be exogenous. This procedure was followed for the other identities involving prices and wages. This treatment means that relative prices and relative wages are exogenous in the model. (Prices relative to wages are not, however, exogenous.) It is beyond the scope of an aggregated model like the present one to explain relative prices and wages, and the foregoing treatment is a simple way of handling these changes. Note, of course, that in actual forecasts with the model, assumptions have to be made about the future values of the ratios.

The last identity of the second type is Eq. 57:

57. $$BR = -g_1 M_b,$$

where BR is the level of bank reserves, M_b is the net value of demand deposits and currency of the financial sector, and g_1 is a "reserve requirement ratio." Data on BR and M_b exist, and g_1 was constructed as $-BR/M_b$. (M_b is negative, since the financial sector is a net debtor with respect to demand deposits and currency, and so the minus sign makes g_1 positive.) g_1 is taken to be exogenous. It varies over time as actual reserve requirements and other features that affect the relationship between BR and M_b change.

4.1.3 Treatment of Unobserved Variables

Expectations

For the most part I have followed the traditional approach in trying to account for expectational effects, namely by the use of lagged dependent variables (see the discussion in Section 2.2.2). A different approach was followed, however, in trying to estimate real interest rates for use as explanatory variables in a number of the stochastic equations. In order to estimate a real interest rate one needs an estimate of the expected rate of inflation over the particular period of the interest rate (for example, five years for a five-year rate). In the present case four different estimates of the expected rate of inflation were tried. Each estimate was taken to be the predicted values from a particular regression. For the first regression the actual rate of price inflation ($\dot{PX}$) was regressed on its first eight lagged values and a constant. For the second regression $\dot{PX}$ was regressed on the first four lagged values of four variables, a constant, and time. The four variables were $\dot{PX}$ itself, the rate of wage inflation ($\dot{W}_f$), the rate of change of import prices ($\dot{PIM}$), and a demand pressure variable (ZZ). For the third regression the actual rate of wage inflation ($\dot{W}_f$) was regressed on its first eight lagged values and a constant. For the fourth regression $\dot{W}_f$ was regressed on the same set of variables used for the second regression. The four equations are as follows (t-statistics are in parentheses).

(4.1)
$$\begin{aligned}
\dot{PX} = {} & \underset{(1.57)}{.458} + \underset{(5.47)}{.526}\ \dot{PX}_{-1} + \underset{(2.30)}{.245}\ \dot{PX}_{-2} + \underset{(0.76)}{.083}\ \dot{PX}_{-3} \\
& + \underset{(1.65)}{.178}\ \dot{PX}_{-4} - \underset{(1.08)}{.120}\ \dot{PX}_{-5} - \underset{(0.33)}{.036}\ \dot{PX}_{-6} - \underset{(0.17)}{.018}\ \dot{PX}_{-7} \\
& + \underset{(0.41)}{.039}\ \dot{PX}_{-8}
\end{aligned}$$

SE = 1.75, R^2 = .731, DW = 1.92, 1954II–1982III

(4.2)
$$\begin{aligned}
\dot{PX} = {} & -\underset{(1.03)}{.548} + \underset{(1.80)}{.0151}\ t + \underset{(1.86)}{.172}\ \dot{PX}_{-1} + \underset{(1.98)}{.187}\ \dot{PX}_{-2} \\
& - \underset{(0.05)}{.004}\ \dot{PX}_{-3} + \underset{(1.14)}{.100}\ \dot{PX}_{-4} + \underset{(1.73)}{.102}\ \dot{W}_{f-1} + \underset{(2.12)}{.127}\ \dot{W}_{f-2} \\
& + \underset{(1.07)}{.062}\ \dot{W}_{f-3} + \underset{(0.36)}{.021}\ \dot{W}_{f-4} + \underset{(0.87)}{.016}\ \dot{PIM}_{-1} \\
& + \underset{(2.11)}{.050}\ \dot{PIM}_{-2} + \underset{(1.81)}{.045}\ \dot{PIM}_{-3} - \underset{(1.41)}{.030}\ \dot{PIM}_{-4} \\
& - \underset{(2.61)}{41.6}\ ZZ_{-1} + \underset{(0.96)}{23.1}\ ZZ_{-2} - \underset{(0.07)}{1.7}\ ZZ_{-3} \\
& + \underset{(0.40)}{6.3}\ ZZ_{-4}
\end{aligned}$$

SE = 1.39, R^2 = .816, DW = 1.85, 1954I–1982III

(4.3)

$$\dot{W}_f = \underset{(2.43)}{1.78} + \underset{(1.40)}{.130}\ \dot{W}_{f-1} + \underset{(1.60)}{.150}\ \dot{W}_{f-2} + \underset{(1.60)}{.149}\ \dot{W}_{f-3} + \underset{(0.91)}{.084}\ \dot{W}_{f-4} + \underset{(1.40)}{.130}\ \dot{W}_{f-5} + \underset{(2.12)}{.196}\ \dot{W}_{f-6} + \underset{(0.99)}{.092}\ \dot{W}_{f-7} - \underset{(2.23)}{.206}\ \dot{W}_{f-8}$$

SE = 2.49, R^2 = .332, DW = 2.05, 1954II–1982III

(4.4)

$$\dot{W}_f = -\underset{(5.27)}{5.10} + \underset{(0.65)}{.0115}\ t + \underset{(1.09)}{.505}\ \dot{PX}_{-1} - \underset{(0.47)}{.208}\ \dot{PX}_{-2} + \underset{(1.54)}{.544}\ \dot{PX}_{-3} - \underset{(0.03)}{.007}\ \dot{PX}_{-4} - \underset{(0.84)}{.080}\ \dot{W}_{f-1} - \underset{(1.24)}{.131}\ \dot{W}_{f-2} - \underset{(0.53)}{.062}\ \dot{W}_{f-3} - \underset{(1.15)}{.124}\ \dot{W}_{f-4} - \underset{(1.43)}{.041}\ \dot{PIM}_{-1} + \underset{(1.64)}{.060}\ \dot{PIM}_{-2} - \underset{(0.72)}{.030}\ \dot{PIM}_{-3} + \underset{(0.49)}{.020}\ \dot{PIM}_{-4} - \underset{(1.00)}{26.1}\ ZZ_{-1} + \underset{(0.02)}{.7}\ ZZ_{-2} - \underset{(0.02)}{1.0}\ ZZ_{-3} - \underset{(0.22)}{6.5}\ ZZ_{-4}$$

SE = 2.18, R^2 = .472, DW = 1.96, 1954I–1982III

Let $\dot{PX}^e$ denote the predicted value from either the first or second equation, and let $\dot{W}_f^e$ denote the predicted value from either the third or fourth equation. If these predicted values are taken to be expected values, then an estimate of a real interest rate is the nominal rate minus the particular predicted value. For example, $RSA - \dot{PX}^e$ or $RSA - \dot{W}_f^e$ is an estimate of the real after-tax short-term interest rate, where *RSA* is the nominal after-tax short-term interest rate. Similarly, $RMA - \dot{PX}^e$ or $RMA - \dot{W}_f^e$ is an estimate of the real after-tax mortgage rate, where *RMA* is the nominal after-tax mortgage rate.

This treatment of expectations is somewhere in between the simple use of lagged dependent variables of the traditional approach and the assumption that expectations are rational. The expectations are not rational because (4.1)–(4.4) are not the equations that the model uses to explain actual wages and prices. The equations are, however (especially Eqs. 4.2 and 4.4), more sophisticated than the simple geometrically declining lag implicit in the traditional approach, and thus the expectations are based on somewhat more information.

The real interest rate was always entered linearly as an explanatory variable in the estimated equations, and therefore any error made in estimating the level of the expected inflation rate that is constant across time is merely absorbed in the estimate of the constant term. This approach does, however, have the problem of not distinguishing between short-term and long-term expected rates of inflation. The same expected inflation variable is subtracted from both the short-term rate and the long-term rates. This is a good example of a situation in which less structure is imposed on the expected rates than would be imposed by the assumption of rational expectations, where the expected inflation rates would in general differ by length of period (since the model would in general predict this).

The attempt to find real interest rate effects in the empirical work is consistent with the theoretical model. Although no mention was made of real interest rates in Chapter 3, their effects are in the model. Consider, for example, the household's maximization problem. The household's response to an interest rate change will be different if, say, the price level in periods 2 and 3 is expected to change than if it is not. Likewise, a firm's response to an interest rate change is a function of what it expects future prices to be.

Labor Constraint Variable for the Household Sector

An important feature of the theoretical model is the possibility that households may at times be constrained in how much they can work. This possible constraint poses a difficult problem for empirical work because the constraints are not directly observed. The approach that I have used is the following.

Let *CSUN* denote the expenditures on services that the household sector would make if it were not constrained in its labor supply, and let *CS* denote the actual expenditures made, where *CS* is observed. Assume that one has specified an equation explaining *CSUN*, that is, an equation explaining the unconstrained decision:

$$CSUN = f(\ldots). \tag{4.5}$$

Assume that all the variables on the RHS of this equation are observed. If the household sector is not constrained, then *CS* equals *CSUN*, and there is no problem. If the household sector is constrained, then *CS* is less than *CSUN* if, as in the theoretical model, binding labor constraints cause the household sector to consume less than it would have consumed unconstrained. If one can find a variable, say *Z*, such that

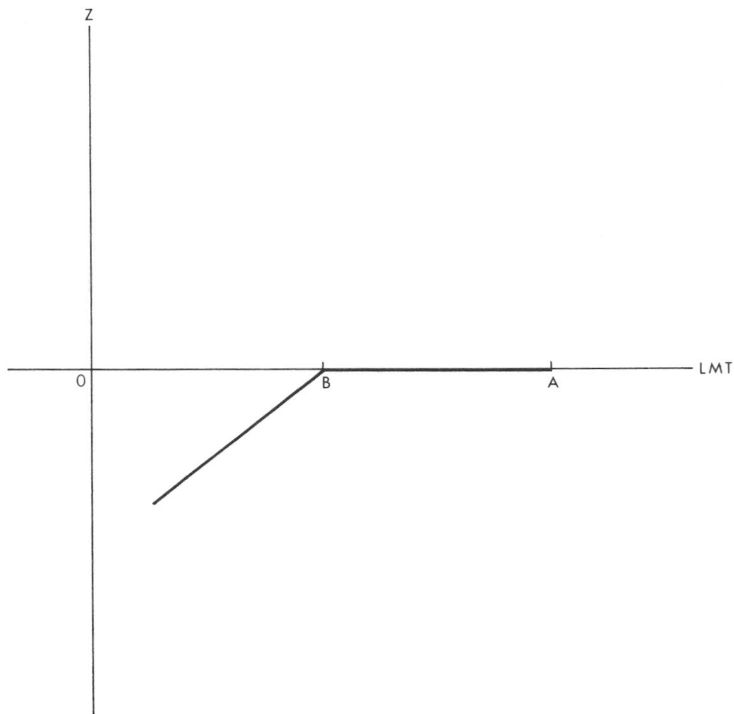

Figure 4-1 Desired shape of the labor constraint variable *(Z)* as a function of the measure of labor market tightness *(LMT)*

$$(4.6) \qquad CS = CSUN + \gamma Z, \qquad \gamma > 0,$$

then one has immediately from (4.5) and (4.6) an equation in observed variables. The problem of accounting for the constraint is thus reduced to a problem of finding a variable Z for which the specification in (4.6) seems reasonable.

The variable Z should take on a value of zero when labor markets are tight and households are not constrained and a value less than zero otherwise. When the variable is less than zero, it should be a linear function of the difference between the constrained and unconstrained decision values of the household sector. Let LMT denote some measure of labor market tightness. The desired shape of Z as a function of LMT is presented in Figure 4-1. Point A is some value that is larger than the largest value of LMT that is ever likely to be observed, and point B is the value of LMT above which it seems reasonable to assume that the household sector is not constrained. An approximation to the curve in Figure 4-1 that was used in the empirical work is the following:

$$(4.7) \qquad Z = 1 - \frac{A}{LMT}.$$

Z is zero when LMT equals A, and it is minus infinity when LMT equals zero.

There are a number of measures of labor market tightness that one might consider in the construction of Z. One obvious possibility is $1 - UR$, where UR is the unemployment rate. In the present case, however, a different measure was used, which is a detrended ratio of total hours paid for in the economy to the total population age 16 and over. This measure is defined by Eqs. 95 and 96 in Table A-5. Equation 95 determines the actual ratio (JJ), and Eq. 96 determines the detrended ratio (JJ^*). (The coefficient $-.00083312$ in Eq. 96 is the estimate of the coefficient of t in the regression of log JJ on a constant and t for the 1952I–1982III period.) Which measure of labor market tightness to use is largely an empirical question; I have found that JJ^* gives slightly better results than does $1 - UR$. The results are not, however, very different, and an example of the use of $1 - UR$ instead of JJ^* for the household sector is presented near the end of this section. The value of A that was used for JJ^* in (4.7) is 337.0, which is slightly larger than the largest value of JJ^* observed in the sample period. Equation (4.7) with this value of A is Eq. 97 in the model.

Demand Pressure Variables

In the theoretical model a firm's price and wage decisions are a function, among other things, of its expectations of the current and future demand curves for its goods and of the current and future supply curves of labor that it faces. These expectations are in turn a function, among other things, of lagged values of the demand for the firm's goods at the prices that it set and of the supply of labor that it received at the wage rates that it set. For the empirical work one needs some way of accounting for these demand and supply effects on prices and wages. A number of "demand pressure" variables were tried in the estimation of the price and wage equations. One might expect there to be a nonlinear relationship between demand and prices in the sense that as demand pressure rises, prices rise at an ever-increasing rate, and therefore a number of nonlinear specifications were tried. However, the data do not appear to be capable of distinguishing among different functional forms and demand pressure variables, and in the end two very simple variables were used, one in the price equation and one in the wage equation.

The demand pressure variable for the price equation, denoted ZZ, was taken to be

$$(4.8) \qquad ZZ = \frac{GNPR^* - GNPR}{GNPR^*},$$

where $GNPR^*$ is an estimate of a high activity level of $GNPR$. ($GNPR$ is real GNP.) $GNPR^*$ was constructed from peak-to-peak interpolations of $GNPR$. The peak quarters are presented in Table A-4. ZZ is simply the percentage difference between the high activity level of $GNPR$ and the actual level. Equation (4.8) is Eq. 98 in Table A-5. The demand pressure variable for the wage equation was taken to be the civilian unemployment rate (UR):

$$(4.9) \qquad UR \equiv \frac{U}{L1 + L2 + L3 - J_m}.$$

Equation (4.9) is Eq. 87 in Table A-5.

Measurement of Excess Labor and Excess Capital

In the theoretical model the amounts of excess labor and excess capital on hand have an effect on the decisions of the firm, particularly the investment and employment decisions. In order to test for this in the empirical work, one needs some way of estimating the amount of excess labor and excess capital on hand in each period. This in turn requires some way of estimating the technology of the firm sector.

Consider first the estimation of the capital stock and the postulation of a production function. The capital stock was constructed to satisfy the following equation:

$$(4.10) \qquad KK = (1 - \delta_K)KK_{-1} + IK_f,$$

where KK is the capital stock of the firm sector and IK_f is gross investment. The measurement of δ_K is discussed in Appendix A. The production function is postulated to be one of fixed proportions:

$$(4.11) \qquad Y = \min[\lambda(J_f H_f^J), \mu(KK \cdot H_f^{KK})],$$

where Y is production, J_f is the number of workers employed, H_f^J is the number of hours worked per worker, KK is the capital stock given above, H_f^{KK} is the number of hours each unit of KK is utilized, and λ and μ are coefficients that may change over time due to technical progress. The variables Y, J_f, and KK are observed; the others are not.

Equations (4.10) and (4.11) are not consistent with the putty-clay technology of the theoretical model; they are at best only good approximations. Each machine in the theoretical model wears out after m periods, but its productivity does not lessen as it gets older. Consequently, even if there were only one type of machine ever in existence, (4.10) would not be true. Rather, $KK - KK_{-1}$ would equal $IK_f - IK_{f-m}$, where IK_{f-m} is the number of machines that wear out at the beginning of the period. It is also the case that no technical change was postulated in the theoretical model, but even if it were, it would not enter in the way specified in (4.11); it would take the form of machines having different λ and μ coefficients according to when they were purchased. One could not write down an equation like (4.11) but instead would have to keep track of when each machine was purchased and what the coefficients were for that machine. This kind of detail is clearly not possible with aggregate data, and therefore one must resort to simpler specifications.

Given the above production function, excess labor was measured as follows. Output per paid-for worker hour, $Y/(J_fH_f)$, was first plotted for the 1952I–1982III period. (Data on hours paid for, H_f, exist, whereas data on hours worked, H_f^J, do not.) The peaks of this series were assumed to correspond to cases in which the number of hours worked equals the number of hours paid for, which implies that values of λ in (4.11) are observed at the peaks. The values of λ other than those at the peaks were then assumed to lie on straight lines between the peaks. Given an estimate of λ for a particular period and given the production function (4.11), the estimate of the number of worker hours required to produce the output of the period (denoted $JHMIN$) is simply Y/λ. (This is Eq. 94 in Table A-5.) The actual number of worker hours paid for can then be compared to $JHMIN$ to measure the amount of excess labor on hand. The exact form that this comparison takes in the model is discussed in Section 4.1.5. The peaks that were used for the interpolations are listed in Table A-4 under the description of λ.

With respect to the measurement of excess capital, there are no data on hours paid for or worked per unit of KK, and thus one must be content with plotting Y/KK. This is, from the production function (4.11), a plot of μH_f^{KK}, where H_f^{KK} is the average number of hours that each machine is utilized. If it is assumed that at each peak of this series H_f^{KK} is equal to the same constant, say $\bar{H}$, then one observes at the peaks $\mu\bar{H}$. Interpolation between peaks can then produce a complete series on $\mu\bar{H}$. If, finally, $\bar{H}$ is assumed to be the maximum number of hours per period that each unit of KK can be utilized, then $Y/(\mu\bar{H})$

is the minimum amount of capital required to produce Y (denoted $KKMIN$). (This is Eq. 93 in Table A-5.) The peaks that were used for the interpolations are listed in Table A-4 under the description of $\mu\overline{H}$.

4.1.4 Stochastic Equations for the Household Sector

The two main decision variables of a household in the theoretical model are consumption and labor supply. The determinants of these variables include the initial value of wealth and the current and expected future values of the wage rate, the price level, the interest rate, the tax rate, and the level of transfer payments. The labor constraint also affects the decisions if it is binding. The aim of the econometric work is to match the decision variables and the determinants of the variables to observed aggregate variables and then to estimate equations explaining the aggregate variables.

Expenditures of the household sector have been disaggregated into four types: consumption of services (CS), consumption of nondurable goods (CN), consumption of durable goods (CD), and investment in housing (IH_h). Four labor supply variables have been used: labor force of prime-age males $(L1)$, labor force of prime-age females $(L2)$, labor force of all others $(L3)$, and the number of people holding more than one job, called "moonlighters" (LM). These eight variables are determined by eight estimated equations.

The explanatory variables that were tried for each equation are the following: (1) the initial value of wealth (AA_{-1}); (2) the after-tax wage rate (WA); (3) the price of the particular good in the case of the expenditure equations and a price index of all the goods in the case of the labor supply equations (PCS, PCN, PCD, PIH, or P_h); (4) the after-tax short-term and long-term interest rates, either nominal (RSA, RMA) or real (RSA or RMA minus an estimate of the expected rate of inflation, where the latter uses the predicted values $\dot{PX}^e$ from Eq. 4.1 or 4.2 or the predicted values $\dot{W}_f^e$ from Eq. 4.3 or 4.4); (5) nonlabor income (YN or YTR); (6) the labor constraint variable (Z); and (7) the lagged dependent variable.

The Searching Procedure

Much searching was done in arriving at the final estimated equations for the household sector. With respect to functional forms, both the linear and logarithmic forms of the equations were tried, and the decision was made fairly early in the process to use the linear form. In general the log form led to fewer significant coefficient estimates than did the linear form, and this was the main reason for dropping it. The results were, however, quite similar using both forms, and the main conclusions regarding the household sector would not be changed if the log form were used. All the equations were estimated in per-capita terms for both forms.

A basic set of explanatory variables was first tried for each equation. A number of changes from this set were then made to see if improvements could be found. The changes consisted of (1) trying each explanatory variable lagged one quarter rather than unlagged, (2) replacing *YN*, which was in the basic set, with *YTR* to see which nonlabor income variable worked better, (3) constraining the wage and price variables to enter the equation as the ratio of the wage rate to the price level rather than separately, (4) trying both the short-term and long-term interest rates together as well as separately, (5) trying both the nominal interest rates and the real interest rates (separately), and (6) estimating the equation under the assumption of first-order serial correlation of the error term. All this searching was done using the 2SLS technique. If in the process a particular variable in an equation continually had the wrong sign, it was finally dropped from the specification. With a few exceptions, the same was also true for variables that were of the right sign but had *t*-statistics less than one in absolute value.

This searching did not result in very many examples in which a variable was significant but of the wrong sign. Had this been true, I would probably not have stopped when I did but instead would have examined the theory and the data further. In order to give the reader a feeling for the kinds of equations that were rejected, some examples will be given later after the basic equations have been presented.

Special Treatment of Housing Investment

Before the estimated equations are presented, the special treatment of housing investment must be noted. Housing investment poses a problem with respect to the links from the theoretical model to the econometric specifications because the theoretical model is not set up to handle investment goods for a household. If consumption of housing services is proportional to the stock of housing, the variables from the theoretical model that affect consumption can be taken to affect the housing stock. If, however, the actual housing stock only adjusts slowly to some desired stock, this use of the theoretical model is incomplete; one needs in addition to specify the lagged adjustments. The following specification, which seems to give reasonable results, was used for this purpose.

Let KH^{**} denote the "desired" stock of housing. If housing consumption is proportional to the housing stock, then the determinants of consumption can be assumed to be the determinants of KH^{**}:

$$KH^{**} = f(\ldots), \tag{4.12}$$

where the arguments of f are the determinants of consumption from the theoretical model. Two types of lagged adjustment were postulated. The first is an adjustment of the housing stock to its desired value:

$$KH^{*} - KH_{-1} = \lambda(KH^{**} - KH_{-1}). \tag{4.13}$$

Given (4.13), "desired" gross investment is

$$IH_h^{*} = KH^{*} - (1 - \delta_H)KH_{-1}, \tag{4.14}$$

where δ_H is the depreciation rate. By definition $IH_h = KH - (1 - \delta_H)KH_{-1}$, and (4.14) is merely the same equation for the desired values. The second type of adjustment is an adjustment of gross investment to its desired value:

$$IH_h - IH_{h-1} = \gamma(IH_h^{*} - IH_{h-1}). \tag{4.15}$$

Combining (4.12)–(4.15) yields:

$$IH_h = (1 - \gamma)IH_{h-1} + \gamma(\delta_H - \lambda)KH_{-1} + \gamma\lambda f(\ldots). \tag{4.16}$$

This treatment thus adds to the housing investment equation both the lagged dependent variable and the lagged stock of housing. Otherwise, the explanatory variables are the same as they are in the other expenditure equations.

This treatment is an example of the ad hoc nature of theory with respect to lagged adjustments. "Extra" theorizing is involved in the specification of the housing investment equation, and the specification is not derived from the assumption of maximizing behavior.

In the empirical work, (4.16) was estimated in per-capita terms. In particular, IH_h was divided by POP, and IH_{h-1} and KH_{-1} were divided by POP_{-1}, where POP is population. If (4.12)–(4.15) are defined in per-capita terms, where current values are divided by POP and lagged values are divided by POP_{-1}, then the present per-capita treatment of (4.16) follows. The only problem with this is that the definition that was used to justify (4.14) does not hold if the lagged housing stock is divided by POP_{-1}. All variables must be divided by the same population variable in order for the definition to hold. This is, however, a minor problem, and it has been ignored. The alternative treatment is to divide all variables in (4.16) by the same population variable, say POP, but this is inconvenient to work with.

The Final Eight Consumption and Labor Supply Equations

All estimates presented in this chapter are two-stage least squares (2SLS) estimates if the equation contains RHS endogenous variables and ordinary least squares (OLS) estimates if it does not. Chapter 6 contains a discussion of all the estimates that have been obtained for the model; it also contains (in Table 6-1) a list of the first-stage regressors that were used for each equation for the 2SLS technique. The estimation period was 1954I–1982III (115 observations) for all equations except Eq. 15, where the period was 1956I–1982III (107 observations).

The final consumption and labor supply equations that were chosen are as follows:

1. $$\frac{CS}{POP} = \underset{(0.06)}{.000188} + \underset{(61.48)}{.986}\left(\frac{CS}{POP}\right)_{-1} + \underset{(2.40)}{.000554}\left(\frac{AA}{POP}\right)_{-1} + \underset{(2.07)}{.0198}\,WA + \underset{(0.36)}{.00714}\,\frac{YN}{POP\cdot P_h} - \underset{(5.87)}{.00126}\,RSA + \underset{(1.92)}{.0231}\,Z$$

$$SE = .00190,\ R^2 = .999,\ DW = 2.45$$

2. $$\frac{CN}{POP} = \underset{(3.96)}{.109} + \underset{(10.03)}{.666}\left(\frac{CN}{POP}\right)_{-1} + \underset{(5.05)}{.00227}\left(\frac{AA}{POP}\right)_{-1} + \underset{(2.48)}{.185}\,WA - \underset{(2.16)}{.0469}\,PCN + \underset{(2.14)}{.0637}\,\frac{YN}{POP\cdot P_h} - \underset{(1.05)}{.000610}\,RSA + \underset{(3.54)}{.0829}\,Z$$

$$SE = .00315,\ R^2 = .994,\ DW = 1.58$$

3. $$\frac{CD}{POP} = \underset{(3.57)}{.0735} + \underset{(5.95)}{.458}\left(\frac{CD}{POP}\right)_{-1} + \underset{(6.18)}{.00235}\left(\frac{AA}{POP}\right)_{-1} + \underset{(4.08)}{.405}\,WA - \underset{(3.12)}{.104}\,PCD + \underset{(1.19)}{.0668}\,\frac{YTR}{POP\cdot P_h} - \underset{(7.96)}{.00617}\,RMA + \underset{(3.38)}{.123}\,Z$$

$$SE = .00445,\ R^2 = .989,\ DW = 1.77$$

4. $$\frac{IH_h}{POP} = \underset{(3.89)}{.0650} + \underset{(9.86)}{.738}\left(\frac{IH_h}{POP}\right)_{-1} - \underset{(3.18)}{.0157}\left(\frac{KH}{POP}\right)_{-1} + \underset{(3.73)}{.00182}\left(\frac{AA}{POP}\right)_{-1} + \underset{(2.61)}{.159}\ WA_{-1} - \underset{(1.88)}{.0178}\ PIH_{-1} + \underset{(0.99)}{.0356}\left(\frac{YN}{POP \cdot P_h}\right)_{-1} - \underset{(5.19)}{.00367}\ RMA_{-1}$$

$\text{SE} = .00243,\ \text{R}^2 = .958,\ \text{DW} = 2.09,\ \hat{\rho} = \underset{(4.65)}{.551}$

5. $$\frac{L1}{POP1} = \underset{(3.67)}{.230} + \underset{(12.20)}{.769}\left(\frac{L1}{POP1}\right)_{-1} - \underset{(3.56)}{.0278}\left(\frac{YN}{POP \cdot P_h}\right)_{-1}$$

$\text{SE} = .00200,\ \text{R}^2 = .972,\ \text{DW} = 2.25$

6. $$\frac{L2}{POP2} = \underset{(3.75)}{.0605} + \underset{(17.98)}{.832}\left(\frac{L2}{POP2}\right)_{-1} + \underset{(3.77)}{.160}\ WA - \underset{(2.95)}{.0200}\ P_h + \underset{(2.86)}{.0364}\ Z$$

$\text{SE} = .00294,\ \text{R}^2 = .999,\ \text{DW} = 2.14$

7. $$\frac{L3}{POP3} = \underset{(5.02)}{.133} + \underset{(17.53)}{.782}\left(\frac{L3}{POP3}\right)_{-1} - \underset{(3.76)}{.00121}\left(\frac{AA}{POP}\right)_{-1} + \underset{(4.14)}{.0930}\ WA - \underset{(4.25)}{.0318}\ P_h + \underset{(4.81)}{.0738}\ Z$$

$\text{SE} = .00258,\ \text{R}^2 = .907,\ \text{DW} = 1.96$

8. $$\frac{LM}{POP} = \underset{(7.17)}{.0150} + \underset{(11.96)}{.634}\left(\frac{LM}{POP}\right)_{-1} + \underset{(0.90)}{.00676}\ WA_{-1} - \underset{(1.48)}{.00374}\ P_{h-1} + \underset{(6.40)}{.0580}\ Z$$

$\text{SE} = .00149,\ \text{R}^2 = .865,\ \text{DW} = 1.95$

It will be useful in discussing these results to consider the effects of each explanatory variable across the eight equations. (1) The results for the asset variable $(AA/POP)_{-1}$ are good in the sense that this variable is significant in all four of the expenditure equations. It is significant (and of the expected negative sign) in one of the four labor supply equations. (2) The wage rate and price variables are significant in all four expenditure equations with the exceptions of the housing investment equation, where the t-statistic for the price variable is 1.88, and the consumption of services equation, where the price variable was dropped because of the wrong sign. The wage and price variables appear in three of the four labor supply equations and are significant in two of these three. (3) With respect to the interest rate variables, the short-term rate is in the first two equations and the long-term rate is in the third and fourth equations. The coefficient estimates are significant except for the estimate in Eq. 2, where the t-statistic is 1.05. (4) The results for the nonlabor income variables are not very strong. The *YN* variable (total nonlabor income) appears in the expenditure equations 1, 2, and 4, but with t-statistics of only 0.36, 2.14, and 0.99. It also appears in one labor supply equation (Eq. 5), with the expected negative sign and with a t-statistic of 3.56. The *YTR* variable (transfer payments) appears in expenditure equation 3, with a t-statistic of 1.19. (5) The labor constraint variable *(Z)* appears in three expenditure equations and three labor supply equations. It is significant in all but equation 1, where the t-statistic is 1.92.

With respect to the housing investment equation, the implied value of γ in (4.15) is $1 - .738 = .262$, which says that the adjustment of gross investment to desired gross investment is 26.2 percent per quarter. Given this estimate and given the value of δ_H of .00655, which was used to construct *KH* and which is the value used in the model, the implied value of λ in (4.13) is .066. This says that the adjustment of the housing stock to its desired value is 6.6 percent per quarter.

In general, these results seem fairly supportive of the theory. With the exception of the nonlabor income variables, the variables that one would expect from the theory to influence household expenditures and labor supply are significant in most of the equations. With respect to the equations themselves, the weakest results are for Eq. 5, which explains the labor force participation of prime-age males. Most prime-age males work, and their participation does not seem to be much affected by economic variables, with the possible exception of nonlabor income.

Other Results from the Searching Procedure

In the process of searching for the final equations to be used in the model, one gets a feeling for what the data do and do not support. This information is not always conveyed to the reader by merely presenting the final set of equations;

it is sometimes helpful to present a few of the intermediate results. This will now be done regarding the results for the household sector.

1. The results are not sensitive to the use of JJ^* as the measure of labor market tightness in the construction of the labor constraint variable Z. Very similar results were obtained using $1 - UR$ as the measure of labor market tightness and defining Z to be $1 - .975/(1 - UR)$, where .975 is slightly larger than the largest value of $1 - UR$ in the sample period. Consider, for example, the first three equations. The t-statistics for Z defined the new way were 1.91, 3.40, and 3.29, which compare to 1.92, 3.54, and 3.38 above. The SEs were .00189, .00318, and .00435, which compare to .00190, .00315, and .00445 above. It is clear that there is little to choose between the two measures, or to put it another way, the data cannot be used to decide between the two.

2. The data do not support the use of real interest rates in the expenditure equations. One way to test for the effects of real interest rates is to include the nominal interest rate and the expected rate of inflation as separate explanatory variables. If the real interest rate is the correct variable to use, the coefficient estimate of the expected rate of inflation variable should be of opposite sign and equal in absolute value to the coefficient estimate of the nominal interest rate variable. To test for this, the four estimates of the expected rate of inflation that were discussed in Section 4.1.3 were added (one at a time) to the four expenditure equations. For 10 of the 16 cases the coefficient estimate of the expected rate of inflation was of the wrong (negative) sign, and for the 6 cases in which it was of the right sign the largest t-statistic was only 0.52. In the 6 cases in which the signs were right, the sizes of the estimates were much smaller in absolute value than the sizes of the estimates of the coefficient of the nominal interest rate, and the other coefficient estimates in the equations changed very little. Two of the 12 negative estimates were significant, with t-statistics of 2.09 and 2.16. Use of the actual rates of inflation in place of the expected rates led to similar poor results.

It is clear that these results do not support the use of real interest rates in the expenditure equations. These negative results may be due, of course, to poor estimates of the expected rate of inflation. It may be, for example, that better estimates would be obtained under the assumption that expectations are rational, and until further work is done, these negative results are very tentative.

3. The data do not support the treatment of consumer durable expenditures as investment expenditures. When KD_{-1}/POP_{-1} was added to Eq. 3, its coefficient estimate was unreasonably small ($-.00968$ with a t-statistic of 2.23). Under the assumption that the treatment of housing investment

discussed earlier also pertains to consumer durable expenditures, the implied value of λ in (4.13) from this regression is .072. (The coefficient estimate of CD_{-1}/POP_{-1} was .525, and the value of the depreciation rate, δ_D, is .0515.) This says that the adjustment of the stock of durable goods to its desired value is 7.2 percent per quarter, which is only slightly larger than the 6.6 percent figure obtained for the housing stock. Given what seemed to be an unreasonably low value of λ, the decision was made to treat consumer durable expenditures like expenditures on services and nondurables.

4. The data provide mild support for the use of the after-tax wage rate rather than the before-tax wage rate in the equations. The wage rate variable that is used, WA, is equal to W_hQ, where $Q = (1 - d^M_{1g} - d^M_{1s} - d_{4g} - d_{4s})$. (This is Eq. 126 in Table A-5.) W_h is the before-tax wage rate. d^M_{1g} and d^M_{1s} are marginal personal income tax rates, and d_{4g} and d_{4s} are employee social security tax rates. To test that the appropriate wage rate variable is W_hQ rather than merely W_h, the wage rate variable can be included in the form αW_hQ^λ, where λ is a coefficient to be estimated along with the regular coefficient α. If the after-tax wage rate is the correct variable to use, the estimate of λ should be close to 1, and if the before-tax wage rate is correct, the estimate of λ should be close to 0.

When λ is estimated, the equation is nonlinear in coefficients. The estimation of such equations is discussed in Chapter 6. For the present results the 2SLS technique was used. The estimates of λ for the four expenditure equations were 2.8, 2.6, 0.3, and 0.7, with standard errors of the respective coefficient estimates of 2.12, 0.86, 0.58, and 1.00. (There is some collinearity between the estimates of α and λ. The t-statistics for the estimates of α changed from 2.07, 2.48, 4.08, and 2.61 to 0.91, 3.48, 2.78, and 2.09 respectively when λ was estimated rather than constrained to be 1. Except for the second equation, the t-statistics are lower in the unconstrained case.) One estimate of λ is significantly different from 0, and none are significantly different from 1. Although the estimates are obviously not precise, three of the four estimates are closer to 1 than to 0, and thus the results provide at least some support to the use of the after-tax wage rate.

5. The data again provide mild support for the use of the after-tax interest rates rather than the before-tax rates. The interest rate variable that is used in Eqs. 1 and 2, RSA, is equal to $RS \cdot Q$, where $Q = (1 - d^M_{1g} - d^M_{1s})$. (This is Eq. 127 in Table A-5.) RS is the before-tax short-term rate. When the interest rate variable was included in these two equations as $\alpha RS \cdot Q^\lambda$, the estimates of λ were -2.6 and 2.5, with standard errors of the coefficient estimates of 4.35 and 11.72. The interest rate variable that is used in Eqs. 3 and 4, RMA, is

equal to $RM \cdot Q$. (This is Eq. 128 in Table A-5.) RM is the before-tax mortgage rate. When the interest rate variable was included in the two equations as $\alpha RM \cdot Q^{\lambda}$, the estimates of λ were 3.0 and 4.6, with standard errors of the coefficient estimates of 1.75 and 1.90. There is again some collinearity between the estimates of α and λ, and the estimates of λ are not precise. One of the four is significantly different from 0, and none are significantly different from 1. Given that three of the estimates are closer to 1 than to 0, there is some support for the use of the after-tax interest rates. The support here is weaker than it was in the wage rate case because the estimated standard errors of λ are larger.

6. It should also be noted with respect to the treatment of taxes that the nonlabor income variable, YN, is after-tax nonlabor income (Eq. 88). This treatment is again in keeping with the theoretical model. Given that the results using YN were not very good, no tests of this variable versus a before-tax version were made. It seemed quite unlikely that the data would be able to discriminate between the two.

The Demand-for-Money Equation

The final estimated equation for the household sector is a demand-for-money equation:

9.
$$\log \frac{M_h}{POP \cdot P_h} = \underset{(3.63)}{.0297} - \underset{(2.64)}{.000698}\, t + \underset{(19.22)}{.835} \log \left(\frac{M_h}{POP \cdot P_h}\right)_{-1} + \underset{(3.13)}{.123} \log \left(\frac{YT}{POP \cdot P_h}\right) - \underset{(3.81)}{.00416}\, RSA$$

$SE = .0140$, $R^2 = .970$, $DW = 2.07$

This is a standard demand-for-money equation in which the per-capita demand for real money balances of the household sector, $M_h/(POP \cdot P_h)$, is a function of per-capita real income, $YT/(POP \cdot P_h)$, and the after-tax short-term interest rate, RSA. A time trend has been added to the equation to account for possible trend changes in the relationship. This equation is consistent with the theoretical model, where the optimal level of money holdings of the household is a negative function of the interest rate.

Summary and Further Discussion

The following paragraphs provide a summary of the general features of the empirical model of household behavior. Not surprisingly, these features are similar to the general features of the theoretical model in Section 3.1.2, since the empirical model was constructed with this similarity in mind. The reader should keep in mind in the following discussion that the smaller the labor constraint, the larger is the labor constraint variable.

1. Household expenditures respond to the following variables: the after-tax wage rate (+), the price level (−), the after-tax short-term or long-term interest rate (−), after-tax nonlabor income (+), the initial value of wealth (+), and the labor constraint variable (+).

2. Labor supply responds to the following variables: the after-tax wage rate (+), the price level (−), after-tax nonlabor income (−), the initial value of wealth (−), and the labor constraint variable (+).

3. A decrease in tax rates (the marginal personal income tax rate and the employee social security tax rate) increases expenditures through the wage rate and nonlabor income variables. A decrease in tax rates also decreases expenditures through the interest rate variables. (A decrease in tax rates, other things being equal, raises the after-tax interest rate, which has a negative effect on expenditures.) The net effect of a decrease in tax rates is thus ambiguous, although it will be seen when the quantitative properties of the model are examined in Section 9.4 that the net effect is positive. Labor supply responds to a decrease in tax rates positively through the wage rate variable and negatively through the nonlabor income variable. It will be seen that the positive effect dominates in the model.

4. Transfer payments are part of nonlabor income, and thus an increase in transfer payments has a negative effect on labor supply. Therefore, a decrease in net taxes through an increase in transfer payments has a negative effect on labor supply, whereas a decrease in net taxes through a decrease in tax rates has a positive effect.

5. An increase in interest rates has a negative effect on expenditures, which, other things being equal, has a positive effect on the household savings rate *(SR)*. The savings rate is thus indirectly a positive function of interest rates.

6. An increase in the savings rate increases wealth *(AA)*, which in turn increases expenditures (with a lag of one quarter). The increase in expenditures in turn decreases the savings rate. There is thus a tendency for a change in the savings rate to reverse itself over time because of the effects of the wealth variable on expenditures.

7. The labor constraint variable is a nonlinear function of hours paid for. When labor markets are tight, this variable has very little effect on expenditures (since its value is close to zero). This is the unconstrained case in which consumption and labor supply decisions are simply a function of wage rates, prices, interest rates, nonlabor income, and wealth. When labor markets are

loose and households are constrained in their labor supply decisions, the labor constraint variable has an effect on expenditures. Because it is a function of hours paid for, its inclusion in the equations means that income is on the RHS of the equations in the form of separate wage-rate and hours-paid-for variables when the constraint is binding. In the constrained case the expenditure equations are thus closer than otherwise to typical consumption equations in which income is an explanatory variable.

8. The labor constraint variable also enters the labor supply equations. Three of the labor supply variables are labor force participation variables, and therefore the inclusion of the labor constraint variable in these equations means that labor force participation is predicted to be less in loose labor markets than in tight labor markets. This effect is sometimes called the "discouraged worker" effect. Given the functional form of the labor constraint variable, this effect is close to zero when labor markets are tight.

4.1.5 Stochastic Equations for the Firm Sector

Sequential Approximation to the Joint Decisions

The maximization problem of a firm in the theoretical model is fairly complicated, which is partly a result of the large number of decision variables. The five main variables are the firm's price, production, investment, demand for employment, and wage rate. In the theoretical model these five decisions are jointly determined, that is, they are the result of solving one maximization problem. The variables that affect this solution include (1) the initial stocks of excess capital, excess labor, and inventories, (2) the current and expected future values of the interest rate, (3) the current and expected future demand schedules for the firm's output, (4) the current and expected future supply schedules of labor facing the firm, and (5) expectations of other firms' future price and wage decisions.

The theoretical model of firm behavior is more difficult to handle empirically than is the theoretical model of household behavior, and, as will be seen, the links from the theory to the econometric specifications are weaker for firms. One of the key approximations that was made was to assume that the five decisions of a firm are made sequentially rather than jointly. The sequence starts from the price decision and then goes to the production decision, to the investment and employment decisions, and finally to the wage rate decision. In this way of looking at the problem, the firm first chooses its optimal price path. This path then implies a certain expected sales path, from which the optimal production path is chosen. Given the optimal production path, the optimal paths of investment and employment are chosen. Finally, given the optimal employment path, the optimal wage path is chosen, which is the path that the firm expects is necessary to attract the amount of labor implied by its optimal employment path.

Seven observed variables were chosen to represent the five decisions: (1) the price level of the firm sector (P_f), (2) production (Y), (3) investment in nonresidential plant and equipment (IK_f), (4) the number of jobs in the firm sector (J_f), (5) the average number of hours paid per job (H_f), (6) the average number of overtime hours paid per job (HO), and (7) the wage rate of the firm sector (W_f).

A Constraint on the Behavior of the Real Wage

Before the estimated equations are discussed, a constraint that was imposed on the relationship between the nominal wage rate (W_f) and the price level (P_f) needs to be explained. It does not seem sensible for the real wage rate (W_f/P_f) to be a function of either W_f or P_f separately, and in order to ensure that this not be true, a constraint on the coefficients of the price and wage equations must be imposed. The relevant parts of the two equations are

$$\text{(4.17)} \qquad \log P_f = \beta_1 \log P_{f-1} + \beta_2 \log W_f + \ . \ . \ . \ ,$$

$$\text{(4.18)} \qquad \log W_f = \gamma_1 \log W_{f-1} + \gamma_2 \log P_f + \gamma_3 \log P_{f-1} + \ . \ . \ . \ .$$

From these two equations, the reduced form equation for the real wage (ignoring the other endogenous variables in the two equations) is

$$\text{(4.19)} \qquad \log W_f - \log P_f = \frac{1}{1-\beta_2\gamma_2}\gamma_1(1-\beta_2)\log W_{f-1} - \frac{1}{1-\beta_2\gamma_2}[\beta_1(1-\gamma_2) - \gamma_3(1-\beta_2)] \log P_{f-1} + \ . \ . \ . \ .$$

In order for the real wage not to be a function of the wage and price levels, the coefficient of $\log W_{f-1}$ in (4.19) must equal the negative of the coefficient of $\log P_{f-1}$. This requires that

$$\text{(4.20)} \qquad 0 = (\gamma_1 + \gamma_3)(1-\beta_2) - \beta_1(1-\gamma_2).$$

This restriction was imposed in the estimation of the model. (The imposition of coefficient restrictions within the context of the various estimation techniques is discussed in Chapter 6.)

The Price and Wage Equations

The main variables that affect the solution of a firm's maximization problem in the theoretical model were mentioned at the beginning of this section. The empirical work for the price and wage equations consisted of trying these variables, directly or indirectly, as explanatory variables. Observed variables were used directly, and unobserved variables were used indirectly by trying observed variables that seemed likely to affect the unobserved variables.

As noted in Section 4.1.3, a number of demand pressure variables were tried in the price and wage equations. In the end the decision was made simply to use ZZ in the price equation and UR in the wage equation. The results of trying other variables are discussed later in this section.

It was argued in Section 3.2.3 that import prices are likely to affect domestic prices, and therefore the import price index *(PIM)* was tried in the price equation. With respect to accounting for the effects of expectations of other firms' price decisions on actual price decisions, the main variable that was tried was simply the lagged price level. It is difficult to think of variables that may help capture the effects of expectations of future price decisions on current decisions. The lagged price level is obviously one possibility; another is the wage rate. If wages are high, this may lead firms to expect prices to be high in the future, which may then affect their current price decisions. It is somewhat unclear whether one should use the current wage rate or the lagged wage rate in the price equation. Given that the data in the model are quarterly, some of the data on wages within the quarter may be used by firms in setting prices within the quarter. In the empirical work both the current wage rate and the wage rate lagged one quarter were tried; the current wage rate gave slightly better results.

The final equation that was chosen is the following:

$$
\begin{aligned}
10.\qquad \log P_f = {} & \underset{(7.32)}{.187} + \underset{(82.62)}{.922} \log P_{f-1} + \underset{(6.95)}{.0339} \log W_f(1 + d_{5g} + d_{5s}) \\
& + \underset{(8.56)}{.0339} \log PIM - \underset{(4.22)}{.0810}\, ZZ_{-1},
\end{aligned}
$$

$$SE = .00406,\ R^2 = .999,\ DW = 1.46$$

where P_f is the price level set by the firm sector, W_f is the wage rate, d_{5g} and d_{5s} are employer social security tax rates, PIM is the import price deflator, and ZZ is the demand pressure variable. The price level is a function of the lagged price level, the wage rate inclusive of employer social security costs, the import price deflator, and the demand pressure variable, ZZ.

In the empirical work for the wage equation, the lagged wage rate and the current and lagged price level were used as proxies for the expectations of future wages of other firms. The unemployment rate, *UR*, was used as a proxy for expectations about the labor supply curve. In addition, a time trend was added to the equation to account for trend changes in the wage rate relative to the price level. The inclusion of the time trend is important, since the time trend is essentially the variable that identifies the price equation. Given that the demand pressure variable *ZZ* and the unemployment rate are highly correlated, the only variable not included in the price equation that is included in the wage equation is essentially the time trend. Another way of looking at the wage equation, especially given the restriction (4.20) that is imposed on the coefficients of the price and wage equations, is that it is a real wage equation.

The estimated wage equation is

$$16. \qquad \log W_f = \underset{(3.52)}{-.423} + \underset{(45.75)}{.929} \log W_{f-1} + .427 \log PX$$

$$- \underset{(3.50)}{.382} \log PX_{-1} + \underset{(4.31)}{.000671}\, t - \underset{(1.53)}{.0760}\, UR.$$

$$SE = .00546,\ R^2 = .999,\ DW = 2.00$$

The wage rate is a function of the lagged wage rate, the current and lagged values of the price level, the time trend, and the unemployment rate. The price variable that is used in the wage equation is PX rather than P_f. PX is the price deflator for sales of the firm sector, and P_f is the price deflator for sales of the firm sector minus farm output. The two deflators are very similar, and for purposes of imposing the real wage constraint discussed above, the two were taken to be the same. Equation 16 was estimated under the coefficient restriction (4.20), where the values used for β_1 and β_2 are the values estimated in Eq. 10. (See Section 6.3.2 for further discussion of this.) The wage equation is numbered 16 rather than 11 to emphasize that in the sequential approximation to the joint decisions, the wage decision is considered to come last.

It is possible from the coefficients of Eqs. 10 and 16 to calculate the coefficients of the real wage equation (4.19). The lagged dependent variable coefficient (that is, the coefficient of $\log W_{f-1} - \log P_{f-1}$ in Eq. 4.19), for example, is .911. When Eq. 16 was estimated without the restriction (4.20) imposed, the fit was essentially unchanged and the coefficient estimates changed very little. The unrestricted estimates of the coefficients of $\log PX$ and $\log PX_{-1}$ were .461 and $-.411$, which compare to the restricted estimates of .427 and $-.382$. An F test accepted the hypothesis at the 95-percent confidence level that the restriction is valid. The F value was 0.12, which compares to the critical value of 3.93 (with 1,109 degrees of freedom).

Movements of the real wage in the model affect the division of income between profits and wages. (The level of profits of the firm sector is determined by a definition, Eq. 67 in Table A-5, where it is a positive function of prices and a negative function of the wage rate.) The coefficient of the current price variable in the wage equation is less than one, and thus when, say, the price level rises by 1 percent in the quarter, the wage rate rises by less than 1 percent, other things being equal. A shock to the price level thus means an initial fall in the real wage. If, for example, the price of imports *(PIM)* rises by 1 percent, this will lead to an increase in the price level of .0339 percent in the current quarter, but to an increase in the wage rate of only about half this amount. An increase in the price of imports thus has a negative effect on the real wage.

The results of searching for the price and wage equations will now be discussed. The only searching that was done for the wage equation was to try alternative measures of demand pressure. The use of $1/UR$ in place of UR led to almost identical results. The fits were essentially the same (SE = .00545 versus .00546 above), and the t-statistic for the coefficient of $1/UR$ was 1.55, which compares to 1.53 above. The use of ZZ in place of UR produced poorer results. The t-statistic for the coefficient of ZZ was only 0.39. The use of log $(ZZ + .04)$, which is a nonlinear transformation of ZZ that takes on a value of minus infinity when $GNPR$ exceeds $GNPR^*$ by 4.0 percent, in place of UR produced similar results to those for ZZ. The t-statistic for the coefficient of log $(ZZ + .04)$ was 0.34.

More searching was done for the price equation. (Results using the one-quarter-lagged values of the demand pressure variables rather than the current values gave better results, and only the results using the lagged values will be reported here.) A nonlinear transformation of ZZ_{-1}, log $(ZZ_1 + a)$, where a is some preassigned number, led to results that were almost identical to those using ZZ_{-1}. For values of a of .01, .04, and .10 the t-statistics were 3.82, 4.03, and 4.12 respectively, which compare to the value of 4.22 given above using ZZ_{-1}. The fits were very close. Three other candidates for the demand pressure variable did not lead to significant coefficient estimates. They were (1) the initial stock of excess labor on hand, (2) the initial stock of excess capital on hand, and (3) the initial ratio of the stock of inventories to the level of sales. The excess capital variable was closest to being significant, with a t-statistic of 1.91.

The use of UR_{-1} or $1/UR_{-1}$ in place of ZZ_{-1} produced slightly better results. The t-statistics were 6.36 and 5.59 respectively, compared to 4.22 for ZZ_{-1}, and the fits were somewhat better (SE = .00376 and .00387 respectively, compared to .00406 above). When UR_{-1} and ZZ_{-1} were both included in the equation, UR_{-1} was significant but ZZ_{-1} was not. A similar result was obtained when $1/UR_{-1}$ and ZZ_{-1} were both included in the equation. In spite of these results, I decided to use ZZ_{-1} as the demand pressure variable in the price equation. The unemployment rate is more difficult to predict than is $GNPR$ (and thus ZZ) because it is more sensitive to errors made in predicting the labor force variables. My general experience is that versions of the price equation that use an unemployment rate variable as the demand pressure variable lead to less accurate predictions of prices within the context of the overall model than do other versions. This is true even though the other versions may not have as good single-equation fits. These differences are generally small, however, and the use of ZZ_{-1} over UR_{-1} or $1/UR_{-1}$ is not an important issue. The results in this book would not be changed very much if UR_{-1} or $1/UR_{-1}$ were used instead.

Two dummy variables were added to the price equation to try to pick up possible effects of the price freeze in 1971IV and the removal of the freeze in 1972I. One dummy variable had a value of 1 in 1971IV and 0 otherwise, and the other had a value of 1 in 1972I and 0 otherwise. Neither of these variables was significant, and their inclusion had little effect on the other coefficient estimates. The coefficient estimates were of the expected signs (negative and positive, respectively), but the t-statistics were only 0.12 and 1.47. The price freeze thus appeared to have too small an effect on P_f to be picked up by an equation like Eq. 10, and therefore no price freeze variables were used. With the current wage rate included in the price equation, the wage rate lagged one quarter was not significant. The latter was thus not included in the final specification.

With respect to employer social security tax rates, the tax rates have a positive effect on the price level through the $W_f(1 + d_{5g} + d_{5s})$ term in Eq. 10. This term is the wage rate inclusive of employer social security taxes. The inclusion of these tax rates in the price equation means that an increase in the rates has a negative effect on the real wage. In other words, at least some of the increase in employer social security taxes is estimated to be passed along to workers in the form of a lower real wage. The inclusion of the social security tax rates in the price equation is not supported by the data. When the terms $\log W_f$ and $\log(1 + d_{5g} + d_{5s})$ are included separately in Eq. 10, the estimate of the tax variable is significant but of the wrong sign (−.529 with a t-statistic of 2.66). The main problem is that there is not much variation in the tax rates. Poor results are thus not surprising and are not necessarily to be trusted as indicating that the tax rates truly do not belong in the equation. The answer to this problem here was merely to assume that the tax rates affect the price level in the same way that the wage rate does.

No evidence could be found that profit taxes affect the price level. When, for example, the variable log $(1 + d_{2g} + d_{2s})$ was added to Eq. 10, its coefficient estimate was insignificant, with a t-statistic of 1.21 (d_{2g} and d_{2s} are the corporate profit tax rates). For the same variable lagged one quarter, the t-statistic was 1.12. Little evidence could thus be found that firms pass on profit taxes in the form of higher prices relative to wages. Again, however, there is not much variation in tax rates, so very little confidence should be placed on this negative result. Unlike the case for the social security tax rates, there is no obvious way to restrict the profit tax rates to enter the price equation, and therefore nothing was tried. The model thus has the property that a change in profit tax rates does not directly affect the real wage.

In previous versions of the US model, two cost-of-capital variables were included in the price equation, the bond rate RB and an investment tax credit variable denoted $TXCR$. In the theoretical model the interest rate affects the firm's decisions, and in the case of experiment 5 in Table 3-3 an increase in the interest rate led the firm to raise its prices in periods 2 and 3. The cost-of-capital variables were thus used to see if there was any empirical support for the proposition that these variables affect prices. When RB and $TXCR$ are included in Eq. 10, they are significant, with t-statistics of 4.69 and 2.17 respectively. The coefficient estimate of RB is positive (.00249) and the coefficient estimate of $TXCR$ is negative (−.00239), both as expected. ($TXCR$ takes on a value of 1.0 when the credit of 7 percent is in full force—1964I–1966III, 1967II–1969I, and 1971IV–1975I; a value of 1.43 when the credit of 10 percent is in force—1975II on; a value of .5 when the credit of 7 percent is estimated to be half in force because of the Long amendment or timing considerations—1962III–1963IV and 1971III; and 0.0 when the credit is not in force.)

With RB included in the price equation, the model has the property that high interest rates, other things being equal, are inflationary. A tight monetary policy defined as high interest rates has a direct positive effect on prices as well as the usual indirect negative effect on prices through the negative effect of high interest rates on demand. The direct positive interest rate effect on prices in this version is large, and for a number of experiments it dominates the indirect negative effect. I finally decided that the effect seems too large, and I have dropped the cost-of-capital variables from the price equation. It may be that some left-out variable from the price equation, such as inflationary expectations, affects both RB and P_f and that RB is spuriously picking up the effects of this variable on P_f. This decision does have a significant effect on the properties of the model, and it should not be taken lightly. If RB actually belongs in the price equation, then excluding it has seriously misspecified the model with respect to a number of policy properties.

The Production Equation

The specification of the production equation is the point at which the assumption that a firm's decisions are made sequentially begins to be used. The equation is based on the assumption that the firm sector first sets its price, then knows what its sales for the current period will be, and from this latter information decides on what its production for the current period will be.

In the theoretical model production is smoothed relative to sales, that is, the optimal production path of a firm generally has less variance than its expected sales path. The reason for this is the various costs of adjustment, which include costs of changing employment, costs of changing the capital stock, and costs of having the stock of inventories deviate from β_1 times sales. If a firm were only interested in minimizing inventory costs, it would produce according to the following equation (assuming that sales for the current period are known):

$$(4.21)\qquad Y = X + \beta_1 X - V_{-1},$$

where Y is the level of production, X is the level of sales, and V_{-1} is the stock of inventories at the beginning of the period. Since by definition, $V - V_{-1} = Y - X$, producing according to (4.21) would ensure that $V = \beta_1 X$. Because of the other adjustment costs, it is generally not optimal for a firm to produce according to (4.21). In the theoretical model there was no need to postulate explicitly how a firm's production plan deviated from (4.21) because its optimal production path just resulted, along with the other optimal paths, from the direct solution of its maximization problem. For the empirical work, on the other hand, it is necessary to make further assumptions.

The estimated production equation is based on the following three assumptions:

$$(4.22)\qquad V^* = \beta X,$$

$$(4.23)\qquad Y^* = X + \alpha(V^* - V_{-1}),$$

$$(4.24)\qquad Y - Y_{-1} = \lambda(Y^* - Y_{-1}),$$

where $*$ denotes a desired value. Equation (4.22) states that the desired stock of inventories is proportional to current sales. Equation (4.23) states that the desired level of production is equal to sales plus some fraction of the difference between the desired stock of inventories and the stock on hand at the end of the previous period. Equation (4.24) states that actual production partially adjusts to desired production each period. Combining the three equations yields

$$Y = (1 - \lambda)Y_{-1} + \lambda(1 + \alpha\beta)X - \lambda\alpha V_{-1}. \quad (4.25)$$

The estimated equation is

$$\text{11.} \quad \underset{(4.36)}{Y = 11.4} + \underset{(3.67)}{.162}\ Y_{-1} + \underset{(19.59)}{1.011}\ X - \underset{(4.44)}{.193}\ V_{-1} - \underset{(1.86)}{2.06}\ D593 + \underset{(0.64)}{.793}\ D594 + \underset{(1.89)}{2.10}\ D601,$$

$$SE = 1.12,\ R^2 = .999,\ DW = 2.20,\ \hat{\rho} = \underset{(6.73)}{.605}$$

where $D593$, $D594$, and $D601$ are dummy variables for the 1959 steel strike. The implied value of λ is $1 - .162 = .838$, which means that actual production adjusts 83.8 percent of the way to desired production in the current quarter. The implied value of α is .230, which means that desired production is equal to sales plus 23.0 percent of the desired change in inventories. The implied value of β is .898, which means that the desired stock of inventories is estimated to equal 89.8 percent of the (quarterly) level of sales.

No searching was done for the production equation other than to try a few strike dummy variables.

The Investment Equation

The investment equation is based on the assumption that the production decision has already been made. In the theoretical model, because of costs of changing the capital stock, it may sometimes be optimal for a firm to hold excess capital. If there were no such costs, investment each period would merely be the amount needed to have enough capital to produce the output of the period. In the theoretical model there was no need to postulate explicitly how investment deviates from this amount, but for the empirical work this must be done.

The estimated investment equation is based on the following three equations:

$$(4.26)\qquad (KK - KK_{-1})^* = \alpha_0(KK_{-1} - KKMIN_{-1}) + \alpha_1 \Delta Y + \alpha_2 \Delta Y_{-1} + \alpha_3 \Delta Y_{-2} + \alpha_4 \Delta Y_{-3},$$

$$(4.27)\qquad IK_f^* = (KK - KK_{-1})^* + \delta_K KK_{-1},$$

$$(4.28)\qquad IK_f - IK_{f-1} = \lambda(IK_f^* - IK_{f-1}),$$

where * again denotes a desired value. IK_f is gross investment of the firm sector, KK is the capital stock, and $KKMIN$ is the minimum amount of capital needed to produce the output of the period. $(KK - KK_{-1})^*$ is desired net investment, and IK_f^* is desired gross investment. Equation (4.26) states that desired net investment is a function of the amount of excess capital on hand and of four change-in-output terms. If output has not changed for four periods and if there is no excess capital, then desired net investment is zero. The change-in-output terms are meant in part to be proxies for expected future output changes. Equation (4.27) relates desired gross investment to desired net investment. $\delta_K KK_{-1}$ is the depreciation of the capital stock during period $t-1$. By definition, $IK_f = KK - KK_{-1} + \delta_K KK_{-1}$, and (4.27) is merely this same equation for the desired values. Equation (4.28) is a stock adjustment equation relating the desired change in gross investment to the actual change. It is meant to approximate cost of adjustment effects.

Combining (4.26)–(4.28) yields

$$(4.29)\qquad IK_f - IK_{f-1} = \lambda\alpha_0(KK_{-1} - KKMIN_{-1}) + \lambda\alpha_1 \Delta Y + \lambda\alpha_2 \Delta Y_{-1} + \lambda\alpha_3 \Delta Y_{-2} + \lambda\alpha_4 \Delta Y_{-3} - \lambda(IK_{f-1} - \delta_K KK_{-1}).$$

Equation (4.29) has two restrictions that were not imposed in the empirical work. First, there is no constant term in (4.29), but one was used in the estimated equation. Second, from the last term in (4.29) the coefficients of IK_{f-1} and $\delta_K KK_{-1}$ are the same, and this constraint was not imposed.

The estimated equation is

$$12.\qquad \Delta IK_f = \underset{(0.11)}{-.0146} - \underset{(2.83)}{.0130}\,(KK - KKMIN)_{-1} + \underset{(5.70)}{.0967}\,\Delta Y + \underset{(0.02)}{.0004}\,\Delta Y_{-1} + \underset{(0.88)}{.0140}\,\Delta Y_{-2} + \underset{(1.24)}{.0196}\,\Delta Y_{-3} - \underset{(2.48)}{.107}\,IK_{f-1} + \underset{(2.59)}{.167}\,\delta_K KK_{-1}.$$

SE = .390, R^2 = .534, DW = 2.13

The estimated value of λ is .107 if taken from the IK_{f-1} term and .167 if taken from the $\delta_K KK_{-1}$ term. This means that gross investment adjusts between about 10.7 and 16.7 percent to its desired value each quarter. The implied value of α_0 is between $-.078$ and $-.121$, which means that between 7.8 and 12.1 percent of the amount of excess capital on hand is desired to be eliminated each quarter.

The estimate of the constant term in Eq. 12 is highly insignificant, and the results were little affected when the constant term was excluded. With respect to the other restriction, when the constraint on the coefficients of IK_{f-1} and $\delta_K KK_{-1}$ was imposed, the estimated value of λ was essentially zero (an estimate of .002, with a t-statistic of 0.12). This is the reason the restriction was not imposed, and it is a good example of the compromises that are sometimes made in empirical work. The theoretical restriction itself is, of course, not very tight in the sense that (4.29) only represents a rough approximation to the investment decision in the theoretical model.

Note that the interest rate does not appear as an explanatory variable in the investment equation. When the after-tax bond rate, *RBA,* was added to the equation, its coefficient estimate was significant but of the wrong sign (.209 with a t-statistic of 3.48). Similar results were obtained by lagging *RBA* one and then two quarters. The coefficient estimates and t-statistics were .223, 3.49 and .277, 3.92, respectively. There is thus no evidence that interest rates negatively affect investment in an equation like Eq. 12. Interest rates do, however, have important negative indirect effects on investment in the model. (See points 2 and 3 at the end of this section.) The investment tax credit variable discussed earlier, *TXCR,* was of the wrong expected sign and not significant when added to Eq. 12. Its coefficient estimate was $-.038$, with a t-statistic of 0.31.

The significance of the excess capital variable in Eq. 12 provides support for the proposition that firms spend time off their production functions. With respect to the output terms in the equation, only the current term is significant, and the results would not be much affected if the other three terms were dropped.

The Three Employment and Hours Equations

The employment and hours equations are similar in spirit to the investment equation. They are also based on the assumption that the production decision has already been made. Because of adjustment costs, it may sometimes be optimal in the theoretical model for firms to hold excess labor. Were it not for the costs of changing employment, the optimal level of employment would merely be the amount needed to produce the ouput of the period. In the theoretical model there was no need to postulate explicitly how employment deviates from this amount, but this must be done for the empirical work.

The estimated employment equation is based on the following three equations:

$$(4.30)\qquad \Delta \log J_f = \alpha_0 \log \frac{J_{f-1}}{J^*_{f-1}} + \alpha_1 \Delta \log Y + \alpha_2 \Delta \log Y_{-1} + \alpha_3 \Delta \log Y_{-2},$$

$$(4.31)\qquad J^*_{f-1} = \frac{JHMIN_{-1}}{H^*_{f-1}},$$

$$(4.32)\qquad H^*_{f-1} = \bar{H}e^{\delta t},$$

where $JHMIN$ is the number of worker hours required to produce the output of the period, H^*_f is the average number of hours per job that the firm would like to be worked if there were no adjustment costs, and J^*_f is the number of workers the firm would like to employ if there were no adjustment costs. The term $\log (J_{f-1}/J^*_{f-1})$ in (4.30) will be referred to as the "amount of excess labor on hand." Equation (4.30) states that the change in employment is a function of the amount of excess labor on hand and three change-in-output terms (all changes are changes in logs). If output has not changed for three periods and if there is no excess labor on hand, the change in employment is zero. As was the case for investment, the change-in-output terms are meant in part to be proxies for expected future output changes. Equation (4.31) defines the desired number of jobs, which is simply equal to the required number of worker hours divided by the desired number of hours worked per job. Equation (4.32) postulates that the desired number of hours worked is a smoothly trending variable, where H and δ are constants.

Combining (4.30)–(4.32) yields

$$(4.33)\qquad \Delta \log J_f = \alpha_0 \log \bar{H} + \alpha_0 \log \frac{J_{f-1}}{JHMIN_{-1}} + \alpha_0 \delta t + \alpha_1 \Delta \log Y + \alpha_2 \Delta \log Y_{-1} + \alpha_3 \Delta \log Y_{-2}.$$

The estimated equation is

$$13.\qquad \begin{aligned} \Delta \log J_f = {} & \underset{(3.76)}{-.885} - \underset{(3.75)}{.141} \log \frac{J_{f-1}}{JHMIN_{-1}} + \underset{(4.28)}{.000176}\, t \\ & + \underset{(8.33)}{.281}\, \Delta \log Y + \underset{(3.03)}{.119}\, \Delta \log Y_{-1} \\ & + \underset{(1.02)}{.033}\, \Delta \log Y_{-2} - \underset{(2.70)}{.00967}\, D593 + \underset{(0.50)}{.00174}\, D594, \end{aligned}$$

$SE = .00335$, $R^2 = .780$, $DW = 2.04$, $\hat{\rho} = \underset{(4.44)}{.447}$

where $D593$ and $D594$ are dummy variables for the 1959 steel strike. The estimated value of α_0 is $-.141$, which means that, other things being equal, 14.1 percent of the amount of excess labor on hand is eliminated each quarter. The implied value of $\overline{H}$ is 531.97, which at a weekly rate is 40.92 hours. The implied value of δ is $-.00125$. The trend variable t is equal to 9 for the first quarter of the sample period (1954I), and so the implied value of H^*_{f-1} for 1954I at a weekly rate is $40.92 \cdot \exp(-.00125 \times 9) = 40.46$. For 1982III t is equal to 123, and therefore the implied value for this quarter is $40.92 \cdot \exp(-.00125 \times 123) = 35.09$. In general these numbers seem reasonable. The significance of the excess labor variable in Eq. 13, like the significance of the excess capital variable in Eq. 12, provides support for the proposition that firms spend some time off their production functions.

The main hours equation is based on (4.31) and (4.32) and the following equation:

$$\Delta \log H_f = \lambda \log \frac{H_{f-1}}{H^*_{f-1}} + \alpha_0 \log \frac{J_{f-1}}{J^*_{f-1}} + \alpha_1 \Delta \log Y. \tag{4.34}$$

The first term on the RHS of (4.34) is the (logarithmic) difference between the actual number of hours paid for in the previous period and the desired number. The reason for the inclusion of this term in the hours equation but not in the employment equation is that, unlike J_f, H_f fluctuates around a slowly trending level of hours. This restriction is captured by the first term in (4.34). The other two terms are the amount of excess labor on hand and the current change in output. Both of these terms have an important effect on the employment decision, and they should also affect the hours decision since the two are closely related. Past output changes might also be expected to affect the hours decision, but these were not found to be significant and thus are not included in (4.34).

Combining (4.31), (4.32), and (4.34) yields

$$\begin{aligned}\Delta \log H_f = {} & (\alpha_0 - \lambda)\log \overline{H} + \lambda \log H_{f-1} + \alpha_0 \log \frac{J_{f-1}}{JHMIN_{-1}} \\ & + (\alpha_0 - \lambda)\delta t + \alpha_1 \Delta \log Y.\end{aligned} \tag{4.35}$$

The estimated equation is

$$\begin{aligned}\text{14.} \quad \Delta \log H_f = {} & \underset{(4.95)}{1.37} - \underset{(5.16)}{.284} \log H_{f-1} - \underset{(3.55)}{.0659} \log \frac{J_{f-1}}{JHMIN_{-1}} \\ & - \underset{(4.94)}{.000250}\, t + \underset{(4.40)}{.120}\, \Delta \log Y.\end{aligned}$$

SE = .00285, R^2 = .398, DW = 2.18

The estimated value of λ is $-.284$, which means that, other things being equal, actual hours are adjusted toward desired hours by 28.4 percent per quarter. The excess labor term is significant, with an estimated value of α_0 of $-.0659$. The implied value of $\bar{H}$ is 534.60, which is 41.12 hours at a weekly rate. This compares closely to the value of 40.92 implied by Eq. 13. The implied value of δ is $-.00115$, which compares closely to the value of $-.00125$ implied by Eq. 13. No attempt was made to impose the restriction that $\bar{H}$ and δ are the same in Eqs. 13 and 14. Given the closeness of the estimates, it is unlikely that imposing this restriction would make much difference. Again, the significance of the excess labor variable is support for the theoretical model.

The second hours equation explains overtime hours *(HO)*. It is of considerably less importance than the employment equation and the other hours equation. One would expect HO to be related to total hours, H_f, in the manner indicated in Figure 4-2. Up to some point A (for example, 40 hours per week), HO should be zero or some small constant amount, and after point A, increases in HO and H_f should be roughly one for one. An approximation to the curve in Figure 4-2 is

$$(4.36) \qquad HO = \exp(\alpha_1 + \alpha_2 H_f),$$

which in log form is

$$(4.37) \qquad \log HO = \alpha_1 + \alpha_2 H_f.$$

The foregoing discussion is based on the implicit premise that H_f has no trend. In practice H_f has a negative trend, which means that A in Figure 4-2 is likely to be shifting left over time. In order to account for this effect, H_f was detrended before being included in (4.37). H_f was regressed on a constant and t for the 1952I–1982III period, which resulted in an estimate of the coefficient for t of $-.56464$. The variable included in the estimated equation was then $H_f + .56464t$, which is denoted H_f^*. (This is Eq. 100 in Table A-5.) The estimated equation is

$$15. \qquad \log HO = \underset{(5.15)}{-8.34} + \underset{(7.38)}{.0223}\ H_f^*.$$

$$SE = .0552,\ R^2 = .905,\ DW = 1.82,\ \hat{\rho} = \underset{(21.38)}{.909}$$

There is considerable serial correlation in this equation ($\hat{\rho} = .909$), but as a rough approximation it seems satisfactory.

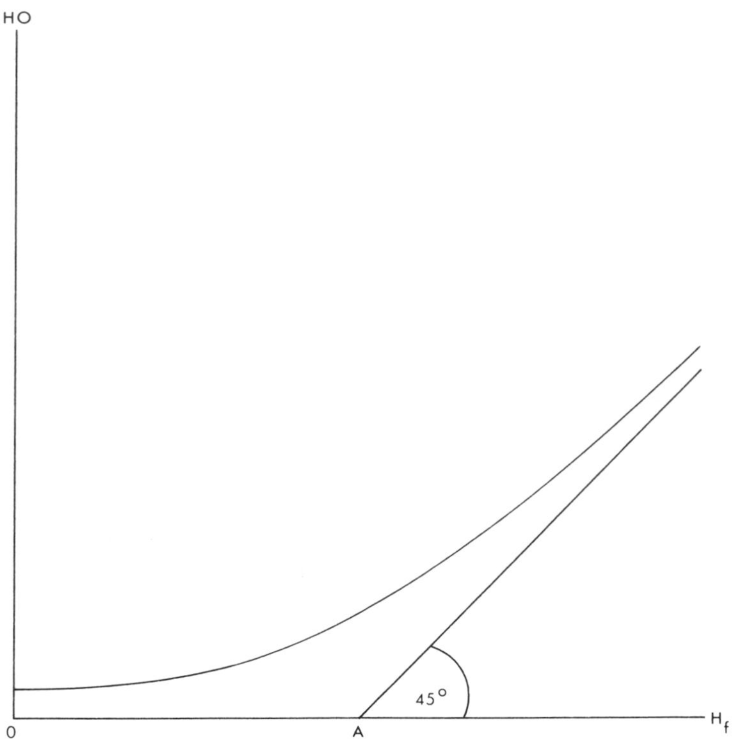

Figure 4-2 Expected relationship between overtime hours *(HO)* and total hours *(H_f)*

The Demand for Money Equation

The estimated demand for money equation for the firm sector is

17. $$\log \frac{M_f}{PX} = \underset{(1.04)}{.106} + \underset{(26.10)}{.920} \log \left(\frac{M_f}{PX}\right)_{-1} + \underset{(2.39)}{.0477} \log X - \underset{(3.26)}{.00700}\, RS(1 - d_{2g} - d_{2s}).$$

$SE = .0237$, $R^2 = .936$, $DW = 2.06$

The demand for real money balances, M_f/PX, is a function of sales, X, and the after-tax short-term interest rate, $RS(1 - d_{2g} - d_{2s})$. The tax rates used here are corporate tax rates, not personal tax rates as in Eq. 9. The level of sales is used as the transactions variable.

The Dividend Equation

The estimated dividend equation is

$$18. \qquad \underset{}{D_f} = \underset{(1.05)}{-.0227} + \underset{(108.28)}{.978}\ D_{f-1} + \underset{(5.64)}{.0201}\ (\pi_f - T_{fg} - T_{fs}),$$

$$SE = .125,\ R^2 = .999,\ DW = 1.58$$

where D_f is the level of dividends and $\pi_f - T_{fg} - T_{fs}$ is the value of after-tax profits. This is a standard dividend equation in which the current level of dividends is a function of current and past values of after-tax profits.

The Interest Payments Equation

The current level of interest payments of the firm sector is a function of its outstanding debt and of the interest rates that were in effect at the times of the relevant debt issues. The estimated equation that attempts to approximate this is

$$19. \qquad INT_f = \underset{(1.96)}{-3.59} + \underset{(8.59)}{.746}\ INT_{f-1} + \underset{(1.91)}{.0200}\ (-A_f) + \underset{(4.25)}{.467}\ RB.$$

$$SE = .364,\ R^2 = .999,\ DW = 2.01,\ \hat{\rho} = \underset{(25.41)}{.954}$$

INT_f is the level of interest payments, A_f is the value of net financial assets of the firm sector, and RB is the bond rate. A_f is negative because the firm sector is a net debtor. Interest payments are estimated to be a function of the debt of the firm sector and the bond rate.

Equation 19 has rather poor statistical properties. The coefficient estimates are not robust to slight changes in the specification, and the estimated serial correlation coefficient is high ($\hat{\rho} = .954$). This is not necessarily unexpected, since the equation does not capture the fact that debt is issued in a variety of maturities at different interest rates. Fortunately, the equation does not have an important effect on the properties of the model except for one of the experiments in Chapter 11, which concerns a version of the model in which there are rational expectations in the bond and stock markets. The results of this experiment indicate that the coefficient estimate of RB in Eq. 19 may be too large. This issue is discussed in Section 11.7.3.

The Inventory Valuation Adjustment Equation

The equation explaining inventory valuation adjustment is

$$\text{20.}\qquad \underset{}{IVA} = \underset{(0.98)}{1.52} - \underset{(3.51)}{95.2}\ PX + \underset{(3.34)}{92.2}\ PX_{-1},$$

$$SE = 1.24,\ R^2 = .865,\ DW = 1.71,\ \hat{\rho} = \underset{(12.45)}{.801}$$

where IVA is the value of the inventory valuation adjustment and PX is the price level. In the theoretical model IVA is equal to $-(PX - PX_{-1})V_{-1}$, and Eq. 20 is an attempt to approximate this. The coefficient estimates for PX and PX_{-1} are of opposite sign and close to each other in absolute value, which is as expected. The variable V_{-1} was added to the equation to see if any effect of the stock of inventories on IVA could be found. Its coefficient estimate was of the wrong sign ($-.0410$, with a t-statistic of 1.92), and therefore V_{-1} was not included in the equation.

The Capital Consumption Equation

The capital consumption of the firm sector (CC_f) is assumed to be a function of the current and past values of nominal investment expenditures $(PIK \cdot IK_f)$, where the lag structure is geometrically declining. The estimated equation is

$$\text{21.}\qquad CC_f = \underset{(3.69)}{-.0930} + \underset{(67.13)}{.966}\ CC_{f-1} + \underset{(4.69)}{.0447}\ PIK \cdot IK_f + \underset{(6.29)}{.562}\ DD811.$$

$$SE = .145,\ R^2 = .999,\ DW = 1.99$$

The dummy variable $DD811$ takes on a value of 1 from 1981I on and a value of 0 otherwise. Equation 21, like Eqs. 19 and 20, is only meant to be a rough approximation. Capital consumption is a function of current and past tax laws and accounting practices (as well as of current and past investment expenditures), both of which have changed over time. Equation 21 ignores these changes except for the inclusion of $DD811$. There appeared to be an important break in the relationship between capital consumption and investment expenditures beginning in 1981I, which could be captured fairly well by merely adding *DD*811 to the equation.

Summary and Further Discussion

The key equations of the firm sector are Eqs. 10–14 and 16. Some of the features of these equations are as follows.

1. Production is smoothed relative to sales. Investment, employment, and hours are smoothed relative to production. The buffer for production is the stock of inventories. The buffer for investment is the amount of excess capital on hand, and the buffer for employment and hours is the amount of excess labor on hand.

2. Although the bond rate is not an explanatory variable in the investment equation, interest rates have indirect negative effects on investment. Interest rates are explanatory variables in the consumer expenditure equations with negative coefficients, and thus an increase in interest rates directly lowers expenditures. This in turn lowers sales *(X)*, which lowers production and then investment and employment. The main channel by which interest rates affect the economy is through their effects on consumer expenditures.

3. Although interest rates affect investment in the manner just discussed, there is no means in the model by which interest rates affect capital-labor substitution. Any changes in the substitution of capital for labor (or vice versa) brought about by changes in the cost of capital relative to the cost of labor are not explained. The effects of long-run changes in the relationship of capital to labor are captured in the model through the peak-to-peak interpolations that are involved in the construction of excess capital and excess labor, in particular of *KHMIN* and *JHMIN*. The interpolations are, however, exogenous, and thus nothing in the model is allowed to affect them.

The spirit of the model is that firms spend much of the time "off" their production functions, which means that for much of the time one is not directly observing the number of capital and labor hours that are actually needed in the production process. If this is true, it is obviously going to be difficult to pick up the effects of, say, interest rate changes on the capital-labor ratio. I have made no attempt to do this in the model. If capital-labor substitution is a fairly slow and smooth process, then little is likely to be lost by the present approach, even with the use of the model for periods as long as, say, five years. If, on the other hand, substitution is fast or erratic, then the present model is likely to be seriously misspecified and should not hold up well in tests.

4.1.6 Stochastic Equations for the Financial Sector

The stochastic equations for the financial sector consist of an equation explaining member bank borrowing from the Federal Reserve, two term structure equations, an equation explaining the change in stock prices, and a demand for currency equation.

The Bank Borrowing Equation

The variable *BO/BR* is the ratio of borrowed reserves to total reserves. This ratio is assumed to be a function of the difference between the three-month Treasury bill rate *(RS)* and the discount rate *(RD)*. The estimated equation is

22. $$\frac{BO}{BR} = \underset{(3.79)}{.0148} + \underset{(1.34)}{.00455}\,(RS - RD).$$

$$\text{SE} = .0162,\ \text{R}^2 = .382,\ \text{DW} = 2.32,\ \hat{\rho} = \underset{(7.93)}{.606}$$

This equation does not fit very well, and the estimate of the serial correlation coefficient is fairly high. There is, however, at least some slight evidence that bank borrowing responds to the interest rate differential.

The Two Term Structure Equations

The expectations theory of the term structure of interest rates states that long-term rates are a function of the current and expected future short-term rates. The two long-term interest rates in the model are the bond rate *(RB)* and the mortgage rate *(RM)*. These rates are assumed to be determined according to the expectations theory, where current and past values of the short-term interest rate are used as proxies for expected future values. The two estimated equations are

23. $$RB = \underset{(2.54)}{.114} + \underset{(53.00)}{.889}\,RB_{-1} + \underset{(10.82)}{.277}\,RS - \underset{(6.48)}{.218}\,RS_{-1} + \underset{(3.48)}{.074}\,RS_{-2},$$

$$\text{SE} = .171,\ \text{R}^2 = .997,\ \text{DW} = 1.74$$

24. $$RM = .343 + .846\ RM_{-1} + .178\ RS + .041\ RS_{-1} - .043\ RS_{-2}.$$
$$\quad (3.36) \quad (29.00) \quad (4.64) \quad (0.80) \quad (1.23)$$

SE = .258, R^2 = .992, DW = 2.23

Note that the lagged dependent variable is included as an explanatory variable in each equation, which implies a fairly complicated lag structure relating each long-term rate to the past values of the short-term rate.

The expected rate of inflation variables that were discussed in Section 4.1.3 were tried in the equations, but no significant results were obtained. The best that was done from all the regressions tried was a *t*-statistic of 1.16 for the first expected wage inflation variable in the *RB* equation. One must thus conclude either that the expected inflation variables are poor measures of expectations or that any effects of expected future inflation rates on expected future nominal short-term interest rates are captured in the current and past short-term rates.

The Capital Gains Equation

The variable *CG* is the change in the market value of stocks held by the household sector. In the theoretical model the aggregate value of stocks is determined as the present discounted value of expected future after-tax cash flow, the discount rates being the current and expected future short term interest rates. The theoretical model thus implies that *CG* should be a function of changes in expected future after-tax cash flow and of changes in current and expected future interest rates. In the empirical work the change in the bond rate, ΔRB, was used as a proxy for changes in expected future interest rates, and the current and one-quarter-lagged values of the change in after-tax cash flow, $\Delta(CF - T_{fg} - T_{fs})$, were used as proxies for changes in expected future after-tax cash flow. The estimated equation is

25. $$CG = 10.9 - 24.4\ \Delta RB + 3.75\ \Delta(CF - T_{fg} - T_{fs}) + 4.07\ \Delta(CF - T_{fg} - T_{fs})_{-1}.$$
$$\quad (2.23) \quad (1.26) \quad (1.49) \quad (2.08)$$

SE = 48.4, R^2 = .145, DW = 1.90

The explanatory power of this equation is low, as would be expected, but at least some effect of interest rates and cash flow on stock prices seems to have been picked up.

The Demand for Currency Equation

The estimated demand for currency equation is

$$26. \quad \log \frac{CUR}{POP \cdot PX} = \underset{(3.87)}{-.106} - \underset{(0.79)}{.000133}\, t + \underset{(32.88)}{.897} \log \left(\frac{CUR}{POP \cdot PX}\right)_{-1}$$

$$+ \underset{(2.36)}{.0801} \log \frac{X}{POP}$$

$$- \underset{(4.00)}{.00313}\, RSA,$$

$$SE = .0103, \; R^2 = .937, \; DW = 2.69$$

where *CUR* is the value of currency. This equation states that the real per-capita demand for currency is a function of the real per-capita level of sales and of the after-tax short-term interest rate. A time trend is also included in the equation, although it is not significant.

4.1.7 The Stochastic Equation for the Foreign Sector

There is one estimated equation for the foreign sector, an equation explaining the demand for imports *(IM)*. Since this demand is demand by the domestic sectors, the position of the equation is somewhat arbitrary. It was put here to highlight the fact that the demand for imports has an important effect on the savings of the foreign sector.

It was argued in Section 3.2.2 that the demand for imports should be a function of the variables that affect a household's maximization problem. For the empirical work, this would mean trying the variables that were used in Section 4.1.4 to explain the expenditure and labor supply decisions of the household sector. The one problem with this is that in practice many imports are for use by the firm sector, and it is not possible to get a breakdown of imports by sector of purchase. As a compromise, I replaced (as possible explanatory variables) the wage rate variable, *WA*, and the labor constraint variable, *Z*, by per-capita domestic sales, *X/POP*. The explanatory variables that were tried included the wealth variable of the household sector, $(AA/POP)_{-1}$, the price of imports, the price of domestic goods, interest rates, and per-capita domestic sales. The wealth variable was not significant and thus was dropped. The equation that was chosen is

$$27. \quad \frac{IM}{POP} = \underset{(4.44)}{-.0277} + \underset{(15.31)}{.752} \left(\frac{IM}{POP}\right)_{-1} + \underset{(4.10)}{.0256} \frac{X}{POP}$$
$$- \underset{(3.90)}{.0114} PIM_{-1} + \underset{(4.64)}{.0393} PX_{-1} - \underset{(2.59)}{.00126} RMA_{-1}$$
$$- \underset{(2.18)}{.00654} D651 + \underset{(1.17)}{.00356} D652 - \underset{(3.65)}{.0109} D691$$
$$+ \underset{(5.42)}{.0166} D692 - \underset{(2.64)}{.00798} D714$$
$$+ \underset{(4.10)}{.0123} D721.$$

$$SE = .00294, R^2 = .994, DW = 1.71$$

The dummy variables are for periods in which there was a dock strike or recovery from a strike.

Equation 27 is similar to the import equations that are estimated for the multicountry model in Section 4.2.5. The demand for imports is a positive function of domestic activity and of the domestic price level and a negative function of the price of imports and of the interest rate. The interest rate in this case is measured by the after-tax mortgage rate, *RMA*. The price variables and the interest rate are lagged one quarter.

4.1.8 The Stochastic Equation for the State and Local Government Sector

The stochastic equation for the state and local government sector explains unemployment insurance benefits *(UB)*. The estimated equation is

$$28. \quad \log UB = \underset{(0.69)}{.369} + \underset{(18.00)}{1.58} \log U + \underset{(6.06)}{.465} \log W_f.$$

$$SE = .0706, R^2 = .992, DW = 1.80, \hat{\rho} = \underset{(12.59)}{.761}$$

Unemployment insurance benefits are a function of the level of unemployment *(U)* and of the nominal wage rate. The inclusion of the nominal wage rate is designed to try to pick up the effects of increases in wages and prices on legislated benefits per unemployed worker.

4.1.9 Stochastic Equations for the Federal Government Sector

There are two estimated equations for the federal government sector: the first is an equation explaining the interest payments of the federal government, and the second is an equation explaining the short-term interest rate. The second equation is interpreted as an interest rate reaction function of the Federal Reserve.

The Interest Payments Equation

The current level of interest payments of the federal government is a function of current and past government security issues and of the values of the interest rates at the time of the issues. The estimated equation that attempts to approximate this is

$$29. \quad \log INT_g = \underset{(4.77)}{-.870} + \underset{(29.65)}{.873} \log INT_{g-1} + \underset{(4.95)}{.148} \log(-A_g) + \underset{(5.54)}{.0572} \log RS + \underset{(2.18)}{.0818} \log RB,$$

$$SE = .0270, \; R^2 = .999, \; DW = 1.89$$

where INT_g is the level of interest payments, A_g is the value of net financial assets of the federal government, RS is the current short-term interest rate, and RB is the current long-term interest rate. The federal government is a net debtor, and therefore A_g is negative. This equation has better statistical properties than does the equation explaining the interest payments of the firm sector (Eq. 19), although it is still only a rough approximation.

The Interest Rate Reaction Function of the Federal Reserve

A key question in any macro model is what one assumes about monetary policy. In the theoretical model monetary policy is determined by an interest rate reaction function, and in the empirical work an equation like this was estimated. This equation is interpreted as an equation explaining the behavior of the Federal Reserve (Fed).

In at least one respect, trying to explain Fed behavior is more difficult than, say, trying to explain the behavior of the household or firm sectors. Since the

Fed is run by a relatively small number of people, there can be fairly abrupt changes in behavior if the people with influence change their minds or are replaced by others with different views. Abrupt changes are less likely to happen for the household and firm sectors because of the large number of decision makers in each sector. Having said this, I have, however, found an equation that seems to explain Fed behavior fairly well from 1954 up to 1979III, which is roughly the beginning of the time of Paul Volcker as chairman of the Fed. Beginning with 1979III there seems to have been an abrupt change in behavior, although, as will be seen, even this change seems capable of being modeled.

The equation explaining Fed behavior has on the LHS the three-month Treasury bill rate (RS). This treatment is based on the assumption that the Fed has a target bill rate each quarter and achieves this target through manipulation of its policy instruments. The RHS variables in this equation are variables that seem likely to affect the target rate. The variables that were chosen are (1) the rate of inflation as measured by the percentage change in the price deflator for domestic sales, $\dot{PD}$, (2) the degree of labor market tightness as measured by JJ^*, (3) the percentage change in real GNP, $GN\dot{P}R$, and (4) the percentage change in the money supply lagged one quarter, $M\dot{1}_{-1}$. What seemed to happen when Volcker became chairman was that the size of the coefficient of $M\dot{1}_{-1}$ increased substantially. This was modeled by adding the variable $DD793 \cdot M\dot{1}_{-1}$ to the equation, where $DD793$ is a dummy variable that is 0 before 1979III and 1 thereafter. The estimated equation is

$$\text{30.} \quad \begin{aligned} RS = & \underset{(2.99)}{-.946} + \underset{(25.55)}{.858}\, RS_{-1} + \underset{(2.11)}{.0687}\, \dot{PD} + \underset{(2.99)}{.0296}\, JJ^* \\ & + \underset{(2.92)}{.0597}\, GN\dot{P}R + \underset{(1.71)}{.032}\, M\dot{1}_{-1} + \underset{(4.20)}{.131}\, DD793 \cdot M\dot{1}_{-1}. \end{aligned}$$

$$SE = .687, \; R^2 = .953, \; DW = 1.91$$

Equation 30 is a "leaning against the wind" equation in the sense that the Fed is predicted to allow the bill rate to rise in response to increases in inflation, labor market tightness, real growth, and money supply growth. What the results show is that the weight given to money supply growth in the setting of the bill rate target is much greater in the Volcker period than before (.032 + .131 = .163 versus .032 before). Aside from the change in the equation when Volcker became chairman, the coefficients do not appear to have changed much over time. A Chow test, for example, accepted the hypothesis that the coefficients are the same (aside from the Volcker change) for the periods before and after 1969I. (The F value was 1.17, which compares to the critical F value with 7,111 degrees of freedom of 2.10 at the 95-percent confidence level.) In other words, the test accepted the hypothesis that there was no structural change in Fed behavior when Arthur Burns became chairman.

4.1.10 Possible Assumptions about Monetary and Fiscal Policies

The main federal government fiscal policy variables in the model are the following:

C_g	Purchases of goods
d_{1g}	Personal income tax parameter
d_{2g}	Profit tax rate
d_{3g}	Indirect business tax rate
d_{4g}	Employee social security tax rate
d_{5g}	Employer social security tax rate
J_g	Number of civilian jobs
J_m	Number of military jobs
TR_{gh}	Transfer payments to households

Some of these variables appear as explanatory variables in the stochastic equations and thus directly affect the decision variables; others indirectly affect the decision variables by influencing variables (through identities) which in turn influence, directly or indirectly, the decision variables. The response of the model to changes in the various fiscal policy variables is examined in Section 9.4.

Monetary policy is less straightforward to discuss. It will be useful for present purposes to list some of the equations that are involved in determining the effects of monetary policy on the economy.

9. $M_h = f_9(RS, \ldots),$

17. $M_f = f_{17}(RS, \ldots),$

26. $CUR = f_{26}(RS, \ldots),$

22. $\frac{BO}{BR} = .0148 + .00455\,(RS - RD),$

57. $BR = -g_1 M_b,$

71. $0 = \Delta M_b + \Delta M_h + \Delta M_f + \Delta M_r + \Delta M_g + \Delta M_s - \Delta CUR,$

77. $$0 = S_g - \Delta A_g - \Delta M_g + \Delta CUR + \Delta(BR - BO) - \Delta Q - DIS_g,$$

81. $$M1 = M1_{-1} + \Delta M_h + \Delta M_f + \Delta M_r + \Delta M_s + MDIF.$$

The other key equation is the interest rate reaction function, Eq. 30, which explains *RS*.

In considering the determination of variables in the model, it is convenient to match variables to equations, and this will be done in the following discussion. It should be remembered, however, that this is done only for expositional convenience. The model is simultaneous, and nearly all the equations are involved in the determination of each endogenous variable.

Consider the matching of variables to equations in the block given above. The demand for money variables, M_h, M_f, and *CUR*, can be matched to the stochastic equations that determine them, 9, 17, and 26. Bank borrowing, *BO*, can be matched to its stochastic equation, 22, and total bank reserves, *BR*, can be matched to its identity, 57. M_b can be matched to Eq. 71, which states that the sum of net demand deposits and currency across all sectors is zero. $M1$ can be matched to its identity, 81. This leaves Eq. 77, the federal government budget constraint; the question is what endogenous variable is to be matched to this equation. The government savings variable, S_g, is determined elsewhere in the model and thus is not a candidate. If Eq. 30 is included in the model (and thus *RS* matched to it), the obvious variable to match to Eq. 77 is A_g, the net financial asset variable of the government. (A_g will be referred to as the "government security" variable. Remember that A_g is negative because the government is a net debtor.) This means that A_g is the variable that adjusts to allow *RS* to be the value determined by Eq. 30. In other words, the target bill rate is assumed to be achieved by the purchase or sale of government securities, that is, by open market operations.

If A_g is taken to be endogenous, the following variables in the block given above are then exogenous: the discount rate, *RD*; the reserve requirement ratio, g_1; demand deposit and currency holdings of the foreign sector, the state and local government sector, and the federal government sector, M_r, M_s, and M_g; gold and foreign exchange holdings of the federal government, *Q*; the discrepancy term, DIS_g; and the variable that is involved in the definition of $M1$, *MDIF*. Instead of treating A_g as endogenous, one could take either *RD* or g_1 to be endogenous and match it to Eq. 77. This would mean that the target bill rate was achieved by changing the discount rate or the reserve requirement ratio instead of the amount of government securities outstanding. Since the main instrument of monetary policy in practice is open market operations, it seems better to treat A_g as endogenous rather than *RD* or g_1.

One can also consider the case in which Eq. 30 is dropped from the model. In this case, RS is matched to Eq. 77 and A_g is taken to be exogenous. The interest rate is "implicitly" determined: it is the rate needed to clear the asset market given a fixed value of A_g. (In the numerical solution of the model in this case, RS is solved using, say, Eq. 9, M_h is solved using Eq. 71, M_b is solved using Eq. 57, and BR is solved using Eq. 77.) When Eq. 30 is dropped, monetary policy is exogenous, and the response of the model to changes in A_g can be examined.

In the exogenous monetary policy case, the main way in which monetary policy affects the economy is by changing interest rates. Changes in A_g change interest rates, which in turn change real variables. The main effects of interest rates on the economy are the direct effects on consumer expenditures (Eqs. 1, 2, 3, and 4). What this means is that the three instruments of monetary policy—A_g, RD, and g_1—all do the same thing, namely, they affect the economy by affecting interest rates. Using all three instruments is essentially no different from using one with respect to trying to achieve, say, some real output target. It also means that in the endogenous monetary policy case where A_g is endogenous and RD and g_1 are exogenous, changes in RD and g_1 have virtually no effect on the economy. Any effects that they might have are simply "undone" by changes in A_g in the process of achieving the target interest rate implied by Eq. 30.

It is also possible in the exogenous monetary policy case to take some variable other than A_g to be exogenous. One possible choice is the money supply, $M1$, and another is the level of nonborrowed reserves, $BR - BO$. Both of these are common variables to take as policy variables in monetary policy experiments. If either of these is taken to be exogenous, A_g must be endogenous.

To return to fiscal policy variables, it should be obvious that fiscal policy effects are not independent of what one assumes about monetary policy. For a given change in fiscal policy, there are a variety of assumptions that can be made about monetary policy. The main possible assumptions are (1) Eq. 30 included in the model and thus monetary policy endogenous, (2) the bill rate exogenous, (3) the money supply exogenous, (4) nonborrowed reserves exogenous, and (5) government securities outstanding, A_g, exogenous. In all but assumption 5, A_g is endogenous. It will be seen in Section 9.4.4 that fiscal policy effects are in fact quite sensitive to what is assumed about monetary policy. The reason for this is that the different assumptions have quite different implications for interest rates, and the latter have large effects on the real side of the economy.

4.1.11 General Remarks about the Transition

1. The links between the theoretical model and the econometric specifications are closer for the household sector than they are for the firm sector, although the specifications of the main equations for the firm sector are in the spirit of the theoretical model. An important simplification for the empirical work is the assumption that the firm sector's decisions are made sequentially, which is contrary to the case in the theoretical model. Also, the restriction that was imposed on the real wage rate in the empirical work, although it seems quite sensible to impose it in the aggregate, is not closely linked to the theoretical work, where the emphasis was on the behavior of individual firms.

2. There is a heavy use of lagged dependent variables in the model, and they are very important explanatory variables. They can be looked upon as accounting in part for expectational effects and in part for lagged adjustment effects, where it is not possible to separate out these two types of effects. This treatment is discussed in Section 2.2.2. The more sophisticated treatment that was tried for the estimation of expectations regarding future inflation rates was not successful. The expectations variables were not significant in the consumer expenditure equations, where they should be if real rather than nominal interest rates affect behavior, or in the term structure equations, where they should be if expected future inflation rates are not adequately captured in the current and lagged values of the short-term interest rate.

3. A number of the stochastic equations are not tied very closely (if at all) to decision variables in the theoretical model. These equations tend to be less important with respect to their effects on the main variables in the model. Equations in this category include the overtime hours equation, 15, the dividend equation, 18, the two interest payments equations, 19 and 29, the inventory valuation adjustment equation, 20, the capital consumption equation, 21, and the unemployment insurance benefits equation, 28. Some of these equations are simply approximations to definitions that would hold if sufficient data were available.

4. Equation 30 is more heroic than the other main behavioral equations in that it is an attempt to model the behavior of a small number of individuals. It can, of course, be dropped from the model and monetary policy taken to be exogenous. In this sense the equation is less important than the others.

5. Since the theoretical model was used to guide the specification of the econometric model, it is likely that the two models have similar qualitative policy effects. The policy properties of the econometric model are examined in Section 9.4, and it is true that the qualitative effects are similar. For

example, the disequilibrium features of the theoretical model are captured in the econometric model through the labor constraint variable, *Z*, and the interest rate effects on households' decisions in the theoretical model are captured in the econometric model through the interest rate variables in the expenditure equations.

6. Two important variables in the model are taken to be exogenous when in fact they should not be. They are the import price deflator, *PIM*, and exports, *EX*. This limitation is eliminated in the next section, where the US model is embedded in the multicountry model. In fact, one way of looking at the multicountry model is that it is a way of making *PIM* and *EX* endogenous.

4.2 The Multicountry (MC) Model

4.2.1 Introduction

The econometric model is extended to a number of countries in this section. Quarterly data have been collected or constructed for 64 countries (counting the United States), and the model contains estimated equations for 43 countries. The basic estimation period is 1958I–1981IV (96 observations). For equations that are relevant only when exchange rates are flexible, the basic estimation period is 1972II–1981IV (39 observations). The theoretical basis of the model was discussed in Section 3.2.

The model differs from previous models in a number of ways, and it will be useful to discuss these briefly here. First, linkages among countries with respect to exchange rates, interest rates, and prices appear to be more important in the present model than they are in previous models, which have been primarily trade linkage models. The LINK model (Ball 1973), for example, is of this kind, although some recent work has been done on making capital movements endogenous in the model. (See Hickman 1974, p. 203, for a discussion of this; see also Berner et al. 1976 for a discussion of a five-country model in which capital flows are endogenous.) Second, the theory on which the model is based differs somewhat from previous theories. This has been discussed in Section 3.2. Third, the number of countries in the model is larger than usual, and the data are all quarterly. Considerable work has gone into the construction of quarterly data bases for all the countries. Some of the quarterly data had to be interpolated from annual data, and a few data points had to be guessed. The collection and construction of the data bases are discussed in subsequent sections.

Finally, there is an important difference between the approach I have taken and an approach like that of Project LINK. I alone have estimated small models for each country and then linked them together, rather than, as Project LINK has done, taking models developed by others and linking them together. The advantage of the LINK approach is that larger models for each country can be used; it is clearly not feasible for one person to construct medium- or large-scale models for each country. The advantage of the present approach, on the other hand, is that the person constructing the individual models knows from the beginning that they are to be linked together, and this may lead to better specification of the linkages. It is unlikely, for example, that the specification of the exchange rate and interest rate linkages in the present model would develop from the LINK approach. Whether this possible gain in the linkage specification outweighs the loss of having to deal with small models of each country is an open question.

4.2.2 Further Theory

The theoretical model as represented by (T1)–(T17) in Section 3.2.5 cannot be implemented in practice. The main problem is that data on bilateral financial flows do not exist. In other words, data on domestic holdings of the securities of a particular foreign country do not exist, and therefore equations like (T13) and (T14) cannot be estimated. Moreover, data on the breakdown of the savings of a country between private and government savings (S_{pt} and S_{gt}) do not always exist. These and other data problems make the transition to a multicountry econometric model particularly difficult. In order to make the transition here, a special case of the theoretical model must be considered. This special case is discussed in this section. Since this discussion is an extension of the discussion of the theoretical model in Section 3.2, the t subscript has been retained for the variables. In the discussion of the econometric model, which begins in Section 4.2.3, the t subscript has been dropped.

Interest Rate Reaction Functions

The two monetary policy variables in the equation set (T1)–(T17) (other than the discount rates RD and rd, which are not of concern here) are A_{gt} and a_{gt}. If these two variables are taken to be exogenous, the two interest rates, R_t and r_t, are "implicitly" determined. An alternative to this treatment is to postulate interest rate reaction functions for both R_t and r_t:

(T18) $R_t = f_{T18}(\ldots)$,

(T19) $r_t = f_{T19}(\ldots)$,

where the arguments in the functions are variables that affect the monetary authorities' decisions regarding the interest rates. In this case A_{gt} and a_{gt} are endogenous.

Exchange Rate Reaction Functions

The policy variable most closely related to the exchange rate, e_t, is Q_t (or q_t), country 1's (or country 2's) holdings of the international reserve. If Q_t is taken to be exogenous, e_t is implicitly determined. An alternative to this is to postulate an exchange rate reaction function:

(T20) $e_t = f_{T20}(. \ . \ .)$,

where the arguments in the function are variables that affect the authorities' decisions regarding the exchange rate. In this case Q_t is endogenous.

Perfect Substitutability and the Forward Rate

The special case of the theoretical model used here includes the interest rate and exchange rate reaction functions. It also includes the assumption that the securities of the two countries are perfect substitutes. Perfect substitution is defined as follows. The covered interest rate from country 1's perspective on the bond of country 2, say r_t', is $(e_t/F_t)(1 + r_t) - 1$, where F_t is the forward rate. If for $R_t = r_t'$ people are indifferent as to which bond they hold, the bonds will be defined to be perfect substitutes. In this case the equation system (T1)–(T17) is modified as follows. First, (T13) and (T14) drop out, since the private sector is now indifferent between the two bonds. Second, arbitrage will ensure that $R_t = r_t'$, and thus a new equation is added:

(T21) $R_t = (e_t/F_t)(1 + r_t) - 1.$

Third, the model is underidentified with respect to A_{pt}, A_{pt}^*, a_{pt}, and a_{pt}^*, and one of these variables must be taken to be exogenous. (This indeterminacy is analogous to the indeterminacy that arises in, say, a two-consumer, two-firm model in which the two consumers are indifferent between the goods produced by the two firms. It is not possible in this model to determine the allocation of the two goods between the two consumers.)

Equation (T21) introduces a new variable, F_t, into the model, and therefore its determination must be specified. If it is assumed that F_t equals the expected future spot rate, one could try to estimate an equation explaining F_t, where the explanatory variables would be variables that one believes affect expectations. Instead of estimating an equation, one could assume that expectations are rational and estimate the model under this constraint. If F_t is determined in either of these two ways, it will be said to play an "active" role in the model.

If F is active, it is not possible to have R_t, r_t, and e_t all implicitly determined or determined by reaction functions. Given (T21) and the equation for F_t (implicit if there are rational expectations, explicit otherwise), only two of the three variables can be implicitly determined or determined by reaction functions. (Also, if F_t is active and exchange rates are fixed, it is not possible to have both R_t and r_t implicitly determined or determined by reaction functions.) An alternative case to F_t being active is the case in which R_t, r_t, and e_t are implicitly determined or determined by reaction functions and F_t is determined by (T21). In this case F_t will be said to play a "passive" role in the model. Given R_t, r_t, and e_t, F_t merely adjusts to ensure that the arbitrage condition holds. The special case of the theoretical model used here is based on the assumption that F_t is passive.

In summary, the special case of the theoretical model used here is based on the assumptions that (1) the interest rates are determined by reaction functions, (2) the exchange rate is determined by a reaction function, (3) the securities of the different countries are perfect substitutes, and (4) the forward rate is passive. The assumption that is most questionable in this choice is probably the assumption that e_t is determined by a reaction function. The alternative assumption is that e_t is implicitly determined, with reserves, Q_t, being exogenous. In practice there is obviously some intervention of the monetary authorities in the exchange markets, and therefore this alternative assumption is also questionable. The assumption that e_t is determined by a reaction function means that intervention is complete: the monetary authority has a target e_t each period and achieves this target by appropriate changes in Q_t. This assumption may not, however, be as restrictive as it first sounds. The monetary authority is likely to be aware of the market forces that are operating on e_t in the absence of intervention (that is, the forces behind the determination of e_t when e_t is implicitly determined), and it may take these forces into account in setting its target each period. If some of the explanatory variables in the reaction function are in part measures of these forces, then the estimated reaction function may provide a better explanation of e_t than one would otherwise have thought. Similar arguments apply to the assumption that R_t and r_t are determined by reaction functions.

The assumption that F_t is passive means that the forward market imposes no "discipline" on the monetary authority's choice of the exchange rate. Again, if the monetary authority takes into account market forces operating on e_t in the absence of intervention, including market forces in the forward market, and if the explanatory variables in the reaction function for e_t are in part measures of these forces, then the estimated reaction function for e_t may not be too poor an approximation.

Given the assumption that F_t is passive and given that F_t does not appear as an explanatory variable in any of the equations, F_t plays no role in the empirical model. For each country it is determined by an estimated version of the arbitrage condition, (T21), but the predictions from these equations have no effect on the predictions of any of the other variables in the model.

Fixed Exchange Rates

The assumption that F_t is passive is not sensible in the case of fixed exchange rates: for most observations F_t is equal to or very close to e_t when e_t is fixed. A different choice was thus made for the fixed rate case. This choice was designed to try to account for the possibility that the bonds of the different countries are not perfect substitutes as well as for the fact that F_t is not passive. The procedure that was followed in the fixed rate case is as follows. The United States was assumed to be the "leading" country with respect to the determination of interest rates. Assume in the above model that the United States is country 1. Consider the determination of r_t, country 2's interest rate. If exchange rates are fixed, bonds are perfect substitutes, and F_t is equal to e_t, then r_t is determined by (T21) and is equal to R_t. In other words, country 2's interest rate is merely country 1's interest rate: country 1 sets the one world interest rate and country 2's monetary authority has no control over country 2's rate. If the bonds are not perfect substitutes, (T21) does not hold and country 2's monetary authority can affect its rate. If, however, the bonds are close to being perfect substitutes, then very large changes in a_{gt} will be needed to change r_t very much.

In the empirical work, interest rate reaction functions were estimated for each country, but with the U.S. interest rate added as an explanatory variable to each equation. If the bonds are close to being perfect substitutes, the U.S. rate should be the only significant variable in these equations and should have a coefficient estimate close to 1.0. If the bonds are not at all close substitutes, the coefficient estimate should be close to zero and the other variables should be significant. The in-between case should correspond to both the U.S. rate and the other variables being significant.

This argument about the U.S. rate in the interest rate reaction functions does not pertain to the flexible exchange rate case. One would thus not expect the interest rate reaction functions to be the same in the fixed and flexible rate cases, and therefore in the empirical work separate interest rate reaction functions were estimated for each country for the fixed and flexible rate periods. The U.S. rate may still be an explanatory variable in the reaction functions for the flexible rate period. This would be, however, because the U.S. rate is one of the variables that affect the monetary authority's interest rate decision, not because the U.S. rate is being used to try to capture the degree of substitutability of the bonds.

Contrary to the case for the other countries, the U.S. interest rate reaction function was estimated over the entire sample period. This procedure is consistent with the assumption made above that the United States is the interest rate leader in the fixed rate period. If it is the leader, then it is not constrained as the other countries are, so there is no reason on this account to expect the function to be different in the fixed and flexible rate periods.

Aggregation

The final issue to consider regarding the special case of the theoretical model is the level of aggregation. The private and government sectors have been aggregated together for this case, and thus there is only one sector per country. In this case the budget constraint for country 1 is the sum of (T5) and (T6):

$$\text{(T5)}' \qquad 0 = S_t - \Delta A_t - e_t \Delta a_t^* - \Delta Q_t.$$

S_t is equal to $S_{pt} + S_{gt}$, ΔA_t is equal to $\Delta A_{pt} + \Delta A_{gt}$, and the p subscript has been dropped from a_t^* since it is now unnecessary. The budget constraint for country 2 is similarly the sum of (T7) and (T8):

$$\text{(T7)}' \qquad 0 = s_t - \Delta a_t - \frac{1}{e_t}\Delta A_t^* - \frac{1}{e_t}\Delta q_t.$$

Equations (T15) and (T16) are now written as follows:

$$\text{(T15)}' \qquad 0 = A_t + A_t^*;$$

$$\text{(T16)}' \qquad 0 = a_t + a_t^*.$$

Consider now a further type of aggregation. Let $\Delta A_t' = \Delta A_t + e_t \Delta a_t^* + \Delta Q_t$ and $\Delta a_t' = \Delta a_t + \frac{1}{e_t}\Delta A_t^* + \frac{1}{e_t}\Delta q_t$. In this notation (T5)′ and (T7)′ are

$$\text{(T5)}'' \qquad 0 = S_t - \Delta A_t',$$

$$\text{(T7)}'' \qquad 0 = s_t - \Delta a_t'.$$

If one adds the first difference of (T15)′, the first difference of (T16)′ multiplied by e_t, and (T17) in Section 3.2.5, the result is

(T17)′ $\quad 0 = \Delta A_t' + e_t \Delta a_t'.$

Equation (T17)′ is redundant, given (T5)″ and (T7)″, because S_t and s_t satisfy the property that $S_t + e_t s_t = 0$.

This aggregation is very convenient because it allows data on A_t' and a_t' to be constructed by summing past values of S_t and s_t from some given base period values. Data on S_t (the balance of payments on current account) are available for most countries, whereas data on A_t, A_t^*, a_t, and a_t^* (that is, bilateral financial data) are generally not available. The cost of this type of aggregation is that capital gains and losses on bonds from exchange rate changes are not accounted for. Given the current data, there is little that can be done about this. The key assumption behind this aggregation is that the securities of the different countries are perfect substitutes. If this were not so, (T13) and (T14) would not drop out, and bilateral financial data would be needed to estimate them.

Final Equations

To summarize, the special case of the theoretical model consists of the following equations:

(T1)′ $\quad S_t = f_{T1'}(\ldots),$ [savings of country 1]

(T3)′ $\quad s_t = f_{T3'}(\ldots),$ [savings of country 2]

(T5)″ $\quad 0 = S_t - \Delta A_t',$ [budget constraint of country 1]

(T7)″ $\quad 0 = s_t - \Delta a_t',$ [budget constraint of country 2]

(T18) $\quad R_t = f_{T18}(\ldots),$ [interest rate reaction function of country 1]

(T19) $\quad r_t = f_{T19}(\ldots),$ [interest rate reaction function of country 2]

(T20) $\quad e_t = f_{T20}(\ldots),$ [exchange rate reaction function]

(T21) $\quad R_t = (e_t/F_t)(1 + r_t) - 1.$ [arbitrage condition]

This is the model that has guided the econometric specifications.

It should finally be noted that although nothing has been said about the determination of S_t and s_t in this section, this determination is a critical part of the model. Equations (T1)′ and (T3)′ are merely a convenient way of summarizing part of the model. In the complete model S_t and s_t are determined by definitions and are affected by nearly every variable in the model.

4.2.3 Data Collection and Choice of Variables and Identities

The discussion in this section relies heavily on the tables in Appendix B, located at the end of the book. It is assumed that these tables will have been studied carefully before this section is read.

The Data and Variables (Tables B-1, B-2, B-7)

The raw data were taken from two of the four tapes that are constructed every month by the International Monetary Fund: the International Financial Statistics (IFS) tape and the Direction of Trade (DOT) tape. The way in which each variable was constructed is explained in brackets in Table B-2 of Appendix B. Some variables were taken directly from the tapes, and some were constructed from other variables. When "IFS" precedes a number in the table, this refers to the variable on the IFS tape with that particular number. Some adjustments were made to the raw data, and these are explained in Appendix B. The main adjustment was the construction of quarterly National Income Accounts (NIA) data from annual data when the quarterly data were not available. Another important adjustment concerns the linking of the Balance of Payments data to the other export and import data. The two key variables involved in this process are S^* and TT^*. The variable S_i^* is the balance of payments on current account, and TT_i^* is the value of net transfers. The construction of these variables is explained in Table B-7 in Appendix B. Most of the data are not seasonally adjusted.

Note that two interest rates are listed in Table B-2, the short-term rate, RS_i, and the long-term rate, RB_i. For many countries only discount rate data are available for RS_i, and this is an important limitation of the data base. The availability of interest data by country is listed in Table B-1 in Appendix B.

The variable A_i^* in Table B-2, which is the net stock of foreign security and reserve holdings, was constructed by summing past values of S_i^* from a base period value of zero. The summation began in the first quarter for which data on S_i^* existed. This means that the A_i^* series is off by a constant amount each period (the difference between the true value of A_i^* in the base period and zero). In the estimation work the functional forms were chosen in such a way that this error was always absorbed in the estimate of the constant term. It is important to note that A_i^* measures only the net asset position of the country vis-à-vis the rest of the world. Domestic wealth, such as the domestically owned housing stock and plant and equipment stock, is not included.

The Identities (Table B-3)

Table B-3 contains a list of the equations for country i. There are up to 11 estimated equations per country, and these are listed first in the table. Equations 12–21 are definitions. This section provides a discussion of these equations except for the specification of the explanatory variables in the stochastic equations, which is discussed in Section 4.2.5.

It will first be useful to consider the matching of the equations in Table B-3 to the equations listed earlier at the end of Section 4.2.2. The level of savings of country i, which is represented by (T1)′ or (T3)′ above, is determined by Eq. 17, a definition, in the table. As noted earlier, the level of savings, S_i^*, is the balance of payments on current account. Almost every variable in the model is at least indirectly involved in its determination. Equation 17 states that S_i^* is equal to export revenue minus import costs plus net transfers. Given S_i^*, the asset variable A_i^* is determined by Eq. 18, which is analogous to (T5)″ or (T7)″ above. This is the budget constraint of country i.

Equations 7a and 7b are the interest rate reaction functions, which are analogous to (T18) or (T19), and Eq. 9b is the exchange rate reaction function, which is analogous to (T20). The "a" indicates that the equation is estimated over the fixed exchange rate period, and the "b" indicates that it is estimated over the flexible rate period. Equation 10b is an estimate of the arbitrage condition, (T21) above. The exchange rate e_i explained by Eq. 9b is the average exchange rate for the period, whereas the exchange rate ee_i in the arbitrage equation 10b is the end-of-period rate. ee_i is end-of-period because the forward rate, F_i, is also end-of-period. Equation 20 links e_i to ee_i, where ψ_{1i} in the equation is the historic ratio of e_i to $(ee_i + ee_{i-1})/2$. ψ_{1i} is taken to be exogenous. As noted in Section 4.2.2, F_i plays no role in the model, and therefore neither does ee_i. Equation 10b is included in the model merely to see how closely the data meet the arbitrage condition.

This completes the matching of the equations in Table B-3 to those at the end of Section 4.2.2. The other equations are as follows. Equation 1 determines the demand for merchandise imports, and Eq. 14 provides the link from merchandise imports to total NIA imports. Equations 2 and 3 determine the demands for consumption and investment, respectively. Equation 16 is the definition for final sales. The level of final sales is equal to consumption plus investment plus government spending plus exports minus imports plus a discrepancy term. Government spending is exogenous. Exports are determined when the countries are linked together. The key export variable is $X75\$_i$, and Eq. 15 links this variable to NIA exports. Equation 4 determines production, and Eq. 12 determines inventory investment, which is the difference between production and sales. Equation 13 defines the stock of inventories. Equation 5, the key price equation in the model, determines the GNP deflator. The other price equation in the model is Eq. 11, which determines the export price index as a function of the GNP deflator and other variables.

Equation 6 determines the demand for money. Even though the money supply does not appear in the budget constraint of the country because it is netted out in the aggregation, it does appear as an explanatory variable in the interest rate reaction functions and thus must be explained. The money supply is netted out in the aggregation because foreign holdings of domestic money are effectively ignored by being included in A_i^*. This had to be done because bilateral data on money holdings do not exist. Equation 8 determines the long-term interest rate, RB_i. It is a standard term structure equation.

Trade and Price Linkages (Table B-4)

The trade and price linkages are presented in Table B-4. Table B-4 takes as input from each country the total value of merchandise imports in 75\$, $M75\$A_i$, the export price index, PX_i, and the exchange rate, e_i. It returns for each country the total value of merchandise exports in 75\$, $X75\$_i$, the import price index, PM_i, and the world price index, $PW\$_i$. These last three variables are used as inputs by each country. The model is solved for each quarter by iterating between the equations for each country in Table B-3 and the equations in Table B-4.

Note from Table B-2 that the data taken from the DOT tape are merchandise exports from i to j in \$, $XX\$_{ij}$. These data were converted to 75\$ by multiplying $XX\$_{ij}$ by $e_i/(e_{i75}PX_i)$ (see $XX75\$_{ij}$ in Table B-2). This could only be done, however, if data on e_i and PX_i existed. Type A countries are countries for which these data exist, and type B countries are the remaining countries. The share variable α_{ji} that is used in Table B-4 is defined in Table B-2. α_{ji} is the share of i's total merchandise imports from type A countries imported from j in 75\$. If j is a type B country, then α_{ji} is zero. Given the definition of $M75\$A_i$ in Table B-2, α_{ji} has the property that $\Sigma_j \alpha_{ji} = 1$. Table B-4 deals only with type A countries. Total merchandise imports of a country from type B countries, $M75\$B_i$ in Table B-2, is taken to be exogenous.

4.2.4 Treatment of Unobserved Variables

Expectations

As discussed earlier, an important expectational assumption in the multicountry model is that the forward rate is passive. No constraint has been imposed that it equals the expected future spot rate, and so in general this will not be true. It is not the case, for example, that the forward rate equals the future spot rate that the model predicts.

As was the case for the US model, expectations are assumed to be accounted for by the use of current and lagged values as proxies for expected future values. Nothing different from the standard procedure discussed in Section 2.2.2 was done.

The Demand Pressure Variable

A demand pressure variable, denoted ZZ_i, was used in the price equation for each country. It was constructed as follows. (Y_i is real gross national product or real gross domestic product, and POP_i is the level of population.) $\text{Log}(Y_i/POP_i)$ was first regressed on a constant, time, and three seasonal dummy variables, and the estimated standard error, $\widehat{\text{SE}}_i$, and the fitted values, $\widehat{\log(Y_i/POP_i)}$, from this regression were recorded. (The results from these regressions are presented in Table 4-13 later in the chapter.) A new series, $(Y_i/POP_i)^*$, was then constructed, where

$$(4.38) \qquad \left(\frac{Y_i}{POP_i}\right)^* = \exp\left[\widehat{\log\frac{Y_i}{POP_i}} + 4 \cdot \widehat{SE_i}\right].$$

ZZ_i was taken to be

$$(4.39) \qquad ZZ_i = \frac{(Y_i/POP_i)^* - Y_i/POP_i}{(Y_i/POP_i)^*}.$$

ZZ_i is similar to the demand pressure variable ZZ in the US model. In the US model ZZ is equal to $(GNPR^* - GNPR)/GNPR^*$, where $GNPR^*$ is constructed from peak-to-peak interpolations of the $GNPR$ series. In the present case, $(Y_i/POP_i)^*$ is not constructed from peak-to-peak interpolations but is instead a variable that is the antilog of a variable whose value each quarter is 4 standard errors greater than the value predicted by the regression of log (Y_i/POP_i) on a constant, time, and three seasonal dummy variables. The use of 4 standard errors in this construction is not critical; similar results would have been obtained had the number been, say, 2 or 3. To put it another way, as is the case for the US model, the data are not capable of discriminating among different measures of demand pressure.

4.2.5 Stochastic Equations for the Individual Countries (Tables 4-1 through 4-13)

The estimated equations for the individual countries are presented in Tables 4-1 through 4-13. Equations 1, 2, 4, 5, 6, and 8 were estimated by 2SLS for most countries; the other equations were estimated by OLS. The estimation technique for each equation is indicated in the tables. The first-stage regressors that were used for each equation estimated by 2SLS are not presented in this book, since this would take up too much space. (The list of these regressors is available from the author upon request.) The selection criterion for the first-stage regressors was the same as that used for the US model, which is explained in Chapter 6. Briefly, the main predetermined variables in each country's model were chosen to constitute a "basic" set for that country, and other variables were added to this set for each individual equation. The variables that were added depended on the RHS endogenous variables in the equation being estimated.

All equations except 10b and 11 were estimated with a constant and three seasonal dummy variables. To conserve space, the coefficient estimates of these four variables are not reported in the tables. Data limitations prevented all equations from being estimated for all countries and also required that shorter sample periods from the basic period be used for many countries. The main part of the model, excluding the United States, consists of the countries Canada through the United Kingdom.

The searching procedure for the stochastic equations was as follows. Lagged dependent variables were used extensively to try to account for expectational and lagged adjustment effects. Explanatory variables were dropped from the equations if they had coefficient estimates of the wrong expected sign. In many cases variables were left in the equations if their coefficient estimates were of the expected sign even if the estimates were not significant by conventional standards. There is considerable collinearity among many of the explanatory variables, especially the price variables, and the number of observations is fairly small for equations estimated only over the flexible exchange rate period. Many of the coefficients are thus not likely to be estimated very precisely, and this is the reason for retaining variables even if their coefficient estimates had fairly large estimated standard errors.

Both current and one-quarter-lagged values were generally tried for the

TABLE 4-1. The 40 demand for import equations

Equation 1: $\log\frac{M_i}{POP_i}$ is the LHS variable

Country	Explanatory variables									
	$\log PY_i$	$\log PM_i$	RS_i or RB_i	$\log\frac{Y_i}{POP_i}$	$\frac{A^*_{i-1}}{PY_{i-1}POP_{i-1}}$	LHS_{-1}	R^2	SE	DW	Sample period
Canada	.097[a] (0.68)	-.099[a] (0.92)	-.0050[ab] (1.20)	.88 (5.96)	.000070 (2.33)	.55 (7.35)	.992	.0366	1.95	581-821
Japan	.080 (0.79)	-.082 (1.60)	-.0028[a] (0.95)	.20 (2.17)	.00031 (1.16)	.81 (12.12)	.996	.0440	1.99	581-822
Austria	.30 (1.29)	-.18 (1.14)	-.011[a] (1.67)	.96 (2.95)	.0042 (1.52)	.45 (4.17)	.991	.0368	2.18	651-821
Belgium	.34 (3.55)	-.38 (5.06)	—	1.05 (6.07)	—	.45 (5.80)	.996	.0344	2.09	581-804
Denmark	.43[a] (4.03)	-.27[a] (3.31)	-.0029[a] (1.27)	.68 (3.59)	.024 (3.24)	.50 (6.59)	.987	.0429	2.33	581-814
France	.18 (1.70)	-.14 (1.96)	—	.65 (4.41)	—	.67 (10.23)	.995	.0416	1.73	581-814
Germany	—	—	-.0050[a] (3.46)	.90 (4.06)	—	.62 (6.54)	.995	.0305	1.87	611-821
Italy	.14 (1.01)	-.04 (0.44)	-.011[ab] (1.33)	1.20 (3.87)	—	.33 (3.21)	.971	.0681	2.13	611-814
Netherlands	.09 (0.77)	-.16 (2.59)	—	.75 (2.60)	—	.58 (5.57)	.991	.0336	2.23	611-814
Norway	.74[a] (3.54)	-.29[a] (2.25)	-.058[ab] (3.84)	.82 (2.77)	.017 (4.06)	.43 (5.16)	.970	.0566	2.38	621-814
Sweden	.16 (1.17)	-.12 (1.28)	-.0035[a] (0.72)	.60 (3.46)	.016 (1.62)	.60 (7.05)	.977	.0509	2.58	581-814
Switzerland	.08[a] (1.54)	-.16[a] (1.77)	-.014[ab] (1.29)	1.57 (7.00)	.021 (3.95)	.31 (3.37)	.994	.0298	2.40	581-814
United Kingdom	—	—	—	1.11 (5.91)	.00022 (1.84)	.40 (3.92)	.981	.0372	2.02	581-804
Finland	—	—	—	1.09 (6.39)	.000047 (3.35)	.38 (4.04)	.964	.0777	2.41	581-814
Greece	.29 (1.13)	-.11 (0.56)	-.012 (1.71)	.93 (5.71)	—	.20 (1.88)	.967	.0970	2.29	581-804
Ireland	.31[a] (2.65)	-.15[a] (1.77)	-.0044[ab] (1.02)	.91 (5.34)	.00042 (2.25)	.48 (6.20)	.988	.0496	2.40	581-804
Portugal	—	—	—	1.30 (7.34)	—	.10 (0.91)	.910	.163	2.20	581-804
Spain	.20 (2.55)	-.14 (1.75)	-.037 (1.76)	.67 (3.41)	—	.58 (6.66)	.980	.0578	2.23	621-794
Turkey[c]	—	—	—	1.28 (3.78)	.16 (3.88)	.48 (4.06)	.891	.109	1.88	691-784

Yugoslavia	—	—	—	.62 (4.52)	.056 (2.63)	.56 (5.84)	.958	.0818	2.04	611-794
Australia	—	—	-.015[ab] (2.58)	.52 (3.43)	.000074 (1.30)	.71 (10.20)	.848	.0632	1.69	603-814
New Zealand	—	—	—	.81 (5.59)	.00011 (3.06)	.52 (6.36)	.829	.0835	2.03	582-811
South Africa	—	—	-.027[a] (4.15)	.55 (3.51)	—	.82 (17.07)	.864	.0772	1.95	621-814
Libya	—	—	—	.12 (0.80)	—	.83 (9.88)	.926	.0739	2.39	721-774
Nigeria[c]	—	—	—	.31 (1.00)	.0022 (4.61)	.75 (12.20)	.977	.0778	1.69	712-781
Saudi Arabia[c]	—	—	—	.56 (2.05)	.043 (4.29)	.45 (3.36)	.994	.0545	2.00	721-792
Venezuela[c]	—	—	—	1.84 (3.64)	.000021 (2.23)	.46 (3.62)	.931	.0668	2.06	711-804
Brazil[c]	—	—	—	.10 (0.51)	.037 (0.35)	.86 (8.79)	.814	.0891	1.65	711-804
Chile[c]	—	—	—	1.29 (2.71)	—	.51 (3.99)	.618	.2344	2.31	711-804
Colombia	—	—	—	—	.000065 (3.51)	.64 (5.85)	.755	.1108	1.94	711-804
Mexico[c]	—	—	—	.66 (3.74)	—	.80 (10.62)	.954	.0525	1.45	711-804
Israel	—	—	—	.18 (0.79)	—	.49 (4.01)	.357	.1269	2.57	691-813
Jordan[c]	.56 (2.62)	-.58 (3.61)	—	.73 (3.09)	.0042 (1.51)	.41 (3.63)	.906	.1174	2.43	731-804
Syria	.68[a] (2.52)	-.24[a] (1.26)	—	.50 (1.73)	.00022 (1.42)	.28 (2.23)	.800	.1450	2.05	641-804
India	—	—	—	—	.32 (1.05)	.40 (3.76)	.252	.1303	2.01	611-794
Korea	.14 (0.89)	-.21 (1.65)	—	.70 (3.41)	.0012 (0.83)	.70 (7.73)	.982	.1077	2.01	641-814
Malaysia[c]	.39[a] (1.59)	-.03[a] (0.24)	—	.62 (2.38)	.00074 (5.91)	.00098 (0.13)	.931	.0506	0.74	711-814
Pakistan[c]	—	—	—	.65 (1.24)	—	.59 (3.29)	.673	.1148	2.59	731-812
Philippines	.95 (5.09)	-.53 (5.22)	-.011 (2.14)	.32 (1.06)	.00034 (3.96)	.30 (3.41)	.703	.0863	2.23	581-802
Thailand	.44 (1.99)	-.32 (2.47)	—	.35 (2.22)	—	.57 (6.36)	.883	.0503	2.08	654-814

Notes: a. Variable is lagged one quarter.
b. RB_i rather than RS_i is used.
c. Equation estimated by OLS rather than 2SLS.
• t-statistics in absolute value are in parentheses.

TABLE 4-2. The 38 consumption equations

Equation 2: $\log\frac{C_i}{POP_i}$ is the LHS variable

Country	Explanatory variables								
	RS_i or RB_i	$\log\frac{Y_i}{POP_i}$	$\frac{A^*_{i-1}}{PY_{i-1}POP_{i-1}}$	LHS_{-1}	$\hat{\rho}_1$	R^2	SE	DW	Sample period
Canada	-.0012 (2.61)	.11 (3.51)	.0000091 (1.55)	.90 (25.78)	—	.998	.00859	2.35	581-821
Japan	-.0026 (4.08)	.16 (2.84)	—	.80 (12.58)	—	.999	.0126	2.32	581-822
Austria	-.0059 (1.95)	.62 (7.49)	—	.36 (4.12)	—	.991	.0185	1.74	651-821
Belgium	-.0017[ab] (0.83)	.55 (9.11)	.00052 (4.41)	.39 (5.37)	—	.997	.0129	1.65	581-804
Denmark	—	.59 (9.19)	.0065 (2.96)	.38 (6.17)	—	.982	.0237	1.28	581-814
France	-.00066[a] (1.22)	.21 (5.40)	—	.80 (19.49)	—	.999	.0105	2.08	581-814
Germany	-.0019 (3.41)	.37 (5.06)	.0047 (1.12)	.66 (10.44)	—	.999	.00807	2.26	611-821
Italy	-.00072 (1.67)	.24 (2.68)	—	.80 (10.53)	—	.998	.0102	1.85	611-814
Netherlands	-.0032[ab] (1.64)	.43 (5.74)	.013 (3.09)	.64 (10.61)	—	.996	.0153	2.25	611-814
Norway	-.0074[b] (3.75)	.66 (10.48)	.00064 (0.82)	.26 (3.79)	—	.991	.0156	1.29	621-814
Sweden	—	.22 (3.24)	.0040 (1.65)	.73 (9.21)	-.70 (7.93)	.969	.0299	1.90	581-814
Switzerland	-.0043 (3.41)	.35 (6.70)	.0019 (2.13)	.70 (15.68)	—	.997	.0103	2.16	581-814
United Kingdom	—	.51 (8.75)	.00020 (4.43)	.40 (5.90)	—	.989	.0132	1.85	581-804
Finland	—	.28 (4.16)	.0000024 (0.52)	.74 (11.38)	—	.993	.0254	2.36	581-814
Ireland	-.0030[ab] (2.38)	.54 (10.69)	.000033 (0.67)	.42 (7.17)	—	.993	.0165	1.44	581-804
Portugal	-.0028[b] (2.45)	.30 (7.46)	—	.47 (7.05)	—	.973	.0306	2.11	581-804
Spain	-.0054 (1.08)	.25 (3.00)	—	.76 (10.86)	—	.989	.0267	2.20	621-794
Turkey[c]	—	.18 (1.93)	.044 (4.26)	.77 (8.79)	—	.965	.0228	1.66	691-784

Yugoslavia	—	.58 (9.16)	—	.35 (5.00)	—	.993	.0219	1.30	611-794
Australia	-.0014 (1.84)	.12 (1.25)	.0000061 (0.56)	.91 (10.43)	—	.997	.00877	1.81	603-814
New Zealand	—	.39 (1.62)	.000026 (1.11)	.67 (3.33)	.76 (4.35)	.986	.0158	1.73	582-811
South Africa	-.0027 (2.56)	.42 (4.47)	—	.74 (12.45)	—	.988	.0136	2.03	621-814
Libya	—	—	.000068 (1.02)	.88 (7.86)	.34 (1.05)	.991	.0322	1.98	651-774
Saudi Arabia[c]	—	.14 (0.34)	.0081 (1.19)	.81 (4.16)	.59 (1.97)	.979	.0503	1.76	721-792
Venezuela	—	.12 (1.24)	.0000025 (0.63)	.95 (22.01)	.50 (3.22)	.996	.0147	1.95	621-804
Argentina[c]	—	.31 (1.78)	—	.79 (10.12)	—	.746	.0711	1.78	671-804
Brazil	—	.17 (2.62)	—	.87 (16.58)	.32 (1.75)	.997	.0221	1.73	641-804
Colombia[c]	-.0029 (2.00)	.34 (2.16)	—	.69 (4.68)	.37 (1.73)	.927	.0165	1.92	711-804
Mexico	—	.53 (9.07)	—	.47 (7.97)	—	.989	.0228	1.64	581-804
Peru	—	.46 (4.29)	—	.65 (8.78)	—	.977	.0196	1.67	611-814
Israel	—	.30 (2.52)	.000045 (1.47)	.73 (7.52)	—	.931	.0300	1.73	691-814
Jordan[c]	—	.64 (6.46)	—	.33 (3.11)	—	.935	.0506	1.23	731-804
Syria	—	.77 (3.47)	—	.08 (0.36)	.85 (9.99)	.957	.0415	1.66	641-804
India[c]	-.0037[a] (3.08)	.33 (3.77)	—	.45 (2.75)	.49 (2.49)	.877	.0166	1.86	611-794
Korea	-.0016 (1.17)	.39 (7.46)	—	.45 (6.10)	—	.969	.0539	1.98	641-814
Malaysia[c]	—	.60 (11.02)	.00021 (7.82)	.38 (6.64)	—	.992	.0136	1.49	711-814
Philippines	-.0023[a] (1.74)	.64 (13.17)	.000053 (2.91)	.26 (4.76)	—	.969	.0252	1.17	581-802
Thailand	-.0037 (1.26)	.42 (1.68)	.012 (0.93)	.58 (2.27)	.41 (1.41)	995	.0113	1.62	654-814

Notes: a. Variable is lagged one quarter.
b. RB_i rather than RS_i is used.
c. Equation estimated by OLS rather than 2SLS.
• t-statistics in absolute value are in parentheses.

TABLE 4-3. The 23 investment equations

Equation 3: ΔI_i is the LHS variable

Country	Explanatory variables									R^2	SE	DW	Sample period
	ΔI_{i-1}	I_{i-1}	ΔY_{i-1}	ΔY_{i-2}	ΔY_{i-3}	ΔY_{i-4}	constant	t	$\hat{\rho}_1$				
Canada	.13 (0.98)	-.104 (2.62)	.12 (1.67)	—	—	—	313.3 (2.54)	9.2 (2.59)	—	.148	190.5	1.86	581-821
Japan	—	-.051 (1.86)	.15 (2.41)	.13 (2.18)	.21 (3.37)	.13 (2.06)	25.1 (0.41)	5.4 (1.29)	—	.285	217.5	2.20	583-822
Belgium	—	-.199 (2.91)	—	.05 (1.64)	.07 (1.99)	—	9.6 (3.27)	.20 (2.65)	—	.151	3.14	1.84	582-804
Denmark	—	-.043 (2.19)	—	.04 (1.33)	.02 (0.73)	.05 (1.68)	.45 (2.15)	—	—	.603	.516	2.14	583-814
France	—	-.049 (1.17)	—	.03 (0.81)	.10 (2.15)	.02 (0.55)	2.0 (1.89)	.026 (0.81)	—	.114	1.48	2.29	583-814
Germany	.08 (0.72)	-.106 (2.46)	—	.09 (1.21)	.07 (0.93)	.18 (2.33)	3.3 (1.99)	.036 (1.99)	—	.191	1.82	1.99	643-821
Italy	.29 (2.87)	-.133 (3.21)	—	.07 (1.66)	.09 (2.22)	—	385.9 (2.89)	6.1 (3.05)	—	.247	159.6	2.05	612-814
Netherlands	—	-.122 (2.40)	—	.05 (1.29)	.13 (2.93)	.08 (1.72)	.83 (2.61)	.0068 (1.64)	—	.187	.354	2.24	613-814
Norway	—	-.106 (2.07)	—	.17 (2.49)	.13 (1.88)	—	.37 (1.55)	.011 (1.62)	—	.146	.573	2.18	623-814
Sweden	—	-.157 (3.32)	—	.22 (8.53)	.14 (5.35)	.27 (10.73)	1.3 (2.88)	.0099 (2.54)	-.36 (3.38)	.900	.681	1.99	583-814
Switzerland	—	-.066 (3.12)	.14 (2.15)	.11 (1.81)	.09 (1.38)	.15 (2.36)	.38 (2.87)	.0017 (1.30)	—	.359	.262	2.13	583-814

United Kingdom	—	-.103 (2.18)	.15 (4.25)	—	—	—	289.9 (2.37)	2.9 (1.83)	-.39 (3.53)	.642	150.9	2.12	581-804
Finland	—	-.160 (3.01)	—	—	.17 (3.12)	.32 (5.84)	383.2 (2.46)	7.7 (2.45)	—	.521	357.8	2.21	583-814
Greece	.16 (1.66)	-.153 (3.16)	—	.07 (2.01)	.03 (0.97)	.20 (5.94)	.80 (1.86)	.066 (2.78)	—	.553	1.66	1.99	583-814
Ireland	—	-.091 (2.19)	—	—	—	.20 (6.04)	2.6 (1.36)	.28 (2.20)	—	.728	7.62	1.91	583-804
Portugal	—	-.277 (3.93)	—	—	.02 (0.79)	.07 (3.12)	.91 (3.25)	.061 (3.89)	—	.299	.790	2.07	583-804
Spain	—	-.031 (0.76)	.03 (0.90)	.06 (1.39)	.08 (2.20)	—	6.7 (1.63)	.023 (0.16)	—	.256	8.15	1.92	622-794
Australia	—	-.071 (1.73)	.16 (2.78)	—	—	—	121.2 (1.67)	2.3 (1.90)	-.32 (2.87)	.137	87.4	1.96	603-814
New Zealand	.45 (4.22)	-.041 (1.93)	.22 (2.10)	—	—	—	12.1 (1.60)	.13 (1.24)	—	.371	14.7	2.04	582-811
South Africa	—	-.062 (1.19)	.07 (0.74)	.11 (1.11)	.07 (0.73)	.21 (2.27)	26.9 (0.96)	.88 (0.85)	-.23 (1.96)	.133	67.0	2.04	623-814
Argentina	.11 (0.62)	-.282 (2.85)	.04 (0.67)	—	—	—	4.2 (1.51)	.26 (2.55)	—	.739	4.49	1.87	671-804
Israel	—	-.243 (2.58)	—	.01 (0.69)	.04 (2.23)	—	107.7 (2.31)	.15 (0.27)	-.26 (1.70)	.395	60.0	2.12	692-814
India	.12 (0.93)	-.064 (1.81)	.07 (2.05)	—	—	—	.65 (1.60)	.022 (1.85)	—	.311	.814	2.05	611-794

Notes: • All equations estimated by OLS.
• t-statistics in absolute value are in parentheses.

TABLE 4-4. The 13 production equations

Equation 4: Y_i is the LHS variable

Country	Explanatory variables				Implied values			R^2	SE	DW	Sample period
	X_i	V_{i-1}	LHS_{-1}	$\hat{\rho}_1$	λ	α	β				
Canada	.62 (6.14)	-.084 (1.49)	.45 (5.59)	.51 (3.78)	.55	.153	.83	.999	249.6	2.07	581-821
Austria	.63 (6.89)	-.055 (1.42)	.47 (5.64)	.18 (1.45)	.53	.104	1.81	.996	2.00	1.96	651-821
Belgium	1.03 (42.91)	-.125 (3.44)	.08 (4.64)	.74 (10.36)	.92	.136	.88	.999	1.90	1.73	581-804
Denmark	1.01 (53.81)	-.058 (1.83)	.03 (1.94)	.79 (10.20)	.97	.060	.69	.999	.218	1.73	581-814
France[a]	1.08 (15.25)	-.129 (2.67)	.13 (2.21)	.57 (5.80)	.87	.148	1.63	.999	2.08	2.12	581-814
Germany	1.01 (13.11)	-.133 (1.99)	.16 (2.90)	.67 (7.74)	.84	.158	1.28	.999	1.50	1.87	611-821
Netherlands	.99 (24.14)	-.064 (1.30)	.07 (2.27)	.83 (10.06)	.93	.069	.94	.999	.266	1.83	611-814
Sweden	.96 (29.90)	-.046 (1.30)	.10 (3.66)	.46 (5.05)	.90	.051	1.31	.996	.847	2.27	581-814
Switzerland	1.00 (11.85)	-.056 (2.45)	.17 (2.72)	.73 (10.01)	.83	.067	3.06	.999	.243	1.83	581-814
United Kingdom	1.00 (11.26)	-.124 (1.91)	.15 (2.52)	.40 (3.62)	.85	.146	1.21	.996	244.8	1.89	581-804
Finland	1.10 (13.09)	-.056 (1.31)	—	.65 (7.14)	1.00	.056	1.79	.993	483.1	1.92	581-814
Spain	.99 (29.01)	-.028 (0.99)	.05 (2.23)	.84 (11.21)	.95	.029	1.45	.999	5.87	1.86	621-794
Korea	1.01 (15.01)	-.156 (2.25)	.11 (1.53)	—	.89	.175	.77	.992	108.5	2.19	641-814

Notes: a. Equation estimated by OLS rather than 2SLS.
• t-statistics in absolute value are in parentheses.

explanatory price and interest rate variables, and the values that gave the best results were used. Similarly, both the short-term and long-term interest rate variables were tried, and the variable that gave the best results was used. A number of the equations were estimated under the assumption of first-order serial correlation of the error term. $\hat{\rho}$ in the tables denotes the estimate of the serial correlation coefficient.

Subject to data limitations, the specification of the stochastic equations follows fairly closely the specification of the equivalent equations in the US model. When it does not, this will be noted. The asset variable, A_i^*, is an important explanatory variable in a number of the equations, and one should be aware of its limitations. As noted earlier, this variable measures only the net asset position of the country vis-à-vis the rest of the world; it does not include the domestic wealth of the country. Also, its value for each country is off by a constant amount, and this required a choice for the functional form of the variable in the equations that one might not have chosen otherwise.

The following subsections present a brief discussion of the results in each table. For a complete picture of the results, the tables should be read carefully along with the discussion.

The 40 Demand-for-Import Equations (Table 4-1)

Equation 1 explains the real per-capita merchandise imports of country *i*. The explanatory variables include the price of domestic goods, the price of imports, the interest rates, per-capita income, and the lagged value of real per-capita assets. The variables are in logarithms except for the interest rates and the asset variable. These demand-for-import equations are similar to the demand-for-import equation in the US model, Eq. 27; the main differences are that Eq. 27 is not in log form and that the asset variable was not found to be significant for the United States and was thus dropped from the equation. The log versus linear difference is not important in that similar results would have been obtained had the US equation been in log form or the present equations in linear form.

The results in Table 4-1 seem fairly good. Most of the variables appear in the equations for the first 18 countries (Canada through Spain). The two price variables ($\log PY_i$ and $\log PM_i$) are expected to have coefficients of opposite signs and of roughly the same size in absolute value, and this was generally found to be the case. For the oil exporting countries Nigeria, Saudi Arabia, and Venezuela, the asset variable is highly significant. This means that as assets increase during rises in oil prices, the countries are predicted to increase their demand for imports, which then lessens their buildup of assets.

The 38 Consumption Equations (Table 4-2)

Equation 2 explains real per-capita consumption. The explanatory variables include the interest rates, real per-capita income, and the lagged value of real per-capita assets. The use of income as an explanatory variable in the consumption equations is inconsistent with the theoretical model of house-

TABLE 4-5. The 36 price equations

Equation 5: log PY_i is the LHS variable

Country	Explanatory variables					R^2	SE	DW	Sample period
	log PM_i	ZZ_i	t	LHS_{-1}	$\hat{\rho}_1$				
Canada	.053[a]	-.22[a]	.00023	.95	—	.999	.00562	1.56	581-821
	(3.67)	(7.02)	(2.45)	(51.91)					
Japan	.027	-.11[a]	.00014	.97	.55	.999	.00869	2.26	581-822
	(1.98)	(2.62)	(0.22)	(21.54)	(5.77)				
Austria	.11[a]	-.20	.0023	.76	—	.997	.0145	2.31	651-821
	(2.45)	(2.10)	(2.82)	(10.24)					
Belgium	.046	-.14[a]	.00068	.93	—	.999	.00644	1.61	581-804
	(3.84)	(5.12)	(4.06)	(46.33)					
Denmark	.065[a]	-.028[a]	.0025	.83	—	.999	.0125	1.98	581-814
	(3.19)	(0.55)	(3.41)	(16.55)					
France	.046[a]	—	.00058	.94	—	.999	.00838	1.81	581-814
	(3.42)		(2.70)	(39.22)					
Germany	.023[a]	-.21[a]	.00026	.96	-.29	.999	.00557	1.95	611-821
	(3.41)	(8.06)	(1.45)	(52.72)	(2.74)				
Italy	.065	-.18	.00042	.92	.39	.999	.00914	1.79	611-814
	(4.79)	(1.69)	(0.86)	(29.26)	(3.32)				
Netherlands	.030[a]	-.12[a]	.0013	.90	—	.999	.00935	1.77	611-814
	(2.03)	(2.42)	(2.58)	(24.07)					
Norway	.050	—	.0013	.90	—	.999	.0111	1.63	622-814
	(1.92)		(2.18)	(17.44)					
Sweden	.072[a]	-.042	.0012	.87	—	.999	.00770	1.73	581-814
	(4.80)	(0.97)	(3.12)	(24.62)					
Switzerland	.042[a]	-.12	.000095	.97	—	.999	.00783	1.86	581-814
	(2.83)	(5.83)	(0.38)	(42.86)					
United Kingdom	.081[a]	—	.00092	.89	—	.999	.0109	1.80	581-804
	(5.96)		(5.73)	(43.13)					
Finland	.056	-.063[a]	.00097	.90	—	.999	.0116	1.62	581-814
	(2.91)	(1.65)	(2.70)	(25.84)					
Greece	.068	-.023[a]	.00074	.92	—	.999	.0157	1.91	581-814
	(3.27)	(0.52)	(2.55)	(27.65)					
Ireland	.079[a]	-.11[a]	.0014	.88	—	.999	.0169	1.88	581-804
	(3.01)	(1.45)	(3.09)	(21.13)					
Portugal	.18	-.059[a]	.0011	.79	—	.999	.0206	2.17	581-804
	(4.08)	(0.97)	(3.23)	(13.99)					

Spain	.059 (5.09)	-.081[a] (1.16)	-.00011 (0.19)	.97 (35.41)	—	.999	.0122	2.10	621-794
Turkey	.071 (1.67)	—	.00033 (0.10)	.94 (12.62)	—	.997	.0287	1.86	691-784
Yugoslavia	—	-.19[a] (1.59)	.0018 (1.13)	.95 (19.21)	.22 (1.78)	.999	.0277	1.93	611-794
Australia	—	-.18[a] (2.36)	.0000059 (0.02)	1.02 (56.19)	—	.999	.0121	2.06	603-814
New Zealand	.049[a] (2.72)	—	.00068 (3.15)	.94 (36.07)	—	.999	.0154	1.95	582-811
South Africa	.031 (1.14)	—	.0012 (2.57)	.93 (18.90)	—	.999	.0169	1.93	621-814
Argentina	.35 (8.31)	—	.0089 (1.60)	.63 (15.32)	—	.999	.0716	1.50	711-804
Brazil	.097 (5.40)	—	.00085 (0.61)	.92 (31.63)	—	.999	.0165	1.56	711-804
Chile	.25 (6.97)	—	.016 (0.41)	.57 (5.20)	.94 (7.45)	.999	.0611	1.73	711-804
Colombia	.026 (0.71)	—	.011 (2.39)	.76 (9.22)	—	.999	.0176	1.94	711-804
Israel	.13 (2.79)	-.080[a] (0.62)	-.00049 (0.36)	.90 (16.48)	—	.999	.0299	2.14	691-813
Jordan	.068 (0.65)	—	.013 (2.81)	.51 (3.31)	—	.923	.0798	1.53	731-804
Syria	.081 (2.42)	—	.0023 (2.25)	.80 (12.18)	—	.992	.0380	2.22	641-804
India	.016[a] (0.72)	—	.0030 (1.80)	.81 (7.38)	.26 (1.54)	.997	.0236	2.12	611-794
Korea	.10 (3.46)	-.28[a] (3.62)	.0088 (3.26)	.70 (8.73)	—	.998	.0411	2.47	641-841
Malaysia[b]	.023 (0.54)	-.42 (2.65)	.0066 (3.54)	.62 (5.56)	—	.989	.0249	2.03	711-814
Pakistan	.058 (2.76)	—	.0036 (2.98)	.78 (15.68)	—	.997	.0147	2.43	731-812
Philippines	.038 (2.74)	-.15[a] (2.20)	.00092 (1.92)	.91 (36.68)	—	.999	.0196	1.53	581-802
Thailand	.019 (0.46)	—	.00099 (2.20)	.94 (13.23)	—	.997	.0189	1.21	654-814

Notes: a. Variable is lagged one quarter.
b. Equation estimated by OLS rather than 2SLS.
• t-statistics in absolute value are in parentheses.

hold behavior in Chapter 3. If a household is choosing consumption and labor supply to maximize utility, income is not the appropriate variable to use in the consumption equation. This procedure can be justified, however, if households are always constrained in their labor supply decision, and this is what must be assumed here. This is an important difference between the US model and the models of the other countries.

The results in Table 4-2 show that the interest rate and asset variables appear in most of the equations through the equations for Spain. It thus appears that interest rate and wealth effects on consumption have been picked up, as well as the usual income effect.

The interest rate variables in both the import and consumption equations are nominal rates. As was done in the estimation of the consumption equations for the US model, various proxies of expected future inflation rates were added to the equations (in addition to the nominal interest rate) to see if their coefficient estimates had the expected positive sign. The proxies consisted of various weighted averages of current and past inflation rates. As in the U.S. case, the results were not very good, which again may be due to the difficulty of measuring expected future inflation rates. More attempts of this kind should be made in future work, but for present purposes the nominal rates have been used.

The 23 Investment Equations (Table 4-3)

The explanation of investment is complicated by the fact that capital stock data were not constructed for the countries. (No benchmark capital stock data were available from the IFS tape.) This means that the specification of the investment equation for the US model, which relied on measures of the capital stock and of the amount of excess capital on hand, could not be used. What was done instead was to specify an investment equation that did not require a measure of the capital stock. The equations are as follows:

$$K_i - K_{i-1} = I_i - DEP_i, \tag{4.40}$$

$$DEP_i = \beta_0 + \beta_1 t, \tag{4.41}$$

$$K_i^* = \alpha_1 Y_{i-1} + \alpha_2 Y_{i-2} + \alpha_3 Y_{i-3} + \alpha_4 Y_{i-4}, \tag{4.42}$$

$$(K_i - K_{i-1})^* = \lambda_1 (K_i^* - K_{i-1}), \qquad 0 < \lambda_1 \leq 1, \tag{4.43}$$

$$I_i^* = (K_i - K_{i-1})^* + DEP_i, \tag{4.44}$$

$$I_i - I_{i-1} = \lambda_2 (I_i^* - I_{i-1}), \qquad 0 < \lambda_2 \leq 1, \tag{4.45}$$

where K_i is the actual value of the capital stock, I_i is gross investment, DEP_i is depreciation, Y_i is the level of output, K_i^* is the desired value of the capital stock, $(K_i - K_{i-1})^*$ is desired net investment, and I_i^* is desired gross investment.

Equation (4.40) is a definition: the change in the capital stock equals gross investment minus depreciation. In the absence of data on depreciation, it is assumed in (4.41) that depreciation is simply a function of a constant and time. The desired capital stock in (4.42) is assumed to be a function of the past four values of output; the past output values are meant as proxies for expected future values. Desired net investment in (4.43) is some fraction λ_1 of the difference between the desired capital stock and the actual capital stock of the previous period. Desired gross investment in (4.44) is equal to desired net investment plus depreciation. Equation (4.44) is the same as the definition (4.40) except that it is in terms of desired rather than actual values. The actual change in gross investment in (4.45) is some fraction λ_2 of the difference between desired gross investment and actual gross investment of the previous period.

This specification is in the spirit of the theoretical model of firm behavior in Chapter 3 in the sense that the lagged adjustment equations (4.43) and (4.45) are meant to reflect costs of adjustment. It seems likely that λ_2 will be much larger than λ_1, and it may in fact be one, which would mean that there are no adjustment costs with respect to changing gross investment.

Combining (4.40)–(4.45) yields the following equation to estimate:

$$\begin{aligned}(4.46)\qquad \Delta I_i = {} & (1-\lambda_2)\Delta I_{i-1} - \lambda_1\lambda_2 I_{i-1} + \lambda_1\lambda_2\alpha_1\Delta Y_{i-1} \\ & + \lambda_1\lambda_2\alpha_2\Delta Y_{i-2} + \lambda_1\lambda_2\alpha_3\Delta Y_{i-3} + \lambda_1\lambda_2\alpha_4\Delta Y_{i-4} \\ & + \lambda_2(\lambda_1\beta_0 - \lambda_1\beta_1 + \beta_1) + \lambda_1\lambda_2\beta_1 t.\end{aligned}$$

If $\lambda_2 = 1$, the lagged dependent variable, ΔI_{i-1}, drops out of the equation. If $\beta_1 > 0$, the coefficient of t is positive, and if $\beta_0 > 0$ and $\beta_1 > 0$, the constant term in the equation is positive. With respect to the stochastic specification, if an error term u_t is added to (4.45), then the error term in (4.46) is $u_t - u_{t-1}$. This means that the error term in (4.46) will be negatively serially correlated unless u_t is first-order serially correlated with a serial correlation coefficient greater than or equal to one. Note that by taking first differences the capital stock variable has been eliminated from (4.46).

The estimates of (4.46) are presented in Table 4-3 for 23 countries. (All these equations were estimated by OLS because there are no RHS endogenous variables.) All the estimates of the constant terms are positive. For most countries the estimate of the coefficient of ΔI_{i-1} was small and insignificant,

TABLE 4-6. The 26 demand for money equations

Equation 6: $\frac{M_i^*}{POP_i}$ is the LHS variable

Country	Explanatory variables				R^2	SE	DW	Sample period
	RS_i	$\frac{PY_iY_i}{POP_i}$	t	LHS_{-1}				
Canada	-8.4 (5.41)	.052 (3.79)	.45 (1.46)	.90 (18.04)	.994	21.0	2.53	581-813
Japan	-1.4 (2.32)	.20 (2.20)	.16 (0.93)	.82 (11.75)	.997	11.6	2.61	581-822
Austria	—	—	.019 (1.65)	.91 (17.58)	.994	.359	1.54	651-821
Belgium	-.37[a] (4.49)	.29 (5.17)	.075 (4.48)	.59 (7.95)	.997	1.09	2.49	581-804
Denmark	-.090 (6.90)	.58 (12.24)	.0027 (1.00)	.33 (5.56)	.997	.229	1.57	581-814
France	-.013[a] (1.35)	.34 (5.28)	.010 (3.37)	.56 (6.10)	.997	.181	2.25	581-814
Germany	-.020 (6.37)	.30 (5.23)	-.00056 (0.49)	.56 (7.49)	.998	.0463	2.51	611-821
Italy	-5.7 (2.01)	.45 (2.24)	2.1 (2.48)	.77 (6.27)	.996	55.8	2.34	611-814
Netherlands	-.039 (6.77)	.52 (7.36)	.0087 (5.30)	.19 (1.92)	.997	.074	2.07	611-814
Norway	-.011[a] (0.42)	.25 (5.33)	.024 (4.15)	.46 (4.70)	.991	.308	2.35	621-814
Sweden	—	.37 (9.55)	-.013 (5.85)	.44 (6.96)	.993	.187	1.75	581-814
Switzerland	-.030 (0.94)	.15 (1.26)	.012 (1.59)	.79 (10.84)	.990	.280	1.59	581-814

United Kingdom	-1.9	.082	.17	.87	.998	5.17	2.18	581-804
	(5.58)	(3.59)	(3.69)	(19.66)				
Finland	-4.2	.21	-1.6	.39	.996	60.6	1.96	581-814
	(0.40)	(7.87)	(2.51)	(4.86)				
Greece	-.039	.59	.015	.09	.997	.507	2.14	581-814
	(0.94)	(9.14)	(2.49)	(0.94)				
Ireland	-1.8	.098	.097	.91	.997	6.60	1.64	581-804
	(4.10)	(3.39)	(1.55)	(18.94)				
Portugal	-.28	.76	.029	.55	.990	1.07	1.94	581-804
	(2.57)	(5.49)	(2.67)	(6.10)				
Spain	-.12[a]	.51	.070	.49	.996	1.58	2.07	621-794
	(0.28)	(4.46)	(2.49)	(4.07)				
Turkey[b]	-.037	.25	-.00076	.76	.997	.0827	1.44	691-784
	(1.20)	(4.15)	(0.21)	(8.46)				
Australia	-7.1	.13	-.042	.79	.997	13.8	1.89	603-814
	(3.72)	(3.84)	(0.21)	(11.05)				
New Zealand	-13.7	.22	-.79	.67	.987	19.7	2.54	582-811
	(4.61)	(5.60)	(3.10)	(10.01)				
South Africa	-1.6	.06	.076	.90	.995	3.60	1.81	621-804
	(3.85)	(3.06)	(1.01)	(14.76)				
Colombia[b]	-7.1	.32	5.0	.29	.994	138.8	1.91	711-804
	(0.51)	(5.28)	(0.73)	(1.83)				
Peru	-.0035	.14	.0091	.78	.998	.344	1.66	611-804
	(0.16)	(5.04)	(2.42)	(13.12)				
Philippines	-.79[a]	.070	.24	.73	.994	7.70	1.72	581-802
	(1.67)	(2.88)	(2.66)	(8.47)				
Thailand	-.0061[a]	.10	.0028	.58	.989	.0351	1.70	654-814
	(1.47)	(3.10)	(3.58)	(4.79)				

Notes: a. Variable is lagged one quarter.
b. Equation estimated by OLS rather than 2SLS.
• t-statistics in absolute value are in parentheses.

and for most countries the variable was dropped. This means that the estimate of λ_2 is one for most countries. All the estimates of the coefficient of I_{i-1} are negative, as expected. The implied estimate of λ_1 ranges from .031 for Spain to .317 for Argentina. Most of the equations showed little evidence of serial correlation of the error term, which means that the error term in (4.45) has a high degree of positive serial correlation. The results for five countries showed enough evidence of negative serial correlation to warrant estimating the equations under the assumption of first-order serial correlation.

The output terms were left in the equations if their coefficient estimates were positive. There is generally a high degree of collinearity among the terms, and thus the coefficient estimates for the individual output terms are generally not very precise.

Although the results in Table 4-3 look reasonable, the results in general of estimating the investment equation are at best fair. There are two main problems: the first is that reasonable results could be found for only 23 countries; the second is that the results are highly sensitive to whether or not the current change in output, ΔY_i, is included in the equation. If the term $\alpha_0 Y_i$ is included in (4.42), so that the desired capital stock is also a function of the current level of output, then the term $\lambda_1\lambda_2\alpha_0\Delta Y_i$ is included in (4.46). When ΔY_i was included in the estimated equations, its coefficient estimate seemed much too large and the other coefficient estimates were substantially changed. Even though most of the equations were estimated by 2SLS, there still appeared to be substantial amounts of simultaneity bias. This problem existed almost without exception across the countries. In the end the decision was made to drop ΔY_i from all the investment equations, but this lack of robustness is not an encouraging feature of the results.

The 13 Production Equations (Table 4-4)

Equation 4 explains the level of production. It is based on the same three equations that were used for the US model—(4.22), (4.23), and (4.24). These equations are repeated here.

(4.22) $V^* = \beta X,$

(4.23) $Y^* \equiv X + \alpha(V^* - V_{-1}),$

(4.24) $Y - Y_{-1} = \lambda(Y^* - Y_{-1}).$

Combining the three equations yields

(4.25) $Y = \lambda(1 + \alpha\beta)X - \lambda\alpha V_{-1} + (1 - \lambda)Y_{-1},$

which is the equation estimated.

The results of estimating (4.25) for 13 countries are presented in Table 4-4. The implied values of λ, α, and β are presented along with the actual coefficient estimates. The estimates of λ range from .53 for Austria to .97 for Denmark. (λ is 1.0 for Finland because Y_{i-1} was dropped from the equation; this variable was dropped because its coefficient estimate was highly insignificant.) The estimates of α range from .029 for Spain to .175 for Korea. The fact that the estimates of λ are much larger than the estimates of α implies that production adjusts much faster to its desired level than does the stock of inventories. Serial correlation of the error terms is quite pronounced in most of the equations.

Equation 4 is essentially an inventory investment equation, and these types of equations are notoriously difficult to estimate. Reasonable results were obtained for the 13 countries in Table 4-4, but only for these 13. Estimating the equation for other countries led to unreasonable implied values of at least one of the three coefficients, λ, α, and β. As with the investment results in the previous subsection, the production results must be interpreted with caution, although there is no equivalent problem here to the robustness problem encountered in the estimation of the investment equation.

The 36 Price Equations (Table 4-5)

Equation 5 explains the GNP deflator. It is the key price equation in the model for each country. The two main explanatory variables in the equation, aside from the lagged dependent variable, are the price of imports, PM_i, and the demand pressure variable, ZZ_i. Equation 5 is similar to the price equation for the US model, Eq. 10 in Table A-5; the main difference is that Eq. 10 includes the wage rate, which Eq. 5 does not. Sufficient data on wage rates do not exist to allow a wage equation to be estimated along with a price equation.

The results of estimating Eq. 5 for 36 countries are presented in Table 4-5. It is clear from the results that import prices have an important effect on domestic prices for most countries. The import price variable appears in 34 of the 36 equations with the expected positive sign. The demand pressure variable appears in the equation for most of the first 18 countries. Serial correlation of the error term is not a problem for most countries, and in general the results seem good.

The 26 Demand-for-Money Equations (Table 4-6)

Equation 6 explains the per-capita demand for money. Both the interest rate and the income variables are generally significant in this equation. For all

TABLE 4-7. The 23 interest rate reaction functions under fixed exchange rates

Equation 7a: RS_i in the LHS variable

Country	US rate: RS_1	German rate: RS_8	$\dot{PY}_{i-1}$	$\frac{\dot{M1}^*_{i-1}}{POP_{i-1}}$	ZZ_i	$\frac{A^*_i}{PY_i POP_i}$	$\frac{A^*_{i-1}}{PY_{i-1} POP_{i-1}}$	t	LHS_{-1}	$\hat{\rho}_1$	R^2	SE	DW	Sample period
	Explanatory variables													
Canada	.82 (4.75)	—	.059 (2.17)	—	—	—	—	.022 (0.62)	.13 (0.80)	.61 (3.88)	.965	.257	1.36	631-701
Japan	—	—	—	.015 (1.43)	-27.9[a] (2.54)	-.21 (3.03)	.22 (2.93)	-.12 (2.33)	.65 (7.76)	—	.762	.825	2.19	581-712
Austria[c]	—	.14 (4.64)	—	—	-7.9[a] (2.12)	—	—	-.017 (2.88)	.20 (1.48)	—	.912	.134	1.82	651-711
Belgium	.37 (4.13)	.20 (2.12)	.034 (1.29)	—	-6.6 (1.62)	-.21[ab] (2.23)	.21[ab] (2.23)	-.012 (0.96)	.56 (3.76)	—	.898	.462	1.91	581-712
Denmark[c]	.19 (3.12)	—	.033 (3.68)	—	-3.1 (1.47)	-.50[ab] (1.33)	.50[ab] (1.33)	-.0096 (1.22)	.74 (10.22)	—	.922	.342	1.50	581-712
France	.35 (3.67)	—	.065 (4.11)	—	—	-2.4[ab] (1.76)	2.4[ab] (1.76)	-.015 (1.71)	.73 (12.94)	—	.925	.494	2.00	581-712
Germany	.46 (3.90)	—	.085 (2.89)	—	-13.4[a] (3.38)	-2.4[ab] (1.33)	2.4[ab] (1.33)	-.015 (0.91)	.68 (11.15)	—	.950	.436	1.70	611-711
Italy[c]	—	.12 (5.91)	—	—	—	-.010 (3.07)	.011 (3.24)	—	.56 (8.47)	—	.937	.167	2.26	611-712
Netherlands	.66 (5.26)	—	.013 (0.72)	.025 (2.10)	—	-4.5[a] (2.15)	3.4[a] (1.75)	-.043 (1.75)	.65 (7.19)	—	.962	.404	1.79	611-711
Sweden[c]	.16 (2.76)	—	—	—	—	-1.5[ab] (2.34)	1.5[ab] (2.34)	.0037 (0.60)	.71 (9.97)	—	.882	.308	2.18	581-712
Switzerland[c]	.04 (1.28)	.04 (2.06)	—	—	—	—	—	.0041 (1.19)	.76 (11.09)	—	.928	.173	2.03	581-711

United Kingdom	.20 (2.28)	—	—	—	-12.7 (2.82)	-.039[a] (3.01)	.031[a] (2.15)	.0044 (0.40)	.67 (7.71)	—	.907	.418	1.69	581-712
Finland[c]	—	—	.017 (2.09)	—	—	—	—	.0018 (0.77)	.45 (2.81)	—	.224	.261	1.59	581-712
Greece[c]	—	—	.024 (3.29)	—	-6.4[a] (3.63)	—	—	-.013 (2.59)	.87 (25.46)	—	.927	.513	2.40	581-751
Ireland[c]	.15 (1.34)	—	—	—	—	—	—	.017 (1.61)	.62 (6.39)	—	.818	.610	1.91	581-712
Portugal[c]	—	—	—	.0027 (1.38)	—	—	—	.0031 (1.64)	.96 (14.80)	—	.940	.118	2.17	581-712
Spain[c]	.12 (3.36)	—	—	—	—	—	—	-.0054 (1.07)	.93 (15.12)	—	.937	.161	2.47	621-712
Australia	.07 (1.66)	—	.014 (1.31)	—	-5.6[a] (3.78)	-.0043[b] (2.86)	.0043[b] (2.86)	-.013 (2.40)	.93 (17.94)	—	.943	.175	2.03	603-712
South Africa	.11 (2.63)	—	—	—	-5.4[a] (1.80)	-.0090[b] (2.25)	.0090[b] (2.25)	.0036 (0.29)	.93 (8.13)	.65 (4.14)	.966	.364	2.06	621-814
Korea[c]	—	—	—	—	-13.8 (3.29)	—	—	-.023 (1.74)	.90 (18.30)	—	.845	2.23	1.75	641-814
Pakistan	—	—	.014 (0.38)	—	—	-.0079 (0.81)	.0057 (0.63)	-.065 (1.02)	.67 (4.75)	—	.742	.751	1.48	731-812
Philippines[c]	.21 (2.70)	—	—	—	—	—	—	-.0092 (1.41)	.86 (17.12)	—	.808	.971	2.01	581-802
Thailand[c]	.20 (4.11)	—	—	—	-3.1 (0.75)	—	—	.020 (2.70)	.59 (7.55)	—	.927	.582	1.79	654-814

Notes: a. Variable is lagged one quarter.
b. Coefficient of $A^*_i/(PY_i POP_i)$ (or its lagged value) constrained to be equal to minus the coefficient of $A^*_{i-1}/(PY_{i-1}POP_{i-1})$ (or its lagged value).
c. Only discount rate data available for RS_i.

- All equations estimated by OLS.
- t-statistics in absolute value are in parentheses.

countries except Austria and Sweden, the estimated coefficient of the interest rate variable is of the expected negative sign.

The per-capita money and income variables in Table 4-6 are nominal rather than real. This is contrary to the case for the money and income variables in the demand-for-money equations in the US model, which are in real terms. Some experimentation was done for the other countries using real variables, but on average the results did not seem to be as good. One of the reasons for this may be errors of measurement in the price deflators. More experimentation should be done in future work, but for present purposes the results in Table 4-6 seem reasonably good.

The Interest Rate Reaction Functions: 23 under Fixed Exchange Rates and 20 under Flexible Exchange Rates (Table 4-7 and 4-8)

The candidates for inclusion as explanatory variables in the interest rate reaction functions are variables that one believes may affect the monetary authorities' decisions regarding short-term interest rates. In addition, the U.S. interest rate may be an important explanatory variable in the equations estimated over the fixed exchange rate period if bonds are close substitutes. The variables that were tried include (1) the lagged rate of inflation, (2) the lagged rate of growth of the money supply, (3) the demand pressure variable, (4) the change in assets, (5) the lagged rate of change of import prices, (6) the exchange rate (Eq. 7b only), and (7) the German interest rate. The form of the asset variable that was tried is $A_i^*/(PY_iPOP_i)$. Except for division by PY_iPOP_i, the change in this variable is the balance of payments on current account. For some countries, depending on the initial results, the current and one-period-lagged values were entered separately. It may be that the monetary authorities respond in part to the level of assets and in part to the change, and entering the current and lagged values separately will pick this up.

The results of estimating Eqs. 7a and 7b are presented in Tables 4-7 and 4-8. Although the equations are estimated over fairly small numbers of observations because of the breaking up of the sample periods, many of the explanatory variables appear in the equations and many are significant. The overall results provide fairly strong support for the proposition that monetary authorities in other countries "lean against the wind." This conclusion is consistent with the results for the US model. The U.S. interest rate, as expected, is a more important explanatory variable in the fixed exchange rate period than it is in the flexible rate period. The variable that is least significant in Tables 4-7 and 4-8 is the lagged growth of the money supply. Contrary to the case for the United States, especially in the Volcker regime, the monetary authorities of other countries do not appear to be influenced very much in their setting of interest rate targets by the money supply growth itself. In other words, money supply growth does not appear to provide independent explanatory power for the interest rate setting behavior of most countries, given the other variables in the equations.

The 17 Term Structure Equations (Table 4-9)

Equation 8 is a standard term structure equation. The current and lagged short-term interest rates in the equation are meant to be proxies for expected future short-term interest rates. This is the same equation as the one that was estimated for the bond and mortgage rates in the US model (Eqs. 23 and 24 in Table A-5). The results of estimating equation 8 for 17 countries are presented in Table 4-9. The 17 countries are the ones for which data on a long-term rate exist. The current short-term rate is significant for all countries except Portugal and New Zealand. In general, the results indicate that current and lagged short-term rates affect long-term rates.

The 22 Exchange Rate Equations (Table 4-10)

Equation 9b explains the spot exchange rate. Candidates for inclusion as explanatory variables in this equation are variables that one believes affect the monetary authority's decision regarding the exchange rate. If, as mentioned in Section 4.2.2, a monetary authority takes market forces into account in choosing its exchange rate target, then variables measuring these forces should be included in the equation. The variables that were tried include (1) the price level of country i relative to the U.S. price level, (2) the short-term interest rate of country i relative to the U.S. rate, (3) the demand pressure variable of country i relative to the U.S. demand pressure variable, ZZ_i, (4) the one-quarter-lagged value of the change in real per-capita net foreign assets of country i relative to the change in the same variable for the United States, and (5) the German exchange rate.

The results of estimating Eq. 9b for 22 countries are presented in Table 4-10. It is clear from the current literature on exchange rates that no one explanation of exchange rates has emerged as being obviously the best. Whether the current explanation as reflected in the results in Table 4-10 turns out to be the best is clearly an open question. The sample period in the flexible exchange rate regime is still fairly short, and more observations are needed before much can be said. In general, the results in Table 4-10 do not seem too

TABLE 4-8. The 20 interest rate reaction functions under flexible exchange rates

Equation 7b: RS_i is the LHS variable

Country	Explanatory variables												R^2	SE	DW	Sample period
	US rate: RS_1	German rate: RS_8	$\dot{PY}_{i-1}$	$\frac{\dot{M1}^*_{i-1}}{POP_{i-1}}$	ZZ_i	$\frac{A^*_i}{PY_i POP_i}$	$\frac{A^*_{i-1}}{PY_{i-1} POP_{i-1}}$	$\dot{PM}_{i-1}$	e_i	t	LHS_{-1}	$\hat{\rho}_1$				
Canada	.70 (8.73)	—	—	.020 (2.30)	-19.3 (1.89)	-.017 (2.94)	.015 (2.70)	—	—	.060 (0.90)	.42 (4.10)	.63 (4.85)	.979	.604	1.99	711-821
Japan	—	—	—	.013 (1.55)	—	-.17 (3.24)	.18 (4.94)	—	9.0 (1.35)	—	.80 (5.50)	.40 (1.72)	.945	.655	1.75	722-822
Austria[c]	.17 (3.64)	—	.035 (2.31)	.011 (1.50)	-5.5 (0.91)	-.65[a] (2.57)	.70[a] (2.67)	—	—	.0047 (0.14)	.69 (8.28)	—	.795	.474	2.03	722-821
Belgium	.12 (0.75)	.13 (1.10)	—	—	-22.8 (2.30)	—	—	.042 (2.46)	187.3 (1.78)	.22 (3.50)	.51 (5.65)	—	.878	1.00	2.14	722-804
Denmark	—	—	.19 (2.94)	—	-22.5 (1.93)	-5.5[a] (2.49)	4.9[a] (2.50)	.047 (2.22)	—	.030 (0.26)	.48 (4.41)	—	.820	1.81	2.22	722-814
France	—	.35 (6.57)	.078 (1.35)	—	-22.6 (1.62)	-2.8[ab] (1.07)	2.8[ab] (1.07)	.017 (1.91)	1384.3 (3.60)	.12 (2.92)	.43 (4.89)	—	.931	.805	1.78	722-814
Germany	.28 (2.31)	—	.049 (0.81)	—	-29.9 (2.90)	-3.5[ab] (1.08)	3.5[ab] (1.08)	—	1091.9 (1.43)	.025 (0.52)	.73 (8.83)	—	.902	.957	2.10	722-821
Italy	—	—	.054 (1.40)	—	-19.3 (1.57)	-.079 (5.03)	.068 (4.31)	—	7.8 (2.90)	.038 (1.03)	.49 (5.37)	—	.944	1.06	1.58	722-814
Netherlands	—	.36 (2.92)	.099 (0.74)	—	-22.7 (1.60)	—	—	.037 (1.71)	—	.15 (2.53)	.39 (3.12)	—	.748	1.85	1.55	722-814
Norway	—	.31 (2.24)	—	—	—	-1.2 (2.21)	1.1 (2.21)	.017 (0.84)	720.2 (0.92)	.11 (1.89)	.32 (2.34)	—	.673	1.46	2.24	722-814

Sweden[d]	—	.09 (1.57)	.046 (1.34)	—	-26.9^a (2.25)	-1.9 (1.52)	.9 (0.74)	.013 (1.50)	—	.041 (1.09)	.61 (6.17)	—	.914	.791	1.67	722-814
Switzerland[c]	.15 (4.93)	—	.026 (2.81)	—	-7.[illegible] (2.52)	.55 (1.08)	-.79 (1.66)	.0070 (2.70)	702.1 (4.58)	.070 (2.40)	.69 (9.18)	—	.982	.217	2.06	722-814
United Kingdom	—	—	—	.040 (2.11)	-14.5^a (1.25)	-.034 (0.94)	.053 (1.41)	.022 (1.36)	—	.15 (2.64)	.68 (3.76)	.44 (1.86)	.892	.965	1.94	722-804
Finland[c]	—	—	—	—	-8.0 (3.74)	—	—	.0024 (0.85)	—	.029 (3.20)	.84 (13.16)	—	.845	.316	1.72	722-814
Greece[c]	—	—	.047 (1.70)	—	-22.3^a (2.57)	—	—	—	—	.28 (3.57)	.71 (5.19)	—	.971	.720	2.53	761-814
Ireland	.28 (1.84)	—	—	—	-8.7 (0.77)	—	—	—	—	.0073 (0.17)	.73 (6.95)	—	.810	1.34	1.28	722-804
Portugal[c]	—	—	.020 (1.73)	—	—	$-.45^b$ (1.06)	$.45^b$ (1.06)	—	196.5 (2.44)	-.041 (0.52)	.73 (6.91)	—	.969	1.00	2.18	722-804
Spain[c]	.09 (3.23)	—	.019 (3.09)	—	—	$-.13^{ab}$ (3.59)	$.13^{ab}$ (3.59)	—	16.8 (2.27)	.014 (0.99)	.66 (6.50)	—	.974	.167	2.28	722-794
Australia	.15 (3.80)	—	—	—	-21.0 (2.87)	$-.0083^b$ (1.83)	$.0083^b$ (1.83)	.0083 (2.30)	—	.064 (2.45)	.71 (8.73)	—	.960	.469	2.02	722-814
New Zealand[c]	—	—	—	—	-10.5 (1.32)	—	—	—	—	.15 (3.41)	.63 (4.23)	—	.953	.613	1.53	732-811

Notes: a. Variable is lagged one quarter.

b. Coefficient of $A_i^*/(PY_i POP_i)$ (or its lagged value) constrained to be equal to minus the coefficient of $A_{i-1}^*/(PY_{i-1} POP_{i-1})$ (or its lagged value).

c. Only discount rate data available for RS_i.

d. Only discount rate data available for RS_i before 743.

- All equations estimated by OLS.
- t-statistics in absolute value are in parentheses.

TABLE 4-9. The 17 term structure equations

Equation 8: RB_i is the LHS variable

Country	Explanatory variables				R^2	SE	DW	Sample period
	RS_i	RS_{i-1}	RS_{i-2}	LHS_{-1}				
Canada	.35 (6.10)	-.28 (3.59)	.07 (1.73)	.83 (18.72)	.985	.334	2.37	581-821
Belgium	.20 (5.69)	-.09 (2.12)	-.00 (0.05)	.89 (21.61)	.982	.222	1.73	581-804
Denmark	.25 (4.76)	-.09 (1.57)	-.06 (1.48)	.92 (23.29)	.975	.641	1.79	581-814
France	.22 (3.05)	-.13 (1.44)	-.03 (0.62)	.97 (24.77)	.988	.299	1.90	581-814
Germany	.26 (4.78)	-.16 (2.31)	.02 (0.41)	.80 (14.53)	.936	.358	1.73	611-821
Italy	.25 (4.72)	-.16 (2.19)	.04 (0.81)	.90 (27.90)	.991	.394	1.25	611-814
Netherlands	.15 (3.43)	-.10 (2.36)	.02 (0.76)	.93 (28.54)	.973	.330	1.92	611-814
Norway	.13 (3.15)	-.04 (1.42)	-.01 (0.27)	.93 (23.12)	.981	.267	1.58	621-814
Sweden	.20 (3.38)	-.14 (1.90)	-.01 (0.22)	.98 (52.62)	.994	.188	1.62	581-814
Switzerland	.44 (7.07)	-.31 (2.97)	-.05 (0.78)	.92 (25.78)	.973	.189	1.31	581-814
United Kingdom	.32 (3.45)	-.27 (2.17)	.02 (0.31)	.94 (29.38)	.982	.452	1.85	581-804
Ireland	.24 (2.07)	-.10 (0.69)	-.03 (0.43)	.92 (23.22)	.972	.670	2.51	581-804
Portugal	.18 (1.80)	.15 (1.54)	-.23 (4.08)	.88 (14.39)	.993	.363	1.80	581-804
Australia	.53 (7.93)	-.31 (3.51)	-.04 (0.81)	.84 (14.98)	.994	.205	1.73	603-814
New Zealand[a]	-.11 (1.67)	.53 (5.87)	-.40 (5.75)	.996 (23.39)	.988	.268	1.95	582-811
South Africa	.46 (3.26)	-.51 (2.19)	.05 (0.42)	.995 (29.15)	.988	.239	1.71	621-814
India[a]	.03 (3.07)	.00 (0.34)	-.01 (0.88)	.91 (36.70)	.980	.099	1.49	611-794

Notes: a. Equation estimated by OLS rather than 2SLS.
• t-statistics in absolute value are in parentheses.

bad. The German exchange rate is an important explanatory variable in the equations for the other European countries, which is as expected. The relative inflation variable appears in all but six of the equations, and it is the next most important variable after the German exchange rate and the lagged dependent variable. The next most important variable is the relative change in assets variable, which appears in half of the equations. (Note with respect to the relative change in assets variable in Table 4-10 that since $\Delta[A^{*}_{i-1}/(PY_{i-1}POP_{i-1})]$ is in 1975 local currency, the respective variable for the United States must be multiplied by the 1975 exchange rate, e_{i75}, to make the units comparable.) The relative interest rate variable and the relative demand pressure variable are of about equal importance, each appearing in 9 of the 22 equations.

Since the LHS variable is the log of the exchange rate, the standard errors are roughly in percentage terms. The standard errors for many European countries are very low—in a number of cases less than 2.0 percent—but this is misleading because of the inclusion of the German exchange rate in the equations. A much better way of examining how well the equations fit is to solve the overall model; the results of doing this are presented and discussed in Section 8.6. The standard error for the German equation in Table 4-10 is 3.94 percent, and the standard error for the Japanese equation, which does not include the German rate as an explanatory variable, is 3.60 percent. These errors do not seem bad, given the variability of exchange rates, but again one should wait for the results of solving the overall model.

The signs of the estimated effects are as follows. (Remember that an increase in the exchange rate is a depreciation and that all changes are relative to changes for the United States. Moreover, not all the effects operate for all countries). (1) An increase in a country's price level has a positive effect on its exchange rate (a depreciation). (2) As real output in a country increases, the demand pressure variable ZZ_i decreases, and a decrease in ZZ_i leads to an increase in the exchange rate. Therefore, an increase in real output has a positive effect on the exchange rate (a depreciation). (3) An increase in a country's short-term interest rate has a negative effect on its exchange rate (an appreciation). (4) An increase in a country's net foreign assets has a negative effect on its exchange rate (an appreciation).

The 13 Forward Rate Equations (Table 4-11)

Equation 10b is the estimated arbitrage condition. Although this equation plays no role in the model, it allows one to see how closely the quarterly data

TABLE 4-10. The 22 exchange rate equations

Equation 9b: $\log e_i$ is the LHS variable

Country	German rate: $\log e_8$	$\log\frac{PY_i}{PY_1}$	$\frac{1}{4}\log\frac{(1+RS_i/100)}{(1+RS_1/100)}$	$ZZ_i - ZZ_1$	$\Delta\frac{A^*_{i-1}}{PY_{i-1}POP_{i-1}} - e_{i75}\Delta\frac{A^*_{1-1}}{PY_{1-1}POP_{1-1}}$	LHS_{-1}	$\hat{\rho}_1$	R^2	SE	DW	Sample period
	Explanatory variables										
Canada	—	.15 (1.92)	-.89 (0.94)	—	—	.92 (16.10)	.33 (2.04)	.974	.0126	1.96	711-821
Japan	—	.10 (0.76)	-2.9 (1.68)	-.41 (1.68)	-.0039 (3.49)	.86 (6.68)	.23 (1.17)	.938	.0360	1.87	722-822
Austria	.95 (47.46)	.072 (0.94)	-.71 (2.04)	—	—	.02 (1.02)	.90 (12.74)	.999	.00566	1.51	722-821
Belgium	.84 (23.61)	—	—	—	-.0033 (1.60)	—	.76 (7.84)	.994	.0106	1.88	722-804
Denmark	.82 (18.71)	—	—	-.16 (1.99)	-.023 (2.45)	.09 (1.74)	.99 (41.25)	.979	.0136	1.22	722-814
France	.60 (8.13)	1.1 (5.94)	—	—	-.072 (1.04)	.35 (4.07)	.69 (5.19)	.938	.0214	1.72	722-814
Germany	—	.94 (2.44)	-3.1 (1.67)	-.45 (0.68)	-.40 (2.58)	.70 (6.26)	—	.949	.0394	1.92	722-804
Italy	.49 (6.49)	.71 (6.86)	—	—	—	.44 (4.44)	.66 (5.08)	.986	.0238	2.10	722-814
Netherlands	.87 (23.95)	—	—	—	—	.08 (2.09)	.85 (10.34)	.994	.0111	1.98	722-814

Norway	.63 (13.61)	—	-.89 (1.99)	—	—	.11 (1.60)	.98 (23.41)	.966	.0145	1.64	722-814
Sweden	.41 (7.52)	.77 (7.18)	-4.3 (4.53)	—	-.041 (1.39)	.56 (6.45)	—	.864	.0246	1.47	722-814
Switzerland	.91 (8.38)	.91 (4.01)	-3.6 (1.77)	-.33 (0.93)	-.084 (1.32)	.08 (0.65)	.75 (5.29)	.988	.0288	1.45	722-814
United Kingdom	.20 (2.67)	.30 (2.91)	—	-.52 (1.85)	-.0011 (1.85)	.82 (10.25)	—	.943	.0326	1.96	711-794
Finland	.52 (10.08)	—	-1.8 (1.81)	—	—	.14 (1.67)	.97 (30.89)	.919	.0161	1.74	722-814
Greece	.31 (2.78)	.70 (4.05)	-2.1 (1.56)	—	-.035 (3.44)	.46 (3.04)	.53 (2.18)	.989	.0166	1.61	761-814
Ireland	.33 (3.97)	.52 (4.03)	—	-.47 (1.95)	—	.70 (8.56)	—	.939	.0312	1.71	722-804
Portugal	.41 (5.43)	.63 (7.24)	—	—	—	.65 (10.62)	—	.991	.0269	1.97	722-804
Spain	.45 (3.66)	.44 (3.68)	—	—	-.0057 (0.93)	.71 (5.24)	—	.926	.0321	1.73	722-794
Australia	—	.21 (3.57)	—	-.22 (1.19)	—	.86 (11.77)	—	.912	.0288	1.75	722-814
New Zealand	—	.15 (1.60)	—	-.48 (2.15)	—	.76 (8.96)	—	.864	.0260	2.13	752-811
Brazil	—	.56 (4.25)	—	—	—	.38 (2.56)	.59 (3.96)	.998	.0414	1.65	641-804
India	—	—	—	-.29 (1.98)	-.12 (2.89)	.70 (8.10)	—	.819	.0238	2.38	722-794

Notes:
- All equations estimated by OLS.
- t-statistics in absolute value are in parentheses.

TABLE 4-11. The 13 forward rate equations

Equation 10b: log F_i is the LHS variable

Country	Explanatory variables: log ee_i	Explanatory variables: $\frac{1}{4}\log\frac{(1+RS_i/100)}{(1+RS_1/100)}$	R^2	SE	DW	Sample period
Canada	.97670 (.00372)	.94 (.08)	.999	.00208	1.84	711-821
Japan	1.00138 (.00178)	1.31 (.28)	.990	.0154	1.18	722-822
Austria	.99966 (.00045)	.92 (.21)	.997	.00847	1.53	722-821
Belgium	.99936 (.00034)	1.33 (.21)	.998	.00648	2.15	722-804
Denmark	.99941 (.00046)	.84 (.19)	.989	.00992	2.08	722-814
France	1.00059 (.00014)	.96 (.11)	.998	.00380	2.00	722-814
Germany	1.00106 (.00014)	.71 (.13)	.999	.00470	1.47	722-821
Netherlands	1.00053 (.00014)	.92 (.13)	.999	.00514	1.88	722-814
Norway	.99894 (.00052)	.99 (.41)	.959	.0162	2.03	722-814
Sweden	.99979 (.00025)	1.08 (.23)	.989	.00765	1.41	722-814
Switzerland	1.00068 (.00029)	.82 (.13)	.999	.00580	1.54	722-814
United Kingdom	1.00046 (.00231)	1.43 (.20)	.998	.00627	1.33	722-804
Finland	1.00578 (.00130)	1.93 (.24)	.966	.0107	1.48	722-814

Notes:
- All equations estimated by OLS.
- Equations do not include a constant term and seasonal dummy variables.
- Standard errors are in parentheses.

match the arbitrage condition. The results are presented in Table 4-11. If the arbitrage condition were met exactly, the coefficient estimates of log ee_i and $\frac{1}{4}\log\frac{(1+RS_i/100)}{(1+RS_1/100)}$ in the table would be 1.0, and the fit would be perfect. As can be seen, the results do indicate that the data are consistent with the arbitrage condition, especially considering the poor quality of some of the interest rate data.

The 32 Export Price Equations (Table 4-12)

Equation 11 provides a link from the GNP deflator to the export price index. Export prices are needed when the countries are linked together (see Table B-4 in Appendix B). If a country produced only one good, then the export price would be the domestic price and only one price equation would be needed. In practice, of course, a country produces many goods, only some of which are exported. If a country is a price taker with respect to its exports, then its export prices would just be the world prices of the export goods. To try to capture the in-between case where a country has some effect on its export prices but not complete control over every price, the export price index was regressed on the GNP deflator and a world price index.

The world price index, $PW\$_i$, is defined in Table B-2 of Appendix B. It is a weighted average of the export prices (in dollars) of the individual countries. Type B countries and oil exporting countries (countries 26 through 35) are excluded from the calculations. The weight for each country is the ratio of its total exports to the total exports of all the countries. The world price index differs for different countries because the individual country is excluded from the calculations for itself.

Since the world price index is in dollars, it needs to be multiplied by the exchange rate to convert it into local currency before being used as an explanatory variable in the export price equation for a given country. (The export price index explained by Eq. 11 is in local currency.) For some countries, depending on the initial results, this was done, but for others the world price index in dollars and the exchange rate were entered separately.

The results of estimating Eq. 11 are presented in Table 4-12. They show, as expected, that export prices are in part linked to domestic prices and in part to world prices. Serial correlation of the error term is quite pronounced in nearly all the equations. It should be kept in mind that Eq. 11 is meant only as a rough approximation. If more disaggregated data were available, one would want to estimate separate price equations for each good, where some goods'

TABLE 4-12. The 32 export price equations

Equation 11: $\log PX_i$ is the LHS variable

Country	Explanatory variables: $\log PY_i$	$\log PW\$_i$	$\log e_i$	constant	$\hat{\rho}_1$	R^2	SE	DW	Sample period
Canada	.82 (8.05)	.33 (4.53)	.15 (1.26)	—	.96 (24.65)	.999	.0152	1.97	581-821
Japan	.86 (4.49)	.25 (2.77)	.57 (8.42)	.62 (3.17)	.98 (70.52)	.992	.0205	1.88	581-822
Austria	.38 (4.67)	.43[a] (4.41)	.43[a] (4.41)	1.7 (4.29)	.73 (9.00)	.989	.0216	2.08	651-821
Belgium	.30 (3.31)	.60[a] (6.42)	.60[a] (6.42)	2.0 (6.41)	.89 (20.07)	.995	.0173	1.83	581-804
Denmark	.09 (2.38)	.83 (17.64)	.55 (9.23)	2.9 (9.34)	.62 (7.40)	.997	.0192	1.82	581-814
France	.26 (7.80)	.69 (20.26)	.48 (14.18)	2.6 (14.27)	.64 (7.86)	.999	.0112	2.09	581-814
Germany	.37 (3.86)	.43 (7.88)	.24 (6.90)	1.4 (6.79)	.94 (28.41)	.998	.0090	1.81	611-821
Italy	.44 (4.41)	.60 (5.82)	.61 (7.29)	.23 (5.18)	.92 (24.17)	.999	.0179	2.27	611-814
Netherlands	.29 (3.27)	.76[a] (10.13)	.76[a] (10.13)	4.6 (10.15)	.93 (22.44)	.997	.0164	1.84	611-814
Norway	.16 (1.29)	1.15 (6.54)	1.00 (6.10)	5.2 (6.17)	.93 (14.79)	.996	.0251	2.06	621-814
Sweden	.46 (6.26)	.64 (9.03)	.32 (5.20)	1.7 (5.14)	.94 (26.93)	.999	.0122	2.00	581-814
Switzerland	.54 (15.17)	.31 (5.45)	.30 (5.54)	1.8 (5.53)	.61 (7.40)	.994	.0163	2.20	581-814
United Kingdom	.53 (11.76)	.56 (10.55)	.33 (8.30)	.30 (7.66)	.94 (24.95)	.999	.0099	2.01	581-804
Finland	.17 (1.71)	1.01 (8.68)	.78 (8.77)	-1.1 (9.09)	.83 (14.08)	.998	.0235	2.03	581-814
Greece	.09 (0.61)	.76 (5.16)	.76 (5.28)	2.6 (5.20)	.25 (2.50)	.982	.0661	2.21	581-814
Ireland	.46 (7.06)	.60 (7.45)	.41 (7.25)	.31 (5.67)	.93 (20.58)	.999	.0151	1.91	581-804

Spain	.10 (1.25)	.73 (5.75)	.66 (5.54)	1.9 (5.72)	.34 (3.11)	.985	.0441	1.94	621-794
Turkey	.18 (1.00)	.97 (3.58)	.61 (4.63)	2.6 (4.76)	.59 (4.32)	.989	.0571	1.59	691-784
Yugoslavia	.21 (3.76)	.75 (9.72)	1.00 (42.50)	4.0 (40.82)	.13 (1.14)	.999	.0369	1.94	611-794
Australia	.46 (2.97)	.46 (2.98)	.12 (0.77)	.077 (1.59)	.90 (19.23)	.994	.0330	1.50	603-814
New Zealand	.68 (4.67)	.24 (1.52)	.24 (1.84)	.19 (3.78)	.91 (18.02)	.995	.0337	1.18	582-811
South Africa	.13 (0.82)	.82 (4.86)	.38 (2.80)	.18 (3.27)	.87 (14.00)	.995	.0326	2.07	621-814
Brazil	—	1.00[a] (31.43)	1.00[a] (31.43)	4.8 (29.81)	.86 (13.37)	.998	.0554	1.78	641-804
Colombia	.68 (1.15)	.16 (0.28)	.60 (0.59)	-2.0 (0.57)	.88 (9.34)	.984	.0968	1.53	711-804
Israel	.02 (0.34)	.93 (7.84)	1.05 (14.49)	-1.9 (20.37)	.87 (13.46)	.999	.0305	1.85	691-814
India	—	.83 (34.44)	.83 (20.72)	4.0 (20.62)	.32 (2.88)	.992	.0415	1.85	611-794
Korea	.04 (0.79)	.76 (8.31)	.96 (16.05)	.82 (13.84)	.89 (14.91)	.998	.0292	1.50	641-814
Malaysia	.47 (1.50)	1.02 (3.50)	.76 (2.06)	-.59 (1.78)	.80 (8.35)	.979	.0593	1.33	711-814
Pakistan	.24 (0.70)	.57 (1.46)	.11 (0.08)	-.070 (0.02)	.79 (5.97)	.950	.0605	1.42	731-812
Philippines	—	.92 (8.01)	.91 (10.56)	-1.9 (10.92)	.87 (15.60)	.993	.0620	1.51	581-802
Thailand	.53 (1.83)	.57 (2.34)	.25 (0.42)	.90 (0.39)	.86 (12.86)	.987	.0498	1.85	654-814
US	.95 (16.83)	.15 (4.16)	—	.23 (12.72)	.93 (25.77)	.999	.0090	1.32	581-822

Notes: a. Coefficient of log $PW\$_i$ constrained to be equal to the coefficient of log e_i.

- All equations estimated by OLS.
- Equations do not include seasonal dummy variables.
- t-statistics in absolute value are in parentheses.

TABLE 4-13. Regressions for the construction of the demand pressure variable

$\log \frac{Y_i}{POP_i}$ is the LHS variable

Country	Explanatory variable: t	Implied value of the growth rate (annual rate)	R^2	SE	DW	Sample period
Canada	.00790 (66.36)	3.2	.978	.0328	0.12	581-821
Japan	.0168 (40.85)	6.9	.945	.115	0.02	581-822
Austria	.00949 (52.73)	3.9	.979	.0298	0.31	651-821
Belgium	.00967 (67.97)	3.9	.981	.0362	0.41	581-804
Denmark	.00758 (40.89)	3.1	.947	.0503	0.55	581-814
France	.00964 (73.71)	3.9	.983	.0355	0.19	581-814
Germany	.00781 (62.31)	3.2	.979	.0283	0.28	611-821
Italy	.00805 (47.61)	3.3	.964	.0375	0.15	611-814
Netherlands	.00825 (51.48)	3.3	.969	.0356	0.33	611-814
Norway	.00905 (79.10)	3.7	.987	.0236	1.20	621-814
Sweden	.00676 (34.53)	2.7	.928	.0531	1.25	581-814
Switzerland	.00541 (28.78)	2.2	.896	.0510	0.07	581-814
United Kingdom	.00554 (65.63)	2.2	.980	.0215	0.76	581-804
Finland	.00994 (54.95)	4.0	.969	.0491	0.47	581-814
Greece	.01345 (48.72)	5.5	.962	.0749	0.51	581-814
Ireland	.00841 (59.54)	3.4	.976	.0359	0.69	581-804
Portugal	.0126 (46.84)	5.1	.960	.0682	0.43	581-804
Spain	.0109 (41.51)	4.4	.960	.0463	0.25	621-794
Turkey	.0103 (37.24)	4.2	.972	.0200	0.13	691-784
Yugoslavia	.0134 (73.05)	5.5	.986	.0351	0.88	611-794

Australia	.00629 (40.81)	2.5	.951	.0355	0.15	603-814
New Zealand	.00453 (37.11)	1.8	.937	.0311	0.06	582-811
South Africa	.00337 (22.77)	1.4	.867	.0306	0.23	621-814
Libya	.0144 (14.62)	5.9	.805	.1061	0.20	651-774
Nigeria	.00847 (13.34)	3.4	.867	.0269	0.25	712-781
Saudi Arabia	.0120 (13.45)	4.9	.858	.0423	0.26	721-792
Venezuela	.00467 (31.17)	1.9	.928	.0286	0.10	621-804
Argentina	.00221 (6.10)	0.9	.733	.0438	0.70	671-804
Brazil	.0157 (53.34)	6.4	.977	.0476	0.16	641-804
Chile	.00127 (0.95)	0.5	.258	.0971	0.49	711-804
Colombia	.00686 (32.62)	2.8	.964	.0153	0.23	711-804
Mexico	.00796 (63.83)	3.2	.978	.0318	1.02	581-804
Peru	.00324 (15.18)	1.3	.733	.0474	0.04	611-814
Israel	.00494 (10.30)	2.0	.672	.0517	0.37	691-814
Jordan	.0205 (12.95)	8.5	.844	.0320	0.65	731-804
Syria	.00994 (14.73)	4.0	.762	.1090	0.18	641-804
India	.00336 (18.13)	1.4	.812	.0354	0.25	611-794
Korea	.0193 (37.05)	7.9	.967	.0916	2.34	641-814
Malaysia	.0118 (34.21)	4.8	.966	.0290	0.35	711-814
Pakistan	.00565 (9.55)	2.3	.909	.0338	1.37	731-812
Philippines	.00649 (34.57)	2.6	.930	.0463	1.07	581-802
Thailand	.0103 (70.72)	4.2	.987	.0220	0.11	654-814

Notes: • All equations estimated by OLS.
• t-statistics in absolute value are in parentheses.

prices would be strongly influenced by world prices and some would not. This type of disaggregation is beyond the scope of the present model.

The world price index for each country, $PW\$_i$, is an endogenous variable in the model because it is a function of other countries' export prices, which are endogenous.

4.2.6 The 2,388 Trade Share Equations

The variable to be explained in this section is α_{jit}, the share of country i's total merchandise imports from type A countries imported from country j (in units of 75\$). (The t subscript has been used for the discussion in this section.) Type A countries are countries for which data on exchange rates and on export prices exist. These data, as can be seen in Table B-2, are needed to construct α_{jit}. There are 47 type A countries out of the total of 64. The α_{jit} obey the property that $\Sigma_{j\epsilon A}\alpha_{jit} = 1$, where the summation is over type A countries. The data are quarterly, and t runs from 1971I through 1981IV for a total of 44 observations per ji pair.

One would expect α_{jit} to be a function of country j's export price relative to an index of export prices of all countries that export to country i. The empirical work consisted of trying to estimate the effects of relative prices on trade shares. A separate equation was estimated for each ji pair, which is the following:

$$(4.44) \quad \alpha_{jit} = \beta_{ji1} + \beta_{ji2}D1_t + \beta_{ji3}D2_t + \beta_{ji4}D3_t + \beta_{ji5}\alpha_{jit-1} + \beta_{ji6}\frac{PX\$_{jt}}{\Sigma_{k\epsilon A}\alpha_{kit}PX\$_{kt}} + u_{jit}, \qquad t = 1, \ldots, 44.$$

$D1_t$, $D2_t$, and $D3_t$ are seasonal dummy variables. $PX\$_{jt}$ is the price index of country j's exports, and $\Sigma_{k\epsilon A}\alpha_{kit}PX\$_{kt}$ is an index of all countries' export prices, where the weight for a given country k is the share of country k's exports to country i in the total imports of country i. The notation $k\epsilon A$ means that the summation is only over type A countries.

If equations for all ji pairs had been estimated, there would have been a total of $47 \times 64 = 3{,}008$ estimated equations. In fact, only 2,388 equations were estimated. Data did not exist for all pairs and all quarters, and if fewer than 21 observations were available for a given pair, the equation was not estimated for that pair. In a few cases observations were excluded from a particular regression because they were extreme; these observations were primarily at the beginning and end of the sample period. It seemed likely in these cases that measurement error was a serious problem, and this was the

TABLE 4-14. Summary results for the 2388 trade share equations

	Percentage of correct and incorrect signs for $\hat{\beta}_{ji6}$	
	All countries	Countries 1-15
Correct sign	72.0	75.3
Correct sign, $t \geq 2.0$	21.9	28.2
Correct sign, $t \geq 1.0$	46.2	53.4
Incorrect sign	28.0	24.7
Incorrect sign, $t \geq 2.0$	3.0	2.3
Incorrect sign, $t \geq 1.0$	10.2	9.2

	Average size of the coefficient estimates that were of the right sign			
			Weighted[a]	
	All countries	Countries 1-15	All countries	Countries 1-15
$\hat{\beta}_{ji6}$	-.0232	-.0100	-.0740	-.0604
$\hat{\beta}_{ji6}/(1 - \hat{\beta}_{ji5})$	-.0587	-.0316	-.2184	-.1818

Note: a. Weight for each ji estimate is $\bar{\alpha}_{ji}$/SUM, where $\bar{\alpha}_{ji} = \frac{1}{T}\Sigma_{t=1}^{T}\alpha_{jit}$ and SUM is the sum of $\bar{\alpha}_{ji}$ over all ji pairs. T is the number of observations in the estimated equation for the particular ji pair.

reason for excluding the observations. The extreme observations were chosen from an examination of the plot of each dependent variable over its potential sample period. About 300 equations had one or more observations excluded by this procedure. Almost all these equations were for *ji* pairs where neither *j* nor *i* was an industrialized country.

I wrote a special computer program to estimate the 2,388 equations, since the use of a package program for this purpose would have been unwieldy. The total time to estimate the equations on an IBM 4341 was about 1.5 minutes.

It is not practical to present all 2,388 estimates of each coefficient, and therefore only a summary of the estimates is given. This summary is presented in Table 4-14. The main coefficient of interest is β_{ji6}, the coefficient of the relative price variable. The significance of the estimate of this coefficient is reported first in the table. Considering all countries, 72.0 percent of the estimates were of the correct sign; 21.9 percent were of the correct sign and had *t*-statistics greater than or equal to 2.0; and 46.2 percent were of the correct sign and had *t*-statistics greater than or equal to 1.0. These numbers are somewhat higher for the first 15 countries alone, which are the main countries in the model. Considering all countries, 3.0 percent were of the incorrect sign and had *t*-statistics greater than or equal to 2.0, and 10.2

percent were of the incorrect sign and had t-statistics greater than or equal to 1.0. These numbers are lower for the first 15 countries.

These results seem to provide some support for the hypothesis that relative prices affect trade shares. The estimates are not very precise, which is at least partly explained by the fairly small number of observations per estimated equation. One would hope for more precise estimates in the future as more observations become available.

Results on the average size of the coefficient estimates are presented in the second half of Table 4-14. For these results only the estimates with the correct sign are used. Both weighted and unweighted estimates are reported in the table. The weights are the means of the LHS variable in the estimated equations, normalized to add to 1.0. The term $\hat{\beta}_{ji6}/(1 - \hat{\beta}_{ji5})$ is the estimated long-run effect of relative prices on trade shares. $\hat{\beta}_{ji5}$ is the coefficient estimate of the lagged dependent variable. The short-run estimates vary from $-.0100$ to $-.0740$, depending on the weighting, and the long-run estimates vary from $-.0316$ to $-.2184$.

The trade share equations with the wrong sign for $\hat{\beta}_{ji6}$ were not used in the solution of the model. Instead, the equations were reestimated with the relative price variable omitted, and these new equations were used. This means that α_{jit} is simply determined by a first-order autoregressive equation if $\hat{\beta}_{ji6}$ is of the wrong sign for the particular ji pair.

It should also be noted regarding the solution of the model that the predicted values of α_{jit}, say, $\hat{\alpha}_{jit}$, do not obey the property that $\Sigma_{j \epsilon A} \hat{\alpha}_{jit} = 1$. Unless this property is obeyed, the sum of total world exports will not equal the sum of total world imports. For solution purposes each $\hat{\alpha}_{jit}$ was divided by $\Sigma_{j \epsilon A} \hat{\alpha}_{jit}$, and this adjusted figure was used as the predicted trade share. In other words, the values predicted by (4.44) were adjusted to satisfy the requirement that the trade shares sum to one. The overall solution of the MC model is discussed in Section 7.5.2.

5 Other Econometric Models

5.1 An Autoregressive Model

5.1.1. The United States Model (ARUS)

An easy model to work with for comparison purposes is one in which each endogenous variable is simply a function of its own lagged values. This model, which will be called an autoregressive model, consists of a set of completely unrelated equations. For the U.S. data I have used a lag length of 8 and have added a constant term and a time trend to the equation. Ten equations were estimated, one each for real GNP (*GNPR*), the GNP deflator (*GNPD*), the unemployment rate (*UR*), the bill rate (*RS*), the money supply (*M*1), the wage rate (W_f), profits (π_f), the savings rate (*SR*), the savings of the federal government (S_g), and the savings of the foreign sector (S_r).

The estimated equations are presented in Table 5-1. The first lag provides most of the explanatory power in these equations, which is typically the case with macro time series data. All the lags of length 1 are significant. Of the other lags, five of length 2 are significant (out of ten), one of length 3, two of length 4, two of length 5, one of length 6, two of length 7, and three of length 8. Five of the coefficient estimates of the time trend are significant.

5.1.2 The Multicountry Model (ARMC)

An autoregressive model was also estimated for the variables in the multicountry model. Each of the variables that appears on the LHS of a stochastic equation in the regular model was regressed on a constant, a time trend, three seasonal dummy variables, and the first four lagged values. The same estimation periods were used for these equations as were used for the equations in the regular model. Equations were not estimated for variables explained by definitions in the regular model. The accuracy of the MC and ARMC models is compared in Section 8.6.

TABLE 5-1. Estimated equations for the ARUS model

Explanatory variables	GNPR	GNPD	UR	RS	M1	W_f	π_f	SR	S_g	S_r
constant	47.5	-.00568	.00171	.0560	.916	-.0000122	.189	.0142	1.06	-.497
	(3.23)	(2.09)	(1.25)	(0.37)	(1.03)	(1.25)	(0.42)	(2.48)	(1.42)	(2.13)
t	.798	.0000406	.0000226	.0131	.0465	.000000298	.0274	.00000571	-.0255	.00470
	(2.90)	(1.42)	(2.15)	(2.85)	(2.13)	(1.45)	(2.06)	(0.29)	(1.79)	(1.54)
Lags:										
-1	1.213	1.542	1.640	1.274	.694	1.113	.901	.645	.945	.614
	(12.92)	(16.83)	(18.22)	(13.61)	(7.28)	(11.77)	(10.75)	(6.98)	(9.35)	(6.01)
-2	-.180	-.394	-.795	-.892	.463	.025	.091	.278	.097	.252
	(1.22)	(2.37)	(4.53)	(5.82)	(4.02)	(0.17)	(0.80)	(2.55)	(0.72)	(1.87)
-3	-.154	.128	.064	1.052	.127	-.037	-.150	-.052	-.132	-.164
	(1.02)	(0.75)	(0.33)	(6.05)	(1.04)	(0.26)	(1.20)	(0.46)	(0.98)	(1.29)
-4	.048	-.337	-.152	-.909	-.125	-.111	.361	-.122	.007	.019
	(0.32)	(1.89)	(0.76)	(4.42)	(1.02)	(0.78)	(2.82)	(1.07)	(0.05)	(0.15)
-5	-.011	-.146	.303	.823	-.208	.100	-.286	.033	-.163	-.178
	(0.07)	(0.81)	(1.47)	(3.69)	(1.64)	(0.69)	(2.27)	(0.29)	(1.16)	(1.40)
-6	.076	.107	-.009	-.733	.197	-.082	.141	.015	.188	.193
	(0.48)	(0.58)	(0.04)	(3.53)	(1.53)	(0.55)	(1.07)	(0.14)	(1.33)	(1.49)
-7	-.056	.104	-.217	.242	.211	.094	.424	-.170	-.038	.329
	(0.35)	(0.56)	(1.18)	(1.29)	(1.57)	(0.61)	(3.03)	(1.59)	(0.27)	(2.34)
-8	-.029	.004	.111	-.031	-.372	-.095	-.572	.166	.031	-.567
	(0.29)	(0.04)	(1.20)	(0.27)	(3.25)	(0.85)	(5.35)	(1.82)	(0.28)	(5.25)
SE	10.6	.00397	.00296	.703	2.44	.0000241	2.04	.00682	3.03	1.06
R^2	.999	.999	.958	.951	.999	.999	.981	.624	.845	.633
DW	1.98	1.99	1.97	2.01	1.85	1.94	1.80	2.04	1.90	1.88

Notes:
- Sample period is 1954 II - 1982 III (114 observations).
- Estimation technique is OLS.
- t-statistics in absolute value are in parentheses.

5.2 Two Vector Autoregressive Models (VAR1US and VAR2US)

Vector autoregressive models are also useful for comparison purposes, and two have been considered here. Both consist of five equations, explaining respectively the log of real GNP (log *GNPR*), the log of the GNP deflator (log *GNPD*), the unemployment rate (*UR*), the bill rate (*RS*), and the log of the money supply (log *M*1). For the first model the explanatory variables in each equation consist of a constant, a time trend, and the first six lagged values of each of the five variables, for a total of 32 coefficients to estimate per equation. For the second model the explanatory variables in each equation consist of a constant, a time trend, the first six lagged values of the own variable, and the first two lagged values of each of the other four variables, for a total of 16 coefficients to estimate per equation. For the second model each equation has a different set of RHS variables.

TABLE 5-2. Summary statistics for the VAR1US and VAR2US models

LHS variable	SE	R^2	DW	SE[a]
VAR1US model:				
log GNPR	.00731	.9993	2.02	.00861
log GNPD	.00270	.9999	1.82	.00318
UR	.00238	.9730	1.98	.00280
RS	.544	.9709	1.98	.640
log M1	.00661	.9997	2.06	.00778
VAR2US model:				
log GNPR	.00804	.9992	1.95	.00867
log GNPD	.00310	.9999	1.79	.00334
UR	.00271	.9649	2.07	.00292
RS	.616	.9626	2.01	.664
log M1	.00790	.9996	2.01	.00851

Notes: a. Adjusted for degrees of freedom.
• Sample period is 1954 I - 1982 III (115 observations).
• Estimation technique is OLS.

The summary statistics for the two models are presented in Table 5-2. The SE's for VAR1US are only slightly lower than the SE's for VAR2US, and thus little explanatory power has been lost by excluding lags 3 through 6 of the variables other than the own variable. VAR2US has the advantage that many fewer coefficients are estimated per equation, and thus the degrees of freedom problem is considerably reduced. Vector autoregressive models in general have the problem of rapidly decreasing degrees of freedom as the number of variables is increased, and one way of dealing with this problem is to exclude all but the first two or so lags of the non-own variables in each equation. As just seen, little explanatory power is lost by following this approach. Another way of dealing with the degrees of freedom problem, which has not been pursued here, is to impose various constraints on the coefficients, either within or across equations.

5.3 A Twelve-Equation Linear Model (LINUS)

The twelve-equation linear model has eight stochastic equations and four identities. With respect to the use of economic theory in the model, it is somewhere between the US model and the autoregressive models; there is some theory behind the specifications, but it is very crude. The model is of interest in providing another basis of comparison for the US model. By comparing it to the US model, one can get an idea of how much gain there is (if any) in going from a simple theory to a more sophisticated one. It is also of interest to see how a model like this compares to the autoregressive models.

The equations are as follows.

1. $$CS = -.447 + .989\ CS_{-1} + .00945\ GNPR - .111\ RS$$
$$\qquad (3.05) \quad (106.37) \qquad (3.24) \qquad (8.19)$$
[consumption of services]

$$SE = .260,\ R^2 = .999,\ DW = 2.13,\ \hat{\rho} = -.229\ (2.58)$$

2. $$CN = 2.69 + .800\ CN_{-1} + .0439\ GNPR - .0772\ RS_{-1}$$
$$\qquad (2.54) \quad (11.09) \qquad (3.05) \qquad (2.03)$$
[consumption of nondurables]

$$SE = .493,\ R^2 = .999,\ DW = 1.94,\ \hat{\rho} = .206\ (2.03)$$

3. $$CD = -2.45 + .760\ CD_{-1} + .0369\ GNPR - .210\ RM_{-1}$$
$$\qquad (3.83) \quad (13.34) \qquad (4.83) \qquad (4.29)$$
[consumption of durables]

$$SE = .768,\ R^2 = .993,\ DW = 2.01$$

4. $$IH_h = 1.97 + .505\ IH_{h-1} + .0259\ GNPR - .442\ RM_{-1}$$
$$\qquad (1.98) \quad (4.17) \qquad (4.37) \qquad (4.75)$$
[housing investment, h]

$$SE = .395,\ R^2 = .975,\ DW = 1.96,\ \hat{\rho} = .816\ (9.10)$$

5. $$Y = 9.93 + .177\ Y_{-1} + .972\ X - .166\ V_{-1}$$
$$\qquad (4.35) \quad (3.64) \qquad (17.20) \qquad (4.32)$$
[production]

$$SE = 1.16,\ R^2 = .999,\ DW = 2.19,\ \hat{\rho} = .535\ (5.82)$$

6. $$IK_f = -1.21 + .822\ IK_{f-1}\ .00760\ KK_{-1} + .0592\ Y$$
$$\qquad (4.53) \quad (17.14) \qquad (4.21) \qquad (2.88)$$
$$- .0200\ Y_{-1}$$
$$(0.79)$$
[investment, f]

$$SE = .424,\ R^2 = .996,\ DW = 1.90$$

7. $$RM = \underset{(3.20)}{.329} + \underset{(28.60)}{.842}\ RM_{-1} + \underset{(7.32)}{.276}\ RS - \underset{(1.31)}{.066}\ RS_{-1} - \underset{(0.72)}{.025}\ RS_{-2}$$ [mortgage rate]

$SE = .261,\ R^2 = .992,\ DW = 2.11$

8. $$RS = \underset{(0.89)}{-.310} + \underset{(14.24)}{.852}\ RS_{-1} + \underset{(1.55)}{.0557}\ GNPR - \underset{(1.41)}{.0527}\ GNPR_{-1} + \underset{(1.76)}{.0387}\ \dot{M1}_{-1} + \underset{(3.92)}{.132}\ DD793 \cdot \dot{M1}_{-1}$$ [bill rate]

$SE = .732,\ R^2 = .947,\ DW = 1.71$

9. $X = CS + CN + CD + IH_h + IK_f + Q_1$ [total sales]

10. $V = V_{-1} + Y - X$ [stock of inventories]

11. $GNPR = Y + Q_2$ [real GNP]

12. $KK = (1 - \delta_K)KK_{-1} + IK_f$ [capital stock]

Equations 1–4 are expenditure equations of the household sector. Each expenditure item is a function of its lagged value, real GNP, and either the short-term or the long-term interest rate. These equations differ from the expenditure equations in the US model in including real GNP and in excluding the price level, the wage rate, the initial value of assets, nonlabor income, and the labor constraint variable. The equations are also not in per-capita terms, and the housing investment equation does not include the lagged stock of housing. The GNP variable in these equations may capture some of the effects of the wage rate and the labor constraint variable in the US model. As discussed in Section 4.1.4, in periods of loose labor markets, when the labor constraint variable is not zero, the wage rate and the labor constraint variable are highly correlated with income.

The production equation, Eq. 5, is the same as Eq. 11 in the US model except for the exclusion here of the strike dummy variables. The investment equation, Eq. 6, is a simplified version of Eq. 12 in the US model. Investment is a function of its lagged value, the lagged value of the capital stock, and current and lagged output. No consideration is given here to the treatment of excess capital, which played an important role in the US model.

Equation 7 is a term structure equation explaining the mortgage rate. It is the same as Eq. 24 in the US model. The coefficient estimates in the two equations differ slightly as a result of the use of different sets of first-stage regressors in the estimation of the equations. Equation 8 explains the short-term interest rate, and it can be interpreted as an interest rate reaction function. It is a simplified version of Eq. 30 in the US model.

Equation 9 defines final sales, X. The variable Q_1, which is taken to be exogenous, is the difference in the data between X and $CS + CN + CS + IH_h + IK_f$. In other words, Q_1 is simply defined to make the definition hold. Equation 10 defines the stock of inventories; it is the same as Eq. 63 in the US model. Equation 11 relates production, Y, to real GNP. Again, the variable Q_2, which is taken to be exogenous, is simply the difference in the data between real GNP and Y. Equation 12 defines the capital stock; it is the same as Eq. 92 in the US model. The depreciation rate δ_K is taken to be exogenous.

The exogenous variables in the model other than Q_1, Q_2, and δ_K are $\dot{M1}_{-1}$ and $DD793 \cdot \dot{M1}_{-1}$. These last two variables, the percentage change in the money supply lagged one quarter and the same variable for the period 1979III and beyond, appear only in the interest rate reaction function.

The equations were estimated by 2SLS for the 1954I–1982III period. Equations 1, 2, 4, and 5 were estimated under the assumption of first-order serial correlation of the error term. The same set of first-stage regressors was used for each equation. The variables in this set in alphabetical order are as follows: constant term, CD_{-1}, CD_{-2}, CN_{-1}, CN_{-2}, CS_{-1}, CS_{-2}, $DD793 \cdot \dot{M1}_{-1}$, $DD793_{-1} \cdot \dot{M1}_{-2}$, $GNPR_{-1}$, $GNPR_{-2}$, IH_{h-1}, IH_{h-2}, IK_{f-1}, IK_{f-2}, KK_{-1}, KK_{-2}, $\dot{M1}_{-1}$, $\dot{M1}_{-2}$, Q_1, Q_2, RM_{-1}, RM_{-2}, RS_{-1}, RS_{-2}, RS_{-3}, V_{-1}, V_{-2}, Y_{-1}, Y_{-2}.

5.4 Sargent's Classical Macroeconomic Model (SARUS)

Sargent's (1976) model is an econometric version of the class of rational expectations models that was discussed in Section 3.1.7. It is an interesting model to consider both because it is the main empirical model of this class and because it incorporates the assumption of rational expectations. The assumption of rational expectations imposes difficult econometric problems, and Sargent's model is good for illustrating the estimation and solution methods presented in Chapter 11.

The model as Sargent estimated it is presented in Table 5-3. Sargent made two econometric mistakes in estimating this model: the first was to include variables in the regression to obtain $E_{t-1}P_t$ and in the first-stage regressions of the 2SLS technique that are not in the model; the second was to fail to note

TABLE 5-3. Sargent's model as originally estimated

Equation number	LHS variable	RHS variables
(1)	Un_t	$1, t, p_t - E_{t-1}p_t, Un_{t-i}$ $(i = 1, \ldots, 4)$
(2)	nf_t	$1, t, p_t - E_{t-1}p_t, Un_t, nf_{t-i}$ $(i = 1, \ldots, 4)$
(3)	y_t	$1, t, n_t, n_{t-i}$ $(i = 1, \ldots, 4)$; filter: $(1 - .6L)^2$
(4)	R_t	$1, t, R_{t-i}$ $(i = 1, \ldots, 4)$
(5c)	$m_t - p_t$	$1, t, R_t, R_{t-i}$ $(i = 1, \ldots, 7)$, y_t, y_{t-i} $(i = 1, \ldots, 7)$; filter: $(1 - .8L)^2$
(6)	n_t	$nf_t - Un_t + pop_t$

Notes:

- $E_{t-1}p_t$ was obtained from a regression of p_t on 1, t, three seasonal dummies, p_{t-i} $(i = 1, \ldots, 4)$, w_{t-i} $(i = 1, \ldots, 4)$, nf_{t-i} $(i = 1, \ldots, 4)$, and Un_{t-i} $(i = 1, \ldots, 4)$.
- The equations were estimated by 2SLS. The explanatory variables used in the first-stage regressions were those variables listed in the above note plus pop_t, m_t, the log of government purchases of goods and services in real terms, government surplus in real terms, and the log of current government employment. The RHS endogenous variables in the structural equations are p_t in equation (1), p_t and Un_t in equation (2), n_t in equation (3), and R_t and y_t in equation (5c).
- The filter $(1 - .6L)^2$ means that each variable z_t in the equation was transformed into $z_t^* = z_t - 1.2z_{t-1} + .36z_{t-2}$ before estimation. For the filter $(1 - .8L)^2$, the transformation is $z_t^* = z_t - 1.6z_{t-1} + .64z_{t-2}$.
- Variables:
  - Un_t = unemployment rate
  - nf_t = log of labor force participation rate
  - y_t = log of real GNP
  - R_t = long-term interest rate (Moody's Baa rate)
  - m_t = log of the money supply
  - p_t = log of the GNP deflator
  - pop_t = log of population
  - n_t = log of employment (approximately)
  - w_t = log of an index of a straight-time manufacturing wage.

that Eq. (5c) is not identified unless one assumes that the error terms in Eqs. (4) and (5c) are uncorrelated. If this assumption is made, then R_t can be treated as predetermined in the estimation of Eq. (5c). Sargent did not treat R_t as predetermined, and he should not have been able to estimate Eq. (5c) by 2SLS. The reason he did not encounter any difficulties is that he used more variables in the first-stage regression for R_t than he should have.

One way of dealing with these mistakes would be to expand the model to

TABLE 5-4. Sargent's model as estimated in this book

i) In place of using the filters, equations (3) and (5c) were estimated under the assumption of first- and second-order serial correlation of the error terms.

ii) The error term in equation (4) was assumed to be uncorrelated with the other error terms in the model, and R_t was taken to be predetermined in the estimation of equation (5c).

iii) There are two exogenous variables in the model, m_t and pop_t. Each of these was regressed on 1, t, and its first eight lagged values, and predicted values, $\hat{m}_t$ and $\widehat{pop}_t$, from these two regressions were taken to be the expected values.

iv) The model was estimated using the method in Chapter 11.

v) Data:

Name in Table 5-3:	Variable(s) in the US model:
Un_t	UR
nf_t	$\log[(L1 + L2 + L3 - J_m)/(POP - J_m)]$
y_t	log GNPR
R_t	RB
m_t	log M1
p_t	log GNPD
pop_t	$\log(POP - J_m)$

include more variables. For those who are interested in this kind of model, this would be interesting work. For present purposes, however, I have not chosen to expand the model; I have instead concentrated on obtaining estimates under the assumption that the model as presented in Table 5-3 is correctly specified.

The model as I have estimated it is presented in Table 5-4. The changes are as follows. (1) The variables that Sargent used in the first-stage regressions that are not in the model were excluded from consideration. (2) The error term in Eq. (4) was assumed to be uncorrelated with the other error terms in the model, and R_t was taken to be predetermined in the estimation of Eq. (5c). (3) In place of using the filters for Eqs. (3) and (5c), the equations were estimated under the assumption of first-order and second-order serial correlation of the error terms. Sargent's use of the filters is equivalent to constraining the first-order and second-order serial correlation coefficients to particular numbers, and thus the approach followed here is less restrictive. (4) The expected values of the two exogenous variables in the model, m_t and pop_t, were taken to be the predicted values from two eighth-order autoregressive equations. (5) Finally, the model was estimated by the method described in Chapter 11. This method, full information maximum likelihood, takes account of all the nonlinear restrictions that are implied by the rational expectations assumption.

It is not convenient to discuss the coefficient estimates of Sargent's model until the method in Chapter 11 has been described, and therefore the estimates will be presented and explained in Chapter 11.

6 Estimation

6.1 Introduction

Macroeconometric models are typically nonlinear, simultaneous, and large. They also tend to have error terms that are serially correlated. The focus of this chapter is on models with these characteristics. The notation that will be used in this chapter and in Chapters 7–10 is as follows. Write the model as

$$(6.1) \qquad f_i(y_t, x_t, \alpha_i) = u_{it}, \qquad i = 1, \ldots, n, \qquad t = 1, \ldots, T,$$

where y_t is an n-dimensional vector of endogenous variables, x_t is a vector of predetermined variables, α_i is a vector of unknown coefficients, and u_{it} is an error term. Assume that the first m equations are stochastic, with the remaining u_{it} $(i = m + 1, \ldots, n)$ identically zero for all t.

Let J_t be the $n \times n$ Jacobian matrix whose ij element is $\partial f_i / \partial y_{jt}$ $(i, j = 1, \ldots, n)$. Also, let u_i be the T-dimensional vector $(u_{i1}, \ldots, u_{iT})'$, and let u be the $m \cdot T$-dimensional vector $(u_{11}, \ldots, u_{1T}, \ldots, u_{m1}, \ldots, u_{mT})'$. Let α denote the k-dimensional vector $(\alpha_1', \ldots, \alpha_m')$ of all the unknown coefficients. Finally, let G_i' be the $k_i \times T$ matrix whose tth column is $\partial f_i(y_t, x_t, \alpha_i)/\partial \alpha_i$, where k_i is the dimension of α_i, and let G' be the $k \times m \cdot T$ matrix,

$$\begin{bmatrix} G_1' & 0 & \cdots & 0 \\ 0 & G_2' & & \\ \vdots & & \ddots & \\ 0 & & & G_m' \end{bmatrix}$$

where $k = \Sigma_{i=1}^{m} k_i$. These vectors and matrices will be used in the following sections.

6.2 Treatment of Serial Correlation

A convenient way of dealing with serially correlated error terms is to treat the serial correlation coefficients as structural coefficients and to transform the equations into equations with serially uncorrelated error terms. This introduces nonlinear restrictions on the coefficients, but otherwise the equations are like any others with serially uncorrelated errors. It will be useful to consider this transformation first because once it has been done, little more needs to be said about serial correlation. Consider the ith equation of (6.1), and assume that u_{it} is first-order serially correlated:

$$(6.2) \qquad u_{it} = \rho_i u_{it-1} + \epsilon_{it}, \qquad t = 2, \ldots, T,$$

where ϵ_{it} is not serially correlated. Lagging (6.1) one period, multiplying through by ρ_i, and subtracting the resulting expression from (6.1) yields

$$(6.3) \qquad f_i(y_t, x_t, \alpha_i) - \rho_i f_i(y_{t-1}, x_{t-1}, \alpha_i) = u_{it} - \rho_i u_{it-1} = \epsilon_{it}, \qquad t = 2, \ldots, T,$$

or

$$(6.4) \qquad f_i^*(y_t, x_t^*, \alpha_i^*) = \epsilon_{it}, \qquad t = 2, \ldots, T,$$

where x_t^* includes the variables in x_t, x_{t-1}, and y_{t-1}, and α_i^* includes both α_i and ρ_i. Equation (6.4) is no more general than (6.1), and thus one can deal directly with (6.1) under the assumption that serial correlation has been eliminated through transformation.

This procedure results in the "loss" of the first observation. This has no effect on the asymptotic properties of the estimators, and it is probably not a problem about which one needs to be concerned in practice. In many cases there are ways of using the first observation more efficiently, but at a considerable cost in complexity relative to the approach just presented.

This procedure can handle serial correlation of higher orders. If, for example, u_{it} is second-order serially correlated:

$$(6.2)' \qquad u_{it} = \rho_{1i} u_{it-1} + \rho_{2i} u_{it-2} + \epsilon_{it}, \qquad t = 3, \ldots, T,$$

the transformation in (6.3) is:

$$(6.3)' \qquad f_i(y_t, x_t, \alpha_i) - \rho_{1i} f_i(y_{t-1}, x_{t-1}, \alpha_i) - \rho_{2i} f_i(y_{t-2}, x_{t-2}, \alpha_i) = \epsilon_{it}, \qquad t = 3, \ldots, T.$$

In this case x_t^* in (6.4) includes the variables in x_t, x_{t-1}, x_{t-2}, y_{t-1}, and y_{t-2}, and α_i^* includes α_i, ρ_{1i}, and ρ_{2i}. Each additional order of the serial correlation process results in the "loss" of one more observation.

With respect to testing for serial correlation, it is well known that the Durbin-Watson (DW) test is biased toward accepting the null hypothesis of no serial correlation if there is a lagged dependent variable in the equation.

Since many equations in macroeconometric models have lagged dependent variables, the DW test is of limited use. My response to this problem is to estimate the equations initially under the assumption of serial correlation (usually first-order) by some consistent technique (usually 2SLS). From this, one can test the hypothesis that the serial correlation coefficients are zero, which is simply a t-test on each coefficient. This test is valid asymptotically if one has correctly estimated the asymptotic covariance matrix of the estimated coefficients, and it is not restricted to equations without lagged dependent variables. It also easily handles serial correlation of higher than first order, since all this requires is estimating the equation under the assumption of the particular order. If a test indicates that a serial correlation coefficient is zero, the equation can be reestimated without this coefficient being included.

Although this is the general procedure that I follow in handling serial correlation problems, I still include the DW statistic in the presentation of the results for a particular equation (see Chapter 4). Since the DW statistic is biased toward acceptance of the hypothesis of no serial correlation when there are lagged dependent variables, a value that rejects the hypothesis indicates that there are likely to be problems. The DW test is thus useful for testing in one direction, and this is the reason I tend to include it in the results.

6.3 Estimation Techniques

6.3.1 Ordinary Least Squares (OLS)

The OLS technique is a special case of the 2SLS technique, where D_i in (6.5) and (6.6) below is the identity matrix. It is thus unnecessary to consider this technique separately from the 2SLS technique.

6.3.2 Two-Stage Least Squares (2SLS)

General Case

2SLS estimates of α_i (say $\hat{\alpha}_i$) are obtained by minimizing

$$u_i'Z_i(Z_i'Z_i)^{-1}Z_i'u_i = u_i'D_iu_i \tag{6.5}$$

with respect to α_i, where Z_i is a $T \times K_i$ matrix of predetermined variables. Z_i and K_i can differ from equation to equation. An estimate of the covariance matrix of $\hat{\alpha}_i$ (say $\hat{V}_{2ii}$) is

$$\hat{V}_{2ii} = \hat{\sigma}_{ii}(\hat{G}_i'D_i\hat{G}_i)^{-1}, \tag{6.6}$$

where $\hat{G}_i$ is G_i evaluated at $\hat{\alpha}_i$ and $\hat{\sigma}_{ii} = T^{-1}\ \Sigma_{t=1}^{T}\ \hat{u}_{it}^2$, $\hat{u}_{it} = f_i(y_t, x_t, \hat{\alpha}_i)$.

The 2SLS estimator in this form is presented in Amemiya (1974). It handles the case of nonlinearity in both variables and coefficients. In earlier work, Kelejian (1971) considered the case of nonlinearity in variables only. Bierens (1981, p. 106) has pointed out that Amemiya's proof of consistency of this estimator is valid only in the case of linearity in the coefficients, that is, only in Kelejian's case. Bierens supplies a proof of consistency and asymptotic normality in the general case.

Linear-in-Coefficients Case

It will be useful to consider the special case in which the equation to be estimated is linear in coefficients. Write equation i in this case as

$$(6.7) \qquad y_i = X_i \alpha_i + u_i,$$

where y_i is the T-dimensional vector $(y_{i1}, \ldots, y_{iT})'$ and X_i is a $T \times k_i$ matrix of observations on the explanatory variables in the equation. X_i includes both endogenous and predetermined variables. Both y_i and the variables in X_i can be nonlinear functions of other variables, and thus (6.7) is much more general than the standard linear model. All that is required is that the equation be linear in α_i. Substituting $u_i = y_i - X_i \alpha_i$ into (6.5), differentiating with respect to α_i, and setting the derivatives equal to zero yields the following formula for $\hat{\alpha}_i$:

$$(6.8) \qquad \hat{\alpha}_i = (X_i' D_i X_i)^{-1} X_i' D_i y_i = (\hat{X}_i' X_i)^{-1} \hat{X}_i' y_i,$$

where $\hat{X}_i = D_i X_i$ is the matrix of predicted values of the regression of X_i on Z_i. Since $D_i' = D_i$ and $D_i D_i = D_i$, $\hat{X}_i' \hat{X}_i = X_i' D_i D_i X_i = X_i' D_i X_i = \hat{X}_i' X_i$, and thus (6.8) can be written

$$(6.9) \qquad \hat{\alpha}_i = (\hat{X}_i' \hat{X}_i)^{-1} \hat{X}_i' y_i,$$

which is the standard 2SLS formula in the linear-in-coefficients case. In this case G_i' is simply X_i', and the formula (6.6) for $\hat{V}_{2ii}$ reduces to

$$(6.10) \qquad \hat{V}_{2ii} = \hat{\sigma}_{ii} (\hat{X}_i' \hat{X}_i)^{-1}.$$

Linear-in-Coefficients Case with Serial Correlation

It will also be useful to consider the linear-in-coefficients case with serially correlated errors. Assume that u_i in (6.7) is first-order serially correlated:

$$(6.11) \qquad u_i = u_{i-1} \rho_i + \epsilon_i.$$

Transforming (6.7) in the manner discussed above yields

(6.12) $$y_i - y_{i-1}\rho_i = (X_i - X_{i-1}\rho_i)\alpha_i + \epsilon_i.$$

Minimizing $\epsilon_i' D_i \epsilon_i$ with respect to α_i and ρ_i results in the following first-order conditions:

(6.13) $$\hat{\alpha}_i = [\widehat{(X_i - X_{i-1}\hat{\rho}_i)}'(X_i - X_{i-1}\hat{\rho}_i)]^{-1}\widehat{(X_i - X_{i-1}\hat{\rho}_i)}'(y_i - y_{i-1}\hat{\rho}_i),$$

(6.14) $$\hat{\rho}_i = \frac{(\hat{y}_{i-1} - \hat{X}_{i-1}\hat{\alpha}_i)'(y_i - X_i\hat{\alpha}_i)}{(\hat{y}_{i-1} - \hat{X}_{i-1}\hat{\alpha}_i)'(y_{i-1} - X_{i-1}\hat{\alpha}_i)},$$

where $\widehat{X_i - X_{i-1}\hat{\rho}_i} = D_i(X_i - X_{i-1}\hat{\rho}_i)$, $\hat{y}_{i-1} = D_i y_{i-1}$, and $\hat{X}_{i-1} = D_i X_{i-1}$. If X_{i-1} is included in Z_i, then $\hat{X}_{i-1} = X_{i-1}$ (since $\hat{X}_{i-1}$ is merely the predicted values from a regression of X_{i-1} on itself and other variables), and therefore $\widehat{X_i - X_{i-1}\hat{\rho}_i} = \hat{X}_i - X_{i-1}\hat{\rho}_i$. If in addition y_{i-1} is included in Z_i, then $\hat{y}_{i-1} = y_{i-1}$, and (6.14) becomes

(6.14)′ $$\hat{\rho}_i = \frac{\hat{u}_{i-1}'\hat{u}_i}{\hat{u}_{i-1}'\hat{u}_{i-1}},$$

where $\hat{u}_{i-1} = y_{i-1} - X_{i-1}\hat{\alpha}_i$ and $\hat{u}_i = y_i - X_i\hat{\alpha}_i$. This is merely the formula for the coefficient estimate of the regression of $\hat{u}_i$ on $\hat{u}_{i-1}$.

Equations (6.13) and (6.14) can easily be solved iteratively. Given an initial guess for $\hat{\rho}_i$, $\hat{\alpha}_i$ can be computed from (6.13), and then given $\hat{\alpha}_i$, $\hat{\rho}_i$ can be computed from (6.14). Given this new value of $\hat{\rho}_i$, a new value of $\hat{\alpha}_i$ can be computed from (6.13), and so on. If convergence is reached, which means that the values of $\hat{\alpha}_i$ and $\hat{\rho}_i$ on successive iterations are within some prescribed tolerance level, the first-order conditions have been solved.

Equations with RHS endogenous variables and serially correlated errors (that is, Eqs. 6.7 and 6.11) occur frequently in practice, and the 2SLS estimator for this case has been widely used. This estimator was discussed in Fair (1970), and I programmed it into the TSP regression package in 1968 under the name TSCORC. ("CORC" refers to the fact that the iterative procedure used to solve Eqs. 6.13 and 6.14 is like the Cochrane-Orcutt [1949] iterative procedure in the nonsimultaneous equations case.) There is an important difference between (6.13) and the formula for $\hat{\alpha}_i$ proposed in Fair (1970), and given the widespread use of the TSCORC command, this difference should be noted. Let $X_i = (Y_i\ X_{2i})$, where Y_i is the matrix of RHS endogenous variables in (6.7) and X_{2i} is the matrix of predetermined variables. Let $\hat{Y}_i = D_i Y_i$ and $\hat{\hat{X}}_i = (\hat{Y}_i\ X_{2i})$. The formula proposed for $\hat{\alpha}_i$ was

(6.13)′ $$\hat{\alpha}_i = [(\hat{\hat{X}}_i - X_{i-1}\hat{\rho}_i)'(\hat{\hat{X}}_i - X_{i-1}\hat{\rho}_i)]^{-1}(\hat{\hat{X}}_i - X_{i-1}\hat{\rho}_i)'(y_i - y_{i-1}\hat{\rho}_i).$$

This is the formula for the coefficient estimates of the regression of $y_i - y_{i-1}\hat{\rho}_i$ on $\hat{X}_i - X_{i-1}\hat{\rho}_i$. Equation (6.13) reduces to (6.13)′ when X_{2i} and $X_{i-1} = (Y_{i-1} \;\; X_{2i-1})$ are included in Z_i, that is, when the exogenous, lagged endogenous, and lagged exogenous variables in the equation being estimated are included among the first-stage regressors. The inclusion of X_{2i} means that $\hat{\hat{X}}_i = \hat{X}_i$, and, as noted earlier, the inclusion of X_{i-1} means that $\widehat{X_i - X_{i-1}\hat{\rho}_i} = \hat{X}_i - X_{i-1}\hat{\rho}_i$. The proposed formula for $\hat{\rho}_i$ was (6.14)′, which, as noted above, is the same as (6.14) only if X_{i-1} and y_{i-1} are included in Z_i. Solving (6.13)′ and (6.14)′ is thus not the same as solving (6.13) and (6.14) unless X_{2i}, X_{i-1}, and y_{i-1} are included in Z_i. It can be shown that if this is not done, solving (6.13)′ and (6.14)′ does not result in consistent estimates. The need to include X_{2i}, X_{i-1}, and y_{i-1} among the first-stage regressors was stressed in Fair (1970), but one should keep in mind that this is not absolutely necessary if the formulas (6.13) and (6.14) are used. In general, however, X_{2i}, X_{i-1}, and y_{i-1} are obvious variables to include among the first-stage regressors, and for most problems this should probably be done even if one is using a program that solves (6.13) and (6.14) rather than (6.13)′ and (6.14)′.

In the case of linearity in the coefficients and first-order serial correlation, $G_i = (X_i - X_{i-1}\rho_i \;\; y_{i-1} - X_{i-1}\alpha_i)$, and the formula (6.6) for $\hat{V}_{2ii}$ can be written

$$(6.15) \quad \hat{V}_{2ii} = \hat{\sigma}_{ii}\begin{bmatrix} (\hat{X}_i - \hat{X}_{i-1}\hat{\rho}_i)'(\hat{X}_i - \hat{X}_{i-1}\hat{\rho}_i) & (\hat{X}_i - \hat{X}_{i-1}\hat{\rho}_i)'(\hat{y}_{i-1} - \hat{X}_{i-1}\hat{\rho}_i) \\ (\hat{y}_{i-1} - \hat{X}_{i-1}\hat{\alpha}_i)'(\hat{X}_i - \hat{X}_{i-1}\hat{\rho}_i) & (\hat{y}_{i-1} - \hat{X}_{i-1}\hat{\alpha}_i)'(\hat{y}_{i-1} - \hat{X}_{i-1}\hat{\alpha}_i) \end{bmatrix}^{-1}.$$

If X_{2i}, X_{i-1}, and y_{i-1} are included in Z_i, then (6.15) becomes

$$(6.15)' \quad \hat{V}_{2ii} = \hat{\sigma}_{ii}\begin{bmatrix} (\hat{\hat{X}}_i - X_{i-1}\hat{\rho}_i)'(\hat{\hat{X}}_i - X_{i-1}\hat{\rho}_i) & (\hat{\hat{X}}_i - X_{i-1}\hat{\rho}_i)'\hat{u}_{i-1} \\ \hat{u}'_{i-1}(\hat{\hat{X}}_i - X_{i-1}\hat{\rho}_i) & \hat{u}'_{i-1}\hat{u}_{i-1} \end{bmatrix}^{-1},$$

where, as above, $\hat{u}_{i-1} = y_{i-1} - X_{i-1}\hat{\alpha}_i$. This is the formula presented in Fair (1970). Remember that $\hat{V}_{2ii}$ in this case is the covariance matrix for $(\hat{\alpha}_i \;\; \hat{\rho}_i)$, not $\hat{\alpha}_i$ alone. It was suggested in Fair (1970, p. 514) that the off-diagonal terms in (6.15)′ be ignored (that is, set to zero) when computing $\hat{V}_{2ii}$, and this was initially done for the TSCORC option in TSP. This is not, however, a good idea, as Fisher, Cootner, and Baily (1972, p. 575, n. 6) first pointed out. The saving in computational costs from ignoring the off-diagonal terms is small, and in general one should not ignore the correlation between $\hat{\alpha}_i$ and $\hat{\rho}_i$ in computing $\hat{V}_{2ii}$. In later versions of TSP the TSCORC option was changed to compute $\hat{V}_{2ii}$ according to (6.15)′, but many copies were distributed before this change was made.

The generalization of the preceding discussion to higher-order serial correlation is straightforward, and this will not be done here except to make one point. As the order of the serial correlation increases, the number of variables that must be included among the first-stage regressors to ensure consistent estimates increases if the higher-order equivalents of (6.13)′ and (6.14)′ are used. In going from first to second, for example, the new variables that must be included are X_{i-2} and y_{i-2}. At some point it may not be sensible, given the number of observations, to include all these variables, in which case the higher-order equivalents of (6.13) and (6.14) should be used for the estimates.

Restrictions on the Coefficients

In the general nonlinear case in which (6.5) is minimized using an algorithm like DFP, restrictions on the coefficients are easy to handle. Minimization is merely over the set of unrestricted coefficients. For each set of unrestricted coefficients tried by the algorithm, the restricted coefficients are first calculated and then the objective function (6.5) is computed. Except for calculating the restricted coefficients given the unrestricted ones, no extra work is involved in accounting for the restrictions.

In the case in which the restrictions are linear and the model is otherwise only nonlinear in variables, an alternative procedure is available for handling the restrictions. To see this, assume that a restriction is

$$(6.16) \qquad R\alpha_i = r,$$

where R is $1 \times k_i$, α_i is $k_i \times 1$, and r is a scalar. R and r are assumed to be known. Let α_{1i} denote the first element of α_i, and assume without loss of generality that the first element of R is nonzero. Given this assumption, (6.16) can be solved for α_{1i}:

$$(6.17) \qquad \alpha_{1i} = R^*\alpha_i^* + r^*,$$

where R^* is $1 \times k_i - 1$ and α_i^* is $k_i - 1 \times 1$. The vector α_i^* excludes α_{1i}.

Given (6.17), (6.7) can be written

$$(6.18) \qquad y_i = X_{1i}\alpha_{1i} + X_{2i}\alpha_i^* + u_i = X_{1i}(R^*\alpha_i^* + r^*) + X_{2i}\alpha_i^* + u_i$$

or

(6.19) $y_i^* = X_i^* \alpha_i^* + u_i$,

where $y_i^* = y_i - X_{1i} r^*$ and $X_i^* = X_{1i} R^* + X_{2i}$. The vector X_{1i} is a $T \times 1$ vector of observations on the variable corresponding to α_{1i}, and X_{2i} is a $T \times k_i - 1$ matrix of observations on the other explanatory variables. Given that R^* and r^* are known, y_i^* and X_i^* are known, and therefore (6.19) can be estimated in the usual way. The original equation has been transformed into one that is linear in the unrestricted coefficients. The extra work in this case is merely to create the transformed variables.

The coefficient restriction in the US model that is represented by (4.20) is a linear restriction on the coefficients of the wage equation (γ_1, γ_2, and γ_3) if the coefficients of the price equation (β_1 and β_2) are given. For all the limited information estimation techniques (that is, all the techniques except 3SLS and FIML), the variables in the wage equation were transformed into an equation like (6.19) before estimation. This required that the price equation be estimated first to get the estimates of β_1 and β_2 to be used in the transformation. This procedure was not followed for the 3SLS and FIML estimates, since the restriction (4.20) is not linear within the context of all the equations of the model.

Choice of First-Stage Regressors

Before estimating an equation by 2SLS, the first-stage regressors (FSRs) must be chosen. Since analytic expressions for the reduced form equations are not available for most nonlinear models, they cannot be used to guide the choice of FSRs. One must choose, given knowledge of the model, FSRs that seem likely to be important explanatory variables in the (unknown) reduced form equations for the RHS endogenous variables in the equation being estimated.

There is considerable judgment involved in the choice of FSRs for a particular equation, and there are only a few rules of thumb that can be given. Consider estimating an equation with y_{2t} and y_{3t} as RHS endogenous variables. Assume that the structural equations that determine y_{2t} and y_{3t} have y_{4t} and y_{5t} as RHS endogenous variables. One obvious choice of FSRs is to use predetermined variables that are in the structural equations that explain y_{2t} and y_{3t}. Another choice is predetermined variables that are in the structural equations that explain y_{4t} and y_{5t}. One can continue this procedure through further layers as desired. (This rule of thumb is discussed in Fisher 1965.)

A rule of thumb about functional forms is to use mostly logarithms of variables if the RHS endogenous variables are in logarithms and to use mostly linear variables if the RHS endogenous variables are linear. Sometimes squares and cubes of variables are used, and sometimes variables multiplied by each other are used. There is no requirement that the same set of FSRs be used for different equations (although the same set must be used for all the RHS endogenous variables in a particular equation), and thus one may want to use different sets across equations, each set depending on the particular RHS endogenous variables in the equation.

The predetermined variables in the equation being estimated should also be included among the FSRs. Not doing so means treating these variables as endogenous. There is, however, an exception to this in the linear-in-coefficients case, which should be explained to avoid possible confusion. Consider (6.7) and let $X_i = (Y_i \quad X_{2i})$, where Y_i is the matrix of RHS endogenous variables and X_{2i} is the matrix of predetermined variables. If $\hat{X}_i$ is defined to be $(\hat{Y}_i \quad X_{2i})$, where $\hat{Y}_i = D_i Y_i$, rather than $D_i X_i$, and if formula (6.8) is used to compute $\hat{\alpha}_i$, then X_{2i} is treated as exogenous even if it is not included in Z_i. Equation (6.8) is the instrumental variables formula for $\hat{\alpha}_i$, and when $(\hat{Y}_i \quad X_{2i})$ is used for $\hat{X}_i$, X_{2i} is serving as its own instrument. When $(\hat{Y}_i \quad X_{2i})$ is used for $\hat{X}_i$, and X_{2i} is not included in X_i, (6.8) and (6.9) are not the same, and (6.9) does not produce consistent estimates. (See McCarthy 1971.) Equations (6.8) and (6.9) are the same only if X_{2i} is included in Z_i.

Covariance Matrix of All the Estimated Coefficients

Some of the stochastic simulation work in Chapters 7, 8, and 9 requires the covariance matrix of all the coefficients estimates, that is, the $k \times k$ covariance matrix of $\hat{\alpha}$, where $\hat{\alpha} = (\hat{\alpha}_1', \ldots, \hat{\alpha}_m')'$. For the completely linear case (linear in both variables and coefficients), this covariance matrix is presented in Theil (1971, pp. 499–500) for the case in which the same set of FSRs is used for each equation. For the more general case of a nonlinear model and a different set of FSRs for each equation, it is straightforward to show that the covariance matrix (say V_2) is

$$V_2 = \begin{bmatrix} V_{211} & \cdots & V_{21m} \\ \vdots & & \vdots \\ V_{2m1} & \cdots & V_{2mm} \end{bmatrix}, \tag{6.20}$$

where

$$(6.21)\qquad V_{2ii} = \sigma_{ii}\left[\operatorname{plim}\frac{1}{T}G_i'D_iG_i\right]^{-1},$$

$$(6.22)\qquad V_{2ij} = \sigma_{ij}\left[\operatorname{plim}\frac{1}{T}G_i'D_iG_i\right]^{-1}\left[\operatorname{plim}\frac{1}{T}G_i'D_iD_jG_j\right]\left[\operatorname{plim}\frac{1}{T}G_j'D_jG_j\right]^{-1}.$$

An estimate of V_{2ii} is $\hat{V}_{2ii}$ in (6.6). An estimate of V_{2ij} (say $\hat{V}_{2ij}$) is

$$(6.23)\qquad \hat{V}_{2ij} = \hat{\sigma}_{ij}(\hat{G}_i'D_i\hat{G}_i)^{-1}(\hat{G}_i'D_iD_j\hat{G}_j)(\hat{G}_j'D_j\hat{G}_j)^{-1},$$

where $\hat{\sigma}_{ij} = T^{-1}\sum_{t=1}^{T}\hat{u}_{it}\hat{u}_{jt}$.

Regarding the proof that V_2 in (6.20) is the correct covariance matrix, the derivation in Theil can easily be modified to incorporate the case of different sets of FSRs. Nonlinearity can be handled as in Amemiya (1974, appendix 1), that is, by a Taylor expansion of each equation. The formal proof that V_2 is as in (6.20), (6.21), and (6.22) is straightforward but lengthy, and it is omitted here. Jorgenson and Laffont (1974, p. 363) incorrectly assert that the off-diagonal blocks of V_2 are zero.

6.3.3 Three-Stage Least Squares (3SLS)

3SLS estimates of α (say $\hat{\alpha}$) are obtained by minimizing

$$(6.24)\qquad u'\,[\hat{\Sigma}^{-1}\otimes Z(Z'Z)^{-1}Z']u = u'Du$$

with respect to α, where $\hat{\Sigma}$ is a consistent estimate of Σ and Z is a $T\times K$ matrix of predetermined variables. An estimate of the covariance matrix of $\hat{\alpha}$ (say $\hat{V}_3$) is

$$(6.25)\qquad \hat{V}_3 = (\hat{G}'D\hat{G})^{-1},$$

where $\hat{G}$ is G evaluated at $\hat{\alpha}$. Σ is usually estimated from the 2SLS estimated residuals. This estimator is presented in Jorgenson and Laffont (1974), and it is further discussed in Amemiya (1977). Both prove consistency and asymptotic normality of 3SLS.

The 3SLS estimator that is based on minimizing (6.24) uses the same Z matrix for each equation. In small samples this can be a disadvantage of 3SLS relative to 2SLS. It is possible to modify (6.24) to include the case of different

Z_i matrices for each equation, and although this modification is not in general practical for large models, it is of some interest to consider. This estimator is the one that minimizes

$$(6.26)\qquad u'\left[\begin{pmatrix} Z_1 & \cdots & 0 \\ \vdots & & \vdots \\ 0 & \cdots & Z_m \end{pmatrix} \begin{pmatrix} \hat{\sigma}_{11}Z_1'Z_1 & \cdots & \hat{\sigma}_{1m}Z_1'Z_m \\ \vdots & & \vdots \\ \hat{\sigma}_{m1}Z_m'Z_1 & \cdots & \hat{\sigma}_{mm}Z_m'Z_m \end{pmatrix}^{-1} \begin{pmatrix} Z_1' & \cdots & 0 \\ \vdots & & \vdots \\ 0 & \cdots & Z_m' \end{pmatrix}\right] u = u'\overline{D}u$$

with respect to α. An estimate of the covariance matrix of this estimator is $(\hat{G}'\overline{D}\hat{G})^{-1}$. (6.26) reduces to (6.24) when $Z_1 = \ldots = Z_m = Z$. The computational problem with this estimator is that it requires inverting the middle matrix in brackets. This matrix is of dimension $K^* = \Sigma_{i=1}^{m} K_i$, which is generally a large number. For small to moderate models, however, it may be feasible to invert this matrix. This estimator has the advantage of being the natural full-information extension of 2SLS when different sets of FSRs are used. This estimator is a special case of one of the 3SLS estimators in Amemiya (1977, p. 963), namely the estimator determined by his equation (5.4), where his S_2 is the first matrix in brackets in (6.26) above.

Choice of First-Stage Regressors

If the estimator that minimizes (6.26) is used, a different set of FSRs can be used for each equation, and the same considerations apply here as apply for the 2SLS estimator. If the estimator that minimizes (6.24) is used, the same set of FSRs must be used for all equations. This set should be roughly equal to the union of the sets that are used (or that would be used) for the 2SLS estimator. The actual set used may have to be smaller than the union if the union contains more variables than seem sensible given the number of observations. Also, some nonlinear functions of the basic variables may be highly collinear (say, x_{1t}, $\log x_{1t}$, and x_{1t}^2), and one or more of these may be able to be excluded without much loss of explanatory power in the first-stage regressions.

6.3.4 Full Information Maximum Likelihood (FIML)

Under the assumption that $(u_{1t}, \ldots, u_{mt})$ is independently and identically distributed as multivariate $N(0,S)$, the density function for one observation is

$$(6.27) \qquad (2\pi)^{-\frac{m}{2}}|S^*|^{\frac{1}{2}}|J_t|\exp\left(-\frac{1}{2}\sum_{i,j} u_{it}s^*_{ij}u_{jt}\right),$$

where $S^* = S^{-1}$ and s^*_{ij} is the ij element of S^*. The Jacobian J_t is defined in Section 6.1. The likelihood function of the sample $t = 1, \ldots, T$ is

$$(6.28) \qquad L^* = (2\pi)^{-\frac{mT}{2}}|S^*|^{\frac{T}{2}}\prod_{t=1}^{T}|J_t|\exp\left(-\frac{1}{2}\sum_{i,j,t} u_{it}s^*_{ij}u_{jt}\right),$$

and the log of L^* is

$$(6.29) \qquad \log L^* = -\frac{mT}{2}\log 2\pi + \frac{T}{2}\log|S^*| + \sum_{t=1}^{T}\log|J_t| - \frac{1}{2}\sum_{i,j,t} u_{it}s^*_{ij}u_{jt}.$$

Since $\log L^*$ is a monotonic function of L^*, maximizing $\log L^*$ is equivalent to maximizing L^*.

The problem of maximizing $\log L^*$ can be broken up into two parts: the first is to maximize $\log L^*$ with respect to the elements of S^*, and the second is to substitute the resulting expression for S^* into (6.29) and to maximize this "concentrated" likelihood function with respect to α. The derivative of $\log L^*$ with respect to s^*_{ij} is

$$(6.30) \qquad \frac{\partial \log L^*}{\partial s^*_{ij}} = \frac{T}{2}s^{*ij} - \frac{1}{2}\sum_{t=1}^{T} u_{it}u_{jt},$$

where s^{*ij} is the ij element of S^{*-1}. This derivative uses the fact that $\dfrac{\partial \log|A|}{\partial a_{ij}} = a^{ij}$ for a matrix A. Setting (6.30) equal to zero and solving for s^{*ij} yields

$$(6.31) \qquad s^{*ij} = \frac{1}{T}\sum_{t=1}^{T} u_{it}u_{jt}.$$

Since $S^* = S^{-1}$, $s^{*ij} = s_{ij}$, and therefore $s_{ij} = \frac{1}{T}\sum_{t=1}^{T} u_{it}u_{jt}$. Substituting (6.31) into (6.29) yields

$$\text{(6.32)} \qquad \log L^* = -\frac{mT}{2}\log 2\pi + \frac{T}{2}\log|S^*| + \sum_{t=1}^{T}\log|J_t| - \frac{Tm}{2}.$$

The $-\frac{Tm}{2}$ term comes from the fact that $-\frac{1}{2}\sum_{i,j,t} u_{it}s^*_{ij}u_{jt} = -\frac{1}{2}\sum_{i,j} s^*_{ij}\sum_{t=1}^{T} u_{it}u_{jt} = -\frac{1}{2}\sum_{i,j} s^*_{ij}Ts^{*ij} = -\frac{Tm}{2}$. The first and last terms on the RHS of (6.32) are constants, and thus the expression to be maximized with respect to α consists of just the middle two terms. Since $\log|S^*| = \log|S^{-1}| = -\log|S|$, the function to be maximized can be written

$$\text{(6.33)} \qquad L = -\frac{T}{2}\log|S| + \sum_{t=1}^{T}\log|J_t|,$$

where, as noted earlier, the ij element of S, s_{ij}, is $\frac{1}{T}\sum_{t=1}^{T} u_{it}u_{jt}$. FIML estimates of α are thus obtained by maximizing L with respect to α. An estimate of the covariance matrix of these estimates (say $\hat{V}_4$) is

$$\text{(6.34)} \qquad \hat{V}_4 = -\left(\frac{\partial^2 L}{\partial\alpha\partial\alpha'}\right)^{-1},$$

where the derivatives are evaluated at the optimum.

Phillips (1982) has pointed out that Amemiya's proof of consistency and asymptotic efficiency (1977) is based on an incorrect lemma. This is corrected in a later paper (Amemiya 1982). Amemiya's article (1977), as corrected, shows that in the nonlinear case FIML is asymptotically more efficient than 3SLS under the assumption of normality. In the linear case FIML is consistent even if the error terms are not normally distributed, where "FIML" means the full information maximum likelihood estimator derived under the assumption of normality. In the nonlinear case this is not in general true, although it sometimes is. Phillips (1982) presents an example of a nonlinear model for which FIML is consistent for a wide class of error distributions. He also proves a "possibility" theorem, which shows that when FIML is consistent under normality it is always possible to find a nonnormal error distribution for which consistency is maintained. The assumption of normality is not necessary for the consistency of 3SLS. Given that 3SLS is consistent under a broader class of error distributions than is FIML, it is in this sense a more robust estimator. There is thus a trade-off between more robustness for 3SLS and more efficiency for FIML if the error terms are normal.

In the linear case Hausman (1975) has shown that FIML can be interpreted as an instrumental variables estimator in which all the nonlinear restrictions on the reduced form coefficients are taken into account in forming the instruments. This is contrary to the case for 3SLS, which forms the instruments from unrestricted estimates of the reduced form equations. FIML thus uses more information about the model than does 3SLS. In the linear case this makes no difference asymptotically because both estimates of the reduced form coefficient matrix are consistent (assuming that 3SLS uses all the explanatory variables in the reduced form equations as first-stage regressors). In the nonlinear case, however, it does make a difference because 3SLS does not obtain consistent estimates of the reduced form equations. In general, analytic expressions for the reduced form equations are not available, and 3SLS must be based on approximations to the equations. No such approximations are involved for FIML, and this is the reason it is asymptotically more efficient.

Another interesting difference between FIML and 3SLS concerns the LHS variable in each equation. Chow (1964) has shown in the linear case that FIML is the natural generalization of least squares in the sense that it minimizes the generalized variance of linear combinations of the endogenous variables. This is not true of 3SLS, which follows the principle of generalized variance but not of linear combinations. What Chow's interpretation shows is that there is no natural LHS variable for FIML: because of the linear combination aspect, each variable in the equation is treated equally. For 3SLS, on the other hand, a LHS variable must be chosen ahead of time for each equation.

For macroeconometric work it is unclear whether the symmetrical treatment of the endogenous variables by FIML is desirable or not. If the equations that are estimated are decision equations, as is the case for the model in Chapter 4, there is a natural LHS variable for each equation. FIML ignores this restriction, whereas 3SLS does not, so this may be an argument in favor of 3SLS. Given this difference and given the fact that 3SLS is more robust to specification errors regarding the distribution of the error terms, the question of which estimator is likely to be better in practice is far from clear.

6.3.5 Least Absolute Deviations (LAD)

LAD estimates of α_i (say $\hat{\alpha}_i$) are obtained by minimizing

$$(6.35) \qquad \sum_{t=1}^{T} |u_{it}|$$

with respect to α_i. For the general nonlinear model the asymptotic distribution of $\hat{\alpha}_i$ is not known. For the standard regression model $y_i = X_i\alpha_i + u_i$, where X_i is a matrix of exogenous variables and u_{it} is independent and identically distributed with distribution function F, Bassett and Koenker (1978) have shown that the asymptotic distribution of $\hat{\alpha}_i$ is normal with mean α_i (thus $\hat{\alpha}_i$ is consistent) and covariance matrix $\omega^2 Q$, where $Q = \lim \frac{1}{T} X_i' X_i$ and ω^2 is the asymptotic variance of the sample median from random samples with distribution F. Amemiya (1982) supplies an alternative proof of this proposition.

The LAD estimator is an example of a robust estimator. An estimator is said to be more robust than another if its properties are less sensitive to changes in the assumptions about the model, particularly assumptions about the distribution of the error terms. In a number of cases the LAD estimator has been shown to be more robust that the OLS estimator to deviations of the error terms from normality. In particular, the LAD estimator seems well suited to cases in which the distribution of the error terms is fat-tailed.

The literature in statistics on robust estimation is now quite extensive, and there are many types of robust estimators. The estimators differ primarily in how error terms that are large in absolute value (that is, outliers) are weighted. These estimators have not been used very much in applied econometric work, so there is little experience to guide the choice of estimator. Since LAD is the simplest of the estimators, it seems to be the best one to start with. An interesting open question is how useful any of the robust estimators are for empirical work in economics.

6.3.6 Two-Stage Least Absolute Deviations (2SLAD)

There are two ways of interpreting the 2SLS estimator that is based on the minimization of (6.5), and these need to be discussed before considering the LAD analogue of 2SLS. For purposes of the discussion in this section and in Section 6.5.4, it will be assumed that the model (6.1) can be written

$$(6.1)' \qquad y_{it} = h_i(y_t, x_t, \alpha_i) + u_{it}, \qquad i = 1, \ldots, n, \qquad t = 1, \ldots, T,$$

where in the ith equation y_{it} appears only on the LHS. Given this and given that $D_i' = D_i$ and $D_iD_i = D_i$, (6.5) can be written

$$(6.36)\qquad \begin{aligned} u_i'D_iu_i &= u_i'D_iD_iu_i \\ &= (y_i' - h_i')D_iD_i(y_i - h_i) \\ &= (y_i'D_i - h_i'D_i)(D_iy_i - D_ih_i) \\ &= (\hat{y}_i' - \hat{h}_i')(\hat{y}_i - \hat{h}_i) \\ &= \hat{y}_i'\hat{y}_i - 2\hat{y}_i'\hat{h}_i + \hat{h}_i'\hat{h}_i, \end{aligned}$$

where $\hat{y}_i = D_iy_i$ and $\hat{h}_i = D_ih_i$. Instead of minimizing (6.36), consider minimizing

$$(6.37)\qquad (y_i' - \hat{h}_i')(y_i - \hat{h}_i) = y_i'y_i - 2y_i'\hat{h}_i + \hat{h}_i'\hat{h}_i.$$

Given that $\hat{y}_i'\hat{h}_i = y_i'D_iD_ih_i = y_i'D_ih_i = y_i'\hat{h}_i$ and given that $\hat{y}_i'\hat{y}_i$ and $y_i'y_i$ are not a function of α_i, minimizing (6.36) with respect to α_i is equivalent to minimizing (6.37). Therefore, the 2SLS estimator can be interpreted as minimizing either $(\hat{y}_i' - \hat{h}_i')(\hat{y}_i - \hat{h}_i)$ or $(y_i' - \hat{h}_i')(y_i - \hat{h}_i)$. The first interpretation is Basmann's (1957) and the second is Theil's (1953).

For the LAD analogue it is unclear which interpretation should be used. Using Basmann's one would minimize

$$(6.38)\qquad \sum_{t=1}^{T} |\hat{y}_{it} - \hat{h}_{it}|,$$

and using Theil's one would minimize

$$(6.39)\qquad \sum_{t=1}^{T} |y_{it} - \hat{h}_{it}|.$$

In this case the choice matters in that minimizing (6.38) and minimizing (6.39) lead to different estimates. Amemiya (1982) has proposed minimizing

$$(6.40)\qquad \sum_{t=1}^{T} |qy_{it} + (1-q)\hat{y}_{it} - \hat{h}_{it}|,$$

where q is chosen ahead of time by the investigator. The estimator that is based on minimizing (6.40) will be called 2SLAD.

For the general nonlinear model the asymptotic distribution of 2SLAD is not known. For the linear model Amemiya (1982) has proved that 2SLAD is consistent. He has also in the linear case derived formulas for the asymptotic covariance matrix of the estimator for particular assumptions about the distributions of the error terms. If all the distributions are normal, he has proved that 2SLAD is asymptotically normal.

6.4 Sample Size Requirements for FIML and the Estimation of Subsets of Coefficients

6.4.1 Sample Size Requirements

For large models there may not be enough observations to estimate all the coefficients by FIML. For a linear model without identities, Sargan (1975) has shown that the FIML likelihood function has an infinite maximum if the number of observations is less than the number of endogenous and exogenous variables. With respect to more general models, Parke (1982b) has derived the FIML sample size requirement for models with identities, nonlinearity in variables, and serial correlation coefficients. It will be useful to consider Parke's main results.

Consider first the case of no identities and no serial correlation coefficients. If the model is only nonlinear in variables, it can be written

$$QA = U, \tag{6.41}$$

where Q is a $T \times q$ matrix of variables that are functions of the basic endogenous and exogenous variables, A is a $q \times m$ matrix of coefficients, and U is a $T \times m$ matrix of error terms. In general the variables in Q are nonlinear functions of the basic endogenous and exogenous variables, although many of them may simply be the basic variables. The total number of variables in the model is q. Under the assumption that each of these variables appears at least once in the model with a nonzero coefficient (a trivial assumption), Parke has shown that the sample size requirement for FIML is $T \geq q$.

Adding identities does not in general change this requirement. One need not include in Q variables that appear in identities but not in the structural equations when one is calculating the sample size requirement. When the identity is what Parke calls a "closed" identity, one that imposes a linear dependency on the columns of Q, the sample size requirement is less. For i closed identities the dependencies can be written

$$QP = 0, \tag{6.42}$$

where P is a $q \times i$ matrix of known coefficients. For i closed identities the sample size requirement is $T \geq q - i$.

An example of a model with a closed identity is the following:

$$Q_{1t} = \alpha_{11} + \alpha_{12}Q_{3t} + \alpha_{13}Q_{4t} + u_{1t}, \tag{6.43}$$

$$Q_{2t} = \alpha_{21} + \alpha_{22}Q_{3t} + \alpha_{23}Q_{5t} + u_{2t}, \tag{6.44}$$

$$Q_{3t} = Q_{1t} + Q_{2t}. \tag{6.45}$$

In this case Q_{3t} could be substituted out of the stochastic equations (6.43) and (6.44) without introducing any new variables, and therefore it is not a variable that needs to be counted against the sample size requirement. Identities of this type are likely to be rare. (There are, for example, no closed identities in the model in Chapter 4.) A much more common identity in the model just presented would be $Q_{3t} = Q_{1t} + Q_{2t} + Q_{6t}$, where Q_{6t} does not appear in the stochastic equations. In this case the identity is "open," and Q_{3t} does count against the sample size requirement.

The treatment of serial correlation is somewhat more involved. Assume that x_{jt} appears in equation i, where equation i has first-order serially correlated errors. After the equation is transformed, the variable appears as $x_{jt}^* = x_{jt} - \rho_i x_{jt-1}$. If x_{jt} and x_{jt-1} appear nowhere else in the model, x_{jt}^* can be counted as only one variable. Otherwise, both x_{jt} and x_{jt-1} must be counted. Even if x_{jt} appears in many equations with first-order serially correlated errors (and in general different serial correlation coefficients), the number of variables to be counted is still only two (x_{jt} and x_{jt-1}). What this says is that the introduction of first-order serial correlation to an equation at most increases the number of variables to be counted by the number of original variables in the equation. The increase is less than this if at least some of the original variables and their one-period-lagged values do not appear elsewhere in the model. If none of the original variables and their lagged values appear elsewhere in the model, the introduction of serial correlation to an equation does not increase the number of variables to be counted. Similar arguments apply to higher-order serial correlation. For example, the introduction of second-order serial correlation at most increases the number of variables to be counted by twice the number of original variables in the equation.

The introduction of a constraint across coefficients does not in general reduce the sample size requirement. If it does, it is sometimes possible to write the model with fewer variables after the constraint is imposed. Brown (1981) shows that this is always the case for a linear constraint across the coefficients in a single equation. As a general rule of thumb, if it is not obvious that a constraint can be used to write the model with fewer variables, it should be assumed that the constraint does not reduce the sample size requirement.

6.4.2 Estimation of Subsets of Coefficients

It is possible to reduce the sample size requirement of FIML by fixing some coefficients at, say, their 2SLS values (or some other consistently estimated values) and estimating the remaining coefficients by FIML. One can fix either all the coefficients in a given equation or only some of them. If all the coefficients are fixed, the equation is still taken to be part of the estimation problem in the sense that the covariance matrix S in (6.33) is still $m \times m$, but none of the coefficients in the equation are estimated by FIML.

Consider the problem by estimating the free coefficients by FIML, and write the relevant subset of the model as

$$(6.46) \qquad Q_1 A_1 = U_1,$$

where Q_1 is $T \times q_1$, A_1 is $q_1 \times m_1$, and U_1 is $T \times m_1$. The matrix A_1 is the matrix of free coefficients, and m_1 is the number of equations in which at least one coefficient is free. q_1, as will be seen, is the number of variables that count for purposes of calculating the sample size requirement. Its determination requires some explanation. Assume that x_{jt} and x_{kt} appear in equation i and that their coefficients (α_{i1} and α_{i2}) are fixed. Assume that $\log y_{it}$ is the LHS variable. This equation can be rewritten with $\log y_{it} - \hat{\alpha}_{i1}x_{jt} - \hat{\alpha}_{i2}x_{kt}$ on the LHS and x_{jt} and x_{kt} eliminated from the RHS. ($\hat{\alpha}_{i1}$ and $\hat{\alpha}_{i2}$ are the consistent estimates of α_{i1} and α_{i2}.) If $\log y_{it}$, x_{jt}, and x_{kt} do not appear elsewhere in the model, this fixing of the coefficients has eliminated two variables. If $\log y_{it}$ does appear elsewhere but x_{jt} and x_{kt} do not, only one variable has been eliminated because the new LHS variable and $\log y_{it}$ count as separate variables. If x_{jt} and x_{kt} appear elsewhere, no variables are eliminated. If all the coefficients in an equation are fixed, a variable in the equation is eliminated if it appears nowhere else in the model. q_1 is the number of variables that remain after all possible eliminations.

Parke has shown that the sample size requirement for this reduced problem is $T \geq q_1 + m_2 - i_1$, where $m_2 = m - m_1$ is the number of equations for which none of the coefficients are estimated and i_1 is the number of closed identities that pertain to the reduced set of equations (that is, the set of equations not counting the m_2 equations for which no coefficients are estimated). Note that one observation is needed for each of the m_2 equations that are not estimated.

Given this result, if the sample size requirement is not met for the complete model, the problem can be reduced by fixing various coefficients until it is met. An example of this procedure is presented in Section 6.5.2.

It should finally be noted that because of computational costs, one may want to restrict the size of the estimation problem even if the sample size requirement is met. The obvious way to do this is to fix some of the coefficients at their 2SLS estimates. This can be done for both the FIML and 3SLS estimators.

When only a subset of the coefficients is estimated by FIML or 3SLS, the easiest thing to do with regard to the estimation of the covariance matrix of all the coefficient estimates is to assume that the coefficient estimates that are fixed with respect to the FIML or 3SLS estimation problem are uncorrelated with the FIML or 3SLS coefficient estimates. This allows the covariance matrix of all the coefficient estimates to be pieced together from the covariance matrix of the fixed estimates and the covariance matrix of the FIML or 3SLS estimates. Since correlation of coefficient estimates across equations is usually small relative to the correlation within an equation, the errors introduced by this procedure are likely to be fairly small in most applications. This is particularly true if the coefficient estimates that are fixed are of lesser importance than the others.

6.5 Computational Procedures and Results

6.5.1 OLS and 2SLS

For equations that are nonlinear in variables only, closed-form expressions exist for the OLS and 2SLS estimators. For 2SLS the expression is (6.9), and for OLS it is (6.9) with X_i replacing $\hat{X}_i$. If the nonlinearity in coefficients is due only to the presence of serially correlated error terms, the estimates can be obtained by solving (6.13) and (6.14) (or Eqs. 6.13′ and 6.14′) or higher-order versions of these iteratively. For general nonlinearities in coefficients, (6.5) must be minimized using some general-purpose algorithm like the DFP algorithm discussed in Section 2.5.

Results for the US Model

The 2SLS estimates of the US model are presented in Chapter 4. The first-stage regressors that were used for these estimates are given in Table 6-1. Two common sets are presented first in Table 6-1, one for equations in which the RHS endogenous variables are primarily linear and one for equations in which the RHS endogenous variables are primarily in logarithms. The additional FSRs that were used for each equation are presented second. These FSRs are primarily variables that appear as explanatory variables in the equation being estimated but that are not part of the common set. The common sets include 34 variables, and the number of additional variables ranges from 0 to 9. The equations that are estimated by OLS have no RHS endogenous variables.

The time taken to estimate the 30 equations by 2SLS was about 3.0 minutes on the IBM 4341 and about 8.4 minutes on the VAX. The estimation of the covariance matrix of all the coefficient estimates, V_2 in (6.20), took about 5.5

TABLE 6-1. First stage regressors for the US model for 2SLS

	Basic sets	
	Linear	Log
1	constant	constant
2	$(AA/POP)_{-1}$	$\log(AA/POP)_{-1}$
3	$C_g + C_s$	$\log(C_g + C_s)$
4	$(CD/POP)_{-1}$	$\log(CD/POP)_{-1}$
5	$(CN/POP)_{-1}$	$\log(CN/POP)_{-1}$
6	$(CS/POP)_{-1}$	$\log(CS/POP)_{-1}$
7	$(1 - d_{1g}^M - d_{1s}^M - d_{4g} - d_{4s})_{-1}$	$\log(1 - d_{1g}^M - d_{1s}^M - d_{4g} - d_{4s})_{-1}$
8	EX	log EX
9	H_{f-1}	$\log H_{f-1}$
10	$(IH_h/POP)_{-1}$	$\log(IH_h/POP)_{-1}$
11	$(IM/POP)_{-1}$	$\log(IM/POP)_{-1}$
12	$(J_f - JHMIN)_{-1}$	$\log(J_f/JHMIN)_{-1}$
13	$(J_gH_g + J_mH_m + J_sH_s)/POP$	$\log[(J_gH_g + J_mH_m + J_sH_s)/POP]$
14	$(KH/POP)_{-1}$	$\log(KH/POP)_{-1}$
15	$(KK - KKMIN)_{-1}$	$\log(KK/KKMIN)_{-1}$
16	$\dot{M1}_{-1}$	$\dot{M1}_{-1}$
17	$\dot{PD}_{-1}$	$\dot{PD}_{-1}$
18	P_{f-1}	$\log P_{f-1}$
19	PIM	log PIM
20	RB_{-1}	RB_{-1}
21	RS_{-1}	RS_{-1}
22	RS_{-2}	RS_{-2}
23	t	t
24	$(TR_{gh} + TR_{sh})/(POP \cdot P_{h-1})$	$\log[(TR_{gh} + TR_{sh})/(POP \cdot P_{h-1})]$
25	V_{-1}	$\log V_{-1}$
26	W_{f-1}	$\log W_{f-1}$
27	Y_{-1}	$\log Y_{-1}$
28	Y_{-2}	$\log Y_{-2}$
29	Y_{-3}	$\log Y_{-3}$
30	Y_{-4}	$\log Y_{-4}$
31	$YN/(POP \cdot P_{h-1})$	$\log[YN/(POP \cdot P_{h-1})]$
32	Z_{-1}	Z_{-1}
33	UR_{-1}	UR_{-1}
34	ZZ_{-1}	ZZ_{-1}

(continued)

TABLE 6-1 (continued)

Equation number	Additional first stage regressors for each equation
1	PCS_{-1}, WA_{-1}
2	PCN_{-1}, WA_{-1}
3	PCD_{-1}, RM_{-1}, WA_{-1}, $[YTR/(POP \cdot P_h)]_{-1}$
4	OLS estimation
5	$(L1/POP1)_{-1}$, P_{h-1}, WA_{-1}
6	$(L2/POP2)_{-1}$, P_{h-1}, WA_{-1}
7	$(L3/POP3)_{-1}$, P_{h-1}, WA_{-1}
8	$(LM/POP)_{-1}$, P_{h-1}, WA_{-1}
9 [a]	$\log[M_h/(POP\ P_h)]_{-1}$, $\log[YT/(POP\ P_h)]_{-1}$
10 [a]	$\log(1 + d_{5g} + d_{5s})$
11	D593, D594, D601, $D601_{-1}$, V_{-2}
12	$\delta_K KK_{-1}$, IK_{f-1}, RBA_{-1}
13 [a]	D593, D594, $D594_{-1}$, $\Delta \log J_{f-1}$, $\log(J_f/JHMIN)_{-2}$
14 [a]	$\log H_{f-2}$, $\log(J_f/JHMIN)_{-2}$
15	OLS estimation
16 [a]	$\log PX_{-1}$
17 [a]	$\log(M_f/PX)_{-1}$, $1 - d_{2g} - d_{2s}$
18	D_{f-1}, $(\pi_f - T_{fg} - T_{fs})_{-1}$, $d_{2g} + d_{2s}$
19	OLS estimation
20	OLS estimation
21	OLS estimation
22	$(BO/BR)_{-1}$, $(RS - RD)_{-1}$
23	no extra
24	RM_{-1}
25	$\Delta(CF - T_{fg} - T_{fs})_{-1}$, CF_{-1}, $d_{2g} + d_{2s}$, $(T_{fg} + T_{fs})_{-1}$
26 [a]	$\log[CUR/(POP \cdot PX)]_{-1}$, $\log(X/POP)_{-1}$
27	PIM_{-1}, PX_{-1}, RMA_{-1}, D651, D652, D691, D692, D714, D721
28 [a]	$\log U_{-1}$, $\log UB_{-1}$
29	OLS estimation
30	$DD793 \cdot \dot{M1}_{-1}$, JJ^*_{-1}

Note: a. Basic set is log.

minutes on the IBM 4341 and about 7.8 minutes on the VAX. The derivatives in the G_i matrices that are needed for the estimation of the covariance matrix were computed numerically.

Eight of the 30 equations were estimated under the assumption of first-order serial correlation of the error terms. The iterative procedure described above was used. The starting value of ρ was always zero, and the number of iterations required for convergence was 10, 7, 11, 4, 13, 6, 4, and 5 respectively. Convergence was defined to take place when successive estimates of ρ were within .001 of each other.

OLS estimation of the 30 equations took about .2 minutes on the IBM 4341 and about .5 minutes on the VAX, which compares to about 3.0 and 8.4 minutes respectively for 2SLS estimation. The number of coefficients estimated in any one equation is small compared to the number estimated in the first-stage regressions, and this is the reason for the considerably larger expense of the 2SLS estimates. The maximum number of coefficients estimated in an equation is 12, whereas the minimum number estimated in a first-stage regression is 34. Nevertheless, the cost of 2SLS estimation is small relative to many other costs reported below.

6.5.2 FIML

Until recently the estimation of large nonlinear models by FIML was not computationally feasible, but this has now changed. The computational problem can be separated into two main parts: the first is to find a fast way of computing L in (6.33) for a given value of α, and the second is to find an algorithm capable of maximizing L.

The main cost of computing L is computing the Jacobian term. Two savings can be made here. One is to exploit the sparseness of the Jacobian. The number of nonzero elements in J_t is usually much less than n^2. For the US model, for example, n is 128 (so $n^2 = 16{,}384$), whereas the number of nonzero elements is only 441. Considerable computer time is saved by using sparse matrix routines to calculate the determinant of J_t.

The second saving is based on an approximation. Consider approximating $\Sigma_{t=1}^{T} \log|J_t|$ by simply the average of the first and last terms in the summation multiplied by T: $\frac{T}{2}(\log|J_1| + \log|J_T|)$. Let S_0 denote the true summation, and let S_1 denote the approximation. It turns out in the applications I have dealt with that $S_0 - S_1$ does not change very much as the coefficients change from their starting values (usually the 2SLS estimates) to the values that maximize the likelihood function. In other words, $S_0 - S_1$ is nearly a constant. This means that S_1 can be used instead of S_0 in computing L, and thus considerable computer time is saved since the determinant of the Jacobian only needs to be computed twice rather than T times for each evaluation of L. For the US model T is 115. Using S_1 in place of S_0 means, of course, that the coefficient values that maximize the likelihood function are not the exact FIML estimates. If one is concerned about the accuracy of the approximation, one can switch from S_1 to S_0 after finding the maximum using S_1. If the approximation is good, one should see little further change in the coefficients; otherwise additional iterations using the algorithm will be needed to find the true maximum.

The choice of algorithm turns out to be crucial in maximizing L for large nonlinear models. My experience is that general-purpose algorithms like DFP do not work, and in fact the only algorithm that does seem to work is the Parke algorithm (1982a), which is a special-purpose algorithm designed for FIML and 3SLS estimation. This algorithm exploits two key features of models. The first is that the mean of a particular equation's estimated residuals is approximately zero for the FIML and 3SLS estimates. For OLS this must be true, and empirically it turns out that it is approximately true for other estimators. The second feature is that the correlation of coefficient estimates within an equation is usually much greater than the correlation of coefficients across equations.

The problem with algorithms like DFP that require numerical first derivatives is that the computed gradients do not appear to be good guides regarding the directions to move in. Gradients are computed by perturbing one coefficient at a time. When a coefficient is changed without the constant term in the equation also being changed to preserve the mean of the residuals, a large change in L results (and thus a large derivative). This result can obviously be quite misleading. The Parke algorithm avoids this problem by spending most of its time perturbing two coefficients at once, namely a given coefficient and the constant term in the equation in which the coefficient appears. The constant term is perturbed to keep the mean of the residuals unchanged. (The algorithm does not, of course, do this all the time, since the means of the residuals must also be estimated). To take advantage of the generally larger correlation within an equation than between equations, the Parke algorithm spends more time searching within equations than between them. General-purpose algorithms do not do this, since they have no knowledge of the structure of the problem.

It should also be noted regarding the computational problem that if only a few coefficients are changed before a new value of L is computed, considerable savings can be made by taking advantage of this fact. If, for example, the coefficients are not in the Jacobian, the Jacobian term does not have to be recomputed. If only a few equations are affected by the change in coefficients, only a few rows and columns in the S matrix have to be recomputed. Since the Parke algorithm spends much of its time perturbing two coefficients at a time, it is particularly suited for these kinds of savings.

The estimated covariance matrix for the FIML coefficient estimates, $\hat{V}_4$ in (6.34), is difficult to compute. It is not part of the output of the Parke algorithm, and thus extra work is involved in computing it once the algorithm has found the optimum. My experience is that simply trying to compute the second derivatives of L numerically does not result in a positive-definite matrix. Although the true second-derivative matrices at the optimum are undoubtedly positive-definite, they seem to be nearly singular. If this is true, small errors in the numerical approximations to the second derivatives may be sufficient to make the matrix not positive-definite.

Fortunately, there is an approach to computing $\hat{V}_4$ that does work, which is derived from Parke (1982a). Parke's results suggest that the inadequate numerical approximations may be due to the fact that the means of the RHS variables in the estimated equations are not zero. If so, the problem can be solved by subtracting the means from the RHS variables before taking numerical derivatives. Let β denote the coefficient vector that pertains to the model after the means have been subtracted, and let α denote the original coefficient vector. The relationship between α and β is

$$\alpha = M \cdot \beta, \tag{6.47}$$

where M is a $k \times k$ square matrix that is composed of the identity matrix plus additional nonzero elements that represent the means adjustments. Unless there are constraints across equations, M is block-diagonal. Assume, for example, that the first equation of the model is

$$y_{1t} = \beta_1 + \beta_2(y_{2t} - m_2) + \beta_3(y_{3t} - m_3) + u_{1t}, \qquad t = 1, \ldots, T, \tag{6.48}$$

where m_2 and m_3 are the sample means of y_{2t} and y_{3t} respectively. This equation can be written

$$\begin{aligned} y_{1t} &= \beta_1 - \beta_2 m_2 - \beta_3 m_3 + \beta_2 y_{2t} + \beta_3 y_{3t} + u_{1t} \\ &= \alpha_1 + \alpha_2 y_{2t} + \alpha_3 y_{3t} + u_{1t}, \qquad t = 1, \ldots, T. \end{aligned} \tag{6.49}$$

In this case the part of (6.47) that corresponds to the first equation is

$$\begin{pmatrix} \alpha_1 \\ \alpha_2 \\ \alpha_3 \end{pmatrix} = \begin{pmatrix} 1 & -m_2 & -m_3 \\ 0 & 1 & 0 \\ 0 & 0 & 1 \end{pmatrix} \begin{pmatrix} \beta_1 \\ \beta_2 \\ \beta_3 \end{pmatrix}. \tag{6.50}$$

Parke found that the covariance matrix of β could easily be computed numerically. Let $\hat{V}_4(\beta)$ denote this matrix:

$$\hat{V}_4(\beta) = -\left[\frac{\partial^2 L(M \cdot \beta)}{\partial\beta\partial\beta'}\right]^{-1}. \tag{6.51}$$

Given $\hat{V}_4(\beta)$, the covariance matrix of α is simply

$$\hat{V}_4 = M \cdot \hat{V}_4(\beta) \cdot M'. \tag{6.52}$$

$\hat{V}_4$ can thus be obtained by first computing the covariance matrix of the coefficients of the transformed model (that is, the model in which the RHS variables have zero means) and then using (6.52) to get the covariance matrix of the original coefficients.

Results for the US Model

The solution of the FIML estimation problem for the US model is reported in Table 6-2. There are 169 unconstrained coefficients in the model; 107 of these were estimated by FIML, with the remaining fixed at their 2SLS estimates. The coefficients that were not estimated by FIML include the dummy variable coefficients in Eqs. 11, 13, and 27 and all the coefficients in Eqs. 5, 6, 7, 8, 15, 18, 19, 20, 21, 25, 28, and 29. These coefficients and equations were judged to be less important than the others, although this is obviously a subjective choice. The sample size requirement for this subset of coefficients is 99. There are 115 observations.

The starting values were the 2SLS estimates. The value of L in (6.34) at these estimates is 5098.66. The change in L after 70 iterations in Table 6-2 is 181.76. On the first iteration the Parke algorithm increased L by 67.07, and on the second and third iterations it increased L by 8.68 and 7.64 respectively. The change after three iterations was thus 83.39, which is 45.9 percent of the total change. This illustrates a general feature of the Parke algorithm: it climbs very quickly for the first few iterations and then slows down considerably for the rest.

TABLE 6-2. Solution of the FIML estimation problem for the US model

L = L in (6.33)
L at start (2SLS estimates) = 5098.66
L after 70 iterations = 5280.42
Total ΔL = 181.76

Iter. no.	ΔL	Iter. no.	ΔL	Iter. no.	ΔL	Iter. no.	ΔL	Iter. no.	ΔL
1	67.07	15	2.23	29	1.60	43	.43	57	.10
2	8.68	16	2.75	30	1.30	44	.31	58 [a]	.08
3	7.64	17	3.21	31	1.05	45	.42	59 [a]	.05
4	4.61	18	3.40	32	1.29	46	.39	60 [a]	.05
5	4.89	19	3.08	33	1.12	47	.30	61 [a]	.06
6	6.84	20	2.58	34	.53	48	.36	62 [a]	.06
7	5.51	21	3.19	35	.47	49	.20	63	.05
8	4.17	22	2.71	36	.70	50	.14	64	.04
9	4.10	23	1.38	37	.57	51	.20	65	.05
10	5.17	24	1.49	38	1.16	52	.23	66	.08
11	5.04	25	2.38	39	.99	53	.10	67	.11
12	2.54	26	1.20	40	.83	54	.20	68	.11
13	3.51	27	1.13	41	.41	55	.10	69	.10
14	3.15	28	1.18	42	.41	56	.10	70 [b]	.06

Notes:

a. 13 Jacobians computed rather than 2. (Computations at observations 1, 10, 19, 28, 37, 46, 55, 64, 73, 82, 91, 100, 115.)

b. Between iterations 69 and 70, 26 coefficients changed by 1.0 percent or more and 4 changed by 5.0 percent or more. The largest 3 changes were 8.1, 12.6, and 18.4 percent.

- Model consists of 169 unconstrained coefficients. 107 coefficients estimated by FIML. Sample period is 1954 I - 1982 III (115 observations).
- Each iteration requires about 462 function evaluations. The time per iteration when 2 Jacobians were computed was about 2.8 minutes on the IBM 4341 and about 7.3 minutes on the VAX. When 13 Jacobians were computed the respective times were 5.4 minutes and 12.3 minutes. The total time on the IBM 4341 for the 70 iterations was thus about 65 × 2.8 minutes + 5 × 5.4 minutes = 3.5 hours.
- The time taken to compute the FIML covariance matrix, $\hat{V}_4$ in (6.34), was about 53 minutes on the IBM 4341 and about 2.1 hours on the VAX.

Between iterations 58 and 62 the number of Jacobians computed to approximate the sum was increased from 2 to 13. When 13 Jacobians were used, the sum was approximated by interpolating between the points. As can be seen in the table, the change in L was little affected by this. If the use of 2 Jacobians in fact provided a poor approximation, it is likely that the Parke algorithm would have increased L by much more than it did on the first few iterations after the switch. That it did not is some evidence in favor of the approximation.

Another way of looking at the 2 versus 13 question is to consider how sensitive the difference in L computed the two ways is to changes in the coefficients. The following results help answer this:

Value of L	*2 Jacobians*	*13 Jacobians*	*Difference*
L at start (2SLS estimates)	5,098.66	5,284.49	−185.83
L after 59 iterations	5,279.53	5,464.04	−184.51
L after 62 iterations	5,279.82	5,464.34	−184.52
L after 70 iterations	5,280.42	5,464.96	−184.54

It is clear that the difference is little affected by the change in the coefficients from the 2SLS estimates to the estimates at the end of iteration 70. It thus seems that the use of 2 Jacobians is adequate. Note that this saves considerable time, since the cost of one iteration of the Parke algorithm increases from about 2.8 minutes to about 5.4 minutes on the IBM 4341 when 13 rather than 2 Jacobians are used.

As discussed earlier, when only one or two coefficients are being changed by the algorithm, many of the calculations involved in computing L do not have to be performed. In the present example, if these cost savings had not been used, the time taken for one iteration of the Parke algorithm would have increased by about a factor of 4.5, which is a considerable difference. As will be seen in the next section, this difference is even more pronounced in the 3SLS estimation problem.

It is a characteristic of the estimation problem that the likelihood function is fairly flat in the vicinity of the optimum. For example, the change in L on iteration 70 was only .06, and yet, as reported in note b in the table, 26 coefficients changed by 1.0 percent or more and 4 changed by 5.0 percent or more. The largest three changes were 8.1, 12.6, and 18.4 percent. The coefficients that change this much are obviously not significant, and they are not coefficients that are very important in the model. Nevertheless, these results do point out one of the reasons the FIML estimation problem is so hard to solve.

As noted in Table 6-2, the total time for the FIML estimation problem was about 3.5 hours on the IBM 4341. The time taken to compute the FIML covariance matrix after the coefficient estimates were obtained was about 53 minutes. The M transformation discussed earlier was used in the calculation of this matrix, and the second derivatives were obtained numerically.

6.5.3 3SLS

The 3SLS estimation problem is to minimize (6.24). The only cost saving to note for this problem is that the D matrix, which is $m \cdot T \times m \cdot T$, need not be calculated anew each time (6.24) is computed if only a few coefficients are changed.

TABLE 6-3. First stage regressors for the US model for 3SLS

From the basic sets for 2SLS	Additional first stage regressors
1. constant	35. WA_{-1}
2. $(AA/POP)_{-1}$	36. RM_{-1}
3. $C_g + C_s$	37. $\log(M_h/(POP \cdot P_h))_{-1}$
4. $(CD/POP)_{-1}$	38. $\log(1 + d_{5g} + d_{5s})$
5. $(CN/POP)_{-1}$	39. V_{-2}
6. $(CS/POP)_{-1}$	40. IK_{f-1}
7. $(1 - d^M_{1g} - d^M_{1s} - d_{4g} - d_{4s})_{-1}$	41. $\delta_K KK_{-1}$
8. EX	42. $\log(J_f/JHMIN)_{-2}$
9. $\log H_{f-1}$	43. $\log(M_f/PX)_{-1}$
10. $(IH_h/POP)_{-1}$	44. $(BO/BR)_{-1}$
11. $(IM/POP)_{-1}$	45. RD_{-1}
12. $\log(J_f/JHMIN)_{-1}$	46. $\log(CUR/(POP \cdot PX))_{-1}$
13. $(J_gH_g + J_mH_m + J_sH_s)/POP$	47. PIM_{-1}
14. $(KH/POP)_{-1}$	48. PX_{-1}
15. $(KK - KKMIN)_{-1}$	49. $DD793 \cdot \dot{MI}_{-1}$
16. $\dot{MI}_{-1}$	
17. $\dot{PD}_{-1}$	
18. $\log P_{f-1}$	
19. $\log PIM$	
20. RB_{-1}	
21. RS_{-1}	
22. RS_{-2}	
23. t	
24. $(TR_{gh} + TR_{sh})/(POP \cdot P_{h-1})$	
25. V_{-1}	
26. $\log W_{f-1}$	
27. Y_{-1}	
28. Y_{-2}	
29. Y_{-3}	
30. Y_{-4}	
31. $(YN/(POP \cdot P_h))_{-1}$	
32. Z_{-1}	
33. UR_{-1}	
34. ZZ_{-1}	

TABLE 6-4. Solution of the 3SLS estimation problem for the US model

F = u'Du in (6.24)
F at start (2SLS estimates) = 1890.33
F after 26 iterations = 1843.78
Total $|\Delta F|$ = 46.55

Iteration number	$\|\Delta F\|$	Iteration number	$\|\Delta F\|$
1	23.90	14	.24
2	9.31	15	.16
3	6.60	16	.10
4	1.91	17	.13
5	.92	18	.12
6	.67	19	.11
7	.62	20	.08
8	.29	21	.06
9	.32	22	.08
10	.22	23	.05
11	.21	24	.07
12	.12	25	.08
13	.16	26 [a]	.05

Notes: a. Between iterations 25 and 26 eight coefficients changed by 1.0 percent or more. The largest three changes were 6.6, 10.5, and 26.7 percent.

- Model consists of 169 unconstrained coefficients. 107 coefficients estimated by 3SLS. Sample period is 1954 I - 1982 III (115 observations).
- Each iteration requires about 444 function evaluations. The time per iteration was about 4 minutes on the IBM 4341 and about 11 minutes on the VAX. The total time on the IBM 4341 was thus about 26 × 4 minutes = 1.7 hours.
- The time taken to compute the 3SLS covariance matrix, $\hat{V}_3$ in (6.25), was about 23 minutes on the IBM 4341 and about 11 minutes on the VAX.

Results for the US Model

The first-stage regressors for this problem are presented in Table 6-3. There are 49 variables in this set. A number of the variables in Table 6-1 that were used for the 2SLS estimates were not used for the 3SLS estimates because of the desire to keep the number relatively small. The 2SLS estimates of the residuals were used to compute $\hat{\Sigma}$ in (6.24), which remained unchanged throughout the solution of the problem.

The same subset of coefficients was estimated by 3SLS as was estimated by FIML. The solution of the 3SLS problem is reported in Table 6-4. This problem was easier to solve than the FIML problem. Again, the 2SLS estimates were used as starting values. The total change in the objective function, F, after 26 iterations was 46.55, of which 39.81 was obtained by the Parke algorithm after 3 iterations. On iteration 26, eight coefficients changed by 1.0 percent or more, and the largest three changes were 6.6, 10.5, and 26.7 percent.

Each iteration requires about 4 minutes on the IBM 4341 and about 11 minutes on the VAX. The total time for the 26 iterations on the IBM 4341 was about 1.7 hours. The D matrix for the US model is 3,450 × 3,450 ($m = 30$, $T = 115$), and considerable time was saved by not computing this matrix from scratch any more times than were absolutely necessary. If the entire matrix had been computed each time that (6.24) was computed, the time per iteration would have increased by about a factor of 17, and thus the total time would have increased from 1.7 hours to 28.9 hours.

The time taken to compute the 3SLS covariance matrix, $\hat{V}_3$ in (6.25), was about 23 minutes on the IBM 4341 and about 11 minutes on the VAX. The derivative matrix $\hat{G}$ that is needed for this calculation was computed numerically. The reason the IBM 4341 time is large relative to the VAX time is that in the calculation of $\hat{V}_3$ much reading and writing from the disk is done, and the IBM 4341 is relatively slow at this.

6.5.4 LAD and 2SLAD

The LAD and 2SLAD computational problem is to minimize

$$(6.53) \qquad \sum_{t=1}^{T} |v_{it}|$$

with respect to α_i, where $v_{it} = u_{it} = y_{it} - h_{it}$ for LAD and $v_{it} = qy_{it} + (1-q)\hat{y}_{it} - \hat{h}_{it}$ for 2SLAD. This computational problem is not particularly easy, especially when v_{it} is a nonlinear function of α_i. I have had no success in trying to minimize (6.53) using the DFP algorithm and Powell's no-derivative algorithm (1964). (When the DFP algorithm was tried, the derivatives were computed numerically. The problem that they do not exist everywhere was ignored.) Both algorithms failed to get close to the optimum in most of the cases that I tried.

Because the standard algorithms do not work, other approaches must be tried. I have used two, one that worked well and one that did not. The one that worked well uses the fact that

$$\sum_{t=1}^{T} |v_{it}| = \sum_{t=1}^{T} \frac{v_{it}^2}{|v_{it}|} = \sum_{t=1}^{T} \frac{v_{it}^2}{w_{it}}, \tag{6.54}$$

where $w_{it} = |v_{it}|$. For a given set of values of w_{it} $(t = 1, \ldots, T)$, minimizing (6.54) is simply a weighted least squares problem. If v_{it} is a linear function of α_i, closed-form expressions exist for $\hat{\alpha}_i$; otherwise a nonlinear optimization algorithm can be used. This suggests the following iterative procedure. (1) Pick an initial set of values of w_{it}. These can be the absolute values of the OLS or 2SLS estimated residuals. (2) Given these values, minimize (6.54). (3) Given the estimate of α_i from step 2, compute new values of v_{it} and thus new values of w_{it}. (4) With the new weights, go back to step 2 and minimize (6.54) again. Keep repeating steps 2 and 3 until successive estimates of α_i are within some prescribed tolerance level. If on any step some value of w_{it} is smaller than some small preassigned number (say ϵ), the value of w_{it} should be set equal to ϵ.

The accuracy of the estimates using this approach is a function of ϵ: the smaller is ϵ, the greater is the accuracy. If v_{it} is a linear function of α_i, the estimates will never be exact because the true estimates correspond to k_i values of w_{it} being exactly zero, where k_i is the number of elements of α_i.

In the case in which the equation to be estimated is linear in coefficients, the closed-form expression for $\hat{\alpha}_i$ for a given set of values of w_{it} is

$$\hat{\alpha}_i = (\hat{X}_i^{*\prime} \hat{X}_i^{*})^{-1} \hat{X}_i^{*\prime} \hat{y}_i^{*}. \tag{6.55}$$

$\hat{X}_i^*$ is the same as $\hat{X}_i$ in (6.9) except that each element in row t of $\hat{X}_i$ is divided by $\sqrt{w_{it}}$. The vector $\hat{y}_i^*$ equals $qy_i + (1 - q)\hat{y}_i$ except that row t is divided by $\sqrt{w_{it}}$. ($\hat{y}_i$ equals $D_i y_i$.)

If the equation is linear in coefficients but has serially correlated errors, v_{it} is not a linear function of the coefficients inclusive of the serial correlation coefficients, and therefore a closed-form expression does not exist. It is possible in his case, however, to solve for the estimates by iteratively solving equations like (6.13) and (6.14). This avoids having to use a general-purpose algorithm like DFP. Assuming that X_{i-1} and y_{i-1} are included in Z_i, the two equations for the first-order serial correlation case are

$$\hat{\alpha}_i = (\hat{X}_i^{**\prime} \hat{X}_i^{**})^{-1} \hat{X}_i^{**\prime} \hat{y}_i^{**}, \tag{6.56}$$

$$\hat{\rho}_i = \frac{\hat{u}_{i-1}^{*\prime} \hat{u}_i^*}{\hat{u}_{i-1}^{*\prime} \hat{u}_{i-1}^*}. \tag{6.57}$$

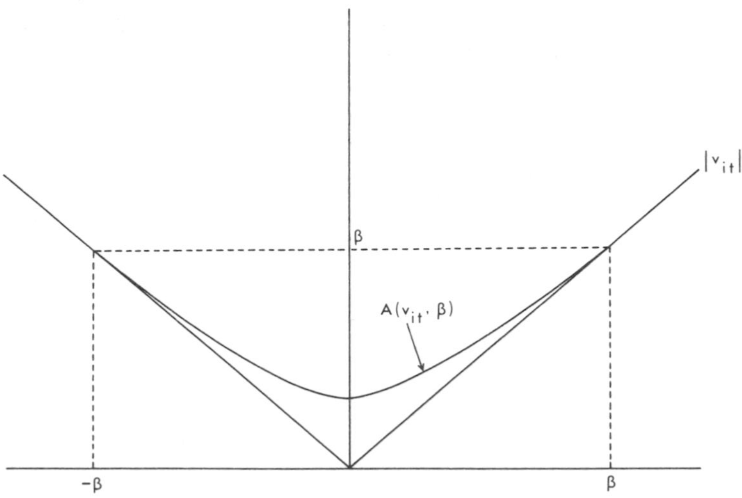

Figure 6-1 Approximation of $A(v_{it}, \beta)$ to $|v_{it}|$

$\hat{X}_i^{**}$ is the matrix $\hat{X}_i - X_{i-1}\hat{\rho}_i$ with each element in row t divided by $\sqrt{w_{it}}$; $\hat{y}_i^{**}$ is the vector $qy_i + (1-q)\hat{y}_i - y_{i-1}\hat{\rho}_i$ with row t divided by $\sqrt{w_{it}}$; $\hat{u}_{i-1}^{*}$ is the vector $y_{i-1} - X_{i-1}\hat{\alpha}_i$ with row t divided by $\sqrt{w_{it}}$; and $\hat{u}_i^{*}$ is the vector $qy_i + (1-q)\hat{y}_i - X_i\hat{\alpha}_i$ with row t divided by $\sqrt{w_{it}}$. For a given set of weights, (6.56) and (6.57) can be solved iteratively.

The second approach is derived from Tishler and Zang (1980). The problem of minimizing (6.53) is changed to a problem of minimizing

$$(6.58) \qquad \sum_{t=1}^{T} A(v_{it}, \beta),$$

where

$$(6.59) \qquad A(v_{it}, \beta) = \begin{cases} -v_{it} & \text{if } v_{it} \leqq -\beta \\ (v_{it}^2 + \beta^2)/2\beta & \text{if } -\beta < v_{it} < \beta \\ v_{it} & \text{if } v_{it} \geq \beta \end{cases}.$$

The value of β is some small preassigned number. Since $\lim_{\beta \to 0} A(v_{it}, \beta) = |v_{it}|$, the smaller is β, the closer is (6.53) to (6.59). The approximation of $A(v_{it}, \beta)$ to $|v_{it}|$ is presented in Figure 6-1. Since $A(v_{it}, \beta)$ is once continuously differentiable, an optimization algorithm like DFP can be used to minimize (6.59) for a given value of β. The smaller is β, the more difficult the minimization problem is likely to be, and thus there is a trade-off between accuracy and ease of solution.

Results for the US Model

Four sets of estimates of the US model were obtained: LAD, 2SLAD using $q = 0.0$, 2SLAD using $q = 0.5$, and 2SLAD using $q = 1.0$. The method of Tishler and Zang did not work well, in the sense that the results were quite sensitive to the value of β chosen, and therefore it was dropped from further consideration fairly early in the calculations. For small values of β the DFP algorithm, which was the algorithm used, failed to converge, and for large values of β the algorithm converged to answers that implied values of the true objective function, (6.53), that were larger than those obtained by the first method. It was difficult to find in-between values of β that worked well.

The first method, on the other hand, worked extremely well. For 2SLAD using $q = 0.5$, for example, the number of iterations required for convergence for the 30 equations ranged from 4 to 145, with an average of 35.6. Convergence was taken to be achieved when successive estimates of each coefficient were within .002 percent of each other. The value used for ϵ was .0000001. The total time for estimating the model by LAD was about 2.2 minutes on the IBM 4341 and about 5.7 minutes on the VAX. The total time for each of the three 2SLAD estimation problems was about 6.5 minutes on the IBM 4341 and about 16.5 minutes on the VAX. Of the 120 equations estimated, none had a residual that was smaller than ϵ in absolute value at the time that convergence was achieved. These results are very encouraging, and they indicate that computational costs are not likely to be a serious problem in the future with respect to LAD and 2SLAD estimation.

6.6 Comparison of the OLS, 2SLS, 3SLS, FIML, LAD, and 2SLAD Results for the US Model

If the model is correctly specified and all the assumptions about the error terms are correct, all but the OLS and LAD estimates of the US model are consistent. They should thus differ from each other only because of a finite sample size. In practice the model is likely to be misspecified, and not all the assumptions about the error terms are likely to be correct. Given this, it is not obvious how the estimates should compare. In this section the quantitative differences among the estimates are examined. The consequences of these differences for the predictive accuracy of the model are discussed in Section 8.5.5, and the consequences for the properties of the model are discussed in Section 9.4.5.

Table 6-5 presents a comparison of the estimates for six equations: the three consumption equations, 1, 2, and 3; the price equation, 10; the production

TABLE 6-5. Comparison of coefficient estimates for selected equations of the US model

Eq. no.	Coeff. no.	2SLS	FIML		3SLS		2SLAD (q = 0.0)		2SLAD (q = 0.5)		2SLAD (q = 1.0)		LAD		OLS	
		a	a	b	a	b	a	b	a	b	a	b	a	b	a	b
1	1	.00019	-.00240	-0.80	-.00042	-0.19	-.00040	-0.18	-.00161	-0.56	.00123	0.32	-.00008	-0.08	.00154	0.42
	2	.98650	.99893	0.77	.99021	0.23	.98920	0.17	.99260	0.38	.97983	-0.42	.98125	-0.33	.98786	0.08
	3	.00055	.00066	0.47	.00058	0.12	.00057	0.07	.00063	0.31	.00062	0.28	.00058	0.12	.00039	-0.72
	4	.01979	.02922	0.99	.02143	0.17	.02051	0.07	.02094	0.12	.02052	0.08	.01183	-0.83	.00936	-1.09
	5	.00714	-.02427	-1.58	-.00118	-0.42	.00265	-0.23	-.00257	-0.49	.01021	0.15	.01490	0.39	.01277	0.28
	6	-.00126	-.00111	0.73	-.00124	0.12	-.00126	0.00	-.00123	0.16	-.00116	0.48	-.00082	2.08	-.00088	1.78
	7	.02312	.01107	-1.00	.01852	-0.38	.02094	-0.18	.01913	-0.33	.02280	-0.03	.00864	-1.21	.01969	-0.29
2	1	.10903	.23997	4.76	.11422	0.19	.10362	-0.20	.08105	-1.02	.07983	-1.06	.11491	0.21	.13478	0.94
	2	.66619	.41164	-3.83	.65620	-0.15	.67928	0.20	.71909	0.80	.73586	1.05	.65734	-0.13	.61356	-0.79
	3	.00227	.00181	-1.04	.00220	-0.15	.00231	0.08	.00235	0.17	.00197	-0.67	.00208	-0.44	.00218	-0.19
	4	.18547	.58420	5.34	.18727	0.02	.19026	0.06	.08513	-1.34	.08915	-1.29	.20575	0.27	.25481	0.93
	5	-.04689	-.16405	-5.40	-.04951	-0.12	-.04648	0.02	-.02047	1.22	-.02517	1.00	-.05775	-0.50	-.06867	-1.00
	6	.06369	.02956	-1.15	.06952	0.20	.05044	-0.45	.08090	0.58	.08117	0.59	.07367	0.34	.06468	0.03
	7	-.00061	.00207	4.59	-.00038	0.39	-.00057	0.06	-.00091	-0.51	-.00054	0.13	-.00005	0.96	-.00004	0.97
	8	.08291	.11018	1.17	.08212	-0.03	.06744	-0.66	.07383	-0.39	.06047	-0.96	.05669	-1.12	.08567	0.12
3	1	.07349	.20807	6.53	.07710	0.18	.05432	-0.93	.06464	-0.43	.07328	-0.01	.06771	-0.28	.06016	-0.65
	2	.45821	.07423	-4.98	.44448	-0.18	.48225	0.31	.51434	0.73	.48472	0.34	.53824	1.04	.49524	0.48
	3	.00235	.00247	0.32	.00222	-0.35	.00238	0.07	.00211	-0.65	.00211	-0.63	.00187	-1.28	.00221	-0.39
	4	.40468	1.03962	6.39	.39950	-0.05	.30037	-1.05	.35109	-0.54	.37741	-0.27	.34360	-0.62	.31159	-0.94
	5	-.10399	-.32751	-6.71	-.10491	-0.03	-.06856	1.06	-.08905	0.45	-.10485	-0.03	-.09862	0.16	-.07811	0.78
	6	.06682	-.11739	-3.27	.08347	0.30	.13503	1.21	.07585	0.16	.08615	0.34	.08378	0.30	.11408	0.84
	7	-.00617	-.00749	-1.70	-.00608	0.12	-.00602	0.19	-.00570	0.60	-.00519	1.27	-.00447	2.20	-.00537	1.04
	8	.12315	.17590	1.45	.12353	0.01	.13739	0.39	.11844	-0.13	.12722	0.11	.11679	-0.17	.13968	0.45
10	1	.18683	.19928	0.49	.18257	-0.17	.16517	-0.85	.18921	0.09	.20110	0.56	.20672	0.78	.18718	0.01
	2	.92214	.90850	-1.22	.91983	-0.21	.93113	0.81	.92353	0.12	.91721	-0.44	.91457	-0.68	.92200	-0.01
	3	.03394	.03672	0.57	.03326	-0.14	.02984	-0.84	.03438	0.09	.03665	0.55	.03771	0.77	.03401	0.01
	4	.03389	.04079	1.74	.03650	0.66	.03192	-0.50	.03210	-0.45	.03482	0.23	.03538	0.38	.03392	0.01
	5	-.08096	-.07402	0.36	-.08966	-0.45	-.07814	0.15	-.07365	0.38	-.07883	0.11	-.08155	-0.03	-.08094	0.00
11	1	11.36381	21.87884	4.04	10.69493	-0.26	8.12354	-1.24	11.64381	0.11	8.81205	-0.98	9.25990	-0.81	10.58937	-0.30
	2	.16209	-.03324	-4.43	.15484	-0.16	.15023	-0.27	.14886	-0.30	.18034	0.41	.17040	0.19	.18002	0.41
	3	1.01142	1.43204	8.15	1.01595	0.09	.98842	-0.45	1.03510	0.46	.97080	-0.79	.98684	-0.48	.98039	-0.60
	4	-.19265	-.43424	-5.57	-.18766	0.11	-.14986	0.99	-.20464	-0.28	-.16538	0.63	-.17028	0.52	-.17797	0.34
	8	.60491	.76119	1.74	.56992	-0.39	.59695	-0.09	.61413	0.10	.60371	-0.01	.58844	-0.18	.58023	-0.27
30	1	-9.45741	-5.60570	1.22	-7.66028	0.57	-9.52105	-0.02	-7.29281	0.68	-8.18864	0.40	-7.91120	0.49	-9.80375	-0.11
	2	.85812	.90573	1.42	.88586	0.83	.83247	-0.76	.89576	1.12	.93716	2.35	.92674	2.04	.86039	0.07
	3	.06872	-.01235	-2.49	.03783	-0.95	.06980	0.03	.05341	-0.47	.02104	-1.46	.03465	-1.05	.06709	-0.05
	4	.02962	.01761	-1.21	.02389	-0.58	.03043	0.08	.02282	-0.69	.02533	-0.43	.02446	-0.52	.03065	0.10
	5	.05974	.06527	0.27	.06069	0.05	.03105	-1.40	.04213	-0.86	.03831	-1.05	.03532	-1.19	.06343	0.18
	6	.03248	.05675	1.28	.04356	0.58	.03640	0.21	.02722	-0.28	.03938	0.36	.04258	0.53	.03166	-0.04
	7	.13149	.11772	-0.44	.10735	-0.77	.14851	0.54	.15053	0.61	.03880	-2.96	.03972	-2.93	.13201	0.02

[illegible] estimate; b = (Coefficient estimate - 2SLS coefficient estimate)/standard error of 2SLS coefficient estimate.

equation, 11; and the interest rate reaction function, 30. The 2SLS estimates are used as the basis of comparison. Each number in a "b" column in the table is the difference between the particular estimate and the 2SLS estimate divided by the standard error of the 2SLS estimate. These numbers thus indicate how many standard errors the estimates are from the 2SLS estimates, where the standard errors that are used are 2SLS standard errors. Table 6-6 provides summary measures for all the coefficient estimates.

The main conclusion to be drawn from these results is that all the estimates are fairly close to each other except for the FIML estimates. Consider Table 6-6: only 3 of the 107 3SLS coefficient estimates are more than 1.5 standard errors away from the 2SLS estimates, whereas 38 of the FIML estimates are. Only 1 of the 169 OLS estimates is more than 1.5 standard errors away. Of the 2SLAD estimates, 7 are more than 1.5 standard errors away for $q = 0.0$, 12 are for $q = 0.5$, and 19 are for $q = 1.0$. For LAD the number is 15. Very few of the estimates changed signs, as can be seen in the bottom half of Table 6-6. Even for FIML, only 6 estimates changed sign.

With respect to the individual estimates in Table 6-5, one important difference between the FIML estimates and the others occurs in Eq. 11, the equation determining production, Y. Coefficient 3 in Eq. 11 is the coefficient for the sales variable, X. For all the estimates except FIML, this coefficient is around 1.0, whereas for FIML it is around 1.4. Also, coefficient 2 in Eq. 11, which is the coefficient of the lagged dependent variable, is around .15 for the other estimates and close to zero for FIML. The FIML estimates of the lagged dependent variable coefficients in two of the three consumption equations (Eqs. 2 and 3) are likewise quite different from the others. In both equations the lagged dependent variable coefficient is number 2. The FIML and 2SLS estimates in the two equations are, respectively, .66619 versus .41164 and .45821 versus .07423.

It should be stressed that the only reason for the present comparison is to get a general idea of how close the estimates are. Of more importance are the comparisons in Sections 8.5.5 and 9.4.5, which examine the estimates within the context of the overall model. What can be said so far is that the FIML estimates differ most from the others when the examination is coefficient by coefficient.

Comparison of Standard Errors

Table 6-7 presents a comparison of the 2SLS, 3SLS, and FIML estimated standard errors. As expected, the 2SLS standard errors are generally larger

TABLE 6-6. Comparison of coefficient estimates of the US model

	Number of coefficient estimates greater than .5, 1.0, 1.5, 2.0 2.5, and 3.0 standard errors away from the 2SLS estimates					
	.5	1.0	1.5	2.0	2.5	3.0
107 total coefficients:						
FIML	81	63	38	25	16	16
3SLS	34	8	3	2	0	0
169 total coefficients:						
2SLAD (q = 0.0)	64	21	7	5	3	1
2SLAD (q = 0.5)	77	33	12	8	3	1
2SLAD (q = 1.0)	98	53	19	12	6	3
LAD	91	40	15	11	4	1
OLS	28	9	1	0	0	0

	Number of sign changes from 2SLS estimates other than those for constant terms
FIML	6
3SLS	2
2SLAD (q = 0.0)	1
2SLAD (q = 0.5)	2
2SLAD (q = 1.0)	1
LAD	1
OLS	2

than the 3SLS standard errors, where the average of the ratios of the two is 1.27. This is not always the case, however, as can be seen for coefficients 1–6 and 8 in Eq. 4, where the 2SLS standard errors are smaller. This difference is due to the different first-stage regressors that are used by 2SLS and 3SLS. As discussed earlier, 2SLS uses different sets of FSRs for different equations, whereas 3SLS uses a common set that is smaller than the union of the 2SLS sets. This can cause the 2SLS standard errors to be smaller. In the present case, Eq. 4 has no RHS endogenous variables, and thus the 2SLS estimates are the OLS estimates. The FSRs in this case include all the explanatory variables in the equation. Not all of these explanatory variables were included in the common set of FSRs for the 3SLS estimates, and therefore some of the variables in the equation were treated as endogenous. This was enough to lead to larger 3SLS standard errors for some of the coefficients.

TABLE 6-7. Ratios of 3SLS and FIML standard errors and of 2SLS and 3SLS standard errors for the US model

Eq. no.	Coeff. no.	$\frac{SE_3}{SE_4}$	$\frac{SE_2}{SE_3}$	Eq. no.	Coeff. no.	$\frac{SE_3}{SE_4}$	$\frac{SE_2}{SE_3}$	Eq. no	Coeff. no.	$\frac{SE_3}{SE_4}$	$\frac{SE_2}{SE_3}$
1	1	.86	1.20	10	1	.75	1.17	17	1	.82	1.16
	2	.78	1.21		2	.72	1.19		2	.77	1.20
	3	.69	1.17		3	.74	1.17		3	.79	1.19
	4	.72	1.19		4	.75	1.18		4	.75	1.20
	5	.82	1.22		5	.75	1.15	22	1	1.03	1.18
	6	.77	1.23	11	1	.32	1.25		2	.67	1.37
	7	.85	1.19		2	.52	1.22		3	.68	1.20
2	1	.63	1.28		3	.40	1.21	23	1	.79	1.12
	2	.68	1.25		4	.27	1.24		2	.70	1.17
	3	.71	1.17		8	.78	1.18		3	.42	1.42
	4	.56	1.30	12	1	.91	1.10		4	.53	1.34
	5	.57	1.32		2	.77	1.22		5	.70	1.22
	6	.79	1.20		3	.66	1.22	24	1	.68	1.18
	7	.65	1.34		4	.74	1.25		2	.65	1.22
	8	.84	1.20		5	.85	1.27		3	.36	1.45
3	1	.26	1.39		6	.82	1.28		4	.49	1.39
	2	.28	1.34		7	.77	1.21		5	.65	1.26
	3	.48	1.25		8	.77	1.21	26	1	.76	1.15
	4	.24	1.41	13	1	.86	1.78		2	.81	1.13
	5	.25	1.40		2	.86	1.78		3	.76	1.15
	6	.43	1.38		3	.87	1.72		4	.82	1.13
	7	.33	1.29		4	.65	1.58		5	.74	1.16
	8	.61	1.33		5	.86	1.66	27	1	.85	1.37
4	1	1.47	.75		6	.83	1.56		2	.87	1.39
	2	1.26	.91		9	.78	1.57		3	.85	1.39
	3	1.09	.95	14	1	.75	1.38		4	.72	1.29
	4	1.32	.87		2	.75	1.45		5	.68	1.28
	5	1.32	.91		3	.77	1.53		6	.67	1.27
	6	1.43	.85		4	.75	1.38	30	1	.82	1.19
	7	1.03	1.17		5	.63	1.51		2	.80	1.22
	8	.99	.96	16	1	.68	1.40		3	.80	1.26
	9	.77	1.40		2	.69	1.41		4	.83	1.19
9	1	.78	1.21		3	.72	1.62		5	.76	1.32
	2	.81	1.20		4	.67	1.36		6	.75	1.29
	3	.77	1.24		5	.81	1.36		7	.73	1.27
	4	.82	1.19								
	5	.72	1.19						AVERAGE	.74	1.27

The more interesting result in Table 6-7 is that the 3SLS standard errors are generally smaller than the FIML standard errors. The average of the ratios of the two is .74. This result has also been obtained, but not discussed, by Hausman (1974). For 10 of the 12 estimated coefficients of Klein's model I that are reported in Hausman's table 1, p. 649, the FIML standard error is larger than the corresponding 3SLS standard error.

My conjecture as to why the 3SLS standard errors are generally smaller is the following. Given the large number of FSRs that are used by 3SLS, the predicted values of the endogenous variables from the first-stage regressions are fairly close to the actual values. For FIML, on the other hand, we know from Hausman's interpretation (1975) of the FIML estimator as an instrumental variables estimator that FIML takes into account the nonlinear restrictions on the reduced form coefficients in forming the instruments. This means that in small samples the instruments that FIML forms are likely to be based on worse first-stage fits of the endogenous variables than are the instruments that 3SLS forms. In a loose sense, this situation is analogous to the fact that in the 2SLS case the more variables that are used in the first-stage regressions, the better is the fit in the second-stage regression.

Possible Use of the Hausman Test

An interesting question is whether Hausman's m-statistic (1978) provides a useful way of examining the differences among the estimates. The m-statistic is as follows. Consider two estimators, $\hat{\beta}_0$ and $\hat{\beta}_1$, where under some null hypothesis both estimators are consistent but only $\hat{\beta}_0$ is asymptotically efficient, while under the alternative hypothesis only $\hat{\beta}_1$ is consistent. Let $q = \hat{\beta}_1 - \hat{\beta}_0$, and let $\hat{V}_0$ and $\hat{V}_1$ denote consistent estimates of the asymptotic covariance matrices (V_0 and V_1) of $\hat{\beta}_0$ and $\hat{\beta}_1$, respectively. Hausman's m-statistic is $\hat{q}'(\hat{V}_1 - \hat{V}_0)^{-1}\hat{q}$, and he has shown that it is asymptotically distributed as χ^2 with k degrees of freedom, where k is the dimension of $\hat{q}$. Note that under the null hypothesis $V_1 - V_0$ is positive-definite.

Consider now comparing the FIML and 3SLS estimates. Under the null hypothesis of correct specification and normally distributed errors, both estimates are consistent, but only the FIML estimates are asymptotically efficient. On the other hand, 3SLS estimates are consistent for a broad class of error distributions, whereas for many distributions FIML estimates are inconsistent. If the alternative hypothesis is taken to be that the error distribution is one that leads to consistent 3SLS estimates but inconsistent FIML estimates, then in principle Hausman's m-statistic can be used to test the null hypothesis of normality against the alternative. Let $\hat{\alpha}^{(3)}$ and $\hat{\alpha}^{(4)}$ denote the 3SLS and FIML estimates of α respectively, and let $\hat{q} = \hat{\alpha}^{(3)} - \hat{\alpha}^{(4)}$. The m-statistic in this case is $\hat{q}'(\hat{V}_3 - \hat{V}_4)^{-1}\hat{q}$, where the estimated covariance matrices $\hat{V}_3$ and $\hat{V}_4$ are defined in (6.25) and (6.34) respectively.

In practice the test cannot be performed if $\hat{V}_3 - \hat{V}_4$ is not positive-definite. For the US model it is clear from Table 6-7 that $\hat{V}_3 - \hat{V}_4$ is not positive-definite, since most of the diagonal elements of $\hat{V}_3$ are smaller than the corresponding elements of $\hat{V}_4$. If anything, $\hat{V}_3 - \hat{V}_4$ is closer to being negative-definite, although this is not true either since some of the diagonal elements of $\hat{V}_4$ are smaller than the corresponding elements of $\hat{V}_3$. The matrix $\hat{V}_3 - \hat{V}_4$ is also not positive-definite for Klein's model I, since, as noted earlier, Hausman's results (1974) show that 10 of the 12 estimated coefficients have larger FIML standard errors than 3SLS standard errors. It thus seems unlikely that $\hat{V}_3 - \hat{V}_4$ will be positive-definite in practice for most models, and therefore the m-statistic is not likely to be useful for testing the normality hypothesis. (If the model is linear, the test obviously has no power, since FIML, like 3SLS, is consistent for a broad class of error distributions.)

The m-statistic can also be used in principle to compare the FIML and 2SLS estimates. Under the null hypothesis of normally distributed errors and correct specification, both estimates are consistent, but only the FIML estimates are asymptotically efficient. Under the alternative hypothesis of normality and misspecification of some subset of the equations, all the FIML estimates are inconsistent, but only the 2SLS estimates of the misspecified subset are inconsistent. The m-statistic can thus be applied to one or more equations at a time to test the hypothesis that the rest of the model is correctly specified. If for some subset the m-statistic exceeds the critical value, the test would indicate that there is misspecification somewhere in the rest of the model.

In practice this test cannot be applied if $\hat{V}_2 - \hat{V}_4$ is not positive definite, and for the US model, as is clear from Table 6-7, $\hat{V}_2 - \hat{V}_4$ is not positive-definite. Many of the diagonal elements of $\hat{V}_2$ are smaller than the corresponding elements of $\hat{V}_4$. It thus also seems unlikely that this test of misspecification will be useful in practice.

Finally, the specification hypothesis can be tested in certain circumstances using the m-statistic on the 2SLS and 3SLS estimates. If both estimators are members of a class of estimators for which 3SLS is asymptotically efficient, the test can be applied. The problem is that when the two estimators are based on different sets of FSRs, as is usually the case with large models, they are not members of the same class. One cannot argue, for example, that the 3SLS estimates given above for the US model are asymptotically efficient relative to the 2SLS estimates, and thus the Hausman test cannot be applied in this case.

In summary, the m-statistic does not seem useful for testing either the normality hypothesis or the correct specification hypothesis. Regarding the latter, my feeling is that it is better simply to assume that the model is misspecified (so that no test is needed) and to try to estimate the degree of misspecification. This is the procedure followed for the comparison method in Chapter 8.

7 Solution

7.1 Definition of Terms

Once the stochastic equations of a model have been estimated and the identities have been written down, the next step is to solve the model. There are various meanings to the word "solve," and it will be useful to begin this discussion with some definitions. "Solve" and "simulate" mean the same thing. A "static" solution or simulation is one in which the actual values of the predetermined variables are used for the solution each period. Predetermined variables include both exogenous and lagged endogenous variables. A "dynamic" simulation is one in which the predicted values of the endogenous variables from the solutions for the previous periods are used for the values of the lagged endogenous variables for the solution for the current period.

"Forecast" and "prediction" are generally used to mean the same thing, and they are so used here. They mean the same thing as solution and simulation. An "outside-sample" forecast or prediction is one for a period that is not included within the estimation period; otherwise the forecast is "within-sample." An "ex post" forecast is one in which the actual values of the exogenous variables are used. An ex post forecast can be outside sample, but it must be within the period for which there are data on the exogenous variables. An "ex ante" forecast is made for a period beyond the period for which data exist; it is a forecast in which guessed values of the exogenous variables are used. In other words, ex ante forecasts are for a period that is truly unknown. Ex ante forecasts must be outside sample and (if the forecast is for more than one period ahead) dynamic. The forecasts must be dynamic because the values of the lagged endogenous variables are only known for the initial period.

In order to solve a model some assumption must be made about the error terms in the stochastic equations. If only one set of values of the error terms is used, the simulation is said to be "deterministic." The expected values of most error terms in most models are zero, and for most deterministic simulations the error terms are set to zero. For linear models the procedure of setting the error terms equal to their expected values and solving the model results in the predicted values of the endogenous variables being equal to their expected values. This is not the case, however, for nonlinear models (see, for example, Howrey and Kelejian 1971), which is simply due to the fact that a nonlinear function of expected values is not equal to the expected value of the nonlinear function. A "stochastic" simulation is one in which many draws of the error terms are made in the process of solving the model. This procedure is discussed in Section 7.3. Aside from sampling error and a few other approximations, solving a nonlinear model by means of stochastic simulation does result in the predicted values being equal to the expected values. As will be seen in Chapters 8 and 9, stochastic simulation is useful for other purposes as well.

7.2 The Gauss-Seidel Technique

Most macroeconometric models are solved using the Gauss-Seidel technique. It is a remarkably simple technique and in most cases works remarkably well. This technique is used for all of the main procedures discussed in the rest of this book. The vast majority of computer time used for any of these procedures is spent solving the model using the Gauss-Seidel technique, and thus the technique is obviously of crucial importance. The technique is easiest to describe by means of an example.

Assume that the model (6.1) consists of three equations, and let x_{it} denote the vector of predetermined variables in equation i. The model is as follows:

$$f_1(y_{1t}, y_{2t}, y_{3t}, x_{1t}, \alpha_1) = u_{1t}, \tag{7.1}$$

$$f_2(y_{1t}, y_{2t}, y_{3t}, x_{2t}, \alpha_2) = u_{2t}, \tag{7.2}$$

$$f_3(y_{1t}, y_{2t}, y_{3t}, x_{3t}, \alpha_3) = u_{3t}, \tag{7.3}$$

where y_{1t}, y_{2t}, and y_{3t} are scalars. The technique requires that the equations be rewritten with each endogenous variable on the LHS of one equation. This is usually quite easy for macroeconometric models, since most equations have an obvious LHS variable. If, say, the LHS variable for (7.2) is $\log(y_{2t}/y_{3t})$, then y_{2t} can be written on the LHS by taking exponents and multiplying the resulting expression by y_{3t}. The technique does not require that each endogenous variable be isolated on the LHS; the LHS variable can also appear on the RHS. It is almost always possible in macroeconometric work, however, to isolate the variable, and this will be assumed in the following example.

The model (7.1)–(7.3) will be written

$$(7.1)' \qquad y_{1t} = g_1(y_{2t}, y_{3t}, x_{1t}, \alpha_1, u_{1t}).$$

$$(7.2)' \qquad y_{2t} = g_2(y_{1t}, y_{3t}, x_{2t}, \alpha_2, u_{2t}),$$

$$(7.3)' \qquad y_{3t} = g_3(y_{1t}, y_{2t}, x_{3t}, \alpha_3, u_{3t}).$$

In order to solve the model, values of the coefficients and the error terms are needed. It is unimportant for now what values are used, as long as some values are available. Given these values and given values of the predetermined variables, the solution proceeds as follows. Initial values of the endogenous variables are guessed. These are usually either actual values or predicted values from the previous period. Given these values, (7.1)′–(7.3)′ can be solved for a new set of values. This requires one "pass" through the model: each equation is solved once. One pass through the model is also called an "iteration." Given this new set of values, the model can be solved again to get another set, and so on. Convergence is reached if for each endogenous variable the values on successive iterations are within some prescribed tolerance level.

There are two main options that can be used when passing through the model. One is to use the values from the previous iteration for all the computations for the current iteration, and the other is to use, whenever possible, the values from the current iteration in solving the remaining equations. Following the second option in the example just given would mean using the current solution for y_{1t} in the solution of y_{2t} and y_{3t} and using the current solutions for y_{1t} and y_{2t} in the solution of y_{3t}. In most cases convergence is somewhat faster using the second option. If the second option is used, the order of the equations obviously matters in terms of the likely speed of convergence. The first option is sometimes called the Jacobi technique rather than the Gauss-Seidel technique, but for present purposes both options will be referred to as the Gauss-Seidel technique.

There is no guarantee that the Gauss-Seidel technique will converge. It is easy to construct examples in which it does not, and I have seen many examples in practice where it did not. The advantage of the technique, however, is that it can usually be made to converge (assuming an actual solution exists) with sufficient damping. By "damping" is meant the following. Let $\hat{y}_{1t}^{(n-1)}$ denote the solution value of y_{1t} for iteration $n-1$ (or the initial value if n is 1), and let $\hat{\hat{y}}_{1t}^{(n)}$ denote the value computed by solving (7.1) on iteration n. Instead of using $\hat{\hat{y}}_{1t}^{(n)}$ as the solution value for iteration n, one can instead adjust $\hat{y}_{1t}^{(n-1)}$ only partway toward $\hat{\hat{y}}_{1t}^{(n)}$:

$$(7.4) \qquad \hat{y}_{1t}^{(n)} = \hat{y}_{1t}^{(n-1)} + \lambda(\hat{\hat{y}}_{1t}^{(n)} - \hat{y}_{1t}^{(n-1)}), \qquad 0 < \lambda \leq 1.$$

If λ is 1, there is no damping, but otherwise there is. Damping can be done for any or all of the endogenous variables, and different values of λ can be used for different variables.

My experience is that one can usually make λ small enough to achieve convergence. The cost of damping is, of course, slow convergence. In some cases I have seen values as low as .05 needed. In the vast majority of the problems that I have solved, however, no damping at all was needed. Two other ways in which one can deal with problems of convergence are to try different starting values and to reorder the equations. This involves, however, more work than merely rerunning the problem with lower values of λ, and I have generally not found it necessary to experiment with starting values and the order of the equations.

Note that nothing is changed in the foregoing discussion if, say, y_{1t} is also on the RHS of (7.1)′. One still passes though the model in the same way. This generally means, however, that it takes longer to converge, and more damping may be required than if y_{1t} is only on the LHS; thus it is better to isolate variables on the LHS whenever possible.

The question of what to use for a stopping rule is not as easy at it might sound. The stopping rule can either be in absolute or percentage terms. In absolute terms it is

$$(7.5) \qquad |\hat{y}_{it}^{(n)} - \hat{y}_{it}^{(n-1)}| < \epsilon_i$$

and in percentage terms it is

$$(7.6) \qquad \left|\frac{\hat{y}_{it}^{(n)} - \hat{y}_{it}^{(n-1)}}{\hat{y}_{it}^{(n-1)}}\right| < \epsilon_i,$$

where ϵ_i is the tolerance criterion for variable i. (If damping is used, $\hat{y}_{it}^{(n)}$ in (7.5) and (7.6) should be replaced with $\hat{\hat{y}}_{it}^{(n)}$.)

The problem comes in choosing the values for ϵ_i. It is inconvenient to have to choose different values of the tolerance criterion for different variables, and one would like to use just one value of ϵ throughout. This is not, however, a sensible procedure if the units of the variables differ and if the absolute criterion is used. Setting the value of ϵ small enough for the required accuracy of the variable with the smallest units is likely to lead to an excess number of iterations, since a large number of iterations are likely to be needed to satisfy the criterion for the variables with the largest units. Setting ϵ greater than this value, on the other hand, runs the risk of not achieving the desired accuracy for some variables. This problem is lessened if the percentage criterion is used, but in this case one must be concerned with variables, like the level of savings of a sector, that can be zero or close to zero.

My experience is that the number of iterations needed for convergence is quite sensitive to the stopping rule. It does not seem to be the case, for example, that once one has converged for most variables, one or two additional iterations increase the accuracy for the remaining variables very much. There is no real answer to this problem. One must do some initial experimentation to decide how many different values of ϵ are needed and whether to use the absolute or percentage criterion for a given variable.

7.3 Stochastic Simulation

7.3.1 The Basic Procedure

Stochastic simulation can be either with respect to the error terms or the coefficient estimates, or both. It requires that an assumption be made about the distributions of the error terms and/or coefficient estimates. In practice these distributions are almost always assumed to be normal, although in principle other assumptions can be made. For the present discussion the normality assumption will be used. In particular, it is assumed that $u_t = (u_{1t}, \ldots, u_{mt})'$ is independently and identically distributed as multivariate $N(0, S)$. This is the same assumption that was used for the FIML estimates in Chapter 6. Given an estimation technique and the data, one can estimate the coefficients, the covariance matrix of the coefficient estimates, and the covariance matrix of the error terms. Denote the estimates of the two covariance matrices $\hat{V}$ and $\hat{S}$ respectively. The dimension of $\hat{S}$ is $m \times m$, and the dimension of $\hat{V}$ is $k \times k$. $\hat{S}$ can be computed as $\frac{1}{T}\hat{U}\hat{U}'$, where $\hat{U}$ is the $m \times T$ matrix of values of the estimated error terms. The computation of $\hat{V}$ depends on the particular estimation technique used. Given $\hat{V}$ and given the normality assumption, an estimate of the distribution of the coefficient estimates is $N(\hat{\alpha}, \hat{V})$, where $\hat{\alpha}$ is the $k \times 1$ vector of coefficient estimates.

Let u_t^* denote a particular draw of the m error terms for period t from the $N(0, \hat{S})$ distribution, and let α^* denote a particular draw of the k coefficients from the $N(\hat{\alpha}, \hat{V})$ distribution. Given u_t^* for each period t of the simulation and given α^*, one can solve the model. This is merely a deterministic simulation for the given values of the error terms and coefficients. Call this simulation a "trial." Another trial can be made by drawing a new set of values of u_t^* for each period t and a new set of values of α^*. This can be done as many times as desired. From each trial one obtains a prediction of each endogenous variable for each period. Let $\tilde{y}^j_{itk}$ denote the value on the jth trial of the k-period-ahead prediction of variable i from a simulation beginning in period t. For J trials, the estimate of the expected value of the variable, denoted $\bar{\tilde{y}}_{itk}$, is

$$\bar{\tilde{y}}_{itk} = \frac{1}{J} \sum_{j=1}^{J} \tilde{y}^j_{itk}. \tag{7.7}$$

Let σ^2_{itk} denote the variance of the forecast error for a k-period-ahead forecast of variable i from a simulation beginning in period t. Given the J trials, a stochastic-simulation estimate of σ^2_{itk} (denoted $\tilde{\sigma}^2_{itk}$) is

$$\tilde{\sigma}^2_{itk} = \frac{1}{J} \sum_{j=1}^{J} (\tilde{y}^j_{itk} - \bar{\tilde{y}}_{itk})^2, \tag{7.8}$$

where $\bar{\tilde{y}}_{itk}$ is determined in (7.7).

It is also possible to treat the coefficients as known and draw only from the distribution of the error terms. For a one-period-ahead forecast and known coefficients, the estimated variance is merely the estimated variance of the reduced form error term.

It should be stressed that these stochastic-simulation estimates of the means and variances are not exact. There are two reasons for this. The first is that the true distributions of the error terms and coefficient estimates are not known; one must always draw from estimated distributions. The second is sampling error that results from taking only a finite number of draws.

7.3.2 The Possible Nonexistence of Moments

It may be the case that the forecast means and variances do not exist, and this problem requires some discussion. For linear models Sargan (1976) has shown that for most overidentified models the 2SLS and 3SLS reduced form estimators have no moments of positive integral order. (A general theorem regarding the nonexistence of moments is given in Phillips 1984, theorem 3.9.1.) For linear models Sargan (1973) has also shown that the FIML reduced form estimates have finite moments of up to order T-K-G, where T is the number of observations, K is the number of exogenous variables in the model, and G is the number of endogenous variables in the model.

In practice, the possible nonexistence of moments is generally ignored: means and variances are estimated as if they always exist. One reason the nonexistence of moments does not appear to arise in practice is that extreme draws of the error terms and coefficient estimates are generally not used. By "extreme" in this case is meant a draw that results in the failure of the Gauss-Seidel technique to find a solution of the model. In many of these cases it may be that with further damping and experimenting with the technique the solution could be found, but in some cases it may be that a solution truly does not exist. By throwing away the extreme draws, one is effectively sampling from truncated distributions, where the moments are likely to exist.

It is possible to compute more robust measures of central tendency and dispersion, such as the median, range, and interquartile range, and for some of the results in Chapter 8 I have reported measures like this. The measure of dispersion that I have used (denoted $\tilde{\delta}_{itk}$) is the following:

$$\tilde{\delta}_{itk} = \frac{\tilde{y}^b_{itk} - \tilde{y}^a_{itk}}{2}. \tag{7.9}$$

$\tilde{y}^a_{itk}$ is the value for which 34.135 percent of the J trial values lie *above* it and *below* the median, and $\tilde{y}^b_{itk}$ is the value for which 34.135 percent of the J trial values lie *below* it and *above* the median. For the normal distribution $\tilde{\sigma}_{itk}$ equals $\tilde{\delta}_{itk}$ except for sampling error, and thus the size of $\tilde{\delta}_{itk}$ is something that one may have some feeling for. Its size is similar to the size of the square root of the variance if the variance exists and if the true error distribution is close to being normal. Another way of looking at $\tilde{\delta}_{itk}$ is that it is like, say, the interquartile range except that $\tilde{y}^b_{itk} - \tilde{y}^a_{itk}$ encompasses 68.270 percent of the values rather than 50.0 percent of the values. If the variance does not exist for a particular problem and if the number of trials is large, one might expect $\tilde{\sigma}_{itk}$ to be considerably larger than $\tilde{\delta}_{itk}$. Therefore, by computing both measures one has at least a loose check on the possible nonexistence of moments.

Another approach to the problem of the possible nonexistence of moments is to modify an estimator in such a way that it is guaranteed to have moments. For linear models, for example, Maasoumi (1978) has proposed an estimator of the reduced form coefficients that is a weighted average of the unrestricted least squares estimator and the 3SLS estimator. The weight on the least squares estimator, which has finite moments, is nonzero when the two sets of estimates are far from each other according to a certain criterion. This way of truncating the 3SLS estimator is enough to ensure that the modified version has finite moments of up to order *T-K-G*, where *T* is the number of observations, *K* is the number of exogenous variables, and *G* is the number of endogenous variables.

It is not clear whether an approach like Maasoumi's can be extended to nonlinear models and whether it will be practical if it can. It may be that the main way in which this problem is dealt with in practice for large nonlinear models is merely to truncate the distributions by not using extreme draws that occur during the stochastic simulations.

7.3.3 Numerical Procedures for Drawing Values

A standard way of drawing values of α^* from the $N(\hat{\alpha}, \hat{V})$ distribution is to (1) factor numerically (using a subroutine package) $\hat{V}$ into PP', (2) draw (again using a subroutine package) k values of a standard normal random variable with mean 0 and variance 1, and (3) compute α^* as $\hat{\alpha} + Pe$, where e is the $k \times 1$ vector of the standard normal draws. Since $Eee' = I$, then $E(\alpha^* - \hat{\alpha})(\alpha^* - \hat{\alpha})' = EPee'P' = \hat{V}$, which is as desired for the distribution of α^*. A similar procedure can be used to draw values of u_t^* from the $N(0, \hat{S})$ distribution: $\hat{S}$ is factored into PP', and u_t^* is computed as Pe, where e is a $m \times 1$ vector of standard normal draws.

An alternative procedure for drawing values of the error terms, derived from McCarthy (1972), has also been used in practice. For this procedure one begins with the $m \times T$ matrix of estimated error terms, $\hat{U}$. T standard normal random variables are then drawn, and u_t^* is computed as $T^{-\frac{1}{2}}\hat{U}e$, where e is a $T \times 1$ vector of the standard normal draws. It is easy to show that the covariance matrix of u_t^* is $\hat{S}$, where, as earlier, $\hat{S}$ is $\frac{1}{T}\hat{U}\hat{U}'$.

An alternative procedure is also available for drawing values of the coefficients. Given the estimation period (say, 1 through T) and given $\hat{S}$, one can draw T values of u_t^* ($t = 1, \ldots, T$). One can then add these errors to the model and solve the model over the estimation period (static simulation, using the original values of the coefficient estimates). The predicted values of the endogenous variables from this solution can be taken to be a new data base, from which a new set of coefficients can be estimated. This set can then be taken to be one draw of the coefficients. This procedure is more expensive than drawing from the $N(\hat{\alpha}, \hat{V})$ distribution, since reestimation is required for each draw, but it has the advantage of not being based on a fixed estimate of the distribution of the coefficient estimates. It is, of course, based on a fixed value of $\hat{S}$ and a fixed set of original coefficient estimates.

7.3.4 Previous Studies and Results

Stochastic simulation has not been widely used in practice, but a few studies do exist. Studies in which only draws from the distribution of the error terms have been made include Nagar (1969); Evans, Klein, and Saito (1972);

Fromm, Klein, and Schink (1972); Green, Leibenberg, and Hirsch (1972); Cooper and Fischer (1972); Sowey (1973); Cooper (1974); Garbade (1975); Bianchi, Calzolari, and Corsi (1976); and Calzolari and Corsi (1977). Studies in which draws from both the distribution of the error terms and the distribution of the coefficient estimates have been made include Schink (1971), (1974); Haitovsky and Wallace (1972); Cooper and Fischer (1974); Muench, Rolnick, Wallace, and Weiler (1974); and Fair (1980a).

One important empirical conclusion that can be drawn from these stochastic simulation studies is that the values computed from deterministic simulations are quite close to the mean predicted values computed from stochastic simulations. In other words, the bias that results from using deterministic simulation to solve nonlinear models appears to be small. This conclusion has been reached by Nagar (1969); Sowey (1973); Cooper (1974); Bianchi, Calzolari, and Corsi (1976); and Calzolari and Corsi (1977) for stochastic simulation with respect to the error terms only and by Fair (1980a) for stochastic simulation with respect to both error terms and coefficients. The results reported in Section 7.5.1 for the US model also confirm this conclusion.

7.4 Subjective Adjustment of Models

In actual forecasting situations most models are "subjectively adjusted" before the forecasts are computed. The adjustments take the form of either using values other than zero for the future error terms or using values other than the estimated values for the coefficients. Different values of the same coefficient are sometimes used for different periods. Adjusting the values of constant terms is equivalent to adjusting the values of the error terms, given that a different value of the constant term can be used each period. Adjustments of this type are sometimes called "add factors." One interpretation of add factors, which is stressed by Intriligator (1978, p. 516), is that they are the user's estimates of the future values of the error terms. With enough add factors it is possible to have the forecasts from a model be whatever the user wants, subject to the restriction that the identities must be satisfied. Most add factors are subjective in that the procedure by which they were chosen cannot be replicated by others. A few add factors are objective; for example, the procedure of setting the future values of the error terms equal to the average of the past two estimated values is an objective one. This procedure, along with another type of mechanical adjustment procedure, is used for some of the results in Haitovsky, Treyz, and Su (1974). (See Green, Liebenberg, and Hirsch 1972 for other examples.)

7.5 Computational Results

7.5.1 The US Model

The US model consists of 30 stochastic equations, 169 unrestricted coefficients, and 98 identities. The covariance matrix of the error terms (S) is thus 30×30, and the covariance matrix of the coefficient estimates (V) is 169×169.

For the solution of the model, the stopping rule for the Gauss-Seidel technique was taken to be in percentage terms and the tolerance value was chosen to be .001 percent. The first 30 equations, which are the stochastic equations, were used for the convergence check. If each of the successive predictions of the first 30 variables were within the tolerance value, convergence was taken to be achieved. Not checking the identities avoided the problem that some of the values of the variables determined by identities are close to zero. Experimentation with alternative (and more precise) stopping rules indicated that the procedure of checking only the first 30 variables provided sufficient accuracy. The number of iterations needed for convergence varied between about 7 and 13 for a typical job. The time taken to solve the model for one quarter was about .2 seconds on the IBM 4341 and about 1.5 seconds on the VAX. No damping was used for any of the variables for the Gauss-Seidel technique.

The results of solving the model for the 1978I–1979IV period are presented in Table 7-1. The 2SLS estimates were used for these results. The values in the 0 rows are predicted values from a deterministic simulation, where the error terms have been set equal to zero. The time for this simulation was about 1.6 seconds on the IBM 4341 (.2 seconds $\times$ 8 quarters) and about 12 seconds on the VAX (1.5 seconds $\times$ 8 quarters). The values in the a rows are predicted values from a stochastic simulation in which only error terms are drawn. Each trial for this simulation consists of 8 draws of 30 values each from the $N(0, \hat{S})$ distribution. A total of 250 trials were made. The cost of each trial is roughly the cost of solving the model once for the eight quarters. The total cost for the 250 trials, as noted at the bottom of Table 7-1, was about 6.7 minutes on the IBM 4341 and 49 minutes on the VAX.

The values in the b and b′ rows are predicted values from a stochastic simulation in which draws of both error terms and coefficients are made. The results in the two rows are based on the same simulation. The b-row values are mean values, and the b′-row values are median values. Each trial for this simulation consists of eight draws of 30 values each from the $N(0, \hat{S})$ distribution and one draw of 169 values from the $N(\hat{\alpha}, \hat{V})$ distribution. A total

TABLE 7-1. Predicted values for the US model: comparison of deterministic and stochastic simulation results

	1978				1979			
	I	II	III	IV	I	II	III	IV
GNPR: Real GNP (billions of 1972 dollars)								
0	1403.6	1425.0	1441.8	1458.6	1467.0	1472.4	1484.0	1490.9
a	1403.4	1427.7	1441.8	1458.1	1466.8	1472.1	1483.2	1489.5
b	1403.2	1424.4	1441.5	1458.6	1465.4	1469.8	1480.3	1487.4
b'	1404.0	1423.8	1441.9	1458.1	1464.1	1469.0	1481.3	1488.6
GNPD: GNP deflator (1972 = 1.0)								
0	1.4589	1.4928	1.5164	1.5494	1.5826	1.6153	1.6506	1.6825
a	1.4590	1.4927	1.5167	1.5499	1.5835	1.6163	1.6521	1.6838
b	1.4590	1.4926	1.5160	1.5489	1.5821	1.6148	1.6493	1.6811
b'	1.4590	1.4931	1.5166	1.5488	1.5823	1.6156	1.6495	1.6826
100•UR: Unemployment rate (percentage points)								
0	6.75	6.76	6.84	6.93	7.00	7.05	7.03	7.20
a	6.77	6.81	6.88	6.98	7.00	7.04	7.02	7.20
b	6.76	6.77	6.83	6.91	7.00	7.09	7.11	7.33
b'	6.75	6.77	6.86	6.92	7.00	7.08	7.05	7.32
RS: Bill rate (percentage points)								
0	6.48	7.06	7.45	7.77	8.13	8.24	10.11	11.01
a	6.42	7.03	7.39	7.79	8.13	8.29	10.21	11.02
b	6.50	7.15	7.58	7.92	8.28	8.36	10.11	10.91
b'	6.46	7.13	7.56	7.99	8.32	8.39	10.20	10.98
M1: Money supply (billions of current dollars)								
0	376.1	383.5	390.1	399.6	406.3	417.0	424.0	432.4
a	376.3	383.8	390.7	400.2	406.9	417.6	424.4	432.7
b	376.0	383.5	390.1	400.1	406.6	416.9	423.9	432.5
b'	376.1	383.1	389.6	399.7	406.0	416.9	423.8	432.5

Notes: 0 = Error terms set equal to zero (no stochastic simulation).
a = Stochastic simulation with respect to error terms only.
b = Stochastic simulation with respect to error terms and coefficient estimates.
b' = Same as b except values are median values rather than mean values.

- Prediction period is 1978 I - 1979 IV. All simulations are dynamic. Number of trials = 250.
- The time for one eight-quarter stochastic simulation of 250 trials was about 6.7 minutes on the IBM 4341 and about 49 minutes on the VAX.

of 250 trials were also made for this simulation. The total cost for the 250 trials was about the same as the cost of the 250 trials for the a-row simulation.

The main conclusion to be drawn from the results in Table 7-1 is that the predicted values from the deterministic simulation are quite close to the corresponding predicted values from the stochastic simulations. This, as noted in Section 7.3, is a common result. The bias that results from solving nonlinear models deterministically appears to be small for most models.

The other important conclusion from the results is that the median values are quite close to the corresponding mean values. In other words, the results are not sensitive to the use of a more robust measure of central tendency. For none of the draws for the results in the table did the Gauss-Seidel technique fail to find a solution, and therefore no draws had to be discarded as being too extreme.

7.5.2 The MC Model

The solution of the MC model is a fairly large computational problem. For each of the 42 countries for which there are estimated equations (not counting the United States), there are up to 11 stochastic equations and 9 identities. In addition, there are 2,388 estimated trade share equations. The model is solved in the following way.

1. Given exports, $X75\$_i$, and the import price index, PM_i, country i's model is solved using the Gauss-Seidel technique. Each model consists of all or some subset of the 20 equations in Table B-3 (Appendix B).

2. Given the solution of each country's model, the calculations in Table B-4 (Appendix B), including the calculations of the trade shares, are performed. Table B-4 takes from each country the predicted value of imports, $M75\$A_i$, the predicted value of the export price index, PX_i, and the predicted value of the exchange rate, e_i. It returns to each country the predicted value of its exports, $X75\$_i$, the predicted value of its import price index, PM_i, and the predicted value of the world price index, $PW\$_i$.

3. Given $X75\$_i$ and PM_i from step 2, each country's model is solved again. The Table B-4 calculations are then performed again. This process is repeated until the successive predicted values from one iteration to the next are within some prescribed tolerance level.

This procedure consists of two types of iterations. The first is the standard Gauss-Seidel type for each country's model separately (step 1), and the second is the iteration between Tables B-3 and B-4 (step 3). The tolerance criterion for the second type of iteration should be greater than that for the first, since otherwise sufficient accuracy may not be achieved for the first type of iteration to achieve the required accuracy for the second.

This procedure worked quite well for the MC model. The average number of iterations for each country's model was usually less than 10, and the number of iterations of the second type varied between about 3 and 15. The total time taken to solve the model for one quarter varied between about 20 and 40 seconds on the IBM 4341 and about 2 and 4 minutes on the VAX. As noted earlier, the times for the US model for one quarter are .2 seconds on the

IBM 4341 and 1.5 seconds on the VAX. The MC model is thus considerably more expensive to solve than the US model. For this reason, no stochastic simulation experiments were performed for the MC model. Deterministic simulations were used to examine both the model's predictive accuracy and its properties. The accuracy is examined in Section 8.6, and the properties are discussed in Section 9.5.

8 Evaluating Predictive Accuracy

8.1 Introduction

This chapter deals with one of the most important issues in macroeconomics: the evaluation and testing of models. The central question in this area is how to decide which model out of a number best approximates the structure of the economy. Although an obvious answer is to choose the model that fits the data best, the problem comes in deciding what criterion to use to judge which model fits the data best. In the next two sections the standard ways in which this problem has been treated are discussed: Section 8.2 considers the evaluation of ex ante forecasts, and Section 8.3 considers the evaluation of ex post forecasts. My method for dealing with this problem is explained in Section 8.4. Results for various models are presented in Sections 8.5 and 8.6.

The three most common measures of predictive accuracy that have been used to evaluate ex ante and ex post forecasts are root mean squared error (RMSE), mean absolute error (MAE), and Theil's (1966, p. 28) inequality coefficient (U). Let $\hat{y}_{it}$ be the forecast of variable i for period t, and let y_{it} be the actual value. $\hat{y}_{it}$ can be a prediction for more than one period ahead. Assuming that observations on $\hat{y}_{it}$ and y_{it} are available for $t = 1, \ldots, T$, the three measures are

$$\text{RMSE} = \sqrt{\frac{1}{T}\sum_{t=1}^{T}(y_{it} - \hat{y}_{it})^2}, \tag{8.1}$$

$$\text{MAE} = \frac{1}{T}\sum_{t=1}^{T}|y_{it} - \hat{y}_{it}|, \tag{8.2}$$

$$\text{U} = \frac{\sqrt{\frac{1}{T}\sum_{t=1}^{T}(\Delta y_{it} - \Delta\hat{y}_{it})^2}}{\sqrt{\frac{1}{T}\sum_{t=1}^{T}(\Delta y_{it})^2}}, \tag{8.3}$$

where Δ in (8.3) denotes either absolute or percentage change. All three measures are zero if the forecasts are perfect. The MAE measure penalizes large errors less than does the RMSE measure. The value of U is one for a no-change forecast ($\Delta\hat{y}_{it} = 0$). A value of U greater than one means that the forecast is less accurate than the simple forecast of no change.

8.2 Evaluation of Ex Ante Forecasts

The procedure followed to evaluate ex ante forecasts is simply to collect the forecast data for a certain period and to compute one or more of the three measures just mentioned. Forecasts from different models are evaluated by comparing the error measures across models. An important practical problem that arises in evaluating ex ante forecasting accuracy is the problem of data revisions. Given that the data for many variables are revised a number of times before becoming "final," it is not clear whether the forecast values should be compared to the first-released values, to the final values, or to some values in between. There is no obvious answer to this problem. If the revision for a particular variable is a benchmark revision, where the level of the variable is revised beginning at least a few periods before the start of the prediction period, then a common procedure is to adjust the forecast value by adding the forecasted change ($\Delta\hat{y}_{it}$), which is based on the old data, to the new lagged value (y_{it-1}). The adjusted forecast value is then compared to the new data. If, say, the revision took the form of adding a constant amount $\bar{y}_i$ to each of the old values of y_{it}, then this procedure merely adds the same $\bar{y}_i$ to each of the forecasted values of y_{it}. This procedure is often followed even if the revisions are not all benchmark revisions, on the implicit assumption that they are more like benchmark revisions than other kinds. Following this procedure also means that if forecast changes are being evaluated, as in the U measure, no adjustments are needed.

A number of studies have examined ex ante forecasting accuracy using one or more of the above measures; some of the more recent ones are McNees (1973, 1974, 1975, 1976) and Zarnowitz (1979). It is usually the case that forecasts from both model builders and non-model builders are examined and compared. A common "base" set of forecasts to use for comparison purposes is the set from the ASA/NBER Business Outlook Survey. A general conclusion from these studies is that there is no obvious "winner" among the various forecasters (see, for example, Zarnowitz 1979, pp. 23, 30). The relative performance of the forecasters varies considerably across variables and length ahead of the forecast, and the differences among the forecasters for a given variable and length ahead are generally small. This means that there is as yet little evidence that the forecasts from model builders are more accurate than, say, the forecasts from the ASA/NBER Survey.

Ex ante forecasting comparisons are unfortunately of little interest from the point of view of examining the predictive accuracy of models. There are two reasons for this; the first is that the ex ante forecasts are based on guessed rather than actual values of the exogenous variables. Given only the actual and predicted values of the endogenous variables, there is no way of separating a given error into that part due to bad guesses and that part due to other factors. A model should not necessarily be penalized for bad exogenous-variable guesses from its users. (More will be said about this in Section 8.4.) The second, and more important, reason is that almost all the forecasts examined in these studies are generated from subjectively adjusted models. (The use of add factors is discussed in Section 7.4.) It is thus the accuracy of the forecasting performance of the model builders rather than that of the models that is being examined.

There is some indirect evidence that the use of add factors is quite important in practice. The studies of Evans, Haitovsky, and Treyz (1972) and Haitovsky and Treyz (1972) analyzing the Wharton and OBE models found that the ex ante forecasts from the model builders were more accurate than the ex post forecasts from the models, even when the same add factors that were used for the ex ante forecasts were used for the ex post forecasts. In other words, the use of actual rather than guessed values of the exogenous variables decreased the accuracy of the forecasts. This general conclusion can also be drawn from the results for the BEA model in table 3 in Hirsch, Grimm, and Narasimham (1974). This conclusion is consistent with the view that the add factors are (in a loose sense) more important than the model in determining the ex ante forecasts: what one would otherwise consider to be an improvement for the model, namely the use of more accurate exogenous-variable values, worsens the forecasting accuracy.

In regard to nonsubjectively-adjusted ex ante forecasts, there is some evidence that their accuracy is improved by the use of actual rather than guessed values of the exogenous variables. During the period 1970III–1973II, I made ex ante forecasts using a short-run forecasting model (Fair 1971b). No add factors were used for these forecasts. The accuracy of these forecasts is examined in Fair (1974b), and the results indicate that the accuracy is generally improved when actual rather than guessed values of the exogenous variables are used.

It is finally of interest to note, although nothing really follows from this, that the (nonsubjectively-adjusted) ex ante forecasts from my forecasting model were on average less accurate than the subjectively adjusted forecasts (McNees 1973), whereas the ex post forecasts (that is, the forecasts based on the actual values of the exogenous variables) were on average of about the same degree of accuracy as the subjectively adjusted forecasts (Fair 1974b).

8.3 Evaluation of Ex Post Forecasts

The RMSE, MAE, and U measures have also been widely used to evaluate the accuracy of ex post forecasts. One of the better-known comparisons of ex post forecasting accuracy is described in Fromm and Klein (1976), where eleven models are analyzed. The standard procedure for ex post comparisons is to compute ex post forecasts over a common simulation period, calculate for each model and variable an error measure, and compare the values of the error measure across models. If the forecasts are outside-sample, there is usually some attempt to have the ends of the estimation periods for the models be approximately the same. It is generally the case that forecasting accuracy deteriorates the further away the forecast period is from the estimation period, and this is the reason for wanting to make the estimation periods as similar as possible for different models.

The use of the RMSE measure, or one of the other measures, to evaluate ex post forecasts is straightforward, and little more needs to be said about it. Sometimes the accuracy of a given model is compared to the accuracy of a "naive" model, which can range from the simple assumption of no change in each variable to an autoregressive moving average (ARIMA) process for each variable. (The comparison with the no-change model is, of course, already implicit in the U measure.) It is sometimes the case that turning-point observations are examined separately; by "turning point" is meant a point at which the change in a variable switches sign. There is nothing inherent in the statistical specification of models that would lead one to examine turning points separately, but there is a strand of the literature in which turning-point accuracy has been emphasized.

Although the use of the RMSE or a similar measure is widespread, there are two serious problems associated with this general procedure. The first concerns the exogenous variables. Models differ both in the number and types of variables that are taken to be exogenous and in the sensitivity of the predicted values of the endogenous variables to the exogenous-variable values. The procedure of comparing RMSEs or similar measures across models does not take these differences into account. If one model is less "endogenous" than another (say that prices are taken to be exogenous in one model but not in another), it has an unfair advantage in the calculation of the error measures. The other problem concerns the fact that forecast error variances vary across time, both because of nonlinearities in the model and because of variation in the exogenous variables. Although RMSEs are in some loose sense estimates of the averages of the variances across time, no rigorous statistical interpretation can be placed on them: they are not estimates of any parameters of the model.

Another problem associated with within-sample calculations of the error measures is the possible existence of data mining. If in the process of constructing a model one has, by running many regressions, searched diligently for the best-fitting equation for each variable, there is a danger that the equations chosen, while providing good fits within the estimation period, are poor approximations to the structure. Within-sample error calculations are not likely to discover this, and thus they may give a very misleading impression of the true accuracy of the model. Outside-sample error calculations should pick up this problem, however, and this is the reason that more weight is generally placed on outside-sample results.

Nelson (1972) used an alternative procedure in addition to the RMSE procedure in his ex post evaluation of the FRB-MIT-PENN (FMP) model. For each of a number of endogenous variables he obtained a series of static predictions using both the FMP model and an ARIMA model. He then regressed the actual value of each variable on the two predicted values over the period for which the predictions were made. If one ignores the fact that the FMP model is nonlinear, the predictions from the model are conditional expectations based on a given information set. If the FMP model makes efficient use of this information, then no further information should be contained in the ARIMA predictions. The ARIMA model for each variable uses only a subset of the information, namely, that contained in the past history of the variable. Therefore, if the FMP model has made efficient use of the information, the coefficient for the ARIMA predicted values should be zero. Nelson found that in general the estimates of this coefficient were significantly different from zero.

This test, although of some interest, cannot be used to compare models that differ in the number and types of variables that are taken to be exogenous. In order to test the hypothesis of efficient information use, the information set used by one model must be contained in the set used by the other model, and this is in general not true for models that differ in their exogenous variables.

8.4 A Method for Evaluating Predictive Accuracy

My method for evaluating predictive accuracy, in contrast to previous procedures, takes account of exogenous-variable uncertainty and of the fact that forecast error variances vary across time. It also deals in a systematic way with the question of the possible misspecification of the model. It accounts for the four main sources of uncertainty of a forecast: uncertainty due to (1) the error terms, (2) the coefficient estimates, (3) the exogenous-variable forecasts, and (4) the possible misspecification of the model. The method relies heavily on the use of stochastic simulation.

8.4.1 Uncertainty from the Error Terms and Coefficient Estimates

Estimating the uncertainty from the error terms and coefficient estimates is simply a matter of computing $\tilde{\sigma}^2_{itk}$ in (7.8). $\tilde{\sigma}^2_{itk}$ is a stochastic-simulation estimate of σ^2_{itk}, the variance of the forecast error for a k-period-ahead forecast of variable i from a simulation beginning in period t. It is based on draws from both the distribution of the error terms and the distribution of the coefficient estimates. If an estimate of the uncertainty from the error terms only is desired, the draws should be only from the distribution of the error terms, with the coefficient estimates fixed at some set of values.

8.4.2 Uncertainty from the Exogenous Variables

There are two polar assumptions that can be made about the uncertainty of the exogenous variables: one is that there is no uncertainty; the other is that the exogenous-variable forecasts are in some way as uncertain as the endogenous-variable forecasts. Under this second assumption one could, for example, estimate an autoregressive equation for each exogenous variable and add these equations to the model. This expanded model, which would have no exogenous variables, could then be used for the stochastic-simulation estimates of the variances. While the first assumption is clearly likely to underestimate exogenous-variable uncertainty in most applications, the second assumption is likely to overestimate it. This is particularly true for fiscal policy variables in macroeconometric models, where government budget data are usually quite useful for purposes of forecasting up to at least about eight quarters ahead. The best approximation is thus likely to lie somewhere in between these two assumptions.

The basic assumption that I have used in my work so far is in between the two polar assumptions. The procedure that I have followed is to estimate an eighth-order autoregressive equation for each exogenous variable (with a constant term and time trend included in the equation) and then to take the estimated standard error from this regression as the estimate of the degree of uncertainty attached to forecasting the variable for each period. This procedure ignores the uncertainty of the coefficient estimates in the autoregressive equations, which is one of the reasons it is not as extreme as the second polar assumption.

A procedure similar to the second polar assumption was used in an earlier stochastic simulation study of Haitovsky and Wallace (1972), where third-order autoregressive equations were estimated for the exogenous variables and then these equations were added to the model. This procedure is consistent with the second polar assumption *except* that for purposes of the stochastic simulations, Haitovsky and Wallace took the variances of the error terms to be one-half of the estimated variances. They defend this procedure (pp. 267–268) on the grounds that the uncertainty from the exogenous-variable forecasts is likely to be less than is reflected in the autoregressive equations.

Another possible procedure that could be used for the exogenous variables would be to gather from various forecasting services data on their ex ante forecasting errors of the exogenous variables (exogenous to the investigator, not necessarily to the forecasting service). From these errors for various periods one could estimate a standard error for each exogenous variable and then use these errors for the stochastic-simulation draws.

For purposes of describing the present method, all that needs to be assumed is that *some* procedure is available for estimating exogenous-variable uncertainty. If equations for the exogenous variables are not added to the model but instead some in-between procedure is followed, then each stochastic-simulation trial consists of draws of error terms, coefficients, and exogenous-variable errors. If equations are added, then each trial consists of draws of error terms and coefficients from both the structural equations and the exogenous-variable equations. In either case, let $\tilde{\tilde{\sigma}}^2_{itk}$ denote the stochastic-simulation estimate of the variance of the forecast error that takes into account exogenous variable uncertainty. $\tilde{\tilde{\sigma}}^2_{itk}$ differs from $\tilde{\sigma}^2_{itk}$ in (7.8) in that the trials for $\tilde{\tilde{\sigma}}^2_{itk}$ include draws of exogenous-variable errors.

The procedure that I have used to estimate exogenous-variable uncertainty is implemented as follows. Let $\hat{s}_i$ denote the estimated standard error from the eighth-order autoregressive equation for exogenous variable i. Let v_{it} be a normally distributed random variable with mean zero and variance $\hat{s}_i^2$: $v_{it} \sim N(0, \hat{s}_i^2)$ for all t. Let $\hat{x}_{it}$ be the "base" value of exogenous variable i for period t. The base values can either be the actual values, if the period in question is within the period for which data exist, or guessed values otherwise. If the values are guessed, they need *not* be the predictions from the autoregressive equations; the latter are used merely to get the values for $\hat{s}_i$. Let x^*_{it} be the value of variable i used on a given trial. Then for a given trial x^*_{it} is taken to be $\hat{x}_{it} + v_{it}$, where v_{it} is drawn from the above distribution. If, say, the simulation period were 8 quarters in length and there were 100 exogenous variables, 800 draws would be taken, one for each of the 100 i's and one for each of the 8 t's. There would be 100 autoregressive equations estimated.

For some of my work I have taken the estimated standard error from the autoregressive equation for each variable to be an estimate of the degree of uncertainty attached to forecasting the *change* in the variable for each period. Given the way that many exogenous variables are forecast, by extrapolating past trends or taking variables to be unchanged from their last observed values, it may be that any error in forecasting the level of a variable in, say, the first period will persist throughout the forecast period. If this is true, the assumption that the errors pertain to the changes in the variables may be better than the assumption that they pertain to the levels. This procedure is implemented as follows. Let quarter 1 be the first quarter of the prediction period, and assume that the prediction period is of length T. The values of x_{it}^* $(t = 1, \ldots, T)$ for a given trial are taken to be

$$\begin{aligned} x_{i1}^* &= \hat{x}_{i1} + v_{i1}, \\ x_{i2}^* &= \hat{x}_{i2} + v_{i1} + v_{i2}, \\ &\vdots \\ x_{iT}^* &= \hat{x}_{iT} + v_{i1} + v_{i2} + \ldots + v_{iT}, \end{aligned} \tag{8.4}$$

where each v_{it} $(t = 1, \ldots, T)$ is drawn from the $N(0, \hat{s}_i^2)$ distribution. Because of the assumption that the errors pertain to changes, the error term v_{i1} is carried along from quarter 1 on. Similarly, v_{i2} is carried along from quarter 2 on, and so forth.

8.4.3 Uncertainty from the Possible Misspecification of the Model

The most difficult and costly part of the method is estimating the uncertainty from the possible misspecification of the model, which requires successive reestimation and stochastic simulation of the model. It is based on a comparison of estimated variances computed by means of stochastic simulation with estimated variances computed from outside-sample forecast errors. As will be seen, the expected value of the difference between the two estimated variances for a given variable and period is zero for a correctly specified model. The expected value is not in general zero for a misspecified model, and this fact can be used to try to account for misspecification effects.

All of the stochastic simulations that are referred to in this section are with respect to error terms and coefficients only. In other words, there is assumed to be no exogenous-variable uncertainty. Section 8.4.4 discusses the way in which the estimates of exogenous-variable uncertainty that were discussed in Section 8.4.2 are combined with the estimates of misspecification effects.

Assume that the prediction period begins one period after the end of the estimation period, and call this period t. From stochastic simulation one obtains an estimate of the variance of the forecast error, $\tilde{\sigma}^2_{itk}$ in (7.8). One also obtains an estimate of the expected value of the k-period-ahead forecast of variable i, $\tilde{\bar{y}}_{itk}$ in (7.7). The difference between this estimate and the actual value, y_{it+k-1}, is the mean forecast error:

$$\hat{\epsilon}_{itk} = y_{it+k-1} - \tilde{\bar{y}}_{itk}. \tag{8.5}$$

If it is assumed that $\tilde{\bar{y}}_{itk}$ exactly equals the true expected value, $\bar{y}_{itk}$, then $\hat{\epsilon}_{itk}$ in (8.5) is a sample draw from a distribution with a known mean of zero and variance σ^2_{itk}. The square of this error, $\hat{\epsilon}^2_{itk}$, is thus under this assumption an unbiased estimate of σ^2_{itk}. One therefore has two estimates of σ^2_{itk}, one computed from the mean forecast error and one computed by stochastic simulation. Let d_{itk} denote the difference between these two estimates:

$$d_{itk} = \hat{\epsilon}^2_{itk} - \tilde{\sigma}^2_{itk}. \tag{8.6}$$

If it is further assumed that $\tilde{\sigma}^2_{itk}$ exactly equals the true value, then d_{itk} is the difference between the estimated variance based on the mean forecast error and the true variance. Therefore, under the two assumptions of no error in the stochastic-simulation estimates, the expected value of d_{itk} is zero.

The assumption of no stochastic-simulation error, that is, $\tilde{\bar{y}}_{itk} = \bar{y}_{itk}$ and $\tilde{\sigma}^2_{itk} = \sigma^2_{itk}$, is obviously only approximately correct at best. As noted in Section 7.3.1, even with an infinite number of draws the assumption would not be correct because the draws are from estimated rather than known distributions. It does seem, however, that the error introduced by this assumption is likely to be small relative to the error introduced by the fact that some assumption must be made about the mean of the distribution of d_{itk}. For this reason, nothing more will be said about stochastic-simulation error. The emphasis instead will be on possible assumptions about the mean of the distribution of d_{itk}, given the assumption of no stochastic-simulation error.

If the model is misspecified, it is not in general true that the expected value of d_{itk} is zero. Misspecification has two effects on d_{itk}. First, if the model is misspecified, the estimated covariance matrices that are used for the stochastic simulation will not in general be unbiased estimates of the true covariance matrices. The estimated variances computed by means of stochastic simulation will thus in general be biased. Second, the estimated variances computed from the forecast errors will in general be biased estimates of the true variances. Since misspecification affects both estimates, the effect on d_{itk} is ambiguous. It is possible for misspecification to affect the two estimates in the same way and thus leave the expected value of the difference between them equal to zero. In general, however, this does not seem likely, and so in general one would not expect the expected value of d_{itk} to be zero for a misspecified model.

Because of the common practice in macroeconometric work of searching for equations that fit the data well, it seems likely that the estimated means of d_{itk} will be positive in practice for a misspecified model. If the model fits the data well within sample, the stochastic-simulation estimates of the forecast error variances will be small. This is because they are based on draws from estimated distributions of the error terms and coefficient estimates that have small (in a matrix sense) covariance matrices. If the model, although fitting the data well, is in fact misspecified, this should result in large outside-sample forecast errors. The estimated mean of d_{itk} is thus likely to be positive: $\tilde{\sigma}^2_{itk}$ is small because of small estimated covariance matrices, and $\hat{\epsilon}^2_{itk}$ is large because of large outside-sample forecast errors.

The procedure described so far uses one estimation period and one prediction period. It results in one value of d_{itk} for each variable i and length ahead k. Since one observation is obviously not adequate for estimating the mean of d_{itk}, more observations must be generated. This can be done by using successively new estimation periods and new prediction periods. Assume, for example, that one has data from period 1 through period 100. The model can be estimated through, say, period 70, with the prediction period beginning with period 71. Stochastic simulation for the prediction period will yield for each i and k a value of d_{i71k} in (8.6). The model can then be reestimated through period 71, with the prediction period now beginning with period 72. Stochastic simulation for this prediction period will yield for each i and k a value of d_{i72k} in (8.6). This process can be repeated through the estimation period ending with period 99. For the one-period-ahead forecast ($k = 1$) the procedure will yield for each variable i 30 values of d_{it1} ($t = 71, \ldots, 100$); for the two-period-ahead forecast ($k = 2$) it will yield 29 values of d_{it2} ($t = 71, \ldots, 99$); and so on. If the assumption of no stochastic-simulation error holds for all t, then the expected value of d_{itk} is zero for all t for a correctly specified model.

The final step in the process is to make an assumption about the mean of

d_{itk} that allows the computed values of d_{itk} to be used to estimate the mean. A variety of assumptions are possible. One is simply that the mean is constant across time. In other words, misspecification is assumed to affect the mean in the same way for all t. If this assumption is made, the mean can be estimated by merely averaging the computed values of d_{itk} for each i and k. Another possible assumption is that the mean is a function of other variables, where the other variables are specified. (A simple example of this is the assumption that the mean follows a linear time trend.) Given this assumption, the mean can be estimated from a regression of d_{itk} on the specified variables. (In the linear trend case, the explanatory variables would be a constant and a time trend.) The predicted value from this regression for period t, denoted $\hat{d}_{itk}$, is the estimated mean for period t. In this case the estimated mean obviously varies over time if the explanatory variables vary. This second assumption would be used if it were felt that the degree of misspecification of the model varies in a systematic way with other variables.

A version of the first assumption is that the mean of d_{itk} is proportional to $\tilde{\tilde{y}}_{itk}^2$, which implies that the mean of $d_{itk}/\tilde{\tilde{y}}_{itk}^2$ is constant across time. d_{itk} is in units of the variable squared, and this assumption is equivalent to the constant mean assumption in percentage terms. For variables with trends it may be more reasonable to couch the assumption in percentage terms, since the mean may vary as a function of the size of the variable.

8.4.4 Total Uncertainty

Given $\hat{d}_{itk}$, the estimate of the mean of d_{itk} for period t, it is possible to estimate the total variance of the forecast error, denoted $\hat{\sigma}_{itk}^2$. This is the sum of $\tilde{\tilde{\sigma}}_{itk}^2$, the stochastic-simulation estimate of the variance due to the error terms, coefficient estimates, and exogenous variables, and $\hat{d}_{itk}$:

$$\hat{\sigma}_{itk}^2 = \tilde{\tilde{\sigma}}_{itk}^2 + \hat{d}_{itk}. \tag{8.7}$$

The use of $\tilde{\tilde{\sigma}}_{itk}^2$ instead of $\tilde{\sigma}_{itk}^2$ in (8.7) is where the estimate of exogenous variable uncertainty is brought into the analysis.

Since the procedure in arriving at $\hat{\sigma}_{itk}^2$ takes into account the four main sources of uncertainty of a forecast, the values of $\hat{\sigma}_{itk}^2$ can be compared across models for a given i, k, and t. If, for example, one model has consistently smaller values of $\hat{\sigma}_{itk}^2$ than another, this would be fairly strong evidence for concluding that it is a more accurate model, that is, a better approximation to the true structure.

It may be useful at this stage to review the steps that are involved in arriving at $\hat{\sigma}_{itk}^2$ in (8.7). Consider the example used in Section 8.4.3, where data are available for periods 1 through 100. Assume that one is interested in estimating the uncertainty of an eight-period-ahead forecast that begins in period 90. In other words, one is interested in computing $\hat{\sigma}_{itk}^2$ for $t = 90$ and $k = 1, \ldots, 8$. Assume that the main set of coefficient estimates of the model is based on an estimation period through period 100. Given (1) these estimates and the associated estimates of the distributions of the error terms and coefficient estimates, (2) the actual values of the exogenous variables for periods 90–97, and (3) some assumption about exogenous-variable uncertainty, $\tilde{\tilde{\sigma}}_{itk}^2$ can be computed using stochastic simulation for $t = 90$ and $k = 1, \ldots, 8$. Each trial consists of one eight-period dynamic simulation beginning in period 90. It requires draws of the error terms, coefficients, and (possibly) exogenous-variable errors. If, say, 250 trials are taken, the model must be solved 250 times for the eight quarters.

Since computing $\tilde{\tilde{\sigma}}_{itk}^2$ requires only one stochastic simulation, this is the relatively inexpensive part of the method. The expensive part consists of the successive reestimation and stochastic simulation that are needed in computing the d_{itk} values. In the example in Section 8.4.3, the model would be estimated 30 times and stochastically simulated 30 times in computing the d_{itk} values. If 250 trials for each stochastic simulation were used, the model would be solved $250 \times 30 = 7{,}500$ times, where each solution is a dynamic eight-period simulation. After the d_{itk} values are computed for, say, periods 70 through 99, $\hat{d}_{itk}$ can be computed for $t = 90$ and $k = 1, \ldots, 8$ using whatever assumption has been made about the distribution of d_{itk}. This procedure then allows $\hat{\sigma}_{itk}^2$ in (8.7) to be computed for $t = 90$ and $k = 1, \ldots, 8$.

8.4.5 General Remarks about the Method

In the successive reestimation of the model, the first period of the estimation period may or may not be increased by one each time. The criterion that one should use in deciding this is to pick the procedure that seems likely to correspond to the chosen assumption about the distribution of d_{itk} being the best approximation to the truth. It is also possible to take the distance between the last period of the estimation period and the first period of the forecast period to be other than one.

Any assumption that one makes about the mean of d_{itk} is at best likely to be only a rough approximation to the truth. It is unlikely that the effects of misspecification on the two estimated variances are so systematic as to lead to any assumption that one might make about the mean of the difference between the two being exactly right. One useful thing that can be done is simply to plot the d_{itk} values over time for a given i and k and see if there are systematic tendencies. One might observe trend or cyclical movements in these plots, which could be useful either in deciding what to assume about the mean of d_{itk} or in deciding how to change the model to try to eliminate the misspecification. If the latter is done, one is using the d_{itk} values to reveal weaknesses in the model that might be corrected rather than to adjust the stochastic-simulation estimates of the variances for misspecification. The individual d_{itk} values may thus be of interest in their own right aside from their possible use in estimating total predictive uncertainty. If the values are used solely to reveal weaknesses of the model, no assumption about the mean of d_{itk} is needed.

Although I have been interpreting the d_{itk} values as measuring the misspecification of the model, this is not exactly right. Since misspecification affects both $\tilde{\sigma}^2_{itk}$ and $\hat{\epsilon}^2_{itk}$ in (8.6), it may be for a particular model that both are affected about the same. In this case the expected value of d_{itk} would be close to zero and yet the model could be seriously misspecified. In other words, misspecification can make both $\tilde{\sigma}^2_{itk}$ and $\hat{\epsilon}^2_{itk}$ larger and leave the difference between the two about the same. The more common case, as discussed in Section 8.4.3, seems likely to be one in which extensive searching for equations that fit the data well has resulted in an estimate of $\tilde{\sigma}^2_{itk}$ that is too small. In this case the d_{itk} values are likely to be on average large. Whatever the case, one should be aware that interpreting the d_{itk} values as measures of misspecification is using the word "misspecification" in a very special way. A better but more awkward way of stating what the d_{itk} values are is that they are a measure of the misspecification of the model that is not already reflected in the stochastic-simulation estimate of the forecast error variance.

It is important to note that the interpretation of the d_{itk} values does not affect the interpretation of $\hat{\sigma}^2_{itk}$ in (8.7) as an estimate of the total variance of the forecast error. If misspecification affects the stochastic-simulation estimate of the variance about as much as it affects the estimate based on the outside-sample forecast error (so that $\hat{d}_{itk}$ is close to zero), misspecification effects will be reflected in $\tilde{\tilde{\sigma}}^2_{itk}$ in (8.7) rather than in $\hat{d}_{itk}$. The term $\hat{d}_{itk}$ is merely the adjustment for the misspecification effects that are not captured by $\tilde{\tilde{\sigma}}^2_{itk}$.

The estimates of the mean of d_{itk} that have been proposed in Section 8.4.3 are not in general efficient because the error term in the d_{itk} regression is in general heteroscedastic. Even under the null hypothesis of no misspecification, the variance of d_{itk} is not constant across time. It is true, however, that

$\hat{\epsilon}_{itk}/\sqrt{\tilde{\sigma}^2_{itk} + \hat{d}_{itk}}$ has unit variance for all t under the null hypothesis, and therefore it is reasonable to assume that $\hat{\epsilon}^2_{itk}/(\tilde{\sigma}^2_{itk} + \hat{d}_{itk})$ has a constant variance for all t. This then suggests the following iterative procedure. (1) For each i and k, calculate $\hat{d}_{itk}$ from the d_{itk} regression, as discussed earlier; (2) divide each observation in the d_{itk} regression by $\tilde{\sigma}^2_{itk} + \hat{d}_{itk}$, run another regression, and calculate $\hat{d}_{itk}$ from this regression; (3) repeat step 2 until the successive estimates of $\hat{d}_{itk}$ are within some prescribed tolerance level. Litterman (1980) has carried out this procedure for a number of models for the case in which the only explanatory variable in the d_{itk} regression is the constant term (that is, for the case in which it is assumed that the mean of the d_{itk} distribution is constant across time).

If one is willing to assume that $\hat{\epsilon}_{itk}$ is normally distributed, which may or may not be a good approximation, Litterman (1979) has shown that the iterative procedure just described produces maximum likelihood estimates. He has used this assumption in Litterman (1980) to test the hypothesis (using a likelihood ratio test) that the mean of d_{itk} is the same in the first and second halves of the sample period. The hypothesis was rejected at the 5-percent level in only 3 of 24 tests. These results thus suggest that the assumption of a constant mean of d_{itk} may not be a bad approximation in many cases. The results for the US model, which are reported in Section 8.5, also suggest that the assumption may be a reasonable approximation.

Another interpretation of the mean of d_{itk} is that it is a measure of the average unexplained forecast error variance (that is, that part not explained by $\tilde{\tilde{\sigma}}^2_{itk}$). Using this interpretation, Litterman (1980) has examined the question of whether the use of the estimated mean of d_{itk} leads to more accurate estimates of the forecast error variance. The results of his tests, which are based on the normality assumption, show that substantially more accurate estimates are obtained using the estimated means.

It should finally be noted that although the method is designed to catch a model that fits the data well within sample but is in fact poorly specified, there is a subtle form of data mining that the method does not account for. If, say, a model is specified in period 100, estimated through period 90, and tested with respect to its outside-sample forecasting accuracy for periods 91–100, it is clear that this is not a strict outside-sample test. Information on what happened between periods 91 and 100 may have been used in the specification of the model, and thus one cannot be sure that the model's "outside-sample" accuracy that is estimated for periods 91–100 will hold for, say, periods 101–110. Within the context of the present method, this means that the computed values of d_{itk} for periods 91–100 are too low, which will result in values of $\hat{d}_{itk}$ that are too low and thus values of $\hat{\sigma}^2_{itk}$ that are too low.

8.5 A Comparison of the US, ARUS, VAR1US, VAR2US, and LINUS Models

In this section five econometric models of the United States are compared using the method in Section 8.4. The main concern is to see how the US model compares to the autoregressive model (ARUS), the two vector autoregressive models (VAR1US and VAR2US), and a simple linear model (LINUS). The US model is discussed in Chapter 4, and the other models are discussed in Chapter 5.

8.5.1 Computing the d_{itk} Values

The primary cost of the method is computing the d_{itk} values. In computing these values, each of the five models was estimated 51 times. The first estimation period ended in 1969III, the second estimation period ended in 1969IV, and so on through 1982I. A stochastic simulation was then run for each of the 51 sets of estimates, where the prediction period began two quarters after the end of the estimation period. The reason for beginning the prediction period two quarters rather than only one quarter after the end of the estimation period is that in practice most of the data for the most recent quarter are preliminary. In my work I use the preliminary data as initial conditions for a forecast but not as observations for estimation. This means that there is always a two-quarter gap between the end of the estimation period and the beginning of the prediction period, and the present procedure is consistent with this practice.

The computations for the US model were as follows. The first of the 51 estimation periods was 1954I–1969III (63 observations). The coefficients were estimated by 2SLS, and the covariance matrix of the coefficient estimates was computed. Let $\hat{\alpha}_2$ denote the coefficient estimates, and let $\hat{V}_2$ denote the estimated covariance matrix. The correct formula for the covariance matrix is (6.20) in Chapter 6, where the off-diagonal blocks of the matrix are not zero. Computing this matrix is fairly expensive in that it requires more time than is required to compute the coefficient estimates. (The times reported in Section 6.5.1 for the IBM 4341 are 3.0 minutes for the coefficient estimates and 5.5 minutes for the covariance matrix.) If the off-diagonal blocks are taken to be zero, there is no extra cost in computing the covariance matrix because the diagonal blocks are available from the estimates of the individual equations. For the work here, the off-diagonal blocks were taken to be zero for all 51 sets of estimates.

Given the coefficient estimates, the covariance matrix of the error terms ($\hat{S}$)

was estimated as $(1/63)\hat{U}\hat{U}'$, where $\hat{U}$ is the 30×63 matrix of values of the estimated error terms. Using $N(0, \hat{S})$ as the distribution of the error terms and $N(\hat{\alpha}_2, \hat{V}_2)$ as the distribution of the coefficient estimates, a stochastic simulation was then run for the 1970I–1971IV period, where both error terms and coefficients were drawn. The number of trials was 50. The results from this simulation allowed values of d_{itk} to be computed for all i, for $k = 1, \ldots, 8$, and for t equal to 1970I. The simulation produces values of $\tilde{\sigma}^2_{itk}$ and $\tilde{\bar{y}}_{itk}$. Given $\tilde{\bar{y}}_{itk}$ and given the actual data on the endogenous variables, $\hat{\epsilon}_{itk}$ can be computed. d_{itk} is then merely $\hat{\epsilon}^2_{itk} - \tilde{\sigma}^2_{itk}$.

The results for one variable in the model (real GNP) from this simulation are presented in the first row of Table 8-1. The first eight values, $100(\tilde{\sigma}_{itk}/\tilde{\bar{y}}_{itk})$, are the stochastic simulation estimates of the standard errors of the forecast, expressed as a percentage of the forecast mean. The second eight values, $100(|\hat{\epsilon}_{itk}|/\tilde{\bar{y}}_{itk})$, are the estimates of the standard errors of the forecast based on the actual outside-sample forecast errors, again expressed as a percentage of the forecast mean.

There are a few dummy variables in the model that are not relevant for the early estimation periods, which means that there are slightly fewer than 169 coefficients to estimate for the early periods. For the first period, for example, there are 165 coefficients to estimate.

The second estimation period was 1954I–1969IV (64 observations), which differs from the first period by the addition of one quarter at the end. The first quarter of the period was left unchanged. The coefficients were estimated by 2SLS for this period, and new estimates of $\hat{V}_2$ and $\hat{S}$ were obtained. Stochastic simulation was then performed for the 1970II–1972I period, which allowed values of d_{itk} to be computed for all i, for $k = 1, \ldots, 8$, and for t equal to 1970II. The results for real GNP from this simulation are presented in the second row of Table 8-1. A total of 50 trials were also used for this simulation.

This process was repeated for the remaining 49 estimation periods. Since only data through 1982III exist, the length of the prediction periods for the last seven sets of estimates was less than eight, as can be seen in Table 8-1. The last estimation period was 1954I–1982I (113 observations), and for this set of estimates the prediction period was merely one quarter, 1982III.

The total time needed to estimate the model 51 times was about 2.1 hours on the IBM 4341. The total time for the 51 stochastic simulations, which consisted of 50 trials each, was about 2.2 hours. The stochastic-simulation work consisted of $50 \times 51 = 2{,}550$ solutions of the model. For none of the draws did the Gauss-Seidel technique fail to solve the model. For the earlier work on the VAX, the model was estimated and stochastically simulated 44 times. The total time for the estimation was about 4.8 hours, and the total time for the stochastic simulation (50 trials each) was about 10.7 hours.

The same calculations were performed for the other models, the only difference being that 100 rather than 50 trials were used for each stochastic simulation for the ARUS, VAR1US, and VAR2US models. (50 trials were used for the LINUS model.) The first quarter of the estimation period was 1954I for all the models except ARUS, where it was 1954II. The estimation times for ARUS, VAR1US, VAR2US, and LINUS were, respectively, 3, 9, 3, and 36 minutes on the IBM 4341 and 5, 16, 5, and 19 minutes on the VAX. The stochastic-simulation times were 15, 28, 13, and 14 minutes on the IBM 4341 and 38, 71, 31, and 35 minutes on the VAX.

8.5.2 Discussion of the d_{itk} Values for the US Model

Since the individual d_{itk} values may be of interest in their own right, they will be examined before proceeding to the estimates of the total variance of the forecast error. Consider the results for real GNP in Table 8-1. If one looks down one of the first eight columns, it can be seen that the standard errors vary considerably across prediction periods (except for perhaps the one-quarter-ahead results in the first column). For the eight-quarter-ahead results, for example, the estimated standard errors vary from 1.43 percent in row 35 to 3.41 percent in row 17. Experimenting with more trials indicated that sampling error contributes very little to this variability. It thus appears that there is considerable variability of forecast-error variances across time (for a fixed k), at least for the US model. This variability is due to different estimated covariance matrices, different initial conditions (that is, different lagged values of the endogenous and exogenous variables), and different values of the exogenous variables. It is interesting to note that some of the largest standard errors occur in the mid-1970s, which was characterized at times by extreme initial conditions and exogenous variable values. In particular, the price of imports *(PIM)*, which is an exogenous variable, took on extreme values during much of this period. It may be that these extreme values help contribute to the larger stochastic-simulation estimates of the standard errors for the mid-1970s.

The values in the last eight columns in Table 8-1 are the absolute values of the outside-sample forecast errors in percentage terms. These values, unlike the values in the first eight columns, use the actual values of the endogenous variables for the prediction period in their calculation, which is the reason they are more erratic. In some cases the forecasts are nearly perfect, and in

TABLE 8-1. Estimated standard errors for 51 estimation periods for real GNP for the US model (each prediction period begins two quarters after the end of the estimation period)

	Estimation period ending in	$100(\tilde{\sigma}_{itk}/\tilde{\bar{y}}_{itk})$								$100(\lvert\hat{\varepsilon}_{itk}\rvert/\tilde{\bar{y}}_{itk})$							
	k :	1	2	3	4	5	6	7	8	1	2	3	4	5	6	7	8
1	1969 III	.55	.82	1.17	1.44	1.82	2.16	2.37	2.69	.31	.55	.17	1.32	.16	.01	.43	.05
2	IV	.39	.75	1.01	1.16	1.34	1.52	1.70	1.81	.03	.56	.43	1.17	1.06	.75	1.15	1.56
3	1970 I	.49	.86	1.20	1.52	1.94	2.34	2.80	3.07	1.03	.41	2.30	2.39	2.11	2.60	2.96	3.97
4	II	.43	.79	1.12	1.40	1.77	2.16	2.53	2.87	1.01	.81	1.01	.95	1.57	2.06	3.22	3.33
5	III	.40	.73	1.09	1.48	1.78	2.11	2.36	2.58	1.23	.26	.91	1.20	1.30	.65	.86	1.01
6	IV	.44	.66	.97	1.27	1.54	1.79	2 16	2.44	1.00	1.98	2.25	2.49	1.91	2.13	2.26	1.90
7	1971 I	.52	.82	1.14	1.44	1.74	2.13	2.50	2.69	1.50	2.07	2.53	2.03	2.50	2.88	2.72	4.64
8	II	.52	.75	1.02	1.46	1.96	2.28	2.71	3.17	.46	.62	1.86	2.08	2.23	2.61	.83	.23
9	III	.35	.67	.92	1.24	1.43	1.77	2.02	2.25	.05	1.10	1.18	1.36	2.04	.45	.10	.34
10	IV	.43	.69	.93	1.19	1.41	1.78	2.04	2.26	.85	.72	.79	1.42	.22	.60	1.11	2.25
11	1972 I	.47	.74	1.04	1.24	1.50	1.83	2.24	2.70	.00	.01	.51	1.42	2.00	2.66	4.16	4.69
12	II	.41	.72	.95	1.27	1.54	2.00	2.32	2.79	.29	.74	1.37	2.18	3.30	5.08	5.88	6.63
13	III	.42	.75	.96	1.25	1.57	2.08	2.53	2.94	.37	1.54	2.32	3.26	4.89	5.75	6.42	7.43
14	IV	.47	.73	1.00	1.31	1.55	1.93	2.45	2.86	1.53	1.92	2.49	3.99	4.60	5.08	5.74	7.73
15	1973 I	.50	.70	.92	1.12	1.32	1.63	1.96	2.37	.45	1.24	2.62	3.24	3.70	4.36	6.33	5.57
16	II	.52	.85	1.15	1.58	1.93	2.35	2.58	2.78	.47	1.50	1.63	1.46	1.73	3.47	2.24	1.67
17	III	.55	1.02	1.40	1.95	2.41	2.85	3.28	3.41	.86	1.17	1.34	2.03	4.19	3.59	3.12	3.80
18	IV	.49	.91	1.38	1.87	2.20	2.61	2.73	2.84	.29	.66	1.24	3.39	2.81	2.45	2.94	1.85
19	1974 I	.57	1.00	1.30	1.76	2.11	2.28	2.49	2.57	.27	.11	1.99	1.47	1.15	1.91	.93	.93
20	II	.43	.77	1.31	1.67	2.01	2.36	2.51	2.65	.41	.77	.45	1.41	1.10	2.30	2.27	1.60
21	III	.54	.97	1.22	1.49	1.79	2.09	2.18	2.29	1.01	.21	1.03	.58	1.73	1.82	1.40	1.33
22	IV	.56	.82	1.12	1.49	1.87	2.19	2.62	2.98	.22	.39	.29	.78	.94	.82	.97	2.27
23	1975 I	.56	.91	1.27	1.73	2.12	2.51	2.80	3.09	.67	1.91	1.29	1.44	1.87	2.01	1.02	.72
24	II	.48	.92	1.27	1.62	1.89	2.27	2.71	2.91	.77	.11	.12	.88	1.42	.93	1.27	1.65
25	III	.38	.68	.97	1.37	1.63	1.85	2.01	2.13	.78	.77	.20	.11	.82	.83	1.03	.18
26	IV	.48	.77	1.10	1.47	1.64	1.77	1.92	2.04	.08	.19	.16	.98	1.11	1.41	.60	.21
27	1976 I	.42	.76	.95	1.16	1.36	1.59	1.67	1.87	.44	.85	.02	.05	.11	.87	1.56	.56
28	II	.44	.67	.92	1.06	1.38	1.66	1.83	1.96	.14	.88	.95	1.02	.10	.68	.11	.59
29	III	.47	.85	1.17	1.34	1.46	1.58	1.72	1.83	.61	.49	.55	.39	.72	.40	.04	.01
30	IV	.45	.64	.91	1.07	1.21	1.26	1.39	1.65	.06	.12	.87	1.34	.37	1.00	1.01	1.60

31	1977	I	.42	.71	.91	1.09	1.13	1.19	1.40	1.62	.29	.67	1.21	.37	.97	.96	1.67	2.59
32		II	.42	.76	1.08	1.34	1.55	1.76	1.92	2.17	.84	1.21	.08	.66	.64	1.27	2.26	2.21
33		III	.40	.57	.88	1.09	1.29	1.51	1.63	1.65	.66	.03	.69	1.01	1.82	2.73	2.69	3.65
34		IV	.39	.56	.75	.92	1.05	1.28	1.37	1.44	1.03	.21	.12	1.14	2.28	2.38	3.31	3.94
35	1978	I	.35	.63	.88	1.10	1.29	1.37	1.39	1.43	.29	.09	.73	1.73	1.87	2.91	3.62	6.26
36		II	.51	.92	1.13	1.26	1.42	1.58	1.59	1.69	.10	.46	1.46	1.46	2.53	3.13	5.91	5.87
37		III	.44	.76	1.03	1.33	1.54	1.78	1.91	2.02	.29	.89	.71	1.58	2.08	4.68	4.64	4.30
38		IV	.45	.70	1.05	1.28	1.34	1.43	1.45	1.48	1.07	1.04	1.79	2.23	4.71	4.54	3.89	2.87
39	1979	I	.39	.57	.77	.94	1.20	1.39	1.51	1.70	.30	1.43	2.05	4.80	4.77	4.34	3.48	4.69
40		II	.39	.63	.89	1.08	1.21	1.30	1.49	1.57	1.30	1.99	4.54	4.40	3.83	2.78	4.02	4.19
41		III	.54	.67	1.05	1.20	1.47	1.70	1.84	1.88	.97	3.79	3.74	3.26	2.29	3.65	3.93	6.23
42		IV	.50	.83	1.05	1.37	1.64	1.77	1.91	1.98	2.59	2.30	1.69	.71	2.11	2.64	4.96	6.25
43	1980	I	.50	.81	1.00	1.14	1.26	1.39	1.45	1.54	.19	.39	.11	1.61	2.21	4.87	6.17	6.39
44		II	.58	.86	.98	1.28	1.50	1.61	1.72	1.73	.57	.24	1.80	2.22	4.78	5.91	5.91	6.15
45		III	.59	.81	1.08	1.35	1.62	1.72	1.79		.85	.42	.99	3.75	5.23	5.57	6.10	
46		IV	.56	.94	1.26	1.48	1.67	1.82			.97	.96	3.34	4.47	4.70	4.97		
47	1981	I	.64	.79	.99	1.33	1.43				.39	1.69	2.79	3.18	3.61			
48		II	.53	.92	1.18	1.42					1.09	1.14	.63	.95				
49		III	.60	.94	1.21						.23	.06	.19					
50		IV	.54	.82							.16	.04						
51	1982	I	.56								.41							

Notes: • Estimation technique was 2SLS. Each of the estimated covariance matrices of the coefficient estimates was taken to be block diagonal.
• 50 trials were used for each stochastic simulation.

others the errors are quite large. The largest error is for the eight-quarter-ahead forecast in row 14, which is 7.73 percent. The results in row 14 are for the prediction period beginning in 1973II, and therefore the eight-quarter-ahead forecast is for 1975I.

The square of an element in the right half of Table 8-1 minus the square of the corresponding element in the left half is equal to $d_{itk}/\tilde{\bar{y}}^2_{itk}$, which is simply d_{itk} in percentage terms. The key question is whether these values have any systematic tendencies. To examine this question, $d_{itk}/\tilde{\bar{y}}^2_{itk}$ is plotted in Figure 8-1 for i equal to real GNP and k equal to 1. The main conclusion from Figure 8-1 is that no systematic tendencies are apparent. The value for 1980II is very large relative to others, but aside from this, the values are not obviously larger for one subperiod than for another, and there is no obvious trend. Plots for many other variables were examined, and the same conclusion was reached.

The only systematic tendency that was apparent was that some of the plots showed evidence of serial correlation for values of k greater than about four or five. This can be explained as follows. If, say, quarter 85 is a difficult quarter to predict, perhaps because of a large unexplained shock in the quarter, then a dynamic simulation that runs through this quarter may also do poorly in predicting quarters 86 and beyond. In other words, the simulation may get thrown off by the bad prediction in quarter 85. This means, for example, that five-quarter-ahead forecasts for quarters 85, 86, 87, 88, and 89 may all be on average poor, thus implying large values for $\hat{\epsilon}^2_{itk}$ ($k = 5$ and $t = 81, \ldots, 85$). The shock in quarter 85 will have no effect on the stochastic-simulation estimates of the variances, since these are not based on the actual data for the endogenous variables for this quarter, and therefore the large values of the outside-sample errors imply large values of d_{itk}. In this way, serial correlation may be introduced into the d_{itk} series for values of k greater than one.

The general impression one gets from examining the plots is thus that the misspecification of the model does not appear to have changed over time or to have been different in any subperiods. One could attempt to examine this question in a less casual way by, say, regressing the d_{itk} values (for a given i and k) on variables that one thinks may be related to the misspecification of the model. Although this might be worth doing in future work, it seems unlikely to me, from having examined the plots, that much would come of it.

The fact that the misspecification of the model does not appear to have changed over time is not in itself encouraging regarding the accuracy of the model. The misspecification may in fact be quite large, even though unchanging, and may have a large effect on total forecasting uncertainty. What is encouraging about the results is that the assumption of a constant mean for d_{itk} or $d_{itk}/\tilde{\bar{y}}^2_{itk}$ (for a given i and k) seems to be a reasonable approximation.

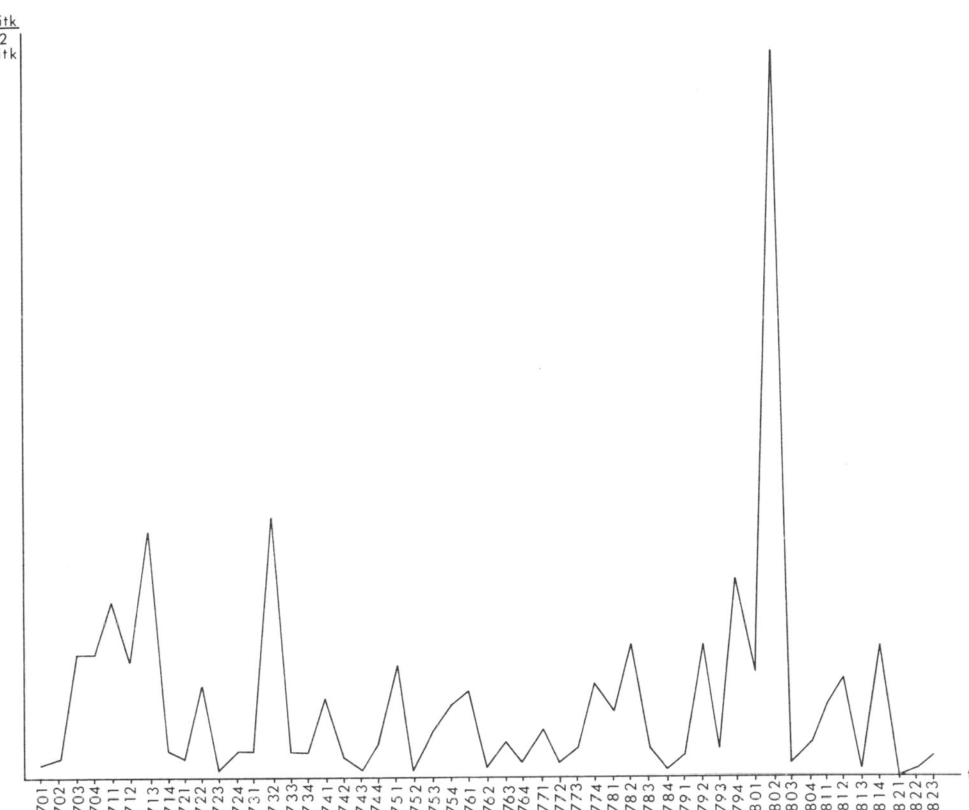

Figure 8-1 Plot of $d_{itk}/\tilde{y}^2_{itk}$ for the US model for i = real GNP, $k = 1$, t = 1970I – 1982III

8.5.3 Computing the Total Variance of the Forecast Error

The total variance of the forecast error is $\hat{\sigma}^2_{itk}$ in (8.7). The computation of $\hat{\sigma}^2_{itk}$ for the five models is discussed in this section. It is easiest to describe these computations by referring to the results in Table 8-2. The prediction period is 1978I – 1979IV. Consider first the results for real GNP for the US model. The values in the a and b rows are from the same two stochastic simulations that were used for the results in Table 7-1. For the a-row results only draws of the error terms were made, whereas for the b-row results draws of both the error terms and coefficients were made. The number of trials for each simulation was 250. The coefficient estimates that were used for these results are the 2SLS estimates for the 1954I – 1982III period (115 observations). These are the

TABLE 8-2. Estimated standard errors of forecasts for 1978 I - 1979 IV for five models

		1978				1979			
		I	II	III	IV	I	II	III	IV
GNPR: Real GNP									
US:	a	.49	.66	.81	.98	1.10	1.14	1.22	1.32
	b	.51	.69	.89	1.03	1.09	1.22	1.30	1.35
	c	.61	.71	.89	1.08	1.24	1.39	1.52	1.60
	d	.87	1.10	1.54	2.00	2.43	2.79	3.09	3.43
ARUS:	a	.78	1.20	1.56	1.81	1.97	2.08	2.14	2.17
	b	.77	1.22	1.57	1.80	2.00	2.12	2.24	2.38
	d	1.25	1.97	2.57	2.94	3.14	3.37	3.68	4.05
VAR1US:	a	.72	1.05	1.24	1.43	1.58	1.71	1.76	1.87
	b	.77	1.20	1.44	1.64	1.91	2.15	2.38	2.59
	d	1.67	2.96	3.71	4.45	5.00	5.63	6.36	7.15
VAR2US:	a	.80	1.14	1.34	1.52	1.68	1.78	1.86	1.96
	b	.85	1.26	1.49	1.80	2.01	2.17	2.44	2.60
	d	1.34	2.35	3.21	3.95	4.30	4.44	4.70	4.93
LINUS:	a	.59	.87	1.07	1.25	1.37	1.47	1.56	1.62
	b	.61	.87	1.03	1.21	1.39	1.55	1.75	1.87
	c	.67	.93	1.12	1.33	1.46	1.65	1.72	1.89
	d	.97	1.53	2.14	2.76	3.38	4.00	4.58	5.13
GNPD: GNP deflator									
US:	a	.35	.51	.64	.72	.79	.87	.90	.93
	b	.37	.52	.63	.77	.84	.93	1.09	1.15
	c	.50	.61	.68	.80	.87	.99	1.10	1.13
	d	.64	1.03	1.46	1.98	2.49	3.03	3.65	4.31
ARUS:	a	.27	.49	.72	.97	1.23	1.43	1.63	1.79
	b	.26	.51	.76	1.08	1.40	1.71	1.99	2.25
	d	.49	.98	1.50	2.09	2.78	3.48	4.16	4.90
VAR1US:	a	.27	.41	.54	.69	.82	.95	1.05	1.13
	b	.29	.45	.59	.78	.96	1.16	1.32	1.46
	d	.56	1.00	1.39	1.82	2.30	2.70	3.03	3.38
VAR2US:	a	.31	.48	.65	.82	.94	1.07	1.17	1.26
	b	.33	.52	.73	.92	1.08	1.24	1.39	1.57
	d	.54	.98	1.41	1.88	2.27	2.57	2.86	3.21
100•UR: Unemployment rate (percentage points)									
US:	a	.24	.38	.48	.54	.61	.65	.65	.68
	b	.26	.42	.52	.61	.70	.77	.78	.80
	c	.27	.41	.52	.61	.66	.76	.81	.82
	d	.45	.69	.92	1.14	1.33	1.52	1.68	1.83
ARUS:	a	.32	.58	.79	.98	1.07	1.10	1.11	1.14
	b	.30	.58	.86	1.09	1.24	1.32	1.38	1.43
	d	.37	.73	1.07	1.39	1.57	1.69	1.78	1.84
VAR1US:	a	.25	.42	.54	.61	.69	.73	.75	.77
	b	.26	.46	.61	.70	.76	.83	.88	.96
	d	.56	1.19	1.71	2.10	2.33	2.47	2.60	2.85
VAR2US:	a	.28	.48	.62	.70	.78	.82	.85	.88
	b	.29	.52	.67	.78	.88	.94	.99	1.02
	d	.44	.90	1.38	1.84	2.17	2.34	2.44	2.50

(continued)

TABLE 8-2 (continued)

		1978				1979			
		I	II	III	IV	I	II	III	IV
RS: Bill rate (percentage points)									
US:	a	.71	1.00	1.07	1.13	1.17	1.21	1.17	1.19
	b	.73	.94	1.04	1.03	1.15	1.25	1.31	1.45
	c	.72	.96	1.07	1.14	1.13	1.27	1.42	1.40
	d	1.20	1.79	1.99	2.15	2.29	2.42	2.50	2.51
ARUS:	a	.72	1.11	1.20	1.35	1.53	1.62	1.70	1.75
	b	.76	1.21	1.37	1.54	1.75	1.96	2.06	2.04
	d	1.36	2.24	2.48	2.85	3.21	3.61	3.83	3.85
VAR1US:	a	.56	.84	.93	1.03	1.07	1.19	1.26	1.22
	b	.59	.96	1.07	1.24	1.39	1.53	1.62	1.70
	d	1.31	2.26	2.59	2.80	3.13	3.64	3.72	3.73
VAR2US:	a	.63	.99	1.10	1.18	1.27	1.39	1.45	1.45
	b	.65	1.08	1.29	1.44	1.61	1.72	1.79	1.81
	d	1.24	2.19	2.71	3.18	3.58	4.01	4.31	4.40
LINUS:	a	.77	.97	1.07	1.19	1.25	1.26	1.33	1.37
	b	.80	1.06	1.18	1.29	1.37	1.42	1.47	1.60
	c	.01	1.05	1.21	1.32	1.40	1.52	1.57	1.70
	d	1.32	1.78	1.96	2.16	2.39	2.64	2.82	2.96
M1: Money supply									
US:	a	.98	1.35	1.49	1.66	1.82	2.00	2.03	1.98
	b	.95	1.37	1.57	1.77	2.11	2.32	2.38	2.54
	c	1.07	1.45	1.64	1.69	2.02	2.00	2.18	2.28
	d	1.41	1.91	2.22	2.68	3.35	3.81	4.62	5.33
ARUS:	a	.66	.77	.97	1.18	1.35	1.50	1.70	1.99
	b	.69	.85	1.09	1.32	1.55	1.74	2.04	2.33
	d	1.22	1.41	1.63	2.08	2.39	2.64	3.07	3.47
VAR1US:	a	.65	.75	.89	.96	1.03	1.11	1.21	1.38
	b	.67	.87	1.04	1.18	1.30	1.48	1.66	1.83
	d	1.25	1.35	1.25	1.10	1.02	.34	1.25	2.02
VAR2US:	a	.77	.93	1.16	1.28	1.40	1.50	1.59	1.76
	b	.82	1.00	1.28	1.53	1.76	1.95	2.09	2.37
	d	1.35	1.71	1.99	2.25	2.33	2.30	2.46	2.71
W_f: Wage rate									
US:	a	.56	.86	1.00	1.13	1.20	1.30	1.32	1.38
	b	.59	.84	1.01	1.15	1.35	1.48	1.70	1.85
	c	.60	.82	1.02	1.17	1.37	1.56	1.80	1.94
	d	.54	.86	1.30	1.81	2.43	3.12	3.96	4.83
ARUS:	a	.38	.55	.69	.81	.95	1.06	1.18	1.29
	b	.40	.58	.73	.92	1.05	1.19	1.33	1.52
	d	.67	1.03	1.35	1.71	2.03	2.36	2.75	3.14
Π_f: Profits									
US:	a	4.98	6.26	7.61	8.75	8.90	10.07	10.91	11.80
	b	5.02	6.55	8.35	9.26	10.27	11.55	13.46	15.11
	c	6.86	7.63	9.21	9.77	10.63	13.22	14.16	15.00
	d	8.49	10.30	12.83	14.59	13.27	13.68	13.29	12.17
ARUS:	a	4.84	6.87	8.21	8.72	9.55	10.33	11.50	13.24
	b	4.82	6.57	8.27	8.67	9.87	10.91	12.57	15.64
	d	9.70	14.79	18.47	20.94	23.92	26.92	32.12	37.88

(continued)

TABLE 8-2 (continued)

		1978 I	1978 II	1978 III	1978 IV	1979 I	1979 II	1979 III	1979 IV
SR: Savings rate of the household sector									
US:	a	6.88	10.05	11.98	14.89	18.41	21.88	22.40	25.99
	b	7.65	10.74	12.33	15.54	20.22	25.08	25.82	30.49
	c	10.73	13.26	14.56	17.34	21.47	26.45	27.28	32.05
	d	11.41	14.58	16.99	21.34	27.08	34.63	40.12	49.01
ARUS:	a	9.46	11.30	12.84	13.71	14.29	15.38	14.94	14.46
	b	9.86	11.88	13.77	13.92	15.18	16.00	16.59	16.58
	d	12.29	14.70	17.21	17.51	19.34	20.65	21.40	21.38
S_g: Savings of the federal government (billions of current dollars)									
US:	a	.72	1.12	1.43	1.69	1.90	2.14	2.38	2.50
	b	.76	1.11	1.45	1.80	1.98	2.33	2.79	2.84
	c	2.29	2.55	2.60	3.07	2.99	3.27	3.52	3.94
	d	2.42	2.82	3.18	3.95	4.37	4.99	5.58	6.31
ARUS:	a	2.84	3.90	4.96	5.65	6.03	6.59	6.77	7.08
	b	3.39	4.54	5.55	6.32	7.12	7.57	8.21	8.66
	d	6.07	8.42	10.26	11.44	12.45	12.89	12.96	12.81
S_r: Savings of the foreign sector (billions of current dollars)									
US:	a	.95	1.27	1.38	1.49	1.61	1.66	1.72	2.09
	b	1.11	1.29	1.45	1.58	1.66	2.05	2.31	2.51
	c	1.64	1.86	1.89	2.18	2.38	2.76	2.85	3.06
	d	2.39	3.39	4.01	4.59	5.22	6.32	7.31	8.35
ARUS:	a	1.07	1.27	1.45	1.46	1.51	1.55	1.60	1.62
	b	1.14	1.41	1.65	1.80	1.77	1.86	1.85	1.89
	d	2.38	2.83	3.44	3.53	3.61	3.61	3.52	3.66

Notes: a = Uncertainty due to error terms.
b = Uncertainty due to error terms and coefficient estimates.
c = Uncertainty due to error terms, coefficient estimates, and exogenous-variable forecasts.
d = Uncertainty due to error terms, coefficient estimates, exogenous-variable forecasts, and the possible misspecification of the model.

• For the unemployment rate, the bill rate, the savings of the federal government, and the savings of the foreign sector, the errors are in the natural units of the variables. These units are indicated in the table. For all other variables the errors are expressed as a percent of the forecast mean (in percentage points).

estimates presented in Chapter 4; they are the basic 2SLS estimates of the model.

The values in Table 8-2 are either estimated standard errors in units of the variable or estimated standard errors in percentage points. For real GNP the errors are in percentage points. The numbers in the b row, for example, are $\tilde{\sigma}_{itk}/\tilde{\bar{y}}_{itk}$, where $\tilde{\bar{y}}_{itk}$ is the stochastic-simulation estimate of the forecast mean (Eq. 7.7) and $\tilde{\sigma}_{itk}$ is the square root of the stochastic-simulation estimate of the variance of the forecast error (Eq. 7.8). The numbers in the a row are the same except that the estimates are based on draws of the error terms only.

The results in the a and b rows are not needed for the computations of the total variance of the forecast error; they are presented merely to show how much of the total variance can be attributed to the uncertainty from the error terms and coefficient estimates. The results that are needed are those from a stochastic simulation with respect to the error terms, coefficients, *and* exogenous variables. These results are presented in the c rows in Table 8-2. The procedure that was used for this stochastic simulation for the US model is as follows.

An eighth-order autoregressive equation (with a constant and time trend included) was estimated for each exogenous variable in Table A-4 (Appendix A) except for the dummy variables, the time trend, and variables whose value never changes or changes only once during the sample period. (These variables are $D593$ through $DD793$, H_m, t, δ_D, δ_H, δ_K, γ_g, and γ_s.) The sample period for each regression was 1954II–1982III. A total of 88 equations were estimated. The estimated standard error from each of these regressions was taken to be the error associated with forecasts of the variable. The procedure discussed in Section 8.4.2 was used for the draws of the exogenous-variable values for the stochastic simulation. The base values of the exogenous variables were taken to be the actual values. Each trial of the stochastic simulation for the c rows consisted of eight draws of 30 values each from the distribution of the error terms, one draw of 169 values from the distribution of the coefficient estimates, and eight draws from each of the 88 distributions of the exogenous-variable errors. A total of 250 trials were taken. For none of the draws did the Gauss-Seidel technique fail to find a solution. The total time taken for this simulation was about the same as the time taken for the a-row and b-row simulations, namely about 6.7 minutes on the IBM 4341 and about 49 minutes on the VAX. (See the note to Table 7-1.)

A stochastic simulation of 250 trials was also performed under the assumption that the exogenous-variable errors pertain to changes in the variables rather than to levels. This procedure is also discussed in Section 8.4.2. The estimated standard errors from this simulation were in general larger than those from the first simulation, but the results were fairly close. These results are not reported in Table 8-2.

The c-row values in Table 8-2 are either $\tilde{\tilde{\sigma}}_{itk}$ or $\tilde{\tilde{\sigma}}_{itk}/\bar{\bar{y}}_{itk}$, where $\tilde{\tilde{\sigma}}_{itk}$ is the square root of $\tilde{\tilde{\sigma}}^2_{itk}$. The final step is to add to $\tilde{\tilde{\sigma}}^2_{itk}$ the estimated mean of d_{itk}. The discussion in Section 8.5.2 indicates that the assumption that the mean of d_{itk} is constant across time may be a reasonable approximation. This assumption was used for variables without trends. For variables with trends it was assumed that the mean of $d_{itk}/\tilde{\bar{y}}_{itk}^2$ is constant across time. Given the first assumption, the estimated mean of d_{itk} is the average of the d_{itk} values (for a fixed i and k); and given the second assumption, the estimated mean of $d_{itk}/\tilde{\bar{y}}_{itk}^2$ is the average of the $d_{itk}/\tilde{\bar{y}}_{itk}^2$ values. There are 51 observations for the one-quarter-ahead forecasts ($k = 1$), 50 observations for the two-quarter-ahead forecasts ($k = 2$), and so on. Let $\hat{d}_{ik}$ denote the estimated mean of d_{itk}, and let $\hat{d}'_{ik}$ denote the estimated mean of $d_{itk}/\tilde{\bar{y}}_{itk}^2$. The t subscript has been dropped from $\hat{d}_{ik}$ and $\hat{d}'_{ik}$ because the estimated means are assumed to be constant across time.

For variables without trends the estimate of the total variance of the forecast error, $\hat{\sigma}_{itk}^2$, is $\tilde{\tilde{\sigma}}_{itk}^2 + \hat{d}_{ik}$. For variables with trends the estimate is $\tilde{\tilde{\sigma}}_{itk}^2 + \hat{d}'_{ik} \cdot \tilde{\bar{y}}_{itk}^2$. For variables without trends the values in the d rows in Table 8-2 are the square roots of $\hat{\sigma}_{itk}^2$, and for variables with trends the values are the square roots of $\hat{\sigma}_{itk}^2/\tilde{\bar{y}}_{itk}^2$. The differences between the d-row and c-row values in the table are measures of the effects of misspecification on predictive accuracy, although this is subject to the qualification discussed in Section 8.4.5 about the interpretation of the word "misspecification."

The same procedure was followed for the other models. There are no exogenous variables in the ARUS, VAR1US, and VAR2US models, and thus there are no c-row values. For the LINUS model there are three exogenous variables for which autoregressive equations were estimated: Q_1, Q_2, and $\dot{M1}$.

8.5.4 Comparison of the Results for the Five Models

The US Model versus the Others

The models can be compared according to the size of the d-row values. In examining the d-row values I usually give more weight to the results the further out the forecast is. In other words, I usually give more weight to the four-quarter-ahead results than to the one-quarter-ahead results, more to the eight-quarter-ahead results than to the four-quarter-ahead results, and so on. The further out a forecast is, the more this is a test of the accuracy of the dynamic properties of the model.

For real GNP it is clear that the US model is substantially better than the other four models. The eight-quarter-ahead standard error is 3.43 percent, which compares to values of 4.05, 7.15, 4.93, and 5.13 percent for the other four models. The US model is also best for the unemployment rate and the bill rate. It is not as good as VAR1US and VAR2US for the GNP deflator. It is substantially worse for the money supply, where the eight-quarter-ahead standard error is 5.33 percent, which compares to values of 3.47, 2.02, and 2.71 for ARUS, VAR1US, and VAR2US respectively.

The poorer results for the money supply mean that the demand-for-money equations in the US model are not as accurate as autoregressive specifications. This is something that I have known for a long time, but it is not easy to remedy. I have so far been unable to find demand-for-money equations that lead to more accurate predictions within the context of the overall model. Fortunately, errors in predicting the money supply have fairly minor consequences for the other variables. Given the use of the interest rate reaction function, the only important way in which errors in predicting the money supply affect the other variables in the model is through their effect on the bill rate predictions. The lagged growth of the money supply is one of the explanatory variables in the bill rate equation, and therefore errors in predicting the money supply affect the bill rate predictions. Although errors in predicting the bill rate have important effects on many other variables in the model, the effect of the money supply on the bill rate is only moderate. The indirect effect of money supply errors on the other variables in the model (through the direct effect of the money supply on the bill rate) is thus fairly minor.

Given that the US model is more accurate for three of the key variables (real GNP, the unemployment rate, and the bill rate), the results seem encouraging for the model. More tests are needed, of course, especially against other structural models, before any strong conclusions can be drawn.

For the remaining five variables in Table 8-2, the comparisons are only between the US and ARUS models. Four of these variables—the level of profits, the savings rate, the savings of the federal government, and the savings of the foreign sector—are "residual" variables. These types of variables are generally hard to predict in structural models, and it is interesting to see how the US model does relative to an autoregressive equation for each variable. The results for the first variable, the wage rate, are about the same for the two models for the first four quarters; after that the ARUS model does somewhat better. For the savings rate of the household sector, the two models are almost the same for the first three quarters, and the ARUS model is substantially better thereafter. The US model is substantially better for profits and the savings of the federal government, and the ARUS model is substantially better for the savings of the foreign sector. The overall results for these five variables are thus mixed. It is encouraging that the US model is better with respect to profits and the savings of the federal government, but it is clear that the model could stand some improvement with respect to the savings rate of the household sector and the savings of the foreign sector.

Comparison of the Other Four Models

Consider first the LINUS model. The main variable that it is designed to explain is real GNP. For this variable it is less accurate than the US model and more accurate than the VAR1US and VAR2US models. It is more accurate than the ARUS model for the first four quarters ahead and less accurate after that. The results are thus mixed, although the fact that the model is not nearly as accurate as the US model is not encouraging in regard to the ability to collapse a large model into a relatively small one without a substantial loss of predictive accuracy.

In the comparison of VAR1US versus VAR2US, VAR2US seems somewhat better: it is more accurate for real GNP, the GNP deflator, and the unemployment rate. It is less accurate for the bill rate and the money supply. In the comparison of ARUS versus VAR2US, ARUS is more accurate for real GNP and the unemployment rate but less accurate for the GNP deflator and the bill rate. The results are mixed for the money supply. There is thus no obvious winner between ARUS and VAR2US.

There is one feature of the money supply results for VAR1US that should be noted. For the four- through seven-quarter-ahead predictions, the d-row values are less than the corresponding b-row values, which means that the estimated means of the $d_{itk}/\tilde{\tilde{y}}^2_{itk}$ values were negative. For the six-quarter-ahead prediction, the estimated mean was almost negative enough to make the d-row value zero. These results are due to the fact that the stochastic-simulation estimates of the variances are large relative to the estimates based on the outside-sample forecast errors. For models like VAR1US, which have a large number of coefficients to estimate relative to the number of observations and thus in general have very imprecise estimates, it sometimes happens that the stochastic-simulation estimates of the variances are very large. It is not clear in these cases whether much confidence should be put in the results; there are just too few observations for much to be said.

Comparison Using Root Mean Squared Errors

Root mean squared errors (RMSEs) for the five models for the 1970I–1982III period are presented in Table 8-3. These errors were computed as follows. Outside-sample forecast errors are available from the 51 stochastic simulations that were involved in computing the d_{itk} values. These errors are the

TABLE 8-3. Root mean squared errors of outside-sample forecasts for 1970 I - 1982 III for five models

	Number of quarters ahead							
	1	2	3	4	5	6	7	8
GNPR: Real GNP								
US	.79	1.15	1.65	2.16	2.65	3.07	3.43	3.83
ARUS	1.21	1.92	2.58	3.04	3.33	3.63	3.97	4.34
VAR1US	1.77	3.06	3.91	4.80	5.49	6.25	7.21	8.29
VAR2US	1.36	2.38	3.29	4.08	4.58	4.98	5.47	6.05
LINUS	.87	1.46	2.16	2.88	3.65	4.42	5.21	5.96
GNPD: GNP deflator								
US	.57	1.05	1.56	2.12	2.70	3.29	3.97	4.71
ARUS	.48	.97	1.49	2.09	2.80	3.55	4.32	5.16
VAR1US	.61	1.08	1.52	2.03	2.60	3.11	3.58	4.09
VAR2US	.56	1.01	1.44	1.94	2.38	2.73	3.09	3.50
100•UR: Unemployment rate (percentage points)								
US	.47	.76	1.01	1.26	1.49	1.69	1.89	2.10
ARUS	.37	.74	1.06	1.36	1.52	1.63	1.73	1.79
VAR1US	.58	1.21	1.72	2.11	2.35	2.49	2.65	2.93
VAR2US	.44	.90	1.39	1.85	2.16	2.34	2.46	2.56
RS: Bill rate (percentage points)								
US	1.10	1.69	1.90	2.08	2.28	2.40	2.45	2.56
ARUS	1.28	2.11	2.34	2.67	2.97	3.30	3.48	3.50
VAR1US	1.30	2.27	2.64	2.87	3.26	3.79	3.89	3.91
VAR2US	1.20	2.13	2.64	3.13	3.53	3.97	4.27	4.39
LINUS	1.19	1.64	1.82	2.03	2.27	2.52	2.72	2.85
M1: Money supply								
US	1.33	1.91	2.42	3.16	3.92	4.68	5.64	6.60
ARUS	1.18	1.40	1.65	2.08	2.37	2.64	3.01	3.38
VAR1US	1.39	1.62	1.82	2.07	2.42	2.64	3.38	4.21
VAR2US	1.36	1.78	2.16	2.52	2.79	3.07	3.57	4.10

Notes:
- The results are based on 51 sets of coefficient estimates for each model.
- Each prediction period began two quarters after the end of the estimation period.
- The predicted values used were the mean values from the 51 stochastic simulations to get the d_{itk} values for each model.
- There are 51 observations for the one-quarter-ahead forecasts, 50 for the two-quarter-ahead forecasts, and so on.
- For the unemployment rate and the bill rate the errors are in the natural units of the variables. For the other variables the errors are expressed as a percent of the forecast mean (in percentage points).

differences between the mean values (the $\tilde{\bar{y}}_{itk}$) and the actual values. They are based on 51 sets of estimates of each model, where each prediction period begins two quarters after the end of the estimation period. From these errors one can compute RMSEs by merely adding the squared errors, dividing by the number of observations, and taking the squared root. For the one-quarter-ahead predictions there are 51 observations, for the two-quarter-ahead predictions there are 50 observations, and so on.

It is of interest to compare the RMSEs in Table 8-3 with the d-row values in

Table 8-2. In some loose sense the RMSEs handle the effects of misspecification because they are based on outside-sample errors only, and thus the main differences between the RMSEs and the d-row values are that the RMSEs do not handle exogenous variable uncertainty and do not account for the fact that forecast error variances vary across time. The RMSEs and the d-row values differ, in some cases by substantial amounts, but the rankings of the models are roughly (but not exactly) the same. One would probably draw similar conclusions as those given above if one looked only at the RMSE results.

The main reason for the similar rankings is that exogenous-variable uncertainty is not much of a problem in any model. For three of the models there are no exogenous variables, and for the US and LINUS models, which have exogenous variables, the differences between the c-row and b-row values in Table 8-2 are not in general very large. The US model in particular does not appear to be heavily tied to hard-to-forecast exogenous variables. For models that are heavily tied and that differ considerably in the number and types of variables that are taken to be exogenous, the difference between the rankings using the RMSEs and those using the d-row values could be substantial.

With respect to the cost of the calculations, the RMSE results are essentially as costly as the d-row results because both are based on 51 sets of estimates and 51 stochastic simulations. The RMSE results could, however, be made less costly by using deterministic simulations to compute the predicted values. As discussed in Section 7.3, predicted values from deterministic simulations are generally close to expected values from stochastic simulations, so little is likely to be lost by using deterministic simulations. In the present case this would save about half the cost, since about half the time was spent computing the estimates and about half in performing the stochastic simulations.

8.5.5 Other Results for the US Model

Comparison across Rows

It should be clear from examining the a and b rows in Table 8-2 that more of the forecasting uncertainty is due to the error terms than to the coefficient estimates: the differences between the b and a rows are small relative to the size of the a-row values. It should also be clear, as noted earlier, that exogenous-variable uncertainty does not contribute very much to total uncertainty: the differences between the c and b rows are small. The variable most affected by exogenous-variable uncertainty in Table 8-2 is the savings of the federal government. This is, of course, as expected, since many of the key exogenous variables in the model are federal government variables.

It should be noted that there is no requirement that each c-row value be greater than its corresponding b-row value. Although this is rare, an increase in the variability of one endogenous variable may be associated with a decrease in the variability of another. In the results for the US model in Table 8-2, one of the c-row values is less than the corresponding b-row value for the GNP deflator, three are less for the unemployment rate, three are less for the bill rate, five are less for the money supply, and one is less for the wage rate.

The d-row values are sometimes more than twice as large as the corresponding c-row values, which means that misspecification contributes substantially to overall uncertainty. For real GNP the d-row value for the eight-quarter-ahead prediction is 3.43 percent, which compares to the c-row value of 1.60 percent. For the GNP deflator the numbers are 4.31 and 1.13 percent. Only one d-row value is less than the corresponding c-row value for the US model, which is for the one-quarter-ahead prediction of the wage rate. When this happens, as noted earlier, it means that the estimated mean of d_{itk} or $d_{itk}/\tilde{\bar{y}}_{itk}^2$ is negative. It is argued in Section 8.4.3 that the estimated means are in general likely to be positive, and the results in Table 8-2 certainly confirm this.

An Alternative Measure of Dispersion

In order to see whether the possible nonexistence of moments is a problem, an alternative measure of dispersion from the variance was computed for some of the variables. This measure, $\tilde{\delta}_{itk}$, is discussed in Section 7.3.2. It is equal to $(\tilde{y}_{itk}^b - \tilde{y}_{itk}^a)/2$, where $\tilde{y}_{itk}^a$ it the value for which 34.135 percent of the trial values lie above it and below the median and $\tilde{y}_{itk}^b$ is the value for which 34.135 percent of the trial values lie below it and above the median. If the nonexistence of moments is a problem, one might expect $\tilde{\sigma}_{itk}$ to be much larger than $\tilde{\delta}_{itk}$.

The results for one stochastic simulation for the US model are presented in Table 8-4. This is the same simulation that was used for the b-row results in Table 8-2. The draws are with respect to the error terms and coefficients. The number of trials was 250. None of the draws resulted in a failure of the Gauss-Seidel technique to find a solution, and therefore no "extreme" draws had to be discarded. The values in the a rows in Table 8-4 are either estimated standard errors, $\tilde{\sigma}_{itk}$, or estimated standard errors as a percentage of the

TABLE 8-4. Stochastic simulation with respect to error terms and coefficient estimates:• two measures of dispersion

	1978				1979			
	I	II	III	IV	I	II	III	IV
GNPR: Real GNP								
a	.51	.69	.89	1.03	1.09	1.22	1.30	1.35
b	.53	.67	.89	1.03	1.11	1.29	1.42	1.33
GNPD: GNP deflator								
a	.37	.52	.63	.77	.84	.93	1.09	1.15
b	.34	.49	.61	.77	.82	.97	1.14	1.24
100•UR: Unemployment rate (percentage points)								
a	.26	.42	.52	.61	.70	.77	.78	.80
b	.26	.43	.55	.58	.69	.76	.73	.74
RS: Bill rate (percentage points)								
a	.73	.94	1.04	1.03	1.15	1.25	1.31	1.45
b	.72	.96	1.03	1.03	1.17	1.20	1.22	1.39
M1: Money supply								
a	.95	1.37	1.57	1.77	2.11	2.32	2.38	2.54
b	.94	1.45	1.55	1.74	2.06	2.41	2.33	2.45

Notes: a = $\tilde{\sigma}_{itk}$ for UR and RS, $\tilde{\sigma}_{itk}/\tilde{\bar{y}}_{itk}$ for the others.
b = $\tilde{\delta}_{itk}$ for UR and RS, $\tilde{\delta}_{itk}/\tilde{y}^m_{itk}$ for the others, where $\tilde{y}^m_{itk}$ is the stochastic-simulation estimate of the median.
• This stochastic simulation is the same as the one used for the b-row results for the US model in Table 8-2.

forecast mean, $\tilde{\sigma}_{itk}/\tilde{\bar{y}}_{itk}$. The values in the b rows are either $\tilde{\delta}_{itk}$ or $\tilde{\delta}_{itk}$ as a percentage of the forecast median, $\tilde{\delta}_{itk}/\tilde{y}^m_{itk}$.

It is clear from Table 8-4 that the results are very close. The measures are almost indistinguishable, and any conclusions drawn from using one measure would also be drawn from using the other. It thus does not appear that the possible nonexistence of moments is a practical problem for models like the US model, and therefore the common practice of ignoring this problem may be justified. It is true, however, that the cost of computing alternative measures is fairly low, and as a check on the results these measures should probably be computed from time to time.

Comparison of the Predictive Accuracy of Eight Sets of Estimates

In Section 6.6 the eight sets of estimates of the US model were compared in various ways. Another way to do this is to see how they compare in terms of predictive accuracy of the overall model. One procedure that could be used would be to compute d-row values like those in Table 8-2 for each estimator, which would require estimating the model 51 times for each estimator and performing 51 stochastic simulations for each estimator. This procedure is too expensive for present purposes, especially given the cost of estimating the model just one time by FIML and 3SLS. One also runs into the problem that the numbers of observations for the early estimation periods are not sufficient to estimate all 107 coefficients that were estimated for the basic period by FIML.

An easier procedure is simply to compute root mean squared errors for each set of estimates for some prediction period, and this is what was done. The prediction period that was used is 1970I–1982III, which is within the estimation period that was used for each set of estimates, 1954I–1982III. Although this procedure is a poor one for comparing alternative models because of possible differences in exogenous variables and the possible misspecification of the models, it is not as bad for comparing alternative estimates of the same model. The exogenous variables are the same for each set of estimates, and the misspecification of the model may not vary too much across the different sets. In future work, however, it would be better to try to use the more expensive procedure to compare the estimates.

The results are presented in Table 8-5. Remember that the main conclusion from the comparisons in Section 6.6 is that all the estimates are fairly close to each other except for the FIML estimates. One of the key questions here, therefore, is how the FIML estimates compare to the others in terms of predictive accuracy.

The main conclusion that one can draw from the results in Table 8-5 is that they are not conclusive. The ranking of the estimates varies across variables and across the length of the prediction period. The biggest difference in the results concerns the one through four quarter ahead results for FIML for real GNP. The one- and two-quarter-ahead FIML errors are much larger than the others, and the three- and four-quarter-ahead FIML errors are smaller. Part of this difference is probably due to the fact, as discussed in Section 6.6, that the FIML estimates of the coefficients of the lagged dependent variables are generally smaller than the other estimates. (See, for example, the results in Table 6.5.) In other words, the FIML results are less dependent on the values of the lagged endogenous variables, which may hurt for the first few quarters ahead and help thereafter.

It is possible that the four LAD estimators (LAD and the three 2SLAD estimators) are hurt by the use of the root mean squared error measure rather than the mean absolute error (MAE) measure. In order to determine this, MAEs were also computed for the eight sets of estimates. The results for real GNP and the GNP deflator are presented in Table 8-6. It is clear from this

TABLE 8-5. Root mean squared errors for eight sets of coefficient estimates for 1970 I - 1982 III for the US model

	Number of quarters ahead							
	1	2	3	4	5	6	7	8
GNPR: Real GNP								
2SLS	.66	.81	1.08	1.25	1.43	1.61	1.73	1.81
FIML	.86	.93	1.03	1.16	1.36	1.58	1.74	1.86
3SLS	.65	.79	1.05	1.20	1.39	1.60	1.76	1.88
2SLAD q = 0.0	.65	.79	1.06	1.24	1.45	1.65	1.77	1.85
2SLAD q = 0.5	.65	.78	1.05	1.19	1.39	1.62	1.77	1.90
2SLAD q = 1.0	.68	.82	1.12	1.28	1.48	1.70	1.84	1.98
LAD	.68	.83	1.15	1.31	1.49	1.68	1.78	1.88
OLS	.67	.84	1.11	1.27	1.43	1.59	1.69	1.77
GNPD: GNP deflator								
2SLS	.44	.69	.88	1.05	1.18	1.23	1.25	1.22
FIML	.45	.70	.90	1.08	1.21	1.26	1.28	1.27
3SLS	.45	.70	.90	1.08	1.21	1.26	1.27	1.24
2SLAD q = 0.0	.45	.71	.91	1.11	1.26	1.35	1.38	1.37
2SLAD q = 0.5	.44	.69	.89	1.08	1.22	1.28	1.31	1.29
2SLAD q = 1.0	.44	.69	.88	1.07	1.21	1.29	1.33	1.33
LAD	.44	.69	.88	1.07	1.21	1.27	1.30	1.29
OLS	.44	.69	.87	1.04	1.16	1.21	1.22	1.20
100•UR: Unemployment rate (percentage points)								
2SLS	.29	.43	.55	.66	.75	.83	.90	.95
FIML	.33	.48	.58	.71	.79	.87	.93	.97
3SLS	.30	.46	.59	.71	.80	.87	.95	1.01
2SLAD q = 0.0	.29	.42	.52	.63	.71	.77	.84	.88
2SLAD q = 0.5	.29	.42	.52	.62	.70	.76	.82	.87
2SLAD q = 1.0	.32	.49	.63	.74	.83	.88	.94	.99
LAD	.30	.44	.56	.67	.76	.82	.87	.91
OLS	.30	.45	.57	.69	.78	.84	.91	.96
RS: Bill rate (percentage points)								
2SLS	.97	1.32	1.37	1.42	1.47	1.47	1.50	1.56
FIML	1.04	1.47	1.55	1.66	1.79	1.82	1.88	1.93
3SLS	.98	1.36	1.41	1.48	1.56	1.58	1.62	1.69
2SLAD q = 0.0	.98	1.35	1.40	1.44	1.49	1.48	1.48	1.54
2SLAD q = 0.5	1.01	1.35	1.39	1.44	1.50	1.50	1.50	1.54
2SLAD q = 1.0	1.03	1.42	1.46	1.56	1.66	1.71	1.77	1.83
LAD	1.03	1.42	1.46	1.57	1.69	1.74	1.81	1.88
OLS	.97	1.33	1.36	1.42	1.49	1.49	1.53	1.60
M1: Money supply								
2SLS	1.07	1.29	1.37	1.63	1.87	1.90	2.05	2.23
FIML	1.05	1.23	1.33	1.64	1.89	1.96	2.15	2.35
3SLS	1.06	1.25	1.35	1.62	1.88	1.94	2.11	2.32
2SLAD q = 0.0	1.05	1.24	1.33	1.60	1.87	1.94	2.11	2.31
2SLAD q = 0.5	1.12	1.41	1.56	1.86	2.14	2.23	2.39	2.59
2SLAD q = 1.0	1.15	1.50	1.72	2.08	2.37	2.46	2.65	2.90
LAD	1.12	1.41	1.56	1.88	2.11	2.14	2.29	2.50
OLS	1.06	1.25	1.32	1.56	1.80	1.82	1.97	2.15

Notes:
- The sample period for all estimates is 1954 I - 1982 III, and so all forecasts are within sample.
- The actual values of the exogenous variables were used for all the forecasts.
- All simulations were deterministic.
- There are 51 observations for the one-quarter-ahead forecasts, 50 for the two-quarter-ahead forecasts, and so on.
- For the unemployment rate and the bill rate the errors are in the natural units of the variables. For the other variables the errors are in percentage points.

TABLE 8-6. Mean absolute errors for eight sets of coefficient estimates for 1970 I - 1982 III for the US model

	Number of quarters ahead							
	1	2	3	4	5	6	7	8
GNPR: Real GNP								
2SLS	.52	.67	.86	1.01	1.10	1.26	1.38	1.48
FIML	.71	.73	.80	.93	1.09	1.28	1.44	1.50
3SLS	.52	.64	.84	.99	1.11	1.30	1.45	1.56
2SLAD q = 0.0	.52	.65	.84	.97	1.13	1.29	1.37	1.44
2SLAD q = 0.5	.52	.64	.84	.98	1.14	1.30	1.41	1.51
2SLAD q = 1.0	.54	.68	.90	1.05	1.22	1.35	1.39	1.54
LAD	.53	.67	.92	1.05	1.17	1.30	1.36	1.47
OLS	.53	.69	.88	1.03	1.10	1.27	1.39	1.47
GNPD: GNP deflator								
2SLS	.34	.55	.72	.85	.95	.95	.97	.95
FIML	.37	.57	.74	.88	.95	.97	.97	.97
3SLS	.36	.57	.74	.89	.97	.97	.97	.93
2SLAD q = 0.0	.35	.57	.75	.88	1.00	1.03	1.09	1.07
2SLAD q = 0.5	.35	.55	.73	.90	1.01	1.05	1.07	1.07
2SLAD q = 1.0	.35	.56	.73	.88	.99	1.03	1.05	1.02
LAD	.35	.56	.73	.88	.99	1.03	1.05	1.00
OLS	.35	.55	.71	.84	.93	.94	.96	.94

Notes:
- The sample period for all estimates is 1954 I - 1982 III, and so all forecasts are within sample.
- The actual values of the exogenous variables were used for all the forecasts.
- All simulations were deterministic.
- There are 51 observations for the one-quarter-ahead forecasts, 50 for the two-quarter-ahead forecasts, and so on.
- The errors are in percentage points.

table that the main conclusion is not changed by the use of the MAE measure: the same inconclusive results are obtained for both measures.

One way of looking at these results is the following. It is clear from the results in Table 8-2 that the US model is misspecified when estimated by 2SLS. Table 8-2 provides quantitative estimates of this misspecification, and for some variables the estimates are fairly large. One might expect that estimating the model by other techniques would change the degree of misspecification, either positively or negatively. The results in Tables 8-5 and 8-6, however, suggest that this is not the case. However the model is misspecified, the size of the misspecification is not sensitive to the use of alternative estimators. An interesting question for future research is whether this conclusion holds for other models and for later versions of the US model.

8.6 A Comparison of the MC and ARMC Models

The cost of solving the MC model is too large for it to be feasible to use the method in Section 8.4 to analyze it. As discussed in Section 7.5.2, the time taken to solve the model for one quarter varies between about 20 and 40 seconds on the IBM 4341, which compares to about .2 seconds for the US model. The MC model is thus between about 100 and 200 times more expensive to solve than the US model, which for present purposes rules out for the MC model many of the experiments that could be performed for the US model. Aside from the cost, the number of observations available for the flexible exchange rate period is also not large enough to allow the method in Section 8.4 to be used. The method requires that a model be successively reestimated over a number of periods, and in the MC case there are barely enough observations to estimate the equations that pertain to the flexible exchange rate period once.

Because the method in Section 8.4 could not be used, the present comparison of the MC and ARMC models is very crude, and not much weight should be placed on the results. What was done is the following. Three eight-quarter periods were chosen: a fixed exchange rate period, 1970II–1972I, and two flexible rate periods, 1974I–1975IV and 1976I–1977IV. For each of these periods both static and dynamic predictions were generated using deterministic simulation, where the error terms were set equal to zero. The actual values of the exogenous variables were used for the MC model; the ARMC model has no exogenous variables. The MC model was solved both for the case in which trade shares are exogenous and for the case in which they are determined by the trade share equations. This allows one to examine how much accuracy is lost by having to predict trade shares rather than knowing them exactly. Given these predictions, RMSEs were computed for each run.

The results are presented in Tables 8-7, 8-8, and 8-9. For the results in Table 8-7 a weighted average of the RMSEs across all countries except the United States was taken for each variable. The RMSEs were weighted by the ratio of the country's real GNP (in 75$) in the last (that is, eighth) quarter of the prediction period to the total real GNP of all the countries. This provides a summary measure of the overall fit of the MC model with respect to each variable. The RMSEs for the individual countries are presented in Table 8-8 for one run, the dynamic simulation for the period 1974I–1975IV. This is the period of the large increase in the price of oil by OPEC, and it is not a particularly easy period to explain. The RMSEs for the United States are presented in Table 8-9.

As mentioned in Section 5.1.2, the ARMC model does not contain estimated equations for variables that are determined by identities in the MC model. Four of the variables listed in Tables 8-7 and 8-8 are determined by identities, *Y, PM, X*75$, and *PW*$, and therefore no ARMC results are presented for these variables.

TABLE 8-7. Weighted RMSEs for all countries except the US

Equation number in Table B-3 or B-4	Variable		1970 II - 1972 I						1974 I - 1975 IV					
			STA			DYN			STA			DYN		
			MC*	MC	ARMC	MC*	MC	ARMC	MC*	MC	ARMC	MC*	MC	ARMC
4	Real GNP	Y	1.54	2.00	—	2.79	2.90	—	1.84	2.58	—	3.25	4.67	—
5	GNP deflator	PY	.88	.89	.93	2.79	2.87	2.68	1.35	1.36	1.55	3.08	3.10	5.24
7a,7b	Interest rate	RS	.58	.60	.69	.82	.94	.97	.89	.94	.97	1.63	1.71	1.73
9b	Exchange rate	e	a	a	a	a	a	a	3.87	3.96	4.16	5.03	5.30	6.22
V	Import price	PM	.98	2.90	—	3.01	5.40	—	2.81	2.89	—	6.55	6.96	—
6	Money supply	M1*	2.74	2.78	2.48	5.21	5.23	4.14	2.83	2.84	2.85	4.78	4.54	4.22
1	Imports	M	4.37	4.65	4.81	7.95	7.22	6.88	4.91	5.11	6.06	6.64	7.94	10.75
2	Consumption	C	1.54	1.59	1.32	2.96	2.83	2.17	2.24	2.34	2.07	3.40	4.08	3.97
3	Investment	I	2.84	2.84	2.72	6.25	5.96	5.35	3.47	3.47	3.62	7.17	7.23	6.84
8	Interest rate	RB	.27	.28	.30	.51	.51	.77	.46	.48	.52	1.02	1.07	1.13
11	Export price	PX	1.90	1.85	2.17	4.83	4.95	6.92	3.84	3.91	3.83	8.16	8.05	11.00
II	Exports	X75$	1.93	7.28	—	5.17	10.45	—	2.27	9.22	—	3.98	14.40	—
VI	World price	PW$	.93	.83	—	3.50	3.70	—	4.06	4.25	—	7.98	7.88	—

Equation number in Table B-3 or B-4	Variable		1976 I - 1977 IV					
			STA			DYN		
			MC*	MC	ARMC	MC*	MC	ARMC
4	Real GNP	Y	1.53	1.90	—	2.41	2.80	—
5	GNP deflator	PY	1.15	1.15	1.18	2.16	2.37	2.75
7a,7b	Interest rate	RS	.86	.85	.96	1.72	1.79	1.81
9b	Exchange rate	e	2.43	2.42	2.51	4.38	4.19	5.73
V	Import price	PM	2.21	2.22	—	4.31	4.23	—
6	Money supply	M1*	2.32	2.34	2.35	3.38	3.48	3.43
1	Imports	M	4.48	4.63	5.04	6.19	7.03	7.16
2	Consumption	C	1.62	1.67	1.48	2.82	3.01	2.33
3	Investment	I	2.82	2.82	2.83	5.01	5.02	4.23
8	Interest rate	RB	.43	.43	.45	.89	1.00	1.00
11	Export price	PX	2.33	2.31	2.42	3.79	3.74	4.98
II	Exports	X75$	1.59	6.87	—	2.83	9.38	—
VI	World price	PW$	1.60	1.56	—	2.46	2.50	—

Notes: a. Fixed exchange rate period for almost all countries.
- STA = Static simulation.
- DYN = Dynamic simulation.
- MC* = MC model with trade shares exogenous.
- All errors are in percentage points.
- Weights are GNP in 75$ in the last quarter of the period.

TABLE 8-8. RMSEs for the individual countries: dynamic simulation, 1974 I - 1975 IV

Country	Real GNP Y MC	GNP deflator PY MC	GNP deflator PY ARMC	Interest rate RS MC	Interest rate RS ARMC	Exchange rate e MC	Exchange rate e ARMC	Import price PM MC	Money supply M1* MC	Money supply M1* ARMC	Imports M MC	Imports M ARMC	Consumption C MC	Consumption C ARMC	Investment I MC	Investment I ARMC	Interest rate RB MC	Interest rate RB ARMC	Export price PX MC	Export price PX ARMC	Exports X75$ MC
Canada	2.4	2.0	3.0	.6	1.3	2.5	2.1	5.2	3.0	3.1	6.7	3.9	1.4	1.8	3.3	3.6	.5	.7	9.1	8.1	16.5
Japan	3.7	1.9	3.5	.7	1.7	3.6	4.2	5.9	6.3	1.7	4.3	21.5	3.1	9.0	8.4	11.0	—	—	7.1	13.1	7.5
Austria	1.7	2.5	3.3	.4	.9	4.2	4.6	7.1	3.7	3.5	9.7	7.1	1.7	1.4	—	—	—	—	8.2	8.2	6.7
Belgium	3.5	4.1	7.0	1.9	1.8	4.1	5.3	7.3	3.6	3.8	10.5	12.4	3.6	2.1	5.5	5.6	.6	.5	8.1	8.5	12.6
Denmark	4.5	3.0	4.4	2.6	4.5	6.4	4.3	5.4	5.0	6.7	8.1	12.9	6.1	5.8	13.2	15.9	.6	1.7	3.6	7.5	5.8
France	3.9	2.3	3.1	2.6	2.2	7.2	8.3	8.0	3.1	4.1	9.0	8.2	2.5	1.2	2.9	3.5	1.1	.9	7.2	9.7	13.3
Germany	4.3	1.6	2.9	3.0	1.7	3.9	5.3	8.7	1.7	3.5	5.9	4.7	1.0	1.6	10.5	6.1	.9	.9	8.5	9.0	9.6
Italy	3.8	1.6	6.8	3.4	4.2	7.0	9.1	4.2	3.0	9.7	8.9	14.1	4.2	3.7	4.0	3.3	1.4	1.5	8.6	11.7	10.4
Netherlands	5.4	1.5	3.5	3.3	2.1	4.5	6.6	5.4	3.1	4.8	8.8	7.2	6.5	2.3	9.5	7.4	.8	.9	8.9	10.5	8.0
Norway	3.9	2.2	2.5	2.3	2.1	6.0	4.6	5.2	8.0	5.2	3.2	4.8	3.1	1.6	9.5	10.8	.5	.6	8.0	9.1	15.9
Sweden	2.4	1.8	3.4	1.5	1.2	6.0	5.7	6.6	7.4	4.8	6.8	6.1	2.2	3.8	7.6	5.5	.8	.3	11.0	9.9	11.6
Switzerland	8.0	4.5	1.9	1.5	.9	10.5	6.7	2.2	8.8	7.2	17.5	15.7	4.9	6.0	18.8	17.1	.6	.7	2.3	6.5	11.6
United Kingdom	3.3	5.0	8.7	.3	.8	2.7	5.2	7.4	6.6	3.9	6.3	4.3	2.8	2.3	4.5	3.9	2.6	2.6	7.8	9.2	8.4
Finland	3.7	6.9	8.5	.2	.3	4.5	5.4	6.1	11.3	10.7	8.1	10.0	3.5	2.3	16.0	9.8	—	—	16.6	18.4	35.1
Greece	3.3	2.9	4.4	1.5	1.3	—	—	7.7	7.6	4.0	10.5	13.5	—	—	20.4	25.2	—	—	10.1	12.1	7.4
Ireland	4.7	4.7	5.0	.9	.7	4.7	5.4	9.9	5.0	5.7	8.1	14.5	3.2	5.6	6.8	8.3	2.2	2.6	5.7	5.5	6.8
Portugal	4.7	6.8	5.3	2.5	1.0	5.9	7.5	12.0	6.6	2.3	17.6	28.4	4.7	5.4	7.9	10.3	1.9	1.0	—	—	17.3
Spain	3.0	1.6	1.3	.2	.3	5.1	7.9	4.8	2.4	2.3	4.1	4.0	2.8	2.5	3.8	4.2	—	—	6.3	8.9	18.0
Turkey	2.2	3.9	5.0	—	—	—	—	7.3	4.1	2.4	8.7	13.5	2.9	9.6	—	—	—	—	9.4	8.2	34.1
Yugoslavia	2.5	4.0	4.6	—	—	—	—	8.5	—	—	6.3	8.2	3.7	3.2	—	—	—	—	7.7	10.9	9.6
Australia	3.1	7.6	6.5	.8	.6	6.9	2.3	12.2	8.5	8.5	7.5	8.8	2.4	2.4	2.3	2.7	.7	1.2	4.7	6.4	8.3
New Zealand	6.2	6.9	5.2	1.8	.6	29.2	18.7	23.4	2.8	6.3	12.9	17.5	7.7	2.0	10.4	18.8	.8	.7	19.9	17.0	24.7
South Africa	12.4	2.1	1.7	1.6	1.5	—	—	8.1	3.4	6.4	7.0	8.5	10.7	1.6	17.3	11.3	.9	.4	5.8	9.6	11.9
Libya	23.7	—	—	—	—	—	—	9.6	—	—	9.8	12.6	6.9	9.2	—	—	—	—	—	—	49.8
Nigeria	9.7	—	—	—	—	—	—	8.5	—	—	5.6	12.1	—	—	—	—	—	—	—	—	32.2
Saudi Arabia	17.3	—	—	—	—	—	—	7.0	—	—	19.9	9.6	17.0	7.3	—	—	—	—	—	—	22.5
Venezuela	8.5	—	—	—	—	—	—	8.0	—	—	20.9	13.9	13.0	11.1	—	—	—	—	—	—	18.1
Argentina	21.0	10.2	38.7	—	—	—	—	8.2	—	—	—	—	33.8	10.2	10.3	10.9	—	—	—	—	23.5
Brazil	4.4	4.9	8.9	—	—	13.6	17.8	8.1	—	—	12.7	13.6	4.5	2.5	—	—	—	—	11.2	29.4	15.7
Chile	3.3	19.2	81.0	—	—	—	—	6.3	—	—	32.9	101.0	—	—	—	—	—	—	—	—	32.0
Colombia	10.1	2.3	2.1	—	—	—	—	7.6	8.0	9.7	12.0	17.1	9.2	3.3	—	—	—	—	8.2	8.5	46.2
Mexico	6.6	—	—	—	—	—	—	7.7	—	—	10.9	8.6	6.5	2.4	—	—	—	—	—	—	74.3
Peru	14.8	—	—	—	—	—	—	7.2	17.7	7.8	—	—	16.6	5.0	—	—	—	—	—	—	24.3
Israel	12.0	7.5	10.4	—	—	—	—	8.3	—	—	10.5	8.7	9.8	5.1	18.4	15.0	—	—	3.7	6.7	17.2
Jordan	11.1	16.3	14.5	—	—	—	—	6.9	—	—	9.9	20.5	15.4	12.5	—	—	—	—	—	—	25.4
Syria	9.7	6.4	8.6	—	—	—	—	8.7	—	—	12.0	13.3	18.4	7.2	—	—	—	—	—	—	26.0
India	4.1	7.5	7.1	—	—	3.3	3.7	3.6	—	—	12.0	10.0	5.3	7.5	6.8	5.4	.1	.3	7.9	12.7	12.5
Korea	3.0	5.6	9.1	2.1	1.8	—	—	5.4	—	—	8.7	10.4	5.2	5.0	—	—	—	—	6.2	4.4	15.7
Malaysia	9.3	4.9	3.3	—	—	—	—	6.3	—	—	4.1	15.3	8.7	6.2	—	—	—	—	9.4	7.9	10.6
Pakistan	2.8	2.5	3.2	1.0	.9	—	—	5.8	—	—	7.5	5.3	—	—	—	—	—	—	14.3	5.8	29.6
Philippines	13.6	5.9	6.1	2.6	2.2	—	—	5.0	5.2	4.7	5.4	6.5	16.8	6.5	—	—	—	—	22.3	21.8	21.2
Thailand	3.7	3.8	3.2	.7	.6	—	—	5.5	3.6	4.7	9.4	18.6	4.3	2.9	—	—	—	—	12.2	9.5	22.0
Weighted	4.7	3.1	5.2	1.7	1.7	5.3	6.2	7.0	4.5	4.2	7.9	10.8	4.1	4.0	7.2	6.8	1.1	1.1	8.0	11.0	14.4

TABLE 8-9. RMSEs for the US with and without the MC model

Variable		1970 II - 1972 I						1974 I - 1975 IV					
		STA			DYN			STA			DYN		
		a	b	c	a	b	c	a	b	c	a	b	c
Real GNP	R	.82	.89	.96	.53	.68	.87	.51	.60	.48	1.45	2.03	2.35
GNP deflator	PY	.49	.46	.51	1.88	1.50	1.45	.56	.63	.63	1.36	2.22	2.19
Interest rate	RS	.62	.64	.68	1.16	1.21	1.27	.42	.47	.47	.72	.81	.86
Import price	PM	—	1.18	4.10	—	4.50	5.76	—	3.23	3.27	—	6.95	7.12
Money supply	M1*	1.17	1.13	1.25	3.09	2.80	2.80	1.17	1.11	1.12	2.37	1.86	1.84
Imports	IM	2.35	2.41	2.38	6.86	7.66	7.76	4.39	4.55	4.58	5.48	8.03	8.39
Interest rate	R	.28	.28	.29	.44	.46	.47	.24	.25	.24	.27	.37	.34
Export price	PX	.99	1.00	1.06	1.20	1.26	1.32	1.78	2.12	2.15	5.45	7.38	7.31
Exports	X75$	—	1.37	9.04	—	2.13	8.57	—	1.70	2.98	—	2.79	5.01
World price	PW$	—	1.06	.90	—	3.96	4.16	—	4.63	4.86	—	8.14	8.03

Variable		1976 I - 1977 IV					
		STA			DYN		
		a	b	c	a	b	c
Real GNP	R	.60	.66	.68	1.56	1.65	1.22
GNP deflator	PY	.54	.56	.54	1.46	1.61	1.69
Interest rate	RS	.36	.36	.39	.57	.59	.73
Import price	PM	—	1.15	1.16	—	2.48	2.88
Money supply	M1*	.97	.99	.97	1.68	1.80	1.80
Imports	IM	2.14	2.16	2.12	3.60	3.91	3.69
Interest rate	R	.11	.11	.11	.16	.17	.24
Export price	PX	1.15	1.28	1.27	2.32	2.82	2.95
Exports	X75$	—	1.44	4.62	—	2.48	7.46
World price	PW$	—	1.78	1.74	—	2.41	2.48

Notes: a = US model alone.
b = MC model with trade shares exogenous (including US model).
c = MC model (including US model).
• STA = Static simulation.
• DYN = Dynamic simulation.
• All errors are in percentage points.

The following general conclusions can be drawn from Table 8-7. (1) MC is generally slightly less accurate than ARMC for consumption and investment. It is generally the same as ARMC or more accurate for other variables: the GNP deflator, the two interest rates, the exchange rate, the money supply, imports, and the price of exports. (2) The best period for the accuracy of MC relative to that of ARMC is probably 1974I–1975IV, the period of the large OPEC price increase, although the relative results across periods are close. (3) The use of the trade share equations increases the RMSEs for the export variable, $X75\$$, by a factor of between about two and four. For the dynamic prediction for 1976I–1977IV, for example, the RMSE increased from 2.83 percent to 9.38 percent. The variable next most affected by the trade share equations is GNP, which is as expected since exports are part of GNP. (4) The largest RMSE for the exchange rate for the MC model is only 5.30 percent (dynamic simulation for the 1974I–1975IV period), which seems fairly good. The largest RMSE for the short-term interest rate is 1.79 percentage points.

The RMSEs in Table 8-8 for the individual countries are generally larger for the smaller countries. This is as expected, given the poor quality of much of the data for the smaller countries and the likelihood that the model approximates less well the structure of these economies. For the first 18 countries in the table (Canada through Spain), the real GNP RMSEs range from 1.7 percent for Austria to 8.0 percent for Switzerland. The range for the GNP deflator is from 1.5 percent for the Netherlands to 6.9 percent for Finland, and the range for the exchange rate is from 2.5 percent for Canada to 10.5 percent for Switzerland.

With respect to the results in Table 8-9 for the United States, the fit of the US model for most variables worsens when it is embedded in the MC model. In the full MC model the two variables that are exogenous in the US model alone, the price of imports (PM) and exports ($X75\$$), are endogenous and thus predicted with error. The RMSEs for PM for the MC model with trade shares endogenous (the c columns) range from 1.16 percent to 7.12 percent, and the RMSEs for $X75\$$ range from 2.98 percent to 9.04 percent. These two additional sources of error generally lead to larger errors for the other variables in the US model, although in some cases the error cancellation is such that the RMSEs are smaller in the full MC model. The largest increase in the RMSE for real GNP occurred for the dynamic simulation for the 1974I–1975IV period, which was from 1.45 percent to 2.35 percent.

As stressed at the beginning of this section, it is not possible to draw any definitive conclusions from the present comparison. In general the MC model seems to do fairly well compared to the ARMC model, and thus the results are at least encouraging. In particular, the exchange rate RMSEs seem small enough for the MC model to warrant at least a small amount of optimism that the exchange rate equations are reasonable approximations.

9 Evaluating Static and Dynamic Properties

9.1 Introduction

A useful way of examining the properties of a model is to consider how the predicted values of the endogenous variables change when one or more exogenous variables are changed. This exercise is usually called multiplier analysis, although the use of the word "multiplier" is somewhat misleading. The output that one looks at from this exercise does not have to be the change in the endogenous variable *divided by* the change in the exogenous variable; it can merely be, for example, the change or percentage change in the endogenous variable itself. Indeed, if more than one exogenous variable has been changed, there is no obvious thing to divide the change in the endogenous variable by. The form of the output that is examined depends on the nature of the problem, and thus the word "multiplier" should be interpreted in a very general way.

The procedure that is usually used to compute multipliers is discussed in Section 9.2. It is based on the use of deterministic simulations. An alternative procedure, which is based on the use of stochastic simulations, is discussed in Section 9.3. The main advantage of using stochastic simulations is that it also allows standard errors of the multipliers to be estimated. Given the obvious importance of knowing how much confidence to place in the results from any given policy experiment in a model, the ability to estimate standard errors is a significant advantage. Results for the US model are discussed in Section 9.4, and results for the MC model are discussed in Section 9.5.

9.2 Use of Deterministic Simulations

Let x_t^a denote a "base" set of exogenous variable values for period t, and let x_t^b denote an alternative set. In most applications the base values are the actual values, although this is not always true. If, for example, the prediction period is beyond the end of the data, the base values must be guessed values. Assume that the prediction period begins in period t and is of length T. Given (1) the initial conditions as of the beginning of period t, (2) the coefficient estimates, (3) a set of exogenous variable values for the entire period, and (4) values of the error terms for the entire period (usually zero), the predicted values of the endogenous variables can be computed using the Gauss-Seidel technique. Let $\hat{y}^a_{itk}$ denote the k-period-ahead predicted value of endogenous variable i from the simulation that uses x^a_{t+k-1} $(k = 1, 2, \ldots, T)$ for the exogenous variable values, and let $\hat{y}^b_{itk}$ denote the predicted value from the simulation that uses x^b_{t+k-1} $(k = 1, 2, \ldots, T)$. The difference between the two predicted values, denoted $\hat{\delta}_{itk}$, is an estimate of the effect on the endogenous variable of changing the exogenous variables:

$$\hat{\delta}_{itk} = \hat{y}^b_{itk} - \hat{y}^a_{itk}. \tag{9.1}$$

If only one exogenous variable is changed, then $\hat{\delta}_{itk}$ is sometimes divided by this change when results are presented. If, say, the exogenous variable is a government spending variable and the change is 5 billion dollars, $\hat{\delta}_{itk}$ would be divided by 5. This procedure is generally followed only if the particular endogenous variable is in the same units as the exogenous variable. For example, if the endogenous variable is GNP in billions of dollars and the exogenous variable is government spending in billions of dollars, then $\hat{\delta}_{itk}$ divided by the change in government spending is an estimate of how much GNP changes for a one-billion-dollar change in government spending.

$\hat{\delta}_{itk}$ is sometimes simply divided by $\hat{y}^a_{itk}$, which converts the change into a percentage change. This percentage change may then be divided by something else, where the something else is problem-specific. Examples of this procedure are presented in Sections 9.4 and 9.5.

The error terms are generally set equal to their expected values for the simulations, where the expected values are almost always zero. For linear models it makes no difference what values are used as long as the same values are used for both simulations. For nonlinear models the choice does make a difference, and in this case the choice of zero values has some problems associated with it. Consider, for example, a model in which inflation responds in a very nonlinear way to the difference between actual output and some high activity level of output: inflation accelerates as output approaches the high activity level. Consider now a period in which output is close to the high activity level, and consider an experiment in which government spending is increased. This experiment should be quite inflationary, but this will not necessarily be the case if the model is predicting a much lower level of output than actually existed. In other words, if the model is predicting that output is not close to the high activity level when in fact it is, the inflationary consequences of the policy change will not be predicted very well.

There is an easy answer to this problem if the simulation period is within the period for which data exist, which is simply to use the actual (historical) values of the error terms rather than the zero values. By "actual" in this case is meant the values of the estimated residuals that result from the estimation of the equations. If these values are used and if the actual values of the exogenous variables are used, the simulation will result in a perfect fit. As the Gauss-Seidel technique passes through the model, each stochastic equation results in a perfect fit. The identities also fit perfectly, and therefore one pass through the equations will simply give back the actual values. (This assumes that the actual values are used as starting values. If this is not the case, the technique will require more iterations to converge to the actual values.) This solution will be called the "perfect tracking" solution. Once the residuals are added to the equations, they are never changed. The same set of values is used for all experiments.

If the actual values of the error terms are used, the problem regarding the response of inflation to output does not exist. The model predicts the actual data before any policy change is made. Note that this procedure is also not inconsistent with the statistical assumptions of the model, since the error terms are assumed to be uncorrelated with the exogenous and lagged endogenous variables. This procedure cannot be followed if the simulation period is beyond the end of the data. In this case no historical residuals are available, and therefore other values, such as zero, must be used.

The use of the actual values of the error terms has the advantage that only one simulation needs to be performed per policy experiment. $\hat{y}^a_{itk}$ is simply the actual value of the variable, and thus a simulation is only needed to get $\hat{y}^b_{itk}$.

9.3 Use of Stochastic Simulations

For nonlinear models $\hat{\delta}_{itk}$ in (9.1) is not an unbiased estimate of the change because the predicted values are not equal to the expected values. This does not, however, seem to be an important problem in practice (see Section 7.3), and so if one were only interested in estimates of the changes, it seems unlikely that stochastic simulation would be needed. The main reason for using stochastic simulation is to compute standard errors of $\hat{\delta}_{itk}$, that is, to estimate the uncertainty attached to the policy effects. The following is a discussion of a procedure that can be used to estimate standard errors of multipliers.

Since multipliers for nonlinear models are a function of the error terms, the treatment of the error terms must be considered. From the discussion in

Section 9.2, the best possibility seems to be to use the actual values of the error terms for all the simulations, where the base run is then simply the perfect tracking solution. The other main possibility is to use zero values for the error terms. Both possibilities will be considered in the description of the procedure.

There are two sources of uncertainty of policy effects in models: one is from the coefficient estimates, and the other is from the possible misspecification of the model. Unlike the procedure in Chapter 8, the present procedure does not account for the possible misspecification of the model. The estimated standard errors are based on the assumption that the model is correctly specified. This is a serious limitation, but the question of how to handle misspecification effects is still open.

The uncertainty from the coefficient estimates is estimated by drawing alternative sets of coefficients from an estimated distribution. As in Chapter 7, let $N(\hat{\alpha}, \hat{V})$ be the distribution of the coefficient estimates, and let α^* be a draw from this distribution. The steps of the procedure for the case in which the actual values of the error terms are used are the following.

1. Draw α^*, and for this draw compute the values of the error terms in the stochastic equations over the prediction period. Let u^* denote these values.
2. Given α^*, u^*, and the base set of exogenous variable values (x^a_{t+k-1}, $k = 1, 2, \ldots, T$), solve the model. Let $\tilde{y}^{aj}_{itk}$ denote the k-period-ahead predicted value of variable i from this solution. If the exogenous variable values are the actual values, this solution does not have to be performed because it is merely the perfect tracking solution.
3. Given α^*, u^*, and the alternative set of exogenous variable values (x^b_{t+k-1}, $k = 1, 2, \ldots, T$), solve the model. Let $\tilde{y}^{bj}_{itk}$ be the k-period-ahead predicted value of variable i from this solution.
4. Compute

$$\tilde{\delta}^j_{itk} = \tilde{y}^{bj}_{itk} - \tilde{y}^{aj}_{itk}. \tag{9.2}$$

5. Repeat steps 1 through 4 J times, where J is the desired number of trials.
6. Given the values from the J trials, compute the mean ($\tilde{\tilde{\delta}}_{itk}$) and variance ($\tilde{s}^2_{itk}$) of $\tilde{\delta}_{itk}$:

$$\tilde{\tilde{\delta}}_{itk} = \frac{1}{J}\sum_{j=1}^{J} \tilde{\delta}^j_{itk}, \tag{9.3}$$

$$\tilde{s}^2_{itk} = \frac{1}{J}\sum_{j=1}^{J} (\tilde{\delta}^j_{itk} - \tilde{\tilde{\delta}}_{itk})^2. \tag{9.4}$$

If zero values of the error terms are used instead of the actual values, step 1 merely consists of drawing α^*. In this case the solution in step 2 must always be performed because there is no perfect tracking solution. Otherwise the steps are the same.

It is important to understand the computation of u^* in step 1. These errors are computed using the actual values of all the variables in the stochastic equations. For $\hat{\alpha}$, the actual vector of coefficient estimates, these errors are simply the residuals from the estimated equations (assuming that the prediction period is within the estimation period). For α^* they are the residuals that would exist if the coefficient estimates had been α^* rather than $\hat{\alpha}$. It is necessary to compute new values of the error terms for each draw to have each base run be the perfect tracking solution.

One final point should be made about this procedure. Consider first the case in which zero values of the error terms are used, where the zero values are the expected values. In this case, for linear models $\tilde{\delta}^j_{itk}$ in (9.2) is the difference between two expected values. For nonlinear models there is the usual problem that the predicted values of the endogenous variables are not the expected values. The bias in the nonlinear case could be corrected by computing both $\tilde{y}^{bj}_{itk}$ and $\tilde{y}^{aj}_{itk}$ using stochastic simulation. In other words, two stochastic simulations could be performed for each pass through steps 1–4, one in step 2 and one in step 3. This procedure is expensive, because it means that two stochastic simulations are being performed within the overall stochastic simulation represented by steps 1–4. Given that the bias in the nonlinear case seems small, these simulations are not likely to be necessary in most applications.

In the case in which u^* is used, stochastic simulation in steps 2 and 3 could also be performed. The errors in u^* would be treated as exogenous variables, and the errors that are drawn for the stochastic simulation would simply be added to the stochastic equations *inclusive* of the errors in u^*. The predicted values computed by the stochastic simulation would be expected values conditional on u^*. In step 2 the predicted values would not be equal to the actual values even if the actual values of the exogenous variables were used, and therefore the solution in step 2 would always have to be performed. Again, however, these stochastic simulations are not likely to be needed.

9.4 Properties of the US Model

The rest of this chapter consists of a discussion of the properties of the US and MC models. The US model is discussed in this section, and the MC model is discussed in Section 9.5. This material provides both an example of the application of the deterministic and stochastic simulation techniques that were discussed in Sections 9.2 and 9.3 and a detailed description of the properties of the models. For purposes of understanding the US and MC models, this section and the next are the most important in the book.

9.4.1 General Remarks about the Properties

Because the theoretical model was used to guide the specification of the econometric model, the qualitative properties of the two models are similar. The properties of the theoretical model were examined by changing various variables from a position of equilibrium. Although this is an artificial starting point in the sense that the model never returns to equilibrium once it is shocked, it is useful for learning about the properties of the model. In particular, it is easy to see how disequilibrium can occur as a result of expectation errors and how multiplier reactions can take place. This artificial environment cannot be set up for the econometric model, and the experiments must be performed over an actual sample period.

The first quarter of the prediction period that is used for the results below, 1977I, was not a high activity quarter. The unemployment rate was 7.5 percent; the labor constraint variable Z was considerably below 0; and the demand pressure variable ZZ was considerably above 0. (Remember that slack times correspond to negative values of Z and positive values of ZZ: see Eqs. 97 and 98 in Table A-5.) This means that an expansionary policy action beginning in this quarter is likely to increase real output and employment. The main way in which this comes about is as follows (all equation numbers refer to Table A-5 in Appendix A).

1. The level of sales of the firm sector (X) is increased, say by an increase in government purchases of goods.
2. The firm sector responds by increasing production (Y): Eq. 11.
3. The increase in Y leads to an increase in plant and equipment investment (IK_f), jobs (J_f), and hours per job (H_f): Eqs. 12, 13, and 14.
4. The increase in J_f and H_f leads to an increase in JJ and JJ^* and then to an increase in the labor constraint variable Z: Eqs. 95, 96, and 97.
5. The increase in Z leads to an increase in consumption: Eqs. 1, 2, and 3.
6. The increase in plant and equipment investment and consumption increases sales (Eq. 60), which leads to a further increase in production, and so on.

If the labor constraint variable is close to 0 and thus not very binding, the expansionary effects in step 5 do not take place since Z will be changed very little. Also, considerable inflation will result from any attempt at expansion because the demand pressure variable will be small. (Values of the labor constraint variable close to zero almost always correspond to small values of the demand pressure variable.) In this situation the price level responds faster initially than does the wage rate, and thus the real wage falls. The fall in the real wage then has a negative effect on consumption and housing investment.

One of the key variables in the econometric model, as in the theoretical model, is the short-term interest rate. The interest rate has important effects on consumption and housing investment, which in turn have important effects on production, plant and equipment investment, and employment as outlined in the steps above. If the interest rate reaction function is part of the model, the interest rate will rise as an expansion takes place (the Fed "leans against the wind"), which means that the expansion will not be as strong as it would be if, say, the interest rate remained unchanged.

Four of the most important equations in the model are the three consumption equations and the housing investment equation. If these are affected by a policy change, this will affect sales, which then affects the economy in the manner outlined above. The explanatory variables in these four equations have been discussed extensively in Chapter 4; they include the price level, the after-tax wage rate, the after-tax interest rate (either short-term or long-term), nonlabor income, the initial value of wealth, and the labor constraint variable. Nonlabor income and the initial value of wealth are the variables through which transfer payments and dividends affect the economy. If, say, transfer payments are increased, this increases nonlabor income, which increases demand. An increase in nonlabor income also increases wealth to the extent that not all of the income is spent in the current quarter. The increase in wealth then has a positive effect on demand in the next quarter.

The link between output and the unemployment rate is not very tight in the model. When output increases by a certain percentage, the number of jobs increases by less than this percentage (Eq. 13). How much the number of jobs increases depends in part on the amount of excess labor on hand, which varies considerably over time. When the number of jobs increases, the number of people holding two jobs increases (Eq. 8), which means that the number of new people employed increases by less than the number of new jobs (Eq. 85). How much the number of people holding two jobs increases depends in part on the value of the labor constraint variable, which also varies considerably over time. Finally, when the number of jobs increases, the number of people in the labor force increases (Eqs. 6 and 7), which means that the unemployment rate falls less than it otherwise would for the given increase in the number of new people employed (Eqs. 86 and 87). How much the number of people in the labor force increases also depends on the value of the labor constraint variable. Because of these three leakages, the unemployment rate will drop less than the percentage change in output. Because the various responses vary depending on factors such as the amount of excess labor on hand and the value of the labor constraint variable, it seems quite unlikely that the relationship between output and the unemployment rate will be stable over time. The model thus does not obey Okun's law.

There are a number of variables other than the demand pressure variable that affect the price level (Eq. 10), and thus one would also not expect a stable relationship between, say, the rate of inflation and the demand pressure variable when they are simply plotted together on a graph. A stable relationship is even less likely to exist between the rate of inflation and the unemployment rate because of the many factors that affect the labor force variables and thus the unemployment rate. An important variable in the price equation is the price of imports, which has a positive effect on prices.

Productivity defined as output per paid-for worker hour (Y/J_fH_f) is procyclical. When Y changes by a certain percentage, J_fH_f changes by less than this percentage in the immediate quarter. The buffer for this is the amount of excess labor held: as output falls, excess labor builds up, and vice versa. Other things being equal, excess labor is gradually eliminated because it has a negative effect on the demand for employment and hours. Similar considerations apply to the amount of excess capital held. Excess capital is gradually eliminated because it has a negative effect on investment.

9.4.2 Estimated Effects for Eight Policy Actions

Construction of Tables 9-1 and 9-2

The procedure in Section 9.3 was used to estimate the uncertainty of eight policy actions for the US model. The 2SLS estimates were used for these results. The period for the policy actions was 1977I–1980IV (16 quarters). The eight policy variables that were changed (one at a time) are (1) C_g, government purchases of goods, (2) d_{1g}, the personal income tax rate, (3) d_{2g}, the profit tax rate, (4) d_{3g}, the indirect business tax rate, (5) d_{4g}, the employee social security tax rate, (6) d_{5g}, the employer social security tax rate, (7) J_g, the employment of the government, and (8) TR_{gh}, the level of transfer payments from the government to the household sector. All these variables are federal government variables.

The change in C_g from its actual value for each quarter was taken to be .25 percent of real GNP, *GNPR*. (*GNPR* is at an annual rate, whereas C_g is at a quarterly rate, and therefore the amount by which C_g was changed each period is .000625 · *GNPR*.) C_g was changed for each of the 16 quarters, not just the first, and the amount by which it was changed varied because *GNPR* varied. Remember that the change is from the actual value for the quarter; it is not the change from quarter to quarter. The results for this experiment are presented first in Table 9-1 for each endogenous variable. The effects on five endogenous variables are presented in the table: real GNP, the GNP deflator, the unemployment rate, the bill rate, and the money supply. The values in the 0 rows are the estimated effects from a deterministic simulation; the values in the a rows are the estimated effects from a stochastic simulation; and the values in the b rows are the estimated standard errors computed from the stochastic simulation. The actual values of the error terms were used for both simulations, and therefore the base run for both simulations was the perfect tracking solution. The number of trials for each experiment was 50.

The units of the results in Table 9-1 are as follows. For real GNP, the GNP deflator, and the money supply, the numbers in the 0 rows are $(1/.0025)(\hat{\delta}_{itk}/\hat{y}^a_{itk})$, where from (9.1) $\hat{\delta}_{itk} = \hat{y}^b_{itk} - \hat{y}^a_{itk}$. The $\hat{y}^a_{itk}$ values are the actual values because the base run is the perfect tracking solution. These numbers are the percentage changes in the variables divided by .0025. Since C_g was changed by .25 percent of real GNP, each number can be interpreted as the percentage change in the variable (in percentage points) that results from an exogenous change in real GNP of 1.0 percent. For the bill rate, which is in units of percentage points (1.0 percent = 1.0), the numbers in the 0 rows are simply $\hat{\delta}_{itk}$. For the unemployment rate, which is in units of percent (1.0 percent = .01), the numbers are $100 \cdot \hat{\delta}_{itk}$.

The numbers in the a rows are $(1/.0025)(\tilde{\bar{\delta}}_{itk}/y^a_{itk})$ for real GNP, the GNP deflator, and the money supply, where $\tilde{\bar{\delta}}_{itk}$ is defined in (9.3) and the y^a_{itk} values are the actual values. For the bill rate the numbers are $\tilde{\bar{\delta}}_{itk}$, and for the unemployment rate the numbers are $100 \cdot \tilde{\bar{\delta}}_{itk}$. The numbers in the b rows are $\tilde{s}_{itk}$ for the bill rate, where $\tilde{s}_{itk}$ is the square root of $\tilde{s}^2_{itk}$, which is defined in (9.4). For the unemployment rate the numbers are $100 \cdot \tilde{s}_{itk}$. For real GNP, the GNP deflator, and the money supply, the b-row numbers are the estimated standard errors of the a-row numbers. In other words, the b-row

TABLE 9-1. Estimated policy effects for the US model for five variables and eight experiments

Policy variable changed		1977 I	II	III	IV	1978 I	II	III	IV	1979 I	II	III	IV	1980 I	II	III	IV	Sum[c]
GNPR: Real GNP																		
C_g	0	1.10	1.31	1.32	1.28	1.20	1.10	1.01	.93	.86	.80	.75	.71	.69	.66	.64	.64	13.4
	a	1.09	1.30	1.32	1.28	1.20	1.10	1.01	.93	.85	.79	.74	.70	.68	.65	.64	.63	13.4
	b	.07	.07	.09	.10	.11	.12	.12	.13	.13	.14	.14	.14	.14	.14	.13	.13	1.5
d_{1g}	0	.23	.47	.63	.75	.80	.81	.81	.78	.76	.74	.71	.69	.68	.70	.71	.72	10.0
	a	.23	.46	.62	.73	.79	.79	.79	.77	.75	.73	.70	.69	.68	.70	.71	.71	9.8
	b	.06	.09	.11	.12	.13	.14	.14	.14	.14	.14	.14	.13	.13	.13	.13	.13	1.7
d_{2g}	0	-.00	.03	.09	.14	.17	.19	.20	.20	.20	.20	.20	.21	.22	.26	.30	.32	2.7
	a	.00	.03	.09	.13	.16	.18	.19	.20	.20	.20	.20	.20	.22	.26	.30	.33	2.6
	b	.00	.02	.05	.07	.09	.10	.11	.11	.12	.13	.13	.13	.14	.15	.16	.17	1.5
d_{3g}	0	.20	.40	.54	.62	.66	.66	.66	.64	.62	.60	.58	.57	.57	.59	.59	.60	8.2
	a	.20	.39	.52	.60	.64	.64	.63	.61	.60	.58	.56	.55	.55	.57	.58	.59	8.0
	b	.04	.07	.09	.09	.10	.10	.10	.10	.10	.10	.10	.10	.11	.11	.11	.12	1.3
d_{4g}	0	.40	.81	1.09	1.26	1.35	1.35	1.35	1.31	1.27	1.23	1.18	1.16	1.16	1.21	1.23	1.25	16.8
	a	.40	.80	1.07	1.25	1.34	1.34	1.34	1.30	1.26	1.23	1.18	1.17	1.17	1.23	1.24	1.26	16.8
	b	.09	.14	.17	.19	.20	.21	.22	.22	.21	.21	.21	.20	.20	.20	.20	.20	2.6
d_{5g}	0	.01	.04	.10	.15	.19	.22	.24	.26	.28	.29	.30	.31	.32	.34	.35	.36	3.4
	a	.01	.04	.10	.15	.19	.22	.24	.26	.27	.29	.29	.31	.32	.34	.35	.36	3.4
	b	.00	.01	.03	.04	.06	.06	.07	.07	.07	.08	.08	.08	.08	.09	.09	.09	.9
J_g	0	1.31	1.38	1.35	1.19	1.10	1.00	.96	.80	.76	.69	.69	.61	.69	.73	.68	.68	13.1
	a	1.31	1.37	1.34	1.18	1.09	.99	.94	.78	.74	.67	.67	.58	.65	.70	.64	.64	12.7
	b	.05	.09	.12	.15	.18	.20	.22	.23	.25	.27	.27	.27	.27	.28	.28	.27	2.9
TR_{gh}	0	.16	.32	.44	.53	.58	.59	.60	.60	.60	.59	.57	.57	.56	.57	.57	.56	7.6
	a	.16	.32	.43	.50	.54	.56	.56	.56	.55	.54	.52	.52	.51	.52	.51	.50	7.1
	b	.07	.12	.16	.19	.21	.22	.23	.23	.23	.24	.23	.24	.24	.25	.26	.27	2.9
GNPD: GNP deflator																		
C_g	0	.04	.18	.27	.33	.40	.46	.54	.57	.61	.63	.67	.71	.77	.80	.80	.85	
	a	.03	.17	.26	.32	.38	.45	.52	.54	.59	.60	.64	.68	.73	.76	.76	.81	
	b	.03	.02	.04	.05	.07	.08	.10	.11	.12	.13	.13	.14	.15	.15	.16	.16	
d_{1g}	0	-.01	.01	.05	.09	.12	.18	.23	.26	.30	.34	.37	.38	.41	.43	.45	.46	
	a	-.01	.01	.05	.09	.12	.17	.22	.25	.28	.32	.35	.36	.39	.41	.43	.44	
	b	.01	.01	.01	.02	.03	.04	.05	.06	.07	.08	.09	.10	.10	.11	.12	.12	
d_{2g}	0	-.00	-.00	.00	.01	.02	.04	.05	.06	.07	.09	.10	.10	.11	.13	.15	.16	
	a	-.00	-.00	.00	.01	.02	.03	.05	.06	.07	.08	.09	.10	.10	.11	.13	.15	
	b	.00	.00	.00	.01	.01	.02	.03	.03	.04	.05	.06	.06	.07	.08	.09	.10	
d_{3g}	0	-1.03	-1.03	-1.00	-.95	-.94	-.88	-.86	-.81	-.79	-.74	-.73	-.73	-.73	-.72	-.68	-.70	
	a	-1.03	-1.03	-1.00	-.96	-.94	-.89	-.87	-.83	-.81	-.77	-.75	-.75	-.76	-.75	-.71	-.74	
	b	.01	.01	.01	.02	.03	.04	.05	.05	.06	.07	.07	.08	.08	.09	.10	.10	
d_{4g}	0	-.02	.02	.09	.16	.22	.32	.40	.46	.51	.58	.63	.65	.69	.72	.76	.78	
	a	-.02	.02	.08	.16	.21	.30	.38	.44	.49	.55	.61	.62	.66	.70	.74	.76	
	b	.01	.01	.02	.04	.05	.07	.09	.10	.12	.13	.14	.15	.16	.17	.18	.19	
d_{5g}	0	-.06	-.12	-.17	-.21	-.24	-.27	-.30	-.32	-.34	-.35	-.37	-.39	-.41	-.42	-.43	-.44	
	a	-.06	-.12	-.17	-.21	-.24	-.28	-.31	-.33	-.35	-.37	-.38	-.40	-.42	-.44	-.44	-.46	
	b	.01	.02	.03	.03	.04	.04	.05	.05	.05	.06	.06	.06	.07	.07	.07	.08	
J_g	0	-.12	-.04	.06	.21	.30	.34	.36	.44	.45	.44	.41	.53	.50	.47	.50	.61	
	a	-.13	-.05	.05	.19	.27	.31	.32	.40	.40	.39	.35	.47	.43	.39	.41	.51	
	b	.01	.03	.05	.08	.09	.11	.13	.15	.17	.18	.20	.21	.23	.25	.26	.28	
TR_{gh}	0	-.00	.01	.04	.08	.11	.15	.19	.23	.26	.30	.34	.36	.39	.42	.45	.47	
	a	-.01	.01	.04	.07	.09	.14	.17	.20	.23	.27	.30	.31	.34	.36	.39	.40	
	b	.01	.01	.02	.03	.04	.06	.07	.09	.10	.11	.13	.13	.14	.15	.17	.18	

(continued)

TABLE 9-1 (continued)

Policy variable changed		1977 I	1977 II	1977 III	1977 IV	1978 I	1978 II	1978 III	1978 IV	1979 I	1979 II	1979 III	1979 IV	1980 I	1980 II	1980 III	1980 IV
100·UR: Unemployment rate (percentage points)																	
C_g	0	-.05	-.10	-.11	-.11	-.11	-.10	-.09	-.09	-.08	-.08	-.08	-.07	-.07	-.07	-.07	-.07
	a	-.05	-.09	-.11	-.11	-.11	-.10	-.09	-.09	-.08	-.08	-.08	-.07	-.07	-.07	-.07	-.07
	b	.01	.01	.01	.01	.02	.02	.01	.01	.01	.02	.02	.02	.02	.02	.02	.02
d_{1g}	0	.02	.02	.02	.02	.03	.03	.04	.04	.05	.05	.05	.06	.06	.06	.06	.06
	a	.02	.02	.02	.02	.03	.03	.04	.04	.05	.05	.05	.06	.06	.06	.06	.07
	b	.01	.01	.02	.02	.02	.02	.02	.02	.02	.02	.02	.02	.02	.02	.02	.02
d_{2g}	0	-.00	-.00	-.01	-.02	-.02	-.03	-.03	-.03	-.03	-.03	-.03	-.03	-.03	-.03	-.03	-.04
	a	.00	-.00	-.01	-.02	-.02	-.03	-.03	-.03	-.03	-.03	-.03	-.03	-.03	-.03	-.04	-.04
	b	.00	.00	.01	.01	.01	.01	.02	.02	.02	.02	.02	.02	.02	.02	.02	.02
d_{3g}	0	.00	-.00	-.01	-.02	-.02	-.02	-.02	-.02	-.02	-.01	-.01	-.01	-.01	-.01	-.01	-.02
	a	.00	-.00	-.01	-.02	-.02	-.02	-.02	-.01	-.01	-.01	-.01	-.01	-.01	-.01	-.01	-.01
	b	.00	.01	.01	.01	.01	.01	.01	.01	.01	.01	.01	.01	.01	.01	.01	.02
d_{4g}	0	.02	.03	.03	.03	.04	.04	.05	.06	.07	.08	.09	.09	.10	.10	.10	.10
	a	.02	.03	.03	.03	.03	.04	.05	.06	.07	.08	.09	.09	.10	.10	.10	.11
	b	.01	.02	.02	.03	.03	.03	.03	.03	.03	.03	.03	.03	.03	.03	.03	.03
d_{5g}	0	.00	-.00	-.01	-.01	-.02	-.02	-.02	-.03	-.03	-.03	-.03	-.03	-.03	-.03	-.03	-.03
	a	.00	-.00	-.01	-.01	-.02	-.02	-.02	-.02	-.03	-.03	-.03	-.03	-.03	-.03	-.03	-.03
	b	.00	.00	.00	.01	.01	.01	.01	.01	.01	.01	.01	.01	.01	.01	.01	.01
J_g	0	-.40	-.36	-.33	-.26	-.24	-.23	-.24	-.20	-.20	-.20	-.22	-.19	-.22	-.23	-.20	-.20
	a	-.40	-.36	-.33	-.27	-.24	-.23	-.24	-.20	-.20	-.20	-.22	-.19	-.22	-.23	-.21	-.20
	b	.01	.01	.02	.02	.02	.02	.02	.02	.03	.03	.03	.03	.03	.03	.03	.03
TR_{gh}	0	-.01	-.03	-.04	-.06	-.07	-.07	-.08	-.08	-.09	-.09	-.09	-.09	-.09	-.10	-.10	-.10
	a	-.01	-.03	-.04	-.06	-.06	-.07	-.07	-.08	-.08	-.08	-.09	-.09	-.09	-.09	-.09	-.10
	b	.00	.01	.01	.02	.02	.02	.02	.02	.02	.02	.02	.02	.02	.02	.02	.02
RS: Bill rate (percentage points)																	
C_g	0	.08	.10	.12	.13	.13	.14	.14	.14	.14	.13	.13	.13	.12	.12	.12	.12
	a	.08	.10	.12	.13	.13	.13	.14	.14	.13	.13	.13	.13	.12	.12	.12	.12
	b	.02	.02	.02	.02	.02	.03	.03	.03	.03	.03	.03	.03	.03	.03	.03	.03
d_{1g}	0	.02	.03	.05	.06	.07	.08	.09	.09	.10	.10	.10	.10	.09	.09	.10	.10
	a	.02	.03	.05	.06	.07	.08	.09	.09	.09	.10	.10	.10	.09	.09	.10	.10
	b	.01	.01	.01	.01	.02	.02	.02	.02	.02	.02	.02	.02	.02	.02	.02	.02
d_{2g}	0	.00	-.00	.00	.00	.00	.00	.01	.01	.01	.01	-.00	-.01	-.03	-.04	-.04	-.04
	a	-.00	-.00	.00	.00	.00	.01	.01	.01	.01	.01	.00	-.01	-.03	-.04	-.04	-.04
	b	.00	.00	.01	.01	.01	.01	.01	.02	.02	.02	.02	.02	.03	.03	.03	.03
d_{3g}	0	.01	.01	.03	.04	.06	.06	.07	.08	.08	.08	.09	.09	.09	.09	.09	.10
	a	.01	.01	.03	.04	.05	.06	.07	.07	.08	.08	.09	.09	.09	.09	.09	.10
	b	.01	.02	.01	.01	.01	.01	.01	.02	.02	.02	.02	.02	.02	.02	.02	.02
d_{4g}	0	.03	.06	.08	.10	.12	.13	.14	.15	.15	.16	.16	.16	.16	.16	.17	.17
	a	.03	.06	.08	.10	.12	.13	.14	.15	.15	.16	.16	.16	.16	.16	.17	.17
	b	.01	.02	.02	.02	.03	.03	.03	.03	.03	.04	.04	.03	.03	.03	.03	.03
d_{5g}	0	-.00	-.01	-.01	-.00	-.00	.00	.00	.01	.01	.01	.01	.01	.02	.02	.02	.02
	a	-.00	-.01	-.01	-.00	-.00	.00	.00	.01	.01	.01	.01	.02	.02	.02	.02	.02
	b	.00	.00	.01	.01	.01	.01	.01	.01	.01	.01	.01	.01	.01	.02	.02	.02
J_g	0	.13	.18	.21	.22	.24	.25	.26	.26	.26	.26	.26	.25	.26	.26	.26	.26
	a	.13	.17	.20	.22	.23	.24	.25	.25	.26	.25	.26	.24	.25	.25	.25	.25
	b	.03	.04	.04	.05	.05	.06	.06	.06	.06	.07	.06	.06	.06	.07	.07	.07
TR_{gh}	0	.01	.02	.04	.05	.05	.06	.07	.07	.08	.08	.08	.09	.09	.09	.09	.10
	a	.01	.02	.04	.04	.05	.06	.06	.07	.07	.08	.08	.08	.08	.09	.09	.09
	b	.01	.01	.02	.02	.02	.03	.03	.03	.03	.04	.04	.04	.04	.04	.04	.04

(continued)

TABLE 9-1 (continued)

Policy variable changed		1977 I	II	III	IV	1978 I	II	III	IV	1979 I	II	III	IV	1980 I	II	III	IV
M1: Money supply																	
C_g	0	-.13	-.10	-.06	-.04	-.02	-.01	-.00	.00	-.01	-.01	-.01	-.02	-.02	-.03	-.02	-.03
	a	-.13	-.10	-.07	-.05	-.03	-.02	-.02	-.01	-.03	-.03	-.03	-.04	-.05	-.05	-.05	-.05
	b	.04	.08	.12	.16	.19	.21	.24	.26	.28	.29	.30	.31	.32	.32	.33	.33
d_{1g}	0	-.03	-.05	-.07	-.08	-.09	-.09	-.10	-.12	-.14	-.16	-.17	-.20	-.22	-.22	-.22	-.25
	a	-.03	-.05	-.07	-.08	-.09	-.10	-.11	-.12	-.14	-.16	-.18	-.20	-.22	-.22	-.22	-.25
	b	.01	.03	.05	.07	.09	.12	.14	.16	.18	.20	.21	.22	.24	.24	.26	.27
d_{2g}	0	-.10	-.18	-.28	-.38	-.47	-.55	-.67	-.76	-.89	-.95	-1.05	-1.20	-1.33	-1.43	-1.50	-1.68
	a	-.10	-.19	-.28	-.40	-.48	-.57	-.69	-.78	-.92	-.98	-1.08	-1.24	-1.38	-1.48	-1.55	-1.74
	b	.03	.05	.07	.10	.12	.15	.17	.20	.23	.25	.27	.30	.33	.36	.37	.42
d_{3g}	0	-.65	-.56	-.48	-.40	-.36	-.32	-.29	-.26	-.25	-.23	-.23	-.23	-.24	-.24	-.21	-.23
	a	-.65	-.56	-.49	-.40	-.37	-.32	-.30	-.26	-.25	-.23	-.23	-.22	-.24	-.23	-.21	-.23
	b	.03	.05	.07	.09	.11	.13	.15	.16	.18	.19	.20	.21	.22	.22	.23	.24
d_{4g}	0	-.13	-.23	-.31	-.35	-.40	-.43	-.46	-.49	-.53	-.57	-.59	-.62	-.64	-.66	-.68	-.71
	a	-.13	-.24	-.32	-.37	-.42	-.45	-.48	-.52	-.55	-.59	-.61	-.64	-.66	-.68	-.70	-.73
	b	.03	.06	.09	.11	.14	.17	.20	.22	.25	.27	.29	.31	.32	.33	.35	.37
d_{5g}	0	-.04	-.08	-.11	-.13	-.15	-.17	-.19	-.21	-.22	-.24	-.26	-.27	-.29	-.30	-.32	-.34
	a	-.04	-.08	-.11	-.14	-.15	-.17	-.19	-.21	-.23	-.25	-.26	-.28	-.29	-.31	-.33	-.35
	b	.01	.02	.02	.03	.04	.04	.05	.06	.07	.08	.08	.09	.10	.10	.11	.12
J_g	0	-.04	-.04	-.06	-.11	-.15	-.22	-.30	-.35	-.44	-.49	-.55	-.60	-.64	-.68	-.71	-.72
	a	-.04	-.05	-.07	-.12	-.17	-.24	-.32	-.38	-.47	-.51	-.58	-.64	-.68	-.72	-.75	-.77
	b	.07	.14	.21	.27	.33	.38	.43	.48	.53	.57	.60	.63	.65	.67	.70	.71
TR_{gh}	0	-.01	-.01	-.01	-.00	.01	.02	.03	.04	.04	.05	.06	.06	.07	.07	.08	.09
	a	-.01	-.01	-.01	-.00	.00	.01	.02	.03	.03	.04	.05	.04	.05	.05	.06	.06
	b	.01	.02	.03	.05	.06	.08	.10	.11	.13	.15	.16	.17	.18	.19	.20	.21

Notes: 0 = Estimated effects from deterministic simulations.
a = Estimated effects from stochastic simulations.
b = Estimated standard errors of the a-row values.
c. Sum of the changes (at quarterly rates) over the 16 quarters, in billions of 1972 dollars.
• See discussion in text for an explanation of the units of the variables.

numbers are estimated standard errors of $\tilde{\delta}^j_{itk}/\tilde{y}^{aj}_{itk}$, where $\tilde{\delta}^j_{itk}$ is defined in (9.2) and the $\tilde{y}^{aj}_{itk}$ values are the actual values. The formulas are

$$\bar{\tilde{\delta}}^*_{itk} = \frac{1}{J}\sum_{j=1}^{J}\frac{\tilde{\delta}^j_{itk}}{\tilde{y}^{aj}_{itk}}, \tag{9.6}$$

$$\tilde{s}^{*2}_{itk} = \frac{1}{J}\sum_{j=1}^{J}\left(\frac{\tilde{\delta}^j_{itk}}{\tilde{y}^{aj}_{itk}} - \bar{\tilde{\delta}}^*_{itk}\right)^2. \tag{9.7}$$

The b-row numbers are the square roots of $\tilde{s}^{*2}_{itk}$. Because of the nonlinearities involved, $\tilde{s}^*_{itk}$ does not equal $\tilde{s}_{itk}/\tilde{y}^a_{itk}$, and thus the latter would not be appropriate to use for the b-row values.

The changes for the other policy variables in Table 9-1 were made to be comparable to the change in C_g with respect to the initial injection of funds into the system. Consider, for example, the change in d_{1g}. The aim is to change d_{1g} so that the change in personal income taxes in real terms is equal to the change in C_g. From Eq. 47 in Table A-5, the variable for personal income taxes, T_{hg}, is equal to $[d_{1g} + (\gamma_g YT)/POP]YT$, where YT is taxable income. Let ΔC_g denote the change in C_g for a given quarter. The aim is to change d_{1g} in such a way that the change in T_{hg} is equal to $P_g \Delta C_g$, where P_g is the price deflator for C_g. The change in d_{1g} for the given quarter is thus $(P_g \Delta C_g)/YT$. The values that were used for P_g and YT for these calculations are the actual values, not the predicted values. The predicted values are, of course, affected by the change in d_{1g}. All this procedure does is to change d_{1g} by an amount that would lead personal income taxes to change by $P_g \Delta C_g$ if nothing else happened.

The changes in the other policy variables are similarly done. For d_{2g} the relevant tax variable is T_{fg}, corporate profit taxes, and the relevant equation in Table A-5 is 49. The other matchings are as follows: d_{3g} to IBT_g and Eq. 51, d_{4g} to SI_{hg} and Eq. 53, d_{5g} to SI_{fg} and Eq. 55, J_g to $W_g J_g H_g$ (no separate equation), and T_{gh} to itself (no separate equation).

In order to understand some of the properties of the model, it is necessary to present results for other than just the five endogenous variables in Table 9-1. Results for eighteen other variables for the C_g experiment are presented in Table 9-2. The results are in percentage terms (like the results for real GNP in Table 9-1) except for RB, S_r, and S_g. The units for S_r and S_g are billions of current dollars. The units for RB are the same as those for RS in Table 9-1.

The results in Table 9-1 are based on 6,400 solutions of the model (6,400 = 50 trials × 8 experiments × 16 quarters). As discussed in Section 7.5.1, each solution of the model takes about .2 seconds on the IBM 4341 and about 1.5 seconds on the VAX. The total time for the 6,400 solutions was thus about 21 minutes on the IBM 4341 and 2.7 hours on the VAX.

The rest of this section consists of a discussion of the results in Tables 9-1 and 9-2. Each experiment will be discussed first without regard to the estimated standard errors, and then the standard errors will be discussed.

The C_g Experiment

The increase in government purchases of goods led to an increase in real GNP, the GNP deflator, and the bill rate and to a decrease in the unemployment rate and the money supply (Table 9-1). The reasons for the increase in output were discussed in Section 9.4.1, and they will not be repeated here. The GNP deflator rose because of the effects of the increase in real GNP on the demand pressure variable. The Fed responded (through Eq. 30, the interest rate reaction function) to the output and inflation increase by raising the bill rate, and this is the reason for the higher values of the bill rate. The money supply fell because of the rise in the interest rate. An increase in output and prices has a positive effect on the demand for money, but this positive effect was outweighed by the negative interest rate effect. In general, the changes in the money supply were quite small.

More detailed results from this experiment are presented in Table 9-2. Either immediately or after a few quarters, two of the three consumption variables and housing investment become lower. This change is due to the increase in the interest rates: the negative effects from the interest rates are larger than the positive effects from the labor constraint variable. The decrease in consumption and housing investment is the main reason that real GNP rose by less than the change in C_g after 8 quarters (Table 9-1).

The wage rate (W_f) rose less than the GNP deflator, and a decrease in the real wage has a negative effect on consumption and housing investment. It also has a negative effect on the two labor force variables $L2$ and $L3$. This negative effect on $L2$ and $L3$ was, however, more than offset by the positive effect from the labor constraint variable: $L2$ and $L3$ both rose.

Plant and equipment investment was higher because of the higher output, as was the number of jobs. The percentage increase in the number of jobs was less than the percentage increase in real output, as expected from the discussion in Section 9.4.1. The demand for money of the firm sector fell as a result of the bill rate increase. The demand for money of the household sector fell for the first three quarters and rose thereafter. The bond rate *(RB)* rose; this occurred because of the bill rate increase. This is the term structure equation 23 in operation. Although it is not shown in Table 9-2, the mortgage rate *(RM)* also rose, for similar reasons. The demand for imports rose because of the increase in output and because of the increase in the domestic price level relative to the price of imports.

The last four variables in Table 9-2 are determined by identities. They are interesting summary variables to consider. The level of profits rose because of the expansion and because of the fall in the real wage. The savings of the foreign sector (S_r), which is the negative of the balance of payments on current account, rose because of the increase in the demand for imports. By the end of the period, however, the change in S_r was essentially zero. S_r is negatively affected by the increase in the price of exports that results from the expansion, and by the end of the period this negative effect roughly offset the positive effect from the increase in imports. The level of savings of the federal

TABLE 9-2. Estimated policy effects for the US model for eighteen variables and one experiment

	1977				1978				1979				1980			
	I	II	III	IV	I	II	III	IV	I	II	III	IV	I	II	III	IV
CS: Consumption of services																
a	-.04	-.07	-.11	-.15	-.19	-.23	-.28	-.32	-.36	-.40	-.43	-.46	-.49	-.52	-.54	-.56
b	.02	.04	.05	.07	.08	.10	.11	.12	.14	.15	.16	.18	.19	.20	.22	.23
CN: Consumption of nondurables																
a	.04	.12	.19	.23	.25	.26	.26	.25	.25	.25	.24	.24	.25	.27	.27	.28
b	.04	.07	.10	.12	.13	.14	.15	.15	.15	.16	.16	.16	.16	.17	.17	.17
CD: Consumption of durables																
a	.10	.16	.12	-.04	-.26	-.46	-.67	-.85	-1.03	-1.19	-1.27	-1.37	-1.44	-1.66	-1.63	-1.58
b	.08	.19	.27	.32	.38	.39	.42	.44	.47	.51	.51	.53	.54	.61	.58	.55
IH_h: Housing investment																
a	.00	-.10	-.39	-.86	-1.37	-1.85	-2.31	-2.76	-3.15	-3.49	-3.74	-3.94	-4.21	-5.04	-5.03	-4.38
b	.00	.10	.23	.37	.49	.59	.69	.80	.91	1.01	1.10	1.18	1.28	1.56	1.58	1.39
L1: Labor force of males 25-54																
a	.00	-.00	.00	.00	.00	.00	.00	-.00	-.00	-.01	-.01	-.01	-.02	-.02	-.02	-.02
b	.00	.00	.00	.00	.00	.00	.01	.01	.01	.01	.01	.01	.01	.02	.02	.02
L2: Labor force of females 25-54																
a	.03	.07	.12	.16	.19	.22	.25	.26	.28	.29	.30	.30	.30	.31	.31	.31
b	.01	.03	.04	.06	.07	.08	.09	.10	.10	.11	.11	.11	.12	.12	.13	.13
L3: Labor force of all others 16 and over																
a	.08	.17	.26	.34	.41	.45	.47	.48	.47	.47	.45	.43	.41	.38	.35	.33
b	.02	.03	.05	.06	.07	.07	.08	.08	.08	.09	.09	.09	.10	.10	.11	.11
M_h: Demand for money, h																
a	-.18	-.11	-.04	.01	.06	.11	.15	.17	.19	.21	.22	.24	.26	.28	.31	.32
b	.05	.11	.16	.20	.24	.28	.31	.34	.36	.38	.39	.41	.42	.43	.43	.44
IK_f; Plant and equipment investment																
a	1.46	2.00	2.58	3.01	3.12	2.90	2.72	2.50	2.28	2.11	1.87	1.72	1.54	1.48	1.33	1.21
b	.25	.34	.37	.38	.42	.41	.42	.43	.43	.44	.43	.44	.43	.45	.44	.42
J_f: Number of jobs in the firm sector																
a	.34	.68	.88	.97	1.01	1.01	1.00	.97	.94	.91	.88	.85	.83	.81	.79	.78
b	.06	.08	.09	.10	.11	.12	.12	.13	.13	.14	.14	.14	.14	.14	.14	.14
W_f: Wage rate																
a	.01	.07	.14	.20	.26	.31	.35	.39	.42	.45	.48	.50	.52	.54	.55	.56
b	.01	.03	.05	.08	.10	.12	.13	.15	.16	.17	.18	.19	.20	.21	.22	.23
M_f: Demand for money, f																
a	-.10	-.13	-.17	-.23	-.29	-.37	-.44	-.51	-.60	-.68	-.76	-.83	-.88	-.94	-1.00	-1.04
b	.05	.11	.17	.21	.26	.30	.33	.37	.41	.45	.48	.52	.54	.57	.60	.63
RB: Bond rate (percentage points)																
a	.02	.03	.04	.06	.07	.08	.09	.10	.10	.11	.11	.12	.12	.12	.12	.13
b	.01	.01	.01	.01	.01	.02	.02	.02	.02	.02	.02	.02	.02	.02	.02	.03
IM: Imports																
a	.42	.69	.91	1.01	1.02	1.02	1.00	.96	.93	.86	.82	.77	.74	.76	.78	.74
b	.10	.18	.25	.30	.34	.38	.42	.45	.50	.52	.56	.58	.60	.66	.72	.69
Π_f: Profits																
a	7.98	8.33	7.23	6.11	5.37	4.47	4.39	3.77	3.68	3.44	3.67	4.21	4.69	6.33	5.88	6.91
b	.80	.58	.71	.81	.91	.09	.97	1.01	1.09	1.18	1.28	1.40	1.39	1.84	1.78	1.85
S_r: Savings of the foreign sector (billions of current dollars)																
a	.05	.07	.09	.09	.09	.08	.07	.06	.05	.04	.03	.02	.01	.00	-.00	-.01
b	.01	.02	.03	.04	.04	.05	.06	.07	.08	.09	.10	.11	.12	.13	.13	.14
S_g: Savings of the federal government (billions of current dollars)																
a	-.89	-.86	-.89	-.92	-1.01	-1.07	-1.16	-1.21	-1.29	-1.34	-1.43	-1.51	-1.64	-1.72	-1.75	-1.88
b	.03	.03	.03	.04	.04	.05	.06	.06	.07	.08	.09	.09	.10	.10	.11	.11
SR: Savings rate																
a	5.29	7.10	7.36	8.35	8.51	10.74	10.75	11.43	11.08	11.01	12.07	14.48	13.57	12.48	11.99	13.52
b	.83	.92	1.09	1.31	1.41	1.81	1.89	2.09	2.13	2.21	2.54	3.17	3.07	2.98	3.04	3.46

Notes: a = Estimated effects from stochastic simulation.
b = Estimated standard errors of the a-row values.

- This experiment is the C_g experiment in Table 9-1.
- Unless otherwise noted, the changes are in percentage points. See discussion in text.

government fell, primarily as a result of the increase in C_g. The deficits are smaller than they otherwise would be because taxes increased as a result of the expansion. The savings rate was higher in all quarters. The increase in the interest rate is the primary reason for the higher savings rate.

The Other Experiments

Given an understanding of the C_g experiment, the other experiments in Table 9-1 are fairly easy to follow. A useful way of comparing the expansionary effects across experiments is to compute the sums of the real GNP changes over the 16 quarters of the prediction period. This has been done in the last column in Table 9-1. The sums are in billions of 1972 dollars rather than in percentage terms.

All the experiments led to an increase in real GNP. The main channels are the following.

1. The decrease in d_{1g}, the personal income tax parameter, increases after-tax nonlabor income (Eq. 88). It also decreases the marginal personal income tax rate (Eq. 90), which in turn increases the after-tax wage rate (Eq. 126) and the after-tax interest rates (Eqs. 127 and 128). The increase in after-tax nonlabor income and the after-tax wage rate has a positive effect on consumption and housing investment, and the increase in the after-tax interest rates has a negative effect. The net effect is positive, and therefore the experiment is expansionary. It is initially less expansionary than the C_g experiment, but by the end of the period it becomes more so. The unemployment rate is higher for this experiment even though output is higher. The decrease in d_{1g} raises the after-tax wage rate *(WA)*, which has a positive effect on the labor force variables $L2$ and $L3$ and thus on the unemployment rate. This effect was large enough to offset the negative effect on the unemployment rate from the increase in employment.

2. The decrease in d_{2g}, the profit tax rate, increases after-tax profits, which increases dividends, which increases nonlabor income of the household sector, which in turn increases consumption and housing investment.

3. The decrease in d_{3g}, the indirect business tax rate, decreases the price deflators for consumption (Eqs. 35, 36, and 37), which has a positive effect on consumption. The GNP deflator is lower in this case because indirect business tax rates are included in it. The unemployment rate is essentially unchanged even though output is higher because there was a positive labor force response to the increase in the real wage.

4. The decrease in d_{4g}, the employee social security tax rate, is similar to the

decrease in d_{1g} in that it increases after-tax nonlabor income, the after-tax wage rate, and the after-tax interest rates. The unemployment rate also is higher in this case because of the increase in the after-tax wage rate.

5. The decrease in d_{5g}, the employer social security tax rate, lowers the cost of labor in the firm sector, which has a negative effect on the price level (Eq. 10). This leads to a rise in the real wage, which stimulates consumption and housing investment. Also, the lower tax rate means that profits are higher (Eq. 67), which leads to an increase in dividends and thus in nonlabor income of the household sector, which stimulates consumption and housing investment.

6. The increase in J_g, the number of jobs of the government, lessens the labor constraint on the household sector and thus leads to an increase in consumption.

7. The increase in TR_{gh}, the level of transfer payments to the household sector, increases nonlabor income, which stimulates consumption and housing investment. The increase in TR_{gh} has a negative effect on the labor force variable $L1$ and thus on the unemployment rate. The unemployment rate thus fell more than it otherwise would have as a result of the increase in transfer payments. This is contrary to the case of the decrease in d_{1g}, where the unemployment rate actually rose.

To summarize the results for the eight experiments, although all are expansionary with respect to real output changes, they differ regarding the effects on variables like the GNP deflator and the unemployment rate. The GNP deflator is lower for the d_{3g} and d_{5g} experiments, and the unemployment rate is higher for the d_{1g} and d_{4g} experiments. There is essentially no change in the unemployment rate for the d_{3g} experiment, where the various effects on it roughly cancel each other out. These results thus reinforce the conclusion stated earlier that the relationships between real output and the unemployment rate and between real output and the inflation rate are not likely to be stable.

The Estimated Standard Errors

The estimated standard errors in Tables 9-1 and 9-2 in general seem fairly small. This conclusion is consistent with the results in Table 8-2, which show that the contribution of the uncertainty of the coefficient estimates to the total uncertainty of the forecast is in general relatively small. If the only concern is with uncertainty from the coefficient estimates, which is true for the standard errors of the multipliers, a fairly high degree of confidence can be placed on the results. Consider, for example, the eight-quarter-ahead prediction of the five variables in Table 9-1 for the C_g experiment. The estimated means and standard errors for the five variables are as follows: .93 and .13 for real GNP, .54 and .11 for the GNP deflator, −.09 and .01 for the unemployment rate, .14 and .03 for the bill rate, and −.01 and .26 for the money supply. Only for the money supply are the results not precise. In the more detailed results in Table 9-2, the only main imprecise results are for the two demand-for-money variables (M_h and M_f). The results for the last four summary variables in the table are even fairly good.

The results are thus encouraging regarding the accuracy of the properties of the model, provided the model is correctly specified. The assumption of correct specification is the key restriction in the present exercise. It was seen in Section 8.5, for example, that misspecification contributes substantially to the total variance of the forecast error for the US model, and therefore it should be taken into account in the estimation of the standard errors of multipliers. It is an open question as to how this can be done, and until it is done, the present estimates of the standard errors must be interpreted as merely lower bounds.

9.4.3 Estimated Effects of a Change in Import Prices

One of the significant economic events of the 1970s was the large change in import prices that occurred for most countries. It is thus of interest to examine the effects of import prices on the endogenous variables. The relevant exogenous variable in the model is *PIM*, the price deflator for imports. For the results in Table 9-3, *PIM* was increased by 10 percent in the first quarter of the period (1977I). For the other quarters of the prediction period it was not changed from its historical values. The same stochastic simulation procedure was followed here as was followed for the results in Table 9-1. The number of trials was 50.

The results in Table 9-3 show that the increase in import prices is contractionary with respect to real output and inflationary with respect to the GNP deflator. *PIM* is an explanatory variable in the price equation, and this is the reason for the increase in domestic prices. The real wage fell as a result of the increase in prices, and this led to a fall in consumption and housing investment. The fall in the real wage also had a negative effect on the labor force, and this is the main reason the unemployment rate fell in the first quarter and rose very little in the other quarters even though output fell. The Fed responded to the initial change in prices by increasing the bill rate, which is another reason for the fall in consumption and housing investment. After

TABLE 9-3. Estimated effects of a change in the import price deflator (PIM) for the US model

	1977				1978				1979				1980				Sum[c]
	I	II	III	IV	I	II	III	IV	I	II	III	IV	I	II	III	IV	
GNPR: Real GNP																	
a	-.95	-.78	-.65	-.54	-.44	-.34	-.28	-.22	-.17	-.13	-.10	-.08	-.06	-.05	-.04	-.04	-4.3
b	.20	.22	.19	.17	.16	.14	.12	.10	.09	.09	.08	.07	.07	.07	.07	.07	1.1
GNPD: GNP deflator																	
a	1.76	.94	.83	.75	.68	.61	.56	.51	.47	.43	.41	.37	.34	.32	.31	.29	
b	.17	.14	.12	.11	.09	.08	.08	.08	.07	.07	.07	.07	.07	.07	.06	.06	
100•UR: Unemployment rate (percentage points)																	
a	-.01	.03	.03	.03	.02	.02	.01	.01	.01	.01	.01	.01	.00	.00	.00	.00	
b	.02	.02	.02	.02	.02	.01	.01	.01	.01	.01	.01	.01	.01	.01	.01	.01	
RS: Bill rate (percentage points)																	
a	.44	.04	-.07	-.06	-.05	-.05	-.05	-.04	-.04	-.04	-.03	-.03	-.03	-.02	-.02	-.02	
b	.23	.08	.03	.02	.02	.02	.02	.02	.01	.01	.01	.01	.01	.01	.01	.01	
M1: Money supply																	
a	3.07	-.28	-.16	-.06	-.00	.05	.09	.12	.15	.16	.18	.19	.19	.19	.20	.19	
b	.40	.29	.22	.18	.16	.14	.14	.13	.13	.13	.12	.12	.11	.11	.11	.10	

Notes: a = Estimated effects from a stochastic simulation.
b = Estimated standard errors of the a-row values.
c = Sum of the changes (at quarterly rates) over the 16 quarters, in billions of 1972 dollars.
• PIM was increased by 10 percent for 1977 I. For the other quarters it was kept unchanged from its historical values.
• The changes for GNPR, GNPD, and M1 are in percentage points.

three quarters, however, the bill rate was lower. The lower values are due primarily to the lower values of real output. (The change in real output is an explanatory variable in the interest rate reaction function.)

This experiment is the best example in the model of a situation in which real GNP and the rate of inflation are negatively correlated. The estimated standard errors are again fairly small except for those for the money supply.

9.4.4 Sensitivity of Fiscal Policy Effects to Assumptions about Monetary Policy

The various assumptions that one can make about monetary policy have been discussed in Section 4.1.10, and the reader should review this material before reading this section. The results in Table 9-4 are for the C_g experiment in Table 9-1 under five assumptions about monetary policy. The row 1 experiment is the same as that in Table 9-1. In this case the Fed is assumed to behave according to the interest rate reaction function. Note that the values of $-A_g$ are positive in row 1 in Table 9-4: the Fed issued securities in response to the increase in purchases of goods of the government. ($-A_g$ will be called the "amount of government securities outstanding.")

TABLE 9-4. Estimated policy effects for the US model under alternative assumptions about monetary policy

	1977 I	1977 II	1977 III	1977 IV	1978 I	1978 II	1978 III	1978 IV
GNPR: Real GNP								
1	1.10	1.31	1.32	1.28	1.20	1.10	1.01	.93
2	1.14	1.42	1.52	1.58	1.59	1.57	1.56	1.53
3	1.15	1.38	1.38	1.32	1.21	1.10	1.00	.91
4	1.15	1.42	1.48	1.48	1.41	1.31	1.22	1.13
5	1.69	2.64	3.15	3.28	3.18	2.97	2.79	2.62
GNPD: GNP deflator								
1	.04	.18	.27	.33	.40	.46	.54	.57
2	.04	.18	.28	.36	.44	.54	.66	.72
3	.04	.18	.28	.35	.42	.48	.56	.58
4	.04	.18	.29	.36	.44	.52	.61	.65
5	.02	.21	.44	.66	.83	1.06	1.25	1.36
RS: Bill rate (percentage points)								
1	.08	.10	.12	.13	.13	.14	.14	.14
2	0	0	0	0	0	0	0	0
3	-.02	.12	.14	.15	.15	.15	.14	.14
4	-.02	.03	.07	.09	.10	.11	.12	.11
5	-1.08	-.74	-.30	.05	.00	.01	-.06	-.08
M1: Money supply								
1	-.13	-.10	-.06	-.04	-.02	-.01	-.00	.00
2	-.03	.13	.29	.46	.61	.76	.89	1.01
3	0	0	0	0	0	0	0	0
4	-.00	.11	.19	.25	.29	.32	.34	.35
5	1.36	2.35	2.76	2.72	2.75	2.81	2.95	3.05
CUR: Currency (billions of current dollars)								
1	.00	.02	.04	.06	.07	.08	.09	.10
2	.02	.06	.11	.16	.21	.26	.31	.35
3	.03	.04	.06	.07	.08	.09	.10	.10
4	.03	.06	.09	.12	.14	.16	.18	.19
5	.25	.46	.61	.66	.74	.80	.88	.95
BR-BO: Nonborrowed reserves (billions of current dollars)								
1	-.03	-.03	-.03	-.04	-.04	-.04	-.04	-.04
2	-.01	.01	.02	.04	.05	.07	.08	.10
3	.00	-.03	-.03	-.04	-.04	-.04	-.04	-.05
4	0	0	0	0	0	0	0	0
5	.34	.38	.31	.27	.27	.28	.30	.34
S_g: Savings of the federal government (billions of current dollars)								
1	-.88	-.85	-.88	-.92	-1.00	-1.06	-1.15	-1.21
2	-.86	-.80	-.79	-.77	-.80	-.80	-.82	-.81
3	-.86	-.82	-.86	-.90	-.99	-1.06	-1.15	-1.21
4	-.86	-.80	-.82	-.83	-.91	-.96	-1.04	-1.08
5	-.59	-.25	-.08	-.01	-.08	-.07	-.11	-.11
$-A_g$: Amount of federal government securities outstanding (billions of current dollars)								
1	.91	1.74	2.60	3.51	4.50	5.56	6.70	7.91
2	.85	1.59	2.31	3.01	3.75	4.48	5.23	5.98
3	.83	1.67	2.51	3.41	4.39	5.45	6.59	7.80
4	.83	1.60	2.38	3.19	4.08	5.01	6.03	7.10
5	0	0	0	0	0	0	0	0

	1979 I	1979 II	1979 III	1979 IV	1980 I	1980 II	1980 III	1980 IV	Sum[a]
GNPR: Real GNP									
1	.86	.80	.75	.71	.69	.66	.64	.64	13.4
2	1.52	1.50	1.47	1.45	1.43	1.41	1.37	1.34	21.1
3	.84	.78	.74	.71	.69	.67	.66	.66	13.6
4	1.05	.98	.92	.88	.84	.81	.78	.77	15.8
5	2.52	2.48	2.43	2.41	2.39	2.40	2.34	2.27	37.4
GNPD: GNP deflator									
1	.61	.63	.67	.71	.77	.80	.80	.85	
2	.80	.87	.97	1.02	1.12	1.20	1.24	1.32	
3	.62	.64	.68	.72	.77	.81	.81	.86	
4	.71	.74	.78	.83	.89	.94	.93	.99	
5	1.48	1.58	1.71	1.80	1.93	2.04	2.12	2.21	
RS: Bill rate (percentage points)									
1	.14	.13	.13	.13	.12	.12	.12	.12	
2	0	0	0	0	0	0	0	0	
3	.13	.13	.12	.12	.12	.12	.12	.12	
4	.11	.11	.11	.11	.10	.10	.10	.10	
5	-.16	-.19	-.18	-.21	-.19	-.17	-.16	-.16	
M1: Money supply									
1	-.01	-.01	-.01	-.02	-.02	-.03	-.02	-.03	
2	1.12	1.20	1.29	1.36	1.42	1.47	1.53	1.55	
3	0	0	0	0	0	0	0	0	
4	.35	.36	.36	.35	.35	.35	.35	.35	
5	3.29	3.46	3.64	3.83	3.97	4.04	4.17	4.21	
CUR: Currency (billions of current dollars)									
1	.10	.10	.11	.11	.11	.11	.11	.11	
2	.40	.44	.49	.52	.56	.60	.63	.67	
3	.10	.11	.11	.11	.11	.12	.12	.12	
4	.20	.21	.22	.23	.23	.24	.24	.25	
5	1.04	1.14	1.23	1.30	1.39	1.47	1.54	1.61	
BR-BO: Nonborrowed reserves (billions of current dollars)									
1	-.05	-.04	-.04	-.05	-.05	-.05	-.05	-.05	
2	.11	.12	.13	.14	.15	.17	.16	.16	
3	-.04	-.04	-.04	-.04	-.05	-.05	-.04	-.04	
4	0	0	0	0	0	0	0	0	
5	.39	.40	.42	.47	.49	.54	.51	.49	
S_g: Savings of the federal government (billions of current dollars)									
1	-1.28	-1.33	-1.43	-1.50	-1.63	-1.71	-1.75	-1.87	
2	-.83	-.82	-.85	-.88	-.92	-.94	-.91	-.97	
3	-1.29	-1.33	-1.42	-1.50	-1.62	-1.70	-1.73	-1.86	
4	-1.16	-1.20	-1.29	-1.36	-1.48	-1.56	-1.59	-1.71	
5	-.13	-.11	-.12	-.12	-.11	-.12	-.04	-.05	
$-A_g$: Amount of federal government securities outstanding (billions of current dollars)									
1	9.20	10.52	11.95	13.45	15.08	16.79	18.53	20.40	
2	6.75	7.52	8.32	9.15	10.02	10.91	11.80	12.74	
3	9.08	10.41	11.83	13.32	14.94	16.64	18.36	20.22	
4	8.25	9.44	10.72	12.08	13.55	15.11	16.69	18.39	
5	0	0	0	0	0	0	0	0	

Notes: a. Sum of the changes (at quarterly rates) over the 16 quarters, in billions of 1972 dollars.
1. Interest rate reaction function.
2. Bill rate exogenous.
3. Money supply exogenous.
4. Nonborrowed reserves exogenous.
5. A_g exogenous.

- The changes for GNPR, GNPD, and M1 are in percentage points.
- This experiment is the C_g experiment in Table 9-1. The values are estimated effects from deterministic simulations.

In examining the results in Table 9-4 it will be useful to keep in mind the government budget constraint, Eq. 77 in Table A-5:

$$77. \qquad 0 = S_g - \Delta A_g - \Delta M_g + \Delta CUR + \Delta(BR - BO) - \Delta Q - DIS_g.$$

This equation states that any decrease in S_g that results from the increase in C_g must result in a change in at least one of the other RHS variables. Since M_g, Q, and DIS_g are exogenous, the other variables are A_g, currency *(CUR)*, and nonborrowed reserves *(BR − BO)*. Subject to rounding error, the values presented in Table 9-4 meet this identity. For example, the first-quarter values for the row 1 experiment are −.88 for S_g, .91 for $-\Delta A_g$, .00 for ΔCUR, and −.03 for $\Delta(BR - BO)$, which sum to zero. The second-quarter values are −.85 for S_g, 1.74 − .91 = .83 for $-\Delta A_g$, .02 − .00 = .02 for ΔCUR, and −.03 − (.03) = .00 for $\Delta(BR - BO)$, which also sum to zero.

For the other four experiments in Table 9-4 the interest rate reaction function was dropped. For the row 2 experiment the bill rate was kept unchanged from its historical values. This experiment is considerably more expansionary than the first, since the bill rate does not rise to choke off some of the increase in demand. The increase in the GNP deflator is larger because of the larger increase in output. The sum of the GNP changes across the 16 quarters is 21.1 in this case versus 13.4 in the first case. The money supply rose rather than fell because there was no negative effect from a higher interest rate. The increase in the amount of government securities outstanding was less, since less was needed to meet the lower bill rate target.

There is an unusual, but not important, feature of the results for the second experiment that needs to be explained before going further. The question is why the money supply falls in the first quarter for the second experiment (the change in $M1$ is −.03). In the first quarter real GNP and the GNP deflator are higher and the bill rate is unchanged, so there appears to be no reason for the money supply to fall. The reason is that the price deflator P_h that is used in the demand-for-money equation of the household sector (Eq. 9) actually falls in the first quarter, which then results in a fall in the demand for money. P_h is a weighted price deflator, and it falls because of a change in weights caused by the change in C_g. It can be seen from Eq. 34 in Table A-5 that P_h is a function of another deflator *(PD)* and the average indirect business tax rate. When C_g increases, the average tax rate falls, and this is the reason for the initial fall in P_h. This feature of the results is not of any quantitative importance.

For the row 3 experiment the money supply, $M1$, was kept unchanged from its historical values. This experiment is slightly more expansionary than the first experiment because in that experiment the money supply fell. The money supply fell in the first experiment because the bill rate rose (the rise in

RS in the first quarter was .08). In the third experiment the bill rate needs to rise less because the money supply is unchanged. The bill rate actually fell in the first quarter for the third experiment (the change in *RS* was −.02), which is due to the feature of the results discussed in the previous paragraph: with the bill rate unchanged the money supply initially falls, and thus the bill rate must fall to prevent the fall in the money supply. Were it not for this feature, the bill rate would have increased in the first quarter for the third experiment, but by less than the increase for the first experiment. The third experiment is not as expansionary as the second experiment, where the bill rate did not change, because some increase in the bill rate (after the first quarter) was needed to choke off the increase in the demand for money that would otherwise have occurred as a result of the increase in income and prices.

For the row 4 experiment the level of nonborrowed reserves, $BR - BO$, was kept unchanged from its historical values. This experiment is more expansionary than the first experiment. In the first experiment nonborrowed reserves decreased, which was caused by both an increase in borrowing (because of the higher bill rate) and a decrease in reserves (because of a lower level of demand deposits). The increase in the bill rate thus choked off all of the increase in nonborrowed reserves that would otherwise have taken place as a result of the expansion *and then some.* For the fourth experiment, where the increase in nonborrowed reserves is constrained to be zero, the "and then some" does not take place. The increase in the bill rate is thus smaller in the fourth experiment because less is choked off. The fourth experiment is, on the other hand, less expansionary than the second experiment, because some increase in the bill rate was needed. The fourth experiment is more expansionary than the third experiment because less of an increase in the bill rate was needed to choke off nonborrowed reserves than was needed to choke off the money supply. The increase in the bill rate in the fourth experiment has two effects, one in decreasing the demand for money and thus bank reserves and the other in increasing borrowing. Both of these result in a drop in nonborrowed reserves. The effect on bank borrowing is not relevant for the third experiment, and therefore the interest rate increase in the third experiment must be larger.

In the row 5 experiment the amount of government securities outstanding, $-A_g$, was kept unchanged from its historical values. This means that the entire deficit of the government is financed by changes in currency and nonborrowed reserves. This requires a large change in the money supply, which requires a large initial fall in the bill rate. This experiment is thus quite expansionary, since it corresponds to both an increase in government pur-

TABLE 9-5. Estimated effects of an exogenous change in the bill rate

	1977				1978				1979				1980				Sum[c]
	I	II	III	IV	I	II	III	IV	I	II	III	IV	I	II	III	IV	
GNPR: Real GNP																	
a	-.12	-.31	-.51	-.71	-.89	-1.02	-1.15	-1.24	-1.33	-1.41	-1.44	-1.48	-1.50	-1.54	-1.54	-1.51	-64.6
b	.03	.06	.09	.12	.15	.18	.20	.22	.25	.28	.30	.32	.35	.38	.41	.43	13.2
GNPD: GNP deflator																	
a	.01	-.00	-.03	-.08	-.11	-.19	-.26	-.33	-.40	-.49	-.60	-.62	-.70	-.78	-.87	-.92	
b	.00	.00	.01	.02	.03	.05	.06	.08	.10	.12	.14	.16	.18	.20	.23	.25	
100•UR: Unemployment rate (percentage points)																	
a	.02	.08	.14	.21	.28	.34	.38	.42	.46	.48	.50	.51	.52	.52	.51	.51	
b	.01	.02	.03	.04	.06	.07	.08	.09	.11	.12	.12	.13	.14	.15	.15	.16	
M1: Money supply																	
a	-.32	-.61	-.89	-1.14	-1.38	-1.62	-1.85	-2.05	-2.26	-2.42	-2.60	-2.76	-2.90	-3.01	-3.16	-3.26	
b	.06	.11	.15	.19	.22	.26	.29	.32	.35	.38	.41	.44	.47	.50	.54	.58	

Notes: a = Estimated effects from a stochastic simulation.
b = Estimated standard errors of the a-row values.
c. Sum of the changes (at quarterly rates) over the 16 quarters, in billions of 1972 dollars.
• The change in the bill rate was 1.0 percentage points for each quarter.
• The changes for GNPR, GNPD, and M1 are in percentage points.

chases of goods and an initial decrease in the bill rate. The change in real GNP over the 16 quarters was 37.4, which is almost double the next largest change. The change in the GNP deflator by the end of the period is also almost double the next largest change. After the first quarter the government deficit ($-S_g$) is small, which is primarily a result of the increased tax collections caused by the more expansionary economy.

It is clear from the results in Table 9-4 that fiscal policy effects are quite sensitive to what is assumed about monetary policy. Monetary policy, in other words, is very important. To give one more example of this, an experiment was run in which the bill rate was raised by one percentage point for all quarters. (The interest rate reaction function is dropped for this experiment.) The results are presented in Table 9-5. This sustained rise in the bill rate of one percentage point led by the end of the period to a decrease in real GNP of 1.51 percent and an increase in the unemployment rate of .51 percentage points. The money supply was 3.26 percent lower, and the GNP deflator was .92 percent lower. This experiment clearly shows the importance of the bill rate in the model.

One last feature of the results in this section that should be emphasized is that the policy of keeping the money supply unchanged is almost the same as the policy implied by the use of the interest rate reaction function. In other words, for all practical purposes the first and third experiments in Table 9-4 are identical.

TABLE 9-6. Estimated policy effects for the US model under alternative sets of coefficient estimates

	1977				1978				1979				1980				
	I	II	III	IV	I	II	III	IV	I	II	III	IV	I	II	III	IV	Sum[a]
GNPR: Real GNP																	
2SLS	1.10	1.31	1.32	1.28	1.20	1.10	1.01	.93	.86	.80	.75	.71	.69	.66	.64	.64	13.41
3SLS	1.12	1.32	1.32	1.28	1.19	1.09	1.00	.93	.86	.81	.76	.73	.70	.67	.65	.64	13.49
FIML	1.97	1.58	1.42	1.30	1.15	1.06	.99	.94	.90	.87	.85	.83	.81	.74	.75	.75	15.08
2SLAD $q = 0.5$	1.14	1.37	1.38	1.35	1.27	1.17	1.08	1.00	.91	.84	.78	.73	.69	.66	.64	.63	13.98
OLS	1.11	1.35	1.38	1.34	1.25	1.15	1.05	.96	.88	.81	.76	.72	.69	.67	.65	.65	13.76
GNPD: GNP deflator (percent)																	
2SLS	.04	.18	.27	.33	.40	.46	.54	.57	.61	.63	.67	.71	.77	.80	.80	.85	
3SLS	.04	.19	.30	.37	.44	.52	.60	.63	.69	.71	.76	.80	.86	.90	.90	.95	
FIML	.26	.25	.34	.39	.47	.51	.58	.60	.65	.66	.70	.74	.80	.84	.83	.89	
2SLAD $q = 0.5$	.05	.17	.26	.32	.39	.45	.53	.55	.60	.62	.66	.70	.75	.79	.78	.83	
OLS	.03	.17	.27	.33	.40	.47	.55	.57	.62	.63	.67	.71	.76	.80	.79	.85	

Notes: a. Sum of the changes (at quarterly rates) over the 16 quarters, in billions of 1972 dollars.
• This experiment is the C_g experiment in Table 9-1. The values are estimated effects from deterministic simulations.
• The changes are in percentage points.

9.4.5 Sensitivity of Policy Effects to Alternative Sets of Coefficient Estimates

The last issue examined in this chapter regarding the US model is the sensitivity of policy effects to the different sets of coefficient estimates. The C_g experiment was run for five sets of estimates; the results are presented in Table 9-6. The five estimators are 2SLS, 3SLS, FIML, 2SLAD for $q = 0.5$, and OLS. The 2SLS results are the same as those in Table 9-1. The procedure followed for the results for the other estimators is the same as that followed for the 2SLS results.

The main difference in the results in Table 9-6 concerns the FIML estimator: the initial increases in real GNP and the GNP deflator are larger for FIML than they are for the other estimators. This is again due to the fact that the FIML estimates of the lagged dependent variable coefficients are in general smaller than the estimates for the other estimators. In other words, the lagged adjustment behavior of the model that is due to the presence of the lagged endogenous variables is less pronounced for the FIML estimates because the coefficients of the lagged endogenous variables are generally smaller.

Aside from this difference for the FIML estimator, the results in Table 9-6 are very close to each other. The properties of the model are clearly not very sensitive to the choice of estimator, including the OLS estimator. This conclusion complements the conclusion in Section 8.5.5 that the overall fit of the model is not very sensitive to the choice of estimator. It is of interest for future research to see if this conclusion holds for other models and for later versions of the US model.

9.5 Properties of the MC Model

9.5.1 General Remarks

As was the case for the US model, it is possible to get some idea of the properties of the MC model without performing simulation experiments. In the following discussion, a variable is said to have a "direct" effect on another variable if it appears on the RHS of the equation (either a stochastic equation or a definition) explaining the other variable. Most endogenous variables have at least an indirect effect on the other endogenous variables—either contemporaneously or with a lag of one quarter. As a result, it is difficult to explain the properties of the model in a very systematic way. This discussion is designed to try to give a general idea of the properties without going into every possible indirect effect. It should also be kept in mind that not all of the effects operate for all countries. All interest rates referred to are short-term rates unless otherwise noted.

Summary of the Stochastic Equations of the Model

For reference purposes it will be useful to provide a summary of the stochastic equations per country. The signs in parentheses in the following list are the expected signs of the coefficient estimates.

Equation number	*Dependent variable*	*Explanatory variables*
1	Merchandise imports	Short-term or long-term interest rate (−), GNP deflator (+), import price index (−), real GNP (+), lagged net foreign assets (+), lagged dependent variable (+)
2	Consumption	Short-term or long-term interest rate (−), real GNP (+), lagged net foreign assets (+), lagged dependent variable (+)
3	Change in investment	Changes in real GNP—current, lagged once, lagged twice, lagged three times—(+), lagged level of investment (−)
4	Real GNP	Final sales (+), lagged stock of inventories (−), lagged dependent variable (+)
5	GNP deflator	Import price index (+), demand pressure variable (−), lagged dependent variable (+)

6	Nominal money supply	Short-term interest rate (−), nominal GNP (+), lagged dependent variable (+)
7a,7b	Short-term interest rate	Lagged rate of inflation (+), lagged rate of growth of the money supply (+), demand pressure variable (−), change in net foreign assets (−), lagged rate of change in the import price index—four countries only—(+), exchange rate—three countries only—(+), lagged dependent variable (+)
8	Long-term interest rate	Short-term interest rates—current, lagged once, lagged twice—(+ or −), lagged dependent variable (+)
9b	Exchange rate	GNP deflator (+), short-term interest rate (−), demand pressure variable (−), lagged change in net foreign assets (−)—all relative to the respective U.S. variables—lagged dependent variable (+)
10b	Forward rate	Exchange rate (+), short-term interest rate relative to the U.S. short-term interest rate (+)
11	Export price index	GNP deflator (+), world price index (+), exchange rate (+)

Trade Effects among Countries

There is a standard trade multiplier effect in the model. An autonomous increase in GNP in country i increases the demand for imports, which increases the exports of other countries and thus their GNP and demand for imports, which then increases the exports of country i and thus its GNP. In short, exports affect imports and vice versa.

Price Effects among Countries

There is also a price multiplier effect in the model. An autonomous increase in country i's domestic price level increases its export prices, which increases the import prices of other countries, which increases their domestic prices, including their export prices, which then increases country i's import prices and thus its domestic and export prices. In short, export prices affect import prices and vice versa.

Direct Interest Rate Effects among Countries

The U.S. short-term interest rate appears as an explanatory variable in the interest rate reaction functions of a number of countries. The U.S. rate is more important in the fixed exchange rate period than it is in the flexible rate period, but even in the flexible rate period it has an effect on some countries.

This means that an increase in the U.S. interest rate directly increases other countries' rates. The German interest rate appears as an explanatory variable in the interest rate reaction functions of a few other European countries, and thus an increase in the German interest rate also directly increases other countries' rates.

Direct Exchange Rate Effects among Countries

The German exchange rate appears as an explanatory variable in the exchange rate equations of the other European countries. The German exchange rate thus directly affects other exchange rates. All exchange rates are relative to the U.S. dollar, and therefore each explanatory variable in the exchange rate equations (other than the lagged dependent variable and the German exchange rate) is the particular variable of the country relative to the same variable for the United States. This means that the following U.S. variables appear as explanatory variables in the exchange rate equations: the GNP deflator, the short-term interest rate, the demand pressure variable, and the change in net foreign assets.

Direct Effects within a Country

The short-term interest rate directly affects the long-term rate in the term structure equation (Eq. 8). The short-term or long-term rate has a direct negative effect on imports and consumption (Eqs. 1 and 2). The short-term rate has a direct negative effect on the demand for money and the exchange rate (Eqs. 6 and 9b). (The reader should remember that an increase in the exchange rate is a depreciation of the country's currency.)

The asset variable, which is the sum of past values of the balance of payments and a measure of the net asset position of the country vis-à-vis the rest of the world, has a direct positive effect on imports and consumption (Eqs. 1 and 2) and a direct negative effect on the short-term interest rate and the exchange rate (Eqs. 7b and 9b).

The exchange rate has a direct positive effect on the local currency price of exports (Eq. 11) and on the local currency price of imports (the equations in Table B-4 involved in linking export and import prices). It also has a direct negative effect on the dollar price of exports (because the coefficient estimate of the exchange rate in Eq. 11, which is in log form, is less than one). It has a direct positive effect on the short-term interest rate for nine countries (Eq. 7b).

The price of imports has a direct negative effect on imports (Eq. 1), a direct positive effect on the GNP deflator (Eq. 5), a direct negative effect on the asset variable (Eqs. 17 and 18), and a direct positive effect on the short-term interest rate (Eq. 7b). The price of exports has a direct positive effect on the asset variable (Eqs. 17 and 18). The GNP deflator has direct positive effects on imports, the demand for money, the short-term interest rate, the exchange rate, and the price of exports (Eqs. 1, 6, 7a, 7b, 9b, and 11).

The level of imports has a direct negative effect on final sales and the asset variable, and the level of exports has a direct positive effect on these two variables (Eqs. 16, 17, and 18). The level of final sales has a direct positive effect on GNP (Eq. 4). Any deviation of GNP from final sales in a period is absorbed by a change in inventories (Eq. 12). The stock of inventories has a direct negative effect on GNP (Eq. 4). GNP has a direct positive effect on imports, consumption, investment, the GNP deflator, the demand for money, the short-term interest rate, and the exchange rate.

The money variable $M1_i^*$ does not play a very important role in the model. It is only a potential explanatory variable in the two interest rate reaction functions, Eqs. 7a and 7b. It appears in 3 of the 23 estimates of Eq. 7a (Table 4-7) and in 4 of the 20 estimates of Eq. 7b (Table 4-8). This means that other than in these few cases, the equation that determines $M1_i^*$, Eq. 6, plays no role in the model. The properties of the model would not be affected if Eq. 6 were dropped for all countries for which $M1_i^*$ is omitted from Eqs. 7a and 7b.

Some Indirect Effects within a Country

It should be clear that there are very few unambiguous indirect effects in the model with respect to sign. The signs depend on the relative sizes of the coefficient estimates. It is useful, however, to consider the likely signs of some indirect effects, even though these signs are not necessarily logical consequences of the model.

Consider first the indirect effect of the exchange rate on GNP. The main direct effect of the exchange rate is on the price of imports, at least in the short run. The price of imports has a direct negative effect on imports, and the level of imports has a direct positive effect on GNP. In other words, an increase in the price of imports causes substitution from imports to domestically produced goods, which raises GNP. The exchange rate thus has an indirect positive effect on GNP through this channel (that is, depreciation increases GNP).

Depreciation also lowers the dollar price of the country's exports, which through the trade-share equations has a positive effect on the other countries' demand for the given country's exports. Therefore, depreciation also increases GNP through this channel.

For some countries the exchange rate is an explanatory variable in the interest rate reaction function, which means that for these countries depreciation leads to an increase in the short-term interest rate. The short-term rate has a negative effect on GNP, and therefore depreciation has a negative effect on GNP through this channel.

Depreciation is likely to have a negative indirect effect on GNP through a fourth channel. The likely initial effect of a depreciation on the balance of payments is negative. Depreciation raises the local currency price of imports more than it does the local currency price of exports, which, other things being equal, has a negative effect on the balance of payments. Depreciation also lowers imports and raises exports, which has a positive effect on the balance of payments. This latter effect is, however, likely to be smaller initially than the price effect, and thus the initial net effect is likely to be negative. (This is the "J-curve" effect.) A decrease in the balance of payments decreases net foreign assets, which directly decreases imports and consumption and directly increases the short-term interest rate. Although the decrease in imports raises GNP, the decrease in consumption and the increase in the interest rate lowers GNP, and the net effect is likely to be negative. Depreciation is thus likely to have an initial indirect negative effect on GNP through this asset effect channel.

Depreciation has two main indirect effects on the GNP deflator, one positive and one ambiguous. The positive effect is through the price of imports, which has a direct positive effect on the GNP deflator. The second effect is through GNP. If the net effect of depreciation on GNP is positive, this will have a positive effect on the GNP deflator through the direct positive effect of demand pressure on the GNP deflator. If the net effect of depreciation on GNP is negative, the indirect effect on the GNP deflator is negative.

There are three main effects of the short-term interest rate on GNP, one negative, one ambiguous, and one positive. The negative effect is through consumption: an increase in the short-term rate increases the long-term rate; an increase in the short-term rate or the long-term rate decreases consumption, which lowers GNP. The ambiguous effect is through the exchange rate: an increase in the short-term rate has a negative effect on the exchange rate (an appreciation), which has an ambiguous effect on GNP. The positive effect is through imports: an increase in the short-term or the long-term rate lowers imports, which, other things being equal, raises GNP. The consumption effect is likely to be the dominant one, and thus the net effect of the short-term rate on GNP is likely to be negative.

An increase in the short-term interest rate has two main effects on the GNP deflator, both negative. The first is the likely negative indirect effect of the short-term rate on GNP and thus on demand. The second is the effect on the exchange rate: the exchange rate appreciates, which lowers the price of imports, which lowers the GNP deflator.

9.5.2 Results for Eleven Experiments: The Construction of Tables 9-7 through 9-17

The results of eleven experiments are reported in this section. The first experiment is for the fixed exchange rate period 1970II – 1972I, and the others are for the flexible rate period 1976I – 1977IV. The experiments are as follows.

1. An increase in U.S. government spending (fixed exchange rate period)
2. An increase in U.S. government spending (flexible exchange rate period)
3. An increase in the U.S. short-term interest rate
4. An increase in German government spending
5. An increase in the German interest rate
6. A depreciation of the German exchange rate
7. An increase in U.K. government spending
8. A depreciation of the U.K. exchange rate
9. An increase in Japanese government spending
10. A depreciation of the Japanese exchange rate
11. An increase in the price of exports of the oil-exporting countries

The results are presented in Tables 9-7 through 9-17. Stochastic simulation is too expensive to perform for the MC model, and thus all of the results in these tables are from deterministic simulations. For all the simulations the estimated residuals were added to the stochastic equations and treated as exogenous. The base path for the experiments is thus the perfect tracking solution. The complete MC model was used for all the experiments except 11, where trade shares were taken to be exogenous. The special treatment for experiment 11 is discussed later in this section.

Results for 15 countries and 13 variables per country are presented in the tables for the two-quarter-ahead and six-quarter-ahead predictions. Except for the numbers for the balance of payments and the two interest rates, each number in the tables is the percentage change in the variable (in percentage

TABLE 9-7. Percentage change in the variable after two and six quarters induced by a sustained 1 percent autonomous increase in US real GNP (initial change in 1970 I)

Country	Real GNP 2	Real GNP 6	GNP deflator 2	GNP deflator 6	Short-term interest rate 2	Short-term interest rate 6	Exchange rate 2	Exchange rate 6	Import price 2	Import price 6	Money supply 2	Money supply 6	Imports 2	Imports 6
JS	1.31	1.05	.10	.44	.39	.53	.00	.00	.02	.15	-.08	.03	1.07	1.34
Canada	.12	.18	.01	.17	.35	.52	.00	-.09	.07	.24	-.69	-2.11	.10	.24
Japan	.05	.15	.00	.05	-.03	-.01	.00	.00	.04	.20	.04	.12	.02	.10
ustria	-.01	-.05	-.00	-.00	.04	.10	.00	.00	.02	.12	-.00	-.00	-.04	-.26
Belgium	.02	-.05	.00	.02	.28	.65	.00	.00	.03	.15	-.14	-.99	.02	-.13
Denmark	.04	.07	.00	.02	.12	.30	.00	.00	.03	.15	-.20	-.56	.01	-.06
rance	.00	-.08	.00	.01	.22	.54	.00	.00	.03	.13	-.03	-.26	.00	-.11
Germany	.01	-.02	.00	.01	.28	.62	.00	.00	.03	.16	-.44	-1.35	-.06	-.57
Italy	.02	.00	.01	.03	.04	.14	.00	.00	.02	.13	-.05	-.29	.02	-.05
etherlands	.01	-.12	.00	-.00	.34	.80	.00	.00	.03	.15	-.75	-1.75	.01	-.17
orway	.00	-.04	.00	.02	.00	.00	.00	.00	.02	.15	.00	-.01	.01	-.03
weden	.02	.05	.00	.03	.10	.22	.00	.00	.03	.16	.02	.09	-.00	-.08
witzerland	.00	-.03	.00	.01	.04	.13	.00	.00	.03	.14	-.02	-.13	-.02	-.29
nited Kingdom	.03	.03	-.00	.02	.12	.27	.00	.00	.03	.16	-.20	-.89	.04	.07
inland	.01	-.01	.00	.02	-.00	.00	.00	.00	.02	.13	.01	.01	.02	-.00
S Alone	1.31	1.07	.10	.43	.40	.53	—	—	0	0	-.08	.02	1.07	1.37

ountry	Consumption 2	Consumption 6	Investment 2	Investment 6	Long-term interest rate 2	Long-term interest rate 6	Export price 2	Export price 6	Exports 2	Exports 6	Balance of payments[a] 2	Balance of payments[a] 6
S	.04	-.11	1.92	2.95	.12	.31	.09	.44	-.00	-.19	-95.072	-130.478
anada	-.04	.12	.03	.10	.13	.30	.02	.19	.78	1.02	27.132	34.395
apan	.02	.08	.01	.15	.00	.00	.01	.09	.44	.54	7.182	9.396
ustria	-.07	-.17	.00	.00	.00	.00	.02	.08	.05	-.08	.019	.043
elgium	.01	-.08	.00	.01	.07	.28	.02	.12	.06	-.13	.043	-.031
enmark	.03	.07	.00	.02	.04	.15	-.04	.16	.14	.04	.002	.009
rance	-.01	-.10	.00	-.01	.06	.21	.03	.13	.05	-.13	.012	-.003
ermany	-.05	-.23	.00	.01	.08	.24	.02	.09	.12	.10	.049	.165
taly	.01	.00	.00	.01	.01	.06	.03	.13	.11	-.07	2.032	.500
etherlands	-.00	-.19	.00	-.01	.06	.24	.03	.14	.04	-.21	.004	-.003
orway	.00	-.03	.00	-.00	.00	.00	.12	.31	.03	-.16	.009	.009
weden	.01	.04	.00	.08	.02	.08	.02	.13	.08	-.01	.006	.003
witzerland	-.04	-.17	.00	-.01	.02	.07	.01	.06	.12	.01	.006	.015
nited Kingdom	.02	.04	.01	.02	.04	.12	.02	.12	.15	.10	1.806	.046
inland	.01	-.00	.00	.01	.00	.00	.04	.19	.05	-.08	1.241	.006
S Alone	.04	-.10	1.92	2.98	.12	.30	.08	.41	0	0	-92.871	-92.480

ote: a. Change is absolute change, not percentage change, in units of local currency.

points) divided by something. For the spending increases (Tables 9-7, 9-8, 9-10, 9-13, and 9-15), the divisor is the change in government spending as a percentage of GNP (in percentage points). In other words, each number is $[(\hat{y}_{jt} - y_{jt})/y_{jt}]/(\Delta G_{it}/Y_{it})$, where $\hat{y}_{jt}$ is the two- or six-quarter-ahead predicted value of y_{jt} after the change, ΔG_{it} is the change in government spending in quarter t, and Y_{it} is the actual value of GNP in quarter t. (Remember that all changes are changes from the actual values, not changes from quarter to quarter.) Each number is thus the percentage change in the variable induced

TABLE 9-8. Percentage change in the variable after two and six quarters induced by a sustained 1 percent autonomous increase in US real GNP (initial change in 1976 I)

Country	Real GNP 2	Real GNP 6	GNP deflator 2	GNP deflator 6	Short-term interest rate 2	Short-term interest rate 6	Exchange rate 2	Exchange rate 6	Import price 2	Import price 6	Money supply 2	Money supply 6	Imports 2	Imports 6
US	1.31	1.07	.15	.64	.42	.59	—	—	.44	1.62	-.08	.10	.84	.8
Canada	.11	.17	.02	.26	.35	.59	.01	-.13	.32	1.20	-.40	-1.45	.08	.0
Japan	.05	.28	-.00	.10	-.06	-.11	-.34	-.20	-.01	1.10	.03	.23	.03	.1
Austria	-.01	.05	.00	.20	.11	.31	-.68	-2.14	.22	1.10	-.00	-.00	-.13	-.6
Belgium	.03	.13	.01	.18	.04	.10	-.64	-1.89	.20	1.27	-.01	.00	-.04	-.4
Denmark	-.05	-.14	-.01	.05	-.09	.09	-.86	-2.18	-.09	.86	.03	-.19	.03	-.3
France	-.04	-.36	.00	-.01	-.01	-.36	-.71	-2.87	.02	-.07	-.02	-.15	-.03	-.4
Germany	-.04	-.23	-.01	-.07	.13	.16	-.75	-2.24	-.05	.55	-.15	-.48	-.09	-.5
Italy	-.01	-.17	.01	.02	-.07	-.45	-.55	-2.34	.16	.30	.04	.30	-.00	-.0
Netherlands	-.02	-.14	-.00	-.00	.05	.10	-.68	-2.09	.02	.59	-.07	-.20	-.01	-.3
Norway	-.00	.00	.02	.19	.03	.04	-.41	-1.44	.27	1.48	.00	.08	-.02	-.4
Sweden	.09	.04	.04	.35	.07	.21	.05	-1.23	.87	1.84	.11	.47	-.07	-.4
Switzerland	-.02	-.24	.01	-.03	.08	.10	-.88	-2.81	-.01	.50	-.04	-.16	-.13	-.7
United Kingdom	.01	-.21	.01	-.18	-.01	-.10	-.79	-3.90	-.13	-1.40	.01	.10	.01	-.0
Finland	-.04	-.43	.04	.30	-.00	-.04	-.22	-1.02	.53	2.20	-.00	-.10	-.04	-.6
US Alone	1.31	1.09	.13	.48	.40	.53	—	—	0	0	-.10	-.01	.87	1.2

Country	Consumption 2	Consumption 6	Investment 2	Investment 6	Long-term interest rate 2	Long-term interest rate 6	Export price 2	Export price 6	Exports 2	Exports 6	Balance of payments[a] 2	Balance of payments[a] 6
US	.02	-.19	2.07	2.92	.13	.33	.20	.99	.14	.51	-294.394	-443.6
Canada	-.05	-.15	.02	.08	.13	.33	.24	1.07	.74	.89	56.762	63.9
Japan	.03	.19	.01	.23	.00	.00	.17	.77	.27	.93	22.569	30.1
Austria	-.09	-.22	.00	.00	.00	.00	-.01	.25	-.00	-.06	-.083	-.2
Belgium	.02	.06	.00	.03	.01	.05	.02	.46	-.01	-.27	-.647	-3.1
Denmark	-.03	-.13	-.00	-.04	-.02	.02	.07	.90	-.12	-.72	.012	-.0
France	-.01	-.13	.00	-.07	-.00	-.11	.43	1.68	-.21	-1.59	.264	.9
Germany	-.05	-.22	.00	-.11	.04	.07	.26	1.02	-.12	-.70	.214	.2
Italy	.01	-.00	.00	-.04	-.02	-.17	.40	1.51	-.05	-.81	17.477	82.5
Netherlands	-.01	-.14	.00	-.05	.01	.03	-.01	.35	-.05	-.44	-.018	-.1
Norway	-.01	-.01	.00	-.00	.01	.02	.35	1.55	-.03	-.58	.003	-.0
Sweden	.02	.04	.00	.24	.01	.07	.45	1.81	.22	-.57	-.048	-.0
Switzerland	-.06	-.28	.00	-.22	.04	.07	.20	.76	-.07	-.84	.034	.0
United Kingdom	.01	.05	.01	-.11	-.00	-.04	.36	1.23	.00	-.99	47.549	249.5
Finland	-.01	-.23	.00	-.12	.00	.00	.67	2.66	-.19	-1.66	-.777	-57.6
US Alone	.03	-.08	2.07	2.95	.12	.31	.07	.40	0	0	-230.193	-290.

Note: a. Change is absolute change, not percentage change, in units of local currency.

by a one-percent autonomous increase in GNP of the country in which the policy change was made.

For the interest rate increases (Tables 9-9 and 9-11), the divisor is the change in the interest rate (in percentage points). The actual change in the interest rate for the experiments was 2.0 percentage points, so the divisor was 2.0. Each number in these tables is thus the percentage change in the variable induced by a 1.0 percentage point increase in the interest rate. For the exchange rate increases (Tables 9-12, 9-14, and 9-16), the percentage change in the exchange rate was 10.0 percent and the divisor was 1.0. Each number in

TABLE 9-9. Percentage change in the variable after two and six quarters induced by a sustained 1 percentage point increase in the US short-term interest rate (initial change in 1976 I)

ountry	Real GNP		GNP deflator		Short-term interest rate		Exchange rate		Import price		Money supply		Imports	
	2	6	2	6	2	6	2	6	2	6	2	6	2	6
S	-.34	-1.13	-.04	-.40	1.00	1.00	—	—	-.67	-1.77	-.67	-1.82	-.29	-2.04
anada	-.10	-.62	-.01	-.33	.95	1.05	.08	.09	-.27	-1.07	-1.22	-3.50	-.21	-1.38
apan	-.04	-.35	.04	.17	.17	.61	1.30	3.03	.95	1.92	-.07	-.51	-.14	-1.12
ustria	-.08	-.24	-.03	-.28	.28	.38	1.00	1.98	-.21	-.99	-.00	-.00	-.26	-.84
elgium	-.10	-.58	-.02	-.26	.30	.39	.77	1.62	-.26	-1.12	-.11	-.70	-.00	-.39
enmark	-.06	-.40	-.02	-.17	-.09	-.14	.83	1.85	-.46	-1.16	.03	-.34	.04	-.04
rance	-.04	-.28	-.01	-.05	.26	.72	.71	2.20	-.22	-.35	-.04	-.36	.02	-.24
ermany	-.08	-.31	-.01	-.14	.50	.83	.91	1.93	-.02	-.62	-.51	-1.50	-.23	-1.33
taly	-.03	-.17	-.04	-.21	.07	.38	.56	1.68	-.32	-.65	-.06	-.50	-.03	-.50
etherlands	-.06	-.49	-.00	-.10	.20	.28	.83	1.80	-.04	-.58	-.26	-.70	-.04	-.47
orway	-.04	-.16	-.04	-.24	.19	.38	.81	1.49	-.50	-1.70	-.04	-.26	-.04	-.52
weden	.02	.00	.04	.24	.21	.68	1.95	3.45	.90	.64	.05	.30	-.19	-.99
witzerland	-.05	-.24	.02	.02	.30	.53	1.62	3.05	.54	.13	-.14	-.52	-.46	-1.74
ited Kingdom	-.03	-.26	-.03	-.15	-.04	.01	.34	2.19	-.54	-.21	.02	-.12	-.03	-.48
inland	-.02	-.12	-.03	-.26	-.00	-.03	1.00	1.65	-.37	-1.58	.03	.32	.05	-.50
Alone	-.34	-1.10	-.01	-.21	1.00	1.00	—	—	0	0	-.62	-1.63	-.36	-2.53

untry	Consumption		Investment		Long-term interest rate		Export price		Exports		Balance of payments[a]	
	2	6	2	6	2	6	2	6	2	6	2	6
	-.41	-1.12	-.50	-2.30	.31	.64	-.20	-.78	-.12	-.81	463.175	1907.530
nada	-.20	-.71	-.02	-.23	.34	.64	-.30	-1.07	-.26	-1.93	-11.473	-102.456
pan	-.06	-.51	-.00	-.25	.00	.00	-.17	-.43	-.12	-.86	-128.978	-275.178
stria	-.26	-.56	.00	.00	.00	.00	.04	-.31	-.13	-.81	.447	1.270
lgium	-.06	-.48	.00	-.12	.08	.20	-.08	-.57	-.11	-.78	.767	2.242
nmark	-.03	-.34	-.00	-.07	-.02	-.09	-.27	-.98	-.13	-.85	.045	-.094
ance	-.02	-.23	.00	-.06	.07	.28	-.59	-1.58	-.13	-.76	-.899	-3.617
rmany	-.17	-.62	.00	-.18	.14	.34	-.35	-1.03	-.09	-.64	-.408	-.160
aly	-.01	-.15	.00	-.06	.02	.15	-.54	-1.48	-.13	-.77	-50.535	-278.212
therlakds	-.03	-.46	.00	-.15	.04	.10	-.05	-.51	-.13	-.87	-.052	-.165
rway	-.06	-.25	.00	-.05	.03	.13	-.22	-1.32	-.10	-.75	.124	.326
eden	-.00	-.13	.00	.08	.05	.22	-.52	-1.37	-.09	-.71	-.673	-.962
itzerland	-.21	-.75	-.03	-.24	.15	.32	-.25	-.71	-.13	-.79	-.131	-.047
ited Kingdom	-.01	-.26	-.00	-.15	-.01	-.00	-.51	-1.36	-.12	-.79	-3.679	-328.702
nland	-.01	-.10	.00	-.04	.00	.00	-.88	-2.39	-.10	-.70	-75.568	-119.221
Alone	-.43	-1.20	-.50	-2.24	.31	.64	-.01	-.18	0	0	212.951	1708.547

te: a. Change is absolute change, not percentage change, in units of local currency.

these tables is thus the percentage change in the variable induced by a 10.0 percent increase in the exchange rate. Finally, for the increase in the export prices (Table 9-17), the percentage change in the prices was 50.0 percent and the divisor was 1.0. Each number in this table is thus the percentage change in the variable induced by a 50.0 percent increase in the export prices.

The numbers for the balance of payments are not in percentage terms and have not been divided by anything; they are merely the actual changes in the balance of payments corresponding to whatever policy change was made. The balance-of-payments variables are in units of nominal local currency, and

TABLE 9-10. Percentage change in the variable after two and six quarters induced by a sustained 1 percent autonomous increase in German real GNP (initial change in 1976 I)

Country	Real GNP 2	Real GNP 6	GNP deflator 2	GNP deflator 6	Short-term interest rate 2	Short-term interest rate 6	Exchange rate 2	Exchange rate 6	Import price 2	Import price 6	Money supply 2	Money supply 6	Imports 2	Imports 6
US	.01	.04	-.01	-.04	-.00	-.01	—	—	-.13	-.48	-.01	-.03	.02	.1
Canada	.01	.04	-.00	-.01	-.00	-.01	.00	.01	-.08	-.30	.00	.02	.01	.1
Japan	.01	.05	-.00	-.01	-.01	-.02	.01	.04	-.08	-.28	.01	.03	.01	.1
Austria	.09	.17	.02	.11	-.01	-.00	.39	1.26	.03	.10	-.00	-.00	.11	.3
Belgium	.22	.27	.02	.13	.18	.59	.34	1.09	.03	.04	-.01	-.23	.28	.5
Denmark	.08	.15	.00	.03	.01	.04	.35	1.15	.05	.17	.06	.13	.07	.1
France	.07	.06	-.00	.02	.28	1.07	.30	1.16	.02	.18	.01	-.17	.06	.0
Germany	1.21	1.67	.20	1.18	.57	1.65	.40	1.30	.14	.34	.45	.62	1.52	2.0
Italy	.07	.14	.01	.10	.02	.22	.26	1.09	-.00	.19	.02	-.02	.10	.1
Netherlands	.28	.44	.02	.16	.32	1.05	.36	1.20	.11	.32	-.16	-.69	.26	.6
Norway	.08	.41	-.00	-.03	.21	.70	.22	.74	-.04	-.21	.01	.07	.02	-.5
Sweden	.05	.12	-.00	-.06	.05	.26	.15	.45	-.14	-.55	.05	.09	.06	.1
Switzerland	.08	.19	.01	.09	.02	.08	.39	1.34	.07	.25	.01	.01	.13	.2
United Kingdom	.05	.10	-.01	-.03	-.01	.04	.12	.71	-.11	-.12	.01	-.01	.07	.1
Finland	.05	.13	-.01	-.03	.00	.02	.22	.74	-.08	-.29	.03	.09	.07	.1

Country	Consumption 2	Consumption 6	Investment 2	Investment 6	Long-term interest rate 2	Long-term interest rate 6	Export price 2	Export price 6	Exports 2	Exports 6	Balance of payments[a] 2	Balance of payments[a] 6
US	.00	.03	.02	.08	-.00	-.00	-.05	-.18	.12	.25	60.253	164.2
Canada	.00	.02	.00	.02	-.00	-.00	-.08	-.29	.06	.22	5.823	18.5
Japan	.01	.03	.00	.05	.00	.00	-.06	-.23	.08	.19	4.285	7.6
Austria	.07	.16	.00	.00	.00	.00	.08	.24	.48	.73	.148	.1
Belgium	.15	.24	.00	.11	.04	.23	.07	.21	.51	.72	.875	1.2
Denmark	.06	.15	-.00	.06	.00	.02	.01	-.02	.30	.45	.021	-.0
France	.01	-.07	.00	.05	.07	.39	-.14	-.51	.38	.56	.067	-.3
Germany	.55	.77	.00	1.96	.16	.61	-.01	.12	.10	.22	-.865	-1.1
Italy	.02	.07	.00	.09	.00	.08	-.12	-.41	.40	.58	9.776	-40.8
Netherlands	.16	.39	.00	.34	.05	.29	.11	.35	.65	.91	.103	.0
Norway	.03	.15	.00	.08	.03	.20	-.04	-.20	.25	.38	.026	.1
Sweden	.02	.08	.00	.18	.01	.08	-.14	-.54	.23	.31	.035	.0
Switzerland	.03	.09	.03	.28	.01	.04	-.06	-.19	.34	.51	.004	-.0
United Kingdom	.03	.08	.02	.07	-.00	.02	-.13	-.45	.19	.34	5.684	-29.[illegible]
Finland	.02	.09	.00	.09	.00	.00	-.22	-.81	.21	.37	-1.367	-26.[illegible]

Note: a. Change is absolute change, not percentage change, in units of local currency.

thus it is not readily apparent from the tables how one country's balance of payments changed relative to another's. For the most part it is unnecessary to know this to understand the rest of the results; when it is necessary, the relative change will be mentioned in the text. The main interest in the balance-of-payments results for a country is the sign of the changes.

For the two interest rates, the changes are absolute changes (in percentage points) rather than percentage changes. The divisors are the same as they are for the other variables.

The exchange rate experiments, 6, 8, and 10, require that the exchange rate reaction function be dropped for the particular country in question. The

TABLE 9-11. Percentage change in the variable after two and six quarters induced by a sustained 1 percentage point increase in the German short-term interest rate (initial change in 1976 I)

ountry	Real GNP		GNP deflator		Short-term interest rate		Exchange rate		Import price		Money supply		Imports	
	2	6	2	6	2	6	2	6	2	6	2	6	2	6
S	-.02	-.09	.03	.13	.01	.03	—	—	.48	1.32	.03	.10	-.06	-.49
anada	-.01	-.09	.01	.08	.01	.05	-.00	-.03	.29	.84	-.02	-.10	-.02	-.27
apan	-.01	-.06	.01	.08	.01	.05	.01	.02	.33	.90	-.00	-.03	-.04	-.25
ustria	-.03	-.08	-.01	.04	.01	.07	-1.29	-2.60	.06	.52	-.00	-.00	-.05	-.46
elgium	-.10	-.17	-.01	-.02	.05	-.04	-1.14	-2.27	-.00	.48	-.05	-.11	-.10	-.58
enmark	-.04	-.09	-.00	.03	-.02	.04	-1.16	-2.39	.02	.39	-.02	-.11	-.02	-.28
rance	-.04	-.18	.00	-.00	.41	.20	-1.01	-2.56	.02	-.01	-.07	-.21	-.04	-.23
ermany	-.11	-.16	-.03	-.15	1.00	1.00	-1.35	-2.68	-.43	-.31	-1.20	-1.77	-.66	-1.50
taly	-.03	-.12	.01	-.01	-.10	-.48	-.83	-2.25	.15	.09	.05	.34	-.03	.07
etherlands	-.15	-.46	-.01	-.14	.44	.44	-1.23	-2.52	-.28	-.19	-.62	-.88	-.06	-.58
orway	.01	.35	.00	.09	.37	.35	-.99	-1.96	.05	.76	-.03	.13	-.22	-.97
weden	-.02	-.12	.01	.05	.13	.03	-.90	-2.30	.18	.32	-.00	-.07	-.07	-.11
itzerland	-.03	-.14	-.01	-.05	-.03	-.12	-1.27	-2.66	-.09	.16	.01	.04	-.02	-.05
ited Kingdom	-.02	-.10	.02	.18	.03	-.02	-.40	-1.57	.48	.65	-.02	.01	-.03	-.14
nland	-.03	-.15	.03	.22	.00	-.01	-.75	-1.59	.45	1.42	.01	.07	-.02	-.03

untry	Consumption		Investment		Long-term interest rate		Export price		Exports		Balance of payments[a]	
	2	6	2	6	2	6	2	6	2	6	2	6
	-.02	-.10	-.02	-.17	.00	.01	.17	.51	-.06	-.30	-234.466	-585.770
nada	-.00	-.04	-.00	-.03	.01	.02	.30	.83	-.07	-.50	-15.258	-85.659
pan	-.00	-.05	-.00	-.04	.00	.00	.24	.66	-.06	-.32	-11.523	-33.452
stria	-.03	-.13	.00	.00	.00	.00	-.21	-.18	-.21	-.57	-.408	-.947
lgium	-.06	-.19	.00	-.07	.02	-.00	-.19	-.07	-.22	-.61	-2.265	-5.240
nmark	-.03	-.09	-.00	-.03	-.00	.02	.04	.47	-.15	-.46	-.028	-.013
ance	-.03	.17	.00	-.06	.12	.14	.54	1.45	-.16	-.44	.815	2.914
rmany	-.39	-.60	.00	-.18	.30	.45	.29	.79	-.04	-.27	1.727	3.142
aly	.00	.01	.00	-.05	-.03	-.19	.50	1.29	-.18	-.51	43.274	196.395
therlands	-.09	-.55	.00	-.25	.08	.17	-.31	-.32	-.28	-.74	-.136	-.164
rway	-.05	.13	.00	.04	.07	.16	-.03	.56	-.11	-.32	.007	.087
eden	-.00	-.01	.00	-.10	.03	.03	.53	1.43	-.12	-.47	.153	.419
itzerland	.00	.01	-.00	-.17	-.01	-.07	.25	.65	-.15	-.46	.063	.071
ited Kingdom	-.01	-.05	-.00	-.06	.01	-.00	.48	1.32	-.09	-.36	-7.329	127.243
nland	-.01	-.07	.00	-.06	.00	.00	.85	2.30	-.11	-.37	42.714	66.408

te: a. Change is absolute change, not percentage change, in units of local currency.

exchange rate is instead taken to be exogenous and then changed by the specified amount. This procedure is somewhat artificial in that the interest rate reaction function for the particular country is not also changed. Presumably exchange rate and interest rate decisions are coordinated, so changing one but not the other is not necessarily realistic. These experiments, however, were performed solely with the aim of trying to understand the properties of the model; they are not meant to be realistic descriptions of actual policy-making decisions. Similar considerations apply to the German interest rate experiment, experiment 5.

The following discussion of the results is somewhat loose. Reference is

TABLE 9-12. Percentage change in the variable after two and six quarters induced by a sustained 10 percent increase in the German exchange rate (depreciation) (initial change in 1976 I)

Country	Real GNP		GNP deflator		Short-term interest rate		Exchange rate		Import price		Money supply		Imports	
	2	6	2	6	2	6	2	6	2	6	2	6	2	6
US	.09	.28	-.21	-.57	-.10	-.09	—	—	-3.24	-4.24	-.20	-.35	.56	2.
Canada	.05	.31	-.09	-.44	-.11	-.14	.03	.12	-2.00	-2.80	.13	.38	.24	1.
Japan	.01	.08	-.11	-.38	-.07	-.13	-.07	-.17	-2.19	-3.02	.01	-.01	.31	.
Austria	-.00	-.39	.04	-.47	-.09	-.27	9.65	9.68	-.34	-1.71	-.00	-.00	.10	.
Belgium	-.01	-.68	.06	-.28	1.20	1.03	8.35	8.35	-.03	-1.64	-.30	-1.51	-.08	-.
Denmark	.08	-.28	.05	-.09	.32	-.07	8.86	8.86	.24	-1.07	-.18	-.19	-.21	.
France	-.03	-.37	-.03	.18	1.03	2.21	8.37	10.56	.81	1.04	-.10	-.72	-.10	-.
Germany	-.10	-.38	.09	.12	.64	1.04	10.00	10.00	2.99	1.19	-.56	-1.65	-.23	-1.
Italy	-.04	-.00	-.10	.03	1.00	2.29	6.96	9.19	-.11	.63	-.65	-2.33	-.20	-1.
Netherlands	.20	-.15	.08	.26	.68	.49	9.36	9.43	2.37	.85	-.54	-.46	-.38	-.
Norway	.01	-.04	-.04	-.42	.50	.72	6.77	6.80	-.64	-2.61	-.05	-.36	-.11	-.
Sweden	-.10	-.11	-.22	-.53	.02	.78	6.07	7.33	-1.64	-2.04	-.26	-.77	.26	-.
Switzerland	.02	-.07	.06	.07	.27	.49	9.64	9.81	.75	-.72	-.11	-.41	-.50	-1.
United Kingdom	.01	-.14	-.26	-.62	-.29	.04	3.46	7.08	-2.58	-.70	.15	-.34	.02	-.
Finland	.03	.15	-.25	-.93	-.02	-.01	5.75	5.87	-2.70	-4.36	-.16	-.72	-.12	-1.

Country	Consumption		Investment		Long-term interest rate		Export price		Exports		Balance of payments[a]	
	2	6	2	6	2	6	2	6	2	6	2	6
US	.14	.41	.13	.57	-.03	-.06	-1.18	-1.79	.09	.26	617.978	510.
Canada	.03	.17	.00	.12	-.04	-.08	-1.99	-2.74	.47	1.73	50.361	127.
Japan	.03	.13	-.00	.07	.00	.00	-1.57	-2.21	.23	.69	28.042	28.
Austria	.06	-.08	.00	.00	.00	.00	1.62	.76	-.09	-.73	1.029	1.
Belgium	.02	-.47	.00	-.15	.31	.59	1.52	.48	-.14	-.80	6.357	7.
Denmark	.04	-.23	-.00	.02	.08	-.02	.13	-1.16	.03	-.60	.007	-.
France	-.04	-.52	.00	-.05	.27	.92	-3.49	-4.44	-.09	-.68	-4.050	-6.
Germany	-.23	-1.02	.00	-.23	.17	.43	-1.96	-2.63	-.04	-.22	-3.607	-2.
Italy	-.11	-.48	.00	-.03	.27	1.06	-3.22	-3.99	-.04	-.41	-287.036	-453.
Netherlands	.14	-.01	.00	.14	.11	.21	2.67	1.56	-.11	-.90	.194	.
Norway	-.07	-.27	.00	.02	.09	.27	.10	-1.68	.02	-.51	.164	.
Sweden	-.04	-.29	.00	-.26	.01	.23	-3.53	-4.60	-.06	-.41	-.534	-.
Switzerland	-.16	-.61	-.02	.01	.13	.29	-1.63	-2.09	-.01	-.42	-.264	-.
United Kingdom	.01	-.40	.00	-.06	-.09	.01	-3.17	-4.06	.03	-.10	-56.048	-378.
Finland	.00	-.01	.00	.08	.00	.00	-5.46	-7.01	.01	-.47	-176.527	-132.

Note: a. Change is absolute change, not percentage change, in units of local currency.

sometimes made to a change in one endogenous variable "leading to" or "resulting in" a change in another endogenous variable. This is not, strictly speaking, correct because the model is simultaneous, but it does help to give a general idea of the model's properties. Not all results in the tables are explained, and not every possible indirect effect is noted. Emphasis is placed on the main results and effects and, as the discussion progresses, on the results in a table that are different from the results in previous tables. In what follows, the terms "GNP" and "income" are used interchangeably, interest rates are always short-term rates unless otherwise noted, and import and export prices are local currency prices unless otherwise noted.

TABLE 9-13. Percentage change in the variable after two and six quarters induced by a sustained 1 percent autonomous increase in United Kingdom real GNP (initial change in 1976 I)

ountry	Real GNP 2	Real GNP 6	GNP deflator 2	GNP deflator 6	Short-term interest rate 2	Short-term interest rate 6	Exchange rate 2	Exchange rate 6	Import price 2	Import price 6	Money supply 2	Money supply 6	Imports 2	Imports 6
s	.01	.03	-.00	-.02	-.00	-.00	—	—	-.05	-.26	-.00	-.02	.01	.10
nada	.02	.04	.00	.01	-.01	-.01	.00	.02	-.03	-.17	.01	.03	.03	.13
pan	.01	.04	-.00	-.00	-.01	-.02	.01	.04	-.02	-.12	.00	.03	.01	.06
stria	.03	.04	.01	-.02	-.00	-.01	.01	.09	-.05	-.25	-.00	-.00	.05	.18
lgium	.07	.06	.00	-.01	.02	.02	.01	.08	-.08	-.38	.01	.02	.13	.35
nmark	.14	.08	.00	-.04	.01	-.14	.03	.09	-.08	-.45	.10	.21	.13	.49
ance	.04	.06	-.00	-.03	.01	.04	.01	.07	-.06	-.32	.02	.02	.04	.17
rmany	.04	.11	.00	.04	.01	.06	.01	.10	-.06	-.28	.02	.06	.05	.16
aly	.03	.06	.00	-.01	-.01	-.01	.01	.08	-.05	-.24	.01	.05	.04	.15
therlands	.11	.15	.01	.04	.03	.07	.01	.09	-.06	-.33	.04	.06	.12	.35
rway	.21	.20	-.00	-.05	-.01	.01	.01	.06	-.08	-.41	.08	.09	.23	.56
eden	.08	.16	.00	-.03	-.01	-.03	.03	.12	-.08	-.43	.08	.17	.08	.41
itzerland	.05	.07	.01	-.00	.01	.01	.02	.11	-.08	-.48	.00	.01	.08	.25
ited Kingdom	1.41	1.19	-.00	.36	.27	.41	.52	2.56	.47	2.29	.12	-.12	2.01	1.76
nland	.09	.15	-.00	-.05	.01	.03	.00	.04	-.10	-.53	.07	.10	.13	.37

ntry	Consumption 2	Consumption 6	Investment 2	Investment 6	Long-term interest rate 2	Long-term interest rate 6	Export price 2	Export price 6	Exports 2	Exports 6	Balance of payments[a] 2	Balance of payments[a] 6
	.00	.02	.02	.06	.00	.00	-.01	-.08	.13	.24	51.303	120.412
ada	.00	.03	.00	.02	-.00	-.00	-.02	-.12	.14	.21	13.296	18.359
an	.00	.03	.00	.04	.00	.00	-.02	-.10	.07	.16	3.468	5.957
tria	.02	.05	.00	.00	.00	.00	-.02	-.13	.17	.26	.060	.104
gium	.05	.07	.00	.04	.01	.01	-.04	-.19	.20	.35	.397	.827
mark	.10	.13	-.00	.07	.00	-.06	-.04	-.27	.52	.53	.059	.038
nce	.01	.03	.00	.03	.00	.01	-.05	-.27	.21	.30	.129	.142
many	.02	.08	.00	.09	.00	.02	-.03	-.16	.18	.31	.103	.195
ly	.01	.04	.00	.04	-.00	-.01	-.04	-.23	.16	.26	9.699	11.272
herlands	.07	.18	.00	.13	.01	.02	-.04	-.22	.27	.36	.045	.042
way	.16	.18	.00	.19	-.00	-.00	-.07	-.38	.75	.85	.051	.035
den	.03	.12	.00	.28	-.00	-.01	-.04	-.26	.36	.48	.066	.070
tzerland	.02	.06	.01	.14	.00	.01	-.02	-.12	.19	.28	.017	.046
ted Kingdom	.91	.56	.88	.74	.09	.20	-.02	-.06	.07	.23	-194.756	-422.917
land	.04	.13	.00	.16	.00	.00	-.07	-.39	.40	.49	18.327	24.275

e. a. Change is absolute change, not percentage change, in units of local currency.

United States Spending Increase: Fixed Exchange Rate Period (Table 9-7)

The increase in U.S. government spending increased U.S. income, which in turn increased U.S. imports. This increased other countries' exports, which in turn increased their income and imports. This is the trade multiplier effect. The increase in U.S. income also led to an increase in the U.S. price level, which increased other countries' import prices. This led to an increase in other countries' export prices, which resulted in further increases in other countries' import prices. This is the price multiplier effect.

The other important effect in this case is the interest rate effect. The

TABLE 9-14. Percentage change in the variable after two and six quarters induced by a sustained 10 percent increase in the United Kingdom exchange rate (depreciation) (initial change in 1976 I)

Country	Real GNP		GNP deflator		Short-term interest rate		Exchange rate		Import price		Money supply		Imports	
	2	6	2	6	2	6	2	6	2	6	2	6	2	6
US	.03	.05	-.05	-.11	-.03	-.01	—	—	-.73	-.75	-.05	-.06	.17	.
Canada	.01	.04	-.03	-.11	-.05	-.03	.02	.03	-.51	-.55	.06	.10	.09	.
Japan	.01	.03	-.02	-.06	-.02	-.02	-.01	.01	-.42	-.46	.01	.02	.07	.
Austria	-.03	-.06	-.12	-.30	-.03	-.05	.03	.12	-.80	-.82	-.00	-.00	.16	.
Belgium	-.21	-.23	-.13	-.37	-.30	-.10	.03	.11	-1.19	-1.20	-.04	-.15	.32	.
Denmark	-.15	-.44	-.11	-.38	-.61	-.38	.01	.05	-1.54	-1.56	.34	-.34	.47	.
France	-.03	-.09	-.05	-.20	-.10	-.08	.04	-.02	-.96	-1.11	-.03	-.15	.20	.
Germany	.04	.04	-.02	-.06	-.01	-.02	.04	.13	-.91	-.91	.03	.02	.05	.
Italy	.01	-.00	-.11	-.28	-.08	-.09	-.02	-.08	-.86	-.97	.01	-.06	.07	.
Netherlands	-.06	-.16	-.04	-.16	-.20	-.10	.03	.12	-.99	-1.11	.14	-.11	.21	.
Norway	-.14	-.46	-.13	-.30	-.11	.00	.04	.09	-1.25	-1.28	-.08	-.38	.29	-.
Sweden	-.05	-.23	-.13	-.42	-.19	-.26	.15	.16	-1.40	-1.47	-.14	-.75	.29	.
Switzerland	-.03	-.15	-.08	-.35	-.04	-.07	.02	-.10	-1.49	-1.86	.00	-.06	.26	.
United Kingdom	-.05	-.62	.73	2.98	1.62	-1.16	10.00	10.00	9.46	9.45	-1.10	.76	-.35	-2.
Finland	.01	-.10	-.17	-.41	-.02	-.02	.02	.08	-1.50	-1.61	-.12	-.46	.05	.

Country	Consumption		Investment		Long-term interest rate		Export price		Exports		Balance of payments[a]	
	2	6	2	6	2	6	2	6	2	6	2	6
US	.04	.08	.04	.12	-.01	-.01	-.21	-.29	.07	.02	166.899	71.
Canada	.01	.05	.00	.02	-.02	-.02	-.35	-.45	.14	.24	32.238	22.
Japan	.01	.04	.00	.04	.00	.00	-.27	-.34	.10	.14	9.478	4.
Austria	-.01	-.01	.00	.00	.00	.00	-.44	-.53	.08	.01	.214	.
Belgium	-.14	-.13	.00	-.07	-.06	-.07	-.59	-.69	.12	-.05	1.832	1.
Denmark	-.06	-.34	-.00	-.14	-.15	-.24	-.77	-.89	.06	-.34	.112	.
France	-.01	-.03	.00	-.03	-.02	-.04	-.67	-.81	.09	-.07	.180	.
Germany	.03	.08	.00	.07	-.00	-.01	-.43	-.51	.15	.02	.376	.
Italy	.01	.03	.00	.01	-.02	-.05	-.61	-.77	.11	.02	35.193	11.
Netherlands	-.03	-.08	.00	-.08	-.03	-.04	-.70	-.78	.10	-.08	.061	.
Norway	-.07	-.37	.00	-.16	-.02	-.01	-1.05	-1.19	.01	-.92	.043	.
Sweden	-.01	-.05	.00	-.22	-.04	-.09	-.65	-.87	.12	-.21	.157	.
Switzerland	.01	-.01	.01	-.18	-.02	-.04	-.33	-.52	.09	-.01	.102	.
United Kingdom	-.30	-2.12	.01	-.39	.53	-.27	.12	1.24	.18	.25	-892.626	-713.
Finland	.01	-.03	.00	-.00	.00	.00	-.96	-1.14	.08	-.29	47.621	36.

Note: a. Change is absolute change, not percentage change, in units of local currency.

increase in U.S. income and prices led to an increase in the U.S. interest rate through the reaction function of the Federal Reserve. This offset some of the increase in U.S. income that would otherwise have occurred and also led to an increase in other countries' interest rates. The interest rates for all countries except Japan were higher after two quarters. This worldwide increase in interest rates offset some of the increase in world income that would otherwise have occurred. For a number of countries the interest rate effect was large enough to lead to a net negative effect on GNP by the sixth quarter. In other words, the U.S. expansion caused GNP for some countries to fall because of the interest rate increase that resulted from the expansion.

TABLE 9-15. Percentage change in the variable after two and six quarters induced by a sustained 1 percent autonomous increase in Japanese Real GNP (initial change in 1976 I)

ntry	Real GNP		GNP deflator		Short-term interest rate		Exchange rate		Import price		Money supply		Imports	
	2	6	2	6	2	6	2	6	2	6	2	6	2	6
	.01	.02	-.01	-.02	-.00	-.00	—	—	-.09	-.20	-.01	-.02	.01	.09
ada	.01	.03	-.00	-.00	-.00	-.01	.00	.01	-.03	-.08	.00	.02	.01	.08
an	1.29	2.29	.10	.65	.10	.38	.49	1.38	.47	1.32	.31	1.08	.36	.85
tria	-.00	.00	-.00	-.02	-.00	-.00	.00	.02	-.04	-.10	-.00	-.00	.01	.03
gium	-.01	-.01	-.00	-.02	-.01	-.00	.00	.02	-.05	-.11	-.00	-.01	.01	.04
mark	.00	.00	-.00	-.02	-.01	-.01	.00	.02	-.05	-.12	.01	-.01	.01	.04
nce	.00	.00	-.00	-.01	-.00	.01	.01	.04	-.03	-.08	-.00	-.00	.01	.03
many	.00	.02	-.00	-.00	.00	.01	.00	.02	-.05	-.12	.00	.00	.00	.02
ly	.00	.01	-.00	-.02	-.00	.00	.00	.02	-.04	-.09	-.00	-.01	.00	.02
herlands	-.00	.00	-.00	-.01	-.00	.00	.00	.02	-.04	-.10	.00	-.00	.01	.03
way	-.00	-.00	-.01	-.03	-.00	-.00	.00	.02	-.08	-.19	-.00	-.01	.01	.04
den	.00	.01	-.00	-.02	-.00	-.00	.01	.03	-.05	-.11	-.00	-.01	.01	.03
tzerland	.00	.01	-.00	-.01	-.00	.00	.00	.03	-.05	-.11	.00	-.00	.01	.05
ted Kingdom	.00	.02	-.00	-.02	-.00	-.00	.00	.00	-.05	-.13	.00	.01	.01	.03
land	.00	.01	-.00	-.02	-.00	.00	-.00	.01	-.05	-.13	-.00	-.01	.00	.01

ntry	Consumption		Investment		Long-term interest rate		Export price		Exports		Balance of payments[a]	
	2	6	2	6	2	6	2	6	2	6	2	6
	.00	.02	.01	.05	-.00	-.00	-.02	-.05	.05	.15	39.366	87.069
da	.00	.01	.00	.01	-.00	-.00	-.02	-.06	.04	.16	5.176	14.273
n	.30	.82	.50	3.05	.00	.00	.07	.53	.01	.07	-36.872	-78.847
ria	-.00	.00	.00	.00	.00	.00	-.03	-.08	.01	.04	.008	.025
ium	-.00	-.01	.00	-.00	-.00	-.00	-.04	-.10	.01	.04	.000	.021
ark	.00	-.00	-.00	.00	-.00	-.01	-.06	-.14	.02	.06	.001	.001
ce	.00	.00	.00	.00	-.00	.00	-.05	-.13	.01	.04	-.012	-.039
any	.00	.01	.00	.01	.00	.00	-.03	-.08	.01	.05	.018	.048
y	.00	.00	.00	.00	-.00	.00	-.04	-.11	.01	.05	.229	-.990
erlands	-.00	-.00	.00	.00	-.00	-.00	-.05	-.12	.01	.04	-.004	-.006
ay	.00	-.00	.00	-.00	-.00	-.00	-.08	-.19	.01	.05	.004	.009
en	.00	.00	.00	.01	-.00	-.00	-.05	-.12	.01	.05	.002	.002
zerland	.00	.01	.00	.02	.00	.00	-.02	-.06	.02	.06	.003	.007
ed Kingdom	.00	.02	.00	.01	-.00	-.00	-.04	-.11	.01	.06	1.266	4.245
and	.00	.01	.00	.00	.00	.00	-.07	-.18	.01	.04	-.653	-.684

a. Change is absolute change, not percentage change, in units of local currency.

The U.S. increase had a negative effect on the U.S. balance of payments and a positive effect on the other countries' balance of payments. Imports declined for some countries even though GNP rose; this is due in part to the effects of higher interest rates and in part to the fact that import prices increased more initially than did domestic prices. An increase in import prices relative to domestic prices leads to a substitution away from imported goods. Note finally that the money supply decreased for many countries. Although income was higher, interest rates were also higher, and in many cases the negative interest rate effect dominated.

This completes the discussion of the first experiment. An interesting

TABLE 9-16. Percentage change in the variable after two and six quarters induced by a sustained 10 percent increase in the Japanese exchange rate (depreciation) (initial change in 1976 I)

Country	Real GNP		GNP deflator		Short-term interest rate		Exchange rate		Import price		Money supply		Import	
	2	6	2	6	2	6	2	6	2	6	2	6	2	
US	.06	.12	-.13	-.31	-.08	-.05	—	—	-1.93	-2.10	-.13	-.18	.38	1
Canada	.02	.09	-.04	-.16	-.10	-.09	.03	.12	-.76	-.92	.12	.29	.11	
Japan	-.14	-.53	.48	1.28	1.57	1.79	10.00	10.00	9.51	9.30	-.63	-1.61	-1.73	-5
Austria	-.03	-.03	-.09	-.34	-.03	-.07	.07	.40	-.85	-1.05	-.00	-.00	.17	
Belgium	-.17	-.15	-.10	-.33	-.23	-.06	.07	.35	-1.00	-1.19	-.03	-.10	.27	
Denmark	-.06	-.12	-.06	-.27	-.22	.00	.05	.33	-1.10	-1.25	.10	-.36	.22	
France	-.02	-.02	-.03	-.15	-.05	.07	.19	.60	-.71	-.78	-.02	-.11	.15	
Germany	.04	.09	-.02	-.07	-.03	-.01	.08	.42	-1.06	-1.20	.04	.05	.05	
Italy	.01	.06	-.09	-.25	.00	.08	.08	.38	-.78	-.87	-.03	-.18	.04	
Netherlands	-.05	-.09	-.03	-.14	-.15	-.06	.07	.39	-.88	-.98	.11	-.09	.17	
Norway	-.10	-.12	-.16	-.38	-.11	-.02	.06	.28	-1.76	-1.89	-.08	-.27	.29	
Sweden	-.02	-.05	-.08	-.34	.08	-.07	.09	.32	-1.07	-1.28	-.08	-.46	.18	
Switzerland	-.01	-.06	-.04	-.23	-.04	-.04	.12	.42	-1.01	-1.15	.01	-.02	.15	
United Kingdom	.03	.08	-.08	-.37	-.11	.01	.05	.14	-1.00	-1.37	.06	-.01	.04	
Finland	.03	.09	-.11	-.32	-.01	.01	.01	.22	-1.12	-1.38	-.07	-.22	.01	-

Country	Consumption		Investment		Long-term interest rate		Export price		Exports		Balance of payments[a]	
	2	6	2	6	2	6	2	6	2	6	2	
US	.10	.24	.09	.27	-.02	-.04	-.37	-.62	-.10	-.39	456.514	177
Canada	.02	.10	-.00	.04	-.04	-.06	-.54	-.76	.18	.48	44.177	39
Japan	-.63	-1.88	-.03	-.56	.00	.00	.21	.78	.24	.55	-437.133	-204
Austria	-.00	.04	.00	.00	.00	.00	-.64	-.77	.08	.18	.124	
Belgium	-.12	-.12	.00	-.06	-.05	-.06	-.88	-1.02	.11	.23	-.103	
Denmark	-.03	-.15	-.00	-.05	-.05	-.04	-1.18	-1.38	.08	.13	-.020	-
France	-.01	-.01	.00	-.01	-.01	.02	-1.03	-1.33	.09	.18	-.351	-
Germany	.03	.11	.00	.08	-.01	-.01	-.68	-.87	.13	.20	.278	
Italy	.00	.02	.00	.02	.00	.03	-.92	-1.23	.10	.25	-1.880	-31
Netherlands	-.04	-.14	.00	-.06	-.02	-.03	-1.08	-1.19	.12	.24	-.093	-
Norway	-.06	-.10	.00	-.11	-.01	-.01	-1.64	-1.92	.09	.21	.059	
Sweden	-.01	-.02	.00	-.07	-.02	-.03	-.97	-1.35	.12	.18	.015	-
Switzerland	.01	.01	.00	-.09	-.02	-.03	-.48	-.70	.06	.09	.036	
United Kingdom	.02	.09	.01	.05	-.03	-.01	-.87	-1.26	.11	.22	17.649	1
Finland	.01	.05	.00	.06	.00	.00	-1.48	-1.92	.10	.18	-15.600	-1

Note: a. Change is absolute change, not percentage change, in units of local currency.

question is how the properties of the model compare to those of other models. It is difficult to make these comparisons because experiments across models generally differ, but some multiplier results for other multicountry econometric models are presented in Fair (1979b, tables 1 and 2) that provide a rough basis of comparison for the results in Table 9-7. In general, the present income multipliers are smaller and the price multipliers are larger than those of the other models. This result is as expected, because the other models are primarily trade multiplier models and thus have weak or nonexistent price multiplier and interest rate effects.

TABLE 9-17. Percentage change in the variable after two and six quarters by a sustained 50 percent increase in the price of exports of the oil-exporting countries (initial change in 1976 I)

untry	Real GNP 2	Real GNP 6	GNP deflator 2	GNP deflator 6	Short-term interest rate 2	Short-term interest rate 6	Exchange rate 2	Exchange rate 6	Import price 2	Import price 6	Money supply 2	Money supply 6	Imports 2	Imports 6
	-.46	-1.10	.66	1.60	.39	.16	—	—	10.22	12.54	.74	.95	-1.92	-6.80
nada	-.25	-1.38	.20	.42	.80	.71	-.25	-1.03	3.69	3.77	-1.02	-2.77	-.89	-4.43
pan	-.23	-.55	.77	1.96	1.75	1.28	-1.18	-2.74	15.21	14.26	-.68	-1.17	-2.60	-7.48
stria	.05	.06	.34	.99	.23	.37	-.39	-2.43	2.49	2.89	-.00	-.00	-.65	-1.57
lgium	.02	-.02	.13	.51	.28	-.02	-.35	-2.06	1.79	3.13	-.01	-.03	-.76	-1.72
nmark	.03	.30	.13	.66	.91	1.28	-.27	-1.93	1.96	4.09	-.67	-.56	-.74	-2.56
ance	.11	-.01	.21	1.01	.63	.13	-.90	-2.94	4.73	3.91	.12	.46	-.93	-1.32
rmany	-.22	-.62	.08	.17	.24	.15	-.41	-2.45	4.41	3.99	-.29	-.76	-.27	-1.51
aly	-.05	.18	.92	2.79	1.45	1.98	-.01	-.55	7.83	9.95	-.65	-.60	-.82	-2.48
therlands	.27	-.57	.17	.74	1.07	.05	-.36	-2.27	5.87	5.18	-.83	.02	-1.10	-2.44
rway	.08	.48	.26	.81	.38	.14	-.26	-1.69	3.39	3.79	.09	.60	-.73	-2.51
eden	-.01	-.20	.17	.74	.42	.52	-.63	-3.53	3.19	2.40	.13	.68	-.65	-1.73
itzerland	-.13	-.20	.02	.14	.08	-.01	-.65	-3.30	1.26	1.24	-.05	-.08	-.46	-1.06
ited Kingdom	-.21	-.68	.51	2.32	1.06	-.88	-.16	-.27	6.74	7.46	-.75	.52	-.45	-2.41
nland	-.11	-.28	.19	.70	.01	-.05	-.04	-1.33	2.20	3.79	.06	.36	-.20	-1.04

untry	Consumption 2	Consumption 6	Investment 2	Investment 6	Long-term interest rate 2	Long-term interest rate 6	Export price 2	Export price 6	Exports 2	Exports 6	Balance of payments[a] 2	Balance of payments[a] 6
	-.60	-1.46	-.68	-2.35	.12	.16	.70	2.11	-.68	-1.21	-3291.746	-2506.534
nada	-.21	-1.06	-.03	-.54	.29	.47	.44	1.35	-1.86	-6.59	-544.729	-654.937
an	.73	-1.75	-.04	-.77	.00	.00	.86	2.50	-.71	-1.19	-722.171	-372.842
tria	-.11	-.29	.00	.00	.00	.00	.36	.79	-.43	-1.05	-1.197	-1.106
gium	-.00	-.26	.00	-.03	.06	.06	.38	.97	-.74	-1.43	-5.575	-8.369
mark	-.05	-.01	-.00	.05	.23	.64	.61	1.82	-.68	-1.85	-.266	-.360
nce	.04	-.07	.00	.05	.14	.15	.65	2.56	-.56	-1.20	-3.475	-1.254
many	-.18	-.85	.00	-.49	.06	.10	.42	1.50	-.71	-1.11	-3.098	-1.618
ly	-.17	-.40	.00	.00	.40	1.05	.96	3.31	-.57	-.36	-716.023	-598.857
herlands	.04	-1.75	.00	.11	.17	.15	.47	1.09	-.56	-1.35	-1.634	-1.116
way	-.01	.27	.00	.13	.06	.11	.83	2.40	-.60	-2.26	-.520	-.308
den	-.02	-.26	.00	-.07	.09	.21	.65	2.51	-.63	-1.76	-.630	-.002
tzerland	-.11	-.29	-.05	-.45	.04	.01	.29	1.12	-.63	-.85	-.111	.044
ted Kingdom	-.30	-1.67	-.04	-.50	.35	-.21	.78	3.18	-.59	-.62	-596.329	-339.250
land	-.04	-.26	.00	-.21	.00	.00	.95	3.62	-.52	-1.27	-116.597	-67.358

e: a. Change is absolute change, not percentage change, in units of local currency.

United States Spending Increase: Flexible Exchange Rate Period (Table 9-8)

The results in Table 9-8 are for the flexible exchange rate period. One key difference between the fixed and flexible rate periods is that in the latter the U.S. interest rate has smaller direct effects on other countries' interest rates. The changes in the other countries' interest rates after two quarters are generally smaller in Table 9-8 than in Table 9-7. This means that there is less initial offset to the trade multiplier effect from higher interest rates in the flexible rate period.

There are four main effects of the U.S. spending increase on the exchange rates, three negative and one positive. The spending increase raised U.S. output and prices relative to those of the other countries, both of which have a negative effect on other countries' exchange rates (an appreciation). The U.S. balance of payments fell relative to those of the other countries (the balance of payments of other countries generally rose), and this also has a negative effect on exchange rates. The positive effect is the interest rate effect. The U.S. short-term interest rate rose relative to other countries' rates, and this has a positive effect on exchange rates (a depreciation). As can be seen in Table 9-8, the net effect is usually negative. Only for the two-quarter-ahead results for Canada and Sweden is the net effect positive (the interest rate effect dominating).

The price of exports of most countries increased. This is the price multiplier effect from the initial increase in U.S. prices. Exports for some countries increased and for other countries decreased. Whether exports for a particular country increase or decrease depends on the *relative* change in the country's export price (the trade share equations). The balance of payments for a number of countries fell. This may at first glance seem puzzling, since the J-curve effect that was discussed earlier implies that an appreciation should initially increase the balance of payments. What should be remembered, however, is that although almost all currencies appreciated relative to the dollar, they obviously did not all appreciate relative to each other. If a country's currency appreciated relative to the dollar but depreciated relative to most of its other trading partners, then its currency has effectively depreciated rather than appreciated, which will have an initial negative effect on the balance of payments.

The price of imports of most countries increased because of the general increase in export prices. For two countries, however, France and the United Kingdom, the change in import prices was negative after six quarters. After six quarters, the United Kingdom's currency had appreciated relative to all others and France's currency had appreciated relative to all others except the United Kingdom's. Appreciation has, other things being equal, a negative effect on the price of imports, and in these two cases it was large enough to dominate the positive effect from the general increase in export prices.

GNP for some countries was lower after two and/or six quarters. The three main things that can cause this are (1) an increase in the interest rates RS and RB in the country, (2) a decrease in exports, and (3) a decrease in the balance of payments. (A decrease in the balance of payments has a negative effect on GNP through the wealth effects.) One or more of these effects are operating for countries that experienced a fall in GNP. With respect to the GNP deflator, there are two main effects operating on it, one through the price of imports and one through GNP. Given that the effects on these last two variables are not the same across countries, one would not expect the effect on the GNP deflator to be the same across countries, and it is in fact not: for some countries the GNP deflator is higher and for some it is lower.

The results at the bottom of Table 9-8 are for the US model alone. In this case the rest of the world is exogenous—in particular, exports and the price of imports are exogenous. One of the main differences in the results is that the increase in the GNP deflator is less for the US model alone. In the complete model the U.S. price of imports rose because of the depreciation of the dollar and the general increase in export prices, which had a positive effect on the GNP deflator. This effect is absent for the US model alone. Another main difference is that the fall in the balance of payments after six quarters is less for the US model alone. This is again due primarily to the fact that the price of imports rose in the complete model. The properties of the US model regarding the change in GNP are not sensitive to the treatment of the rest of the world: the GNP changes are almost identical in the two cases.

United States Interest Rate Increase (Table 9-9)

For this experiment, the U.S. interest rate reaction function is dropped and the U.S. interest rate is taken to be exogenous. The results of an increase in the U.S. interest rate are presented in Table 9-9. This increase lowered U.S. income and imports and led to a general contraction in world income and exports (trade multiplier effect).

The interest rate increase also led to a depreciation of the other countries' exchange rates. The depreciation of the German exchange rate after six quarters, for example, was 1.93 percent. For some countries, such as Japan and Sweden, the depreciation was large enough to lead to an increase in their import prices and then to their GNP deflators. The U.S. interest rate increase thus led for some countries to an increase in their inflation rates through the depreciation of their exchange rates.

The balance of payments of some countries (other than the United States) increased. In these cases the change in export revenue (export price times exports) was greater than the change in import costs (import price times imports). Exports fell for all countries, and except for the two-quarter-ahead results for Austria, export prices also fell. In almost all cases imports fell, and in most cases import prices fell.

The results at the bottom of Table 9-9 are for the US model alone. The fall in the U.S. GNP deflator is less in this case because there is no negative effect from a fall in import prices. The differences in the effects on GNP are again quite small.

German Spending Increase (Table 9-10)

This experiment corresponds to an increase in German government spending on German goods. It led to a worldwide increase in exports and income. The increase in German income led to an increase in the German GNP deflator. This increase and the increase in income led to a fairly large increase in the interest rate through the reaction function (1.65 percentage points after six quarters). This increase had a negative effect on the exchange rate, but it was more than offset by the positive price, output, and balance of payments effects: the German exchange rate depreciated. The German exchange rate has a positive effect on the exchange rates of the other European countries, and this resulted in a depreciation of the other European rates.

The Canadian and Japanese exchange rates, which are not tied to the German rate, changed very little. This means that these two rates, along with the U.S. exchange rate, appreciated relative to the European rates. This led to a fall in the import prices of Canada, Japan, and the United States, which led to a fall in their GNP deflators. The German expansion thus led to a fall in prices for some countries because of the exchange rate effect on prices.

German Interest Rate Increase (Table 9-11)

For this experiment, the German interest rate reaction function was dropped and the German interest rate was taken to be exogenous. The results of an increase in the German rate are presented in Table 9-11. This increase lowered German income and imports and led to a general contraction in world exports and income.

The relative increase in the German interest rate and balance of payments led to an appreciation of the mark, which in turn led to an appreciation of the other European currencies. The GNP deflator for Germany was lower because of the appreciation and the fall in income. Contrary to the case for the other countries, GNP for Norway rose. The Norwegian currency appreciated relative to the dollar but depreciated relative to the most European currencies, which resulted in an increase in Norway's price of imports. This led to a substitution away from imported goods that was large enough to lead to a net increase in GNP.

German Exchange Rate Increase (Table 9-12)

For this experiment, the German exchange rate reaction function was dropped and the German exchange rate was taken to be exogenous. The results in Table 9-12 are for an increase in the exchange rate of 10 percent (a depreciation).

It was argued earlier that the initial effect of a depreciation on the balance of payments is likely to be negative, and this is the case for Germany in Table 9-12, even after six quarters. The depreciation led to a decrease in German GNP. As already noted, the effect of a depreciation on GNP can go either way. In this case the negative effects from the increase in the interest rates and the fall in the balance of payments more than offset the positive effects from the rise in the price of imports and the relative fall in the price of exports. German exports actually decreased slightly in response to the depreciation, which seems unusual. There are two main reasons for this. The first is that the German depreciation is not large relative to the other European countries because the other countries' exchange rates are fairly closely tied to the German rate. This means that the German price of exports does not fall very much relative to the others, and in fact for some countries the price of exports fell more than it did for Germany. As a result, the German gain in trade shares through the trade share equations is not very large. The second reason is the general contraction in world exports that resulted from the German depreciation. Even though Germany gained some trade share, the total size of the export base was less. The increase in share was small enough and the decrease in the export base large enough to lead to a slight fall in German exports.

The depreciation of the German exchange rate led to a decrease in the U.S. GNP deflator. This is due to the fall in the U.S. price of imports, which in turn is due to the general appreciation of the dollar. The Canadian and Japanese GNP deflators fell for similar reasons. This experiment also resulted in an increase in GNP for the United States, Canada, and Japan, primarily because of the decreases in the short-term interest rates in the three countries. For the United States the main reason for the decrease in the interest rate was the decrease in the GNP deflator. For Canada and Japan the main reason was the increase in the balance of payments. The main reason for the increase in the balance of payments of the two countries (as well as of the United States) was the fall in the price of imports that resulted from the general appreciation of the currencies. The exports of the three countries increased, primarily as a result of the fact that all three countries expanded and all three trade considerably with each other.

United Kingdom Spending Increase (Table 9-13)

This experiment corresponds to an increase in U.K. government spending on U.K. goods. As in the German case in Table 9-10, the increase in spending in Table 9-13 led to a worldwide increase in exports and income. The U.K. exchange rate depreciated, as did the German exchange rate in Table 9-10. The other European exchange rates appreciated relative to the dollar, although only slightly; this is due primarily to the balance-of-payments effect on the exchange rate. The European countries benefited more from the U.K. expansion than did the United States with respect to the increase in exports, and thus their balance of payments improved more. The increase in U.K. income led to an increase in U.K. imports, and the depreciation of the U.K. exchange rate led to an increase in the U.K. price of imports. Both of these factors contributed to the decrease in the U.K. balance of payments.

United Kingdom Exchange Rate Increase (Table 9-14)

For this experiment, the U.K. exchange rate reaction function was dropped and the U.K. exchange rate was taken to be exogenous. The results in Table 9-14 are for an increase in the exchange rate of 10 percent (a depreciation).

As in the German case in Table 9-12, the depreciation led to a decrease in the balance of payments and a decrease in GNP. In contrast to the German case, the effects on the other European exchange rates were slight. The depreciation led, as in the German case, to a decrease in the GNP deflator and an increase in GNP for the United States, Canada, and Japan, although the effects in the U.K. case are smaller.

Japanese Spending Increase (Table 9-15)

This experiment corresponds to an increase in Japanese government spending on Japanese goods. As in the German and U.K. cases, the exchange rate depreciated in response to the expansion and the balance of payments decreased. The increase in imports of Japan in Table 9-15 is less than the increase in imports of Germany in Table 9-10 and of the United Kingdom in Table 9-13, which resulted in smaller effects on the rest of the world in Table 9-15.

Japanese Exchange Rate Increase (Table 9-16)

For this experiment, the Japanese exchange rate reaction function was dropped and the Japanese exchange rate was taken to be exogenous. The results in Table 9-16 are for an increase in the exchange rate of 10 percent (a depreciation).

In this case, as in the German and U.K. cases, the depreciation led to a decrease in the balance of payments and a decrease in GNP. The European exchange rates depreciated relative to the dollar, primarily because the U.S. balance of payments benefited more from the Japanese depreciation than did the European balance of payments. The United States benefited more because the price of imports fell more; the price of imports fell more because the United States is a larger trading partner of Japan. U.S. GNP was higher and the U.S. GNP deflator was lower as a result of the Japanese depreciation.

Increase in the Price of Exports of the Oil-Exporting Countries (Table 9-17)

The oil-exporting countries in the model are Algeria, Indonesia, Iran, Iraq, Kuwait, Libya, Nigeria, Saudi Arabia, United Arab Emirates, and Venezuela. The price of exports is exogenous for these countries. The experiment corresponded to a 50-percent increase in the price of exports of all these countries.

This experiment approaches, if not exceeds, the aggregation limits of the model. There is no specific treatment of oil in the model other than the fact that almost all of the exports of the oil-exporting countries are oil. If the ability of countries to substitute away from oil is less than it is for the other goods, the model has not adequately captured the effects of oil price changes. In particular, the degree of substitution implicit in the trade-share equations may be too high for oil. The trade share equations were thus not used for this experiment, and the shares were taken to be exogenous. This may underestimate the degree of substitution possible, but it is probably closer to the truth than is the other case. At any rate, because of this problem, the results of this experiment should be interpreted with considerable caution.

Different countries were affected quite differently in this experiment. The exchange rates of all countries appreciated relative to the dollar. This is due in large part to the generally larger decrease in the U.S. balance of payments relative to the decreases for the other countries. The price of imports rose for most countries, as expected, although part of the increase that would otherwise have occurred was offset by the appreciation of the exchange rates. The increase in import prices led to an increase in the GNP deflators, and thus there was a general worldwide increase in inflation.

GNP fell for many countries. This is due in part to the increase in the interest rate in many countries (because of the increase in inflation and the decrease in the balance of payments) and in part to the decrease in net foreign assets (because of the decrease in the balance of payments). There was, in other words, both a negative interest rate effect and a negative asset effect on GNP. Imports fell for all countries because of the increase in the price of imports relative to the GNP deflator. For some countries this substitution effect was large enough to lead to an increase in GNP.

Although this is not shown in the table, the balance of payments of the oil-exporting countries rose substantially, as expected. This increase in net foreign assets then led to an increase in imports of the countries for which there are import equations (Libya, Nigeria, Saudi Arabia, and Venezuela). In some cases these increases were quite large. The six-quarter-ahead increases for Nigeria and Saudi Arabia, for example, were 20.6 and 57.2 percent, respectively. These increases were not, of course, large enough to offset completely the increases in the balance of payments of these countries (and thus the decreases in the balance of payments of the oil-importing countries).

9.5.3 Estimates of the Exchange Rate Effect on Inflation (Table 9-18)

The MC model can be used to estimate what will be called the "exchange rate effect" on inflation. One of the ways in which monetary and fiscal policies may affect a country's inflation rate is by first influencing its exchange rate, which in turn influences import prices, which in turn influence domestic prices. This is what is called the exchange rate effect on inflation. In order to estimate the size of this effect, one needs a model linking monetary and fiscal policies to exchange rates, exchange rates to import prices, and import prices to domestic prices; the MC model provides these links.

Exchange rates have an effect on domestic inflation in the model through their effects on import prices. The 10.0 percent depreciation of the mark in Table 9-12 resulted in an increase in the German GNP deflator of .12 percent after six quarters. For the U.K. results in Table 9-14 the increase was 2.98 percent, and for the Japanese results in Table 9-16 the increase was 1.28 percent.

The question considered in this section is how much of the change in inflation that results from a monetary or fiscal policy change can be attributed to the change in the exchange rate that results from the policy change. Estimates of this exchange rate effect on inflation are presented in Table 9-18. The results in the a rows are from the experiments discussed in Section 9.5.2. For the results in the b rows, the same experiments were performed except that all exchange rates were taken to be exogenous. Exchange rates, in other words, were assumed to be fixed. The difference in the two rows for a given

TABLE 9-18. Estimated effects of monetary and fiscal policies on inflation through their effects on exchange rates (results are for the country initiating the policy)

	US spending increase (Table 9-8)		German spending increase (Table 9-10)		UK spending increase (Table 9-13)		Japanese spending increase (Table 9-15)	
	2	6	2	6	2	6	2	6
GNP deflator:								
a	.15	.64	.20	1.18	.00	.36	.10	.65
b	.13	.49	.19	1.15	.00	.00	.08	.53
c	.13	.23	.05	.03	—	1.00	.20	.18
Price of imports:								
a	.44	1.62	.14	.34	.47	2.29	.47	1.32
b	.01	.08	.01	.10	.00	.02	.00	.03
Real GNP:								
a	1.31	1.07	1.21	1.67	1.41	1.19	1.29	2.29
b	1.31	1.08	1.20	1.63	1.39	1.25	1.29	2.28
Exchange rate:								
a			.40	1.30	.52	2.56	.49	1.38

	US interest rate increase (Table 9-9)		German interest rate increase (Table 9-11)	
	2	6	2	6
GNP deflator:				
a	-.04	-.40	-.03	-.15
b	-.00	-.22	-.00	-.05
c	1.00	.45	1.00	.67
Price of imports:				
a	-.67	-1.77	-.43	-.31
b	-.00	-.09	-.00	-.02
Real GNP:				
a	-.34	-1.13	-.11	-.16
b	-.35	-1.17	-.11	-.18
Exchange rate:				
a			-1.35	-2.68

Notes: a = Exchange rates endogenous.
b = Exchange rates exogenous.
c = (row a - row b)/row a.

quarter for the GNP deflator is an estimate of the exchange rate effect on inflation for the quarter. These differences as a percentage of the a row values are presented in the c row.

The estimates in Table 9-18 vary considerably across countries and type of experiment. Consider the c-row values for the six-quarter-ahead predictions for the spending experiments. For the United States, 23 percent of the increase in the GNP deflator that resulted from the U.S. spending increase is attributed to the exchange rate effect. With the exchange rates endogenous the increase in the GNP deflator is .64 percent, and with the exchange rates exogenous the increase is .49 percent. For Germany, only 3 percent of the increase in the GNP deflator is attributed to the exchange rate. This small number is due to the fact that the other European exchange rates are closely tied to the German rate, and therefore a depreciation of the German exchange rate of, say, 10 percent is not much of a depreciation. For the United Kingdom, all of the increase in the GNP deflator is attributed to the exchange rate. The price equation for the United Kingdom (Eq. 5, Table 4-5) does not include the demand pressure variable (it was of the wrong sign), so the U.K. GNP deflator is not directly affected by GNP changes. Therefore, the only inflation that results from the U.K. spending increase is from the exchange rate effect. Japan is similar to the United States: 18 percent of the increase in the GNP deflator is attributed to the exchange rate effect.

With respect to the interest rate experiments, the estimates after six quarters are 45 percent for the United States and 67 percent for Germany. These estimates are higher than the corresponding estimates for the spending experiments. This is as expected, since interest rate changes in general have large effects on exchange rates.

9.5.4 Summary

It is difficult to summarize the MC results because they vary considerably across countries. Theoretically there are few unambiguous effects, and the empirical results show that there are few unambiguous empirical effects either. Regarding the effects on other countries from a policy change in one country, they depend considerably on relative positions, and thus it is common to find some countries affected one way and other countries affected the other way for a given policy experiment.

A few of the unambiguous empirical effects are the following. (1) Spending increases in a given country lead to a depreciation of the country's exchange rate. The interest rate effect, which works in favor of an appreciation, is dominated by the other effects discussed above. (2) Spending increases in a given country also lead to a decrease in its balance of payments. (3) Depreciation in a given country leads to an initial fall in its balance of payments and to a fall in its GNP. (4) An increase in a country's interest rate leads to an appreciation of its currency and to a decrease in its GNP.

One obvious feature of the results is that price, interest rate, and exchange rate linkages are quantitatively quite important. There are many channels; a key one is exchange rates affecting import prices, import prices affecting domestic prices and thus export prices, and export prices affecting other countries' import prices. Interest rates affect exchange rates directly, and they are in turn affected by many other variables. Another important effect in the model is the wealth effect from changes in the balance of payments.

Another way of looking at the overall results is the observation that if the MC model is at all a good approximation of the economic linkages among countries, attempts to use very simple models (with unambiguous effects) for policy purposes are not likely to be very successful. Trade multiplier models, for example, seem likely to be quite misleading in this regard. In short, the world economy seems complicated, and insights gained from simple models may be misleading.

10 Optimal Control Analysis

10.1 Introduction

Optimal control techniques have a number of potentially important uses in macroeconometrics. Solving optimal control problems for a particular model may yield insights about the model that one would not pick up from multiplier calculations. Depending on the objective function, the solutions of optimal control problems are sometimes extreme in that they result in the predicted values being considerably away from the historical values, and this sometimes conveys new information about the properties of the model. Optimal control techniques can also be used to evaluate past policies in the light of particular objective functions. The techniques may also be useful in the long run in helping to make actual policy decisions, depending on how good an approximation to the structure of the economy models eventually become.

10.2 A Method for Solving Optimal Control Problems

10.2.1 The Method

Optimal control problems have historically been formulated in continuous time and have been looked upon as problems in choosing *functions* of time to maximize an objective function. This is particularly true in the engineering literature. Fairly advanced mathematical techniques are required to solve these problems. For discrete time models, however, which include virtually all macroeconometric models, optimal control problems can also be looked upon as problems in choosing *variables* to maximize an objective function. The number of variables to be determined is equal to the number of control variables times the number of time periods chosen for the problem. From this perspective, optimal control problems are straightforward maximization problems, and one can attempt to solve them using algorithms like the DFP algorithm discussed in Section 2.4.

Let the model be represented by (6.1), which is repeated here:

$$f_i(y_t, x_t, \alpha_i) = u_{it}, \qquad i = 1, \ldots, n. \tag{6.1}$$

The variables in the x_t vector include both exogenous and lagged endogenous variables. Among the exogenous variables are variables that are under the control of the government and variables that are not. It will be useful to redefine x_t to include only noncontrolled exogenous variables. Let z_t denote the vector of control variables, and let q_{t-1} denote the vector of all lagged endogenous variables in the model, even variables lagged more than one period. Rewrite (6.1) to include these changes:

$$(10.1) \qquad f_i(y_t, q_{t-1}, x_t, z_t, \alpha_i) = u_{it}, \qquad i = 1, \ldots, n.$$

In the following discussion the coefficients α_i are assumed to be known with certainty.

The first step in setting up an optimal control problem is to postulate an objective function. Assume that the period of interest is $t = 1, \ldots, T$. A general specification of the objective function is

$$(10.2) \qquad W = h(y_1, \ldots, y_T, x_1, \ldots, x_T, z_1, \ldots, z_T),$$

where W, a scalar, is the value of the objective function corresponding to values of y_t, x_t, and z_t $(t = 1, \ldots, T)$. In most applications the objective function is assumed to be additive across time, which means that (10.2) can be written

$$(10.3) \qquad W = \sum_{t=1}^{T} h_t(y_t, x_t, z_t),$$

where $h_t(y_t, x_t, z_t)$ is the value of the objective function for period t. The function h has a t subscript to note the fact that it may vary over time. This will be true, for example, if future periods are discounted.

The optimal control problem is to choose values of $z_1, \ldots, z_T$ so as to maximize the expected value of W in (10.2) subject to the model (10.1). Consider first the deterministic case where the error terms in (10.1) are all zero. Assume that z_t is of dimension k, so that there are kT control values to determine, and let z be the kT-component vector denoting these values: $z = (z_1, \ldots, z_T)$. For each value of z one can compute a value of W by first solving the model (10.1) for $y_1, \ldots, y_T$ and then using these values along with the values for $x_1, \ldots, x_T$ and z to compute W in (10.2). Stated this way, the optimal control problem is a problem in choosing variables (the elements of z) to maximize an *unconstrained* nonlinear function. By substitution, the constrained maximization problem is transformed into the problem of maximizing an unconstrained function of the control variables:

$$(10.4) \qquad W = \phi(z),$$

where ϕ stands for the mapping $z \rightarrow z, y_1, \ldots, y_T, x_1, \ldots, x_T \rightarrow W$. For nonlinear models it is generally not possible to express y_t explicitly in terms of z_t and x_t, which means that it is generally not possible to write W in (10.2) explicitly as a function of z and $x_1, \ldots, x_T$. Nevertheless, given values for $x_1, \ldots, x_T$, values of W can be obtained numerically for different values of z.

Given this setup, the problem can be turned over to a nonlinear maximization algorithm like DFP. For each iteration, the derivatives of ϕ with respect to the elements of z, which are needed by the algorithm, can be computed numerically. Each iteration will thus require kT function evaluations for the derivatives plus a few more for the line search. Each function evaluation requires one solution (dynamic simulation) of the model for T periods plus the computation of W in (10.2) after $y_1, \ldots, y_T$ are determined.

There is one important cost-saving feature regarding the method that should be noted. Assume that there are two control variables and that the length of the period is 30. The number of unknowns is thus 60, and therefore 60 function evaluations will have to be done per iteration to get the numerical first derivatives. In perturbing the control values to get the derivatives, one should start from the end of the control period and work backward. When the control values for period 30 are perturbed, the solution of the model for periods 1 through 29 remains unchanged from the base solution, so these calculations can be skipped. The model only needs to be resolved for period 30. Similarly, when the control values for period 29 are perturbed, the model only needs to be resolved for periods 29 and 30, and so on. This cuts the cost of computing the derivatives roughly in half.

10.2.2 Stochastic Simulation Option

Consider now the stochastic case where the error terms in (10.1) are not zero. It is possible to convert this case into the deterministic case by simply setting the error terms to their expected values (usually zero). The problem can then be solved as above. In the nonlinear case this does not lead to the exact answer because the values of W that are computed numerically in the process of solving the problem are not the expected values. In order to compute the expected values correctly, stochastic simulation would have to be done. In this case each function evaluation (that is, each evaluation of the expected value of W for a given value of z) would consist of the following.

1. A set of values of the u_{it} error terms in (10.1) would be drawn from an estimated distribution.

2. Given the values of the error terms, the model would be solved for $y_1, \ldots, y_T$ and the values of W corresponding to this solution would be computed from (10.2). Let $\tilde{W}^j$ denote this value.
3. Steps 1 and 2 would be repeated J times, where J is the number of trials.
4. Given the J values of $\tilde{W}^j$ $(j = 1, \ldots, J)$, the expected value of W would be taken to be the mean of these values.

$$(10.4) \qquad \tilde{\bar{W}} = \frac{1}{J} \sum_{j=1}^{J} \tilde{W}^j.$$

This procedure increases the cost of solving the control problem by roughly a factor of J, since the maximization algorithm spends most of its time doing function evaluations. It is probably not worth the extra cost for most applications. It was seen in Chapter 7 that the bias in predicting the endogenous variables that results from using deterministic rather than stochastic simulation seems to be small for most models, and thus the bias in computing the expected value of W is also likely to be small. At any rate, the stochastic simulation option is always open if computer time is no constraint.

10.2.3 Comparison of the Method to Other Procedures

There are two main advantages of the method just described. One is that it can handle very general objective functions; the objective function need not be quadratic and need not even be additive across time. The second is that the method is extremely easy to use. Assuming that a program is available for solving the model, which is almost always the case, all that needs to be supplied is a subroutine that computes W in (10.2) for a given set of RHS values. In a program that is structured like the Fair-Parke program in Appendix C, which allows one to move automatically from estimation to solution, this is an important advantage. Given a subroutine that computes W, one can move automatically from estimation to solving control problems. There are thus virtually no extra setup costs involved in using the method.

The method described above is "open-loop." The alternative type of method is "closed-loop," where closed-loop feedback control equations are derived. A feedback control equation is one that relates the current value of a control variable to the lagged values of the endogenous variables. In the case of a linear model and a quadratic objective function, it is relatively easy to compute the feedback equations. (Chow 1975 is a good reference for this.) One of the advantages of obtaining feedback equations is that they can be used to compute the optimal control values for all future periods without having to solve any further problems. Given the realizations of the endogenous variables for a given period, the optimal control values for the next period can simply be computed from the feedback equations. For open-loop methods, on the other hand, a new optimization problem has to be solved after each period's realization. Consider, for example, the problem presented above, where optimal values for periods 1 through T were computed. If this solution were used in practice, the optimal values for period 1 would be used, but the values for periods 2 through T would not. The latter values are needed only to compute the period 1 values. After the realization in period 1, where in general the endogenous variable values will not equal the values that were expected at the time the control problem was solved, a new control problem would have to be solved to get the optimal values for period 2.

In the linear-quadratic case, open-loop methods with reoptimization after each realization and closed-loop methods lead to the same control values being used each period. This is the certainty equivalence theorem. In the general nonlinear case, analytic expressions for the feedback equations are not available, so there is no known closed-loop solution. An interesting question is whether the current open-loop method with stochastic simulation to eliminate the bias in computing the expected value of W and with reoptimization after each realization leads to the correct answer aside from errors introduced by the stochastic simulation procedure. The answer is no. Maximizing the expected value of W simultaneously with respect to $z_1, \ldots, z_T$ fails to account for the fact that the optimal strategy is sequential rather than simultaneous. (See Chow 1975, pp. 295–296, for a discussion of this.) This is a subtle point, and it is an open question whether it is important quantitatively.

Chow (1975, chap. 9) has proposed an alternative method for solving optimal control problems in the nonlinear case. He suggests obtaining a linear approximation to the model and a quadratic approximation to the objective function and then solving the resulting linear-quadratic problem by standard methods. One then iterates on the approximations. This method also does not lead to the correct answer, although for a different reason than in the case of the open-loop method. The linearization of the model must be around the solution path of the deterministic control problem (since the future values of the error terms are not known), and therefore the linearization is not quite right. The computed optimal values are thus not truly optimal. The method has the advantage that feedback equations are obtained, although this is not as much of an advantage as it might at first appear. Even given the feedback equations, one may want to reoptimize after the realization for a given period because the linearization will change. One will not get the same optimal values for the period using the old feedback equations as one would get by reoptimizing based on an updated linearization.

From a computational point of view, Chow's method is somewhat messy because of the linear approximations. These approximations require considerable storage space for the matrices, and it is not as easy to adjust for changes in the model because for each adjustment the linearization must also be adjusted. In addition, if the model is large, a large matrix must be inverted in calculating the optimal values. An advantage of the method over the open-loop method is that the computational costs only increase linearly in T, the length of the control period, whereas they increase roughly as the square of T for the open-loop method. (The cost for the open-loop method increases as the square of T because an increase in T increases both the number of control values to determine and the cost of solving the model for a given function evaluation.) There are thus likely to be some applications for which Chow's method is better and some for which the open-loop method is better. Whether one will end up dominating for most applications remains to be seen.

The discussion so far has been based on the assumption that the coefficients are known with certainty. The question of how to handle coefficient uncertainty in the nonlinear case is difficult, and no exact solutions are available. This issue will be not be explored here; the interested reader is referred to Chow (1976), who presents an approximate solution.

The discussion so far has also been based on the assumption that the model is not a rational expectations model. The solution of optimal control problems for rational expectations models is discussed in Section 11.5.

10.2.4 Steps that a Policymaker Would Follow

For purposes of the discussion in the next section, it will be useful to review the steps that a policymaker would follow if he or she were setting policies by solving control problems. Assume that a policy decision is to be made at the beginning of period 1 and that at this time data for period 0 and all prior periods are available. Given the model (10.1) and, say, a horizon of length T, the steps that could be followed are:

1. Estimate the coefficients of the model over the sample period ending in 0.
2. Form expectations of the exogenous variables (other than the control variables) for periods 1 through T.
3. Form expectations of the values of the error terms for periods 1 through T.

4. Decide on the objective function (10.2) to be maximized.
5. Using some maximization algorithm (like DFP), maximize (10.2) with respect to $z_1, z_2, \ldots, z_T$. Let $z_1^*, z_2^*, \ldots, z_T^*$ denote the optimum values.
6. Use z_1^* as the vector of policy values for period 1.

After the values for period 1 have been realized, steps 1–6 can be repeated for period 2. As noted in Section 10.2.3, the optimal value of z_2 that is computed at this time is not in general equal to z_2^* in step 5. The actual values of the endogenous variables for period 1 are in general different from what they were predicted to be, and therefore the initial conditions for the problem beginning in period 2 are different from what the solution at the beginning of period 1 implied that they would be. Also, the coefficient estimates will have changed because of the reestimation through period 1. The actual values of the exogenous variables for period 1 will in general be different from what they were expected to be, and the expectations for periods 2 and beyond are likely to have changed.

If stochastic simulation is used, step 3 is replaced by a step in which the distribution of the error terms is chosen. This distribution is then used in step 5 in the manner discussed in Section 10.2.2.

If Chow's procedure is used to solve the control problem, step 5 is replaced with this procedure. It is still necessary in this case to form expectations of the error terms for periods 1 through T (step 3), because this is needed for the linearization. Also, as noted in Section 10.2.3, steps 1 through 6 would be performed again after the values for period 1 have taken place because these values affect the linearization and thus the feedback equations. The different coefficient estimates and exogenous variable values will also affect the linearization.

The reestimation of the model in step 1 means that the coefficient estimates are always based on the latest available data. This does not mean, however, that by doing this one has accounted for coefficient uncertainty in solving the optimal control problem. Nothing in this procedure informs the method in step 5 that the coefficient estimates are to be reestimated in the future, and so this information is not taken into account.

10.3 Use of Optimal Control Analysis to Measure the Performance of Policymakers

It is common practice in political discussions to hold policymakers accountable for the state of the economy that existed during their time in power.

Policymakers are generally blamed for high unemployment, low real growth, and high inflation rates during their time in power and praised for the opposite. Although at first glance this may seem to be a reasonable way of evaluating the economic performances of policymakers, there are at least two serious problems with it. The first is that this kind of evaluation does not take into account possible differences in the degree of difficulty of controlling the economy in different periods. The economy may be more difficult to control at one time than another either because of more unfavorable values of the uncontrolled exogenous variables or because of a more unfavorable initial state of the economy (or both). The second problem with the evaluation is that it ignores the effects of a policymaker's actions on the state of the economy beyond its time in power. If, for example, a policymaker strongly stimulates the economy in the year of an election, in, say, the belief that this might improve its chances of staying in power, most of the inflationary effects of this policy might not be felt until after the election. Any evaluation of performance that was concerned only with the time before the election would not, of course, pick up these effects.

A measure of performance is proposed in this section that takes account of these problems. It is based on the solutions of optimal control problems. This performance measure requires that a welfare function be postulated and that the economy be represented by an econometric model. The welfare function must be additive across time. It will be convenient to take the objective function to be a loss function to be minimized rather than a welfare function to be maximized.

Let P denote either the entire period that policymaker p is in power or some subset of this period. The measure, denoted M, is as follows (low values of M are good):

(10.5) M = expected loss in P given p's actual behavior
− expected loss in P if p had behaved optimally
+ expected loss beyond P given p's actual behavior and given optimal behavior of future policymakers
− expected loss beyond P if p had behaved optimally and given optimal behavior of future policymakers
$= a - b + c - d.$

The term $a - b$ is the expected loss that could have been avoided during P if p had behaved optimally. The term $c - d$ is the potential expected loss to future policymakers from the fact that p did not behave optimally. If P is a subset of the entire period that p is in power, then "future policymakers" in the definition above may include p.

M takes account of the two problems mentioned earlier. If the economy is difficult to control for p, then b will be large, which will offset more than otherwise a large value of a. The term $c - d$ measures the effects of p's policies on the economy beyond period P, where these effects are measured under the assumption that future policymakers behave optimally.

The Computation of M

If a policymaker follows steps 1–6 in Section 10.2.4, he or she will be said to behave optimally. Remember, however, that the policy choice z_1^* in step 6 is not truly optimal because (1) the solution method is open-loop, (2) coefficient uncertainty has not been taken into account, and (3) deterministic rather than stochastic simulation has been used to compute the expected value of the objective function. As in (10.3), let $h_t(y_t, x_t, z_t)$ denote the objective function for period t, but now assume that it is a loss function rather than a welfare function. The loss function for the control problem is thus $\Sigma_{t=1}^{T} h_t(y_t, x_t, z_t)$.

In order to compute M, the period beyond P must be specified. Let 1 be the first period of P, and let P' be the length of P. The period beyond P will be assumed to run from $P' + 1$ to T'. The symbol T will continue to be used to denote the length of the horizon for the control problem. T is assumed to be larger than T'. It should be a number that is large enough so that further increases in T have a negligible effect on the optimal values for the first period of the horizon. Since only the values for the first period ever get used, the only criterion that needs to be used in deciding on the length of the horizon is the effect of this choice on the first-period values.

The procedure for computing M is as follows. (Steps 1–6 always refer to the steps in Section 10.2.4)

(i) Perform steps 1–6 for period 1. This requires choosing values for the expectations of the exogenous variables and error terms for periods 1 through T. These values should be estimates of what the policymaker actually knew at the beginning of period 1. The optimal values $z_1^*, z_2^*, \ldots, z_T^*$ minimize the expected value of $\Sigma_{t=1}^{T} h_t(y_t, x_t, z_t)$, where the expected value is computed by means of deterministic simulation. Let $\hat{h}_1^*$ denote the first term in the optimal sum, let x_1^e denote the values chosen for the expectations of the exogenous variables for period 1, and let u_1^e denote the values chosen for the expectations of the error terms for period 1. $\hat{h}_1^*$ is computed by solving the model for period 1 using z_1^*, x_1^e, u_1^e, and q_0 and then using these solution values (denoted $\hat{y}_1^*$) plus x_1^e and z_1^* to compute $\hat{h}_1^*$. The vector q_0 is the vector of initial conditions. $\hat{h}_1^*$ is h_1 evaluated at $\hat{y}_1^*$, x_1^e, and z_1^*. It is the part of b in (10.5) that corresponds to period 1.

(ii) Let z_1 denote the actual value of the control vector for period 1. Given z_1, x_1^e, u_1^e, and q_0, solve the model for period 1 and then use these solution values (denoted $\hat{y}_1$) plus x_1^e and z_1 to compute the value of the loss function for period 1 (denoted $\hat{h}_1$). $\hat{h}_1$ is h_1 evaluted at $\hat{y}_1$, x_1^e, and z_1. It is the part of a in (10.5) that corresponds to period 1.

(iii) Let u_1 denote the actual values of the error terms for period 1, and let x_1 denote the actual values of the exogenous variables for period 1. Given z_1^*, x_1, u_1, and q_0, solve the model for period 1. These solution values (denoted y_1^*) are estimates of what would have been observed in period 1 had the policy-maker behaved optimally. Let q_1^* denote the vector that includes y_1^*. (If there are lagged control variables in the model, then these variables should also be in q_{t-1} in Eq. 10.1. In this case z_1^* is in q_1^*.)

(iv) Perform steps 1–6 for period 2 using q_1^* as the vector of initial conditions. This will in general require choosing new values for the expectations of the exogenous variables. Given z_2^*, x_2^e, u_2^e, and q_1^*, solve the model for $\hat{y}_2^*$ and then compute $\hat{h}_2^*$. $\hat{h}_2^*$ is the part of b in (10.5) that corresponds to period 2.

(v) Given z_2, x_2^e, u_2^e, and q_1, solve the model for period 2 and then compute $\hat{h}_2$. q_1 is the vector of actual values of the initial conditions. $\hat{h}_2$ is the part of a in (10.5) that corresponds to period 2.

(vi) Repeat steps (iii), (iv), and (v) for periods 3 thrugh P'.

(vii) a in (10.5) is equal to $\Sigma_{t=1}^{P'} \hat{h}_t$, and b is equal to $\Sigma_{t=1}^{P'} \hat{h}_t^*$.

(viii) Given the optimal values for period P' from step (vi), $z_{P'}^*$, and given $x_{P'}$, $u_{P'}$, and $q_{P'-1}^*$, solve the model for period P'. Denote the solution values $y_{P'}^*$, and let $q_{P'}^*$ denote the vector that includes $y_{P'}^*$.

(ix) Perform steps 1–6 for period $P' + 1$ using $q_{P'}^*$ as the vector of initial conditions. Given $z_{P'+1}^*$, $x_{P'+1}^e$, $u_{P'+1}^e$, and $q_{P'}^*$, solve the model for $\hat{y}_{P'+1}^*$ and then compute $\hat{h}_{P'+1}^*$. $\hat{h}_{P'+1}^*$ is the part of d in (10.5) that corresponds to period $P' + 1$. This step is the same as step (iv) except for a different period.

(x) Repeat step (viii) for period $P' + 1$, and then repeat step (ix) for period $P' + 2$. Keep repeating through period T'. d in (10.5) is equal to $\Sigma_{t=P'+1}^{T'} \hat{h}_t^*$.

(xi) Perform steps 1–6 for period $P' + 1$ using the actual value of $q_{P'}$ as the vector of initial conditions. To distinguish these optimal values from the optimal values computed in step (ix), let $z_{P'+1}^{**}$ rather than $z_{P'+1}^*$ denote them. Given $z_{P'+1}^{**}$, $x_{P'+1}^e$, $u_{P'+1}^e$, and $q_{P'}$, solve the model for $\hat{y}_{P'+1}^{**}$ and then compute $\hat{h}_{P'+1}^{**}$. $\hat{h}_{P'+1}^{**}$ is the part of c in (10.5) that corresponds to period $P' + 1$.

(xii) Given $z_{P'+1}^{**}$, $x_{P'+1}$, $u_{P'+1}$, and $q_{P'}$, solve the model for period $P' + 1$. Denote the solution values $y_{P'+1}^{**}$, and let $q_{P'+1}^{**}$ denote the vector that includes $y_{P'+1}^{**}$.

(xiii) Perform steps 1–6 for period $P' + 2$ using $q^{**}_{P'+1}$ as the vector of initial conditions. Given $z^{**}_{P'+2}$, $x^{e}_{P'+2}$, $u^{e}_{P'+2}$, and $q^{**}_{P'+1}$, solve the model for $\hat{y}^{**}_{P'+2}$ and then compute $\hat{h}^{**}_{P'+2}$.

(xiv) Repeat step (xii) for period $P' + 2$, where $q^{**}_{P'+1}$ is used as the vector of initial conditions, and then repeat (xiii) for period $P' + 3$. Keep repeating through period T'. c in (10.5) is equal to $\Sigma^{T'}_{t=P'+1} \hat{h}^{**}_{t}$.

This completes the computational steps. M is equal to $a - b + c - d$, where a and b are defined in step (vii), c is defined in step (xiv), and d is defined in step (x). The only difference between the steps involved in computing c and those involved in computing d is that for d the series of control problems begins from the initial conditions that would have prevailed had optimal policies been followed during P, whereas for c the series of control problems begins from the initial conditions that actually prevailed.

It is clear that the work involved in computing M is substantial. Assume, for example, that one is interested in measuring the performance of a presidential administration in the United States during its four-year period in office. If the model is quarterly, then 16 control problems need to be solved to compute b in (10.5). If the period beyond P is taken to be, say, 24 quarters, then 24 control problems need to be solved to compute c and 24 need to be solved to compute d. Computing M thus involves solving $16 + 24 + 24 = 64$ control problems, each of length T, where T should probably be some number like 40 (a 10-year horizon). Each of the 16 problems and each pair of the 24 problems require choosing values of the expectations of the exogenous variables. Even though this is a substantial amount of work, it is not completely out of the question. It might not be unreasonable to use autoregressive equations to generate the expectations of at least some of the exogenous variables, which would mechanize this part of the problem. The cost then would merely be the computer time to solve the 64 control problems. Although it is not feasible to do this for the results in this book, it should be possible in the future with faster and cheaper computers.

Since the first step of steps 1–6 is to estimate the coefficients over the latest available data, computing M also requires that the model be estimated a number of times. The model was estimated a number of times for the results in Chapter 8, and this is not that expensive. Note with respect to steps (iv), (ix), (xi), and (xiii) that the estimation must be over the actual data, not the data that would have existed had the policymaker behaved optimally. This is one unavoidable difference between what a policymaker could do in practice and what can be done after the fact in measuring performance. Note also that reestimation can occur right before steps (iii), (viii), (x), and (xii) rather than right after them. In other words, the model can be reestimated before the "actual" values of the error terms are computed. If this were done, u_1 in step (iii) would be based on the model estimated through period 1 rather than through period 0.

The problem of data revisions that was discussed in Section 8.2 regarding the evaluation of ex ante forecasts is also a problem here. A policymaker must make decisions on the basis of preliminary data, not the latest revised data that are generally used in econometric work. One possible solution to this would be to construct separate data sets for each starting point (that is, for the solution of each control problem), where each data set contains the preliminary data that were used as initial conditions and estimated data for the future periods that are consistent with the preliminary data. This is, however, a very tedious task, and it is unlikely to be done very often in practice. Most often it will merely be assumed that the latest revised data are good approximations to the data that the policymakers actually used.

Comparison to Chow's Measure

Chow (1978) has proposed a measure of performance that is almost identical to M if the model is linear and P consists of only one period. If the length of P is greater than one period, the two measures differ more. For P length 2, Chow's measure in words is as follows.

(10.6) M' = expected loss in period 1 given p's actual behavior in period 1
- − expected loss in period 1 if p had behaved optimally in period 1
- + expected loss in periods 2 and beyond given p's actual behavior in period 1 and given optimal behavior in periods 2 and beyond
- − expected loss in periods 2 and beyond if p had behaved optimally in period 1 and given optimal behavior in periods 2 and beyond
- + expected loss in period 2 given p's actual behavior in periods 1 and 2
- − expected loss in period 2 if p had behaved optimally in period 2 but not in period 1
- + expected loss in periods 3 and beyond given p's actual behavior in periods 1 and 2 and given optimal behavior in periods 3 and beyond

— expected loss in periods 3 and beyond if p had behaved optimally in period 2 but not in period 1 and given optimal behavior in periods 3 and beyond.

The first four terms in (10.6) are the same as those in (10.5) if P is of length 1, and therefore in this case M and M' are identical if the expected losses are computed in the same way. In fact, however, Chow bases his computations of expected loss on the closed-loop approach, whereas the computations for M are based on the open-loop approach with reoptimization. This means that the expected losses are computed slightly differently even in the linear-quadratic case. This difference is fairly subtle, and it is not likely to be of much practical importance.

For P length of 2 it is clear that M and M' differ more than merely in how the expected losses are computed. Although there is no right or wrong answer regarding which measure is better, the question that M′ answers does not seem to be as relevant for policy evaluation as the question that M answers. Consider a presidential administration and a 16-quarter period. M compares the administration's actual behavior over the 16 quarters to the behavior that it would have followed had it optimized over the 16 quarters. M' compares first the administration's actual behavior in quarter 1 to the behavior that it would have followed in quarter 1 had it optimized, then its actual behavior in quarter 2 to the behavior that it would have followed had it started optimizing in quarter 2, then its actual behavior in quarter 3 to the behavior that it would have followed had it started optimizing in quarter 3, and so on through quarter 16. M seems more relevant for policy evaluation since it simply compares how well an administration did to how well it could have done had it optimized from the beginning. The question that M' answers is more complicated and also seems to resemble less the kinds of questions that are asked in practice about an administration's performance.

10.4 Solution of an Optimal Control Problem for the US Model

This section contains an example of solving an optimal control problem for the US model. The example is not realistic in the sense that the postulated loss function is too simple to approximate well the preferences of policymakers. The example is primarily meant to illustrate the properties of the model regarding the trade-off between real output and inflation.

10.4.1 The Loss Function and the Experiments

The period considered is 1973I–1977IV, and the loss function is

$$L = \sum_{t=1973I}^{1977IV} \left\{ \left[\frac{GNPR_t - GNPR_t^*}{GNPR_t^*} \right]^2 + \lambda \left[\left(\frac{GNPD_t}{GNPD_{t-1}} \right)^4 - 1 \right]^2 \right\}. \tag{10.7}$$

This loss function is additive across periods and is quadratic. The first term is the square of the percentage deviation of real GNP from the high-activity-level $GNPR^*$, and the second term is the square of the percentage change in the GNP deflator at an annual rate. $GNPR^*$ is defined in Table A-4 in Appendix A. The parameter λ is the weight attached to inflation in the loss function.

One control variable was used: C_g, federal government purchases of goods. Monetary policy was assumed to be accommodating in the sense that the bill rate was taken to be exogenous and equal to its actual value each quarter. This means that the interest rate reaction function is not used. The Fed, for example, does not respond to any fiscal policy stimulus by raising short-term interest rates. Actual values for the exogenous variables and zero values for the error terms were used.

The objective is to choose C_g to minimize L subject to the US model. There are 20 values of C_g to determine, one per quarter. The problem was solved using the DFP algorithm. Actual values of C_g were used as starting values. Two problems were solved, one for $\lambda = 1$ and one for $\lambda = 2$. The results are presented in Table 10-1.

10.4.2 The Results

The first column in Table 10-1 presents the actual values of C_g, and the next two columns present the predicted values of the output gap and the rate of inflation that are based on the use of the actual C_g values. The predicted values are not equal to the actual values because zero error terms have been used. The 1974–1975 period was one of low output and high inflation, and the predicted values in the table are consistent with this.

The first set of optimal values is for $\lambda = 1$. The value of the loss function was lowered from .1470 to .1411. The output part of the loss was lowered from .0179 to .0069, and the inflation part was raised from .1291 to .1342. The optimal values of the output gap (the numbers in the a columns) are smaller than the base values for the 1974–1976 period, and the optimal inflation values are larger except for 1974I and 1976IV. The optimal values of C_g are

TABLE 10-1. Results of solving an optimal control problem for the US model

	Predicted values using actual C_g			Predicted values using optimal C_g					
				λ = 1			λ = 2		
	C_g	a	b	C_g	a	b	C_g	a	b
1973 I	12.45	-.81	7.15	11.36	-1.22	7.16	8.28	-2.34	7.20
II	11.65	-.29	8.70	9.80	-1.12	8.60	7.63	-2.14	8.26
III	11.45	-.78	8.60	13.18	-.44	8.17	12.16	-1.04	7.84
IV	12.12	-.78	6.72	11.73	-.90	7.01	9.69	-1.81	6.88
1974 I	11.67	-1.63	7.51	13.71	-.88	7.27	12.46	-1.65	7.10
II	12.10	-2.00	7.24	12.39	-1.63	7.81	9.46	-2.95	7.45
III	12.07	-3.22	9.17	15.84	-1.78	9.25	12.21	-3.41	8.70
IV	12.23	-4.78	9.05	19.39	-1.86	9.57	16.17	-3.46	9.19
1975 I	12.07	-5.34	7.24	18.85	-2.26	7.98	14.50	-4.17	7.54
II	12.03	-5.19	9.31	17.33	-2.49	10.71	12.59	-4.63	10.03
III	12.45	-4.32	9.05	16.46	-2.14	9.79	12.48	-4.06	9.26
IV	12.47	-3.45	7.98	16.68	-1.34	8.51	14.74	-2.56	8.13
1976 I	12.00	-3.30	6.14	14.93	-1.83	6.64	10.55	-3.53	6.38
II	11.95	-3.47	8.01	16.27	-1.72	8.19	12.57	-3.28	7.87
III	12.07	-3.18	6.47	15.55	-1.62	6.94	12.30	-3.04	6.59
IV	12.20	-2.83	6.63	11.84	-2.72	6.62	5.64	-4.95	6.23
1977 I	12.27	-2.41	10.14	12.14	-2.52	9.49	6.58	-4.78	8.90
II	12.92	-1.54	7.31	12.05	-1.76	7.19	9.64	-3.26	6.90
III	13.37	-.95	7.47	7.70	-3.22	6.71	-.71	-6.02	6.31
IV	13.25	-.85	9.27	12.99	-1.36	8.57	11.96	-2.60	8.27

	Value of L			
	λ = 1		λ = 2	
	Actual	Optimal	Actual	Optimal
Output loss	.0179	.0069	.0179	.0244
Inflation loss	.1291	.1342	.2582	.2448
Total loss	.1470	.1411	.2761	.2692

Notes: $a = 100 \cdot (GNPR - GNPR^*)/GNPR^*$.
$b = 100 \cdot [(GNPD/GNPD_{-1})^4 - 1]$.
• Cg is in units of billions of 1972 dollars.

larger for this period except for 1976IV. The overall results thus say that given the particular loss function and model, the optimal policy would have been for more stimulus in 1974–1976 than actually existed.

The optimal C_g values in the last two or three quarters are not to be taken seriously because they are trading on the fact that there is no tomorrow after the end of the horizon. These values have very little effect on the optimal value for C_g for the first quarter, which is the only quarter that matters for carrying out actual policy.

The optimal C_g values show fairly large fluctuations from quarter to quarter, and this is one of the reasons the example is not realistic. In practice there are constraints on the degree to which fiscal policy variables can be changed. The way in which this would be handled in the present context would be to add a term like $\gamma(C_{gt} - C_{gt-1})^2$ to the loss function. This would penalize large quarter-to-quarter changes in C_g. If this were done, other fiscal policy variables might also be taken as control variables (with similar penalties in the loss function) to increase the ability to minimize the loss with respect to the basic target variables. With no penalties on the control variables in the loss function, little is gained by using more than one control variable. The fiscal policy variables work roughly the same way with respect to their effects on output and inflation, and thus the use of one to minimize a loss function in output and inflation does about as well as the use of many. In this sense the control variables are collinear if there are no penalties on them in the loss function.

The second set of optimal values is for $\lambda = 2$, which is a higher weight on inflation in the loss function. The value of the loss function was lowered from .2761 to .2692. The output part of the loss was raised from .0179 to .0244, and the inflation part was lowered from .2582 to .2448. On average the optimal values of the output gap for 1974 and 1975 are not much different from those for the base run. The second loss function is thus one for which the optimal policy is not for more stimulus than actually existed in these two years. Overall, the optimal policy is for less stimulus, since the output part of the loss increases from the base solution to the optimal solution. The comments made above about the fluctuations in C_g pertain to both sets of optimal values, as do the comments about the values at the end of the horizon.

It should be stressed again that this example is not realistic, not only because no penalty on C_g fluctuations was imposed, but also because of the use of the actual values of the exogenous variables. If one were trying to approximate what could have been done during this period, estimated values should be used. In addition, the model should be estimated only up to the beginning of the control period, and separate control problems should be solved at the beginning of each quarter. In other words, this example is not what would be done if one were trying to compute the measure of performance discussed in Section 10.3.

10.4.3 Computational Experience

The program that I wrote for the DFP algorithm, which is discussed in Section 2.5, was used to solve the optimal control problem. The accuracy of the answer depends on the tolerance criteria used for the Gauss-Seidel technique in solving the model. The criteria that are discussed in Section 7.5.1 were used. Given this, the DFP algorithm essentially converged after six iterations for the $\lambda = 1$ problem. The use of two-sided derivatives resulted in a value of the loss function of .141150 after six iterations. Further iterations did not lower this value. The use of one-sided derivatives resulted in a value of the loss function of .141175 after six iterations, and further iterations did not lower this value. The use of two-sided derivatives thus gave a slightly more accurate answer. Each iteration required about 50 function evaluations when two-sided derivatives were used, 40 for the derivatives and 10 for the line search. The number of function evaluations was 20 less per iteration when one-sided derivatives were used.

The procedure that was discussed at the end of Section 10.2.1 for saving computer time was not used for the present results, which means that each function evaluation required solving the model for 20 periods. Although the cost-saving procedure was not used, the problem was programmed in such a way that the starting values for the Gauss-Seidel algorithm were always the solution values from the previous function evaluation. These are generally very good starting values in the sense of being close to the final answer. (When, for example, the derivative with respect to the control value for quarter 10 is being computed, with the derivative with respect to the quarter 9 control value having been computed in the previous function evaluation, the number of passes through the model per quarter for the first 8 quarters is merely one, since the solution for the first 8 quarters is the same for both derivatives.) As a result, the Gauss-Seidel technique required on average fewer passes through the model to achieve convergence for a given quarter than are required for other problems. The average cost per solution per quarter for the control problem was about .1 seconds on the IBM 4341, which compares to about .2 seconds for other problems. The cost per function evaluation was thus about .1 seconds $\times$ 20 quarters = 2 seconds, and so the cost per iteration of the DFP algorithm when two-sided derivatives were used was about 2 seconds $\times$ 50 function evaluations = 1.67 minutes.

The BFGS algorithm was also used to solve the control problem, and the results were almost identical to those for the DFP algorithm. The BFGS algorithm also converged to the allowed accuracy after six iterations.

The computational experience for the $\lambda = 2$ problem was almost identical to that for the $\lambda = 1$ problem. The only notable difference is that seven rather than six iterations were needed for convergence.

11 Models with Rational Expectations

11.1 Introduction

The model considered in this chapter is one in which expectations of future values of endogenous variables appear as explanatory variables in the stochastic equations and the expectations are assumed to be rational in the Muth (1961) sense. This means that given a set of expectations of the exogenous variables, the expectations of the endogenous variables are equal to the model's predictions of these variables. The model (6.1) that was used for Chapters 6–10 must be modified for this chapter. The model will be written

$$f_i\left(y_t, y_{t-1}, \ldots, y_{t-p}, \underset{t-1}{E}\, y_t, \underset{t-1}{E}\, y_{t+1}, \ldots, \underset{t-1}{E}\, y_{t+h}, x_t, \alpha_i\right) = u_{it}, \quad i = 1, \ldots, n, \quad t = 1, \ldots, T, \tag{11.1}$$

where y_t is an n-dimensional vector of endogenous variables at time t, x_t is a vector of exogenous variables at time t, $\underset{t-1}{E}$ is the conditional expectations operator based on the model and on information through period $t-1$, α_i is a vector of unknown coefficients, and u_{it} is an error term. Compared to the notation in (6.1), x_t now includes only exogenous variables rather than both exogenous and lagged endogenous variables. As was the case for (6.1), the first m equations in (11.1) are assumed to be stochastic, with the remaining u_{it} $(i = m+1, \ldots, n)$ identically zero for all t.

The key difference between (6.1) and (11.1) is the assumption that the expectations are rational. If they are not, but are instead, say, a function of the current and lagged values of a few variables, they can be substituted out of (11.1) to end up with a model like (6.1). This may introduce restrictions on the coefficients, but (6.1) already encompasses such restrictions. An example of this type of substitution is presented in Section 2.2.2, (2.1)–(2.3). In this case the expectation is only a function of the lagged values of the own variable. Another example is presented in Section 4.1.3, where expectations of price and wage inflation are assumed to be functions of a few lagged values.

An example of (11.1) is Sargent's model in Section 5.4, where the expectations variable $E_{t-1}p_t$ appears as an explanatory variable in the first two equations. Another example is presented later in this chapter in Section 11.7, where the US model is modified to incorporate the assumption that there are rational expectations in the bond and stock markets.

The question of how to estimate and solve (11.1) is not easy. The next three sections are concerned with this question. A numerical method for solving the model for a given set of coefficients is discussed in Sections 11.2.1 and 11.2.2. A simple example is presented in Section 11.2.3 to motivate the method and to relate it to analytic techniques that have been used in previous research for solving and estimating rational expectations models. A numerical method for obtaining the full information maximum likelihood estimate of the coefficients is presented in Section 11.3. The possible use of stochastic simulation is discussed in Section 11.4, and the solution of optimal control problems for rational expectations models is considered in Section 11.5. Examples of using the methods are presented in Sections 11.6–11.8.

The solution method is an extension of the iterative technique used in Fair (1979d). In addition to dealing with serial correlation and multiple viewpoint dates, the extension involves an iterative procedure (called type III in the following discussion) designed to ensure numerical convergence to the rational expectations solution.

The estimation method is an extension to the nonlinear case of full information maximum likelihood techniques designed for linear rational expectations models, as described by Wallis (1980) and Hansen and Sargent (1980, 1981). Applications to particular economic problems are found in Sargent (1978) and Taylor (1980). The connection between the estimation problem considered in this chapter and the one considered by Hansen and Sargent appears in the f_i functions in (11.1), which for Hansen and Sargent would represent first-order conditions for the linear-quadratic optimization problem that they consider. Chow (1980) has proposed an alternative approach that leads to the same functional relationship between the structural parameters and the likelihood function as does the Hansen and Sargent approach.

Full information estimation techniques are particularly useful for rational expectations models because of the importance of cross-equation restrictions, where most of the testable implications of the rational expectations hypothesis lie. For linear models one can explicitly calculate a reduced form of model (11.1) in which the expectations variables are eliminated and nonlinear restrictions are placed on the coefficients. Under the assumption that the u_{it} are normally distributed, this restricted reduced form can be used to evaluate the likelihood function in terms of the structural coefficients. The maximum of the likelihood function with respect to the structural coefficients is found using some maximization algorithm like DFP.

For nonlinear models the reduced form cannot be calculated explicitly, but it can be calculated numerically. The estimation strategy here is to replace the calculation of the restricted reduced form in linear models with the numerical solution in nonlinear models. This permits one to evaluate the likelihood function in terms of the unknown structural coefficients much like in the linear case.

Although the solution and estimation methods described here should expand the range of empirical problems that can be approached using rational expectations, there is a limitation that may affect their general applicability. Because of computational costs, it is necessary in some applications to approximate the conditional expectations that appear in (11.1) by setting the future disturbances u_{it} equal to their conditional means in a deterministic simulation of the model. In nonlinear rational expectations models, the conditional expectations will involve higher-order moments of the u_{it} in addition to their means. (See Lucas and Prescott 1970, for example.) Although it is possible, as discussed in Section 11.4, to use stochastic simulation to obtain the conditional forecasts, this is computationally expensive. The results in Chapter 7 suggest that the bias introduced by using deterministic rather than stochastic simulation to solve models is small for typical macroeconometric models, and thus for many applications the use of stochastic simulation for rational expectations models is not likely to be needed. For other applications, however, the deterministic approximation may not be accurate, and stochastic simulation will be needed even though it is expensive.

With respect to (11.1), it should be noted that the model can include expectations of nonlinear functions of the endogenous variables. For example, if $y_{2t} = y_{1t}^2$, then the appearance of $\underset{t-1}{E}\, y_{2t}$ in one of the equations indicates that agents are concerned with the conditionally expected variance of y_{1t}. The model does not, however, include expectations based on current period *(t)* information. The incorporation of such variables does not cause difficulties for the solution of the model (as described below), but it does cause difficulties for estimation since the Jacobian of the transformation from the u_t to the y_t is altered.

11.2 A Solution Method

The numerical solution of (11.1) for a particular period s and for a given set of values of the α_i coefficients is considered in this section. The model without serial correlation of the errors is considered first, and then the modifications needed for the serial correlation case are discussed.

In the following discussion $\underset{t-1}{E}\, x_{t+j}$ will be used to denote the expected value of x_{t+j} based on information through period $t-1$. Both the actual realizations of x_t and the expected values are assumed to be known. If there are any exogenous variables that are not known but can be described by a known stochastic process, these are treated as endogenous and incorporated in the y_t vector. In this section, all simulations of the model are deterministic and are subject to the approximation mentioned in Section 11.1.

11.2.1 Models without Serial Correlation: The Basic Method

If one were given numerical values for the expected endogenous variables in (11.1) for all periods from s on, then it would be straightforward to solve the model for period s using the Gauss-Seidel iterative technique. The numerical method described here entails a series of iterations that converge from an arbitrary initial path of values for these expectations to a path that is consistent with the forecasts of the model itself. Let the initial set of values for the expected endogenous variables, $\underset{s-1}{E}\, y_{s+r}$, be represented as g_r, $r = 0, 1, \ldots$. Since in general the model will have no natural termination date, an infinite number of these values need to be specified in principle. In practice, however, only a finite number will be used in obtaining a solution with a given finite tolerance range. The initial values are required to be bounded: $|g_r| < M$ for every r, where M is not a function of r.

The solution method can be described in terms of five steps.

1. Choose an integer k, which is an initial guess at the number of periods beyond the horizon h for which expectations need to be computed in order to obtain a solution within a prescribed tolerance level δ. Set $\underset{s-1}{E}\, y_{s+r}$ equal to g_r, $r = 0, 1, \ldots, k + 2h$. For the purpose of describing the iterations, call these initial values $e_r(1,k)$, $r = 0, 1, \ldots, k + 2h$; the values at later iterations will then be called $e_r(i,k)$, $i > 1$.

2. Obtain a new set of values for $\underset{s-1}{E}\, y_{s+r}$, $r = 0, 1, \ldots, k + h$, by solving the model dynamically for y_{s+r}, $r = 0, 1, \ldots, k + h$. This is done by setting the disturbances to their expected values (usually zero), using the values $\underset{s-1}{E}\, x_s, \ldots, \underset{s-1}{E}\, x_{s+h+k}$ in place of the actual x's, and using the values $e_r(i,k)$ in place of $\underset{s-1}{E}\, y_{s+r}$. Call these new guesses $e_r(i+1, k)$, $r = 0, 1, \ldots, k + h$. If the model is nonlinear, the solution for each period requires a series of Gauss-Seidel iterations. Call each of these a type I iteration.

3. Compute for each expectations variable and each period the absolute value of the difference between the new guess and the previous guess, that is, compute the absolute value of the difference between each element of the $e_r(i+1, k)$ vector and the corresponding element of the $e_r(i,k)$ vector for $r = 0, 1, \ldots, h+k$. If any of these differences are not less than a prescribed tolerance level (that is, if convergence has not been achieved), increase i by 1 and return to step 2. If convergence has been achieved, go to step 4. Call this iteration (performing steps 2 and 3), a type II iteration. (The type II tolerance level should be smaller than δ, which is the overall tolerance level. Similarly, the type I tolerance level should be smaller than the type II tolerance level.) Let $e_r(k)$ be the vector of the convergent values of a series of type II iterations $(r = 0, 1, \ldots, k+h)$.

4. Repeat steps 1 through 3 replacing k by $k+1$. Compute the absolute value of the difference between each element of the $e_r(k+1)$ vector and the corresponding element of the $e_r(k)$ vector, $r = 0, 1, \ldots, h$. If any of these differences are not less than δ, increase k by 1 and repeat steps 1 through 4. If convergence has been achieved, go to step 5. Call this iteration (performing steps 1 through 4) a type III iteration. Let e_r be the vector of the convergent values of a series of type III iterations $(r = 0, 1, \ldots, h)$.

5. Use e_r for $\underset{s-1}{E}\, y_{s+r}$, $r = 0, 1, \ldots, h$, and the actual values for x_t to solve the model for period s. This gives the desired solution, say $\hat{y}_s$, and concludes the solution method.

To summarize, the method just outlined iterates on future *paths* of the expected endogenous variables, $\underset{s-1}{E}\, y_{r+s}$. Starting from an initial guess at the path g_r, $r = 0, 1, 2, \ldots, k+2h$, the path is *extended* beyond $k+2h$ until further extensions do not affect the solution by more than δ.

Note with respect to step 3 that in the process of achieving type II convergence, the initial guesses $e_r(1,k)$, $r = k+h+1, \ldots, k+2h$, never get changed. These guesses are needed to allow the model to be solved through period $s+h+k$. Also note that when one is repeating steps 1 through 3 for $k+1$, it may be possible to speed convergence by using some information from iteration k. The most obvious thing to do is to use as initial guesses $e_r(1,k+1) = e_r(k)$, $r = 0, 1, \ldots, k+h$. The values g_r would then be used for $e_r(1, k+1)$, $r = k+h+1, \ldots, k+2h+1$.

Computational costs for the method are determined by the total number of passes through the model required for convergence. A pass is simply a single evaluation of the LHS endogenous variables in terms of the RHS variables. Let N_1 be the number of type I iterations required for convergence, and let N_2

be the number of type II iterations required for convergence. Then the number of passes through the model required for one type III iteration is given by the product of the number of passes for one type II iteration, $N_1 \times (h + k + 1)$, and the number of type II iterations required for convergence, N_2. The total number of passes through the model to obtain type III convergence is given by the sum of this expression from k to $k + N_3 - 1$, where N_3 is the number of type III iterations required for convergence. In other words, the number of passes through the model required by type III convergence is approximately

$$\sum_{q=k}^{k+N_3-1} [N_2 \times N_1 \times (h + q + 1)].$$

This formula is only approximate because it is based on the assumption of the same number of type I iterations for each period and the same number of type II iterations for each type III iteration. In practice this is usually not the case.

Two points about the solution method should be noted. First, it can be easily modified to handle the case in which the expectations are based on information through period s rather than through period $s - 1$: one just replaces $\underset{s-1}{E}$ by $\underset{s}{E}$ everywhere. Second, if the expectations horizon is infinite ($h = \infty$), then it must be truncated first. For most models the error introduced by this truncation for reasonably large values of h is likely to be small. A large value of h means, of course, that a large number of calculations are required per type II iteration, and thus in practice there may be a trade-off between truncation error and computational cost.

For a general nonlinear model there is no guarantee that any of the iterations will converge. If convergence is a problem, it is sometimes helpful to damp the successive solution values. "Damping" means to take the value of a variable at, say, the start of iteration n to be some fraction of the difference between the value actually computed on iteration $n - 1$ and the value used at the start of iteration $n - 1$. (See the discussion of damping in Section 7.2.)

In special cases a problem may have terminal conditions. If, say, the values $\underset{s-1}{E} y_{s+r}$, $r = k + h + 1, \ldots, k + 2h$, are known, then the present method gives the correct answer after type II convergence. No type III convergence tests are needed because the values for periods $s + k + h + 1$ through $s + k + 2h$ are known. Cases with terminal conditions are referred to as two-point boundary value problems. They have been used to study rational expectations models when one can approximate the terminal conditions with steady-state values, which may be derived in certain situations. (See Lipton et al. 1982, who use a "multiple shooting" method to solve the two-point boundary value problem.) The approximation that comes from equating the terminal conditions with the steady-state values does not arise with the present method. Moreover, the method does not require that one compute steady-state values beforehand.

One final point about the solution method should be noted. If the model either has no exogenous variables or if the actual values of the exogenous variables are used for all periods, the solution values of the expectations—$\underset{s-1}{E}\, y_{s+r}$, $r = 0, 1, \ldots, h$—are the final predicted values of the model. This means that $\hat{y}_s$ in step 5 is simply $\underset{s-1}{E}\, y_s$, and therefore step 5 does not have to be done. It also means that if a dynamic simulation is to be run for, say, periods s through $s+q$, the model only needs to be solved once in the above manner (for period s) to get all the predicted values if q is less than or equal to h.

For purposes of the following discussion, the method presented in this section will be called the "basic method."

11.2.2 Models with Serial Correlation

Forecasting and Policy Applications

The case of first-order serial correlation is considered in this section:

$$(11.2) \qquad u_{it} = \rho_i u_{it-1} + \epsilon_{it}, \qquad i = 1, \ldots, n,$$

where the ρ_i are serial correlation coefficients. The solution method is first modified for applications in which there are enough data prior to the solution period s to permit calculation of the solution values with only a negligible effect of the errors prior to period $s-1$. This situation is likely to occur in forecasting or policy applications, where a large sample prior to the simulation period is usually available. The method is then modified for estimation applications, where sufficient prior data are generally not available.

First note that (11.1) and (11.2) can be combined to yield

$$(11.3) \qquad f_i(y_t, y_{t-1}, \ldots, y_{t-p}, y_{t-p-1}, \underset{t-1}{E}\, y_t, \underset{t-1}{E}\, y_{t+1}, \ldots, \underset{t-1}{E}\, y_{t+h}, \underset{t-2}{E}\, y_{t-1}, \underset{t-2}{E}\, y_t, \ldots, \underset{t-2}{E}\, y_{t+h-1}, x_t, x_{t-1}, \alpha_i, \rho_i) = \epsilon_{it}, \qquad i = 1, \ldots, n,$$

where the ρ_i can be thought of as structural coefficients. For solution purposes the important difference between (11.1) and (11.3) is the addition in (11.3) of an extra viewpoint data ($t-2$). This requires an additional type of iteration, denoted type IV.

If one were given values for the expectations with viewpoint date $s-2$, then (11.3) could be solved using the basic solution method in Section 11.2.1. The expectations with viewpoint date $s-2$ could be obtained by solving the model one period earlier at time $s-1$, but this in turn would require values for the expectations with viewpoint data $s-3$, and so on. By working backward in this way, however, it is possible to ensure that these initial values have negligible influence on the current period s.

The procedure is as follows.

(a) Choose an integer j, which is an initial guess at the number of periods before period s for which the model needs to be solved in order to achieve the prescribed tolerance level. Set $\underset{s-j-2}{E}\, y_{s-j-1+r}$, $r=0, 1, \ldots, h$, to an initial set of values. (As with the basic method, the initial guesses are required to be bounded.)

(b) Given the values from (a), solve the model for period $s-j$ using the basic method. For this solution the viewpoint date for the expectations for x_{s-j} and beyond is $s-j-1$. Actual values are used for x_{s-j-2}. The solution yields values for $\underset{s-j-1}{E}\, y_{s-j+r}$, $r=0, 1, \ldots, h$.

(c) Given the expectations with viewpoint date $s-j-1$ from (b), solve the model for period $s-j+1$ using the basic method. For this solution the viewpoint date for the expectations for x_{s-j+1} and beyond is $s-j$. Actual values are used for x_{s-j-1}. This solution yields values for $\underset{s-j}{E}\, y_{s-j+1+r}$, $r=0, 1, \ldots, h$. Continue this procedure (using the basic method to solve for the next period, given the solved-for expectations from the previous period) through period s. The solution for period s yields values for $\underset{s-1}{E}\, y_{s+r}$, $r=0, 1, \ldots, h$.

(d) Increase j by 1 and repeat (a) through (c). This yields new values for $\underset{s-1}{E}\, y_{s+r}$, $r=0, 1, \ldots, h$. Compare these values to the values obtained by using the smaller j. If any new value is not within the prescribed tolerance level of the old value, increase j by 1 and repeat steps (a) through (c). Keep doing this until convergence is reached. Call this iteration (performing steps a through c) a type IV iteration. (The tolerance level for the type IV iterations should be greater than δ, the tolerance level for the type III iterations.)

(e) After type IV convergence one has final values of $\underset{s-1}{E}\, y_{s+r}$ and $\underset{s-2}{E}\, y_{s-1+r}$, $r=0, 1, \ldots, h$. Use these values and the actual values of x_s and x_{s-1} to solve the model for period s.

Each type IV iteration requires solving the model for $j + 1$ starting points (that is, achieving type III convergence $j + 1$ times). The serial correlation case is thus considerably more expensive than the nonserial correlation case when one is solving the model for one period. However, no additional type IV iterations are required for solving the model for periods later than s, once the solution for period s has been obtained. The predictions with viewpoint date $s - 1$ are known after solving for period s, for example, and they can be used in solving for period $s + 1$.

It should be emphasized that type IV iterations can handle problems that are more general than the case of first-order autoregressive errors. In particular, the expectations variables with viewpoint dates $t - 2$ need not arise solely from the presence of autoregressive errors, and there can be more than two viewpoint dates. If, say, viewpoint date $t - 3$ were also included in the model, the only change in the procedure would be the addition of initial guesses for $\underset{s-j-3}{E}$ values in step (a). One would merely need to keep track of three sets of expectations instead of two as the solutions proceeded from period $s - j$ to period s.

Estimation Applications

Type IV iterations require sufficient data prior to the solution period that the initial guesses have a negligible effect on the solution. In most estimation problems one would not want to lose as many observations from the beginning of the sample as would be required for type IV convergence. Fortunately, there is a way around this problem, which is based on an assumption that is usually made when one is estimating multiple equation models with moving average residuals. This assumption is that the last presample *uncorrelated* error is zero; in particular that $\epsilon_{is-1} = 0$ in (11.2) when one is solving for period s. As before, the case of first-order serial correlation is considered; generalization to higher orders is fairly straightforward. The method requires data for period $s - 1$. (Data before period $s - 1$ will be needed if there are lagged endogenous or lagged exogenous variables in the model. It is implicitly assumed here that sufficient data for the lagged variables are available for the solution for period $s - 1$.) Rather than first transforming (11.1) into (11.3), the method works directly with (11.1), treating (11.2) as another set of equations.

If u_{is-2} were known, then (11.1) could be solved for period $s - 1$ and all subsequent periods using the basic method and the fact that $\underset{s-2}{E}\, u_{is+r} = \rho_i^{(r+2)} u_{is-2}$. In other words, in the dynamic simulations that underlie the basic method, one would use $\rho_i^{(r+2)} u_{is-2}$ on the RHS of (11.1). The problem then becomes one of choosing an appropriate value for u_{is-2}. This is where the assumption about ϵ_{is-1} comes in. The idea is to choose u_{is-2} in such a way that when the model is solved for period $s-1$, it generates a value of $\epsilon_{is-1}=0$; that is, $u_{is-1}=\rho_i u_{is-2}$. The rationale for this choice is simply that 0 is the unconditional mean of ϵ_{is-1}, and thus the actual value is likely to be relatively close to this value.

An iterative procedure for choosing u_{is-2} so that $\epsilon_{is-1}=0$ can be described as follows (note that each calculation is performed for each equation $i=1, \ldots, m$).

(i) Guess values for the error terms u_{is-2}.

(ii) Given the values from (i), solve the model for period $s-1$ using the basic method. Note that $\underset{s-2}{E}\, u_{s+r}$ is set to $\rho_i^{(r+2)} u_{is-2}$ in calculating the predicted values.

(iii) Given the predicted value of y_{is-1} ($\hat{y}_{is-1}$) from step (ii), calculate $\hat{\epsilon}_{is-1}=y_{is-1}-\hat{y}_{is-1}$ and $\hat{u}_{is-1}=\rho_i u_{is-2}+\hat{\epsilon}_{is-1}$, where u_{is-2} is the initial guess. If $\hat{\epsilon}_{is-1}$ is not within a prescribed tolerance level of 0, then convergence has not been reached, (that is, the solution is not consistent with the assumption that $\epsilon_{is-1}=0$).

(iv) If convergence is not reached in (iii), set the new value of u_{is-2} equal to $\hat{u}_{is-1}/\rho_i$ and do (ii) and (iii) over for these new values. Repeat this until convergence is reached.

(v) Using the converged iterate u_{is-2}, compute $u_{is-1}=\rho_i u_{is-2}$. Given these values, solve for period s using the basic method, where in this case $\underset{s-1}{E}\, u_{s+r}=\rho_i^{(r+1)} u_{is-1}$ is used in calculating the predicted values. This completes the solution for period s.

Once the solution for period s has been obtained, the solutions for periods $s+1$ and beyond do not require further iterations from those used by the basic method. The reason for this is that the forecasts with viewpoint date $s-1$ are known after solving for period s.

11.2.3 A Simple Example

The conditions under which the solution method just presented will converge from an arbitrary set of initial guesses to the rational expectations solution are examined for a simple linear model in this section. The aim is to motivate the method and relate it to existing analytic techniques.

A scalar linear version of (11.1) with serial correlation is given by

$$(11.4) \qquad y_t = \alpha \underset{t-1}{E}\, y_{t+1} + \gamma \underset{t-1}{E}\, x_t + u_{1t},$$

$$(11.5) \qquad x_t = \lambda x_{t-1} + \epsilon_{2t},$$

$$(11.6) \qquad u_{1t} = \rho u_{1t-1} + \epsilon_{1t},$$

where α, γ, λ, and ρ are scalar parameters and $(\epsilon_{1t}, \epsilon_{2t})$ is a serially uncorrelated vector. It is assumed that $|\lambda| < 1$ and $|\rho| < 1$. Equations (11.4) and (11.5) correspond to (11.1) when the exogenous variable x_t is assumed to follow a known stochastic process, and (11.6) corresponds directly to the autoregressive error assumption made in (11.2).

The rational expectations solution of (11.4) through (11.6) in period s is given by

$$(11.7) \qquad \underset{s-1}{E}\, y_s = \sum_{i=0}^{\infty} \alpha^i \lambda^{i+1} x_{s-1} + \sum_{i=0}^{\infty} \alpha^i \rho^{i+1} u_{1s-1}$$
$$= \frac{\gamma\lambda}{1-\alpha\lambda} x_{s-1} + \frac{\rho}{1-\alpha\rho} u_{1s-1}.$$

(See Hansen and Sargent 1981 and Taylor 1980 for discussion of an analytic solution method.) Note that the last equality in (11.7) requires that $|\alpha\lambda| < 1$ and $|\alpha\rho| < 1$, which will be satisfied if $|\alpha| < 1$. The objective is to show that the numerical solution method generates the same solution value as that given in (11.7). For now take u_{1s-1} as given; a procedure for calculating u_{1s-1} is described subsequently. Recall that $e_r(i,k)$ is the guess of $\underset{s-1}{E}\, y_{s+r}$ on type II iteration i and type III iteration k. Each type III iteration is started with an initial set of guesses $e_r(1,k)$, $r = 0, 1, \ldots, k+2$ ($h = 1$ in this example). The aim is to show that $\lim_{i,k \to \infty} e_0(i,k)$ equals the RHS of (11.7).

For a fixed k the type II iterations can be described by the set of equations

$$(11.8) \qquad e_r(i+1, k) = \alpha e_{r+1}(i,k) + \gamma\lambda^r x_{s-1} + \rho^r u_{1s-1},$$

where $r = 0, 1, \ldots, k+1$. By repeated substitution

$$(11.9) \qquad e_0(k+3, k) = (\alpha)^{k+2} e_{k+2}(1, k) + \gamma\lambda \sum_{h=1}^{k+1} (\alpha\lambda)^h x_{1s-1}$$
$$+ \rho \sum_{h=1}^{k+1} (\alpha\rho)^h u_{1s-1},$$

which is the converged iterate of the type II iterations for a fixed k. Equation (11.9) is not equal to the RHS of (11.7). However, if $|\alpha| < 1$, then the limit of

$e_0(k+3, k)$ as $k \to \infty$ is equal to the RHS of (11.7). This motivates the requirement that the initial values $e_{k+2}(1,k) \equiv g_{k+2}$ are bounded, and it shows that type III iterations converge to the rational expectations solution. Note that in this model the solution is independent of all g_r values. Given that the g_r values are bounded, type III iterations ensure convergence to the correct answer.

Note that the condition for this convergence ($|\alpha| < 1$) is identical to the condition needed to obtain a unique solution in rational expectations models (see Taylor 1977). This suggests that the numerical method will converge in the class of rational expectations models for which the uniqueness conditions hold, although a general proof is still open.

This example will now be used to illustrate the relationship between the procedure described in Section 11.2.2 (designed to choose initial conditions for estimation applications) and the conditional maximum likelihood estimates of linear ARMA models.

Substituting (11.7) into (11.4) results in

$$(11.10) \qquad y_t = \frac{\gamma\lambda}{1-\alpha\lambda} x_{t-1} + \frac{\rho}{1-\alpha\rho} u_{1t-1} + \epsilon_{1t}.$$

Subtracting the lagged value of (11.10) multiplied by ρ from (11.10) results in the "quasi-differenced" expression

$$(11.11) \qquad y_t = \rho y_{t-1} + \frac{\gamma\lambda}{1-\alpha\lambda}(x_{t-1} - \rho x_{t-2}) + \frac{\alpha\rho^2}{1-\alpha\rho} \epsilon_{1t-1} + \epsilon_{1t},$$

which when combined with (11.5) gives a two-dimensional vector ARMA(2,1) model with nonlinear constraints on the parameters. For estimation of the parameters of this ARMA model it is necessary to calculate the residuals $(\epsilon_{1t}, \epsilon_{2t})$ in terms of the data and the parameters. For "conditional" maximum likelihood estimates, this calculation is started by setting $\epsilon_{1s-1} = 0$ and taking y_{s-1}, x_{s-1}, and x_{s-2} as given, where s is the beginning of the estimation period. The residual ϵ_{1s} is then computed by subtracting (11.11) with these values from the actual observation y_s. The residuals for later periods are calculated recursively using this computed residual ϵ_{1s}.

The procedure described in Section 11.2.2 is designed to calculate these "conditional" residuals numerically for linear as well as nonlinear models. This can be illustrated by showing that

$$(11.12) \qquad \hat{y}_s = \rho y_{s-1} + \frac{\gamma\lambda}{1-\alpha\lambda}(x_{s-1} - \rho x_{s-2})$$

when the value u_{1s-1} in (11.7) is chosen according to the procedure outlined in steps (i) through (v) in Section 11.2.2. It is known from (11.7) that the basic numerical solution method will generate

$$(11.13)\qquad \hat{y}_{s-1} = \frac{\alpha\lambda}{1-\alpha\lambda} x_{s-2} + \frac{\rho}{1-\alpha\rho} u_{1s-2}$$

when applied in period $s-1$, as indicated in step (ii). Iterating steps (iii) and (iv) will yield a converged iterate of u_{1s-2} that has the property that $y_{s-1} - \hat{y}_{s-1} \equiv \epsilon_{1s-1} = 0$ to within the tolerance level. From (11.13) this value of u_{1s-2} is given by

$$(11.14)\qquad u_{1s-2} = \frac{1-\alpha\rho}{\rho}\left(y_{s-1} - \frac{\gamma\lambda}{1-\alpha\lambda} x_{s-2}\right)$$

and therefore

$$(11.15)\qquad u_{1s-1} = \rho u_{1s-2} = (1-\alpha\rho)\left(y_{s-1} - \frac{\gamma\lambda}{1-\alpha\lambda} x_{s-2}\right).$$

Substituting (11.15) into (11.17) yields (11.12), which is what is to be shown. Note that when analytic techniques can be used, it is trivial to choose u_{1s-2} according to (11.14), but when the solutions are calculated numerically, it is necessary to search for the value u_{1s-2} that gives $\epsilon_{1s-1} = 0$.

11.3 FIML Estimation

11.3.1 Evaluating and Maximizing the Likelihood Function

FIML estimates of the coefficients are obtained by maximizing L in (6.33), which is repeated here:

$$(6.33)\qquad L = -\frac{T}{2}\log|S| + \sum_{t=1}^{T}\log|J_t|.$$

S is the $m \times m$ matrix whose ij element is $\frac{1}{T}\sum_{t=1}^{T} u_{it}u_{jt}$, and J_t is the $n \times n$ Jacobian matrix whose ij element is $\partial f_i/\partial y_{jt}$. Because the expectations in (11.1) are based only on information through period $t-1$ (and thus not on y_{jt}), the derivatives of the expectations with respect to the y_{jt} $(j = 1, \ldots, n)$ are zero. The expectations are thus like the exogenous variables with respect to the Jacobian calculations.

Given the solution method in Section 11.2, it is straightforward to compute

L for a given value of α for rational expectations models. If there is no serial correlation, then for a given value of α one can solve for $\underset{s-1}{E} y_s$, $\underset{s-1}{E} y_{s+1}$, . . . , $\underset{s-1}{E} y_{s+h}$ for $s = 1, 2, \ldots, T$ using the solution method. These values can then be used in conjunction with the y and x data to compute values of u_{is} $(s = 1, 2, \ldots, T)$ and thus the matrix S. The Jacobian determinants can be computed in the usual way, thereby completing the determination of L. The extra work involved in the calculation of L for rational expectations models thus consists of using the solution method to compute the expected values for each of the T viewpoint dates. For models without rational expectations none of these calculations are needed. Given this extra work, however, FIML estimates can be obtained in the usual way by maximizing L numerically with respect to α. For small models an algorithm like DFP may be sufficient to maximize L, but for other models the Parke algorithm is likely to be needed.

When the u_{it} follow a first-order autoregression process, only one main change to the procedure given above is necessary. In this case steps (i) through (iv) in Section 11.2.2 are needed to calculate the expected values for the first sample point (say, period 2). Given these expected values, which have viewpoint date 1, the expected values for period 3 can be obtained using the solution method. These expected values can then be used in the calculation of the expected values for period 4, and so on through the end of the sample period. The only extra work in the serial correlation case pertains to the first sample point. Numerical maximization in this case is with respect to both the structural coefficients and the serial correlation coefficients.

11.3.2 A Less Expensive Method for Maximizing the Likelihood Function

The procedure in Section 11.3.1 is expensive because many evaluations of L are needed in the process of maximizing the likelihood function, and the model must be solved T times for each evaluation of L. This requires a very large number of passes through the model for a given estimation problem. In this section a way of modifying the estimation method is considered that requires fewer calls to the solution method. This modification is as follows.

(A) Given the initial value of α, solve for $\underset{s-1}{E} y_s$, $\underset{s-1}{E} y_{s+1}$, . . . , $\underset{s-1}{E} y_{s+h}$ for $s = 1, 2, \ldots, T$ using the solution method. This requires doing steps 1–5 in Section 11.2.1 T times. Call the solution values from this step the "base" values.

(B) Perturb each coefficient (one at a time) from its initial value and use the solution method to get a new set of solution values. From these values and the base values, calculate numerically the derivatives of the expectations with respect to the coefficients. This step requires doing steps 1 – 5 T times for each coefficient.

(C) In the procedure that calculates L for a given value of α, use the base values and the derivatives to calculate new expected values for each new value of α. This eliminates the need to use the solution method in computing new values of L.

(D) Once the maximization algorithm has found the value of α that maximizes L, compute a new set of base values using the new value of α and a new set of derivatives. Given the new derivatives, use the maximization algorithm again to find the value of α that maximizes L. Keep doing this until the successive estimates of α from one use of the maximization algorithm to the next are within a prescribed tolerance level.

The advantage of this modification is that once the problem is turned over to the maximization algorithm, the solution method is no longer needed. The use of the base values and derivatives in the calculation of L is very inexpensive relative to the use of the solution method, and given that algorithms require many calculations of L, this modification is likely to result in a considerable saving of time. There is, of course, no guarantee that the procedure will converge. If the expectations are not a well-behaved function of α, then computing the derivatives at a given point may not be very helpful. It may be, in other words, that using the base values and derivatives to calculate new expected values yields values that are far from the (correct) values that would be computed by the solution method.

Once the estimates have been obtained, the covariance matrix in (6.34) can be calculated by taking numerical derivatives of L with respect to α (at the optimum). It may be possible to use the derivatives of the expectations with respect to α in the calculation of the values of L. This would allow the covariance matrix to be computed without using the solution method.

For the serial correlation case one must also calculate in step (B) the derivative of $\hat{u}_{is-1}$ with respect to α (for each i), where s is the first sample point. $\hat{u}_{is-1}$ is a function of α, and therefore if steps (i) – (iv) are to be bypassed in the calculation of L, the derivative of $\hat{u}_{is-1}$ with respect to α must also be calculated and used.

11.4 Solution and Estimation Using Stochastic Simulation

The use of stochastic simulation to estimate and solve rational expectations models is discussed in this section. The case of (11.1) with no serial correlation will be considered.

Consider first the problem of solving a rational expectations model. Suppose that both the α coefficients in (11.1) and S are known, where S is the covariance matrix of the disturbances u_{it}. Assume that the u_{it} are normally distributed. The solution procedure is modified as follows. First, the expected values computed in step 2— $\underset{s-1}{E}\, y_{s+r}$, $r = 0, 1, \ldots, k+h$—are computed by stochastic rather than deterministic simulations. Instead of setting the disturbances to their expected values and solving once, one solves the model for many different trials. Each trial consists of a set of draws of the disturbances u_{is+r}, $r = 0, 1, \ldots, k+h$, from the $N(0,S)$ distribution (assuming the expected values of all the disturbances are zero). Each expected value is computed as the average across all the trials. Second, the final solution value $\hat{y}_s$ computed in step 5 is also computed by a stochastic rather than a deterministic simulation. In this case only draws of the disturbances for period s are needed.

Stochastic simulation can also be used to obtain FIML estimates of the coefficients. In contrast to the deterministic case, however, the likelihood function cannot be "concentrated" as it is in (6.33). In the fully stochastic case, changes in S affect the solution of the model and thereby the computed residuals. Instead, one works directly with the "unconcentrated" (log) likelihood function, which except for a constant can be written

$$(11.16) \qquad L^* = \sum_{t=1}^{T} \log|J_t| - \frac{T}{2}\log|S| - \frac{1}{2}\sum_{t=1}^{T} u_t' S^{-1} u_t,$$

where $u_t = (u_{1t}, \ldots, u_{mt})'$. FIML estimates can be obtained by maximizing L^* with respect to the parameters (α,S). Each evaluation of L^* for a given set of values of α and S requires computing the expected values, $\underset{t-1}{E}\, y_{t+r}$, $r = 0, 1, \ldots, k+h$, by means of stochastic simulation, where each trial consists of draws of the disturbances from the $N(0,S)$ distribution. The expected values are computed for each sample point $t = 1, \ldots, T$, which then allows u_t to be computed for each point. The determinants of the J_t can be obtained, and thus the function L^* can be evaluated in terms of the parameters (α,S). Nonlinear maximization routines can then be used to maximize L^*.

Because this estimation procedure requires maximization over the $(m+1)m/2$ independent elements of S in addition to the elements of α and because of the stochastic simulation costs, the method is likely to be extremely expensive in practice. Given this, experiments with the method on small representative nonlinear models would be useful to try to gauge how much accuracy is likely to be gained by using stochastic simulation.

11.5 Solution of Optimal Control Problems for Rational Expectations Models

The method for solving optimal control problems in Section 10.2 merely requires the ability to solve the model for a given set of values of the control variables. Given this, the problem is turned over to a maximization algorithm like DFP to find the optimum. The method in Section 11.2 provides the ability to solve rational expectations models, and thus optimal control problems can be solved for these models by using this solution method within the context of the overall method in Section 10.2.

Since rational expectations models are forward-looking, future values of the control variables affect current decisions, and therefore more values of the control variables have to be determined in this case than in the standard case. Values of the control variables must be chosen far enough into the future so that adding another future period has a negligible effect on the solutions for the actual control problem. The solution method in Section 11.2 ensures that the predicted values in the last future period have a negligible effect on the predicted values for the current period, and thus the requirement for the optimal control problem is merely to choose the number of control values that are required by the solution method in the course of solving the model.

There is a potential problem of time inconsistency in solving optimal control problems for rational expectations models, which has been pointed out by Kydland and Prescott (1977). Consider a deterministic setting, and assume that a control problem has been solved using the above procedure for periods 1 through T. This yields optimal values $z_1^*, z_2^*, \ldots, z_T^*$. Now wait for one period, and consider the solution of the problem at the beginning of period 2. Since the setting is deterministic, nothing unexpected has happened, and therefore one might think that the same optimal values $z_2^*, \ldots, z_T^*$ would be determined. If the model is forward-looking, this is not necessarily the case, and when it is not, the optimal policy is said to be time-inconsistent. The model does not have to be a rational expectations model in order for this problem to arise; it only needs to have the property that future values of the control variables affect current decisions.

The problem of time inconsistency does not mean that the above solution of the control problem is not optimal. It is optimal if it is believed and carried out. The problem is that the policymakers have an incentive to do something different in the future, and therefore agents may not believe that the original plan will be carried out. If it is not possible for the policymakers to convince agents that the plans will be carried out, other policies may be better. Even in this case, however, it is of some interest to solve the control problem in the above manner in order to have a benchmark to which other policies can be compared.

11.6 Results for a Small Linear Model

11.6.1 Model without Serial Correlation

For purposes of testing the solution and estimation methods, a small linear model has been analyzed. This model can be solved and estimated using existing linear techniques, and thus it provides a useful check for the nonlinear methods. The model is a version of the wage-contracting model in Taylor (1980). It can be represented as

$$(11.17)\quad y_{1t} = \alpha_{11}y_{1t-1} + \alpha_{12}y_{1t-2} + \alpha_{13}\underset{t-1}{E}\,y_{1t+1} + \alpha_{14}\underset{t-1}{E}\,y_{1t+2} + \alpha_{15}\underset{t-1}{E}\,y_{2t} + \alpha_{16}\underset{t-1}{E}\,y_{2t+1} + \alpha_{17}\underset{t-1}{E}\,y_{2t+2} + u_{1t},$$

$$(11.18)\quad y_{2t} = \alpha_{21}y_{1t} + \alpha_{22}y_{1t-1} + \alpha_{23}y_{1t-2} + u_{2t},$$

with restrictions $\alpha_{11} = \alpha_{13} = \frac{1}{3}$, $\alpha_{12} = \alpha_{14} = \frac{1}{6}$, $\alpha_{15} = \alpha_{16} = \alpha_{17}$, $\alpha_{21} = \alpha_{22} = \alpha_{23}$. There are two free coefficients to estimate, α_{15} and α_{21}. The data for this model were generated by simulating the model using normally distributed serially independent errors with zero correlation between equations. Values of α_{15} and α_{21} of .0333333 and $-.333333$ were used for this purpose.

The model was first solved and estimated using the technique described in Taylor (1980), which is based on a factorization procedure that calculates a restricted ARMA version of the model. The ARMA version is used for the likelihood function calculations. Because of its small size, the model does not require the use of the Parke algorithm for the FIML estimation, so the DFP algorithm was used. Using a sample of 50 observations, the estimated coefficients were $\hat{\alpha}_{15} = .02601$ and $\hat{\alpha}_{21} = -.3916$, with t-statistics of 1.18 and 6.33, respectively. Each evaluation of the likelihood function took about .004 seconds on an IBM 360/91 at Columbia University using this factorization technique. The DFP algorithm required 90 function evaluations starting from the true values (.0333333 and $-.333333$).

The model was next solved using the method in Section 11.2. The model was solved for all 50 observations, and the value of the likelihood function was computed. When evaluated at the same coefficient values, the method gave the same value of the likelihood function as did the factorization

TABLE 11-1. Computational summary of the likelihood function evaluations for the small linear model

---

Model with no serial correlation ($h = 2$):

1. The initial value of k was taken to be 15. Type III convergence was almost always achieved after 2 iterations (i.e., for $k = 16$).
2. The average number of Type II iterations per Type III iteration was about 15.
3. Given the expectations, the model is recursive, so only one Type I iteration was needed for convergence each period. The average length of the simulation period for a Type II iteration was 18.5 periods, so the total number of Type I iterations for the solution for the 50 observations was about (50 obs.) × (1 Type I iteration) × (15 Type II iterations) × (18.5 periods per Type II iteration) × (2 Type III iterations) = 27750.
4. One Type I iteration requires about 10 multiplications and 7 additions.

Model with serial correlation ($h = 2$):

1. Call the first period of the sample period, period s. Steps i)–iv) were first used to calculate u_{1s-1}. The initial guess for u_{1s-2} was zero. A damping factor of .25 was used. Convergence took 18 iterations to obtain u_{1s-1}. For these calculations the initial value of k was taken to be 15, and Type III convergence was always achieved after 2 iterations. The average number of Type II iterations per Type III iteration was about 15. Given the expectations, the model is recursive, and so only one Type I iteration was needed for convergence each period. The number of passes for these calculations was thus about (18 iterations) × (1 Type I) × (15 Type II) × (18.5 periods per Type II) × (2 Type III) = 9990.
2. Given u_{1s-1}, step v) was used to solve for period s. This required 21 Type II iterations. The starting values for this step were the values computed in 1., and convergence was achieved after 1 Type III iteration. The number of passes for this step was thus (21 Type II) × (18 periods per Type II) = 378.
3. Given the solution for period s, the calculations for the remaining 49 periods are essentially the same as those above for the model with no serial correlation. These calculations thus required about 49 × 1 × 15 × 18.5 × 2 = 27195 passes.
4. The total number of passes through the model was thus about 9990 + 378 + 27195 = 37563.

---

technique, which serves as a useful check on both procedures. The details of the iterations of the method when solving the model are summarized in the upper section of Table 11-1. A total of about 27,750 passes through the model were required for one function evaluation, which is estimated to take about 1 second on an IBM 360/91. This is about 250 times slower than the factorization technique. (The actual computations were done on a computer at Yale University, and the estimated time for the IBM 360/91 is only approximate.)

Had the same DFP program been used to maximize the likelihood function as was used for the factorization technique, the same 90 function evaluations would have been required to find the maximum. The reason for this is that the solution method and the factorization technique give the same value of the likelihood function for the same set of coefficient values, and this is all the information that the DFP algorithm takes from the methods. The total time needed to estimate the model would thus be about 90 seconds. The DFP calculations were not repeated, but instead an attempt was made to maximize the likelihood function using the less expensive method discussed in Section 11.3.2. These calculations will now be described.

The calculations using the less expensive method are summarized in Table 11-2. Using the true values of the coefficients as starting values, the model was first solved for each of the 50 observations. As noted in Table 11-1, this requires about 27,750 passes through the model. The model was then solved two more times to calculate the derivatives of the expectations with respect to the two coefficients. The problem was then turned over to the DFP algorithm. The computer program of the DFP algorithm used here was different from the program used above for the factorization technique, and the performance of the algorithm for a given problem does vary across programs. The following results thus differ in two respects from the results using the factorization technique: the derivatives are used in one case but not in the other, and the computer programs differ. It is not possible to say which of these factors is more important regarding the performance of the DFP algorithm, but this is not of great concern here. The question of interest is whether the use of the derivatives results in the optimum being found. (The program of the DFP algorithm used here is also not the one that I wrote and used for the results in Section 10.4. The work for the present section was done before I wrote the DFP program that is now part of the overall Fair-Parke program.)

As indicated in Table 11-2, the first DFP iteration required 45 calls to the subroutine that calculates L for a given value of the coefficient vector. Convergence was essentially achieved after the first iteration. The program was allowed to run for three more iterations, where for each iteration the model was solved three times: once to get the base values and twice more to get the derivatives. The results in Table 11-2 show that the use of the derivatives provides a close approximation to the "true" value of L obtained by solving the entire model. Given that the DFP algorithm required 45 evaluations of L (for the first iteration), the use of the derivatives saved a considerable amount of time. The derivatives were also used in the calculation of the covariance matrix after the optimum was reached.

TABLE 11-2. Results of estimating the small linear model using the less expensive method

	$\hat{\alpha}_{15}$	$\hat{\alpha}_{21}$	Value of L using expected values computed from derivatives	Value of L using expected values computed from steps 1-4	Number of times L was computed by the DFP algorithm
Initial values	.0333333	-.333333		508.6022686	
Iteration 1	.0252715	-.391654	509.0471277	509.0460742	45
Iteration 2	.0260208	-.391609	509.0466651	509.0466725	39
Iteration 3	.0260044	-.391616	509.0466727	509.0466724	20
Iteration 4	.0260076	-.391612	509.0466725		71

Notes:
- Estimated standard error of $\hat{\alpha}_{15}$ = 0.0221141.
- Estimated standard error of $\hat{\alpha}_{21}$ = 0.0618044.

11.6.2 Model with Serial Correlation

The linear model was also solved and estimated for the case where u_{1t} in (11.17) follows a first-order autoregressive process, with $\rho_1 = .7$. Steps (i)–(v) were used with a damping factor of .25 to solve for the first observation, with steps 1–4 used thereafter. Some initial experimentation with no damping factor for calculating the initial condition indicated that convergence would either not be achieved or would be very slow. Again, for the same set of coefficient values, the same likelihood value was obtained using both the factorization technique and the method in Section 11.2. A summary of the calculations for the method is presented in the lower section of Table 11-1. The required number of passes in this case was about 37,563, which is about 35 percent greater than the number required for the model without serial correlation.

An attempt was made to use the less expensive method to estimate this version of the model, but this was not successful. The expectations did not appear to be well-behaved functions of the coefficients, and quite different derivatives were obtained for different step sizes. The values of L computed using the derivatives were generally not very close to the values of L computed by solving the entire model. It appears for this version that the entire model has to be solved for each new evaluation of L.

The use of the less expensive method for the small linear model thus produced mixed results. More estimation of alternative models is needed before one can determine whether the difficulties with the serial correlation case are specific to the example and, if so, whether the example is representative of the type of model that is likely to be estimated in practice.

11.7 Results for the US Model with Rational Expectations in the Bond and Stock Markets (USRE1 and USRE2)

An interesting exercise with the US model is to consider how its policy properties would differ if it were specified to be consistent with the assumption of rational expectations in the bond and stock markets. The method in Section 11.2 can be used to solve the model in this case. The modifications of the model to incorporate the rational expectations assumption are discussed first, and then the policy properties of the different versions are compared.

11.7.1 The Two Term Structure Equations

The two term structure equations in the model, Eqs. 23 and 24, are discussed in Section 4.1.6. In each equation the long-term rate, *RB* or *RM*, is a function of current and lagged values of the short-term rate, *RS*. The theory on which these equations are based is the expectations theory of the term structure of interest rates. According to this theory, the return from holding an n-period security is equal to the expected return from holding a series of one-period securities over the n periods. Let RS^e_{t+i} denote the expected one-period rate of return for period $t + i$, the expectation being conditional on information available as of the beginning of period t, and let R_t denote the yield to maturity in period t on an n-period security. Then according to the expectations theory,

$$(11.19) \quad (1 + R_t)^n = (1 + RS^e_t)(1 + RS^e_{t+1}) \;.\;.\;.\; (1 + RS^e_{t+n-1}).$$

When considered by themselves, Eqs. 23 and 24 are consistent with the expectations theory in the sense that the current and lagged values of *RS* are proxies for the expected future values in (11.19). When these equations are considered as part of the overall model, however, they are not consistent with the expectations theory *if* expectations of the future values of *RS* are rational. The reason for this is that in simulations of the model, the predicted values of the long-term rates and the short-term rates do not in general satisfy (11.19).

The US model can be modified to be consistent with the rational expectations assumption by dropping Eqs. 23 and 24 from the model and requiring instead that the solution values of *RS, RB,* and *RM* satisfy (11.19), where R_t in (11.19) represents *RB* and *RM*. The resulting model, which will be called

USRE1, is then consistent with the assumption of rational expectations in the bond market *if* (1) people believe that USRE1 is the true model and know how to solve it and (2) people at any one time have the same set of forecasts regarding the future values of the exogenous variables and the same set of expectations regarding the future values of the error terms. Given these assumptions, the solution values of the endogenous variables are people's expectations of these values (ignoring the bias due to the nonlinearity of the model). Since three of the endogenous variables in the model are *RS, RB,* and *RM*, if the solution values of these variables satisfy (11.19), then people's expectations are consistent with this equation.

11.7.2 The Stock-Price Equation

The stock-price or capital-gains equation, Eq. 25, is also discussed in Section 4.1.6. The capital-gains variable, *CG*, is a function of the change in *RB*, the change in after-tax cash flow, and the one-quarter-lagged value of the change in after-tax cash flow. The theory on which this equation is based is that the value of stocks is the present discounted value of expected future after-tax cash flow, the discount rates being the expected future short-term interest rates. Let $\pi_t = CF_t - T_{fgt} - T_{fst}$ denote the actual value of after-tax cash flow for period t, and let π^e_{t+i} denote the expected value for period $t+i$, the expectation being conditional on information available as of the beginning of period t. Let SP_t denote the value of stocks for period t based on information as of the beginning of period t. Then according to the theory

$$(11.20)\quad SP_t = \frac{\pi^e_t}{1 + RS^e_t} + \frac{\pi^e_{t+1}}{(1 + RS^e_t)(1 + RS^e_{t+1})} + \ . \ . \ . \ + \frac{\pi^e_{t+T}}{(1 + RS^e_t)(1 + RS^e_{t+1}) \ . \ . \ . \ (1 + R^e_{t+T})},$$

where T is large enough to make the last term in (11.20) negligible. By definition

$$(11.21)\quad CG_t = SP_t - SP_{t-1},$$

where *CG* is the capital-gains variable used on the LHS of Eq. 25.

When considered by itself, Eq. 25 is consistent with (11.20) and (11.21) in the sense that the change in the bond rate is a proxy for expected future interest rate changes and the changes in after-tax cash flow are proxies for expected future changes. When considered as part of the overall model, Eq.

25 is not consistent with (11.20) and (11.21) if expectations of the future values are rational; this is because in simulations of the model the predicted values of *CG* do not in general satisfy (11.20)–(11.21).

The US model can also be modifid to be consistent with the rational expectations assumption regarding stock prices by dropping Eq. 25 and requiring instead that the solution values of *CG* satisfy (11.20)–(11.21). If this modification is made in conjunction with the modification regarding the term structure of interest rates, the resulting model, which will be called USRE2, is consistent with the assumption of rational expectations in both the bond and stock markets. Note in this case that because *RS* is used as the discount rate in (11.20), the expected return on stocks is the same as the expected return on bonds. There are no arbitrage opportunities in USRE2 between bonds and stocks, just as there are none in either USRE1 or USRE2 between bonds of different maturities.

RS is in units of percentage points at an annual rate, and for use in (11.19) and (11.20) in the following experiments, each *RS* term was divided by 400. This puts *RS* in units of percent at a quarterly rate.

11.7.3 The Policy Experiments

Unanticipated Change

Since both USRE1 and USRE2 have expected future values on the RHS of some equations, the solution method in Section 11.2 must be used to solve the models. Before they can be solved, however, some assumption must be made about n in (11.19) and T in (11.20). For present purposes both n and T were taken to be 32 quarters. The policy experiment consisted of a permanent increase in C_g (from its historical values) of 1.0 percent of real GNP. This is the same experiment as the first experiment in Table 9-1 except for a different period. The period here is 1958I–1960IV; this early period was chosen so that enough future data would be available to avoid having to make any assumptions about values of variables beyond the end of the data.

The value of h in (11.1) for both models is 31. The initial value of k in step 1 was chosen to be 67. This required initial guesses of the expectations of the future values of *RS* and of after-tax cash flow for 1958I through 1990II, although the values for the last 31 quarters are not changed during the solution process. For all but the last 31 quarters the initial expected values were taken to be the actual values. For the last 31 quarters (1982IV–1990II) the values were taken to be the 1982III values.

An important question for the experiment is how to handle the fact that (11.19) and (11.20)–(11.21) do not fit the data perfectly. The present experiment is not meant to be a test of the assumption of rational expectations in the bond and stock markets, but merely to examine the sensitivity of the properties of the model to this assumption. Given this, the easiest thing to do is to add error terms to (11.19) (for both *RB* and *RM*) and to (11.20) in such a way that the equations fit perfectly when the expected values are taken to be the actual values. If the actual values of the error terms are also used for the other equations, the solution of the model using the actual values of the exogenous variables (including C_g) is the perfect tracking solution. The base values for the C_g experiment are thus the actual values, which is the same as for the experiments in Chapter 9. The actual values of the exogenous variables were used for the experiment.

The error terms in (11.19) and (11.20) are not assumed to be serially correlated, which means that steps (a)–(e) in Section 11.2.2 do not have to be used. Even though some of the stochastic equations in the model have serially correlated errors, steps (a)–(e) do not have to be used unless the serial correlation occurs in equations with explanatory expectations variables.

The estimated policy effects are presented in Table 11-3. The solution method in Section 11.2 worked quite well in solving USRE1 and USRE2. For USRE2, for example, the number of type II iterations required for convergence was 28 for $k = 67$. When k was increased by one, the required number was 17. Type III convergence was achieved at this point. In other words, the initial value of k was chosen large enough so that increasing it by one more had negligible effects on the solution values for the first 32 quarters. For $h = 31$ and $k = 67$, each type II iteration requires solving the model for $31 + 67 + 1 = 99$ quarters. The solution for each quarter requires about .2 seconds on the IBM 4341, so the solution time for one type II iteration is about 19.8 seconds. The total time for the 28 type II iterations was thus about 9.2 minutes. For k increased by one, the time per type II iteration is only .2 seconds longer. The time for the other 17 type II iterations was thus about 20 seconds $\times$ 17 = 5.7 minutes. The total time required for the solution for USRE2 was thus about 14.9 minutes. The times for USRE1 were similar. If one compares these times to the time required to solve the regular version of the US model for the 12 quarters in Table 11-3 of 12 $\times$ .2 seconds = 2.4 seconds, the USRE1 and USRE2 models are about 373 times more expensive to solve than the US model.

It is important to note with respect to solution times that the model only had to be solved once for each set of results in Table 11-3. The reason for this

TABLE 11-3. Estimated effects of an unanticipated increase in C_g for US, USRE1, and USRE2

	1958				1959				1960				Sum[a]
	I	II	III	IV	I	II	III	IV	I	II	III	IV	
GNPR: Real GNP													
US	1.12	1.34	1.34	1.27	1.15	1.02	.88	.77	.67	.60	.54	.50	4.95
USRE1	.99	1.04	.97	.90	.84	.78	.74	.72	.71	.71	.70	.69	4.34
USRE2	1.00	1.04	.96	.89	.83	.77	.73	.70	.69	.67	.66	.64	4.25
GNPD: GNP deflator													
US	.04	.19	.26.	.33	.42	.47	.50	.53	.54	.55	.56	.56	
USRE1	.01	.12	.16	.20	.27	.31	.35	.38	.41	.45	.47	.49	
USRE2	.02	.12	.16	.20	.28	.32	.36	.39	.41	.44	.47	.49	
100·UR: Unemployment rate (percentage points)													
US	-.06	-.11	-.12	-.11	-.10	-.10	-.08	-.07	-.06	-.05	-.05	-.05	
USRE1	-.05	-.08	-.09	-.08	-.07	-.07	-.06	-.06	-.06	-.06	-.06	-.07	
USRE2	-.05	-.08	-.08	-.07	-.07	-.06	-.06	-.06	-.06	-.06	-.06	-.06	
RS: Bill rate (percentage points)													
US	.07	.10	.11	.12	.13	.13	.13	.13	.12	.12	.11	.11	
USRE1	.06	.07	.08	.09	.10	.10	.11	.11	.11	.11	.12	.12	
USRE2	.06	.07	.08	.09	.10	.10	.10	.11	.11	.11	.11	.11	
RB: Bond rate (percentage points)													
US	.02	.03	.04	.05	.06	.07	.08	.09	.10	.10	.10	.11	
USRE1	.11	.12	.12	.12	.12	.12	.12	.13	.13	.13	.14	.14	
USRE2	.10	.10	.10	.11	.11	.11	.11	.11	.11	.11	.12	.12	
RM: Mortgage rate (percentage points)													
US	.01	.03	.05	.06	.08	.09	.10	.10	.11	.11	.12	.12	
USRE1	.10	.10	.10	.11	.11	.11	.11	.11	.11	.12	.12	.12	
USRE2	.09	.09	.09	.09	.10	.10	.10	.10	.10	.10	.10	.10	
CG: Capital gains variable (billions of current dollars)													
US	-.11	-.06	-.68	-.45	-.34	-.30	-.26	-.20	-.18	-.14	-.12	-.09	
USRE1	-2.50	-.20	-.52	-.21	-.14	-.06	-.08	-.07	-.10	-.13	-.16	-.14	
USRE2	-3.40	-.26	-.16	-.15	-.15	-.15	-.17	-.18	-.19	-.17	-.17	-.17	
CF: Cash flow (billions of current dollars)													
US	.18	.11	.07	.04	.02	-.01	-.03	-.05	-.07	-.08	-.09	-.10	
USRE1	.11	-.00	-.07	-.10	-.12	-.13	-.15	-.16	-.17	-.18	-.19	-.20	
USRE2	.12	.01	-.05	-.08	-.09	-.11	-.12	-.13	-.13	-.14	-.15	-.15	
INT_f: Interest payments of the firm sector (billions of current dollars)													
US	.01	.02	.03	.04	.06	.08	.10	.12	.13	.15	.16	.17	
USRE1	.05	.09	.12	.15	.17	.19	.21	.22	.24	.25	.26	.28	
USRE2	.05	.08	.11	.13	.15	.17	.18	.19	.20	.21	.22	.24	

Notes: a. Sum of the changes (at quarterly rates) over the 12 quarters, in billions of 1972 dollars.
- C_g was increased by 1.0 percent of GNPR beginning in 1958 I (sustained increase).
- The changes for GNPR and GNPD are in percentage points.

is that the actual values of the exogenous variables were used and that the length of the simulation period of interest (12 quarters) was less than h. (See the discussion at the end of Section 11.2.1 for an explanation of this.)

The results in Table 11-3 are fairly easy to understand. For all three versions, the Fed responded to the increase in C_g by raising RS. In the regular version this had a gradual effect over time on RB and RM through the term structure equations. In the other two versions, however, knowledge that the

Fed was going to raise *RS* in the future was incorporated immediately into the long-term rates, and therefore the initial changes in *RB* and *RM* were greater for USRE1 and USRE2 than for the US model. This led to lower initial increases in real GNP and to smaller initial decreases in the unemployment rate. The lower initial increases in real GNP led to smaller increases in the GNP deflator.

Because of the lower initial increases in real GNP for USRE1 and USRE2, the initial increases in *RS* were also lower. In other words, the Fed responded less with respect to increasing *RS* in these two cases. The higher initial values of *RB* and *RM* for USRE1 and USRE2 required less of an increase in *RS* in order to lessen the expansionary impact of the increase in C_g.

One puzzling feature of the results in Table 11-3 is why the initial change in stock prices (*CG*) is negative for USRE2. It is more negative for USRE2 than it is for USRE1, which through the wealth effects in the model leads to a slightly more expansionary economy for USRE1 than for USRE2. If future values of cash flow are higher because of the expansion, this information should be reflected immediately in higher stock prices for USRE2. There are, of course, two effects on stock prices, a positive one through higher future values of cash flow and a negative one through higher future values of the discount rates. It may merely be that the negative discount rate effect dominates for USRE2. This is not, however, the case. The problem is that future values of cash flow are smaller rather than larger. (This can be seen for the first 12 quarters in Table 11-3.) The reason for this is that interest payments of the firm sector, which are subtracted from cash flow, are larger because of the higher bond rate. (This can also be seen for the first 12 quarters in Table 11-3).

The puzzling result is thus due to the higher interest payments of the firm sector. Interest payments are determined by Eq. 19 in the model. This equation, as discussed in Section 4.1.5, does not have good statistical properties, and in particular it may be that the bond rate coefficient in the equation is too large. The USRE1 versus USRE2 results thus unfortunately depend on a questionable equation. In order to see how sensitive the results in Table 11-3 are to the interest payments equation, the experiments were done over with the interest payments equation dropped and interest payments taken to be exogenous. The results of these experiments are presented in Table 11-4. The results for US and USRE1 are not much affected, but it is now the case that future values of cash flow are positive. The initial change in stock prices for USRE2 is now positive. *CG* increased by 1.28 in the first quarter for USRE2, whereas it decreased by 1.96 for USRE1. The decrease for USRE1 is a result

TABLE 11-4. Estimated effects of an unanticipated increase in C_g for US, USRE1, and USRE2 with INT_f exogenous

	1958				1959				1960				
	I	II	III	IV	I	II	III	IV	I	II	III	IV	Sum[a]
GNPR: Real GNP													
US	1.12	1.33	1.33	1.25	1.12	.98	.83	.70	.60	.52	.45	.40	4.69
USRE1	1.00	1.07	1.00	.93	.86	.79	.73	.69	.67	.65	.63	.60	4.27
USRE2	.97	1.09	1.07	1.04	1.00	.96	.92	.89	.88	.86	.84	.83	5.05
GNPD: GNP deflator													
US	.04	.18	.26	.32	.41	.46	.49	.51	.52	.53	.53	.53	
USRE1	.02	.13	.17	.22	.30	.34	.38	.41	.43	.46	.48	.50	
USRE2	.01	.12	.17	.23	.32	.37	.43	.47	.51	.55	.58	.61	
100 UR: Unemployment rate (percentage points)													
US	-.06	-.10	-.12	-.11	-.10	-.09	-.07	-.06	-.05	-.04	-.04	-.03	
USRE1	-.05	-.08	-.09	-.08	-.07	-.07	-.06	-.05	-.05	-.05	-.05	-.05	
USRE2	-.05	-.09	-.10	-.10	-.09	-.09	-.09	-.09	-.09	-.09	-.09	-.08	
RS: Bill rate (percentage points)													
US	.07	.10	.11	.12	.13	.13	.12	.12	.11	.11	.10	.10	
USRE1	.06	.08	.08	.09	.10	.10	.10	.10	.10	.11	.11	.10	
USRE2	.06	.08	.09	.10	.11	.11	.12	.12	.13	.13	.13	.13	
RB: Bond rate (percentage points)													
US	.02	.03	.04	.05	.06	.07	.08	.09	.09	.10	.10	.10	
USRE1	.09	.10	.10	.10	.10	.10	.10	.10	.10	.10	.10	.10	
USRE2	.12	.12	.12	.12	.12	.12	.12	.12	.12	.12	.13	.13	
RM: Mortgage rate (percentage points)													
US	.01	.03	.05	.06	.07	.09	.09	.10	.10	.11	.11	.11	
USRE1	.08	.08	.09	.09	.09	.09	.09	.09	.09	.09	.09	.09	
USRE2	.10	.10	.11	.11	.11	.11	.11	.11	.11	.11	.11	.11	
CG: Capital gains variable (billions of current dollars)													
US	-.10	-.03	-.64	-.39	-.26	-.21	-.17	-.11	-.09	-.05	-.03	-.00	
USRE1	-1.96	.05	-.33	-.06	.01	.06	.04	.04	.01	-.01	-.03	-.01	
USRE2	1.28	-.00	.07	.09	.10	.10	.09	.09	.10	.10	.09	.08	
CF: Cash flow (billions of current dollars)													
US	.19	.13	.10	.08	.07	.06	.06	.06	.06	.06	.07	.07	
USRE1	.17	.09	.06	.05	.06	.06	.06	.07	.07	.08	.08	.08	
USRE2	.16	.10	.07	.06	.07	.07	.07	.08	.08	.08	.09	.09	
INT_f: Interest payments of the firm sector (billions of current dollars)													
US	0.	0.	0.	0.	0.	0.	0.	0.	0.	0.	0.	0.	
USRE1	0.	0.	0.	0.	0.	0.	0.	0.	0.	0.	0.	0.	
USRE2	0.	0.	0.	0.	0.	0.	0.	0.	0.	0.	0.	0.	

Notes: a. Sum of the changes (at quarterly rates) over the 12 quarters, in billions of 1972 dollars.

- C_g was increased by 1.0 percent of GNPR beginning in 1958 I (sustained increase).
- The changes for GNPR and GNPD are in percentage points.

of the higher value of *RB*, which appears as an explanatory variable in the *CG* equation. The economy is now more expansionary for USRE2 than it is for USRE1.

This feature of the results regarding the difference between USRE1 and USRE2 is thus sensitive to the interest payments equation. The results in Tables 11-3 and 11-4 bound the differences in the sense that interest payments are probably too sensitive to interest rates in Table 11-3 and not sensitive enough in Table 11-4. For purposes of illustrating the properties of the two versions of the US model, these results are sufficient.

An interesting aspect of the results is that the sums of the GNP changes across the 12 quarters are quite close. The timing of the GNP changes differs between the US model and the two rational expectations versions, but this is to some extent the only substantial difference among the results.

Anticipated Change

The experiment just reported is an unanticipated increase in C_g beginning in 1958I. If the increase had been announced before this time, the quarters prior to the enactment would have been affected in models USRE1 and USRE2. To investigate this, a second experiment was run in which it was assumed that the announcement of the C_g increase beginning in 1958I was made at the beginning of 1956I. The results of this experiment are reported in Table 11-5. (The interest payments equation was used for these results.) The initial value of k was taken to be 75 for this experiment rather than 67, and the starting quarter was 1956I rather than 1958I. Otherwise, the procedure for this experiment was the same as that for the first. Convergence was achieved in two type III iterations for each model, and the solution times were similar to those for the first experiment.

The results for the US model in Table 11-5 are the same as those in Table 11-3. The announcement has no effect on this model since it is not forward-looking. For the other two models, knowledge that the Fed will raise *RS* in the future gets incorporated immediately into *RB* and *RM*, which has a negative effect on real output. Real GNP is lower in 1956 and 1957 because of the higher long-term interest rates. *RS* is lower in these two years because of the contractionary economy; *RS* begins to rise after the increase in C_g actually takes place.

The sum of the output changes across the 20 quarters is 4.95 for the US model, 3.96 for USRE1, and 3.44 for USRE2. The difference between the US model and the others is larger here than it is in the first experiment, which is due to the negative effects in the first two years for USRE1 and USRE2. The reason the economy is less expansionary for USRE2 than for USRE1 is again because of the interest payments equation. The opposite result would be obtained if the interest payments equation were dropped.

Conclusions

These experiments give a good indication of the sensitivity of the policy properties of the model to the assumption of rational expectations in the bond

TABLE 11-5. Estimated effects of an anticipated increase in C_g for US, USRE1, and USRE2

	1956				1957				1958				1959				1960				Sum[a]
	I	II	III	IV	I	II	III	IV	I	II	III	IV	I	II	III	IV	I	II	III	IV	
GNPR: Real GNP																					
US	0.	0.	0.	0.	0.	0.	0.	0.	1.12	1.34	1.34	1.27	1.15	1.02	.88	.77	.67	.60	.54	.50	4.95
USRE1	-.12	-.30	-.43	-.52	-.56	-.57	-.57	-.56	.58	.89	1.01	1.08	1.10	1.10	1.10	1.09	1.09	1.09	1.08	1.07	3.96
USRE2	-.09	-.29	-.44	-.54	-.59	-.61	-.61	-.61	.53	.83	.94	1.00	1.03	1.03	1.02	1.01	1.00	.99	.97	.94	3.44
GNPD: GNP deflator																					
US	0.	0.	0.	0.	0.	0.	0.	0.	.04	.19	.26	.33	.42	.47	.50	.53	.54	.55	.56	.56	
USRE1	-.03	-.08	-.13	-.19	-.24	-.28	-.32	-.35	-.33	-.20	-.13	-.06	.05	.13	.21	.28	.35	.42	.47	.52	
USRE2	-.02	-.07	-.12	-.18	-.23	-.28	-.32	-.35	-.34	-.21	-.15	-.07	.03	.11	.18	.24	.31	.37	.42	.46	
100•UR: Unemployment rate (percentage points)																					
US	0.	0.	0.	0.	0.	0.	0.	0.	-.06	-.11	-.12	-.11	-.10	-.10	-.08	-.07	-.06	-.05	-.05	-.05	
USRE1	.01	.02	.04	.05	.06	.06	.06	.06	-.01	-.06	-.09	-.10	-.10	-.10	-.10	-.10	-.11	-.11	-.11	-.11	
USRE2	.01	.02	.04	.06	.06	.07	.07	.07	.00	-.05	-.07	-.08	-.08	-.09	-.09	-.09	-.09	-.09	-.09	-.09	
RS: Bill rate (percentage points)																					
US	0.	0.	0.	0.	0.	0.	0.	0.	.07	.10	.11	.12	.13	.13	.13	.13	.12	.12	.11	.11	
USRE1	-.01	-.02	-.03	-.04	-.05	-.06	-.06	-.07	.01	.03	.06	.08	.10	.11	.12	.13	.14	.15	.15	.16	
USRE2	-.01	-.02	-.03	-.05	-.06	-.06	-.07	-.07	-.00	.03	.05	.07	.09	.10	.11	.12	.13	.13	.14	.14	
RB: Bond rate (percentage points)																					
US	0.	0.	0.	0.	0.	0.	0.	0.	.02	.03	.04	.05	.06	.07	.08	.09	.10	.10	.10	.11	
USRE1	.09	.09	.10	.10	.11	.11	.12	.13	.14	.15	.15	.15	.16	.16	.16	.16	.17	.17	.18	.18	
USRE2	.07	.07	.08	.08	.09	.09	.10	.10	.11	.12	.12	.12	.12	.13	.13	.13	.13	.13	.14	.14	
RM: Mortgage rate (percentage points)																					
US	0.	0.	0.	0.	0.	0.	0.	0.	.01	.03	.05	.06	.08	.09	.10	.10	.11	.11	.12	.12	
USRE1	.08	.08	.09	.09	.10	.10	.11	.11	.12	.13	.13	.14	.14	.14	.15	.15	.15	.15	.16	.16	
USRE2	.06	.07	.07	.07	.08	.08	.09	.09	.10	.10	.11	.11	.11	.11	.11	.11	.11	.12	.12	.12	
CG: Capital gains variable (billions of current dollars)																					
US	0.	0.	0.	0.	0.	0.	0.	0.	-.11	-.06	-.68	-.45	-.34	-.30	-.26	-.20	-.18	-.14	-.12	-.09	
USRE1	-2.27	-.35	-.29	-.22	-.26	-.26	-.22	-.31	-.02	-.09	-.48	-.24	-.19	-.10	-.11	-.10	-.13	-.17	-.20	-.17	
USRE2	-3.71	-.21	-.20	-.20	-.20	-.21	-.21	-.22	-.22	-.28	-.18	-.18	-.18	-.18	-.21	-.22	-.23	-.21	-.20	-.20	
CF: Cash flow (billions of current dollars)																					
US	0.	0.	0.	0.	0.	0.	0.	0.	.18	.11	.07	.04	.02	-.01	-.03	-.05	-.07	-.08	-.09	-.10	
USRE1	-.06	-.12	-.15	-.18	-.21	-.23	-.25	-.27	-.11	-.18	-.23	-.26	-.27	-.29	-.31	-.32	-.33	-.35	-.36	-.38	
USRE2	-.05	-.10	-.13	-.15	-.17	-.19	-.21	-.23	-.06	-.12	-.16	-.19	-.20	-.21	-.22	-.23	-.24	-.25	-.26	-.27	
INT_f: Interest payments of the firm sector (billions of current dollars)																					
US	.0	.0	.0	.0	.0	.0	.0	.0	.01	.02	.03	.04	.06	.08	.10	.12	.13	.15	.16	.17	
USRE1	.04	.08	.11	.13	.16	.18	.20	.22	.25	.27	.29	.31	.33	.35	.37	.39	.40	.42	.45	.47	
USRE2	.03	.06	.08	.10	.12	.14	.16	.18	.19	.21	.23	.24	.26	.27	.29	.30	.31	.33	.34	.35	

Notes: a. Sum of the changes (at quarterly rates) over the 20 quarters, in billions of 1972 dollars.

- C_g was increased by 1.0 percent of GNPR beginning in 1958 I (sustained increase). The increase was announced in 1956 I.
- The changes for GNPR and GNPD are in percentage points.

and stock markets. It is clear that there are some important quantitative policy differences, especially with respect to timing and anticipated changes. The rational expectations assumption is clearly of some quantitative importance.

It should be stressed again that the results in this section provide no tests of the rational expectations assumption. For purposes of the experiments, (11.19) and (11.20) have been made to fit perfectly by merely adding the actual errors to them before they are solved. These errors are in fact quite large relative to the errors in the estimated term structure and capital gains equations. This is not, however, evidence against the specification of (11.19) and (11.20). Some of the reasons for this are the following.

1. The *RB* and *RM* rates are not eight-year rates, as assumed here, and therefore a closer matching of the rate data to n would be needed in any tests.
2. The value of T used for (11.20), 32 quarters, is not large enough to make the last term in the equation negligible.
3. The data on cash flow after taxes and stock prices do not match exactly.
4. The use of actual values of *RS* and π for the expected future values in the construction of the error terms for (11.19) and (11.20) is not appropriate.

None of these problems are important for the sensitivity experiments performed in this section, but they are obviously so for testing. If better data were collected so that 1 and 3 were taken care of and if a larger value of T were used so that 2 was taken care of, then the rational expectations assumption with respect to the bond and stock markets could be tested by, say, comparing the accuracy of the predictions from USRE2 and US, especially the predictions of *RB, RM,* and *CG*. For USRE2 one would have to choose for each beginning quarter of a prediction period a set of future values of the exogenous variables that one believes were expected at the time. The predictions for each different beginning quarter would be based on a different set of future values of the exogenous variables. The joint hypothesis that would be tested by this procedure is that (a) people know USRE2 and believe it to be true, including (11.19) and (11.20); (b) the chosen exogenous variable values and error terms correctly reflect the expectations at the time; and (c) expectations with respect to future values of *RS* and cash flow after taxes are rational.

11.8 Results for Sargent's Model (SARUS)

The estimation of Sargent's model is somewhat involved, as is true of any rational expectations model, and it will be easiest to discuss the estimation of

TABLE 11-6. Coefficient estimates of Sargent's model for 1954 II - 1982 III

Equation (1): Un_t is the LHS variable

	constant	t	$p_t - E_{t-1}p_t$	Un_{t-1}	Un_{t-2}	Un_{t-3}	Un_{t-4}	SE
2SLS	.00169 (1.32)	.0000232 (2.25)	—	1.635 (18.09)	-.800 (4.52)	.005 (0.03)	.105 (1.16)	.00304
FIML	.00192 (1.39)	.0000245 (2.30)	—	1.648 (17.76)	-.806 (4.34)	.016 (0.09)	.082 (0.90)	
FIML	-.00007	.0000173	-.380	1.633	-.767	.053	.066	

Equation (2): nf_t is the LHS variable

	constant	t	$p_t - E_{t-1}p_t$	Un_t	nf_{t-1}	nf_{t-2}	nf_{t-3}	nf_{t-4}	SE
2SLS	-.0033 (0.22)	.0000336 (1.82)	—	-.047 (1.58)	.945 (10.39)	.057 (0.46)	-.059 (0.47)	.048 (0.51)	.00330
FIML	-.0366 (2.70)	.0000614 (3.30)	—	-.002 (0.07)	.963 (10.65)	.041 (0.34)	-.056 (0.50)	-.014 (0.18)	
FIML	-.0393	.0000660	.207	-.015	.960	.036	-.057	-.012	

Equation (3): y_t is the LHS variable

	constant	t	n_t	n_{t-1}	n_{t-2}	n_{t-3}	n_{t-4}	$\hat{\rho}_1$	$\hat{\rho}_2$	SE
2SLS	3.04 (2.26)	.00123 (0.29)	1.833 (7.28)	-.466 (1.99)	-.225 (1.19)	-.289 (1.56)	.054 (0.33)	.930 (8.39)	.054 (0.49)	.00774
FIML	.98 (0.80)	.00024 (0.11)	2.147 (5.16)	-.539 (1.73)	-.186 (1.06)	-.199 (1.15)	.147 (1.08)	.870 (9.17)	.096 (1.00)	
FIML	1.08	.00022	2.190	-.619	-.188	-.156	.123	.872	.099	

Equation (5c): $m_t - p_t$ is the LHS variable

	constant	t	R_t	R_{t-1}	$R_{t-2}\cdots R_{t-7}$	y_t	y_{t-1}	$y_{t-2}\cdots y_{t-7}$	$\hat{\rho}_1$	$\hat{\rho}_2$	SE
2SLS	-.282 (0.20)	.0043 (1.82)	.0078 (2.67)	.0037 (1.08)	-.0005 (0.12)	-.667 (4.43)	.189 (1.67)	-.091 (0.90)	.841 (7.88)	.070 (0.66)	.00834
FIML	-3.623 (1.46)	-.0009 (0.24)	.0058 (2.01)	.0066 (2.08)	.0026 (0.71)	-.122 (0.37)	.039 (0.30)	-.088 (0.92)	.890 (8.95)	.072 (0.72)	
FIML	-2.747	-.0009	.0079	.0075	.0062	-.447	.061	-.098	.895	.060	

Equation (4): R_t is the LHS variable

	constant	t	R_{t-1}	R_{t-2}	R_{t-3}	R_{t-4}	SE
OLS	.105 (1.46)	.00643 (2.77)	1.269 (14.53)	-.518 (3.86)	.632 (4.62)	-.460 (4.82)	.289

Equation (6): $n_t = nf_t - Un_t + pop_t$

Notes:
- FSRs for 2SLS, all equations: constant, t, Un_{t-1}, Un_{t-2}, Un_{t-3}, Un_{t-4}, nf_{t-1}, nf_{t-2}, nf_{t-3}, nf_{t-4}, n_{t-1}, n_{t-2}, n_{t-3}, n_{t-4}, n_{t-5}, n_{t-6}, R_t, R_{t-1}, ..., R_{t-9}, y_{t-1}, y_{t-2}, ..., y_{t-9}, pop_t, m_t, $m_{t-1} - p_{t-1}$, $m_{t-2} - p_{t-2}$.
- 2SLS for equation (1) is OLS because there are no RHS endogenous variables.

it in steps. The model is presented in Section 5.4, and the reader should review this material before reading this section, in particular the material in Tables 5-3 and 5-4. The model consists of five stochastic equations and one identity. These equations are listed in Table 11-6. The first thing to remember about the model is that the error term in Eq. (4) is assumed to be uncorrelated with the other error terms in the model. This means that Eq. (4) can be treated separately from the rest and simply estimated by OLS.

The key variable in Sargent's model is $p_t - E_{t-1}p_t$, which is an explanatory variable in Eqs. (1) and (2). Without this variable, the model is not a rational expectations model and can thus be estimated by standard techniques. The first step in the estimation work was to estimate the model by 2SLS without the $p_t - E_{t-1}p_t$ variable included. These estimates are presented first in Table 11-6. The first-stage regressors that were used for these estimates are listed at the bottom of the table. The next step was to estimate this same version of the model by FIML. These estimates are presented next in Table 11-6. The 2SLS estimates were used as starting values. The value of L (see Eq. 6.33) at the starting point was 2438.49. The Parke algorithm was allowed to run for 40 iterations, which increased L by 10.37 to 2448.86. Near the end of the 40 iterations, L was increasing by about .01 per iteration. Each iteration corresponds to about 180 function evaluations and takes about 65 seconds on the IBM 4341. At the stopping point the covariance matrix of the coefficient estimates was computed ($\hat{V}_4$ in Eq. 6.34), and this is where the t-statistics for the first set of FIML estimates in Table 11-6 come from.

The next step was to add the expectations variable to the model and estimate it using the method in Section 11.2. The solution of the model is fairly easy because there are no expectations variables for periods $t+1$ and beyond, only for period t. This means that no type II or type III iterations have to be performed. In order to get the values for $E_{t-1}p_t\,(t = 1, \ldots, T)$ that are needed for the computation of L, the model is simply solved each period using the expected values of the exogenous variables. The predicted values of p_t from this solution are the values used for $E_{t-1}p_t$. For purposes of estimation there are three exogenous variables: m_t, pop_t, and R_t. As noted in Table 5-4, the expected values of m_t and pop_t were taken to be predicted values from eighth-order autoregressive equations. The expected values of R_t were taken to be the predicted values from Eq. (4).

In this third step each evaluation of L requires that the model be solved for each of the 114 observations of the sample period. This solution takes about 10.5 seconds on the IBM 4341. As noted earlier, the number of function evaluations required per iteration of the Parke algorithm is about 180, which takes about 65 seconds for the nonrational expectations version of the model. The total time per iteration for the complete model is thus about 10.5 seconds $\times$ 180 + 65 seconds = 32.6 minutes. Because of the cost per iteration, the Parke algorithm was only allowed to run for eight iterations. The FIML estimates of the nonrational expectations version were used as starting values. The value of L was increased from the starting value of 2448.86 to 2475.16, which is a change of 26.30 points.

The set of estimates at this point is the third set presented in Table 11-6. The key result in this table is that both coefficient estimates for $p_t - E_{t-1}p_t$ are of the expected sign (negative in Eq. 1 and positive in Eq. 2). According to the theory behind the model, positive price surprises should lead to a fall in the unemployment rate and a rise in labor supply, and the results are consistent with this theory.

The covariance matrix of the third set of coefficient estimates was not computed because of the expense, but it is the case that the two coefficient estimates for $p_t - E_{t-1}p_t$ are jointly significant. This can be seen by performing a likelihood ratio test. Let L^* denote the optimal value of L and let L^{**} denote the value of L obtained by maximizing the likelihood function subject to the constraint that both coefficients are zero. Then $2(L^* - L^{**})$ has an asymptotic χ^2 distribution with two degrees of freedom. The value of L^{**} is 2448.86 from the above results. A lower bound for the value of L^* is the final value of 2475.16. (This is only a lower bound because the Parke algorithm was not allowed to run long enough to obtain the maximum.) Twice the difference between the lower bound for L^* and L^{**} is 52.60, which is clearly greater than the critical χ^2 value at the 95-percent confidence level of 5.99. Therefore, even using this conservative value, the two coefficient estimates are highly significant.

Because of the expense of estimating Sargent's model, it was not feasible to use the method in Chapter 8 to examine the accuracy of the model. It did seem worthwhile, however, to try to get a rough idea of its accuracy. This was done by computing within-sample root mean squared errors (RMSEs). RMSEs were computed for one- through eight-quarter-ahead predictions for the 1970I–1982III period. This was done for the three estimates of Sargent's model in Table 11-6, for the ARUS model, and for the US model. The results are presented in Table 11-7. The results in Table 11-7 for the US model are the same as those in Table 8-5 (2SLS estimates).

Before discussing the results in Table 11-7, one should be clear about how the rational expectations version of Sargent's model is solved when the simulation is dynamic. (The simulations that were used in the above estima-

TABLE 11-7. Root mean squared errors of within-sample forecasts for 1970 I - 1982 III for SARUS, ARUS, and US

	Number of quarters ahead							
	1	2	3	4	5	6	7	8
GNPR = e^y: Real GNP								
SARUS[a]	1.07	1.72	2.08	2.37	2.45	2.56	2.67	2.77
SARUS[b]	1.02	1.66	2.12	2.49	2.71	2.92	3.08	3.24
SARUS[c]	1.09	1.79	2.33	2.75	3.03	3.31	3.52	3.73
ARUS	1.04	1.60	2.05	2.37	2.56	2.73	2.85	3.01
US	.66	.81	1.08	1.25	1.43	1.61	1.73	1.81
GNPD = e^p: GNP deflator								
SARUS[a]	.75	1.04	1.25	1.50	1.83	2.02	2.29	2.56
SARUS[b]	1.00	1.35	1.71	2.12	2.59	2.88	3.22	3.59
SARUS[c]	1.09	1.54	1.93	2.35	2.89	3.18	3.48	3.83
ARUS	.38	.69	1.00	1.27	1.57	1.87	2.07	2.26
US	.44	.69	.88	1.05	1.18	1.23	1.25	1.22
100·UR = 100·Un: Unemployment rate (percentage points)								
SARUS[a]	.36	.68	.92	1.10	1.13	1.12	1.13	1.14
SARUS[b]	.33	.62	.84	1.04	1.12	1.16	1.19	1.22
SARUS[c]	.33	.63	.86	1.06	1.15	1.20	1.24	1.27
ARUS	.32	.61	.84	1.03	1.12	1.17	1.21	1.24
US	.29	.43	.55	.66	.75	.83	.90	.95

Notes: a. Second set of FIML estimates in Table 11-6 (complete model).
b. First set of FIML estimates in Table 11-6 ($p_t - E_{t-1}p_t$ excluded).
c. 2SLS estimates in Table 11-6.
• There are 51 observations for the one-quarter-ahead forecasts, 50 for the two-quarter-ahead forecasts, and so on.
• For the unemployment rate the errors are in the natural units of the variables. For real GNP and the GNP deflator the errors are percentage errors (in percentage points).

tion of the model were all static.) Remember that the model is actually solved two times per quarter to get the final solution values. The model is first solved using the expected values of the exogenous variables, which gives a solution value for $E_{t-1}p_t$. The model is then solved again using this solution value plus the actual values of the exogenous variables. For both the static and dynamic simulations the expected values of the two exogenous variables, m_t and pop_t, were taken to be static predictions from the two estimated eighth-order autoregressive equations. It would not be appropriate to use dynamic predictions for this purpose because of the exogeneity of m_t and pop_t themselves. For solution purposes, in contrast to estimation purposes, R_t is an endogenous variable, and therefore the above procedure for m_t and pop_t is not followed for R_t. The R_t equation, Eq. (4), is simply added to the model for solution purposes.

The results in Table 11-7 indicate that Sargent's model is not very accurate.

All three versions are considerably less accurate than the US model for all three variables. All versions are less accurate than the ARUS model for the GNP deflator. The three versions and ARUS are of about the same degree of accuracy for the unemployment rate. The rational expectations version of Sargent's model is slightly more accurate than ARUS for real GNP for the five- through eight-quarter-ahead predictions. The other two versions are less accurate than ARUS for real GNP. Although these results are subject to the reservations discussed in Chapter 8 regarding within-sample RMSE comparisons, they are clearly not encouraging regarding Sargent's model.

Sargent's model was the first serious attempt to construct an econometric version of the class of rational expectations models discussed in Section 3.1.7, and thus it is obviously very preliminary in nature. The negative results achieved here should thus be interpreted with some caution. It may be that with more work on models of this type, the accuracy will be much improved. It is really too early to judge this type of model. One discouraging feature about this work, however, is that there have been no attempts to follow up on Sargent's model or models like it. Unless more econometric work is done on this class of rational expectations models, it may lose by default.

12 Conclusions

Because of the "wait and see" theme of this book, no strong conclusions are drawn here. The following is a summary of some of the main results in the book and a discussion of problems that I think are in particular need of future research.

12.1 Methodology

One of the three main goals of this book has been to argue for a particular methodology. The methodology centers around the testing of econometric models using the method in Section 8.4. An example of the use of the method is presented in Section 8.5. I am under no illusions that the method can be easily used to decide which model best approximates the structure of the economy. The problem is not that the method is expensive to use, since, as seen in Section 8.5, the method is not prohibitively expensive now and it will be considerably less expensive in the future with cheaper and faster computers. Rather, the problem is that it is in general difficult to use macroeconomic data to distinguish among alternative hypotheses or models. Given the smoothness of much of the data, the size of the sample that one is dealing with is to some extent small. Many more observations are needed before much can be said. I am also aware of the possibility, as discussed in Section 2.4, that the structure of the economy is not stable enough for any model in the future to be very good. If this is the case, any attempt to find the "best" model is futile. Whether the methodology emphasized here will in fact help to advance our knowledge of the structure of the economy is clearly an open question. Since the method presented here can be easily used within the context of the Fair-Parke program, the hope is that this book will stimulate more comparisons and testing of models as well as more work on the method itself.

12.2 Specification

Another goal of this book has been to present my theoretical and econometric macro models. This modeling exercise is my attempt at approximating the structure of the economy, and it provides an example of the transition from theoretical to econometric models.

12.2.1 The US Model

The theoretical model on which the US econometric model is based is one in which disequilibrium can occur because of expectation errors. Contrary to the work of Barro and Grossman (1976) and the related work on fixed price equilibria, the model provides an explanation of market failures. Firms determine prices and wages (along with other variables) within the context of their multiperiod maximization problems, and because of expectation errors, these prices and wages are not always market clearing. Whether the key assumption in the model regarding expectations, namely that expectations are not rational, is the best approximation to the truth is one of the most important current issues in macroeconomics. If expectations are in fact rational, many of the features of the theoretical model are not likely to be good approximations, and thus the econometric model that is based on this model should not, other things being equal, perform well in tests against models in which expectations are rational.

Another important feature of the theory is the idea that firms may spend time "off" their production functions. Because of adjustment costs, it may be optimal for firms to hold excess labor, excess capital, or both during periods of slack demand. If this is true, it has important implications for empirical work: it means that attempts to estimate the degree of substitution between capital and labor that are based on the assumption that the observed inputs are the utilized inputs are not trustworthy. The same holds for attempts to estimate the effects of the cost of capital on investment behavior.

Another characteristic of both the theoretical and econometric models is the accounting for all flow-of-funds and balance-sheet constraints. This implies that the government budget constraint is accounted for, and it makes clear the various assumptions about monetary policy that are possible. These issues are discussed in Sections 4.1.10 and 9.4.4.

The results that have been obtained for the econometric model so far are encouraging. With respect to the disequilibrium issue, the key disequilibrium variable in the model (the Z variable) appears in the three consumption equations and in three of the four labor supply equations. It is significant in the three labor supply equations and in two of the three consumption equations (Section 4.1.4). Regarding the question of whether firms spend time off their production functions, the excess labor variable is significant in the employment and hours equations and the excess capital variable is significant in the investment equation (Section 4.1.5). The tests of the overall model in Section 8.5 show that it is more accurate than the ARUS, VAR1US, VAR2US, and LINUS models for a number of the key variables, and the results of the comparisons in Section 11.8 show that it is more accurate than Sargent's model.

Some of the open questions or problems about the US model as I see them are the following.

1. The method in Chapter 8 has not been used to compare the model to other large-scale structural models. Also, the results in Section 8.5 show that the model is less accurate than at least one of the other models for some variables, and therefore more work is needed regarding the explanation of these variables.

2. Interest rates have a very large effect on consumption and housing investment (and thus on GNP). This can be seen best in Tables 9-4 and 9-5, especially the latter. It may be that these effects are too large. Trying both the short-term and the long-term rates, current and lagged, in each equation and then choosing the one that was most significant may have resulted in an upward bias in the estimated effects.

3. The interest rate reaction function appears to have changed when Volcker became chairman of the Fed, although not enough observations are available to know whether the way in which this change has been modeled is a good approximation. It may be that the entire equation will have to be replaced by a reaction function with a different LHS variable.

4. Some of the minor equations of the model, such as the equation explaining the interest payments of the firm sector, have fairly poor statistical properties and are thus in need of further work.

5. No evidence could be found for the effects of real as opposed to nominal interest rates in the household expenditure equations, which could be because of poor estimates of expected future inflation rates. More work is needed here.

Within the next ten years or so these problems should be worked out one way or another. One should also have by this time a good idea of how the model compares to other structural models. If the problems have not been adequately dealt with or if other features of the model are poor approximations, the comparisons should reveal this. In particular, if the Lucas point is a serious quantitative problem for the model, this should be revealed in poor performances. Likewise, if the Brainard-Tobin pitfalls criticism regarding the treatment of financial securities in models like the US model is important quantitatively, this should show up.

12.2.2 The MC Model

The MC model is in a much more preliminary state than is the US model, and it will take more than ten years to decide if it has formed the basis for a model that provides a good approximation of the economic linkages among countries.

One of the key features of the theoretical model is that there is no stock-flow distinction with respect to the determination of the exchange rate. Because the model accounts for the flow-of-funds and balance-sheet constraints, the stock and flow effects are completely integrated. The other features of the theoretical model are essentially those of the single-country model, since the two-country model is conceived of as two single-country models put together.

For the econometric work, data limitations required that a special version of the theoretical model be considered. This is a version in which (1) the short-term interest rates are determined by interest rate reaction functions, (2) the exchange rate is determined by an exchange rate reaction function, (3) the forward rate is passive, and (4) the bonds of the two countries are perfect substitutes. In addition, the sectors are aggregated into just one sector per country. This version guided the econometric specifications.

The results of comparing the MC and ARMC models in Section 8.6 are encouraging regarding the MC model. In general, it does better than the ARMC model, and variables like the exchange rates seem to be explained fairly well so far. These results are, of course, very preliminary, and for variables like consumption and investment more work on the specification of the equations is needed.

The discussion and results in Section 9.5 give a good idea of the properties of the MC model. It is clear from these results that the effects of a given change vary considerably across countries and that the trade effects by no means dominate the price, interest rate, and exchange rate effects. Although sufficient observations in the flexible exchange rate regime are not yet available to allow much weight to be placed on these results, they do suggest that models that are primarily trade multiplier models are likely to be poor approximations.

12.3 Estimation and Analysis

The final main goal of this book has been to discuss the techniques needed to estimate and analyze large nonlinear macroeconometric models. The Fair-Parke program, which is discussed in Appendix C, provides a fairly easy way of implementing these techniques.

12.3.1 Estimation Techniques

The results in Chapter 6 show that it is becoming feasible to estimate large-scale models by full information techniques and by robust techniques like 2SLAD. If one takes the view that all models are at least slightly misspecified, and thus that the standard statistical properties of the estimators are not valid, the key question is which estimator yields a model that is the best approximation of the structure. The results in Chapter 6 and in Section 8.5.5 are inconclusive on this matter, but to some extent they show that the choice of estimator does not make much difference. An important question for future research is whether this conclusion holds for other models and for later versions of the US model.

12.3.2 Testing and Analysis

The results in Chapters 7, 8, and 9 show that stochastic simulation can now be a fairly routine matter in analyzing models. The use of stochastic simulation allows one to compare models by means of the method in Chapter 8 and to estimate standard errors of multipliers. The method in Chapter 8 requires that a model be estimated a number of times, which is clearly feasible for the limited information techniques. This is still not feasible for 3SLS and FIML, although in a few years even these techniques may be capable of being used routinely.

The method in Chapter 8 is based on the premise that all models are misspecified. It is not designed to test the null hypothesis of correct specification, since this hypothesis is already assumed to be false, but instead to *estimate* the degree to which a model is misspecified. An important conclusion from the results in Table 8-2 is that all the models tested appear to be misspecified by a fairly large amount. More precisely, the estimated contribution of misspecification to the total variance of the forecast error is fairly large for most variables. This conclusion has important implications for the estimation of the standard errors of multipliers in Chapter 9. The method in Chapter 9 that is used to estimate these standard errors does not account for misspecification effects, and thus the estimated standard errors are merely lower bounds. An important question for future research is how to account for misspecification effects in this context.

The results in Chapter 10 show that it is feasible to solve optimal control problems for large models. Until models become more accurate, it is unlikely that optimal control techniques will be used in a serious way for actual policy purposes. The techniques can also be used, however, to help analyze the properties of the models, and in this respect they are of current interest. They are also of current interest in helping to evaluate past policies in the light of particular welfare functions.

12.4 Rational Expectations Models

The methods in Chapter 11 now allow nonlinear rational expectations models to be estimated and solved. The methods are expensive for large models, but not necessarily prohibitively so on fast and cheap computers. The estimation method is, as far as I know, the only method available for estimating a nonlinear rational expectations model by FIML. Given the widespread use of the rational expectations assumption and the important implications it has for policy, it is important in future research that the assumption be tested. The methods in Chapter 11 allow this to be done.

The solution method in Chapter 11 is used in Section 11.7 to analyze two versions of the US model, one with rational expectations in the bond market and one with rational expectations in the bond and stock markets. These versions are not realistic because they have not been estimated, but this exercise provides a good example of the way in which the solution method can be used. The exercise is also useful in determining how sensitive the properties of the US model are to alternative specifications. The estimation method is used in Section 11.8 to estimate Sargent's model.

It may be that it will become feasible to test econometric rational expectations models before these models are actually developed. Very little work has been done in this area since Sargent's model in 1976. Now that the methods in Chapter 11 are available, it may be that work will proceed more rapidly. One would hope that within the next ten years or so, well-developed rational expectations models will be available to compare to other models.

Appendixes

Notes

References

Index

Appendix A: Data and Identities for the United States Model

The data and identities for the US model are discussed in this appendix. Tables A-1 through A-4 describe the construction of the variables, and Table A-5 contains the identities. The stochastic equations of the model, which are presented in Chapter 4, are repeated in Table A-5. (The tables are grouped together at the end of this appendix.) Some of the material in these tables was discussed in Section 4.1.2, and the discussion will not be repeated here.

The FFA data were taken from a Flow of Funds tape of data through 1982III. The NIA data prior to 1977I were taken from an NIA tape. The tape consisted of data through 1981I, but the data from 1977I on were preliminary and subject to revision. NIA data for the 1977I–1982I period were taken from the July 1982 issue of the *Survey of Current Business*. In addition, data for a few variables for 1973I–1976IV were taken from this issue (table 3, pp. 131–132) to replace the data taken from the tape. NIA data for 1982II and 1982III were taken from an advance copy of the *Survey of Current Business* tables dated December 1982.

Table A-1 lists the sectors of the model. The notation on the RHS of the table (*H*1, *FA*, and so on) is used in Table A-2 in the description of the FFA data. The notation on the LHS (*h, f*, and so on) is used in the model.

Table A-2 contains a description of all the raw-data variables. These variables are used in Table A-4 to construct the actual variables in the model. The units quoted in Table A-2 are the units used for the construction of the variables in Table A-4; they are not necessarily the units from the original sources. The raw-data variables are listed in alphabetic order at the end of Table A-2. This makes it easier to find particular raw-data variables, which one needs to do to see how the variables in Table A-4 are constructed.

The source for the interest rate data is the *Federal Reserve Bulletin*, denoted FRB in the table. Listed in the table for each interest rate variable is the table number in the November 1982 issue of the FRB where the variable can be found. Some of the past data were obtained directly from the Federal Reserve.

The main source for the employment and population data is *Employment and Earnings,* denoted EE in the table. Listed in the table for each variable is the table or page number in the February 1982 issue of EE where the variable can be found. Some of the past data were obtained directly from the Bureau of Labor Statistics (BLS). For two variables, *JF* and *HF*, the relevant data are not published in EE, and they were obtained directly from the BLS.

A few adjustments were made to the raw data, and these are also presented in Table A-2. The quarterly social insurance variables 171–176 were constructed from the annual variables 73–78 and the quarterly variables 33, 54, and 66. Only annual data are available on the breakdown of social insurance contributions between the federal and the state and local governments with respect to the categories "personal," "government and government enterprises employer," and "other employer." It is thus necessary to construct the quarterly variables using the annual data. It is implicitly assumed in this construction that as employers, state and local governments do not contribute to the federal government and vice versa.

The tax variables 177 and 178 concern the breakdown of corporate profit taxes of the financial sector between federal and state and local. Data on this breakdown do not exist. It is implicitly assumed in this construction that the breakdown is the same as it is for the total corporate sector.

Regarding the tax and transfer variables 51 and 56, the tax surcharge of 1968III–1970III and the tax rebate of 1975II were taken out of personal income taxes (*TPG*) and put into personal transfer payments (*TRGH*). The tax surcharge numbers were taken from Okun (1971, table 1, p. 171). The rebate was 7.8 billion dollars at a quarterly rate.

The multiplication factors in Table A-2 pertain to the population, labor force, and employment variables. Official adjustments to the data on *POP*, *POP*1, *POP*2, *CL*, *CL*1, *CL*2, and *CE* were made a few times, and these must be accounted for. This was done as follows. Consider as an example the adjustments to *POP*. In January 1972 the BLS added 787 thousand to *POP* (a .547 percent increase), and in March 1973 it added 13 thousand (a .009 percent increase). To account for the first change, the old data on *POP* for the 1952I–1971IV period were multiplied by 1.00547. To account for the second change, the old data on *POP* ("old" now including the first change) for the 1952I–1972IV period were multiplied by 1.00009 and the old data for 1973I were multiplied by 1.00006. Since the second change occurred in March 1973, the adjustment to the old data for 1973I was only two-thirds of the adjustment for the earlier quarters. The same procedure was followed for the other variables. For four of the variables (*CL*, *CL*1, *CL*2, and *CE*), there was also an official adjustment in January 1978. All the multiplication factors are presented in Table A-2. The official adjustments are discussed in *Employment and Earnings,* February 1972, April 1973 (note to Table A-1), and February 1978. Some of the official adjustment numbers were obtained directly from the BLS. In the February 1983 issue of *Employment and Earnings* the household data were revised back to 1970 to reflect the information from the 1980 Census. These revisions did not eliminate the need to make the above adjustments, but they did otherwise make the pre- and post-Census data comparable.

Table A-3 contains the checks on the consistency of the NIA and FFA data. The financial savings of the sectors are defined in Eqs. (1)–(6). The savings must sum to zero across sectors, which is Eq. (7). The savings variables are based on NIA data, and they must match the corresponding variables based on FFA data—Eqs. (8)–(13). Equations (14)–(16) are adding-up checks on the FFA data alone.

Table A-4 presents all the variables in the model. With a few exceptions, the variables are either defined in terms of the raw-data variables in Table A-2 or are determined by identities. The construction of each variable is given in brackets. If the variable is determined by an identity, the notation "Def., eq." appears, where the equation number is the identity in Table A-5 that defines the variable. In a few cases the identity that defines an endogenous variable is not the equation that determines it in the model. For example, Eq. 85 defines *LM*, whereas stochastic equation 8 determines *LM* in the model. Equation 85 instead determines *E*, *E* being constructed directly from raw-data variables. Also, some of the identities define exogenous variables. For example, the exogenous variable d_{2g} is defined by Eq. 49. In the model Eq. 49 determines T_{fg}, T_{fg} being constructed directly from raw-data variables.

The financial stock variables in the model that are constructed from flow identities need a base quarter and a base quarter starting value. The base quarter values are indicated in the table. The base quarter was taken to be 1971IV, and the stock values for this quarter were taken from the Flow of Funds tape.

There are also a few internal checks on the data in Table A-4. The variables for which there are both raw data and an identity available are *GNP, GNPR,* M_b, PU_g, PU_s, and π_f. In addition, the savings variables in Table A-3 (*SAH, SAF,* and so on) must match the savings variables in Table A-4 (S_h, S_f, and so on). The checks on the savings variables are strong because many variables affect savings. Finally, there is one redundant equation in the model, Eq. 80, which the variables must satisfy.

There are a few variables in Table A-4 whose construction needs some explanation. They are discussed in the following sections.

The Variable H_f^*

H_f^* is H_f detrended. The trend factor was obtained from a regression of H_f on a constant and t for the 1952I–1982III period. The estimate of the coefficient of t was $-.56464$, and this is the coefficient that is used in the definition of H_f^* (Eq. 100).

The Variable *HO*

Data are not available for *HO* for the first 16 quarters of the sample period (1952I–1955IV). The equation that explains *HO* in the model has log *HO* on the LHS and a constant and H_f^* on the RHS. This equation was estimated for the 1956I–1982III period, and the predicted values from this regression for the (outside sample) 1952I–1955IV period were taken to be the actual data. For this work the equation was estimated under the assumption of no serial correlation of the error term. The equation that is actually used in the model is estimated under the assumption of first-order serial correlation.

The Variable *JJ**

*JJ** is *JJ* detrended. The trend factor was obtained from a regression of log *JJ* on a constant and t for the 1952I–1982III period. The estimate of the coefficient of t was $-.00083312$, which is the coefficient that is used in the definition of *JJ** (Eq. 96).

The Parameter γ_g

γ_g is the progressivity tax parameter in the personal income tax equation for g. It was obtained as follows. The sample period was divided into 15 subperiods, each subperiod corresponding roughly to a period in which there were no major changes in the federal tax laws. The 15 subperiods are 1954I–1963IV, 1964I–1965I, 1965II–1968II, 1968III–1969IV, 1970I–1970IV, 1971I–1971IV, 1972I–1972IV, 1973I–1975I, 1975II, 1975III–1976IV, 1971I, 1977II, 1977III–1980IV, 1981I–1981IV, and 1982I–1982III. Two assumptions were then made about the relationship between T_{hg}, personal income taxes, and *YT*, taxable income. The first is that within a subperiod T_{hg}/POP is equal to $[d_1 + \gamma_g(YT/POP)](YT/POP)$ plus a random error term, where d_1 and γ_g are constants. The second is that changes in the tax laws affect d_1 but not γ_g. These two assumptions led to the estimation of the following equation:

$$\text{(A.1)} \quad \frac{T_{hg}}{POP} = \underset{(3.39)}{-.0187} + \sum_{i=1}^{15} \hat{a}_i DUMG_i \frac{YT}{POP} + \underset{(8.84)}{.015513}\left(\frac{YT}{POP}\right)^2$$

$$\hat{a}_1 = \underset{(15.12)}{.123},\ \hat{a}_2 = \underset{(14.98)}{.108},\ \hat{a}_3 = \underset{(16.85)}{.108},\ \hat{a}_4 = \underset{(18.52)}{.112},$$

$$\hat{a}_5 = \underset{(18.23)}{.109},\ \hat{a}_6 = \underset{(17.15)}{.101},\ \hat{a}_7 = \underset{(18.77)}{.108},\ \hat{a}_8 = \underset{(17.77)}{.100},$$

$$\hat{a}_9 = \underset{(16.13)}{.095},\ \hat{a}_{10} = \underset{(16.12)}{.092},\ \hat{a}_{11} = \underset{(16.44)}{.098},\ \hat{a}_{12} = \underset{(15.59)}{.093},$$

$$\hat{a}_{13} = \underset{(14.43)}{.090},\ \hat{a}_{14} = \underset{(12.67)}{.088},\ \hat{a}_{15} = \underset{(11.26)}{.080}$$

SE = .00355, R^2 = .999, DW = 1.74, 1954I–1982III

$DUMG_i$ is a dummy variable that takes on a value of one in subperiod i and zero otherwise. $\hat{a}_i$ is an estimate of d_1 for subperiod i. The estimate of the coefficient of $(YT/POP)^2$, .015513, is the estimate of γ_g. Since (A.1) is only a rough approximation, a constant term was included in the estimated equation even though the above two assumptions do not call for it. When YT is zero, T_{hg} ought to be zero, but the zero-zero point is so far removed from any observation in the sample period that it seemed unwise from the point of view of approximating the tax system to constrain the equation to pass through this point.

Given γ_g, d_{1g} is defined to be $T_{hg}/YT - (\gamma_g YT)/POP$ (see Table A-4). d_{1g} is taken to be exogenous, and T_{hg} is explained (Eq. 47) as $[d_{1g} + (\gamma_g YT)/POP]YT$. This treatment allows a marginal tax rate to be defined (Eq. 90): $d_{1g}^M = d_{1g} + (2\gamma_g YT)/POP$.

The Parameter γ_s

γ_s is the progressivity tax parameter in the personal income tax equation for s. The same procedure was used to estimate this parameter as was used to estimate γ_g. There were 19 subperiods: 1954I–1964IV, 1965I–1965IV, 1966I–1966IV, 1967I–1967IV, 1968I–1968IV, 1969I–1969IV, 1970I–1970IV, 1971I–1971IV, 1972I–1972IV, 1973I–1973IV, 1974I–1974IV, 1975I–1975IV, 1976I–1976IV, 1977I–1977IV, 1978I–1978IV, 1979I–

1979IV, 1980I–1980IV, 1981I–1981IV, and 1982I–1982III. The estimated equation was

$$\text{(A.2)}\quad \frac{T_{hs}}{POP} = \underset{(12.93)}{-.0157} + \sum_{i=1}^{19} \hat{b}_i DUMS_i \frac{YT}{POP} + \underset{(2.38)}{.0022626}\left(\frac{YT}{POP}\right)^2$$

$$\hat{b}_1 = \underset{(16.79)}{.0352},\ \hat{b}_2 = \underset{(17.35)}{.0344},\ \hat{b}_3 = \underset{(17.53)}{.0344},\ \hat{b}_4 = \underset{(17.91)}{.0351},$$

$$\hat{b}_5 = \underset{(18.44)}{.0362},\ \hat{b}_6 = \underset{(18.75)}{.0371},\ \hat{b}_7 = \underset{(19.18)}{.0383},\ \hat{b}_8 = \underset{(19.78)}{.0398},$$

$$\hat{b}_9 = \underset{(20.93)}{.0431},\ \hat{b}_{10} = \underset{(19.05)}{.0408},\ \hat{b}_{11} = \underset{(18.01)}{.0398},\ \hat{b}_{12} = \underset{(18.10)}{.0408},$$

$$\hat{b}_{13} = \underset{(17.60)}{.0415},\ \hat{b}_{14} = \underset{(16.56)}{.0413},\ \hat{b}_{15} = \underset{(14.90)}{.0401},\ \hat{b}_{16} = \underset{(13.09)}{.0380},$$

$$\hat{b}_{17} = \underset{(12.32)}{.0379},\ \hat{b}_{18} = \underset{(10.99)}{.0368},\ \hat{b}_{19} = \underset{(10.82)}{.0375}$$

SE = .000780, R^2 = .999, DW = 1.82, 1954I–1982III

As can be seen, the estimate of γ_s is .0022626. d_{1s} is defined to be $T_{hs}/YT - (\gamma_s YT)/POP$ (see Table A-4). The marginal tax rate is defined to be (Eq. 91): $d_{1s}^M = d_{1s} + (2\gamma_s YT)/POP$.

The Variable *V*

The base quarter for the stock of inventories, V, was taken to be 1980IV. The base quarter value was 340.6, which was taken from the *Survey of Current Business,* July 1981, p. 17.

The Variable *KH*

KH is an estimate of the stock of housing of the household sector. It is defined by Eq. 59:

59. $\quad KH = (1 - \delta_H)KH_{-1} + IH_h.$

Given IH_h, which is constructed from the raw data, KH can be constructed once a base quarter value and a value for the depreciation rate δ_H are chosen. Annual estimates of the stock of housing are available through 1975 from the *Survey of Current Business,* April 1976. The base quarter for KH was taken to be 1963IV, and the base quarter value was taken to be 657.1. This number is the sum of the last four numbers in the 1963 row in table 8, p. 52, of the April 1976 issue of the *Survey*. Given this starting point, alternative values of δ_H were used to generate different *KH* series from Eq. 59. The aim was to find a value that led to fourth-quarter values of *KH* that were close to the published values. The value of δ_H that was chosen was .00655, which is a depreciation rate of .655 percent per quarter. The generated value of *KH* for 1973IV was 905.4, which compares almost exactly to the published value of 905.9. (Again, the 905.9 number is the sum of the last four numbers in table 8, p. 52, of the *Survey*.) The generated value for 1974IV was 928.1, which compares to the published value of 923.3.

The Variable *KD*

KD is an estimate of the stock of durable goods. It is determined by Eq. 58, which is similar to Eq. 59 for *KH*. Annual estimates of *KD* are available through 1979 from the *Survey*, April 1981. The base quarter was taken to be 1964IV, and the base quarter value was taken to be 249.6, which is the 1964 value in table 4, p. 65, of the April 1981 issue of the *Survey*. The value of the depreciation rate, δ_D, that led to a good approximation to the published series was .0515. The generated value of *KD* for 1979IV was 599.7, which compares to the published value of 598.3.

The Variable *KK*

KK is an estimate of the stock of capital of the firm sector. It is determined by Eq. 92, which is similar to Eqs. 58 and 59 for *KD* and *KH*. Annual estimates of *KK* are available through 1979 from the *Survey*, February 1981. In this case no one depreciation rate could be found that adequately approximated the published data, and in the end two rates were used. The first rate, .0247, was used from 1952I through 1963IV, and the second rate, .0263, was used from 1964I on. The first base quarter was 1952IV, with a value of 290.3, and the second base quarter was 1963IV, with a value of 413.0. The first value is the 1952 value in table 4, p. 60, of the February 1981 issue of the *Survey* under the column heading "Corporate Nonfinancial." The second value is the value of *KK* generated for 1963IV using the first depreciation rate. This value compares closely to the published value of 411.3. The value of *KK* generated for 1979IV (using the second rate) was 812.5, which compares to the published value of 806.0.

TABLE A-1. The six sectors in the model

Sector in the model	Corresponding sector(s) in the Flow of Funds accounts
1. Household (h)	1a. Households, Personal Trusts, and Nonprofit Organizations (H1)
	1b. Farms, Corporate and Noncorporate (FA)
	1c. Nonfarm Noncorporate Business (NN)
2. Firm (f)	2. Nonfinancial Corporate Business, Excluding Farms (F)
3. Financial (b)	3a. Commercial Banking (B1):
	(1) U.S. Chartered Commercial Banks
	(2) Domestic Affiliates of Commercial Banks
	(3) Foreign Banking Offices in U.S.
	(4) Banks in U.S. Possessions
	3b. Private Nonbank Financial Institutions (B2):
	(1) Savings and Loan Associations
	(2) Mutual Savings Banks
	(3) Credit Unions
	(4) Life Insurance Companies
	(5) Private Pension Funds
	(6) State and Local Government Employee Retirement Funds
	(7) Other Insurance Companies
	(8) Finance Companies
	(9) Real Estate Investment Trusts
	(10) Open-End Investment Companies (Mutual Funds)
	(11) Money Market Mutual Funds
	(12) Security Brokers and Dealers
4. Foreign (r)	4. Foreign Sector (R)
5. Federal Government (g)	5a. U.S. Government (US)
	5b. Federally Sponsored Credit Agencies and Mortgage Pools (CA)
	5c. Monetary Authority (MA)
6. State and Local Government (s)	6. State and Local Governments (S)

TABLE A-2. The raw-data variables

NIA data from the <u>Survey of Current Business</u>

Variable	Table	Line	Units	Description
1 GNP	1.1	1	SAQR$	Gross National Product
2 CDZ	"	3	"	Personal Consumption Expenditures, Durable Goods
3 CNZ	"	4	"	Personal Consumption Expenditures, Nondurable Goods
4 CSZ	"	5	"	Personal Consumption Expenditures, Services
5 IKZ	"	8	"	Nonresidential Fixed Investment
6 IHZ	"	11	"	Residential Fixed Investment
7 IVZ	"	15	"	Change in Business Inventories
8 EXZ	"	19	"	Exports
9 IMZ	"	20	"	Imports
10 GNPR	1.2	1	SAQR	Gross National Product
11 CD	"	3	"	Personal Consumption Expenditures, Durable Goods
12 CN	"	4	"	Personal Consumption Expenditures, Nondurable Goods
13 CS	"	5	"	Personal Consumption Expenditures, Services
14 IK	"	8	"	Nonresidential Fixed Investment
15 IH	"	11	"	Residential Fixed Investment
16 IV	"	15	"	Change in Business Inventories
17 EX	"	19	"	Exports
18 IM	"	20	"	Imports
19 PURG	"	22	"	Federal Government Purchases of Goods and Services
20 PURS	"	25	"	State and Local Government Purchases of Goods and Services
21 FAZ	1.5	7	SAQR$	Farm Gross Product
22 PROGZ	"	13	"	Federal Government Gross Product
23 PROSZ	"	14	"	State and Local Government Gross Product
24 FA	1.6	7	SAQR	Farm Gross Product
25 PROG	"	13	"	Federal Government Gross Product
26 PROS	"	14	"	State and Local Government Gross Product
27 CCT	1.7	2	SAQR$	CC, Total
28 STAT	"	8	"	Statistical Discrepancy
29 WLDF	"	14	"	Wage Accruals less Disbursements
30 DPER	"	17	"	Personal Dividend Income, Total
31 TRFH	"	18	"	Business Transfer Payments
32 COMPT	1.11	2	SAQR$	Compensation of Employees, Total
33 SIT	"	7	"	Employer Contributions for Social Insurance, Total
34 DC	"	25	"	Dividends, Corporate
35 INTF	"	29	"	Net Interest, Corporate
36 CCCB	1.13	2	SAQR$	CC, Corporate Business
37 PIECB	"	10	"	Profits before Tax, Corporate Business
38 TCB	"	11	"	Profits Tax Liability, Corporate Business
39 DCB	"	13	"	Dividends, Corporate Business
40 IVA	"	15	"	Inventory Valuation Adjustment, Corporate Business
41 CCADCB	"	16	"	Capital Consumption Adjustment, Corporate Business
42 CCCBN	"	20	"	CC, Nonfinancial Corporate Business
43 PIECBN	"	28	"	Profits Before Tax, Nonfinancial Corporate Business
44 TCBN	"	29	"	Profits Tax Liability, Nonfinancial Corporate Business
45 DCBN	"	31	"	Dividends, Nonfinancial Corporate Business
46 CCADCBN	"	34	"	Capital Consumption Adjustment, Nonfinancial Corporate Business
47 PRI	2.1	9	SAQR$	Proprietors' Income with Inventory Valuation and Capital Consumption Adjustments
48 RNT	"	12	"	Rental Income of Persons with Capital Consumption Adjustment
49 UB	"	17	"	Government Unemployment Insurance Benefits
50 TRHR	"	29	"	Personal Transfer Payments to Foreigners (net)

(continued)

TABLE A-2 (continued)

Variable	Table	Line	Units	Description
51 TPG	3.2	2	SAQR$	Personal Tax and Nontax Receipts, Federal Government (See below for adjustments.)
52 TCG	"	6	"	Corporate Profits Tax Accruals, Federal Government
53 IBTG	"	7	"	Indirect Business Tax and Nontax Accruals, Federal Government
54 SIG	"	11	"	Contributions for Social Insurance, Federal Government
55 PURGZ	"	13	"	Purchases of Goods and Services, Federal Government
56 TRGH	"	17	"	Transfer Payments to Persons, Federal Government (See below for adjustments.)
57 TRGR	"	18	"	Transfer Payments to Foreigners, Federal Government
58 TRGS	"	19	"	Grants in Aid to State and Local Governments, Federal Government
59 INTG	"	20	"	Net Interest Paid, Federal Government
60 INTGR	"	23	"	Interest Paid to Foreigners, Federal Government
61 SUBG	"	25	"	Subsidies less Current Surplus of Government Enterprises, Federal Government
62 WLDG	"	28	"	Wage Accruals less Disbursements, Federal Government
63 TPS	3.3	2	SAQR$	Personal Tax and Nontax Receipts, State and Local Government (S&L)
64 TCS	"	6	"	Corporate Profits Tax Accruals, S&L (Note: TCS = TCB - TCG.)
65 IBTS	"	7	"	Indirect Business Tax and Nontax Accruals, S&L
66 SIS	"	11	"	Contributions for Social Insurance, S&L
67 PURSZ	"	14	"	Purchases of Goods and Services, S&L
68 TRRSH	"	17	"	Transfer Payments to Persons, S&L
69 INTS	"	18	"	Net Interest Paid, S&L
70 SUBS	"	22	"	Subsidies Less Current Surplus of Government Enterprises, S&L
71 WLDS	"	25	"	Wage Accruals less Disbursements, S&L
72 COMPMIL	3.7	8	SAQR$	Federal Government Compensation of Employees, Military
73 SIHGA	3.13	3	YEAR$	Personal Contributions for Social Insurance to the Federal Government
74 SIQGA	"	5	"	Government and Government Enterprises Employer Contributions for Social Insurance to the Federal Government
75 SIFGA	"	6	"	Other Employer Contributions for Social Insurance to the Federal Government
76 SIHSA	"	14	"	Personal Contributions for Social Insurance to the S&L Governments
77 SIQSA	"	16	"	Government and Government Enterprises Employer Contributions for Social Insurance to the S&L Governments
78 SIFSA	"	17	"	Other Employer Contributions for Social Insurance to the S&L Governments

Data from the Flow of Funds tape.

(All flow data are SAQR$. All stock data are end of quarter in billions of current dollars.)

Variable	Code	Description
79 CDDCF	103020001	Change in Demand Deposits and Currency, F
80 NFIF	105000005	Net Financial Investment, F
81 IHMF	105012205	Residential Construction, Multi-family Units, Nonfinancial Corporate Business
82 IH1F	105012405	Residential Construction, 1-4 Family Structures, Change in Work in Process on Corporate Nonfarm
83 MRS	105030003	Mineral Rights Sales
84 PIEF1	106060005	Profits before Tax, F
85 DISF	107005005	Discrepancy, F
86 CDDCNN	113020003	Change in Demand Deposits and Currency, NN
87 NFINN	115000005	Net Financial Investment, NN
88 IKNN	115013005	Nonresidential Fixed Investment, NN
89 IVNN	115020000	Inventory Investment, NN
90 CCNN	116300005	Capital Consumption, NN. Also, Current Surplus = Gross Saving, NN
91 CDDCFA	133020003	Change in Demand Deposits and Currency, FA
92 NFIFA	135000005	Net Financial Investment, FA

(continued)

TABLE A-2 (continued)

Variable	Code	Description
93 IKFA	135013003	Nonresidential Fixed Investment, FA
94 IVFA	135020003	Inventory Investment, FA
95 PIEFA	136060003	Corporate Profits, FA
96 DFA	136120003	Dividends, FA
97 TFA	136231003	Tax Accruals, FA
98 CCFA	136300103	Capital Consumption, FA
99 CCADFA	136310103	Capital Consumption Adjustment, FA
100 CDDCH1	153020005	Change in Checkable Deposits and Currency, H1
101 MVCE,CCE	153064005	Net Purchases of Corporate Equities of Households MVCE is the market value of the stock. CCE is the change in the stock excluding capital gains and losses.
102 NFIH1	155000005	Net Financial Investment, H1
103 IKH1	155013003	Nonresidential Fixed Investment, Nonprofit Institutions
104 DISH1	157005005	Discrepancy, H1
105 NFIS	205000005	Net Financial Investment, S
106 DISS	207005005	Discrepancy, S
107 CDDCS	213020005	Change in Demand Deposits and Currency, S
108 RET	224090005	Retirement Credits to Households, S
109 CGLDR	263011005	Change in Gold and SDR's, R
110 CDDCR	263020001	Change in U.S. Demand Deposits, R
111 CFXUS	263111005	Change in U.S. Official Foreign Exchange and Net IMF Position
112 NFIR	265000005	Net Financial Investment, R
113 PIEF2	266060001	Net Corporate Earnings Retained Abroad
114 DISR	267005005	Discrepancy, R
115 CGLDFXUS	313011005	Change in Gold, SDR's, and Foreign Exchange, US
116 CDDCUS	313020001	Change in Demand Deposits and Currency, US
117 INS	313154005	Insurance Credits to Households, US
118 NFIUS	315000005	Net Financial Investment, US
119 DISUS	317005005	Discrepancy, US
120 CDDCCA	403020000	Change in Demand Deposits and Currency, CA
121 NIACA	404090005	Net Increase in Financial Assets, CA
122 NILCA	404190005	Net Increase in Liabilities, CA
123 SURCA	406006003	Current Surplus of CA
124 DISCA	407005005	Discrepancy, CA
125 NIDDLB2	493127005	Net Increase in Liabilities in the form of Checkable Deposits, B2
126 IHBZ	645012205	Residential Construction, Multi-family Units, Reits
127 CGD	656120000	Capital Gains Dividend
128 CDDCB2	693020005	Change in Demand Deposits and Currency, B2
129 NIAB2	694090005	Net Increase in Financial Assets, B2
130 NILB2	694190005	Net Increase in Liabilities, B2
131 DISB2	697005005	Discrepancy, B2
132 CGLDFXMA	713011005	Change in Gold and Foreign Exchange, MA
133 CFRLMA	713068000	Change in Federal Reserve Loans to Domestic Banks, MA
134 NILBRMA	713113001	Change in Member Bank Reserves, MA
135 NIDDLRMA	713122605	Change in Liabilities in the form of Demand Deposits and Currency due to Foreign of the MA
136 NIDDLGMA	713123101	Change in Liabilities in the form of Demand Deposits and Currency due to U.S. Government of the MA
137 NILCMA	713125001	Change in Liabilities in the form of Currency Outside Banks of the MA
138 NIAMA	714090005	Net Increase in Financial Assets, MA
139 NILMA	714190005	Net Increase in Liabilities, MA
140 SURMA	716006003	Current Surplus of MA
141 CVCBRB1	723020005	Change in Vault Cash and Member Bank Reserves, B1
142 NILVCMA	723025000	Change in Liabilities in the form of Vault Cash of Commercial Banks of the MA
143 DISB1	727005005	Discrepancy, B1
144 NIDDAB1	743020003	Net Increase in Financial Assets in the form of Demand Deposits and Currency of Banks in U.S. Possessions
145 NIDDLB1	763120005	Net Increase in Liabilities in the form of Checkable Deposits, B1
146 NIAB1	764090005	Net Increase in Financial Assets, B1
147 NILB1	764190005	Net Increase in Liabilities, B1
148 IKBZ	795013003	Nonresidential Fixed Investment, Financial Corporations
149 MAILFLT1	903023105	Mail Float, U.S. Government
150 MAILFLT2	903029205	Mail Float, Private Domestic Nonfinancial

(continued)

TABLE A-2 (continued)

Interest rate data

Variable	Description
151 RS	Three-Month Treasury Bill Rate (Auction Average), percentage points [FRB, A28. Quarterly average of monthly data.]
152 RM	Mortgage Rate, percentage points. [FRB, A40. FHA mortgages (HUD series), secondary markets. Quarterly average of monthly data. Linear interpolation for missing monthly observations.]
153 RB	Aaa Corporate Bond Rate, percentage points. [FRB, A28. Quarterly average of monthly data.]
154 RD	Discount Rate, percentage points. [FRB, A7. Rate at F.R. Bank of N.Y. Quarterly average, inclusive of any surcharge.]

Employment and population data

Variable	Description
155 CE	Civilian Employment, SA in millions. [EE, A-33. Quarterly average of monthly data. See below for adjustments.]
156 CL	Civilian Labor Force, SA in millions. [EE, A-33. Quarterly average of monthly data. See below for adjustments.]
157 CL1	Civilian Labor Force of Males 25-54, SA in millions. [EE, p. 132. Quarterly average of monthly data. See below for adjustments.]
158 CL2	Civilian Labor Force of Females 25-54, SA in millions. [EE, p. 133. Quarterly average of monthly data. See below for adjustments.]
159 AF	Armed Forces, millions. [EE, A-33. Quarterly average of monthly data.]
160 AF1	Armed Forces of Males 25-54, millions. [EE, A-3. Total labor force - Civilian labor force. Quarterly average of monthly data.]
161 AF2	Armed Forces of Females, 25-54, millions. [EE, A-3. Total labor force - Civilian labor force. Quarterly average of monthly data.]
162 POP	Total noninstitutional population 16 and over, millions. [EE, A-3. Quarterly average of monthly data. See below for adjustments.]
163 POP1	Noninstitutional population of males 25-54, millions. [EE, A-3. Total labor force + Not in labor force. Quarterly average of monthly data. See below for adjustments.]
164 POP2	Noninstitutional population of females 25-54, millions. [EE, A-3. Total labor force + Not in labor force. Quarterly average of monthly data. See below for adjustments.]
165 JF	Employment, Total Private Sector, All Persons, SA in millions. [BLS, unpublished, "Basic Industry Data for the Total Private Sector, All Persons." November 29, 1982.]
166 HF	Average Weekly Hours, Total Private Sector, All Persons, SA. [BLS, unpublished, "Basic Industry Data for the Total Private Sector, All Persons." November 29, 1982.]
167 HO	Average Weekly Overtime Hours in Manufacturing, SA. [EE, C-6. Quarterly average of monthly data.]
168 JQ	Total Government Employment, SA in millions. [EE, B-4. Quarterly average of monthly data.]
169 JG	Federal Government Employment, SA in millions. [EE, B-4. Quarterly average of monthly data.]
170 JHQ	Total Government Employee Hours, SA in millions of hours per quarter. [EE, C-9. Quarterly average of monthly data.]

(continued)

TABLE A-2 (continued)

Adjustments to the raw data

171 SIHG = (SIHGA/(SIHGA + SIHSA))(SIG + SIS - SIT)
[Contributions for Social Insurance, h to g.]
172 SIHS = SIG + SIS - SIT - SIHG
[Contributions for Social Insurance, h to s.]
173 SIFG = (SIFGA/(SIFGA + SIQGA))(SIG - SIHG)
[Contributions for Social Insurance, f to g.]
174 SIGG = SIG - SIHG - SIFG
[Contributions for Social Insurance, g to g.]
175 SIFS = (SIFSA/(SIFSA + SIQSA))(SIS - SIHS)
[Contributions for Social Insurance, f to s.]
176 SISS = SIS - SIHS - SIFS
[Contributions for Social Insurance, s to s.]

177 TBG = (TCG/(TCG + TCS))(TCB - TCBN)
[Corporate Profit Tax Accruals, b to g.]
178 TBS = TCB - TCBN - TBG
[Corporate Profit Tax Accruals, b to s.]

51 TPG = TPG from raw data - TAXADJ
56 TRGH = TRGH from raw data + TAXADJ
[TAXADJ: 1968 III = 1.525, 1968 IV = 1.775, 1969 I = 2.675,
1969 II = 2.725, 1969 III = 1.775, 1969 IV = 1.825,
1970 I = 1.25, 1970 II = 1.25, 1970 III = .1,
1975 II = -7.8.]

Multiplication factors (See the discussion in Appendix A.)

	1952 I - 1971 IV	1952 I - 1972 IV	1973 I	1952 I - 1977 IV
POP	1.00547	1.00009	1.00006	—
POP1	.99880	1.00084	1.00056	—
POP2	1.00251	1.00042	1.00028	—
CL	1.00391	1.00069	1.00046	1.00239
CL1	.99878	1.00078	1.00052	1.00014
CL2	1.00297	1.00107	1.00071	1.00123
CE	1.00375	1.00069	1.00046	1.00268

Abbreviations

BLS Bureau of Labor Statistics
CC Capital Consumption Allowances with Capital Consumption Adjustment
EE _Employment and Earnings_, February 1982
FRB _Federal Reserve Bulletin_, November 1982
SA Seasonally Adjusted
SAQR Seasonally Adjusted at Quarterly Rates in Billions of 1972 Dollars
SAQR$ Seasonally Adjusted at Quarterly Rates in Billions of Current Dollars
YEAR$ Annual Data, Billions of Current Dollars.
For the construction of variables 171 - 176, the same yearly observation was used for each quarter of the year.

See Table A-1 for abbreviations: B1, B2, CA, F, FA, H1, MA, NN, R, S, US.

(continued)

TABLE A-2 (continued)

Alphabetical listing of the raw-data variables

Variable	Number	Variable	Number	Variable	Number	Variable	Number
AF	159	DISCA	124	MAILFLT1	149	RB	153
AF1	160	DISF	85	MAILFLT2	150	RD	154
AF2	161	DISH1	104	MRS	83	RET	108
CCADCB	41	DISR	114	MVCE	101	RM	152
CCADCBN	46	DISS	106	NFIF	80	RNT	48
CCADFA	99	DISUS	119	NFIFA	92	RS	151
CCCB	36	DPER	30	NFIH1	102	SIFG	173
CCCBN	42	EX	17	NFINN	87	SIFGA	75
CCE	101	EXZ	8	NFIR	112	SIFS	175
CCFA	98	FA	24	NFIS	105	SIFSA	78
CCNN	90	FAZ	21	NFIUS	118	SIG	54
CCT	27	GNP	1	NIAB1	146	SIGG	174
CD	11	GNPR	10	NIAB2	129	SIHG	171
CDDCB2	128	HF	166	NIACA	121	SIHGA	73
CDDCCA	120	HO	167	NIAMA	138	SIHS	172
CDDCF	79	IBTG	53	NIDDAB1	144	SIHSA	76
CDDCFA	91	IBTS	65	NIDDLB1	145	SIQGA	74
CDDCH1	100	IH	15	NIDDLB2	125	SIQSA	77
CDDCNN	86	IHBZ	126	NIDDLGMA	136	SIS	66
CDDCR	110	IHMF	81	NIDDLRMA	135	SISS	176
CDDCS	107	IHZ	6	NILBRMA	134	SIT	33
CDDCUS	116	IH1F	82	NILB1	147	STAT	28
CDZ	2	IK	14	NILB2	130	SUBG	61
CE	155	IKB2	148	NILCA	122	SUBS	70
CFRLMA	133	IKFA	93	NILCMA	137	SURCA	123
CFXUS	111	IKH1	103	NILMA	139	SURMA	140
CGD	127	IKNN	88	NILVCMA	142	TBG	177
CGLDFXMA	132	IKZ	5	PIECB	37	TBS	178
CGLDFXUS	115	IM	18	PIECBN	43	TCB	38
CGLDR	109	IMZ	9	PIEFA	95	TCBN	44
CL	156	INS	117	PIEF1	84	TCG	52
CL1	157	INTF	35	PIEF2	113	TCS	64
CL2	158	INTG	59	POP	162	TFA	97
CN	12	INTGR	60	POP1	163	TPG	51
CNZ	3	INTS	69	POP2	164	TPS	63
COMPMIL	72	IV	16	PRI	47	TRFH	31
CS	13	IVA	40	PROG	25	TRGH	56
CSZ	4	IVFA	94	PROGZ	22	TRGR	57
CVCBRB1	141	IVNN	89	PROS	26	TRGS	58
DC	34	IVZ	7	PROSZ	23	TRHR	50
DCB	39	JF	165	PURG	19	TRRSH	68
DCBN	45	JG	169	PURGZ	55	UB	49
DFA	96	JHQ	170	PURS	20	WLDF	29
DISB1	143	JQ	168	PURSZ	67	WLDG	62
DISB2	131					WLDS	71

TABLE A-3. Links between the NIA and FFA data

1.1	HH	None
1.2	FH	COMPT - PROGZ - PROSZ - (SIT - SIGG - SISS) - WLDF - SUBG - SUBS + PRI + RNT + INTF + TRFH + DCBN + DC - DFA - DCB + PIEFA + CCT - CCCB + CCFA
1.3	BH	DCB - DCBN + CGD
1.4	RH	None
1.5	GH	PROGZ - SIGG - WLDG + TRGH + INS + INTG - INTGR + SUBG
1.6	SH	PROSZ - SISS - WLDS + TRRSH + RET + INTS + DP - DC + SUBS
2.1	HF	CSZ + CNZ + CDZ - IBTG - IBTS - IMZ - PIECB + PIECBN - CCCB + CCCBN - CCADCB + CCADCBN + IHZ - IH1F - IHMF - IHBZ + IKH1 + IKFA + IKNN + IVFA + IVNN
2.2	FF	IH1F + IHMF + IKZ - IKH1 - IKFA - IKNN - IKBZ + IVZ - IVFA - IVNN
2.3	BF	IHBZ + IKBZ
2.4	RF	EXZ
2.5	GF	PURGZ - PROGZ
2.6	SF	PURSZ - PROSZ
3.1	HB	PIECB - PIECBN + CCCB - CCCBN + CCADCB - CCADCBN
3.2	FB	None
3.3	BB	None
3.4	RB	None
3.5	GB	None
3.6	SB	None
4.1	HR	IMZ + TRHR
4.2	FR	None
4.3	BR	None
4.4	RR	None
4.5	GR	TRGR + INTGR
4.6	SR	None
5.1	HG	TPG + TFA + IBTG + SIHG
5.2	FG	TCG - TFA - TBG + MRS + SIFG
5.3	BG	TBG + SURCA + SURMA
5.4	RG	None
5.5	GG	SIGG
5.6	SG	None
6.1	HS	TPS + IBTS + SIHS
6.2	FS	TCS - TCG - TBS + SIFS
6.3	BS	TBS
6.4	RS	None
6.5	GS	TRGS
6.6	SS	SISS

Savings of the sectors:

(1) SAH = FH + BH + GH + SH - (HF + HB + HR + HG + HS)
(2) SAF = HF + FF + BF + RF + GF + SF - (FH + FF + FG + FS)
(3) SAB = HB - (BH + BF + BS + BG)
(4) SAR = HR + GR - RF
(5) SAG = HG + FG + BG + GG - (GH + GF + GR + GS + GG)
(6) SAS = HS + FS + BS + GS + SS - (SH + SF + SS)

Checks:

(7) 0 = SAH + SAF + SAB + SAR + SAG + SAS

(8) SAH = NIFIH1 + NFIFA + NFINN + DISH1
(9) SAF = NFIF + DISF + WLDF + STAT
(10) SAB = NIAB1 - NILB1 + NIAB2 - NILB2 + DISB1 + DISB2
(11) SAR = NFIR + DISR
(12) SAG = NFIUS + NIACA - NILCA + NIAMA - NILMA + DISUS + DISCA
(13) SAS = NFIS + DISS

(14) 0 = -NIDDLB1 + NIDDAB1 + CDDCB2 - NIDDLB2 + CDDCF + MAILFLT1 + MAILFLT2 + CDDCUS + CDDCCA - NIDDLRMA - NIDDLGMA + CDDCH1 + CDDCFA + CDDCNN + CDDCR + CDDCS - NILCMA

(15) 0 = CVCBRB1 - NILBRMA - NILVCMA
(16) 0 = CGLDR - CFXUS + CGLDFXUS + CGLDFXMA

Notes:
- IJ = receipts from I to J; I, J = H, F, B, R, G, S.
- See Table A-2 for the definitions of the variables.

TABLE A-4. The variables of the model in alphabetical order

Name	Equation number	Description
A_b	73	Net financial assets, b, B$. [Def., eq. 73. Base Period = 1971 IV, Value = 250.697.]
A_f	70	Net financial assets, f, B$. [Def., eq. 70. Base Period = 1971 IV, Value = -240.261.]
A_g	77	Net financial assets, g, B$. [Def., eq. 77. Base Period = 1971 IV, Value = -214.404.]
A_h	66	Net financial assets, h, B$. [Def., eq. 66. Base Period = 1971 IV, Value = 1321.270.]
A_r	75	Net financial assets, r, B$. [Def., eq. 75. Base Period = 1971 IV, Value = -31.570.]
A_s	79	Net financial assets, s, B$. [Def., eq. 79. Base Period = 1971 IV, Value = -105.872.]
AA	89	Total net wealth, h, B72$. [Def., eq. 89.]
BO	22	Bank borrowing from the Fed, B$. [Sum of CFRLMA. Base Period = 1971 IV, Value = .039.]
BR	57	Total bank reserves, B$. [Sum of CVCBRB1. Base Period = 1971 IV, Value = 35.329.]
C_g	0	Purchases of goods, g, B72$. [PURG - PROG]
C_s	0	Purchases of goods, s, B72$. [PURS - PROS]
CC_b	0	Capital consumption, b, B72$. [(CCCB + CCADCB - CCCBN - CCADCBN)/PX. See below for PX.]
CC_f	21	Capital consumption, f, B$. [CCCBN + CCADCBN - CCFA - CCADFA]
CC_h	0	Capital consumption, h, B$. [CCT - CCCB + CCFA]
CD	3	Consumer expenditures for durable goods, B72$. [CD]
CF	68	Cash flow, f, B$. [Def., eq. 68.]
CG	25	Capital gains (+) or losses (-) on corporate stocks held by the household sector, B$. [MVCE - $MVCE_{-1}$ - CCE]
CN	2	Consumer expenditures for nondurable goods, B72$. [CN]
CS	1	Consumer expenditures for services, B72$. [CS]
CUR	26	Currency held outside banks, B$. [Sum of NILCMA. Base Period = 1971 IV, Value = 53.438.]
d_{1g}	0	Personal income tax parameter, g. [Def., eq. 47.]
d_{1g}^M	90	Marginal personal income tax rate, g. [Def., eq. 90.]
d_{1s}	0	Personal income tax parameter, s. [Def., eq. 48.]
d_{1s}^M	91	Marginal personal income tax rate, s. [Def., eq. 91.]
d_{2g}	0	Profit tax rate, g. [Def., eq. 49.]
d_{2s}	0	Profit tax rate, s. [Def., eq. 50.]
d_{3g}	0	Indirect business tax rate, g. [Def., eq. 51.]
d_{3s}	0	Indirect business tax rate, s. [Def., eq. 52.]
d_{4g}	0	Employee social security tax rate, g. [Def., eq. 53.]
d_{4s}	0	Employee social security tax rate, s. [Def., eq. 54.]
d_{5g}	0	Employer social security tax rate, g. [Def., eq. 55.]
d_{5s}	0	Employer social security tax rate, s. [Def., eq. 56.]
D593	0	1 in 1959 III; 0 otherwise.
D594	0	1 in 1959 IV; 0 otherwise.
D601	0	1 in 1960 I; 0 otherwise.
D651	0	1 in 1965 I; 0 otherwise.
D652	0	1 in 1965 II; 0 otherwise.
D691	0	1 in 1969 I; 0 otherwise.
D692	0	1 in 1969 II; 0 otherwise.

(continued)

TABLE A-4 (continued)

Name	Equation number	Description
D714	0	1 in 1971 IV; 0 otherwise.
D721	0	1 in 1972 I; 0 otherwise.
DD793	0	1 from 1979 III on; 0 otherwise.
DD811	0	1 from 1981 I on; 0 otherwise.
D_b	0	Dividends paid, b, B$. [DCB - DCBN + CGD]
D_f	18	Dividends paid, f, B$. [DC - DFA - (DCB - DCBN)]
DIS_b	0	Discrepancy for b, B$. [DISB1 + DISB2]
DIS_f	0	Discrepancy for f, B$. [DISF]
DIS_g	0	Discrepancy for g, B$. [DISUS + DISCA]
DIS_h	0	Discrepancy for h, B$. [DISH1]
DIS_r	0	Discrepancy for r, B$. [DISR]
DIS_s	0	Discrepancy for s, B$. [DISS]
DR_s	0	Dividends received by s, B$. [DC - DPER]
E	85	Total employment, civilian and military, millions. [CE + AF]
EX	0	Exports, B72$. [EX]
EXP_g	106	Total expenditures, g, B$. [Def., eq. 106.]
EXP_s	113	Total expenditures, s, B$. [Def., eq. 113.]
FA	0	Farm gross product, B72$. [FA]
g_1	0	Reserve requirement ratio. [Def., eq. 57.]
GNP	82	Gross National Product, B$. [Def., eq. 82, or GNP.]
GNPD	84	GNP deflator. [Def., eq. 84.]
GNPR	83	Gross National Product, B72$. [Def., eq. 83, or GNPR.]
GNPR*	0	High activity level of GNPR, B72$. [Peak to peak interpolation of GNPR. Peak quarters are 1952 I - 1953 II, 1955 III, 1960 I, 1962 II, 1966 I, 1968 II - 1969 II, 1973 I, and 1978 IV.]
H_f	14	Average number of hours paid per job, f, hours per quarter. [13•HF]
H_f^*	100	H_f detrended. [Def., eq. 100.]
H_g	0	Average number of hours paid per civilian job, g, hours per quarter. [JHQ/JQ]
H_m	0	Average number of hours paid per military job, g, hours per quarter. [520.]
H_s	0	Average number of hours paid per job, s, hours per quarter. [JHQ/JQ]
HN	62	Average number of non overtime hours paid per job, f, hours per quarter. [Def., eq. 62.]
HO	15	Average number of overtime hours paid per job, f, hours per quarter. [13•HO. Constructed values for 1952 I - 1955 IV. See the discussion in Appendix A.]
IBT_g	51	Indirect business taxes, g, B$. [IBTG]
IBT_s	52	Indirect business taxes, s, B$. [IBTS]
IH_b	0	Housing investment, b, B72$. [IHBZ/(IHZ/IH)]
IH_f	0	Housing investment, f, B72$. [(IH1F + IHMF)/(IHZ/IH)]
IH_h	4	Housing investment, h, B72$. [(IHZ - IH1F - IHMF - IHBZ)/(IHZ/IH)]

(continued)

TABLE A-4 (continued)

Name	Equation number	Definition
IK_b	0	Plant and equipment investment, b, B72$. [IKBZ/(IKZ/IK)]
IK_f	12	Plant and equipment investment, f, B72$. [(IKZ - IKH1 - IKFA - IKNN - IKBZ)/(IKZ/IK)]
IK_h	0	Plant and equipment investment, h, B72$. [(IKH1 + IKNN + IKFA)/(IKZ/IK)]
IM	27	Imports, B72$. [IM]
INS	0	Insurance credits to households from g, B$. [INS]
INT_f	19	Interest payments, f, B$. [INTF]
INT_g	29	Interest payments, g, B$. [INTG]
INT_{gr}	0	Interest payments to r from g, B$. [INTGR]
INT_s	0	Interest payments, s, B$. [INTS]
IV_f	117	Inventory investment, f, B72$. [(IVZ - IVFA - IVNN)/PIV]
IV_h	0	Inventory investment, h, B72$. [(IVFA + IVNN)/PIV]
IVA	20	Inventory valuation adjustment, B$. [IVA]
J_f	13	Number of jobs, f, millions. [JF]
J_g	0	Number of civilian jobs, g, millions. [JG]
J_m	0	Number of military jobs, g, millions. [AF]
J_s	0	Number of jobs, s, millions. [JQ - JG]
JHMIN	94	Number of worker hours required to product Y, millions. [Def., eq. 94.]
JJ	95	Ratio of the total number of worker hours paid for to the total population 16 and over. [Def., eq. 95.]
JJ^*	96	JJ detrended. [Def., eq. 96.]
KD	58	Stock of durable goods, B72$. [Def., eq. 58. Base Period = 1964 IV, Value = 249.6, Dep. Rate = .0515.]
KH	59	Stock of housing, h, B72$. [Def., eq. 59. Base Period = 1963 IV, Value = 657.1, Dep. Rate = .00655.]
KK	92	Stock of capital, f, B72$. [Def., eq. 92. Base Period 1 = 1952 IV, Value = 290.3, Dep. Rate = .0247; Base Period 2 = 1963 IV, Value = 413.0, Dep. Rate = .0263.]
KKMIN	93	Amount of capital required to produce Y, B72$. [Def., eq. 93.]
L1	5	Labor force of males 25-54, millions. [CL1 + AF1]
L2	6	Labor force of females, 25-54, millions. [CL2 + AF2]
L3	7	Labor force of all others, millions. [CL + AF - CL1 - AF1 - CL2 - AF2]
LM	8	Number of "moonlighters": difference between the total number of jobs (establishment data) and the total number of people employed (household survey data), millions. [Def., eq. 85.]
M_b	71	Net demand deposits and currency, b, B$. [Def., eq. 71. Also sum of -NIDDLB1 + NIDDAB1 + CDDCB2 - NIDDLB2. Base Period = 1971 IV, Value = -189.409.]
M_f	17	Demand deposits and currency, f, B$. [Sum of CDDCF + MAILFLT1 + MAILFLT2. Base Period = 1971 IV, Value = 64.905.]
M_g	0	Demand deposits and currency, g, B$. [Sum of CDDCUS + CDDCCA - NIDDLRMA - NIDDLGMA. Base Period = 1971 IV, Value = 10.530.]
M_h	9	Demand deposits and currency, h, B$. [Sum of CDDCH1 + CDDCFA + CDDCNN. Base Period = 1971 IV, Value = 149.448.]
M_r	0	Demand deposits and currency, r, B$. [Sum of CDDCR. Base Period = 1971 IV, Value = 6.503.]

(continued)

TABLE A-4 (continued)

Name	Equation number	Description
M_s	0	Demand deposits and currency, s, B$. [Sum of CDDCS. Base Period = 1971 IV, Value = 11.966.]
MDIF	0	Net increase in demand deposits and currency of banks in U.S. possessions plus change in demand deposits and currency of private nonbank financial institutions plus change in demand deposits and currency of federally sponsored credit agencies and mortgage pools minus mail float, U.S. government, B$. [NIDDAB1 + CDDCB2 + CDDCCA - MAILFLT1]
MRS	0	Mineral rights sales, B$. [MRS]
M1	81	Money supply, B$. [Def., eq. 81. Base Period = 1971 IV, Value = 247.136.]
P_f	10	Price deflator for X - FA. [Def., eq. 31.]
P_g	40	Price deflator for C_g. [(PURGZ - PROGZ)/(PURG - PROG)]
P_h	34	Price deflator for domestic sales exclusive of indirect business taxes. [Def., eq. 34]
P_s	41	Price deflator for C_s. [(PURSZ - PROSZ)/(PURS - PROS)]
PCGNPD	122	Percentage change in GNPD, annual rate, percentage points. [Def., eq. 122.]
PCGNPR	123	Percentage change in GNPR, annual rate, percentage points. [Def., eq. 123.]
PCM1	124	Percentage change in M1, annual rate, percentage points. [Def., eq. 124.]
PCD	37	Price deflator for CD. [CDZ/CD]
PCN	36	Price deflator for CN. [CNZ/CN]
PCS	35	Price deflator for CS. [CSZ/CS]
PD	33	Price deflator for X - EX + IM (domestic sales) [Def., eq. 33.]
PEX	32	Price deflator for EX. [EXZ/EX]
PFA	0	Price deflator for FA. [FAZ/FA]
PIH	38	Price deflator for housing investment. [IHZ/IH]
PIK	39	Price deflator for plant and equipment investment. [IKZ/IK]
PIM	0	Price deflator for IM. [IMZ/IM]
PIV	42	Price deflator for inventory investment, adjusted. [IVZ/IV. The following adjustments were made: 1953 III = .7637, 1958 III = .7981, 1959 III = .7956, 1975 III = 1.4110, 1975 IV = 1.4110, 1979 IV = 1.5000, 1980 I = 1.5000, 1980 II = 1.5000, 1981 I = 3.0000.]
POP	120	Noninstitutional population 16 and over, millions. [POP. POP is the sum of three exogenous variables and so it is in fact exogenous.]
POP1	0	Noninstitutional population of males 25-54, millions. [POP1]
POP2	0	Noninstitutional population of females 25-54, millions. [POP2]
POP3	0	Noninstitutional population of all others, millions. [POP - POP1 - POP2]
PROD	118	Output per paid for worker hour ("productivity"). [Def., eq. 118.]
PU_g	104	Purchases of goods and services, g, B$. [Def., eq. 104, or PURGZ.]
PU_s	110	Purchases of goods and services, s, B$. [Def., eq. 110, or PURSZ.]
PX	31	Price deflator for X. [(CDZ + CNZ + CSZ + IHZ + IKZ + PURGZ - PROGZ + PURSZ - PROSZ + EXZ - IMZ - IBTG - IBTS - IVFA + IVNN)/(CD + + CN + CS + IH + IK + PURG - PROG + PURS - PROS + EX - IM + (IVFA + IVNN)/PIV)]
Q	0	Gold and foreign exchange, g, B$. [Sum of CGLDFXUS + CGLDFXMA. Base Period = 1971 IV, Value = 12.167.]

(continued)

TABLE A-4 (continued)

Name	Equation number	Definition
RB	23	Bond rate, percentage points. [RB]
RD	0	Discount rate, percentage points. [RD]
REC_g	105	Total receipts, g, B$. [Def., eq. 105.]
REC_s	112	Total receipts, s, B$. [Def., eq. 112.]
RET	0	Retirement credits to households from s, B$. [RET]
RM	24	Mortgage rate, percentage points. [RM]
RMA	128	After tax mortgage rate, percentage points. [Def., eq. 128.]
RNT	0	Rental income, h, B$. [RNT]
RS	30	Three month bill rate, percentage points. [RS]
RSA	130	After tax bill rate, percentage points. [Def., eq. 130.]
S_b	72	Savings, b, B$. [Def., eq. 72.]
S_f	69	Savings, f, B$. [Def., eq. 69.]
S_g	76	Savings, g, B$. [Def., eq. 76.]
S'_g	107	NIA surplus (+) or deficit (-), g, B$. [Def., eq. 107.]
S_h	65	Savings, h, B$. [Def., eq. 65.]
S_r	74	Savings, r, B$. [Def., eq. 74.]
S_s	78	Savings, s, B$. [Def., eq. 78.]
S'_s	114	NIA surplus (+) or deficit (-), s, B$. [Def., eq. 114.]
$SHR\pi_f$	121	Ratio of after tax profits to the wage bill net of employer social security taxes. [Def., eq. 121.]
SI_g	103	Total social insurance contributions to g, B$. [SIG]
SI_s	109	Total social insurance contributions to s, B$. [SIS]
SI_{fg}	55	Social insurance contributions, f to g, B$. [SIFG]
SI_{fs}	56	Social insurance contributions, f to s, B$. [SIFS]
SI_{gg}	0	Social insurance contributions, g to g, B$. [SIGG]
SI_{hg}	53	Social insurance contributions, h to g, B$. [SIHG]
SI_{hs}	54	Social insurance contributions, h to s, B$. [SIHS]
SI_{ss}	0	Social insurance contributions, s to s, B$. [SISS]
SP	-	Stock price, B$. [Sum of CG. Base Period = 1971 IV, Value = 832.806. This variable is only used for the USRE2 model in Section 11.7. See equation (11.21).]
SR	116	Savings rate, h. [Def., eq. 116.]
STAT	0	Statistical discrepancy, B$. [STAT]
SUB_g	0	Subsidies less current surplus of government enterprises, g, B$. [SUBG]
SUB_s	0	Subsidies less current surplus of government enterprises, s, B$. [SUBS]
SUR	0	Current surplus of federally sponsored credit agencies and mortgage pools and of the monetary authority, B$. [SURCA + SURMA]
t	0	1 in 1952 I, 2 in 1952 II, etc.

(continued)

TABLE A-4 (continued)

Name	Equation number	Definition
T_{bg}	0	Corporate profit taxes, b to g, B$. [TBG]
T_{bs}	0	Corporate profit taxes, b to s, B$. [TBS]
T_{fg}	49	Corporate profit taxes, f to g, B$. [Def., eq. 102.]
T_{fs}	50	Corporate profit taxes, f to s, B$. [Def., eq. 108.]
T_{hg}	47	Personal income taxes, h to g, B$. [Def., eq. 101.]
T_{hs}	48	Personal income taxes, h to s, B$. [TPS]
TC_g	102	Corporate profit tax receipts, g, B$. [TCG]
TC_s	108	Corporate profit tax receipts, s, B$. [TCS]
TFA	0	Farm taxes, B$. [TFA]
TP_g	101	Personal income tax receipts, g, B$. [TPG]
TR_{fh}	0	Transfer payments, f to h, B$. [TRFH]
TR_{gh}	0	Transfer payments, g to h, B$. [TRGH]
TR_{gr}	0	Transfer payments, g to r, B$. [TRGR]
TR_{gs}	0	Transfer payments, g to s, B$. [TRGS]
TR_{hr}	0	Transfer payments, h to r, B$. [TRHR]
TR_{sh}	0	Transfer payments, s to h, excluding unemployment insurance benefits, B$. [Def., eq. 111.]
TRR_{sh}	111	Total transfer payments, s to h, B$. [TRRSH]
U	86	Number of people unemployed, millions. [Def., eq. 86.]
UB	28	Unemployment insurance benefits, B$. [UB]
UBR	125	Unborrowed reserves, B$. [Def., eq. 125.]
UR	87	Civilian unemployment rate. [Def., eq. 87.]
V	63	Stock of inventories, f, B72$. [Def., eq. 117. Base Period = 1980 IV, Value = 340.6.]
W_f	16	Average hourly earnings excluding overtime of workers in f. [(COMPT - PROGZ - PROSZ - (SIT - SIGG - SISS) - WLDF + PRI)/(JF(HF + .5HO))]
W_g	44	Average hourly earnings of civilian workers in g. [(PROGZ - COMPMIL - SIGG - WLDG)/(JG(JHQ/JQ))]
W_h	43	Average hourly earnings excluding overtime of all workers. [Def., eq. 43.]
W_m	45	Average hourly earnings of military workers. [COMPMIL/(520·AF)]
W_s	46	Average hourly earnings of workers in s. [(PROSZ - SISS - WLDS)/((JQ - JG)(JHQ/JQ))]
WA	126	After tax wage rate. [Def., eq. 126.]
WLD_f	0	Wage accruals less disbursements, f, B$. [WLDF]
WLD_g	0	Wage accruals less disbursements, g, B$. [WLDG]
WLD_s	0	Wage accruals less disbursements, s, B$. [WLDS]
WR	119	Real wage rate of workers in f. [Def., eq. 119.]
X	60	Total sales, f, B72$. [Def., eq. 60.]

(continued)

TABLE A-4 (continued)

Name	Equation number	Definition
XX	61	Total sales, f, B$. [Def., eq. 61.]
Y	11	Production, f, B72$. [Def., eq. 63.]
YD	115	Disposable income, h, B$. [Def., eq. 115.]
YN	88	After tax nonlabor income, h, B$. [Def., eq. 88.]
YT	64	Taxable income, h, B$. [Def., eq. 64.]
YTR	99	Transfer payments, g and s to h, B$. [Def., eq. 99.]
Z	97	Labor constraint variable. [Def., eq. 97.]
ZZ	98	Demand pressure variable. [Def., eq. 98.]
π_b	0	Before tax profits, b, B$. [(PIECB - PIECBN)/PX. See above for PX.]
π_f	67	Before tax profits, f, B$. [Def., eq. 67, or PIEF1 + PIEF2.]
π_h	0	Before tax profits, h, B$. [PIEFA]
δ_D	0	Physical depreciation rate of the stock of durable goods, rate per quarter. [.0515]
δ_H	0	Physical depreciation rate of the stock of housing, rate per quarter. [.00655]
δ_K	0	Physical depreciation rate of the stock of capital, rate per quarter. [.0247 through 1963 III, .0263 thereafter.]
λ	0	Amount of output capable of being produced per worker hour. [Peak to peak interpolation of $Y/(J_f H_f)$. Peak quarters are 1952 I, 1953 II, 1955 I, 1966 I, 1973 I, and 1977 I.]
$\mu\bar{H}$	0	Amount of output capable of being produced per unit of capital. [Peak to peak interpolation of Y/KK. Peak quarters are 1953 II, 1966 I, 1973 I, and 1978 IV.]
ψ_1	0	Ratio of PEX to PX. [Def., eq. 32.]
ψ_2	0	Ratio of PCS to $(1 + d_{3g} + d_{3s})$PD. [Def., eq. 35.]
ψ_3	0	Ratio of PCN to $(1 + d_{3g} + d_{3s})$PD. [Def., eq. 36.]
ψ_4	0	Ratio of PCD to $(1 + d_{3g} + d_{3s})$PD. [Def., eq. 37.]
ψ_5	0	Ratio of PIH to PD. [Def., eq. 38.]
ψ_6	0	Ratio of PIK to PD. [Def., eq. 39.]
ψ_7	0	Ratio of P_g to PD. [Def., eq. 40.]
ψ_8	0	Ratio of P_s to PD. [Def., eq. 41.]
ψ_9	0	Ratio of PIV to PD. [Def., eq. 42.]
ψ_{10}	0	Ratio of W_g to W_f. [Def., eq. 44.]
ψ_{11}	0	Ratio of W_m to W_f. [Def., eq. 45.]
ψ_{12}	0	Ratio of W_s to W_f. [Def., eq. 46.]
ψ_{13}	0	Ratio of gross product of g and s to total employee hours of g and s. [(PROG + PROS)/(JHQ + 520•AF)]
γ_g	0	Progressivity tax parameter in personal income tax equation for g. [Determined from a regression. See the discussion in Appendix A.]
γ_s	0	Progressivity tax parameter in personal income tax equation for s. [Determined from a regression. See the discussion in Appendix A.]

Note: 0 = Variable is exogenous.

TABLE A-5. The equations of the US model

Stochastic equations (2SLS estimates in Chapter 4. Estimation period = 1954 I - 1982 III.)

Household sector:

1. CS:

$$\frac{CS}{POP} = \underset{(0.06)}{.000188} + \underset{(61.48)}{.986}\left(\frac{CS}{POP}\right)_{-1} + \underset{(2.40)}{.000554}\left(\frac{AA}{POP}\right)_{-1} + \underset{(2.07)}{.0198}\,WA + \underset{(0.36)}{.00714}\,\frac{YN}{POP\cdot P_h} - \underset{(5.87)}{.00126}\,RSA + \underset{(1.92)}{.0231}\,Z$$

[consumer expenditures for services]

2. CN:

$$\frac{CN}{POP} = \underset{(3.96)}{.109} + \underset{(10.03)}{.666}\left(\frac{CN}{POP}\right)_{-1} + \underset{(5.05)}{.00227}\left(\frac{AA}{POP}\right)_{-1} + \underset{(2.48)}{.185}\,WA - \underset{(2.16)}{.0469}\,PCN + \underset{(2.14)}{.0637}\,\frac{YN}{POP\cdot P_h} - \underset{(1.05)}{.000610}\,RSA + \underset{(3.54)}{.0829}\,Z$$

[consumer expenditures for nondurable goods]

3. CD:

$$\frac{CD}{POP} = \underset{(3.57)}{.0735} + \underset{(5.95)}{.458}\left(\frac{CD}{POP}\right)_{-1} + \underset{(6.18)}{.00235}\left(\frac{AA}{POP}\right)_{-1} + \underset{(4.08)}{.405}\,WA - \underset{(3.12)}{.104}\,PCD + \underset{(1.19)}{.0668}\,\frac{YTR}{POP\cdot P_h} - \underset{(7.96)}{.00617}\,RMA + \underset{(3.38)}{.123}\,Z$$

[consumer expenditures for durable goods]

4. IH_h:

$$\frac{IH_h}{POP} = \underset{(3.89)}{.0650} + \underset{(9.86)}{.738}\left(\frac{IH_h}{POP}\right)_{-1} - \underset{(3.18)}{.0157}\left(\frac{KH}{POP}\right)_{-1} + \underset{(3.73)}{.00182}\left(\frac{AA}{POP}\right)_{-1} + \underset{(2.61)}{.159}\,WA_{-1} - \underset{(1.88)}{.0178}\,PIH_{-1} + \underset{(0.99)}{.0356}\left(\frac{YN}{POP\cdot P_h}\right)_{-1} - \underset{(5.19)}{.00367}\,RMA_{-1}, \quad \hat{\rho} = \underset{(4.65)}{.551}$$

[housing investment, h]

5. L1:

$$\frac{L1}{POP1} = \underset{(3.67)}{.230} + \underset{(12.20)}{.769}\left(\frac{L1}{POP1}\right)_{-1} - \underset{(3.56)}{.0278}\left(\frac{YN}{POP\cdot P_h}\right)_{-1}$$

[labor force of males 25-54]

6. L2:

$$\frac{L2}{POP2} = \underset{(3.75)}{.0605} + \underset{(17.98)}{.832}\left(\frac{L2}{POP2}\right)_{-1} + \underset{(3.77)}{.160}\,WA - \underset{(2.95)}{.0200}\,P_h + \underset{(2.86)}{.0364}\,Z$$

[labor force of females 25-54]

7. L3:

$$\frac{L3}{POP3} = \underset{(5.02)}{.133} + \underset{(17.53)}{.782}\left(\frac{L3}{POP3}\right)_{-1} - \underset{(3.76)}{.00121}\left(\frac{AA}{POP}\right)_{-1} + \underset{(4.14)}{.0930}\,WA - \underset{(4.25)}{.0318}\,P_h + \underset{(4.81)}{.0738}\,Z$$

[labor force of all others 16 and over]

8. LM:

$$\frac{LM}{POP} = \underset{(7.17)}{.0150} + \underset{(11.06)}{.634}\left(\frac{LM}{POP}\right)_{-1} + \underset{(0.90)}{.00676}\,WA_{-1} - \underset{(1.18)}{.00374}\,P_{h-1} + \underset{(6.10)}{.0580}\,Z$$

[number of moonlighters]

9. M_h:

$$\log\frac{M_h}{POP\cdot P_h} = \underset{(3.63)}{.0297} - \underset{(2.64)}{.000698}\,t + \underset{(19.22)}{.835}\,\log\left(\frac{M_h}{POP\cdot P_h}\right)_{-1} + \underset{(3.13)}{.123}\,\log\frac{YT}{POP\cdot P_h} - \underset{(3.81)}{.00416}\,RSA$$

[demand deposits and currency, h]

(continued)

Firm sector:

10. P_f: $$\log P_f = \underset{(7.32)}{.187} + \underset{(82.62)}{.922} \log P_{f-1} + \underset{(6.95)}{.0339} \log W_f(1 + d_{5g} + d_{5s}) + \underset{(8.56)}{.0339} \log PIM - \underset{(4.22)}{.0810} ZZ_{-1}$$

[price deflator for X-FA]

11. Y: $$Y = \underset{(4.36)}{11.4} + \underset{(3.67)}{.162} Y_{-1} + \underset{(19.59)}{1.011} X - \underset{(4.44)}{.193} V_{-1} - \underset{(1.86)}{2.06} D593 + \underset{(0.64)}{.793} D594 + \underset{(1.89)}{2.10} D601, \quad \hat{\rho} = \underset{(6.73)}{.605}$$

[production, f]

12. IK_f: $$\Delta IK_f = \underset{(0.11)}{-.0146} - \underset{(2.83)}{.0130} (KK - KKMIN)_{-1} + \underset{(5.70)}{.0967} \Delta Y + \underset{(0.02)}{.0004} \Delta Y_{-1} + \underset{(0.88)}{.0140} \Delta Y_{-2} + \underset{(1.24)}{.0196} \Delta Y_{-3} - \underset{(2.48)}{.107} IK_{f-1} + \underset{(2.59)}{.167} \delta_K KK_{-1}$$

[plant and equipment investment, f]

13. J_f: $$\Delta \log J_f = \underset{(3.76)}{-.885} - \underset{(3.75)}{.141} \log \frac{J_{f-1}}{JHMIN_{-1}} + \underset{(4.28)}{.000176} t + \underset{(8.33)}{.281} \Delta \log Y + \underset{(3.03)}{.119} \Delta \log Y_{-1} + \underset{(1.02)}{.033} \Delta \log Y_{-2} - \underset{(2.70)}{.00967} D593 + \underset{(0.50)}{.00174} D594, \quad \hat{\rho} = \underset{(4.44)}{.447}$$

[number of jobs, f]

14. H_f: $$\Delta \log H_f = \underset{(4.95)}{1.37} - \underset{(5.16)}{.284} \log H_{f-1} - \underset{(3.55)}{.0659} \log \frac{J_{f-1}}{JHMIN_{-1}} - \underset{(4.94)}{.000250} t + \underset{(4.40)}{.120} \Delta \log Y$$

[average number of hours paid per job, f]

15. HO: $$\log HO = \underset{(5.15)}{-8.34} + \underset{(7.38)}{.0223} H_f^*, \quad \hat{\rho} = \underset{(21.38)}{.909}$$

[average number of overtime hours paid per job, f]

16. W_f: $$\log W_f = \underset{(3.52)}{-.423} + \underset{(45.75)}{.929} \log W_{f-1} + .427 \log PX - \underset{(3.50)}{.382} \log PX_{-1} + \underset{(4.31)}{.000671} t - \underset{(1.53)}{.0760} UR$$

[average hourly earnings excluding overtime of workers in f]

17. M_f: $$\log \frac{M_f}{PX} = \underset{(1.04)}{.106} + \underset{(26.10)}{.920} \log\left(\frac{M_f}{PX}\right)_{-1} + \underset{(2.39)}{.0477} \log X - \underset{(3.26)}{.00700} RS(1 - d_{2g} - d_{2s})$$

[demand deposits and currency, f]

18. D_f: $$D_f = \underset{(1.05)}{-.0227} + \underset{(108.28)}{.978} D_{f-1} + \underset{(5.64)}{.0201} (\Pi_f - T_{fg} - T_{fs})$$

[dividends paid, f]

19. INT_f: $$INT_f = \underset{(1.96)}{-3.59} + \underset{(8.59)}{.746} INT_{f-1} + \underset{(1.91)}{.0200} (-A_f) + \underset{(4.25)}{.467} RB, \quad \hat{\rho} = \underset{(25.41)}{.954}$$

[interest payments, f]

20. IVA: $$IVA = \underset{(0.98)}{1.52} - \underset{(3.51)}{95.2} PX + \underset{(3.34)}{92.2} PX_{-1}, \quad \hat{\rho} = \underset{(12.45)}{.801}$$

[inventory valuation adjustment]

21. CC_f: $$CC_f = \underset{(3.69)}{-.0930} + \underset{(67.13)}{.966} CC_{f-1} + \underset{(4.69)}{.0447} PIK \cdot IK_f + \underset{(6.29)}{.562} DD811$$

[capital consumption, f]

(continued)

TABLE A-5 (continued)

Financial sector:

22. BO: $$\frac{BO}{BR} = \underset{(3.79)}{.0148} + \underset{(1.34)}{.00455}\,(RS-RD)\;,\quad \hat{\rho} = \underset{(7.93)}{.606}$$

[bank borrowing from the Fed]

23. RB: $$RB = \underset{(2.54)}{.114} + \underset{(53.00)}{.889}\,RB_{-1} + \underset{(10.82)}{.277}\,RS - \underset{(6.48)}{.218}\,RS_{-1} + \underset{(3.48)}{.074}\,RS_{-2}$$

[bond rate]

24. RM: $$RM = \underset{(3.36)}{.343} + \underset{(29.00)}{.846}\,RM_{-1} + \underset{(4.64)}{.178}\,RS + \underset{(0.80)}{.041}\,RS_{-1} - \underset{(1.23)}{.043}\,RS_{-2}$$

[mortgage rate]

25. CG: $$CG = \underset{(2.23)}{10.9} - \underset{(1.26)}{24.4}\,\Delta RB + \underset{(1.49)}{3.75}\,\Delta(CF - T_{fg} - T_{fs})$$

$$+ \underset{(2.08)}{4.07}\,\Delta(CF - T_{fg} - T_{fs})_{-1}$$

[capital gains or losses on corporate stocks held by h]

26. CUR: $$\log\frac{CUR}{POP\cdot PX} = \underset{(3.87)}{-.106} - \underset{(0.79)}{.000133}\,t + \underset{(32.88)}{.897}\,\log\left(\frac{CUR}{POP\cdot PX}\right)_{-1}$$

$$+ \underset{(2.36)}{.0801}\,\log\frac{X}{POP} - \underset{(4.00)}{.00313}\,RSA$$

[currency held outside banks]

Foreign sector:

27. IM: $$\frac{IM}{POP} = \underset{(1.11)}{-.0277} + \underset{(15.31)}{.752}\,\frac{IM}{POP}_{1} + \underset{(1.10)}{.0256}\,\frac{X}{POP} - \underset{(3.00)}{.0114}\,PIM_{-1} + \underset{(1.61)}{.0393}\,PX_{-1}$$

$$- \underset{(2.59)}{.00126}\,RMA_{-1} - \underset{(2.18)}{.00654}\,D651 + \underset{(1.17)}{.00356}\,D652 - \underset{(3.65)}{.0109}\,D691$$

$$+ \underset{(5.42)}{.0166}\,D692 - \underset{(2.64)}{.00798}\,D714 + \underset{(4.10)}{.0123}\,D721$$

[imports]

S&L government sector:

28. UB: $$\log UB = \underset{(0.69)}{.369} + \underset{(18.00)}{1.58}\,\log U + \underset{(6.06)}{.465}\,\log W_f\;,\quad \hat{\rho} = \underset{(12.59)}{.761}$$

[unemployment insurance benefits]

Federal government sector

29. INT_g: $$\log INT_g = \underset{(4.77)}{-.870} + \underset{(29.65)}{.873}\,\log INT_{g-1} + \underset{(4.95)}{.148}\,\log(-A_g) + \underset{(5.54)}{.0572}\,\log RS$$

$$+ \underset{(2.18)}{.0818}\,\log RB$$

[interest payments, g]

30. RS: $$RS = \underset{(2.99)}{-9.46} + \underset{(25.55)}{.858}\,RS_{-1} + \underset{(2.11)}{.0687}\,\dot{PD} + \underset{(2.99)}{.0296}\,JJ^{*} + \underset{(2.92)}{.0597}\,\dot{GNPR}$$

$$+ \underset{(1.71)}{.032}\,\dot{M1}_{-1} + \underset{(4.20)}{.131}\,DD793\cdot\dot{M1}_{-1}$$

[three month bill rate]

(continued)

Identities

31. $PX = \dfrac{P_f(X-FA) + PFA \cdot FA}{X}$ [price deflator for X]

32. $PEX = \psi_1 PX$ [price deflator for EX]

33. $PD = \dfrac{PX \cdot X - PEX \cdot EX + PIM \cdot IM}{X - EX + IM}$ [price deflator for domestic sales]

34. $P_h = PD + \dfrac{IBT_g + IBT_s}{X - EX + IM}$ [price deflator for domestic sales exclusive of indirect business taxes]

35. $PCS = \psi_2(1 + d_{3g} + d_{3s})PD$ [price deflator for CS]

36. $PCN = \psi_3(1 + d_{3g} + d_{3s})PD$ [price deflator for CN]

37. $PCD = \psi_4(1 + d_{3g} + d_{3s})PD$ [price deflator for CD]

38. $PIH = \psi_5 PD$ [price deflator for housing investment]

39. $PIK = \psi_6 PD$ [price deflator for plant and equipment investment]

40. $P_g = \psi_7 PD$ [price deflator for C_g]

41. $P_s = \psi_8 PD$ [price deflator for C_s]

42. $PIV = \psi_9 PD$ [price deflator for inventory investment]

43. $W_h = 100\dfrac{W_f J_f(HN + 1.5HO) + W_g J_g H_g + W_m J_m H_m + W_s J_s H_s}{J_f(HN + 1.5HO) + J_g H_g + J_m H_m + J_s H_s}$ [average hourly earnings excluding overtime of all workers]

44. $W_g = \psi_{10} W_f$ [average hourly earnings of civilian workers in g]

45. $W_m = \psi_{11} W_f$ [average hourly earnings of military workers]

46. $W_s = \psi_{12} W_f$ [average hourly earnings of workers in s]

47. $T_{hg} = \left[d_{1g} + \dfrac{\gamma_g YT}{POP}\right]YT$ [personal income taxes, h to g]

48. $T_{hs} = \left[d_{1s} + \dfrac{\gamma_s YT}{POP}\right]YT$ [personal income taxes, h to s]

49. $T_{fg} = d_{2g}\pi_f$ [corporate profits taxes, f to g]

50. $T_{fs} = d_{2s}\pi_f$ [corporate profits taxes, f to s]

51. $IBT_g = \dfrac{d_{3g}}{1 + d_{3g}}(PCS \cdot CS + PCN \cdot CN + PCD \cdot CD - IBT_s)$ [indirect business taxes, g]

52. $IBT_s = \dfrac{d_{3s}}{1 + d_{3s}}(PCS \cdot CS + PCN \cdot CN + PCD \cdot CD - IBT_g)$ [indirect business taxes, s]

53. $SI_{hg} = d_{4g} W_f J_f(HN + 1.5HO)$ [social insurance contributions, h to g]

(continued)

54. $SI_{hs} = d_{4s}W_fJ_f(HN + 1.5HO)$	[social insurance contributions, h to s]
55. $SI_{fg} = d_{5g}W_fJ_f(HN + 1.5HO)$	[social insurance contributions, f to g]
56. $SI_{fs} = d_{5s}W_fJ_f(HN + 1.5HO)$	[social insurance contributions, f to s]
57. $BR = -g_1M_b$	[total bank reserves]
58. $KD = (1 - \delta_D)KD_{-1} + CD$	[stock of durable goods]
59. $KH = (1 - \delta_H)KH_{-1} + IH_h$	[stock of housing, h]
60. $X = CS + CN + CD + IH_h + IK_f + EX - IM + C_g + C_s + IK_h + IK_b + IH_f + IH_b + IV_h - \pi_b - CC_b$	[total sales, f]
61. $XX = PCS \cdot CS + PCN \cdot CN + PCD \cdot CD + PIH \cdot IH_h + PIK \cdot IK_f + PEX \cdot EX - PIM \cdot IM + P_gC_g + P_sC_s + PIK(IK_h + IK_b) + PIH(IH_f + IH_b) + PIV \cdot IV_h - PX(\pi_b + CC_b) - IBT_g - IBT_s$	[total nominal sales, f]
62. $HN = H_f - HO$	[average number of non overtime hours paid per job, f]
63. $V = V_{-1} + Y - X$	[stock of inventories, f]
64. $YT = W_fJ_f(HN + 1.5HO) + W_gJ_gH_g + W_mJ_mH_m + W_sJ_sH_s + D_f + D_b - DR_s + INT_f + INT_g - INT_{gr} + INT_s + RNT + TR_{fh} + \pi_h + SI_{hg} + SI_{hs}$	[taxable income, h]
65. $S_h = YT - SI_{hg} - SI_{hs} + CC_h - PCS \cdot CS - PCN \cdot CN - PCD \cdot CD - PIH \cdot IH_h - PIK \cdot IK_h - PIV \cdot IV_h - TR_{hr} - T_{hg} - SI_{hg} + TR_{gh} - T_{hs} - SI_{hs} + TR_{sh} + UR + INS + RET$	[savings, h]
66. $0 = S_h - \Delta A_h - \Delta M_h + CG - DIS_h$	[budget constraint, h: determines A_h]
67. $\pi_f = XX + PIV(V - V_{-1}) - W_f(1 + d_{5g} + d_{5s})J_f(HN + 1.5HO) - RNT - TR_{fh} - \pi_h - CC_h + SUB_g + SUB_s - INT_f - CC_f - IVA - WLD_f - STAT$	[before tax profits, f]
68. $CF = XX - W_f(1 + d_{5g} + d_{5s})J_f(HN + 1.5HO) - RNT - TR_{fh} - \pi_h - CC_h + SUB_g + SUB_s - INT_f - PIK \cdot IK_f - PIH \cdot IH_f - MRS$	[cash flow, f]
69. $S_f = CF - T_{fg} - T_{fs} - D_f$	[savings, f]
70. $0 = S_f - \Delta A_f - \Delta M_f - DIS_f - WLD_f - STAT$	[budget constraint, f: determines A_f]
71. $0 = \Delta M_b + \Delta M_h + \Delta M_f + \Delta M_r + \Delta M_g + \Delta M_s - \Delta CUR$	[demand deposit identity: determines M_b]
72. $S_b = PX(\pi_b + CC_b) - PIK \cdot IK_b - PIH \cdot IH_b - D_b - T_{bg} - T_{bs} - SUR$	[savings, b]
73. $0 = S_b - \Delta A_b - \Delta M_b - \Delta(BR\text{-}BO) - DIS_b$	[budget constraint, b: determines A_b]
74. $S_r = PIM \cdot IM + TR_{hr} + TR_{gr} + INT_{gr} - PEX \cdot EX$	[savings, r]

(continued)

75. $0 = S_r - \Delta A_r - \Delta M_r + \Delta Q - DIS_r$ [budget constraint, r: determines A_r]

76. $S_g = T_{hg} + IBT_g + T_{fg} + T_{bg} + SUR + SI_{hg} + SI_{fg} + MRS - P_gC_g - W_gJ_gH_g - W_mJ_mH_m - INT_g - TR_{gr} - TR_{gh} - TR_{gs} - SUB_g - INS$ [savings, g]

77. $0 = S_g - \Delta A_g - \Delta M_g + \Delta CUR + \Delta(BR\text{-}BO) - \Delta Q - DIS_g$ [budget constraint, g: determines A_g unless equation 30 is not included in the model]

78. $S_s = T_{hs} + IBT_s + T_{fs} + T_{bs} + SI_{hs} + SI_{fs} + TR_{gs} + DR_s - P_sC_s - W_sJ_sH_s - INT_s - SUB_s - TR_{sh} - UB - RET$ [savings, s]

79. $0 = S_s - \Delta A_s - \Delta M_s - DIS_s$ [budget constraint, s: determines A_s]

80. $0 = \Delta A_h + \Delta A_f + \Delta A_b + \Delta A_g + \Delta A_s + \Delta A_r - CG + DIS_h + DIS_f + DIS_b + DIS_g + DIS_s + DIS_r + WLD_f + STAT$ [asset identity: redundant equation]

81. $M1 = M1_{-1} + \Delta M_h + \Delta M_f + \Delta M_r + \Delta M_s + MDIF$ [money supply]

82. $GNP = 4\cdot\left(XX + PIV(V - V_{-1}) + IBT_g + IBT_s + W_gJ_gH_g + W_mJ_mH_m + W_sJ_sH_s + WLD_g + WLD_s + PX(\pi_b + CC_b) + SI_{gg} + SI_{ss}\right)$ [nominal GNP, annual rate]

83. $GNPR = 4\cdot\left(Y + \pi_b + CC_b + \psi_{13}(J_gH_g + J_mH_m + J_sH_s)\right)$ [real GNP, annual rate]

84. $GNPD = \dfrac{GNP}{GNPR}$ [GNP deflator]

85. $E = J_f + J_g + J_m + J_s - LM$ [total employment, civilian and military]

86. $U = L1 + L2 + L3 - E$ [number of people unemployed]

87. $UR = \dfrac{U}{L1 + L2 + L3 - J_m}$ [civilian unemployment rate]

88. $YN = \left(1 - d_{1g} - d_{1s} - \dfrac{(\gamma_g + \gamma_s)YT}{POP}\right)(D_f + D_b - DR_s + INT_f + INT_g - INT_{gr} + INT_s + RNT + TR_{fh} + \pi_h) + TR_{gh} + TR_{sh} + UB$ [after tax nonlabor income, h]

89. $AA = \dfrac{A_h + M_h}{P_h} + KH$ [total net wealth, h]

90. $d^M_{1g} = d_{1g} + \dfrac{2\gamma_g YT}{POP}$ [marginal personal income tax rate, g]

91. $d^M_{1s} = d_{1s} + \dfrac{2\gamma_s YT}{POP}$ [marginal personal income tax rate, s]

92. $KK = (1 - \delta_K)KK_{-1} + IK_f$ [stock of capital, f]

93. $KKMIN = \dfrac{Y}{\mu\bar{\bar{H}}}$ [amount of capital required to produce Y]

94. $JHMIN = \dfrac{Y}{\lambda}$ [number of worker hours required to produce Y]

(continued)

95. $JJ = \frac{J_f H_f + J_g H_g + J_m H_m + J_s H_s}{POP}$	[ratio of the total number of worker hours paid for to the total population 16 and over]
96. $JJ^* = \frac{JJ}{\exp(-.00083312t)}$	[JJ detrended]
97. $Z = 1 - \frac{337.0}{JJ^*}$	[labor constraint variable]
98. $ZZ = \frac{GNPR^* - GNPR}{GNPR^*}$	[demand pressure variable]
99. $YTR = TR_{gh} + TR_{sh} + UB$	[transfer payments, g and s to h]
100. $H_f^* = H_f + .56464t$	[H_f detrended]
101. $TP_g = T_{hg} - TFA$	[personal income tax receipts, g]
102. $TC_g = T_{fg} + TFA + T_{bg}$	[corporate profit tax receipts, g]
103. $SI_g = SI_{hg} + SI_{fg} + SI_{gg}$	[total social insurance contributions to g]
104. $PU_g = P_g C_g + W_g J_g H_g + W_m J_m H_m + SI_{gg} + WLD_g$	[purchases of goods and services, g]
105. $REC_g = TP_g + TC_g + IBT_g + SI_g$	[total receipts, g]
106. $EXP_g = PU_g + TR_{gh} + TR_{gr} + TR_{gs} + INT_g + SUB_g - WLD_g$	[total expenditures, g]
107. $S'_g = REC_g - EXP_g$	[NIA surplus or deficit, g]
108. $TC_s = T_{fs} + T_{bs}$	[corporate profit tax receipts, s]
109. $SI_s = SI_{hs} + SI_{fs} + SI_{ss}$	[total social insurance contributions to s]
110. $PU_s = P_s C_s + W_s J_s H_s + SI_{ss} + WLD_s$	[purchases of goods and services, s]
111. $TRR_{sh} = TR_{sh} + UB$	[total transfer payments, s to h]
112. $REC_s = T_{hs} + TC_s + IBT_s + SI_s + TR_{gs}$	[total receipts, s]
113. $EXP_s = PU_s + TRR_{sh} + INT_s + DR_s + SUB_s - WLD_s$	[total expenditures, s]
114. $S'_s = REC_s - EXP_s$	[NIA surplus or deficit, s]
115. $YD = W_f J_f(HN + 1.5HO) + W_g J_g H_g + W_m J_m H_m + W_s J_s H_s + RNT + D_f + D_b - DR_s + INT_f + INT_g - INT_{gr} + INT_s + TR_{fh} + TR_{gh} + TR_{sh} + UB - SI_{hg} - SI_{hs} - T_{hg} - TFA - T_{hs} - TR_{hr}$	[disposable income, h]
116. $SR = \frac{YD - PCS \cdot CS - PCN \cdot CN - PCD \cdot CD}{YD}$	[savings rate, h]

(continued)

TABLE A-5 (continued)

117. $IV_f = V - V_{-1}$	[inventory investment, f]
118. $PROD = \frac{Y}{J_f H_f}$	[output per paid for worker hour: "productivity"]
119. $WR = \frac{W_f}{PX}$	[real wage rate of workers in f]
120. $POP = POP1 + POP2 + POP3$	[noninstitutional population 16 and over]
121. $SHR\pi = \frac{(1 - d_{2g} - d_{2s})\pi_f}{W_f J_f(HN + 1.5HO)}$	[ratio of after tax profits to the wage bill net of employer social security taxes]
122. $PCGNPR = 100\left[\left(\frac{GNPR}{GNPR_{-1}}\right)^4 - 1\right]$	[percentage change in GNPR]
123. $PCGNPD = 100\left[\left(\frac{GNPD}{GNPD_{-1}}\right)^4 - 1\right]$	[percentage change in GNPD]
124. $PCM1 = 100\left[\left(\frac{M1}{M1_{-1}}\right)^4 - 1\right]$	[percentage change in M1]
125. $UBR = BR - BO$	[unborrowed reserves]
126. $WA = W_h(1 - d^M_{1g} - d^M_{1s} - d_{4g} - d_{4s})$	[after tax wage rate]
127. $RSA = RS(1 - d^M_{1g} - d^M_{1s})$	[after tax bill rate]
128. $RMA = RM(1 - d^M_{1g} - d^M_{1s})$	[after tax mortgage rate]

Appendix B: Data and Identities for the Multicountry Model

The data for all the countries were obtained from the International Financial Statistics (IFS) tape (November 1982) and the Direction of Trade (DOT) tape (November 1982). The following steps were involved in the construction of the data base.

1. A program was written to read the IFS tape and create for each country all the variables in Table B-2 except the variables for which DOT data are needed: $M75\$A_i$, $M75\$B_i$, PM_i', $XX\$_{ij}$, $XX75\$_{ij}$, α_{ji}, and ψ_{2i}. Most of the work in constructing the data base was writing this program. Since no two countries were exactly alike with respect to the availability of the data, separate subroutines were written for each country. (Before these subroutines were written, a program was written to print the IFS data in a convenient format. The information needed to write the individual subroutines was taken from this printout. I am indebted to William Parke for help in writing the initial program that read the tape.) The individual treatment of the countries is discussed below. The output from this program was stored by country on a tape called IFS1.
2. A program was written to read the DOT tape and create the $XX\$_{ji}$ data (the bilateral trade data). The output from this program was stored by country on a tape called DOT1.
3. The IFS1 and DOT1 tapes were sorted to store the data by quarter. The sorted tapes were then used together to create the variables mentioned in step 1. This completed the construction of the data base.

The individual treatment of the data for each country is outlined in Table B-1. The comments in the table discuss any special treatment of the country. If no comments appear for a particular country, then all the data were available and nothing special needed to be done. Two standard procedures were followed for all the countries, and it is necessary to discuss these before considering the comments in Table B-1. First, if no quarterly National Income Accounts (NIA) data were available, quarterly data were interpolated from annual data using quarterly data on the industrial production index (*IP*). If quarterly data on *IP* were not available, the procedure in Table B-6 was used to create the quarterly data. One can thus tell from Table B-1 how the quarterly NIA data were constructed (if they were) by noting whether or not *IP* data were available.

The second standard procedure concerns the construction of the Balance of Payments (BOP) data; this procedure is presented in Table B-7. The key variable that is created in this process is S_i^*, the balance of payments on current account. It is used in the construction of the asset variable, A_i^*, for each country. Quarterly BOP data do not generally begin as early as the other data, and the procedure in Table B-7 allows data on S_i^* to be constructed as far back as the beginning of the data for merchandise imports and exports ($M\$_i$ and $X\$_i$). When all data are available, the procedure is a way of linking the BOP and non-BOP data.

Most of the comments in Table B-1 are self-explanatory. Data for a variable were "made up" if there was a relatively small gap in an otherwise good series. In these cases the data were usually made up by linearly interpolating between the closest two available observations. In a few cases quarterly data on the consumer price index (*CPI*) were used for quarterly interpolations of annual data, and for France and Switzerland quarterly data on employment (*EMPL*) rather than on industrial production were used for the quarterly interpolation of the NIA data. For many countries only discount rate data were available for the short-term interest rate (*RS*), and these cases are mentioned in the table. For a few countries the NIA year began at a time other than January 1, and this had to be taken into account in the quarterly interpolations. These cases are also mentioned in the table. For a few countries data on real GNP (*Y*) were not available, but data on the nominal NIA variables were. In these cases, as indicated in the table, *CPI* data were used for the GNP deflator. Real GNP was then taken to be nominal GNP divided by the GNP deflator.

Quarterly population data were not available for any country, and the procedure in Table B-6 was used to construct quarterly from annual data. See in particular the note at the bottom of the table.

Quarterly DOT data began only in 1970I, and no attempt was made to construct DOT data before this quarter. Instead, the variables in the model were constructed in such a way (with one exception noted below) that no DOT data were needed in the estimation of the model. In other words, no DOT data were used for the estimates in Tables 4-1 through 4-13 in Chapter 4. This allowed the estimation periods for most countries to be much longer than would otherwise have been the case. The DOT data are needed, of course, for the solution of the model, and therefore the earliest quarter for which the model can be solved is 1970I. In a few cases annual but not quarterly DOT data were available, and in these cases the procedure in Table B-6 was used to construct the quarterly data. In a few cases no DOT data existed, and in these cases the observations were assumed to be zero.

For a few countries no data on import prices were available, and for these countries the data were constructed as indicated in the fifth note to Table B-2. This construction required the existence of DOT data, and this is the exception mentioned in the previous paragraph where DOT data were needed for the estimation work. For countries for which DOT data were used in the construction of the import price index, the estimation period had to begin no earlier than 1970I for the equations that relied on these data.

The links to and from the US model are listed in Table B-5. The two key exogenous foreign sector variables in the US model are the real value of exports (EX) and the import price deflator (PIM). When the US model is embedded in the overall model, these two variables become endogenous. The US endogenous variables in Table A-4 that affect the rest of the model are the real value of imports (IM), the bill rate (RS), the GNP deflator ($GNPD$), real GNP ($GNPR$), and the demand pressure variable (ZZ). The data base for the US model is different from the data base for the United States on the IFS tape (among other things, the real variables in the US model are in 72$, whereas the real variables for the United States on the IFS tape are in 75$), and the δ_i variables in Table B-5 are used to link the two data sets. As noted in the table, when the US model is part of the MC model, the equation determining PEX is no longer Eq. 32 in Table A-5. Instead, Eq. 11 in Table 4-12 for the United States is used to determine PX_1, and PEX is then linked to PX_1.

The sample periods that were used for the estimation work are listed in the tables in Chapter 4. The beginning of the sample period was usually taken to be four quarters after the beginning of the data, and the end of the sample period was usually taken to be the last quarter of the data. One can thus tell from the tables in Chapter 4 approximately how many observations are available for each country.

TABLE B-1. Individual treatment of the data per country

	Country	Local currency	Quar. NIA data?	Comments
1.	United States	U.S. Dollars (mil.)	yes	See Appendix A.
2.	Canada	Can. Dollars (mil.)	yes	Splice in M1* series at 673.
3.	Japan	Yen (bil.)	yes	RB from 681.
4.	Austria	Schillings (bil.)	yes	Discount rate data for RS. RB from 701. Made up quarterly data from annual data for PX and PM for 611-633.
5.	Belgium	Bel. Francs (bil.)	no	Made up quarterly data from annual data for RB for 631-633.
6.	Denmark	Den. Kroner (bil.)	no	Discount rate data for RS prior to 721.
7.	France	Fr. Francs (bil.)	most	Interpolated data for IFS71IV for 571-614 using IFS73. Quarterly interpolations for NIA data prior to 651 using EMPL.
8.	Germany	D. Mark (bil.)	yes	---
9.	Italy	Lire (bil.)	most	Discount rate data for RS prior to 711. Quarterly C, ΔV, and G data interpolated using quarterly Y data for 601-694 and 811-814.
10.	Netherlands	Guilders (bil.)	no	---
11.	Norway	Nor. Kroner (bil.)	no	Discount rate data for RS prior to 714.
12.	Sweden	Swe. Kroner (bil.)	some	Discount rate data for RS prior to 743. Made up quarterly data from annual data for M1* for 571-594. Some quarterly interpolations for NIA data; used EMPL prior to 691 and Y thereafter.
13.	Switzerland	Swiss Francs (bil.)	no	Discount rate data for RS. EMPL used for quarterly interpolations for NIA data. Made up quarterly data from annual data for PX and PM for 601-604.
14.	United Kingdom	U.K. Pounds (mil.)	yes	---
15.	Finland	Markkaa (mil.)	some	Discount rate data for RS. No RB.
16.	Greece	Drachmas (bil.)	no	Discount rate data for RS. No F. No RB. Table B-6 procedure for PM for 571-594.
17.	Ireland	Irish Pounds (mil.)	no	Discount rate data for RS prior to 702. No F.
18.	Portugal	Escudos (bil.)	no	Discount rate data for RS. No F. No PX. Made up data for RB for 742-754. Made up quarterly data from annual data for IP for 743 and 744. PY data for PX.
†19.	Romania	Lei	no	Only e data collected from IFS.
20.	Spain	Pesetas (bil.)	no	Discount rate data for RS. No RB.
21.	Turkey	Liras (bil.)	no	Discount rate data for RS. No F. No RB. No IP. PX and PM from 681 on.
22.	Yugoslavia	Dinars (bil.)	no	No RS. No F. No RB. Quarterly PX and PM data interpolated using quarterly CPI data.
23.	Australia	Aust. Dollars (mil.)	yes	---
24.	New Zealand	N.Z. Dollars (mil.)	no	Discount rate data for RS. No F. No IP. NIA year begins April 1.
25.	South Africa	Rand (mil.)	yes	No F.
†26.	Algeria	Alg. Dinars (mil.)	no	No RS. No F. No RB. No IP. No PM. Made up quarterly data from annual data for IFS70 for 711-713 and for IFS71V for 711-733. PX data from 721.
†27.	Indonesia	Rupiahs (bil.)	no	No RS. No F. No RB. No IP. No PM. No ΔV. CPI to deflate IM.
†28.	Iran	Rials (bil.)	no	Discount rate data for RS. No F. No RB. No IP. No PM. NIA year begins March 21. No V1. CPI to deflate IM.
†29.	Iraq	Iraq Dinars (mil.)	no	No RS. No F. No RB. No IP. No PM. CPI to deflate IM.
†30.	Kuwait	Ku. Dinars (mil.)	no	No RS. No F. No RB. No IP. No PM. NIA year begins April 1.
31.	Libya	Lib. Dinars (mil.)	no	No RS. No F. No RB. No IP. No PM. CPI to deflate IM.
32.	Nigeria	Naira (mil.)	no	Discount rate data for RS. No F. No RB. No PM. CPI to deflate IM. No ΔV. NIA year begins April 1.
33.	Saudi Arabia	Riyals (bil.)	no	No RS. No F. No RB. No IP. No PM. CPI to deflate IM. Table B-6 procedure for IFS71IV for 571-674 and 721-734. NIA year begins July 1.
†34.	United Arab Emirates	Dirham (bil.)	no	No RS. No F. No RB. No IP. No PM. No BOP data.
35.	Venezuela	Bolivares (mil.)	no	Discount rate data for RS. No F. No RB. No PM. No IP. CPI to deflate IM.
36.	Argentina	Arg. Pesos (bil.)	no	No RS. No F. No RB. No PM. No PX. CPI to deflate IM. PY data for PX.

(continued)

TABLE B-1 (continued)

Country	Local currency	Quar. NIA data?	Comments
37. Brazil	Cruzerios (bil.)	no	Discount rate data for RS prior to 711. No F. No RB. PM from 721 on. CPI to deflate IM. Set ΔV = 0 for 801-804. IFS71V for 711-784 interpolated using IFS71.VO.
38. Chile	Chile Pesos (mil.)	no	No RS. No F. No RB. PX from 754 on. Made up quarterly data from annual data for M$ for 671-674. Set ΔV = 0 for 771-774. PY to deflate EX. PY data for PX prior to 754.
39. Colombia	Col. Pesos (mil.)	no	Discount rate data for RS. No F. No RB. No IP. IFS70..D for X$ from 781 on.
40. Mexico	Mex. Pesos (bil.)	no	No RS. No F. No RB. No PM. No PX. CPI to deflate IM. PY data for PX.
41. Peru	Soles (bil.)	no	Discount rate data for RS. No F. No RB. No IP. No PM. CPI to deflate IM. PY data for PX for 601-624 and 783 on.
†42. Egypt	Egy. Pounds (mil.)	no	Discount rate data for RS. No F. No RB. No IP. No PM. No PX. CPI to deflate IM. PY data for PX.
43. Israel	Isr. Pounds (mil.)	yes	No RS. No F. No RB. No ΔV.
44. Jordan	Jor. Dinars (mil.)	no	Discount rate data for RS. No F. No RB. No Y data. Used CPI data for PY. Table B-6 procedure for PX and PM.
†45. Lebanon	Leb. Pounds (mil.)	no	Only data on e, MP*, X$, and POP.
46. Syria	Syr. Pounds (mil.)	no	No RS. No F. No RB. No IP. Table B-6 procedure for PX and PM. Set ΔV = 0 prior to 701.
†47. Bangladesh	Taka (mil.)	no	No RS. No F. No RB. No IP. No PX. No PM.
†48. Republic of China (Taiwan)	N.T. Dollars (bil.)	no	Eliminated from the IFS and DOT tapes.
†49. Hong Kong	H.K. Dollars (bil.)	no	Only X$ data collected from IFS.
50. India	Ind. Rupees (bil.)	no	No F. NIA year begins April 1.
51. Korea	Won (bil.)	yes	Discount rate data for RS. No F. No RB. PY to deflate C.
52. Malaysia	Ringgit (mil.)	no	No RS. No F. No RB. PY to deflate IM for 701-704. No ΔV.
53. Pakistan	Pak. Rupees (mil.)	no	No F. NIA year begins July 1.
54. Philippines	Phil. Pesos (mil.)	no	Discount rate data for RS. No F. No RB.
†55. Singapore	Sing. Dollars (mil.)	no	No RS. No F. No RB. No EX. No IM.
56. Thailand	Baht (bil.)	no	Discount rate data for RS. No F. No RB. No IP.
†57. Bulgaria		no	No IFS data.
†58. China (Mainland)		no	No data collected from IFS.
†59. Cuba		no	No IFS data.
†60. Czechoslovakia		no	No IFS data.
†61. E. Germany		no	No IFS data.
†62. Hungary		no	No data collected from IFS.
†63. Poland		no	No IFS data.
†64. USSR		no	No IFS data.
†65. Rest of World		no	No IFS data.

Note: † No estimated equations for this country.

TABLE B-2. The variables for country i in alphabetical order

Equation number	Variable	Description
18	A^*_i	= net stock of foreign security and reserve holdings, end of quarter, in lc. [$= A^*_{i-1} + S^*_i$. Base value of zero was used for the quarter prior to the beginning of the data.]
2	C_i	= personal consumption in 75 lc. [IFS96F/CPI_i.]
	††CPI_i	= consumer price index, 1975 = 1.0. [= (IFS64 or IFS64X)/100.]
	†e_{i75}	= average exchange rate in 1975, lc per \$. [= IFSRF for 1975.]
9b	e_i	= exchange rate, average for the quarter, lc per \$. [= IFSRF.]
20	ee_i	= exchange rate, end of quarter, lc per \$. [= IFSAE.]
	††$EMPL_i$	= industrial or manufacturing employment index, 1975 = 100. [IFS67 or various 67 options.]
15	EX_i	= total exports (NIA) in 75 lc. [= (IFS90C or IFS90N)/PX_i.]
	†$EXDIS_i$	= discrepancy between NIA export data and other export data in 75 lc. [$= EX_i - e_{i75}X75\$_i - XS_i$.]
10b	F_i	= three-month forward rate, lc per \$. [= IFSB.]
	†G_i	= government purchases of goods and services in 75 lc. [= (IFS91F or IFS91FF)/PY_{it}.]
3	I_i	= gross fixed investment in 75 lc. [= IFS93/PY_i.]
14	IM_i	= total imports (NIA) in 75 lc. [= IFS98C/PM_i.]
	†$IMDIS_i$	= discrepancy between NIA import data and other import data in 75 lc. [$= IM_i - M_i - MS_i$.]
	††IP_i	= industrial production index, 1975 = 100. [= IFS66 or various 66 options.]
1	M_i	= merchandise imports (fob) in 75 lc. [= IFS71V/PM_i.]
	†MS_i	= other goods, services, and income (debit) in 75 lc. BOP data. [= (IFS77ADD$\cdot e_i$.]
	††$M\$_i$	= merchandise imports (fob) in \$. [= IFS71V/e_i.] [Also equals $(PM_iM_i)/e_i$.]
19	$M75\$A_i$	= merchandise imports (fob) in 75\$ from Type A countries. [$= \sum_j XX75\$_{ji}$.]
	†$M75\$B_i$	= merchandise imports (fob) in 75\$ from Type B countries. [$= M_i/e_{i75} - M75\$A_i$.]
6	$M1^*_i$	= money supply in lc. [= IFS34 or IFS34..B.]
V	PM_i	= import price index, 1975 = 1.0. [IFS75/100.]
IV	PM'_i	= import price index from DOT data. [$= \{e_i\sum_j(PX\$_jXX75\$_{ji})\}/\{e_{i75}\sum_j XX75\$_{ji}\}$.]
	†POP_i	= population in millions. [= IFS99Z.]
VI	$PW\$_i$	= world price index, \$/75\$. [$= \sum^*_{j\neq i}(PX\$_jX\$_j) \,/\, \sum^*_{j\neq i} X\$_j$, where $\sum^*$ denotes summation that excludes Type B countries and countries 26-35.]
11	PX_i	= export price index, 1975 = 1.0. [= IFS74/100.]
III	$PX\$_i$	= export price index, \$/75\$. [$= (e_{i75}PX_i)/e_i$.]
5	PY_i	= GNP or GDP deflator, 1975 = 1.0. [= (IFS99A or IFS99B)/Y_i.]
8	RB_i	= long-term interest rate, percentage points. [= IFS61 or IFS61A.]
7a,7b	RS_i	= three-month interest rate, percentage points. [= IFS60, IFS60B, IFS60C, or IFS60X.]
17	S^*_i	= total net goods, services, and transfers in lc. Balance of Payments on current account. Savings of the country. [See Table B-7.]

(continued)

TABLE B-2 (continued)

Equation number	Variable	Description
	$^{\dagger}TT^*_i$	= total net transfers in lc. [See Table B-7.]
12	ΔV_i	= inventory investment in 75 lc. [= IFS93I/PY_i.]
13	V_i	= stock of inventories, end of quarter, in 75 lc. [= $V_{i-1} + \Delta V_i$. Base value of zero was used for the quarter prior to the beginning of the data.]
16	X_i	= final sales in 75 lc. [= $Y_i - \Delta V_i$.]
	$^{\dagger}XDIS_i$	= discrepancy in real NIA data (in 75 lc) due to use of different deflators. [= $X_i - C_i - I_i - G_i - EX_i + IM_i$.]
	$^{\dagger}XS_i$	= other goods, services, and income (credit) in 75 lc. BOP data. [= (IFS77ACD$\cdot e_i$)/PX_i.]
	$^{\dagger}X\$_i$	= merchandise exports (fob) in \$. [= IFS70/e_i.]
	$^{\dagger\dagger}XX\$_{ij}$	= merchandise exports (fob) from i to j in \$. [DOT tape.] [$XX\$_{i65} = X\$_i - \sum_{j\neq 65} XX\$_{ij}$ and $XX\$_{65i} = M\$_i - \sum_{j\neq 65} XX\$_{ji}$.] [$XX\$_{ij}$ = 0 if i = j.]
I	$XX75\$_{ij}$	= merchandise exports (fob) from i to j in 75\$. [= $(e_i XX\$_{ij})/(e_{i75} PX_i)$ if i is a Type A country; = 0 if i is a Type B country.]
II	$X75\$_i$	= merchandise exports (fob) in 75\$. [= $\sum_j XX75\$_{ij}$.] [Also equals $X\$_i PX\$_i$.] [Equals 0 and is not used if i is a Type B country.]
4	Y_i	= real GNP or GDP in 75 lc. [= IFS99A.P, IFS99B.P, IFS99A.R, or IFS99B.R.]
21	ZZ_i	= demand pressure variable. [= $\{(Y_i/POP_i)^* - (Y_i/POP_i)\}/(Y_i/POP_i)^*$. See equation (4.38) in Chapter 4 for the definition of $(Y_i/POP_i)^*$.]
	α_{ji}	= share of i's total merchandise imports from Type A countries imported from j in 75\$. [= $XX75\$_{ji}/M75\$A_i$.]
	$^{\dagger}\psi_{1i}$	= $((ee_i + ee_{i-1})/2)/e_i$.
	$^{\dagger}\psi_{2i}$	= PM_i/PM'_i.

Notes:
- lc = local currency. All prices are in lc. e and F are in units of lc per \$.
- * denotes that the variable is in units of lc.
- † denotes exogenous variable.
- †† denotes that the variable is used only in the construction of the data.
- For countries with no PM data, PM_i was taken to be PM'_{it} (so that $\psi_{2i} = 1$) and M_{it} was taken to be $[e_i \sum_j (PX\$_j XX75\$_{ji})]/PM_i$. For these countries is it not the case that $M\$_i = (PM_i M_i)/e_i$ because the summation $\sum_j (PX\$_j XX75\$_{ji})$ is only over Type A countries. $M\$_i$ pertains to all countries.
- For the oil exporting countries (countries 26-35), CPI was used in place of PY to deflate IFS91F or IFS91FF for G_i, IFS93E for I_i, and IFS93I for ΔV_i.

TABLE B-3. The list of equations for country i

Stochastic equations	
1. $M_i = f_1(PY_i, PM_i, RS_i \text{ or } RB_i, Y_i, A^*_{i-1}, M_{i-1})$	[merchandise imports in 75 lc]
2. $C_i = f_2(RS_i \text{ or } RB_i, Y_i, A^*_{i-1}, C_{i-1})$	[private consumption in 75 lc]
3. $\Delta I_i = f_3(\Delta I_{i-1}, I_{i-1}, \Delta Y_{i-1}, \Delta Y_{i-2}, \Delta Y_{i-3}, \Delta Y_{i-4}, t)$	[change in gross fixed investment in 75 lc]
4. $Y_i = f_4(X_i, V_{i-1}, Y_{i-1})$	[GNP in 75 lc]
5. $PY_i = f_5(PM_i, ZZ_i, t, PY_{i-1})$	[GNP deflator]
6. $M1^*_i = f_6(RS_i, PY_iY_i, t, M1^*_{i-1})$	[money supply in lc]
7a. $RS_i = f_{7a}(RS_1, RS_8, \dot{PY}_{i-1}, \dot{M1}^*_{i-1}, ZZ_i, A^*_i, A^*_{i-1}, t, RS_{i-1})$	[three-month interest rate]
7b. $RS_i = f_{7b}(\text{same as 7a plus } \dot{PM}_{i-1}, e_i)$	[three-month interest rate]
8. $RB_i = f_8(RS_i, RS_{i-1}, RS_{i-2}, RB_{i-1})$	[long-term interest rate]
9b. $e_i = f_{9b}(e_8, PY_i, PY_1, RS_i, RS_1, ZZ_i, ZZ_1, \Delta A^*_{i-1}, \Delta A^*_{1-1}, e_{i-1})$	[exchange rate, average for the quarter]
10b. $F_i = f_{10b}(ee_i, RS_i, RS_1)$	[three-month forward rate]
11. $PX_i = f_{11}(PY_i, PW\$_i, e_i)$	[export price index]
Identities	
12. $\Delta V_i = Y_i - X_i$	[inventory investment in 75 lc]
13. $V_i = V_{i-1} + \Delta V_i$	[stock of inventories in 75 lc]
14. $IM_i = M_i + MS_i + IMDIS_i$	[total imports (NIA) in 75 lc]
15. $EX_i = e_{i75} \cdot X75\$_i + XS_i + EXDIS_i$	[total exports (NIA) in 75 lc]
16. $X_i = C_i + I_i + G_i + EX_i + IM_i + XDIS_i$	[final sales in 75 lc]
17. $S^*_i = PX_i(e_{i75} \cdot X75\$_i + XS_i) - PM_i(M_i + MS_i) + TT^*_i$	[balance of payments on current account in lc]
18. $A^*_i = A^*_{i-1} + S^*_i$	[net stock of foreign security and reserve holdings in lc]
19. $M75\$A_i = M_i/e_i - M75\$B_i$	[merchandise imports in 75$ from Type A countries]
20. $ee_i = 2\psi_{1i}e_i - ee_{i-1}$	[exchange rate, end of quarter]
21. $ZZ_i = [(Y_i/POP_i)^* - (Y_i/POP_i)]/(Y_i/POP_i)^*$	[demand pressure variable]
Variables explained when the countries are linked together (Table B-4)	
22. $X75\$_i$	[merchandise exports in 75$]
23. PM_i	[import price index]
24. $PW\$_i$	[world price index]

TABLE B-4. Equations that pertain to the trade and price linkages among countries

	Equation	Description
I	$XX75\$_{ji} = \alpha_{ji} M75\$A_i$	[merchandise exports from j to i in 75$.] [= 0 if j is a Type B country.]
II	$X75\$_i = \sum_j XX75\$_{ij}$	[merchandise exports of i in 75$.] [= 0 if i is a Type B country.]
III	$PX\$_{it} = (e_{i75} PX_i)/e_i$	[export price index of i, $/75$.] [= 0 if i is a Type B country.]
IV	$PM_i' = \dfrac{e_i \sum_j (PX\$_j XX75\$_{ji})}{e_{i75} \sum_j XX75\$_{ji}}$	[import price index of i from DOT data.]
V	$PM_i = \psi_{2i} PM_i'$	[import price index of i.]
VI	$PW\$_i = \dfrac{\sum^*_{j \neq i} (PX\$_j X\$_j)}{\sum^*_{j \neq i} X\$_j}$	[world price index facing i.]

Notes:
- α_{ji} = share of i's total merchandise imports from Type A countries imported from j in 75$.
- The determination of α_{ji} is explained in Section 4.2.6.
- $\sum^*$ denotes summation that excludes Type B countries and countries 26-35.

TABLE B-5. Links to and from the US model

A. When the US model is part of the MC model, equation 32 in Table A-5, which determines PEX, is dropped. Instead, equation 11 in Table 4-12 for the US is used to determine PX_1, and PEX is determined as:

$$PEX = \delta_3 PX_1 \, .$$

B. Relevant endogenous variables in the US model (see Table A-4):

IM = imports (NIA), B72$.

RS = three month bill rate, percentage points.

GNPD = GNP deflator, 1972 = 1.0.

GNPR = GNP, B72$.

ZZ = demand pressure variable.

Links from the endogenous variables in the US model to the variables that affect the rest of the world:

$$M75\$_1 = IM/\delta_2 - M75\$_1 - IMDIS_1 \, .$$ [merchandise imports in 75$ from Type A countries]

$$PY_1 = GNPD/\delta_6 \, .$$ [GNP deflator, 1975 = 1.0]

$$RS_1 = RS \, .$$ [three month interest rate]

$$Y_1 = GNPR/\delta_5 \, .$$ [real GNP in 75$]

C. Relevant exogenous variables in the US model:

EX = exports (NIA), B72$.

PIM = price deflator for imports (NIA), 1972 = 1.0.

Links from the rest of the world to the exogenous variables in the US model:

$$EX = \delta_1 EX_1 = \delta_1 (X75\$_1 + XS_1 + EXDIS_1) \, .$$

$$PIM = \delta_4 PM_1 \, .$$

D. New exogenous variables:

$$\delta_1 = EX/EX_1 = EX/(X75\$ + XS_1 + EXDIS_1) \, .$$

$$\delta_2 = IM/(M75\$A_1 + M75\$B_1 + MS_1 + IMDIS_1) = IM/IM_1 \, .$$

$$\delta_3 = PEX/PX_1 \, .$$

$$\delta_4 = PIM/PM_1 \, .$$

$$\delta_5 = GNPR/Y_1 \, .$$

$$\delta_6 = GNPD/PY_1 \, .$$

E. Other relevant equations:

$$M_1 = M75\$A_1 + M75\$B_1 \, .$$

$$S_1^* = PX_1(X75\$_1 + XS_1) - PM_1(M_1 + MS_1) + TT_1^* \, .$$

$$A_1^* = A_{1-1}^* + S_1^* \, .$$

TABLE B-6. Procedure used to create quarterly data from annual data when no quarterly interpolation variables were available

---

Let:

y_t = (observed) average value of the variable for year t,

y_{it} = (unobserved) average value of the variable for quarter i of year t (i = 1, 2, 3, 4).

Then:

$$\text{(i)} \quad y_{1t} + y_{2t} + y_{3t} + y_{4t} = \lambda y_t,$$

where $\lambda = \begin{cases} 1 \text{ for flow variables (at quarterly rates)} \\ 4 \text{ for stock variables and price variables.} \end{cases}$

Assume that the annual data begin in year 1, and let $\lambda y_1 = a_1$, $\lambda y_2 = a_2$, $\lambda y_3 = a_3$, ... The key assumption is that the four quarterly changes within the year are the same:

$$\text{(ii)} \quad y_{1t} - y_{4t-1} = y_{2t} - y_{1t} = y_{3t} - y_{2t} = y_{4t} - y_{3t} = \begin{cases} \delta_2 \text{ for } t = 1, 2 \\ \delta_t \text{ for } t \geq 3 \end{cases} .$$

Given (i) and (ii) for t = 1, 2, one can solve for y_{40} and δ_2 in terms of a_1 and a_2:

$$y_{40} = \frac{13}{32} a_1 - \frac{5}{32} a_2,$$

$$\delta_2 = \frac{a_2 - a_1}{16} .$$

Using y_{40} and δ_2, one can then construct quarterly data for years 1 and 2 using (ii). Given y_{42} from these calculations and given (i) and (ii) for t = 3, one can solve for δ_3 in terms of a_3 and y_{42}:

$$\delta_3 = \frac{a_3 - 4y_{42}}{10} .$$

Using y_{42} and δ_3, one can then construct quarterly data for year 3. One can then solve for δ_4 in terms of y_{43} and a_4, and so on.

Note: • The annual population data that were collected for the model are mid-year estimates. In order to apply the above procedure to these data, the assumption was first made that each mid-year value is the same as the average value for the year.

TABLE B-7. Construction of the balance of payments data: data for S_i^* and TT_i^*

Let:

$M\$_i'$ = merchandise imports (fob) in \$, BOP data. [= IFS77ABD.]

$M\$_i$ = merchandise imports (fob) in \$. [In Table B-2.]

$X\$_i'$ = merchandise exports (fob) in \$, BOP data. [= IFS77AAD.]

$X\$_i$ = merchandise exports (fob) in \$. [In Table B-2.]

$MS\$_i$ = other goods, services, and income (debit) in \$. BOP data. [= IFS77ADD.]

$XS\$_i$ = other goods, services, and income (credit) in \$. BOP data. [= IFS77ACD.]

$PT\$_i$ = private unrequited transfers in \$. BOP data. [= IFS77AED.]

$OT\$_i$ = official unrequited transfers in \$. BOP data. [= IFS77AGD.]

A. When quarterly data on all the above variables were available, then:

(i) $S\$_i = X\$_i' + XS\$_i - M\$_i' - MS\$_i + PT_i + OT\$_i$,

(ii) $TT\$_i = S\$_i - X\$_i - XS\$_i + M\$_i + MS\$_i$,

where $S\$_i$ is total net goods, services, and transfers in \$ (balance of payments on current account) and $TT\$_i$ is total net transfers in \$.

B. When only annual data on $M\$_i'$ were available, interpolated quarterly data were constructed using $M\$_i$. Similarly for $MS\$_i$.

When only annual data on $X\$_i'$ were available, interpolated quarterly data were constructed using $X\$_i$. Similarly for $XS\$_i$, $PT\$_i$, and $OT\$_i$.

When no data on $M\$_i'$ were available, then $M\$_i'$ was taken to be $\lambda \cdot M\$_i$, where λ is the last observed annual value of $M\$'/M\$$. Similarly for $MS\$_i$ (where λ is the last observed annual value of $MS\$/M\$$).

When no data on $X\$_i'$ were available, then $X\$_i'$ was taken to be $\lambda \cdot X\$_i$, where λ is the last observed annual value of $X\$'/X\$$. Similarly for $XS\$_i$ (where λ is the last observed annual value of $XS\$/X\$$), for $PT\$_i$ (where λ is the last observed annual value of $PT\$/X\$$), and for $OT\$_i$ (where λ is the last observed annual value of $OT\$/X\$$).

Equations (i) and (ii) were then used to construct quarterly data for $S\$_i$ and $TT\$_i$.

C. After data on $S\$_i$ and $TT\$_i$ were constructed, data on S_i^* and TT_i^* were constructed as:

(iii) $S_i^* = e_i S\$_i$,

(iv) $TT_i^* = e_i TT\$_i$.

D. Notice from MS_i and XS_i in Table B-2 and from $MS\$_i$ and $XS\$_i$ above that

$$MS\$_i = (PM_i MS_i)/e_i,$$

$$XS\$_i = (PX_i XS_i)/e_i.$$

Notice also from Table B-2 that

$$M\$_i = (PM_i M_i)/e_i,$$

$$X\$_i = (e_{i75} PX_i X75\$_i)/e_i.$$

Therefore, from equations (ii)-(iv), the equation for S_i^* can be written

$$S_i^* = PX_i(e_{i75}X75\$_i + XS_i) - PM_i(M_i + MS_i) + TT_i^*,$$

which is equation 17 in Table B-3.

E. For countries with no PM data it is not the case that $M\$_i = (PM_i M_i)/e_i$. (See the fifth note to Table B-2.) For these countries TT_i^* was taken to be

$$TT_i^* = S_i^* - PX_i(e_{i75}X75\$_i + XS_i) - PM_i(M_i + MS_i),$$

where PM_i and M_i are defined in the fifth note to Table B-2.

Appendix C: The Fair-Parke Program for the Estimation and Analysis of Nonlinear Econometric Models

The Fair-Parke program allows all the techniques discussed in this book to be used automatically once the necessary information on a model has been read by the program. The necessary information consists of a few FORTRAN subroutines and a few data sets to present the stochastic equations and the identities. Once the program has this information, almost all the techniques can be used with no further programming. (In a few cases, such as FIML estimation, the user must supply additional information. In the FIML case, for example, information on the Jacobian must be supplied. These exceptions are discussed later in this appendix.) This has the obvious advantage of allowing many things to be done with only one setup, and it also means that the model only needs to be debugged once. It is quite easy, as will be seen, to check coding errors, and once these errors have been corrected, one need not worry about further coding errors for any of the techniques.

The model is represented by (6.1), which is repeated here:

$$(6.1)\qquad f_i(y_t, x_t, \alpha_i) = u_{it}, \qquad i = 1, \ldots, n.$$

The program requires that the stochastic equations of the model be rewritten,

$$(\text{C}.1)\qquad f_i(z_t, \alpha_i) = u_{it}, \qquad i = 1, \ldots, m,$$

where z_t is a vector of variables that are transformations (generally nonlinear) of the variables in y_t and x_t. If, for example, one of the variables in an equation is $\log(y_{2t}/x_{3t-1})$, then one of the variables in z_t would equal this. A variable in z_t can simply be a variable in y_t or x_t, and thus no generality is lost in going from (6.1) to (C.1). In this notation the stochastic equations are assumed to come first in the model, although the program does not require this.

The heart of the program consists of four subroutines: ZFYX, YFZX, IDENT, and RESID. RESID is internal to the program, and the other three are user-supplied. ZFYX calculates the z variables as a function of the y and x variables. It consists of statements like Z(J,1) = DLOG(Y(J,2)/X(J − 1,3)), where J is the time index. YFZX contains the reverse transformations from the z and x variables to the y variables that are matched to the stochastic equations. If, say, $z_{1t} = \log(y_{2t}/x_{3t-1})$ is the LHS variable of equation 1 and if y_{2t} is matched to this equation, then YFZX would contain the expression $y_{2t} = e^{z_{1t}} \cdot x_{3t-1}$, which in FORTRAN is Y(J,2) = DEXP(Z(J,1))*X(J − 1,3). YFZX contains m such statements. The z variables pertain only to the stochastic equations; they are not needed and are not used for the identities. IDENT calculates the identities. It contains the code for the identities in terms of the y and x variables, such as Y(J,6) = Y(J,5) + Y(J,4) + X(J,3). IDENT contains $n - m$ such statements.

RESID calculates the LHS z variable for each stochastic equation. If an equation is linear in coefficients except for the possible presence of serial correlation coefficients, RESID only needs to know which z variables appear in the equation. These variables can simply be listed in a data set, and therefore in this case RESID does not have to be touched by the user. If an equation is nonlinear in coefficients, RESID has to be modified for the equation. Since most equations in macroeconometric models are linear in coefficients, RESID seldom needs to be adjusted.

The reason these four subroutines are the heart of the model is that they are used by the Gauss-Seidel technique to solve the model. In the solution of the model for a given period, ZFYX is first called to get initial values for the z variables. The problem is then turned over to the Gauss-Seidel technique. One iteration (that is, one "pass" through the model) consists of successive calls to RESID, YFZX, IDENT, and ZFYX. RESID computes the LHS z variables in the stochastic equations; YFZX computes the y variables corresponding to these z variables; IDENT computes the y variables that are determined by the identities; and ZFYX computes the z variables that were not computed by RESID. The four calls are then repeated, and the process continues until convergence is reached or there is an abnormal termination. (With respect to the call to ZFYX, it does not make any difference if ZFYX computes the z variables that were already computed by RESID. Given that YFZX is called right after RESID, ZFYX merely computes the values computed by RESID back again. It is, of course, wasteful of computer time to do this, and ZFYX has an option for the relevant z variables to be skipped.) The order of the equations matters for solution purposes in that once a z or y variable is computed, this value is used in any subsequent calculations involving the variable on the RHS of the equations. The order is determined by the user in the coding of subroutines YFZX, IDENT, and ZFYX and in the numbering of the stochastic equations.

Since the techniques discussed in this book require little, if anything, more from the user than a way of solving the model, once the four subroutines are available, the rest of the programming for a technique requires little or no user intervention. One of the advantages of this feature is that one can move automatically from estimation to the use of other techniques. It is easy in the program to modify a stochastic equation (or to create a new one) and then estimate it, and the program always stores the last estimate of each equation. This means that one can modify a model, reestimate it, and then go immediately to the solution of the modified version with no extra programming.

Debugging subroutines is always a problem for large models, but the program allows this to be done fairly easily. First, given the actual data for the y and x variables, a call to IDENT should result in the predicted values of the identity-determined y variables being equal to the actual values. Since, as noted earlier, order matters in this subroutine, if an error has been made in one equation so that the predicted value of the y variable corresponding to the equation is not equal to the actual value, this error will affect the calculations of subsequent identities that use this variable. This sometimes makes it difficult to determine if an error is a coding error or the result of a previous error, and the easiest thing to do is to correct the obvious errors and run the test again. Debugging of IDENT can usually be accomplished with two or three sets of corrections.

Second, RESID can be tested in the following way. There is an option in RESID to compute either the LHS z variables in the stochastic equations or the residuals. In other words, RESID will compute either the LHS variable in equation i in (C.1) or the error term u_{it}. If the residuals are computed over the estimation period and if the actual values of the z variables are used for these calculations, then the sum of these residuals squared for each equation should equal the sum of squared residuals computed by the estimation technique at the time of estimation. This latter sum is printed by the program at the time of estimation, and thus one can check to see if the two sums are the same for each equation. To some extent this check is unnecessary, since RESID does not have to be debugged, but it is useful to make sure that the set of coefficients being used is what the user thinks it is and that no changes have been made between estimation and solution time that affect these calculations.

Finally, the entire solution process can be tested as follows. If RESID is called and if the residual computation option is used, the program computes and stores the residuals. A second call to RESID to compute the z variables will then result in the computed values of the z variables being equal to the actual values. A call to YFZX should then produce actual values of the y variables corresponding to the stochastic equations, and a call to IDENT should produce the actual values of the y variables determined by the identities. In short, the solution values should equal the actual values when the estimated residuals are used in RESID for the solution of the z variables. If not, and if RESID and IDENT have been checked previously, then YFZX must contain one or more errors.

These three tests do not catch all errors. There may, for example, be an error in ZFYX in computing a z variable that is not a LHS variable of a stochastic equation, and this will not necessarily be caught. The tests do, however, catch most errors, so once these tests are passed, one can have some confidence that no coding errors are involved in the use of the various techniques.

Note with respect to the third test that because RESID computes residuals as well as z variables, perfect tracking solutions are easy to create and then use as a base for other experiments. This is accomplished by one call to RESID using the residual option and the actual values of the z variables. The residuals are stored and treated as exogenous for any future experiments.

The extra subroutines are that needed for some of the techniques will now be discussed. For FIML estimation, one must supply information on the Jacobian. This is done by creating a data set that consists of FORTRAN code for the nonzero derivatives (in any order). A program that accompanies the main Fair-Parke program reads this data set and creates two FORTRAN subroutines, which are then added to the main program. The program automatically takes account of the sparse structure of the Jacobian, so the user need not worry about this. Debugging the Jacobian code is a serious problem, however. If errors have been made in the code, it may still be the case that the subroutines compile and the determinants of the Jacobian are computed with no error messages. There is no obvious way to test that all the derivatives are correct. It is easy to make small errors in the code, and my suggestion is to have two people each take and code the derivatives. Two separate setup jobs can then be run, and two separate initial values of the likelihood function can be computed. If the two values are not the same, then at least one error has been made, which then requires checking the two sets of code line by line.

If there are constraints on the coefficients, such as $\alpha_{18} = \alpha_{17}\alpha_{25}$, a subroutine must be supplied that codes these constraints. The constrained coefficients are not estimated, but they are used in RESID in computing the z variables and residuals. Given the subroutine for the constraints, RESID does not have to be modified to account for them.

If an equation is nonlinear in coefficients for reasons other than because of serial correlation problems and if the equation is to be estimated by OLS or 2SLS, a subroutine must be supplied that computes the residuals for a given set of coefficients. The program uses the residuals to compute $u_i'D_iu_i$ in (6.5), which is then turned over to the DFP algorithm.

For the solution of optimal control problems, a subroutine must be supplied that computes the value of the objective function for a given set of values of the y and x variables. In other words, the user must supply a subroutine that computes W in (10.2).

Two additional subroutines are needed if the model is a rational expectations model. One subroutine creates the expectations variables from the Y and X variables. The user-supplied part of this subroutine consists merely of one line of code per expectation variable, so it requires very little work to construct. The other subroutine creates the expectations of the exogenous variables, where the assumptions that are used for this are left to the user. This subroutine does not have to be supplied if the expectations of the exogenous variables are assumed to be equal to the actual values for all variables.

These are the main additional subroutines. A few others are required for some of the options, but they are not of general interest here. A final point to emphasize about the program is that it allows successive reestimation and stochastic simulation to be done with virtually no extra work on the part of the user. One number indicates how many times the estimation or simulation is to be done. Because of the emphasis in this book on the comparison method in Chapter 8, which requires successive reestimation and stochastic simulation, the program was written to make this as easy as possible.

Notes

3. A Theoretical Model

The single-country model in Section 3.1 is similar to the model in Fair (1974d). The main differences between the two models are the following. (1) The earlier model took account of both labor and loan constraints, whereas the present model considers only labor constraints. I have been unable to find in my empirical work much evidence of the effects of loan constraints on the economy, and this is the main reason they have been dropped from the theoretical model. Eliminating the loan constraints greatly simplifies the model. The household and firm maximization problems are easier to specify, and it is no longer necessary to specify a maximization problem for banks. If financial markets always clear, as is assumed here, banks can be specified to play a passive role in the economy. In the earlier model a rather complicated model of bank behavior had to be specified to explain the possible existence of credit rationing. Also, a bond dealer had to be postulated in the earlier model, which is now no longer necessary. (2) The model of household behavior now includes another decision variable, the amount of time spent taking care of money holdings. It provides a choice-theoretic explanation of the interest sensitivity of the demand for money. (3) Some slight changes in the specification of adjustment costs in the model of firm behavior have been made. (4) An option has been added to allow monetary policy to be endogenous, which is to postulate the possible existence of an interest rate reaction function of the government. In my empirical work I have estimated and used such a function, and it is now part of the theoretical model. (5) The length of the decision horizon for the solution of the household and firm maximization problems is now taken to be three rather than thirty. This change lessens the cost of solving the model, and it allows more accurate algorithms to be written. The first-order conditions have been obtained explicitly for the household problem, and a more accurate algorithm has been written for the firm problem. The cost of solving the earlier model was large enough to require that a "condensed" version of the model be used for many of the simulations. In the present case a condensed version is not needed. The use of three periods is enough to capture the multiperiod nature of the maximization problems, so nothing is really lost by lessening the length of the horizon. (6) Because of the foregoing changes, the values used for the parameters and variables in the simulation work are generally different between the two models. This is not very important, however, because the only things of interest from the simulation experiments are the qualitative results.

The discussion of the class of rational expectations models in Section 3.1.7 is similar to that in Fair (1978c). The discussion in this paper relied on a "static-equilibrium" version of the basic model in Fair (1974d). I have not used this version in the present case. The main points about the class of rational expectations models can be made without reference to this version, of which I have never been particularly fond. It is an attempt to collapse the basic version, which is dynamic and has disequilibrium features, to one with no dynamics and no disequilibrium. So much of the basic version is lost in this process, however, that the resulting model is not very useful for comparison purposes.

The two-country model in Section 3.2 is similar to the theoretical model in Fair (1979a). In this paper a "quasi-empirical" two-country model was also presented, which consisted of my US econometric model linked to a model exactly like it. This model, which was called Model A, has not been used here. I look on Model A as a help in the transition from the theory to the multicountry econometric model in Chapter 4, but it is now no longer of much interest.

Although this note has concentrated on the differences between the models in Sections 3.1 and 3.2 and those in Fair (1974d) and (1979a), the general premises and main features are the same. In particular, the discussion of the models in Sections 3.1.1 and 3.2.1 pertains to both the earlier work and the present work.

4. An Econometric Model

The US model in Section 4.1 is similar to the model in Fair (1976), with the addition of the interest rate reaction function in Fair (1978b). The idea that firms may at times be off their production functions and hold excess labor, which is part of both the theoretical and econometric models, was first explored in Fair (1969). The employment and hours equations in Section 4.1.5 are similar to those in this earlier work. The specification of the production equation has been in part influenced by the results in Fair (1971a).

The US model has been updated and changed slightly over the years, but the basic structure and features have remained the same. One of the more important minor changes that has been made is the imposition of the real wage constraint in Section 4.1.5. A change that expanded the size of the model, but otherwise had little effect, was the disaggregation of the government sector into federal and state & local.

The US model is not a revised or extended version of my original forecasting model (Fair 1971b). The only stochastic equation that is similar between the two models is the employment equation, which, as just noted, is derived from the work in Fair (1969). The forecasting model was intended to be used for very short run forecasting purposes, which meant that a number of expectations variables, such as a variable measuring plant and equipment investment expectations, were taken to be exogenous. In this sense the forecasting model is not structural, whereas the US model is.

The MC model in Section 4.2, aside from the trade share equations, is presented in an unpublished working paper (Fair 1981a). The model in this paper took trade shares to be exogenous. The endogenous treatment of trade shares in Section 4.2.6 is new. This treatment is different from an earlier one presented in another unpublished working paper (Fair 1981b), where constraints were imposed on the coefficients across equations.

5. Other Econometric Models

The discussion of Sargent's model in Section 5.4 is similar to the discussion in section II in Fair (1979c). An iterative 2SLS procedure was used in this paper to estimate Sargent's model, but this has not been done here. A much better technique for rational expectations models is full information maximum likelihood (FIML), and it is now possible to estimate Sargent's model by FIML. This is discussed in Chapter 11.

6. Estimation

The method discussed in Section 6.3.2 for the linear-in-coefficients case with serial correlation is presented in Fair (1970). The formulas in (6.20)–(6.23) for the 2SLS covariance matrix are presented in Fair and Parke (1980). The 3SLS estimator that is based on the minimization of (6.26) is also presented in this paper. The 2SLAD estimator in Section 6.3.6 for $q = 1.0$ is suggested in Fair (1974c).

The FIML cost savings with respect to the Jacobians that are considered in Section 6.5.2 are discussed in Fair (1976, chap. 3). The estimation of subsets of coefficients by FIML is also discussed in this chapter. The DFP algorithm was used for this earlier FIML work, and it turned out that the "FIML" estimates that are reported in Fair (1976) are not the true FIML estimates. Parke later found using his algorithm a larger value of the likelihood function.

The computational method for the LAD and 2SLAD estimators in Section 6.5.4 is discussed in Fair (1974c).

The possible use of the Hausman test in Section 6.6 to compare the 2SLS, 3SLS, and FIML estimates is discussed in Fair and Parke (1980). The discussion in this paper is misleading in one respect: we failed to point out that the alternative hypothesis that is tested when the 3SLS and FIML estimates are compared for a nonlinear model is that the distribution of the error terms is such as to lead to inconsistent FIML estimates. It was implicitly assumed that any nonnormal distribution meets this requirement, which, as Phillips (1982) has pointed out, is not the case. The Hausman test was used in this paper to compare the 2SLS and 3SLS estimates even though, as we pointed out, the comparison is not valid because of the different sets of first-stage regressors used by 2SLS and 3SLS. The test was applied, where possible, to try to get a feeling for the results, but very little weight was placed on them. For purposes of this book, no attempts have been made to use the Hausman test.

7. Solution

Part of the discussion in this chapter is taken from Fair (forthcoming).

8. Evaluating Predictive Accuracy

The discussion in Sections 8.2 and 8.3 is taken from Fair (forthcoming). The original discussion of the method in Section 8.4 is contained in Fair (1980a). Further discussion of the method and its use can be found in Fair (1979c) and (1982b). The discussion of the d_{itk} values in Section 8.5.2 is similar to that in Fair (1982b), and the comparison of the models in Section 8.5.4 is similar to that in Fair (1979c). The comparison of the MC and ARMC models in Section 8.6 is similar to that in Fair (1981a).

9. Evaluating Static and Dynamic Properties

The original discussion of the stochastic simulation method in Section 9.3 for estimating the uncertainty of policy effects is contained in Fair (1980b). The empirical analysis in Section 9.4.2 is similar to that in Fair (1980b); the analysis in Section 9.4.4 is similar to that in Fair (1978b); and the analysis in Section 9.4.5 is similar to that in Fair and Parke (1980). The empirical results in these sections are not exactly the same as those in the original papers because the US model has been updated for the purposes of this book.

The discussion of the properties of the MC model in Section 9.5 is similar to that in Fair (1982a). The results in this section are not exactly the same as those in the paper because the US and MC models have been updated and because a different set of trade share equations has been used. For the results in the paper the trade share equations in Fair (1981b) were used, whereas for the results in this book the trade share equations in Section 4.2.6 have been used.

10. Optimal Control Analysis

The original discussion of the method in Section 10.2 is in Fair (1974a). The measure of performance in Section 10.3 was first proposed in Fair (1978a). Chow's (1978) comment on this measure contains an error. Chow asserts that because the measure is based on the open-loop approach it assumes that "decisions . . . [are] made once for all four years at the beginning of each administration" (p. 314). This statement is incorrect because the measure is based on the open-loop approach *with* reoptimization each period. Furthermore, Chow is not explicit in pointing out that his measure also requires that a new optimization problem be solved each period for a nonlinear model because the linearization changes with each new realization. An attempt was made in Fair (1978a) to approximate the measure of performance by solving fewer control problems than are actually needed in the complete case. These approximations were then used to compare past U.S. presidential administrations. No attempt has been made to do this here, since it is not clear how good the approximation is.

11. Models with Rational Expectations

The discussion in Sections 11.2, 11.3, 11.4, and 11.6 is based on Fair and Taylor (1983). The analysis in Section 11.7 is similar to that in Fair (1979d). The results in Section 11.7 do not match exactly the results in this paper because the US model has been updated for present purposes and because the experiments are not exactly the same. The experiments differ in the prediction periods used, in the choice of a value of T in (11.20), in the treatment of the initial value of stock prices, and in the treatment of the variable values beyond the end of the data. The discussion of the solution of optimal control problems in Section 11.5 and the estimation of Sargent's model by FIML in Section 11.8 are new.

References

Allen, Polly Reynolds. 1973. A portfolio approach to international capital flows. *Journal of International Economics 3*:135–160.

Amemiya, Takeshi. 1975. The nonlinear two-stage least squares estimator. *Journal of Econometrics 2*:105–110.

——— 1977. The maximum likelihood and the nonlinear three-stage least squares estimator in the general nonlinear simultaneous equations model. *Econometrica 45*:955–968.

——— 1982a. The two stage least absolute deviations estimators. *Econometrica 50*:689–711.

——— 1982b. Correction to a lemma. *Econometrica 50*:1325–28.

Athans, Michael. 1972. The discrete time linear-quadratic-Gaussian stochastic control problem. *Annals of Economic and Social Measurement 1*:449–491.

Ball, R. J., ed. 1973. *The international linkage of national economic models.* Amsterdam: North-Holland.

Barro, Robert J. 1976. Rational expectations and the role of monetary policy. *Journal of Monetary Economics 2*:1–32.

Barro, Robert J., and Herschel I. Grossman. 1971. A general disequilibrium model of income and employment. *American Economic Review 61*:82–93.

——— 1976. *Money, employment and inflation.* Cambridge: Cambridge University Press.

Basmann, R. L. 1957. A generalized classical method of linear estimation of coefficients in a structural equation. *Econometrica 25*:77–83.

Bassett, Gilbert, Jr., and Roger Koenker. 1978. Asymptotic theory of least absolute error regression. *Journal of the American Statistical Association 73*:618–622.

Berner, Richard, Peter Clark, Howard Howe, et al. 1976. Modeling the international influences on the U.S. economy: A multi-country approach. International Finance Discussion Paper no. 93, Board of Governors of the Federal Reserve System.

Bianchi, Carlo, Giorgio Calzolari, and Paolo Corsi. 1976. Divergences in the results of stochastic and deterministic simulation of an Italian non linear econometric model. In *Simulation of systems,* ed. L. Dekker. Amsterdam: North-Holland.

Bierens, Herman J. 1981. *Robust methods and asymptotic theory in nonlinear econometrics.* Lecture Notes in Economics and Mathematical Systems, vol. 192. Berlin, Heidelberg, and New York: Springer-Verlag.

Black, Stanley W. 1973. *International money markets and flexible exchange rates.*

Studies in International Finance, no. 32. Princeton, N.J.: Princeton University Press.

Brainard, William C., and James Tobin. 1968. Pitfalls in financial model building. *American Economic Review 58*:99–122.

Branson, William H. 1974. Stocks and flows in international monetary analysis. In *International aspects of stabilization policies,* ed. A. Ando, R. Herring, and R. Martson, 27–50. Boston: Federal Reserve Bank of Boston.

Brown, Bryan W. 1981. Sample size requirements in full information maximum likelihood estimation. *International Economic Review 22*:443–459.

Calzolari, Giorgio, and Paolo Corsi. 1977. Stochastic simulation as a validation tool for econometric models. Paper presented at IIASA Seminar, September 13–15, Laxenburg, Vienna.

Chow, Gregory C. 1964. A comparison of alternative estimators for simultaneous equations. *Econometrica 32*:532–553.

——— 1975. *Analysis and control of dynamic economic systems.* New York: Wiley.

——— 1976. The control of nonlinear econometric systems with unknown parameters. *Econometrica 44*:685–695.

——— 1978. Evaluation of macroeconomic policies by stochastic control techniques. *International Economic Review 19*:311–319.

——— 1980. Estimation of rational expectations models. *Journal of Economic Dynamics and Control 2*:241–255.

——— 1981. *Econometric analysis by control methods.* New York: Wiley.

Chow, Gregory C., and Ray C. Fair. 1973. Maximum likelihood estimation of linear equation systems with auto-regressive residuals. *Annals of Economic and Social Measurement 2*:17–28.

Chow, Gregory C., and An-loh Lin. 1971. Best linear unbiased interpolation, distribution, and extrapolation of time series by related series. *Review of Economics and Statistics 53*:372–375.

Christ, Carl F. 1968. A simple macroeconomic model with a government budget restraint. *Journal of Political Economy 76*:53–67.

Clower, Robert W. 1965. The Keynesian counterrevolution: A theoretical appraisal. In *The theory of interest rates,* ed. F. H. Hahn and F. P. R. Brechling. London: Macmillan.

Cochrane, Donald, and Guy Orcutt. 1949. Application of least squares regression to relationships containing autocorrelated error terms. *Journal of the American Statistical Association 44*:32–61.

Cooper, J. P. 1974. *Development of the monetary sector, prediction and policy analysis in the FRB-MIT-Penn model.* Lexington, Mass.: D. C. Heath.

Cooper, J. P., and Stanley Fischer. 1972. Stochastic simulation of monetary rules in two macroeconometric models. *Journal of the American Statistical Association 67*:750–760.

——— 1974. Monetary and fiscal policy in the fully stochastic St. Louis econometric model. *Journal of Money, Credit and Banking 6*:1–22.

Davidon, W. C. 1959. Variable metric method for minimization. A. E. C. Research and Development Report ANL-5990 (revised).

Dennis, J. E., Jr., and Jorge J. More. 1977. Quasi-Newton methods, motivation, and theory, *SIAM Review 19*:46–89.

Dornbusch, Rudiger. Capital mobility, flexible exchange rates and macroeconomic equilibrium. In *Recent developments in international monetary economics,* ed. E. Claassen and P. Salin, 261–278. Amsterdam: North-Holland.

Evans, Michael K., Yoel Haitovsky, and George I. Treyz, assisted by Vincent Su. 1972. An analysis of the forecasting properties of U. S. econometric models. In *Econometric models of cyclical behavior,* ed. B. G. Hickman, 949–1139. New York: Columbia University Press.

Evans, Michael K., Lawrence R. Klein, and Mitsuo Saito. 1972. Short-run prediction and long-run simulation of the Wharton model. In *Econometric models of cyclical behavior,* ed. B. G. Hickman, 139–185. New York: Columbia University Press.

Fair, Ray C. 1969. *The short-run demand for workers and hours.* Amsterdam: North-Holland.

——— 1970. The estimation of simultaneous equation models with lagged endogenous variables and first order serially correlated errors. *Econometrica 38*:507–516.

——— 1971a. Sales expectations and short-run production decisions. *Southern Economic Journal 37*:267–275.

——— 1971b. *A short-run forecasting model of the United States economy.* Lexington, Mass.: D. C. Heath.

——— 1974a. On the solution of optimal control problems as maximization problems. *Annals of Economic and Social Measurement 3*:135–154.

——— 1974b. An evaluation of a short-run forecasting model. *International Economic Review 15*:285–303.

——— 1974c. On the robust estimation of econometric models. *Annals of Economic and Social Measurement 3*:667–677.

——— 1974d. *A model of macroeconomic activity.* Vol. 1, *The theoretical model.* Cambridge, Mass.: Ballinger.

——— 1976. *A model of macroeconomic activity.* Vol. 2, *The empirical model.* Cambridge, Mass.: Ballinger.

——— 1978a. The use of optimal control techniques to measure economic performance. *International Economic Review 19*:289–309.

——— 1978b. The sensitivity of fiscal policy effects to assumptions about the behavior of the Federal Reserve. *Econometrica 46*:1165–79.

——— 1978c. A criticism of one class of macroeconomic models with rational expectations. *Journal of Money, Credit and Banking 10*:411–417.

——— 1979a. A model of the balance of payments. *Journal of International Economics 9*:25–46.

——— 1979b. On modeling the economic linkages among countries. In *International economic policy: Theory and evidence,* ed. R. Dornbusch and J. A. Frenkel, 209–245. Baltimore: The Johns Hopkins University Press.

——— 1979c. An analysis of the accuracy of four macroeconometric models. *Journal of Political Economy 87*:701–718.

——— 1979d. An analysis of a macro-econometric model with rational expectations in the bond and stock markets. *American Economic Review 69*:539–552.

——— 1980a. Estimating the expected predictive accuracy of econometric models. *International Economic Review 21*:355–378.

——— 1980b. Estimating the uncertainty of policy effects in nonlinear models. *Econometrica 48*:1381–91.

——— 1981a. A multicountry econometric model. Cowles Foundation Discussion Paper no. 541R, April 30, 1981.

——— 1981b. The effects of relative prices on trade shares. Cowles Foundation Discussion Paper no. 597, June 10, 1981.

——— 1982a. Estimated output, price, interest rate, and exchange rate linkages among countries. *Journal of Political Economy 90*:507–535.

——— 1982b. The effects of misspecification on predictive accuracy. In *Evaluating the reliability of macro-economic models,* ed. G. Chow and P. Corsi, 193–213. New York: Wiley.

——— Forthcoming. Evaluating the predictive accuracy of models. In *Handbook of Econometrics,* ed. Z. Griliches and M. D. Intriligator. Amsterdam: North-Holland.

Fair, Ray C., and William R. Parke. 1980. Full-information estimates of a nonlinear macroeconometric model. *Journal of Econometrics 13*:269–291.

——— 1981. The Fair-Parke program for the estimation and analysis of nonlinear econometric models. Mimeo.

Fair, Ray C., and John B. Taylor. 1983. Solution and maximum likelihood estimation of dynamic rational expectations models. *Econometrica 51*:1169–85.

Fisher, Franklin M. 1965. Dynamic structure and estimation in economy-wide econometric models. In *The Brookings quarterly econometric model of the United States,* ed. J. S. Duesenberry, G. Fromm, L. R. Klein, and E. Kuh. Amsterdam: North-Holland.

Fisher, Franklin, M., Paul H. Cootner, and Martin Neil Baily. 1972. An Econometric Model of the World Copper Industry. *The Bell Journal 3*:568–609.

Fletcher, R., and M. J. D. Powell. 1963. A rapidly convergent descent method for minimization. *Computer Journal* 6:163–168.

Frenkel, Jacob A., and Harry G. Johnson, eds. 1976. *The monetary approach to the balance of payments.* Toronto: University of Toronto Press.

Frenkel, Jacob A., and Carlos A. Rodrigues. 1975. Portfolio equilibrium and the balance of payments: A monetary approach. *American Economic Review 65*:674–688.

Friedman, Milton. 1953. *Essays in positive economics.* Chicago: The University of Chicago Press.

——— 1968. The role of monetary policy. *American Economic Review 58*:1–17.

Fromm, Gary, and Lawrence R. Klein. 1976. The NBER/NSF model comparison seminar: An analysis of results. *Annals of Economic and Social Measurement 5*:1–28.

Fromm, Gary, Lawrence R. Klein, and George R. Schink. 1972. Short- and long-term simulations with the Brookings model. In *Econometric models of cyclical behavior*, ed. B. G. Hickman, 201–292. New York: Columbia University Press.

Garbade, Kenneth D. 1975. *Discretionary control of aggregate economic activity*. Lexington, Mass.: D. C. Heath.

Girton, Lance, and Dale W. Henderson. 1976. Financial capital movements and central bank behavior in a two-country portfolio balance model. *Journal of Monetary Economics 2*:33–61.

Goldfeld, Stephen M., Richard E. Quandt, and Hale F. Trotter. 1966. Maximization by quadratic-hill-climbing. *Econometrica 34*:541–551.

Grandmont, Jean Michel. 1977. Temporary general equilibrium theory. *Econometrica 45*:535–572.

Green, George R., M. Liebenberg, and Albert A. Hirsch. 1972. Short- and long-term simulations with the OBE econometric model. In *Econometric models of cyclical behavior*, ed. B. G. Hickman, 25–123. New York: Columbia University Press.

Grossman, Herschel I. 1971. Money, interest and prices in market disequilibrium. *Journal of Political Economy 79*:943–961.

——— 1972a. Was Keynes a "Keynesian"? A review article. *Journal of Economic Literature 10*:26–30.

——— 1972b. A choice-theoretic model of an income investment accelerator. *American Economic Review 62*:630–641.

Haitovsky, Yoel, and George Treyz. 1972. Forecasts with quarterly macroeconometric models, equation adjustments, and benchmark predictions: The U. S. experience. *Review of Economics and Statistics 54*:317–325.

Haitovsky, Yoel, George Treyz, and Vincent Su. 1974. *Forecasts with quarterly macroeconometric models*. New York: National Bureau of Economic Research, Columbia University Press.

Haitovsky, Yoel, and Neil Wallace. 1972. A study of discretionary and nondiscretionary monetary and fiscal policies in the context of stochastic macroeconometric models. In *The business cycle today*, ed. V. Zarnowitz. New York: Columbia University Press.

Hansen, Lars P., and Thomas J. Sargent. 1980. Formulating and estimating dynamic linear rational expectations models. *Journal of Economic Dynamics and Control 2*:7–46.

——— 1981. Linear rational expectations models for dynamically interrelated variables. In *Rational expectations and econometric practice*, ed. R. E. Lucas, Jr., and T. J. Sargent. Minneapolis: University of Minnesota Press.

Hausman, Jerry A. 1974. Full information instrumental variables estimation of simultaneous equations systems. *Annals of Economic and Social Measurement* *3*:641–652.

——— 1975. An instrumental variable approach to full-information estimators for linear and certain nonlinear econometric models. *Econometrica* *43*:727–738.

——— 1978. Specification tests in econometrics. *Econometrica 46*:1251–71.

Hickman, Bert G. 1974. International transmission of economic fluctuations and inflation. In *International aspects of stabilization policies,* ed. A. Ando, R. Herring, and R. Martson. Boston: Federal Reserve Bank of Boston.

Hirsch, Albert A., Bruce T. Grimm, and Gorti V. L. Narasimham. 1974. Some multiplier and error characteristics of the BEA quarterly model. *International Economic Review 15*:616–631.

Howrey, E. P., and Harry H. Kelejian. 1971. Simulation versus analytical solutions: The case of econometric models. In *Computer simulation experiments with models of economic systems,* ed. T. H. Naylor. New York: Wiley.

Huang, H. Y. 1970. Unified approach to quadratically convergent algorithms for function minimization. *Journal of Optimization Theory and Applications* *5*:405–423.

Intriligator, Michael D. 1978. *Econometric models, techniques, and applications.* Amsterdam: North-Holland.

Jorgenson, Dale W., and Jean-Jacques Laffont. 1974. Efficient estimation of nonlinear systems of simultaneous equations with additive disturbances. *Annals of Economic and Social Measurement 3*:615–640.

Kelejian, Harry H. 1971. Two stage least squares and econometric models linear in the parameters but nonlinear in the endogenous variables. *Journal of the American Statistical Association 66*:373–374.

Klein, Laurence R. 1971. Forecasting and policy evaluation using large scale econometric models: The state of the art. In *Frontiers of quantitative economics,* ed. M. D. Intriligator. Amsterdam: North-Holland.

Korliras, Panayotis G. 1972. A disequilibrium macroeconomic model. Mimeo.

Kouri, Penti J. K. 1976. The exchange rate and the balance of payments in the short run and in the long run. *Scandinavian Journal of Economics 2*:280–304.

Kydland, Finn E., and Edward C. Prescott. 1977. Rules rather than discretion: The inconsistency of optimal plans. *Journal of Political Economy 85*:473–491.

Leijonhufvud, Axel. 1968. *On Keynesian economics and the economics of Keynes.* New York: Oxford University Press.

——— 1973. Effective demand failures. *Swedish Journal of Economics 65*:27–48.

Lipton, David, James Poterba, Jeffrey Sachs, and Lawrence Summers. 1982. Multiple shooting in rational expectations models. *Econometrica 50*:1329–33.

Litterman, Robert B. 1979. Techniques of forecasting using vector autoregression. Working Paper no. 115, Federal Reserve Bank of Minneapolis.

——— 1980. Improving the measurement of predictive accuracy. Mimeo.

Lucas, Robert E., Jr. 1973. Some international evidence on output-inflation tradeoffs. *American Economic Review 63*:326–334.

——— 1976. Econometric policy evaluation: A critique. In *The Phillips curve and labor markets,* ed. K. Brunner and A. H. Meltzer, 19–46. Amsterdam: North-Holland.

——— 1980. Methods and problems in business cycle theory. *Journal of Money, Credit and Banking 11*:696–715.

——— 1981. Tobin and monetarism: A review article. *Journal of Economic Literature 19*:558–567.

Lucas, Robert E., Jr., and E. C. Prescott. 1970. Investment under uncertainty. *Econometrica 39*:659–681.

Lucas, Robert E., Jr., and Leonard A. Rapping. 1969. Real wages, employment, and the price level. *Journal of Political Economy 77*:721–754.

Maasoumi, Esfandiar. 1978. A modified Stein-like estimator for the reduced form coefficients of simultaneous equations. *Econometrica 46*:695–703.

Maccini, Louis J. 1972. The dynamic behavior of prices, output, and inventories. Mimeo.

Malinvaud, Edmond. 1977. *The theory of unemployment reconsidered.* Oxford: Basil Blackwell.

——— 1980. *Profitability and unemployment.* Cambridge: Cambridge University Press.

Mansur, Ahsan, and John Whalley. 1981. Numerical specification of applied general equilibrium models: Estimation, calibration, and data. Center for the Study of International Economic Relations, Working Paper no. 8106C, The University of Western Ontario.

McCallum, Bennett T. 1980. Rational expectations and macroeconomic stabilization policy: An overview. *Journal of Money, Credit and Banking 11*:716–746.

McCarthy, Michael D. 1971. Notes on the selection of instruments for two stage least squares and k class type estimators. *Southern Economic Journal 37*:251–259.

——— 1972. Some notes on the generation of pseudo-structural errors for use in stochastic simulation studies. In *Econometric models of cyclical behavior,* ed. B. G. Hickman, 185–191. New York: Columbia University Press.

McNees, Stephen K. 1973. The predictive accuracy of econometric forecasts. *New England Economic Review* (Sept./Oct.): 3–22.

——— 1974. How accurate are economic forecasts? *New England Economic Review* (Nov./Dec.): 2–19.

——— 1975. An evaluation of economic forecasts. *New England Economic Review* (Nov./Dec.): 3–39.

——— 1976. An evaluation of economic forecasts: Extension and update. *New England Economic Review* (Sept./Oct.): 30–44.

Mortensen, Dale T. 1970. A theory of wage and employment dynamics. In E. S.

Phelps et al., *Microeconomic foundations of employment and inflation theory,* 167–211. New York: Norton.

Muench, Thomas, Arthur Rolnick, Neil Wallace, and William Weiler. 1974. Tests for structural change and prediction intervals for the reduced forms of the two structural models of the U.S.: The FRB-MIT and Michigan quarterly models. *Annals of Economic and Social Measurement 3*:491–519.

Muth, John F. 1961. Rational expectations and the theory of price movements. *Econometrica 29*:315–335.

Myhrman, Johan. 1976. Balance-of-payments adjustment and portfolio theory: A survey. In *Recent developments in international monetary economics,* ed. E. Claassen and P. Salin, 203–237. Amsterdam: North-Holland.

Nagar, A. L. 1969. Stochastic simulation of the Brookings econometric model. In *The Brookings model: Some further results,* ed. J. S. Duesenberry, G. Fromm, L. R. Klein, and E. Kuh. Chicago: Rand McNally.

Nelson, Charles R. 1972. The prediction performance of the FRB-MIT-PENN model of the U. S. economy. *American Economic Review 62*:902–917.

Okun, Arthur M. 1971. The personal tax surcharge and consumer demand, 1968–70. *Brookings Papers on Economic Activity 1*:167–204.

Parke, William R. 1982a. An algorithm for FIML and 3SLS estimation of large nonlinear models. *Econometrica 50*:81–95.

——— 1982b. Two modified FIML estimators for use in small samples. Mimeo.

Patinkin, Don. 1956. *Money, interest, and prices.* New York: Harper & Row.

Phelps, Edmund S. 1967. Phillips curves, expectations of inflation and optimal unemployment over time. *Economica 34*:254–281.

——— 1970. Money wage dynamics and labor market equilibrium. In E. S. Phelps et al., *Microeconomic foundations of employment and inflation theory,* 124–166. New York: Norton.

Phelps, Edmund S., and Sidney G. Winter, Jr. 1970. Optimal price policy under atomistic competition. In E. S. Phelps et al., *Microeconomic foundations of employment and inflation theory,* 309–337. New York: Norton.

Phelps, Edmund S., et al. 1970. *Microeconomic foundations of employment and inflation theory.* New York: Norton.

Phillips, A. W. 1959. Estimation of parameters in a system of stochastic differential equations. *Biometrika 46*:67–76.

Phillips, P. C. B. 1982. On the consistency of non-linear FIML. *Econometrica 50*:1307–24.

——— 1984. Exact small sample theory in the simultaneous equations model. In *Handbook of econometrics,* ed. Z. Griliches and M. C. Intriligator. Amsterdam: North-Holland.

Powell, M. J. D. 1964. An efficient method for finding the minimum of a function of several variables without calculating derivatives. *Computer Journal 7*:155–162.

Sargan, J. D. 1973. The tails of the FIML estimates of the reduced form coefficients. Mimeo.

——— 1975. Asymptotic theory and large models. *International Economic Review 16*:75–91.

——— 1976. Existence of the moments of estimated reduced form coefficients. London School of Economics Discussion Paper no. A6.

Sargent, Thomas J. 1973. Rational expectations, the real rate of interest, and the natural rate of unemployment. *Brookings Papers on Economic Activity 2*:429–480.

——— 1976. A classical macroeconomic model for the United States. *Journal of Political Economy 84*:207–237.

——— 1978. Estimation of dynamic labor demand schedules under rational expectations. *Journal of Political Economy 86*:1009–44.

Sargent, Thomas J., and Neil Wallace. 1975. "Rational" expectations, the optimal monetary instrument, and the optimal money supply rule. *Journal of Political Economy 83*:241–254.

Schink, George R. 1971. Small sample estimates of the variance—covariance matrix forecast error for large econometric models: The stochastic simulation technique. Ph.D. diss., University of Pennsylvania.

——— 1974. Estimation of small sample forecast error for nonlinear dynamic models: A stochastic simulation approach. Mimeo.

Sims, Christopher A. 1980. Macroeconomics and reality. *Econometrica 48*:1–48.

Smith, Gary, and William C. Brainard. 1976. The value of a priori information in estimating a financial model. *Journal of Finance 31*:1299–1322.

Solow, Robert M., and Joseph E. Stiglitz. 1968. Output, employment, and wages in the short run. *Quarterly Journal of Economics 82*:537–560.

Sowey, E. R. 1973. Stochastic simulation for macroeconomic models: Methodology and interpretation. In *Econometric studies of macro and monetary relations*, ed. A. A. Powell and R. W. Williams. Amsterdam: North-Holland.

Stigler, George J. 1961. The economics of information. *Journal of Political Economy 69*:213–225.

Taylor, John B. 1977. Conditions for unique solutions in stochastic macroeconomic models with rational expectations. *Econometrica 45*:1377–86.

——— 1980. Output and price stability: An international comparison. *Journal of Economic Dynamics and Control 2*:109–132.

Theil, Henri. 1953. Repeated least-squares applied to complete equations systems. The Hague: Central Planning Bureau.

——— 1966. *Applied economic forecasting*. Amsterdam: North-Holland.

Tishler, Asher, and Israel Zang. 1981. An absolute deviations curve fitting algorithm for non-linear models. Mimeo.

Tobin, James. 1969. A general equilibrium approach to monetary theory. *Journal of Money, Credit and Banking 1*:15–29.

——— 1980. *Asset accumulation and economic activity.* Chicago: The University of Chicago Press.

——— 1982. Money and finance in the macroeconomic process. *Journal of Money, Credit, and Banking 14*:171–204.

Tucker, Donald P. 1968. Credit rationing, interest rate lags, and monetary policy speed. *Quarterly Journal of Economics 82*:54–84.

——— 1971a. Macroeconomic models and the demand for money under market disequilibrium. *Journal of Money, Credit, and Banking 3*:57–83.

——— 1971b. Expansion-contraction asymmetry in disequilibrium adjustments to monetary policy. Paper presented at Econometric Society summer meetings, August 23–27, Boulder, Colorado.

Wallis, Kenneth F. 1980. Econometric implications of the rational expectations hypothesis. *Econometrica 48*:49–74.

Zarnowitz, Victor. 1979. An analysis of annual and multiperiod quarterly forecasts of aggregate income, output, and the price level. *Journal of Business 52*:1–33.

Index